COMMENTARY ON ACTS 4

COMMENTARY ON ACTS 4

STEPHEN MANLEY

COMMENTARY ON ACTS 4
© 2021 by Stephen Manley

Published by Cross Style Press
Lebanon, Tennessee
CrossStyle.org

All rights reserved. No part of this book may be reproduced in any form without prior permission from the publisher, except for brief quotations.

Scripture taken from the New King James Version®. Copyright © 1982 by Thomas Nelson, Inc. Used by permission. All rights reserved.

Edited by Delphine Manley

ISBN-13: 978-0-9987265-8-8

Printed in the United States of America.

CrossStyle.org

CONTENTS

The Announced Resurrection – Acts 4:1-4

Acts 4:1	The Alliance	3
Acts 4:1	Alignment	11
Acts 4:2	I Am Disturbed	19
Acts 4:2	Teaching and Preaching	27
Acts 4:2	Resurrection Fusion	35
Acts 4:2	Resurrection Facilitator	43
Acts 4:3	Imprisoning the Truth	51
Acts 4:3	Illuminating Truth	59
Acts 4:3-4	Independent Truth	67
Acts 4:4	Those Who Heard	75
Acts 4:4	Those Who Believe	83

The Analytical Response – Acts 4:5-12

| Acts 4:5-12 | Let the Contest Begin! | 93 |
| Acts 4:5 | The Sanhedrin | 102 |

Acts 4:6	The Congregation	110
Acts 4:7	The Confrontation	118
Acts 4:7	Life's Question	126
Acts 4:8-12	The Communication	135
Acts 4:8	Who is Speaking?	144
Acts 4:8	Filled with the Holy Spirit	152
Acts 4:9	Judged	160
Acts 4:9	The Heart of God	168
Acts 4:10	The Total Message	176
Acts 4:10	A Powerful Name	184
Acts 4:10-12	The Consistency	192
Acts 4:10-12	The Attitude Involved	200
Acts 4:10-12	The Action Response	209
Acts 4:10-12	The Agents	218
Acts 4:10-12	In His Name	226
Acts 4:10-12	By	234
Acts 4:12	Salvation	242
Acts 4:12	Exclusive	250

The Absolute Ratification – Acts 4:13-22

Acts 4:13-22	They Saw	261
Acts 4:13	Am I Ignorant?	270

Acts 4:13	A Spiritual Mind	278
Acts 4:13	With Jesus	286
Acts 4:13	The Great Commission	294
Acts 4:14	The Annex	303
Acts 4:15	Rejection	311
Acts 4:16	Can I Really Choose?	319
Acts 4:16	Spiritual Eyes	327
Acts 4:17	All About the Heart	335
Acts 4:17	Superimposing	343
Acts 4:18	Eliminate	351
Acts 4:19	Discernment	359
Acts 4:19	What is Right	367
Acts 4:20	A Knowing Belief	375
Acts 4:21	Where is the Devil?	383
Acts 4:21	Punishing	391
Acts 4:22	Forty Years Old	399

The Absolute Reign – Acts 4:23-31

Acts 4:23-31	God is Sovereign	409
Acts 4:23	I Need You	418
Acts 4:24	Oneness in Akouo	426
Acts 4:24	Oneness in Admiration	434

Acts 4:24	Oneness in Articulation	442
Acts 4:24	Master/Despot	450
Acts 4:25	Our Sovereign Speaks	459
Acts 4:25-26	Snorting Horses	467
Acts 4:25-26	Kiss the Son	477
Acts 4:27	Holy Incarnate Jesus	486
Acts 4:27-28	Declaration of the Case	494
Acts 4:27-28	Dilemma of the Case: His Suffering	503
Acts 4:28	Dilemma of the Statement Freewill	513
Acts 4:27-28	Determination of the Plan	521
Acts 4:29	Crisis Management	530
Acts 4:29	Praying to Continue	539
Acts 4:29-30	Momentum	548
Acts 4:29-30	My Desperate Desire	557
Acts 4:30	Jesus in Sovereignty	566
Acts 4:31	The Place	575
Acts 4:31	Filled Again	584
Acts 4:31	A Filled Speaking	593

The Agreed Resolve – Acts 4:32-37

Acts 4:32-37	A Common Thing	605
Acts 4:32	A Believing Church	614

Acts 4:32	Stewardship	623
Acts 4:33	Looking Ressurrected	632
Acts 4:33	With Great Power	642
Acts 4:33	Great Power – Involvement	652
Acts 4:33	Great Power –Indulgent	661
Acts 4:33	I Am A Debtor	670
Acts 4:34	Spiritual Fellowship	679
Acts 4:33	Great Grace	688
Acts 4:35	Divine Nature Expressed	697
Acts 4:36	Son of Encouragement	706
Acts 4:37	Attitude of Encouragement	715

## About the Author					725

PART ONE
ACTS 4:1-4

THE ANNOUNCED RESURRECTION

Acts 4:1

THE ALLIANCE

"Now as they spoke to the people, the priests, the captain of the temple, and the Sadducees came upon them" (Acts 4:1).

Our chapter is a continuation of the story about the lame beggar. He was more than forty years of age (Acts 4:22). He developed the skills and mentality of a beggar; he acquired the best location for begging at the gate of the temple called Beautiful (Acts 3:2). When he asked for alms from Peter and John, he received much more than he expected. In the name of Jesus Christ of Nazareth, he received ***"perfect soundness"*** (Acts 3:16).

Because he came daily to the Gate Beautiful at the hour of prayer, the temple attendees knew him well. When he received his healing, he caused such a commotion by leaping, walking, and praising God that more than five thousand men gathered at Solomon's Porch (Acts 3:11). By holding onto Peter, he identified the one through whom this miracle occurred. This miracle established an opportunity for Peter to address the Jews about Jesus. What an exhortation it was! As we begin our chapter, Peter is just finishing his discussion with this crowd.

Our chapter shows the continual involvement of the healed beggar and the consequences of Peter's exhortation. The first section is APPREHENDED BY THE GOSPEL (Acts 4:1-4). The leaders of Israel were much disturbed by what happened, and they apprehended Peter and John. The Gospel message of Jesus appealed to five thousand men, and they became believers. The next morning the leaders of Israel convened to interrogate these Gospel preachers. The second section's focus is AUTHORITY QUESTIONED (Acts 4:5-12). The leaders of Israel were quite mystified by the apostles' knowledge and depth of spiritual insight that produced quite an ARGUMENT IN THE PLOT (Acts 4:13-22). They could not dispute the miracle of the healed beggar who stood before them. These leaders severely threatened and warned the apostles not to speak of Jesus. After returning to the early church, the apostles reported all that the chief priests and elders said to them. In worship and praise, the early church experienced an ANOINTING IN DIFFICULTIES (Acts 4:23-31). It spurred them into AGGRESSIVE MINISTRY (Acts 4:32-37) and generosity.

Peter's exhortation occurred at Solomon's porch and created a significant stir in Jerusalem. The captain of the temple responsible for policing the temple with the priests and Sadducees *"came upon them"* (Acts 4:1). This confrontation introduces the first section of our chapter, APPREHENDED BY THE GOSPEL (Acts 4:1-4). The main verb of the sentence is the Greek verb "ephistemi," translated *came upon*. This word appears twenty- one times in the New Testament. All appearances are in Luke's writings except 1 Thessalonians 5:3 and 2 Timothy 4:2 and 4:6. It appears as a compound word seven times in Luke's Gospel account and eleven times in the Book of Acts. The word "epi," meaning "by, near, or upon" and "histemi," saying "to stand," describes the appearance of the angel announcing the birth of Jesus to the shepherds (Luke 2:9). However, it is also translated to describe violence and threat. Envious Jews selected evil men from the marketplace and formed a mob. They incited uproar in Thessalonica and *"attacked"* (ephistemi) the home of Jason to persecute the Christians (Acts 17:5). The strength and tone of the word must be translated in light of its context. In our passage, the Jewish leaders are *"greatly disturbed"* (Acts 4:2).

Their activity resulted in threatening the apostles and placing them in jail. Thus, they did not *"come upon"* (ephistemi) like an angel announcing good news; instead, they came in attack mode.

The focus of the verse is the ALLIANCE of people involved in this "attack." This alliance consisted of ***"the priests, the captain of the temple, and the Sadducees"*** (Acts 4:1). Why does Luke specifically mention these three groups or individuals? Perhaps it is as simple as they were present on this occasion. As they brought the apostles out of jail to interrogate, others joined this alliance.

The Levitical priests were the qualified males of the tribe of Levi. Egypt enslaved Israel. The final plague bringing Egypt and Pharaoh to submission was the killing of all the firstborn. This day of deliverance took place on the Passover. The Israelites placed the blood of a lamb on the doorposts and lintels of their houses, and God spared their firstborn (Exodus 12). God claimed the Levites as His substitute for the firstborn (Numbers 1:47-53). The Levites became the priests of Israel. They devoted their lives to maintaining and enforcing the worship of God both in the tabernacle and temple.

Personhood
(Association)

The most profound dynamic of the priesthood was not what they did, but who they were; it was not their function; it was their identity! This dynamic was the position of the firstborn. Again let me remind you of God's deliverance of Israel from Egyptian bondage. Every Egyptian family was affected. Their wails and cries were heard throughout Egypt because their firstborn was dead. The death angel accomplished his intent except in the homes of Israelites. God instructed them that on the tenth day of the month, each household was to take an

Part One: The Announced Resurrection

unblemished, male of the first year lamb. On the fourteenth day of the month, they were to kill it at twilight. The blood of the lamb was to be smeared on the doorpost and on the lintel of the houses where they were to eat. They must roast the lamb and eat it, providing energy for their march out of Egyptian bondage. The death angel passed over the houses with the blood saving the firstborn.

The Lord spoke to Moses, **"Consecrate to Me all the firstborn, whatever opens the womb among the children of Israel, both the man and beast; it is Mine"** (Exodus 13:1). The firstborn (the Levitical tribe) belong exclusively to God. They did not receive an inheritance of land because God was their inheritance. They did not have "rights" because the blood of the lamb saved them. Their lives were not their own. Their identity was in their relationship with God. Their functions as priests were to be an expression of this unity and oneness with God. They were not His because they functioned as priests; they functioned as priests because they were His.

What happened to them? In our passage, they attacked the ones who preached the message when they should have embraced and proclaimed the message. God ordained them for this hour! If anyone knew the heart of God and the fulfillment of His plan, it was the priests. What kind of role did they play in preparing people for the one and final sacrificial Lamb? They could have led the way to the redemption of the world. Five thousand men came to believe in Christ despite their negligence (Acts 4:4). His power changed lives, miracles happened in His name, and the world knew the truth despite their failure. What happened to them? How could they have missed their identity, who are they?

Personification
(Assignment)

The assignment of the Levitical priests is an expression of their identity. They expressed who they were through what they did! God enabled them to perform their functions because of their oneness with Him. The functions of the priest were significant in the religious order of their day. The biblical principle consistently revealed in our studies is that our nature determines our actions! Actions do not determine our nature. All the priestly functions flowed from those of the Levitical tribe because of who they were in God. They were not priests because they did priestly functions; they did priestly functions because they were priests.

The priest's identity focused on holiness. Holiness was their distinguishing characteristic; they were "set apart." God said, **"They shall be holy to their God and not profane the name of their God, for they offer the offerings of the Lord made by fire, and the bread of their God; therefore they shall be holy"** (Leviticus 21:6). Their inner purity reflected in their outward physical demonstration. The physical standard required the priest's inner purity (Leviticus 21:17-21).

Aaron's instructions from God to establish the priesthood and the tabernacle revealed a strong connection between the priest and the tabernacle. The color and structure of the priest's garment corresponded closely to the tabernacle's design (Exodus 28). Anointing the priest with oil (Exodus 40:13) symbolized the anointing of God, which paralleled the glory of God filling the tabernacle (Exodus 40:34). The priest was a physical human form of the tabernacle. He was a miniature tabernacle.

What went wrong? How can the priest, the symbol of God's presence among His people, possibly be **"greatly disturbed that they taught the people and preached in Jesus the resurrection from the dead"** (Acts 4:2)? The priest arrayed in all the right garments met the physical requirements. He represented the dwelling place of God of whom Jesus was the visible image. How did they miss it?

In this anointing and representation of God's fullness, the priest became adequate to represent "God to People." This representation was a primary function flowing from the priest's identity. When the priest received sacrifices and offerings, he signified God's acceptance. When the priest ate the peace offering with those who offered it, he signified God feasting in fellowship with them. The priest is the symbol of God's presence, ministering to His people (Exodus 30:7-10). The climactic activity was the priest sprinkling blood on the ark once a year on the Day of Atonement (Leviticus 16). He represented the people of God. He would gather two goats at the door of the tabernacle of meeting and select one of the goats by casting lots. The chosen goat was the scapegoat, and the remaining goat was a sin offering. After the priest confessed the sins of the people over the scapegoat, he chased the goat was into the wilderness. But the goat for the sin offering was brought into the Holy of Holies. God said, *"For on that day the priest shall make atonement for you, to cleanse you, that you may be clean from all your sins before the Lord"* (Leviticus 16:30).

How did the sacredness of this function get so perverted? An individual set apart by the command of God missed the plan of God. Instead of drawing the people to God, the priest hindered the people from embracing God. What went wrong? Peter finished his exhortation tracing God's design of redemption through the prophets of old. The priests were at the heart of this plan. Now they rushed to dispute, attack, and silence the proclamation of the plan. Why did they not assist? What happened to them?

Eli was an aged priest of the Old Testament. He had sons in the priesthood who **"were corrupt; they did not know the Lord"** (1 Samuel 2:12). Their identity was not in God. This corruption was the root of the iniquity, causing all their priestly functions to be evil. Eli cried to his sons, *"No, my sons! For it is not a good report that I hear. You make the Lord's people transgress. If one man sins against another, God will judge him. But if a man sins against the Lord, who will intercede for him?"* (1 Samuel 2:24-25). The sins of the priest were not just sins against a fellow human, but against God Himself. In such an evil manner, they caused the Lord's people to sin! What happened to them?

God established significant parallels for us throughout the Scriptures. The firstborn delivered from the death angel through the blood of the lamb belongs exclusively to the Lord. The priestly tribe of Levi became the firstborn of Israel. A priest's identity was in his relationship with God. He became responsible for the sacrifices and worship to God. The nation of Israel, as the people of God, became the priestly nation to lead the world into a relationship with God. The status of a holy and redeemed people gave them free access to God's service. The prophet Zechariah said, *"Thus says the Lord of hosts: 'If you will walk in My ways, and if you will keep My command, then you shall also judge My house, and likewise have charge of My courts; I will give you places to walk among those who stand here'"* (Zechariah 3:7).

The parallel continues to us. Adam was a prototype of the priest with dominion over all living things. He was to fill the earth and subdue it (Genesis 1:28). He was to defend the Garden of Eden (Genesis 2:15). These were all priestly functions. In other words, a priest is what a person ought to be! In the New Covenant, God restored us to this priestly position. *"But you are a chosen generation, a royal priesthood, a holy nation, His own special people, that you may proclaim the praises of Him who called you out of darkness into His marvelous light"* (1 Peter 2:9). Again the principle is clear; we are not priests because of what we do but because of our relationship with

Part One: The Announced Resurrection

Him. We are to bring people to Jesus and bring Jesus to people.

We must view ourselves in light of our passage (Acts 4:1). Are we any better than they were? How could they have missed it? How do we miss it? As priests to our God, we are to present our ***"bodies a living sacrifice, holy, acceptable to God, which is your reasonable service"*** (Romans 12:1). We do not wear priestly garments made from our own doing, but we ***"put on the Lord Jesus Christ, and make no provisions for the flesh, to fulfill its lusts"*** (Romans 13:14). We are His firstborn; He sets us aside to be exclusively His. Our function is the priestly privilege of bringing God and man together in oneness. We must not miss it!

Acts 4:1

ALIGNMENT

"Now as they spoke to the people, the priests, the captain of the temple, and the Sadducees came upon them" (Acts 4:1).

An alliance was formed. It consisted of **the priests, the captain of the temple, and the Sadducees.** They forcibly pushed their way through the crowd at Solomon's porch to surround Peter and John. The time at this setting, the size and enthusiasm of the crowd, and the content of the message delivered by Peter and John stirred this alliance into action.

We should not be surprised that the priests were involved and concerned about a major activity in the temple that might affect those who come for the hour of prayer. At least twenty-four thousand priests were permanently stationed in Jerusalem during this time. In the event recorded in our passage, there were hundreds of priests serving in the temple, and it was not only the hour of prayer but also the hour of the evening sacrifice.

Five thousand men became believers because of Peter's exhortation (Acts 4:4). Thousands of people were in the temple during this time. One of the priests' duties was to guard and protect the temple. **The captain of the temple** was a priest over the group of priests assigned to this function. He was second in position and responsibility only to the high priest. His term of service was indefinite and uninterrupted. His duty was to maintain order in the temple and its surrounding area.

Part One: The Announced Resurrection

The Sadducees were an elite and wealthy group. They compromised and established a link with Rome to maintain their wealth. Because of their wealth and priestly descent, they controlled the position of the high priest and the Sanhedrin. The temple treasury, which included the temple taxes and money changing tables, all came under their supervision. Many priests and the captain of the temple would have been Sadducees, and they were in charge of the temple and its activities. A reasonable assumption is that this alliance consisted of Sadducees or at least its members were under their control.

It might surprise you to know that those leading the persecution of Jesus and His disciples were different from those who plotted Christ's death. The Pharisees were the bitterest enemies of Jesus. They were so infuriated by their many conflicts with Him that they *plotted against Him, how they might destroy Him* (Matthew 12:14). Our passage reveals that the Sadducees are the ones who threatened the disciples. Their alliance with the priests and the captain of the temple moved them to arrest, threaten, and later release the disciples. After that release *many signs and wonders were done among the people. And they were all with one accord in Solomon's Porch* (Acts 5:12). The disciples did not heed the threats of the Sadducees; instead, they became instruments of increased demonstrations in the same location. These demonstrations resulted in *the high priest rose up, and all those who were with him (which is the sect of the Sadducees), and they were filled with indignation, and laid their hands on the apostles and put them in the common prison* (Acts 5:17-18). During this trial *one in the council stood up, a Pharisee named Gamaliel, a teacher of the law held in respect by all the people,* and intervened to save them from threatened death (Acts 5:34-39). The Sadducees, only mildly interested in the opposition against Jesus, aggressively led the attack on the apostles. A leader of the Pharisees who crucified Jesus spoke on the apostles' behalf.

This highlights an unexpected change in the leadership of the persecution against Jesus and His Church.

When we give this closer examination, the reason for this shift becomes clear. The Pharisees were focused on the law as constituted in the six hundred and thirteen oral traditions. The Sadducees did not embrace the strictness of these traditions but held only to what was plainly stated in the writings of Moses (the first five books of the Old Testament). Jesus' ministry among the people was consistently undermining the oral traditions on which the Pharisees based their righteousness. From the Sermon on the Mount to the last public message (Matthew 23), Jesus exposed the hypocrisy of the Pharisees who hid behind their oral traditions. The "seven woes to the Pharisees" form a strong denunciation unmatched in all literature. The Sadducees stood back in amusement over the exposure of the Pharisees.

The relationship of the apostles with the Pharisees and Sadducees was naturally reversed. ***And with great power the apostles gave witness to the resurrection of the Lord Jesus*** (Acts 4:33). The primary role of the apostles in the early Church was to give witness to the resurrection of Jesus. The distinctive doctrine of the Pharisees was their belief in a resurrection from the dead, which confirmed the testimony of the apostles. Thus the force of their preaching was leveled at the Sadducees disbelief in a resurrection. This preaching stirred the Sadducees to an activity not exhibited toward Jesus. They rushed to arrest Peter and John ***being greatly disturbed that they taught the people and preached in Jesus the resurrection from the dead*** (Acts 4:2). The priests officiating in the temple at the time joined in the arrest while the people were drawn away from the activities in the temple. The ***captain of the temple*** with his guard was subject to the orders of the officiating priest. This alliance was what arrested the apostles.

DISTRACTION is the single issue found in each member of the alliance. Whatever the cause, they were all distracted from their role's calling. Each group or individual represented a function of ministry to which God called him. However, something went drastically wrong, became twisted, or was set aside. They became distracted from the focus of their calling. Discovering the focus of their calling might enable us to identify their distraction.

Jesus, the Messiah, was to be the dwelling place in which every member of this alliance was to function. The permanent physical structure of the temple had an interesting beginning. God used King David to bring peace and prosperity to all of Israel. David felt guilty as he viewed his **house of cedar, but the ark of God dwells inside tent curtains** (2 Samuel 7:2). King David discussed this with the prophet Nathan who gave him the following encouragement. **"Go, do all that is in your heart, for the Lord is with you"** (2 Samuel 7:3). However, that night the Lord spoke to Nathan with a message to give to King David. All this time, from Israel's deliverance from Egyptian bondage to the present peace in the Promised Land, God never requested or even hinted at a desire to have a permanent dwelling place. God's focus was to give Israel a home. He was building a house for His people! God rejected David's plan, but told him He would build a house for David. His house would be a dynasty, **"And your house and your kingdom shall be established forever before you. Your throne shall be established forever"** (2 Samuel 7:16).

This verse is a prophecy about Jesus! Jesus would be the house of God among the people of which the temple was a symbol. Jesus would be the first human being to experience the indwelt presence of God. He would be the King. The structure of the Kingdom was to be an individual made in His image and filled with His presence. A human being filled with the Spirit of Jesus forms the Kingdom. He is the temple of God. Jesus would be the beginning of a new dynasty in which God would reign. Jesus proposed this in His discourse in the upper room.

He said, *"In my Father's house* (household or family) *are many mansions* (dwelling places or homes); *if it were not so, I would have told you. I go to prepare a place for you* (I go to prepare you to be a place)" (John 14:2).

Each member of this alliance served in this physical symbol awaiting the coming of Christ. He arrived, but they were distracted and missed Him! I am convinced it is one of the devil's major tricks. The devil's concern is not about evil deeds, being a bad person, or deadly habits. His concern is not about religious versus irreligious. His goal is simple. He wants to distract you from Jesus. He wants you to concentrate on offering sacrificial lambs instead of embracing the Lamb. He wants you to stress over keeping laws and rules rather than embracing the fulfillment of the Law. He wants you to focus your energy on ministry instead of resting in Jesus so He can minister through you. Rules instead of Jesus, deeds of ministry instead of Jesus, ceremonies instead of Jesus, feelings instead of Jesus, gifts of the Spirit instead of Jesus, positions instead of Jesus, performance instead of Jesus, prosperity instead of Jesus are some of the devil's distractions.

The temple of the Old Testament was the symbol and imagery of the arrival of the New Covenant established by Jesus. Jesus is the fullness of the presence of God in bodily form. A rumor reached the high priest that Jesus acclaimed the destruction of the temple, and He would build another temple *made without hands* (Mark 14:58). A new species of humanity would be found in Jesus. These humans would be the houses in which God would dwell! This dwelling was to be the focus of this alliance. Yet, He came, He was preached and proclaimed, and they were distracted is a message to us!

The PROTECTOR is one member of the alliance. He is not a member of the nation's military. He is the priest who is to protect the temple. He was the superintendent of the guard of priests and Levites who kept watch by night in the temple.

This responsibility is traceable back to the Old Testament's early days. They were the ***priests who kept the door*** (2 Kings 12:9 and 25:18). Their function was obvious. They were to settle any disturbance among the worshippers. As thousands of Israelites moved throughout the temple, all sorts of arguments and incidents occurred. They must protect the valuable fixtures of the temple from thievery. The temple's offering boxes were readily available for all to give donations. The buying, selling, and exchanging secular money for temple money produced large amounts of cash in the temple. Protection of this cash was a high priority. Areas of the temple were restricted, and many attempted to enter these areas. The handicapped, poor, and Gentiles were barred even from the Court of the Gentiles. The men had their section, and the women had another. The captain of the temple's job was to protect the temple.

There is no dispute that this protection was necessary. However, if their focus was protection, they were distracted from the central issue. Protecting the people from the New Covenant was not their business. They were not to cause the people to miss the reality of God's presence indwelling them. Every item in the temple had a purpose, and each was a symbolic prophecy of the Christ Messiah who would lead them into the Holy of Holies. In our passage Jesus was preached, and five thousand men were filled with His presence! Being filled with His presence was the purpose of the temple. Those who were to keep the people from missing the reality were keeping them from the reality. They were distracted.

I have been guilty of the same! I have been more concerned about the carpet in our temple than our people being embraced by Jesus. Quality of program has captured my attention more than the movement of the Spirit. The amount of the offerings had been a greater concern than a little one becoming the dwelling place of God. The style of music has been of greater value than the indwelling of the Spirit. Through these distractions I have protected the worshippers from Jesus instead of protecting them from missing the reality of His embrace.

The Sadducees were the POLITICIANS. They were distracted. They were focused on the comfort of their lifestyle. They pushed aside the oral traditions established by the Pharisees to maintain a link with Rome. This link enabled them to maintain their financial status. In other words, they adjusted their moral and religious standards to fit their desired lifestyle. It seems this also occurred in their theology. They differed from the Pharisees in their position about the resurrection of the dead. The resurrection proposes eternal life. If we dismiss this, the focus of life can be on the present good life. After all, now is all we have left.

The apostles **preached in Jesus the resurrection from the dead** (Acts 4:2). Their message was not limited to the resurrection of Jesus, but it expanded to our resurrection. This belief would require a radical change of focus for the Sadducees. Although they may have tolerated the ministry of Jesus, this message of the resurrection struck at the core of their existence. This must be stopped.

It amazes me how much of our theology is shaped by our preferred lifestyle. This approach is filled with self! We focus on what satisfies our self-centered desires and shape our belief system accordingly. In reality, the truth must be our focus. This truth should shape our desires and determine our life's activities. Jesus is the truth! The Sadducees were called by God to help people embrace the truth; therefore, their lives would be shaped by this truth. But they were distracted. They not only missed the truth for their lives, but they stood in the way of others discovering the truth.

The PRIESTS served an important role in our passage. We investigated them carefully in our previous study. They missed the calling they had from the beginning. Their function was to bring people to God and bring God to the people. The significance of being selected for this role cannot be overrated. How could more than twenty-four thousand priests stationed in Jerusalem for this purpose get so distracted?

It was the hour of prayer and the time of sacrifice at the temple (Acts 3:1). This crowd had a purpose. They were present to encounter God. The priests were there to facilitate them in this endeavor. Ceremonies and rituals were designed to aid the people in this encounter. How could anyone with such a calling become engulfed in the provision of ceremonies and miss their highest calling?

What occurred on Solomon's porch that attracted everyone's attention? No ceremonies or rituals were provided at Solomon's porch. Whatever happened interfered with the activities of the priests. The people were distracted and did not participate in the rituals of sacrifices and prayers. That could not be allowed. The priests became a part of the alliance to bring the crowd back into focus with their distraction.

Isn't it interesting that God moved to distract this crowd from the priest's distraction? He broke through with His presence and brought them back to His purpose of intimacy. Because of their distraction, God set aside the normal pattern He had established. He came in an unorthodox manner to accomplish His plan. I wonder whether this is true for our lives as well! Have our religious programs become a distraction from the original purpose God designed for us? Is God sidestepping that design in order to bring us back to Himself?

Acts 4:2

I AM DISTURBED

"Being greatly disturbed that they taught the people and preached in Jesus the resurrection from the dead" (Acts 4:2).

Our verse is not an independent or a complete sentence, but it is a continuation of the first verse. Luke gives a description and additional details to the actions of the alliance coming on the apostles. The subject of the sentence is **the priests, the captain of the temple, and the Sadducees** who formed the alliance. Luke describes them as those who **came upon,** the verb of the sentence. The Greek word "ephistemi," translated **came upon**, appears twenty-one times in the New Testament. Seventeen of the appearances are in the writings of Luke. "Ephistemi" is a compound word, "eip" meaning "by, near, or upon," and "histemi" meaning "to stand." It can be used in a positive sense, or in a violent and threatening sense. The strength of the word must be translated in light of its context. In our passage, the result of their action is that the disciples are violently put in jail and threatened the next day. Thus, **came upon** is a violent, attacking action.

Another strong indication of the violence of their attack on the disciples is the Greek participle "diaponeo," translated ***being greatly disturbed***. This word is an adjective modifying the subject because it is in the nominative. "Diaponeo" is a compound word; "dia" meaning "through," and "poneo" meaning, "to labor."

However, the root word of "poneo" is "ponos" meaning "toil with the idea of pain." One translation says, "Vexed through and through." The alliance was weary or grieved by the continual teaching and preaching of the apostles. One Greek lexicon defines this word as "to be very angry." The word is used only twice in the New Testament. Once slave girl possessed by a spirit of divination made large profits for her masters by her fortune telling. For many days, she followed Paul and Silas crying they were servants of the Most High God. But Paul, greatly annoyed (diaponeo), turned and said to the spirit, *"I command you in the name of Jesus Christ to come out of her." And he came out that very hour* (Acts 16:18).

What is it that aggravates you to the point you take action? I am not asking what irritates you because you do not like it. What causes your blood pressure to rise, and you cannot stand it. If you do not vent you will explode? We are discussing anger! Biblically it is difficult to say that all anger is wrong or sinful. If you view the list of Scripture references under the word "wrath" in an exhaustive concordance, there are many references to God's wrath. How can God be allowed anger and man is not? Several Greek words are translated in the New Testament for wrath or anger; "thumos," which refers to passion, meaning "heavy breathing," and "orge" meaning "desire, and excitement of the mind." These two words are used together in several important passages (Romans 2:8; Ephesians 4:31: Colossians 3:8; Revelation 19:15). Rage is the definition of "parorgismos" (Ephesians 4:26).

Mark records Jesus healing a man with a withered hand on the Sabbath. The Pharisees were there to accuse Him. *"And when He had looked around at them with anger* (orge), *being grieved by the hardness of their hearts, He said to the man, 'Stretch out your hand'"* (Mark 3:5). Aristotle suggests, "orge anger is desire with grief." Anger promoted by the Spirit of God is against sin and its consequences. Who could love good without hating evil? This demands that love and hate must be present in the individual. You must do both or neither.

Let us return to our discussion of the Greek word in the passage. The alliance, under the jurisdiction of the Sadducees, was **being greatly disturbed** (diaponeo). This word is a participle used as an adjective to modify the subject, the three elements making up the alliance. This adjectival participle gives content to their attitude and motive in the action of the verb **came upon**. The apostles are threatened and put in jail because of the alliance's upset and anger.

This word use is in contrast with the only other time our word (diaponeo) is used in the New Testament. Paul and Silas were in Philippi during their missionary endeavors. A woman named Lydia was converted through the preaching of Paul. She invited Paul and his group to come to her house for prayer. As they journeyed to Lydia's home, a slave girl possessed by a spirit of divination followed them. Her owners made a profit by her fortune telling. She was crying out, "*'these men are the servants of the Most High God, who proclaim to us the way of salvation.' And this she did for many days. But Paul greatly annoyed* (diaponeo) *turned and said to the spirit, 'I command you in the name of Jesus Christ to come out of her.' And he came out that very hour"* (Acts 16:17-18).

The anger (diaponeo) responses demonstrated on these two occasions are very different. In the situation of Paul and Silas in Philippi, the young girl was demon possessed, involved in paganism and idol worship. In the anger of the alliance, these men were at the heart of the nation of Israel through which the Messiah came. These leaders of Israel represented the ultimate in righteousness. What a contrast! Each response affects the work of the Kingdom. Paul's anger promoted the Kingdom of God; the alliance's anger hindered the Kingdom. Paul's anger brought freedom from bondage to a young girl, but the alliance's anger brought imprisonment to the apostles. The Spirit of Jesus worked despite the alliance's anger, and the Spirit of Jesus worked through the anger of Paul. Jesus was glorified through Paul's anger while the alliance attempted to discredit the glory of Jesus through their anger.

Let us look closely at these two demonstrative scenes.

Span of Anger

As the alliance *came upon them,* there is no apparent timespan in the beginning of the anger. Our Greek word "diaponeo," translated *being greatly disturbed* is in the present tense. This tense indicates the present with continuing action, and the future becomes the present. The anger of the alliance began when they recognized the preaching and teaching of the apostles. The rest of the chapter's tone continues with upset, anger, threats, and hatred. The highest officials of the Sanhedrin were called to a meeting (Acts 4:6). They asked accusatory questions (Acts 4:7). Their frustration increased as the evidence and reality of the miracle spread (Acts 4:14). All Jerusalem was a witness to the power of God in the lame beggar.

The opposite happened for Paul and Silas. The Greek word "disponeo," translated *greatly annoyed*, is in the aorist tense (Acts 16:18). This tense is a focus on the action of the upset rather than the time of occurrence. As the story unfolds, Luke highlights the fact that the young girl followed Paul and Silas for several days (Acts 16:18). As they went from place to place ministering in the city, she followed them. The distress element was in her constant announcement, *"These men are the servants of the Most High God, who proclaim to us the way of salvation"* (Acts 16:17). At first we might think this announcement is good advertisement. However, this could harm to the truth of the Gospel. The people of Philippi might consider the ministry of Paul and Silas an extension of the demonic, pagan world possessing this young girl. Therefore, the anger of Paul was not easily provoked but was quickly used for Divine action.

This "slow to anger" is an interesting contrast! The alliance experienced immediate anger, and it lasted throughout the next day. They expressed this in a variety of acts as they tried to satisfy their anger. They acted with punishment to eliminate and destroy the message of Jesus. Paul and Silas' anger took several days to build. They focused their anger on spiritual deliverance. It promoted the name of Jesus and helped establish a church in Philippi.

In each scene, the same Greek word describes what happened in the key people. One group was wrong, and the other group was right. We despair at the state of the alliance, but we rejoice at the spiritual life and victory of Paul and Silas. What is it that aggravates you? I don't mean what simply irritates you or what you prefer or like against what you do not like. What moves you to action? What so aggravates you that you must act? You cannot stand it. Something has to change. Does it come on you gradually and do the results focus on redemption? Is it a heated anger that flares in your heart and you need instant gratification? What determines the difference between these two possibilities? This brings us to the next part of our discussion.

Source of Anger

Remember that the first word in our verse is the Greek word "diaponeo," translated ***being greatly disturbed***. The word is a verb in the nominative case used as an adjectival participle to give content to the main subject, ***the priests, the captain of the temple, and the Sadducees***. This verb is in the middle voice, which means it is a personal preference. In the rest of our verse, Luke writes, ***that they taught the people and preached in Jesus the resurrection from the dead***. The two verbs ***taught*** and *preached* are infinitives giving purpose to the main verb *came upon*. Why was the alliance so angry? According to this verse, they were angry because of what they thought to be deception in the teaching and preaching of the apostles. However, the middle voice of "diaponeo" gives us the source of their anger. They chose as their preference not to be open to what God was speaking through the apostles.

Paul's anger in Philippi was different. The Greek word "diaponeo," translated *greatly annoyed*, is also a verb used as an adjective to give content to the main subject, "***Paul***." This verb is in the passive voice, which indicates that Paul is not responsible for the anger, but God is acting on him. The young girl being used by the evil spirit is not the focus of his anger. Paul *turned and said to the spirit*. The interaction occurred in the spiritual world. Paul did not address the issue in the physical realm. He did not respond as the alliance responded. They *came upon* the apostles and physically put them in jail. They responded to their self-sourced anger in a fleshly manner, the only avenue self-sourced anger has to appease its motivation. Paul immediately invoked the name of Jesus. This put Jesus in charge of the situation. Paul's anger was sourced and appeased by the Spirit of Jesus!

We do not have control over the circumstances that come to us, and we argue that we have no control over our response to those circumstances. The alliance responded to what the apostles were doing in the only way they knew how. Paul responded to the activity of the demonic forces in the only way he knew how. Neither situation was about physical activities but spiritual powers. Therefore, our response to life's circumstances reveals our spiritual condition. When adverse circumstances arise we should thank those involved for being used by God to reveal who we are. Whether the intent is for good or for harm, God allows these circumstances to strengthen and reveal your spirit.

Solution of Anger

When adverse circumstances afflict your life, your inner being responds. This inner response is never isolated to the inner person; there must be a physical response! If anger is concealed and suppressed, it will automatically reveal itself physically in illness, depression, addictions, and so forth.

The teaching and preaching of the apostles caused the alliance to experience inner turmoil. They quickly demonstrated this turmoil with physical acts. They rushed on the apostles, putting them in jail for the night. They did everything possible to eliminate the threat. This drama, continued throughout the Book of Acts, characterized by guard, protect, and self-focus. In this scene, the alliance is frustrated. They had no way to satisfy their desire and eliminate their anger. *So when they had further threatened them, they let them go, finding no way of punishing them, because of the people, since they all glorified God for what had been done* (Acts 4:21). The healed lame man stood in their presence (Acts 4:14). They could not deny that something miraculous had happened. How could they openly express their anger when all Jerusalem attributed the miracle to God? But this is always true of self-sourced anger, and there is no physical solution! What you do in physical action never appeases or satisfies the anger. Revenge and punishment do not satisfy the heart. The lack of a physical solution increases the anger.

But the Spirit-sourced anger is vastly different. Paul's anger was immediately focused on deliverance in the spiritual realm. He focused his physical act on spiritual results. He turned to the spirit possessing the girl and commanded an immediate departure (Acts 16:18). The solution to the anger was found in the spiritual results; however, there were physical consequences to the spiritual actions. The young girl was delivered from the evil spirit's domination. She could no longer profit her masters.

Part One: The Announced Resurrection

They immediately dragged Paul and Silas to the authorities in the market place. They were beaten with many rods and thrown in jail. Did Paul's anger increase? Surely this unfair treatment would accelerate his anger. ***But at midnight Paul and Silas were praying and singing hymns to God, and the prisoners were listening to them. Suddenly there was a great earthquake, so that the foundations of the prison were shaken; and immediately all the doors were opened and everyone's chains were loosed*** (Acts 16:25-26). The Philippi jailor and his household were converted.

Is it possible to have the mind of Christ? Can His mind and your mind be joined in such unity of thought that you see things as He does? Can self-sourcing be crucified? Can we be Spirit-sourced? This means Jesus' anger becomes your anger. The focus of His anger becomes your focus. The solution flowing from His anger engages your being. You become a part of the solution that satisfies the heart of God. What a privilege!

Acts 4:2

TEACHING AND PREACHING

"Being greatly disturbed that they taught the people and preached in Jesus the resurrection from the dead" (Acts 4:2).

The healed lame man created a major stir in the temple (Acts 3:9). He held onto Peter and John as the crowd gathered at Solomon's Porch (Acts 3:11). He had received a miracle. The temple crowd knew his previous condition because he had begged at the Gate Beautiful daily for nearly forty years. Not everyone was pleased with the results of this miracle. The alliance, **the priests, the captain of the temple, and the Sadducees**, were annoyed. They were so deeply disturbed that they acted against the apostles. They **"*came upon them*"** (Acts 4:1).

Luke described them as **greatly disturbed**. Why are they so disturbed? What drove them to such violence? The answer appears in the last half of our verse, **"*that they taught the people and preached in Jesus the resurrection from the dead*"** (Acts 4:2). Teaching and preaching was not a new methodology of evangelism and discipleship. Jesus did each. He trained His disciples in these methods and sent them to minister. Peter and John did what was normal and natural for them. Peter preached a great sermon on the Day of Pentecost (Acts 2:14+). Now he is at Solomon's Porch exhorting the crowd with astounding results.

Luke attributes teaching and preaching to the situation of our passage. Through the years of ministry, I have tried to discover the fine line between teaching and preaching. Is teaching about facts and knowledge, while preaching is about emotion and feelings? Is preaching teaching with an emotional flair? Is teaching the activity of discipleship, while preaching is the activity of evangelizing the unchristian? We can adequately say that a person can teach without preaching. However, is it possible to preach without teaching? You and I realize that the answers to these questions are confined to how we define the terms, teaching and preaching.

Perhaps the Scriptures can teach us something about the interaction of our inner beings with truth. This might mean that the Scriptures teach us and preach in Jesus the reality of truth! The Greek word "didasko," translated "*they taught*," is an infinitive verb, a statement of cause or purpose in the action of the main verb. The main verb is "*came upon*" in the previous verse. If the apostles resisted teaching the people, the alliance would have left them alone. The verb "didasko" is in the present tense. In the Greek grammar, continuous action is contained in the present tense. The persistent and continual teaching of the apostles got them into trouble.

What is this teaching? The Greek word "didasko" has the intent to influence the understanding of the student inherit in it. In other words, teaching in this context contains the motive for convincing and changing the perspective of an individual through the truth. Teaching is never the act of speaking data or about information. Instead, it is about presenting life-changing truth to change the one being taught.

"Akuou" is a counterpart to "didasko." It means to hear and understand. Also "manthano" means, "to learn." From this word, "mathetes," learner, pupil, or disciple is derived. Jesus said, *"A disciple* (mathetes) *is not above his teacher* (didaskei)" (Matthew 10:24). Therefore, the teacher (didaskei) teaches; the disciple (mathetes) learns or assimilates what he learns as part of himself. Biblical teaching is never on a mere academic level or the imparting of information and data to be recorded later on a test for an academic grade. In the scheme of the world, there is teaching that merely shares information, and there is teaching that trains people with job skills. But biblical teaching is always aimed at the assimilation of Truth (Jesus) into the character and nature of the person learning.

In discussing "didasko," the **Theological Dictionary of the New Testament** suggests that the Gospels present an unusual emphasis from their present cultural environment. Everywhere else among Greek writers the emphasis is on the intellectual understanding of the information being taught. This was so strongly stressed in the Greek culture that in some cities studying the law was ranked higher than keeping the law. The biblical teaching of the Gospels presents an absence of intellectual emphasis; it focuses on the character and nature of the person being changed by the truth. It produces such a radical change that the truth becomes a flow of action in the life and character of the student.

Paul gave a new dimension to this concept when he wrote, *"But concerning brotherly love you have no need that I should write to you, for you yourselves are taught by God to love one another"* (1 Thessalonians 4:9). The phrase, *"taught by God,"* is one Greek word coined by Paul. He combined "God" (Theos) and "teach" (didasko) into "theodidaktos." Only here in the New Testament writings is it used. The alliance *came upon* the apostles for teaching, and they violently put them in jail. They released them under the threat of death never to teach again. The alliance could not understand what was happening through the apostles. Jesus taught through them, and truth beyond intellectual information was imparted to the crowd at Solomon's Porch. Truth went to the heart of the crowd and changed their nature and character.

The New Testament teaching of the New Covenant was unknown among the teachers of the world. The teaching started in Jesus and now was present in the believers. It was not a teaching about mere facts but of truth. It became the revelation of God's heart to the individual who assimilated the character and nature into Him. It demanded change not just in the addition of intellectual knowledge, but also in the mannerisms of lifestyle. No wonder the alliance was ***greatly disturbed*** with the teaching of the apostles. The "Truth" was setting the people free (John 8:32).

We must adopt using this emphasis in our approach to the Living Word and the Written Word of God. Every time we use the Word of God to prove our point, win our argument, or manipulate for our benefit, we abuse and crucify the Living Word of God. The moment the Living Word is separated from the Written Word, we cease to teach the Scriptures. We present mere data and information. We must unite the Living Word with the Written Word in a flow of truth by which our lives can be shaped and changed by God into His likeness. We may say that we teach His Word, but without His presence flowing in and through the teaching, we are not experienced biblical teachers. The Scriptures without His presence become an academic study. God's presence without the Scriptures becomes an emotional involvement for self-pleasure. We must experience biblical teaching in our lives.

However, the apostles not only *"taught the people,"* but they also *"preached in Jesus the resurrection from the dead"* (Acts 4:2). The Greek word "kakagello," is translated *"preached."* This Greek word is used eleven times in the Book of Acts and used an additional seven times in Paul's writings. The prefix "kata" is placed there to intensify; "aggello" is the root word meaning "to announce or proclaim." In our passage, the subject of the resurrection is the primary announcement or proclamation. This proclamation was the fundamental role of the apostle. In this chapter, Luke explains, *"And with great power the apostles gave witness to the resurrection of the Lord Jesus"* (Acts 4:33). The primary responsibility of the apostle was not church planting, overseeing of the missionary movement, or correction of doctrinal matters. Instead, it was to be a witness of the resurrection.

It is in this context we begin to understand the view and definition of preaching. Teaching is the informing of truth not merely facts, allowing learners to assimilate this truth into their lives. Truth involves the interaction of the Living Word being revealed in the Written Word. Preaching is the proclamation of truth not an announcement of information. When a person is filled with the Living Word and proclaims the Written Word, it is because the Living Word flows through him. Therefore, preaching is in a category far beyond a speech, lecture, or exhortation. In our passage, preaching comes from the apostle filled with the resurrected Lord, proclaiming the reality of the resurrected Lord through the resurrected Lord's power. If the risen Lord is not present, it is a lecture.

Both dynamics of teaching and preaching took place in our passage. Does this mean there were several sessions? Does it mean they broke into small groups for more personal interaction? Was there a time of questions and answers at the end of Peter's exhortation? Answering any of these questions with "yes" means adding to the presentation of the passage. Teaching and preaching happened simultaneously as Peter unfolded the Scriptures about Jesus, the risen Lord!

We must be careful about our perspective and attitude toward preaching. We must not allow anything to be called preaching that does not contain the above elements! We must not come Sunday after Sunday experiencing preaching and take it casually. The writer of the Book of Hebrews paints a clear picture of preaching for us. He begins chapter four of his book with a picture of the "rest," a ceasing from our works as God did from His (Hebrews 4:10). He relates to us the creation scene. God did creative works for six days and proclaimed the seventh day as a day of rest. Mankind's first day of living was a day of

Part One: The Announced Resurrection

rest. This is our example. Let us rest! Then the writer describes the "Word of God." It is *"**living and powerful, and sharper than any two-edged sword, piercing even to the division of soul and spirit, and of joints and marrow, and is a discerner of the thoughts and intents of the heart**"* (Hebrews 4:12).

If we are to rest, what is our resting place? We are to rest on the Word of God. A lazy-boy recliner, a fluffy pillow, or a comfortable mattress, it is not. It is a sharp surgical knife in the hands of a skilled surgeon. As the preacher rests on the surgical table, the Living Word cuts deep into his spiritual life for healing and correction. In this bleeding and wounded state, the preacher goes to the pulpit. He exposes all the Surgeon has done to him. The congregation comes to rest on the same surgical table and allows the same Surgeon to cut into their lives. They experience the same surgical knife transformation. This surgery is called preaching.

Let us go back to our passage with this awareness. The alliance, "*came upon them being greatly disturbed that they taught the people and preached in Jesus the resurrection from the dead*" (Acts 4:1-2). If we view these verses only on the surface, we might think it was teaching and preaching that greatly disturbed the alliance. With that thought process, we would miss the truth of the passage. Jerusalem was filled with teachers and their selected disciples. The schools directed by Hillel and Shammai were popular and influential. The temple and the synagogues were places of continual teaching and preaching. This communication was not the issue behind the alliance coming on the apostles.

Perhaps it was the subject of the resurrection. The most prominent doctrine of the Sadducees, which dominated this alliance, was the denial of the soul's immortality and the resurrection of the body. The Pharisees believed Moses delivered these doctrines to the elders; in turn, they handed them to their successors. The Sadducees rejected all these traditions. Their focus was on materialism and the comfort of this life. This focus influenced them to compromise with Rome to eliminate anything that might disturb their relationship with the authorities.

Paul was brought before the council in Jerusalem. The council was equally divided between the Pharisees and Sadducees. In his testimony, *he cried out to the council, "Men and brethren. I am a Pharisee, the son of a Pharisee; concerning the hope and resurrection of the dead I am being judged!" And when he had said this, a dissension arose between the Pharisees and the Sadducees; and the assembly was divided. For Sadducees say that there is no resurrection – and no angels or spirits; but the Pharisees confess both* (Acts 23:6-8). Josephus distinctly said that the Sadducees believed the soul dies with the body. The Sadducees deny Divine providence. But surely the Sadducees did not rush on everyone who taught the resurrection from the dead and put them in jail. They tolerated the Pharisees and worked with them in the council. In our passage the problem was greater than a difference in doctrinal belief.

The issue of Jesus disturbed the alliance! All kinds of ideas being taught and some began to use preaching as their avenue of teaching. However, when the Spirit-sourced apostles preached the resurrection of Jesus in the power of the resurrected Lord, the alliance felt pressure they could not tolerate. These men were not just lecturing a concept they hoped was true. They were filled with the resurrected Lord. They were not proposing words but experiencing a Presence.

After the alliance put the apostles in jail for the night, they assembled with others in the morning feeling the pressure again. Peter was filled with the Holy Spirit (Acts 4:8). When he finished preaching, the alliance was amazed and marveled. They knew Peter and John were *"uneducated and untrained men"* (Acts 4:13). They were simple fishermen. Yet they had boldness about them. *"They realized they had been with Jesus"* (Acts 4:13). The statement is somewhat stronger than indicated.

Part One: The Announced Resurrection

The Greek word "sun," translated *with*, denotes union. It is a stronger connection than the Greek word "para" or "meta." "Sun" expresses the idea of instrumentality, resemblance, possession, or companionship. In other words, the alliance sensed the strange presence of the Jesus they had crucified.

Let us return to the teaching and preaching in the biblical context. Something new was happening. It began in Jesus, the first Spirit-sourced man. Now it was happening in those were filled with the Spirit. This Spirit-sourcing was the power promised by Jesus to those who tarried in Jerusalem. He said, ***"But you shall receive power when the Holy Spirit has come upon you, and you shall be witnesses to Me in Jerusalem, and in all Judea and Samaria, and to the end of the earth"*** (Acts 1:8). This witnessing was not about training sessions or academic degrees. This was about the distinct presence of Jesus. As the apostles taught about Jesus, His presence confronted those who heard. As the apostles preached about Jesus, His presence was proclaimed and experienced by the people.

This presence is the heart of the Christian faith. Our world will accept various doctrines and religious beliefs, but the presence of Christ ministering through the heavenly realms into our lives brings amazing pressure for response (John 16:8-11). When Jesus is present, everything in me unlike Him begins to be uncomfortable. Jesus stretches and challenges me to a new level of living in His power. In other words, teaching and preaching will not allow me to remain as I am. For seekers it is life, but it irritates those who want to maintain. In our scene five thousand men believed, but the alliance was disturbed. We must teach and preach in Person; we must respond to teaching and preaching in openness.

Acts 4:2

RESURRECTION FUSION

"Being greatly disturbed that they taught the people and preached in Jesus the resurrection from the dead" (Acts 4:2).

The alliance rushed on the apostles with force and fervor. This attach was not just a momentary disturbance because they continually persecuted the early Church. They put the apostles in jail and made threats against them. The elimination of teaching and preaching became their goal. The apostles' teaching and preaching had elements far beyond their day and was not a presentation of facts or data. They presented the Truth! All facts and data may be truthful, but a truth does exist beyond the memorization of facts. We cannot ultimately understand truth without embracing Jesus. Thus, the teaching of the apostles pushed everyone to ASSIMILATION. The Greek word "didasko," translated "teaching," has the intent to influence the understanding of the student. The teacher presents life-changing truth to affect change in an individual's life. This was a radical change as we discovered in a previous study. The Greek culture focused on intellectual understanding of information. This understanding was such a big thing in Greek culture that some thought studying the law was a higher level than keeping the law! The apostles were teaching truth that contained the anointing of a Presence!

We distinguish preaching from teaching by AWARENESS.

Part One: The Announced Resurrection

When the Truth (Jesus) is proclaimed in preaching, only then is the proclamation experienced. In our passage, preaching is the proclamation from an apostle filled with the resurrected Lord, and he proclaims the reality of the resurrected Lord through the power of the Presence. The alliance was compelled to stop such teaching and preaching. The combination of truth being taught and preached changes the thinking in a person, allowing him to experience the presence of Jesus. The Truth cannot be ignored!

Luke uses words to express the core of what irritated the alliance. The Greek word "en" is the pivotal word. He says, ***"being greatly disturbed that they taught the people and preached in Jesus the resurrection from the dead"*** (Acts 4:2). This highlights the ASSOCIATION between Jesus and the resurrection. The Pharisees and Sadducees did not agree theologically. The Sadducees dominated the alliance, and they denied the immortality of the soul and the resurrection from the dead. The Pharisees believed in the soul's immortality and the resurrection from the dead, and that Moses delivered these doctrines to the elders, who in turn handed them to their successors. The Sadducees rejected all these traditions and focused on the comforts of life.

The Jews held a general belief in the resurrection but had messianic overtones that focused on the end of the world. The Jews of Jesus' day thought Messiah meant revolution. They believed the Messiah would overthrow the foreign power of Rome and restore the Davidic kingdom. The Jews revolted many times over the years, but Rome eliminated each revolution and punished them. In AD66 war was declared by Rome, creating horrible consequences for the Jews. The threat of political disturbance upset the Sadducees, but their focus on materialism forced them into compliance and cooperation with Roman rule. The teaching and preaching of the apostles alarmed them because the resurrection, the Prince of life (Acts 3:15), and fulfilled prophecy were revolutionary ideas. This teaching and preaching contained the seed of political change. The alliance carried out their acts against the apostles because they could not allow this to continue.

Fusion

In the ASSOCIATION between Jesus and the resurrection is the idea of fusion. Fusion is the process or act of joining two or more things together to form one entity. Luke is radical in his proposal of this joining in our passage. The apostles preached ***"in Jesus the resurrection from the dead."*** They connected Jesus to the resurrection and the resurrection to Jesus. In the New Testament, Jesus and the resurrection cannot be divided. They form a single entity, fusion, and it is impossible to experience one without the other!

A major insight from our passage is the idea of something fixed that is a key in the fusion. The Greek word "en," translated ***in***, is small but profound. The King James Version translates it "through." The New King James translates it "in" as do most modern translations. The Greek word "en" is a primary preposition denoting a fixed position in place, time, or state. It can also indicate the instrument through which something happens. Each meaning is implied in our verse; however, its primary meaning is one of rest! This meaning is in contrast with two small words. "Ek" means "out of" or "from." "Eis" means "into" or "unto." These last two words are movement terms. "En" means "in" or "remaining in place."

The apostles were teaching and preaching that the ***resurrection from the dead*** was "in" and remains "in" the person of Jesus! The ***resurrection from the dead*** was not momentary for Jesus. Although God raised Jesus from the dead in a resurrection, everything about the resurrection continuously abides and rests in Jesus. The resurrection is intimately connected and identified with His person. When the apostle John began his presentation of Jesus in his Gospel account, he said, *"In Him was life"* (John 1:4). The Greek word "en," translated "in," is the same word in our passage. *"Life"* is fixed in *"Him."*

Peter preached a sermon to the Jews explaining Pentecost. He could not ignore the resurrection in his explanation. He cried, *"whom God raised up, having loosed the pains of death, because it was not possible that He should be held by it"* (Acts 2:24). Peter highlighted the Easter resurrection of Jesus and proposed the indwelling, fixed, resting, and consistent resurrected life working in Jesus. He explained what it was to be filled with the Spirit of God. His example was *"Jesus of Nazareth, a Man"* (Acts 2:22). This Man was indwelt with the life of the Spirit. Death in all its fullness was pictured as large fingers reaching out to trap and contain Jesus. Even though Jesus entered Hades and damnation, death could not hold Him. The roaring resurrection life of the Spirit of God permeated the entirety of Jesus. Death could not seize Him anymore than a pregnant woman can keep a baby in her womb. *"Pains of death"* means "birth pangs." Peter explained the resurrection was not a result of outside acts of God's magic but the inside presence of God's eternal nature and life. To be filled with the Spirit of God is to be filled with resurrection life.

Jesus was the *"firstborn from the dead"* (Colossians 1:18). He was the first man to be filled with the Spirit and nature of God. He had the nature of life, the resurrected life! This applies to us. We are His brothers (Hebrews 2:11). His life indwells us. Life bursts forth through our beings. It does not visit us at the second coming of Christ. Resurrected life is present tense and fixed in us. No wonder Jesus said, *"And whoever lives and believes in Me shall never die"* (John 11:26). Jesus continually told us that we "have" eternal life (John 3:16, 36; 4:14; 5:24; 6:40, 47). Eternal life is not received at the moment of resurrection but is fixed in Jesus, and Jesus is fixed in us.

The idea of "focused" is also contained in our statement. The resurrection was fixed in Jesus; therefore, it is focused on Jesus. Jesus is the resurrection. This focus is what irritated the alliance about the teaching and preaching of the apostles. They identified the resurrection with the person of Jesus. If the apostles taught the resurrection as the Pharisees did, without mentioning Jesus, the Sadducees would have tolerated them. The apostles never mentioned the resurrection without speaking of Jesus. The resurrection of Jesus was so real in their experience that they seldom spoke of Jesus without reference to the resurrection. Jesus and the resurrection were synonymous. Jesus equaled the resurrection, and the resurrection equaled Jesus and cannot be divided.

Some members of the Corinthian Church were confused about the resurrection. Paul wrote, **"But if there is no resurrection of the dead, then Christ is not risen"** (1Corinthians 15:13). It seemed some of them believed the resurrection of Jesus, but did not believe there was a resurrection from the dead. The resurrection from the dead was intimately connected to Jesus, and Jesus was intimately connected to the resurrection from the dead. To end one, the other would need to be abolished. He continued to explain that everything was focused on Jesus' resurrection. If Jesus were not raised from the dead, preaching was meaningless and faith is stupid. Paul continued with a long list of things that became untrue. If Jesus were not raised from the dead, we would be false witnesses and remaining in our sin. Those who died in Christ perished. **"We are of all men the most pitiable"** (1 Corinthians 15:14-19). But the truth is **"Christ is risen from the dead, and has become the firstfruits of those who have fallen asleep"** (1 Corinthians 15:20). **"For since by man came death, by Man also came the resurrection from the dead"** (1 Corinthians 15:21). Jesus is the *Man*!

This brings us to the next part of our investigation. Because the resurrection from the dead is "fixed" on Jesus, it is "focused" on Jesus. Because it is "focused" on Jesus, it is "fused" with Jesus. Jesus and the resurrection are the same! If you embrace Jesus, you embrace the resurrection. If you want to embrace the resurrection, you must embrace Jesus!

The multitudes surrounded Jesus. He politely told them that they did not come seeking truth; they came seeking free bread, because He had just fed five thousand men. He inquired about why they sought after food that perishes instead of food, *"which endures to everlasting life"* (John 6:27). The discussion then became a debate. The crowd wanted a sign and presented the suggestion that their forefathers ate manna in the desert. Jesus answered, *"Most assuredly, I say to you, Moses did not give you the bread from heaven, but My Father gives you the true bread from heaven. For the bread of God is He who comes down from heaven and gives life to the world"* (John 6:32-33). Jesus called Himself the nutrient for life, and there is no life found outside Him. He is life! He boldly pronounced, *"Most assuredly, I say to you, unless you eat the flesh of the Son of Man and drink His blood, you have no life in you. Whoever eats My flesh and drinks My blood has eternal life, and I will raise him up at the last day"* (John 6:53-54).

God fused the resurrection from the dead and Jesus together, and they became one union that cannot be separated. The details of the resurrection are of no concern. Our focus must be on Him. In the embrace and intimacy of His person, life and resurrection are naturally experienced, and there is no need to look elsewhere! As resurrected life roared through His being, because of the fullness of the Spirit, this life permeates our lives through the fullness of the Spirit of Jesus.

A reference to the *"tree of life"* is at the beginning and the end of the Scriptures. The *"tree of life"* is one of two named trees in the Garden of Eden. Humanity had free access to the *"tree of life"* but the fruit of the *"tree of knowledge of good and evil"* was not to be eaten (Genesis 2:9, 17). After their disobedience,

Adam and Eve were expelled from the garden (Genesis 3:22-24). God barred their access to the *"tree of life;"* not as a punishment but as an act of mercy because to eat of that tree would doom them to endless physical life in a fallen world.

In the Book of Revelation, John refers to the *"tree of life"* in three places (Revelation 2:7; 22:2, 14). His first reference contains a promise from Jesus. ***"To him who overcomes I will give to eat from the tree of life, which is in the midst of the Paradise of God"*** (Revelation 2:7). In his picture of the New Jerusalem, the river of life has the *"tree of life"* on either side (Revelation 22:2). Its leaves never fade, and its monthly fruits never fail. Food and medicine are supplied freely to all. Everyone will enjoy the highest possibilities of activity and blessedness.

The Greek word "xulon," translated *tree,* is used with wood for human violence, such as a cross, club, or stocks for the feet. In speaking to Nicodemus, Jesus used this image from the Old Testament. ***"And as Moses lifted up the serpent in the wilderness, even so must the Son of Man be lifted up, that whoever believes in Him should not perish but have eternal life"*** (John 3:14-15). Snakes bit the people of Israel, and they were dying. God commanded Moses to put a brazen serpent on a "xulon." Everyone who looked at the serpent would live. Jesus compared Himself to such an act. Paul said, ***"Christ has redeemed us from the curse of the law, having become a curse for us (for it is written, 'Cursed is everyone who hangs on a tree'*** (xulon)***"*** (Galatians 3:13).

Life is fused with Jesus, both before the fall of humanity and in the eternal realm. Is He not our resurrection in this present age as well? No one can approach Jesus without sensing life! Embracing Jesus means abundant life. Jesus said, ***"I am the resurrection and the life. He who believes in Me, though he may die, he shall live. And whoever lives and believes in Me shall never die. Do you believe this?"*** (John 11:25-26). Jesus does not give us life! He is life, and there is no life apart from Him, only death!

Part One: The Announced Resurrection

Resurrection from the dead is "fixed" in Jesus; therefore, it is "focused" on Jesus. Because it is "focused" on Jesus, it is "fused" with Jesus. Thus, the apostles proposed the only solution to death. They were not speaking exclusively of physical death but death in all its entanglements. Eternal damnation, present destruction of all good, ruination of relationships, and decaying of spiritual values are in death. Everything the opposite of life is found in death. Jesus is the only chance we have! Therefore, we must be "fixed" in Jesus. He must be our resting and constant abiding place. If we are "fixed" in Jesus, we must be "focused" on Jesus. We must have a single eye. He is our vision. If we are "focused on Jesus, we are "fused" with Jesus. We were created to be in oneness with Him. We become a single entity in His fullness. God and man become the Kingdom of Heaven, and they are also the "new creature" of the New Testament. The Christian life is an "us" relationship, not God alone or man alone. It is "we"! I must rest in Him!

Acts 4:2

RESURRECTION FACILITATOR

"Being greatly disturbed that they taught the people and preached in Jesus the resurrection from the dead" (Acts 4:2).

The Sadducees were **"*greatly disturbed*"** by the teaching and preaching of the apostles. **"*The priests, the captain of the temple, and the Sadducees*"** formed an alliance to stop the apostle's proclamation. Jerusalem was in Judea, and it presented the Jewish culture with the finest of the arts, schools of theology, and education for the children. Galilee was nothing like Jerusalem and had more Gentiles living there. Few, if any, scholars were training disciples in Galilee. The apostles were Jews, but they were from Galilee instead of Judea. The leaders of Israel labeled them **"*uneducated and untrained men*"** (Acts 4:13). These apostles were inferior on every level compared with the Sadducees, socially, educationally, and economically, and they posed little threat. Then why were these leaders irritated?

One reason, assumed and stated in these passages, was the apostle's AGGRESSIVENESS! The alliance put the apostles in jail for the night, and the next morning the council assembled to interrogate them. Their question was, **"*By what power or by what name have you done this?*"** (Acts 4:7). Peter was filled with the Spirit, and his answer focused on Jesus. **"*Now when they saw the boldness of Peter and John, and perceived that they were uneducated and untrained men, they marveled*"** (Acts 4:13).

Part One: The Announced Resurrection

After the crucifixion and resurrection of Jesus, these apostles were radically changed. They had fled at the approach of danger, and after the crucifixion they denied any connection with Jesus. They had walked with the resurrected Jesus for 40 days, and now without shrinking they showed their attachment to their risen Lord. During the seven to ten days after the ascension of Jesus and their experience of Pentecost, they **were continually in the temple praising and blessing God**. They boldly proclaimed the resurrection of Christ!

Peter's sermon on the Day of Pentecost declared his confidence and certainty about the words he spoke (Acts 2:14-16). The crowd was amazed as Peter proclaimed Jesus. As changed man, he did not debate or argue but testified boldly about what happened in his own life. His exhortation at Solomon's Porch was filled with unwavering certainty (Acts 3:12-26). This crowd that cried for Jesus' crucifixion was now captured by the presence of the risen Lord flowing in confidence through Peter.

This scene contains AFFIRMATION. The physical evidence of a miracle was indisputable. Luke repeatedly highlights this fact in his writing of this story. The beggar was crippled from birth, and he was greater than 40 years (Acts 4:22). He was lame from his mother's womb and was daily carried to beg at the temple gate called Beautiful (Acts 3:2). Everyone who came daily to the temple for the hour of prayer knew this beggar. When he received his healing, he entered the temple for the first time. He was leaping and praising God, and all the people saw him (Acts 3:9). They knew he was the beggar at the Gate Beautiful (Acts 3:10). This healed man held onto Peter and John as they were teaching and preaching (Acts 3:11). Possibly he too was put in jail for the night with the apostles (Acts 4:3). The rulers of Israel came together the following morning to deal with this situation (Acts 4:5-6). After Peter gave his explanation and testimony, the council **could say nothing against it**. This healed beggar stood with the apostles (Acts 4:14). As the council discussed this matter, they asked, *"What shall we do to these men? For indeed, that a notable miracle has been done through them is evident to all who dwell in Jerusalem, and we cannot deny it"* (Acts 4:16).

The people of Jerusalem showed AMENABILITY. During this time, the early church was using the temple for evangelism. Luke wrote, *"So continuing daily with one accord in the temple, and breaking bread from house to house, they ate their food with gladness and simplicity of heart, praising God and having favor with all the people"* (Acts 2:46-47). The lame beggar received his miracle amid of the temple crowd. Luke wrote, *"all the people saw him walking and praising God. Then they knew that it was he who sat begging alms at the Beautiful Gate of the temple; and they were filled with wonder and amazement at what had happened to him"* (Acts 3:9-10). The council's concern was that everyone dwelling in Jerusalem knew of the miracle and could not deny it. The alliance could not allow this news to spread further (Acts 4:16-17). This resistance describes the setting in which the apostles delivered the message of the risen Lord.

Is there any wonder why the alliance was so irritated? These apostles were no longer scattering in fear. The miracle of the lame beggar's healing could not be denied. Everyone in Jerusalem was talking about the healed man. He stood before the council. They could not deny the evidence of God's power in the risen Christ. The people of Jerusalem were open to the message of Christ. Evangelism happened and *"the Lord added to the church daily those who were being saved"* (Acts 2:47).

The resurrected Jesus is the explanation for all that was experienced in this story! This explanation is the reason the alliance was *"greatly disturbed."* They could tolerate the boldness of the apostles, and they could rejoice over the miracle of the lame beggar, but their difficulty was with the source being the resurrected Jesus. The language Luke used to describe this is *"they taught the people and preached in Jesus the resurrection from the dead"* (Acts 4:2). Everything about this is contained in the person of Jesus.

What is the content of the apostle's statement?

Firstborn

The word firstborn appears often in the New Testament in relationship to Jesus. Paul expressed it to the Romans, *"For whom He foreknew, He also predestined to be conformed to the image of His Son, that He might be the firstborn among many brethren"* (Romans 8:29). Paul indicated there is an abundant flow of God's loving heart, which causes us to make significant adjustments in our lives. The Spirit of God makes *"intercession for us with groaning which cannot be uttered"* (Romans 8:26). This intercession is always in agreement with the will of God for our lives (Romans 8:27), and it produces an abiding hope and knowledge that God brings all things under the domination of His love, causing everything to *"work together for good"* (Romans 8:28). Because He foreknew us in this manner, God focuses His redemptive power to make us like Jesus! Jesus is the prototype of all that God wants us to be! He is the *"Firstborn."*

Paul described Jesus as *"the firstborn over all creation"* (Colossians 1:15). He went further in his description by saying, *"the firstborn from the dead, that in all things He may have the preeminence"* (Colossians 1:18; also see Hebrews 1:6; Revelation 1:5). Jesus was the first man to come through death into the eternal state designed for all redeemed people. He was the first man to be filled with the Spirit of God, and He was the beginning of the New Covenant. As a man filled with the Spirit, He entered death and it could not hold Him (Acts 2:24). The powerful Spirit of God indwelt Jesus and flowed life through Him. He is the first man on the other side of the grave filled with the Spirit of

God. He is the first Spirit sourced Man who experiences the resurrection body of the New Covenant.

The apostles proclaimed the same message. They *"taught the people and preached in Jesus the resurrection from the dead."* All God's dreams for us are in Jesus. Our eternal future in heaven is in Jesus. He is not merely the agent who makes provision for us, and He is not the supply clerk who grants our requests. Jesus is everything we need. What is the will of God for our lives? The answer is "everything you see in Jesus!" We see the content of "resurrection from the dead" in Jesus.

We must highlight that everyone is raised from the dead, Christians and unbelievers, to avoid any misunderstanding (John 5:29). Jesus indicated there is a *"resurrection of life"* and *"resurrection of condemnation."* The problem of eternity for believers and unbelievers is not living forever. The problem is quality of life. Everyone will live forever, but those only in Jesus will be like Him!

No wonder the Sadducees were irritated. The apostles preached that there was a *resurrection from the dead*, but they took the resurrection to a new level in Jesus. Jesus is the Man who had already experienced the eternal state, quality of life, and intimacy that the Trinity God wants for us. They *"taught the people and preached in Jesus* (the Firstborn) *the resurrection from the dead."*

Frontiersman

We must not overlook a second factor, and its understanding comes from this short expression in the Greek text. The apostles presented two basic ideas. Jesus relates to the resurrection in two ways. He rose from the dead, and He is the "Firstborn" of all that God wants for us. He has proved that we can also enter into all that happened in His resurrection. He is the "Frontiersman" of all God's dreams for us.

Part One: The Announced Resurrection

A variety of words express this reality. The content of this idea is in the Greek compound word "archegos" made of "arche" meaning "beginning to rule" and "argo" meaning "to lead." The word is used four times in the New Testament (Acts 3:15; 5:31; Hebrews 2:10; 12:2). Originator, founder, leader, chief, first, and prince are words used to translate "archegos." However, we must distinguish these words from the idea of being the cause. We can be the cause of something and not the beginning. "Arche' identifies the founder as the first cause, ruler, or dispenser.

Jesus began something new in the resurrection. Although the Pharisees proposed the idea of the resurrection, they were unrealistic and vague. The Old Testament idea of "Sheol" was the abode for the dead, a shadowy place of soul sleeping. The resurrection of Jesus brought an abrupt end to this vagueness. The disciples experienced the resurrected presence of Jesus for forty days (Acts 1:3). They could now teach and preach with authenticity the reality of eternal existence.

A part of the apostles' teaching and preaching that irritated the alliance was their description of Jesus as **"the Prince** (Archegos) *of life"* (Acts 3:15). Life happened in Jesus in the resurrection, but the resurrection did not produce Jesus. In the fullness of the Spirit, Jesus originated the resurrection, and He caused it to happen for humanity. Everything began with Jesus.

The writer of the Book of Hebrews described what the Triune God did in Jesus. He said, **"For it was fitting for Him, for whom are all things and by whom are all things, in bringing many sons to glory, to make the captain** (archegos) *of their salvation perfect through sufferings"* (Hebrews 2:10). That verse is a bold statement of reality! What God did in Jesus fits the nature and character of God, and it is not a surprise. God wants many sons, not one, two, or a dozen. By what method does God achieve His dream? The Greek word "ago," translated *"to make,"* meaning "to lead or bring forth." The Greek word translated *"captain"* is our word "archegos." The Triune God led Jesus into suffering, and His suffering enabled us to become sons of God. In other words, the fullness of the Spirit in Jesus brought Him to death and resurrection. He originated the experience of the New Covenant that we might be intimate with God. He is the first in this new category not the cause of it. What is originated in Him is so powerful that those of us who experience it are called His brothers (Hebrews 2:11). Jesus produced the possibility for us to be sons of God.

Foremost

The phrase *"in Jesus the resurrection from the dead"* proposes one last idea. Jesus was the first human being to experience *"the resurrection from the dead."* The reality of the resurrection is Jesus. In the fullness of the Spirit, Jesus established the possibility for us to experience the resurrection just as He did. Jesus, the Firstborn, began the resurrection, and He made it possible for all humanity. Everything God did in the resurrected Jesus, He wants to do in you. Because Jesus is the originator, He is indeed the "Foremost."

Paul made a strong statement in his description of Jesus to the Colossians. He proclaimed the resurrected Jesus as King of the Kingdom and linked various elements to prove this. Jesus *"is the image of the invisible God"* (Colossians 1:15). In the fullness of God's nature, humanity becomes the revelation of God. Jesus is *"the firstborn over all creation"* (Colossians 1:15). He became the "second Adam" for the humanity. After all, it is *"through Him and for Him"* that creation occurred. This creation includes all that we can conceive and everything in heaven and everything on Earth, those things visible and invisible. The thrones, dominions, principalities, and powers come from Him (Colossians 1:16). I say this to you that you might understand, *"He is before all things and in Him all things consist"* (Colossians 1:17).

Part One: The Announced Resurrection

Jesus is creator, and we acclaim His preeminence, but this is not the base establishing it among us. Jesus ***"is the beginning, the firstborn from the dead"*** (Colossians 1:18). He was the first human being, through the fullness of the Spirit, to march into the realm of death in its full definition. God then raised Jesus from the dead and established the full definition of the resurrection through the fullness of the Spirit. The Trinity God made Jesus the King of the Kingdom of Heaven. He is our King, the first man of the New Covenant, the "Firstborn." Jesus is preeminent because He blazed the trail for all humanity to follow, the "Frontiersman." Now Jesus is "Foremost," the King of the Kingdom. What a privilege to be intimate with Him and filled with His Spirit!

Acts 4:3

IMPRISONING THE TRUTH

"And they laid hands on them, and put them in custody until the next day, for it was already evening" (Acts 4:3).

Luke makes a transitional statement in one brief paragraph (Acts 4:1-4). He highlights the results of Peter's exhortation at Solomon's Porch (Acts 3:12-26). In the rest of chapter four, Luke establishes the platform of the alliance's actions against the apostles (Acts 4:5-37), which introduces the first persecution of the early church. The difficulty lay not with the populace of Jerusalem but with the leadership of the temple, the alliance. The first four verses contain the following sections: THE ALLIANCE (Acts 4:1), THE AGGRAVATION (Acts 4:2), THE ARREST (Acts 4:3), and THE AFTERMATH (Acts 4:4-37).

Our verse describes the alliance's actions and holds many underlying truths. If you casually read this verse, you may not see it, but it is ready to be revealed to the seeking heart! These truths are "Imprisoning the Truth," "Illuminating the Truth," and "Independent Truth." For this study we are focusing on "Imprisoning the Truth." The word "truth" is not found in any of these verses, which may cause you to question our heavy emphasis on it. Yet in the previous verse, the main problem that causes the alliance's disturbance is Jesus (Acts 4:2), therefore, we declare Him as "the Truth" (John 14:6).

The alliance's response to "the Truth" follows the standard

Part One: The Announced Resurrection

pattern of spiritual warfare. Truth wages no war, has no special weapons, and defines no particular strategy. Truth does not defend, puff out its chest, or increase it warriors. Truth does not yell louder to drown deception, and it does not paint itself with alluring imagery to entice. Truth is simply a state of being! Jesus, the Truth, revealed this simple reality in His life. He did not defend Himself, and He did not depend on His followers to deliver Him. Jesus, the Truth, was content to allow deception to do whatever it desired, knowing His state of existence and reality would be forever. He will win! He was crucified on the cross with clouds of destruction rising from the stomping feet of the military's deception, yet Truth lived on in triumph.

"The truth shall make you free" (John 8:32) is declared again in our passage. Truth does not need to wage war because it is a state of existence that cannot be defeated. When Truth appears, falsehood melts, and deception cannot stand in its presence. Anyone who embraces Truth will experience immediate liberation, the trap of deception released, prisons of non-truth opened, and war immediately stopped. These experiences are Truth!

None of thee experiences is true for deception. Deception must always defend, trick, and attack. When Truth appears, deception will always aggressively act, distract the listeners, and move to silence the voice of truth. Deception heightens its imagery to overshadow Truth. This resistance is a picture of our passage. Truth appeared and **taught the people and preached in Jesus the resurrection from the dead** (Acts 4:2). The Spirit of Jesus, through the apostles, confronted this Jewish crowd in this simple presentation of truth. Deception could not allow this teaching and preaching to continue. The alliance (deception) rushed in and **"laid hands on them, and put them in custody until the next day, for it was already evening"** (Acts 4:3). When Truth appears, deception attacks!

This picture appears repeatedly in the Scriptures. John the

Baptist was amid revival. Jerusalem, all Judea, and the region around the Jordan experienced John's ministry (Matthew 3:5). Herod, the tetrarch, came to see the prophet. John boldly proclaimed the truth and rebuked him for his adulterous affair with Herodias, his brother's wife (Luke 3:19). This exposure became a national scandal. In his Gospel Luke wrote Herod's response and stated his unique perspective of his action. **"But Herod the tetrarch, being rebuked by him concerning Herodias, his brother Philip's wife, and for all the evils which Herod had done, also added this, above all, that he shut John up in prison"** (Luke 3:19-20).

We can only imagine the evil things **Herod had done**. His father, Herod the Great, was responsible for the slaughter of all baby boys in Bethlehem and the surrounding district (Matthew 2:16). He was filled with a self-induced insanity that he must have passed on to his son. Luke did not list all his evil deeds, but he highlights this one act above them all. Herod *shut John up in prison*. The Greek word "katekleio," translated *shut up*, is a compound word. "Kata" refers to "down," and "kleio" means "to shut." Herod "shut down" John. The action of Herod was physical, but the implication was far beyond the physical. John the Baptist was the voice of Truth to Herod as God spoke directly to him. Herod rejected the Truth by "shutting it down." The focus is not on a physical act (although there); it is on the attitude of the heart. Rejection happened in the core of Herod's being.

The alliance did the same thing in our passage. A physical action took place when they put Peter and John in jail until the next day. They wanted to silence them permanently but were afraid of the apostles' popularity. They threatened them not to speak the truth about Jesus ever again (Acts 4:17-21). The heart of their sin is not in persecuting the apostles but in their rejection of the truth. The heart of their sin is not in their false imprisonment of Peter and John, but in their stubborn hearts that rebelled against the Truth. They imprisoned the Truth!

Part One: The Announced Resurrection

Personal Perception

The stubborn rejection in the hearts of the alliance was not based on misunderstanding, lack of comprehension, or ignorance. They knew exactly what they were doing. You might argue that their culture led to their lack of understanding because their forefathers so twisted the prophetic truth of the Old Testament and perverted the Messianic picture. Jesus was the opposite of all they expected the Anointed One to be. Even though they had been taught this from early childhood, their argument was weak. The training we receive in our childhood does not relieve us from responsibility in our adult lives. The thundering truth of God coming to our lives daily should correct the fallacies of our training. What about the abundant prevenient grace of God that comes to a man's spirit to correct him and point him to Christ? Paul made forceful statements to the Romans on this subject. God planted a revelation of Himself in human life and in the creation around us. Therefore, the outward and inward revelation of God leaves all humanity without excuse (Romans 1:19-20).

This revelation was true for the pagan world, but it was much more for the alliance! Think of the insight offered to them through prophecies and of the privilege they had being witnesses to the fulfillment of those prophecies. They had waited to hear the voice proclaim the wisdom of God to them but did not recognize it. How could they have witnessed Christ's physical death and its results and not questioned their rebellion? The veil of the temple was torn from top to bottom, the Earth quaked, and the rocks were split (Matthew 27:51). Did this not merit their investigation into the Truth? Appearances of resurrected saints in the area around Jerusalem would leave us to think this should have caused doubts about the teachings against the resurrection from the dead (Matthew 27:52-53).

So many events experienced by these rebellious Jews cause us to wonder how they could miss the Messiah. They witnessed the continued ministry of the Holy Spirit at Pentecost in the temple (Acts 2:1-4). Countless miracles continued through the apostles, which gave evidence and validity to everything Jesus did. Now we come to this occasion. The lame beggar stood healed in front of them (Acts 4:14). How could they deny this? They thought Peter and John were responsible for this, but these apostles refused to take the credit saying the resurrected Jesus healed this man (Acts 4:10)! God opened the door to faith as wide as possible for them. What else could or should He do to include them?

These rebellious hearted Jews took the Truth and "shut it down." In other words there was no additional revelation they could be given, and no other appearances or miracles that would change their point of view. God gave them everything necessary to bring them to faith, but they voluntarily choose to put the apostles in jail and close the voice of Truth speaking to them.

Is this not also true of our lives? What else can God do to convince you? How many times does He need to speak to you or intervene in your life? If you list the sins of your life, would not the "above all this" sin be your lack of response to Him now? Perhaps you and I are in the position where we do not deserve one more moment of revelation. We have had enough! The time is to break down the walls of resistance and not be distracted, ignoring, or silencing His voice. Now is the moment of Truth, and we must respond! The writer of the Book of Hebrews said it is, **"Today"** (Hebrews 3:7, 15; 4:7).

Perpetual Proclamation

The alliance imprisoned the truth, but the patience of God was continuous and His grace was amazing. Everything about their resistance from the perspective of God's grace shows us this. It seems as if God ignored their work against the apostles. He did not punish them or withdraw from them. He aggressively planned and maneuvered how He would invade their attempts to block His revealing grace, and He did not seem to have a deadline in His determination. He perpetually ministered, wooed, and called them to Himself.

The Jews were the most blessed people of the world. God chose them to be the nation through which He would bring the Redeemer. They were the closest to His birth, were the ones who experienced the fulfillment of the prophecies of incarnation, and knew the testimony of the angelic hosts. They handled the symbols of the Messiah's coming daily. Everything they did in temple worship pointed to the Messianic presence. The herald of the Messiah, John the Baptist, got their attention as he announced Jesus' arrival. They were exposed to the fruitful ministry of Jesus as miracles and revelation freely flowed from Him. Would you not think their rejection would cause God to withdraw His invitation to them? Did they not imprison the Truth? They tried to destroy and eliminate the revelation God sent to them (Jesus) through the crucifixion.

But God did not stop His amazing grace for them! Pentecost happened in their presence. God came into the temple. They were among hundreds of Jews who witnessed this amazing fulfillment of prophecy (Acts 2:16-21). Surely they knew of the hundreds of transformed lives and the continual growth of the Church. The continuation of miracles through the apostles was a duplication of Jesus, which certainly caused them to wonder. Now, Peter was again proclaiming the resurrection of the dead in Jesus. Would they listen? No! They again imprisoned the Truth.

The alliance captured the apostles and put them in jail (Acts 4:4) for the evening. Until the next day, there was no decision about what they would do with them. God manipulated the alliance's circumstances of rejection, allowed them to sleep on the revelation He had already given them, and gave them time to reconsider. The following morning when they gathered to interrogate the apostles, Peter was used by God to give a powerful witness, forcing the rebellious Jews to acknowledge the presence and influence of Jesus (Acts 4:13). The healed beggar was with the apostles giving his testimony! The council dismissed the apostles that they might discuss the problem. When the apostles returned, the council threatened them, and then had to listen to another testimony. Will it ever end? The prevenient grace of God will not be silenced. God will not be pressured by their rejection. His love is strong, and His nature is unrelenting and cannot be dismissed. Will the love of Jesus continue to flow until the moment of destruction? Will God ever wipe His hands in disgust and judgment? Does His mercy endure forever (Psalms 136)?

Prolonged Process

In the idea of prolonged process, everything we have already talked about is restated, but we must add one special thought to its reality. All the evidence that declares the truth will be proclaimed without hesitation repeatedly in the presence of all. In fact, Paul declared, **"Therefore God also has highly exalted Him and given Him the name which is above every name, that at the name of Jesus every knee should bow, of those in heaven, and of those on earth, and of those under the earth, and that every tongue should confess that Jesus Christ is Lord, to the glory of God the Father"** (Philippians 2:9-11). This declaration removes any supposition that God will allow the proclamation of the Truth to be removed. Everyone, in all generations regardless of his or her location, will be forced to acknowledge the Truth. This acknowledgment will not be forced by stronghold tactics but will be forced by the indisputable reality of the Truth. All humanity will eventually be convinced that Jesus is Lord. The

Trinity God will not be deterred from the proclamation of the Truth.

God is not broadcasting the message of Truth around the world for the general population to hear. His amazing grace is selective toward each person. We can see this clearly in our story. The Trinity God is concerned and in love with this alliance. He tailors His grace to custom fit those of the alliance. He adjusts His grace to fit their schedule, their culture, their prejudices, their theology, and their physical circumstances. Was God not involved in the timing of the apostles' arrest? Although He may not have caused the delay in their interrogation, He certainly used it for the furtherance of His "grace expression"!

Peter and John interacted with the lame beggar at the ninth hour, the hour of prayer (Acts 3:1) and the hour of sacrifice. This hour attracted the largest crowd of the day in the temple. This miracle extended the opportunity for the exhortation at Solomon's Porch during the late afternoon, the three o'clock hour. By the time Peter finished with his exhortation and the alliance began to react to the response of the crowd, the council's meeting was completed. They met daily to deal with any problems that might have arisen in the temple. This meeting time is why the interrogation was detained until the following day. The influence of the message, the testimony of the healed beggar, and the commitment of the crowd were still valid. This ministry was not a momentary emotional stir. A night in jail did not weaken the force of the grace of God flowing through the apostles. It became stronger! This was God's thought out plan for these particular individuals.

The Trinity God is doing the same for you. His grace is designed for your circumstances. He knows how your mind thinks, your emotions respond, and your will is determined. He is so in love with you that He shapes His grace to give the maximum influence on you. Do not miss the embrace of His love! Do not resist and imprison the Truth!

Acts 4:3

ILLUMINATING TRUTH

"And they laid hands on them, and put them in custody until the next day, for it was already evening" (Acts 4:3).

The impact of Truth is immeasurable. I discovered this repeatedly as a mathematics student when I could not find the right answer to a problem. Then someone came with "truth," about one aspect of the calculation and changed everything. It proves true in mechanics. I spent hours trying to get my truck started when a mechanic came along with "truth" and in a few moments I was driving down the road. This is consistently so in the realm of electronics. I can search for hours to correct a problem, but when someone or something reveals "truth" the problem is eliminated.

Would this apply to human life? Would you agree that the greatest need of the human being is "Truth?" The difficulty with people is our ability to reject truth. Paul had a close relationship with the Galatians, and he wrote to them with sincerity that he knew they would be willing to pluck out their eyes and give them to him (Galatians 4:15). Then he said, **"Have I therefore become your enemy because I tell you the truth?"** (Galatians 4:16). Truth is so illuminating that we resist its clarity.

"Truth" is constant exposure, and it promotes consistent change. Then why would anyone want to come to church weekly and be confronted with "truth"? That "truth" will always reveal the wrong, highlighting all my flaws and faults. If I am open and seeking, I will embrace the "truth," but if I am self-centered and closed, I will reject the "truth." Paul spoke of the pagans as those, ***"who exchanged the truth of God for a lie, and worshiped and served the creature rather than the Creator"*** (Romans 1:25). The only way they could "exchange the truth" was whether they possessed the truth. In fact, Paul said, ***"Because, although they knew God, they did not glorify Him as God"*** (Romans 1:21).

In the Gospel of John (chapters 14-16), Jesus talked to His disciples about the heart of the New Covenant, the fullness of the Holy Spirit, the Spirit of Jesus indwelling the believer. Jesus called Him ***"The Spirit of Truth"*** (John 14:17), and He was definite about His purpose. ***"However, when He, the Spirit of truth, has come, He will guide you into all truth; for He will speak on His own authority, but whatever He hears He will speak; and He will tell you things to come"*** (John 16:13). As Christians, we are continually exposed to "truth;" it indwells us! Every action, thought, and motive always comes under the light of Truth, bringing consistent correction and change. In this state no one becomes superior and capable of judging others.

All are under the shaping fingers of "Truth."

This is the pattern of our passage. The early Church had a strong influence in Jerusalem. At the outset of Pentecost, three thousand Jews were filled with the Spirit of Jesus (Acts 2:41). Luke does not report numbers or time until this passage. He said, ***"And the Lord added to the church daily those who were being saved"*** (Acts 2:47). The Spirit of Jesus used Peter's exhortation and the miracle of the lame beggar to attract five thousand men (Acts 4:4). But this does not seem to be the motivation of the alliance. What disturbed them was that the apostles ***taught the people and preached in Jesus the resurrection from the dead*** (Acts 4:2). It is significant that the Greek verbs "didasko" and "katagello," translated ***taught*** and ***preached*** respectfully, are each significantly in the infinitive mood. Infinitive mood means they are adverbs stating the purpose of the main verb *came upon*, located in the previous verse, (Acts 4:1). In other words, what ***greatly disturbed*** them and caused them to come upon the apostles was "Truth!" Their disturbance was not church growth, crowds, or proposing a resurrection. They were disturbed by "truth" of *"in Jesus the resurrection from the dead"* (Acts 4:2).

I want to offer you a proposition for our study. A series of connected thoughts will bring us to a proper conclusion. Actions exposed by truth expose the person who exposes the judgment.

Truth Exposes Actions

The feet of the alliance are pounding the corridor of the temple, rushing to capture and silence the apostles and the truth that they are teaching and preaching. This alliance is no small crowd, ***the priests, the captain of the temple, and the Sadducees*** united. Although they intended to capture only the two apostles, they had to face the crowd of five thousand gathered. The alliance came ready to defend and protect, but the crowd and the apostles offered no resistance. The decisive action of the alliance was quickly accomplished. ***And they laid hands on them, and put them in custody until the next day, for it was already evening*** (Acts 4:3).

Was the alliance's action right or wrong? Were they justified or condemned for their action? Should we support or disapprove what they did? The alliance was not stepping outside the boundaries of their jurisdiction. They were required by their positions in the temple to disperse any crowd that may propose a threat to the purpose of this structure, and they were obeying the laws established by temple policy. No doubt was in the minds of the people that the deed of the alliance was correct.

The deed of the alliance was not the standard for measuring right or wrong, and this was the difficulty. The action acceptable by law was exposed by truth as wrong. Legalism is never a guide to purity and holiness. We must judge all actions according to truth! What is truth? That was the discussion between Pilate and Jesus. *"What is truth?"* (John 18:38) was the raging question in the heart and mind of Pilate. His main concern was Jesus' position. *"Are you the King of the Jews?"* was his question (John 18:33). Jesus quizzed him about the source of his question. Was this a personal concern for truth or just a curiosity spawned by rumors he heard? Pilate was not a Jew and had no concern, but Jesus pointed out that he should be concerned. He spoke of a kingdom not of this world, and it affected Pilate's life and destiny. Pilate demanded an answer to his question, *"'Are you a king then?' Jesus answered, 'You say rightly that I am a king. For this cause I was born, and for this cause I have come into the world, that I should bear witness to the truth. Everyone who is of the truth hears My voice.' Pilate said to Him, 'What is truth?'"* (John 18:37-38).

Everything Pilate did to Jesus appeared right, and the Law said he was right. His position required him to make decisions to protect the Roman Empire and maintain peace with the Jews. To crucify someone who proposed an unauthorized kingly position would be right! But it was not about the Law; it was about truth. Then what is the answer to Pilate's question, *"What is truth?"* (John 18:38). All deeds must be judged not by the actions contained in the deed, but by how they appeared in light of Jesus.

This judgment is true for our lives. How easy it is to justify our actions as right, especially if we think we are in our rights. We operate within the laws of our temple structure. Could the disturbance within our temple be the presence of Jesus coming to bring light to our actions? Maybe I have been so right in my actions that I am wrong! How can I know? All my actions must be exposed by "Truth"! Will I allow Jesus to determine my life? Instead of bringing an accomplished deed to Him for approval, will I allow Him to prompt the deed? Can He, "the Truth" source my deed?

Actions Exposed by Truth Expose the Person

A large group of men, called the alliance, rushed down the temple courtyard at Solomon's Porch to capture the apostles. They were disturbed about a healed beggar, five thousand men yielded to Jesus, and the proclamation, *"in Jesus the resurrection from the dead"* (Acts 4:2). The **priests** of the temple administered the sacrifices for this day. The ninth hour of prayer was also the hour of sacrifice. **The Sadducees** had a vested interest in all the activities of the temple, and they could not afford any upset with the Roman authority. Within the boundaries of the law and the duty of the alliance, the setting was perfect for their attack!

On the other hand, Jesus, the Truth, exposed their actions. The alliance immediately revealed their motives and hidden agenda. They revealed who they were in their hearts. Their actions were seen as wrong because their hearts were wrong.

Jesus uses this approach in the Sermon on the Mount, validating the Scriptures (Matthew 5:17-20). Twice He highlighted His focus not on destroying the Scriptures but on fulfilling them. God took the dreams of His heart and wrote them into the Scriptures. Then He leapt from His sovereign position and yielded Himself to the Scriptures. He allowed the Scriptures to be the craftsman that shaped and determined His living. Jesus is not only the fulfillment of the Scriptures, but He is the truth of the Scriptures!

The leaders of Israel were academic in their approach to the Scriptures. Their conclusion was, *"You shall not murder, and whoever murders will be in danger of the judgment"* (Matthew 5:21). However, the moment the Written Word interacts with Jesus, the Living Word, Truth is revealed. You must not simply abstain from murder, but you cannot even hate. The abstention focuses on the activity of the deed, and the second focuses on the motive of the heart. The law said, *"You shall not commit adultery"* (Matthew 5:27). The heart of lust surfaces when the Truth becomes involved. Specific laws governing the right to divorce existed, but when Jesus, the Truth, appeared the motive of the heart became visible. The same is true when swearing falsely (Matthew 5:33). Honesty depended on the object a person swore on. How ridiculous! Integrity is not about objects or ceremonies of swearing, but it is about Truth indwelling your inner being. The leaders of Israel could tolerate revenge (Matthew 5:38), but it had to be administered within the boundaries of the law. But Jesus, the Truth, reveals the attitude of revenge. Truth is in being sons of God and having His heart. He calls us to *"be perfect, just as your Father in heaven is perfect"* (Matthew 5:48).

The alliance felt fully justified in silencing the apostles and putting them in jail for the night. They threatened them not to preach in Jesus' name, but the apostles would not follow their instructions and had to bear the consequences of their misdeeds. But everything changes when you see this in the light of Truth. Truth exposed the alliance's actions and the motive for those actions, which unmasked who they were. Those attending the temple might have applauded the alliance for keeping them safe, but Jesus appeared and uncovered the attitude of the alliance, which caused their wrongful actions. Luke was specific about this in writing that the disturbance of the alliance was about the teaching and preaching *"in Jesus the resurrection from the dead"* (Acts 4:2). These rebellious men could tolerate the teaching of the resurrection, the special group meetings, and the distraction of one miracle. But Jesus, the Truth, brought revelation they could not abide.

Do you want the truth about your actions, your

circumstances, and your life? Will you risk coming to Jesus? His revelation is not condemning; instead it is healing! He does not want to destroy you; instead, He wants to fulfill you. You can trust Him!

Actions Exposed by Truth Expose the Person Who Exposes Judgment

The alliance put the apostles in jail because it was already evening. The council met daily in a designated area, but they had already dismissed for the day. The next morning they gathered in full force. The focus of the interrogation was, *"By what power or by what name have you done this?"* (Acts 4:7). Peter answered their inquiry without hesitation. He boldly clarified the source of the miracle. The healed beggar stood with them stopping a denial of the miracle (Acts 4:14). All of Jerusalem discussed the many miracles, and they could not be dismissed as inconsequential (Acts 4:16).

Peter was extremely bold! He realized that they were judged (anakrino) for a good deed to a helpless man. The problem the alliance had was how this miracle was done. Peter said without hesitation that it was *"by the name of Jesus Christ of Nazareth, whom you crucified, whom God raised from the dead"* (Acts 4:10). He highlighted the presence of the resurrected Lord. The Greek word "anakrino," translated *judged*, is from the emphatic "an" and "krino" that means "to judge, discern, examine, or question." Peter said that this good deed must be judged by the source, Jesus *raised from the dead*.

You might wonder who was on trial here. The alliance thought they had Peter and John on trial, and Peter and John knew that it was the council facing trial. This is characterizes Jesus. When He appears, He exposes every action, reveals every person, and makes known the source of his or her life. The action of the deed does not determine judgment. The position of the person does not determine the judgment, but the presence of the living Lord exposes and judges. He does not judge the deed but the source of the inner heart! If Jesus is not the source of the deed, it is not righteous.

The following is the procedure and consistent pattern I desire for my life. The action of every deed must come under the scrutiny of Jesus, the Truth. I do not speak about laws or even statements Jesus may have said in the New Testament, but I speak of the Living Word revealed in the Written Word. Jesus must be present. The moment He appears He will expose the heart of my deed. Is He the source of my life? Am I a living product of His flow and resource? This flow requires intimacy with Him. My life and His life must become one. Judgment is in Him, the Truth!

Acts 4:3-4

INDEPENDENT TRUTH

"And they laid hands on them, and put them in custody until the next day, for it was already evening. However, many of those who heard the word believed; and the number of men came to be about five thousand" (Acts 4:3-4).

"The priests, the captain of the temple, and the Sadducees" (Acts 4:1) formed the alliance. They came to Solomon's Porch as a group of resistance. The main verb of this sentence describes their action. They ***"came upon"*** (ephistemi) the apostles, which can be interpreted as positive or negative. In our passage, it is a definite attack on the apostles. The alliance was ***"greatly disturbed"*** and ***"they laid hands on them, and put them in custody until the text day"*** (Acts 4:3). They revealed their attitude by their clearly expressed threats, which they gave to the apostles in the rest of the chapter.

The three opening verses of this chapter present a shocking interruption to the positive flow of God's movement through the early Church. The believers had been accepting and shown favor from the people of Jerusalem (Acts 2:47). The response of the alliance was the first hint of persecution! What happened?

Our next verse begins with ***"However"*** (Acts 4:4) that is a translation of the Greek word "de." This Greek word is a contrasted conjunction primarily translated as "but." Luke contrasts these aggressive attacks from the alliance with the

Part One: The Announced Resurrection

movement of God on the Jews. He writes, *"**However, many of those who heard the word believed; and the number of the men came to be about five thousand**"* (Acts 4:4). Luke did not give the details that other Gospel writers gave, and he does not include a call to commitment from Peter to the crowd. Peter's exhortation is interrupted by the attack of the alliance. The Jews gathered at Solomon's Porch have been under the leadership of Israel for years, and they participated in the crucifixion. The Jewish leadership came to arrest Peter and John, and they dispersed the crowd with a sense of disapproval, placing condemnation on all Peter had preached. ***"However,"*** five thousand men still responded to the Gospel message. No altar call existed, so how did they become believers? They must have taken great initiative to become a part of the early Church.

This contrast is made repeatedly in the Scriptures. Although it may not be seen in the grammar of the sentence, it is definitely shown in the picture painted by the writer. For instance, angels filled the sky with the announcement of the Christ Child's birth. The shepherds spread the news over the surrounding countryside. Wise men traveled for two years to find the new King and announced His birth to Jerusalem. King Herod ***was troubled, and all Jerusalem with him*** (Matthew 2:3). He had a private interview with the wise men and sent them to Bethlehem to find the new King. When they did not report to him, he was angry. In a demonic rage, he pronounced an edict ordering the destruction of all baby boys two and younger. The King was angry, baby boys were dead, and families were mourning. *"**Now** (de) (however) **when Herod was dead**"* (Matthew 2:19), God continued His redemptive program. Joseph and Mary brought Jesus back to Nazareth from Egypt. Thirty years later John the Baptist appeared on the banks of the Jordan River, and the ministry of Jesus announced the New Covenant. What a contrast!

Jesus experienced the fullness of the Holy Spirit *"alighting upon Him"* (Matthew 3:16). This Spirit brought Jesus (was responsible) to the wilderness, apparently to test Him. The spiritual war between God and Satan was severe. For 40 days and nights, the battle raged with all thought of food pushed aside. When the battle lulled, the body of Jesus screamed for food. The devil leaped to the occasion with temptation, ***"If you are the Son of God, command that these stones become bread"*** (Matthew 4:3). When body drives rage, and objectivity is gone, the ability to make a rational decision is absent, and you might be destined to submit to those drives. ***"But*** (de) (however) ***He answered and said"*** (Matthew 4:4). Jesus fell into the arms of the Father seeking to evaluate and discern the mind of God. ***"He answered"*** is a translation of the Greek word "apokrimo." It indicates a change in location to evaluate and discern. The Father gave Jesus insight about what to do!

The complete picture is never one of dismay or distress. Despite what you may experience, there is a great ***"However."*** The darkness of the storm must not hide the reality of the ***"However."*** Circumstances can be devastating, and your spirit can be crushed, but hope is not lost. In our passage, we do not see the complete picture of the alliance's attack. Despite their mighty force, five thousand men still came to know Jesus!

A description of the alliance presents a force you would not want to confront. They represented the POLITICAL POWER of their hour. The government of Israel rests in this alliance and their attack on the apostles. The next day, Peter and John were interrogated by ***"Annas the high priest, Caiaphas, John, and Alexander, and as many as were of the family of the high priest"*** (Acts 4:6). This elite group was in addition to ***"rulers, elders, and scribes"*** (Acts 4:5). Peter recognized this and addressed them as, ***"Rulers of the people and elders of Israel"*** (Acts 4:8). These apostles, low-ranking fishermen, could not compete with the political power represented by this group.

Part One: The Announced Resurrection

The alliance represented the council of Israel, and they were the PRONOUNCEMENT POWER of their hour. The power of life and death rested in the alliance, and they were the decision-making body that would determine the fate of the apostles. Peter and John were captured by the alliance and brought before the council. After hearing Peter's report ***they had commanded them to go aside out of the council, they conferred among themselves*** (Acts 4:15). The decision about the apostles' fate rested in the hand of the council, and there was no one else to consult.

Everything we have discussed thus far would eliminate all hope, but above all this the alliance controlled the PRAYER POWER. The religious power was in their hands, and they could ban a person from all religious contact with God. All access to sacrifices, proper prayer, and any association with the temple worship were in their control. If God's blessing was on Israel, and you were banned from that fellowship, how would you know God's blessings? With such power residing in the alliance, what chance do two lowly fishermen have? But Luke thunders forth with ***"However"***! This is not the complete story. However, much stress is on us, we must look beyond our circumstance. Amid the spiritual battle, we must raise our heads and see the truth! Five thousand men gave their lives to Jesus!

The cross of Jesus is the greatest picture of this truth. The two disciples on the Emmaus Road were filled with distress and disappointment, and they did not recognize the resurrected Lord. As they walked with the unknown man, they expressed their dismay openly. The hope of deliverance was overcome with ***how the chief priests and our rulers delivered Him to be condemned to death, and crucified Him*** (Luke 24:20). Hope was gone. ***"However,"*** (de) (but) the resurrected Lord was walking with them! This is the picture of Kingdom relationship. This relationship is the cross style!

The Principle of the Cross

Life is found in death! I know that it sounds ridiculous, but it is true! In fact, life is found only in death, and it is the fundamental truth of the cross style that must never be discarded. Any attempt to live outside of death is futile. What a strange message. Jesus pounded this message daily to His disciples during the last six months of His ministry. His call was ***"If anyone desires to come after Me, let him deny himself, and take up his cross, and follow me. For whoever desires to save his life will lose it, and whoever loses his life for My sake will find it"*** (Matthew 16:24-25). The word *"anyone"* eliminates the exclusion of anyone! *"Desires"* (thelo) is the deep heart's cry of our system and expresses the focus of our being. God plants the desire there, and it is a part of the creation of our lives. We are destined with this longing for Him. If we respond to our heart's cry, three things will happen to us. We will deny ourselves, no longer focus on our existence, and Jesus becomes more important to us than we are to ourselves. This self-denial enables Him to bring us to His death, and His death becomes our death. Death empowers us with the resource of His life to live a life that always goes to the cross. Life is never found outside death.

Now I ask you to put this principle in our passage. Why do five thousand men believe in Jesus? Is it because two apostles have experienced death? They have denied themselves, taken up the cross, and followed Jesus. They could have cried, "What we have told you is untrue!" The alliance would have spared them all the trouble of capturing them, putting them in jail for the night, and threatening them. But five thousand men would not have believed, and all would have entered spiritual death. Amid the cross style, the living dying, life is produced in the lives of others.

Paul went into detail to express this principle. He testified to the reality of *"death is working in us, but life in you"* (2 Corinthians 4:12). He viewed himself as *"always carrying about in the body the dying of the Lord Jesus, that the life of Jesus also may be manifested in our body"* (2 Corinthians 4:10). His idea of *"death is working in us"* and *"carrying about in the body the dying of the Lord Jesus"* had nothing to do with symbols or ceremonies. It had to do with their focus and priorities. In this chapter Paul consistently focused on Jesus. He said, *"For we do not preach ourselves, but Christ Jesus the Lord"* (2 Corinthians 4:5). He expounded the treasure placed in earthen vessels. The reason for such a placement is *"that the excellence of the power may be of God and not of us"* (2 Corinthians 4:7). Paul knew that Jesus was released in him (life) in the absolute surrender of self (death). Life is found amid death!

Practice of the Cross

The timeframe of this principle is more than a moment. You cannot die to yourself in a moment and expect to be resurrected after that death. Death to self is not a fleeting memory of the past as you live in the resurrection. Life comes "amid" death not after death. If you think you can endure death's suffering for a moment to receive life forever, you are deceived. Remember these words of Paul, *"always carrying about in the body the dying of the Lord Jesus, that the life of Jesus also may be manifested in our body"* (2 Corinthians 4:10). The verb of *"are...delivered"* is in the present tense. In the Greek grammar, present tense means continual action. Paul puts the word *"always"* with this emphasis.

A critical time period is in our passage (Acts 4:1-4). This time was the first persecution the early Church experienced. They had to practice death continuously, the style of the cross. The alliance puts them in jail for the night, and the following morning they were interrogated by the council of Israel. The alliance could not do what they would have liked with the apostles because of their popularity caused by the healing of the lame beggar, so they settled for threatening them. Amid their persecution, the early Church was filled with the Spirit and spoke the Word of God with boldness. As they embraced their "bleeding, suffering, and dying," their witness was empowered. The council later arrested the apostles another time, but Peter and John continued to practice the cross style.

While suffering this persecution from the council, the early Church quickly discovered there were those in the Church who would not embrace the style of the cross (Acts 5:1-13). Ananias and Sapphira held back their possessions from the Holy Spirit. They practiced the appearance of cross style, but inwardly they resisted. The spiritual world will not tolerate such practice. The cross style must be experienced in every area of life and practiced moment by moment.

Projection of the Cross

Although this may be evident in our passage, it happened some two thousand years ago. The world has dramatically changed through the years, and our generation is different. We have a new culture and philosophy, and there is hardly anything of today that compares with then. Knowledge and understanding have increased, and what worked then will not work now. Yet, this change is not true of the cross style. This style is an eternal principle!

The alliance came on the apostles, and the early Church experienced their first persecution. *"However,"* life appeared in five thousand new believers. This new life did not occur without the "bleeding, suffering, and dying" of the apostles. This truth is also the reality for our generation. We do not have a Solomon's Porch, the alliance, or the Jerusalem council, but the cross style principle remains the foundation of the Kingdom of God. The persecution of Christianity may not be the same now as then, but the truth pervades this period. "Bleeding, suffering, and dying" is the only means to invade the demonic kingdom. Until someone introduces you to the cross, you will never be able to push back sin.

The depth of ridicule that Jesus suffered at the crucifixion was not known even by those gathered around that cross. The chief priests, scribes, and elders joined the by-passers in slandering the King of the Jews. They cried, **"He saved others; Himself He cannot save"** (Matthew 27:42). Without knowing it, these people were expressing the principle of the cross. You cannot save yourself and save others simultaneously. If you choose to save yourself, others will be lost. Jesus said, **"For whoever desires to save his life will lose it, but whoever loses his life for My sake will find it"** (Matthew 16:25). Life is found only amid of death.

Everyone in the Kingdom of Heaven lives this principle. Two thousand years ago it is true, today it is true, and in the eternal realm it is true. Heaven is the experience of the cross, and the cross is how we go to heaven and live there. The cross is the style of the heavenly realms because it is the nature of God. If we are filled with Jesus, if He is living His life through us, and if we have the mind of Christ, "living dying" is the essence of all we are.

The great **"however"** can be possible in our lives only through the cross style. The reason we rejoice in persecution (Matthew 5:10-12) is this style. Our children and spouse are redeemed this style. The Church grows and we win our community to Christ through this style. You and I must lose our lives to live!

Acts 4:4

THOSE WHO HEARD

"However, many of those who heard the word believed; and the number of the men came to be about five thousand" (Acts 4:4).

We have titled this final verse in our passage THE AFTERMATH (Acts 4:4). The Spirit-sourced apostles acted through the power of the Spirit, and here are the results. The first three verses are in some sense an interruption to the flow of the story. The early Church was growing, and the impact of the Gospel was tremendous. Miracles like the lame beggar's healing gained the attention of all Jerusalem. This miracle set the stage for an explanation of the Gospel in which the Spirit drew people to Himself. Suddenly, the alliance caused a major interruption. Peter's message to those gathered at Solomon's Porch brought everything to a standstill. You would think the impact of the moment would have been lost. The alliance achieved their intent.

"However" that is not so! Luke brings us back to the climax of the ministry at Solomon's Porch. The Word of God could not be silenced. Not only do we view the results of the proceeding ministry, but also the influence continued into the interrogation by the council. Not only does this verse serve as a suitable climax to Peter's exhortation, but it also serves as an introduction to the trial scene (Acts 4:5-22).

In our verse, Luke presents the link between the event at Solomon's Porch and the addition of men to the Church. The two elements presented are "hearing" and "believing." A distinct interplay is between these two elements. We must investigate this interaction.

An Emphasis on Hearing
(Catching)

To grasp the truth that Luke presented, we need an understanding of our verses' grammar. The main verb is **believed** (epiteusan) in the aorist tense, active voice, and indicative mood. The aorist tense focuses on the action of the verb, not on when it happened. Luke highlighted the wonder of those who responded to the message of the apostles. Contained in the verb is the subject, a third-person pronoun (he, she, it, they). The verb is plural and refers to "they." Luke said, "they believed." **"Those who heard"** is a translation of the Greek word, "akousanton," a verb in the participle form, the nominative case, and acting as an adjective that modifies the subject, "they." Luke was saying, "The hearing ones believed." The one thing Luke wanted us to know about those who believed was that they heard. **"Many (polloi)"** is an adjective in the nominative case, and it modifies the subject, "they." Luke was saying, "Many hearing ones believed," highlighting the "hearing"!

Something we must note is in the Gospel accounts. "Hearing" is important, while there is little attention paid to physical "seeing." For instance, we were given no physical details of Jesus' crucifixion, which does not allow us to visualize what was actually done to Him. Matthew's Gospel has two long chapters of the events happening around the cross (Matthew 26 & 27), and he gives details of the interaction with Jesus but nothing about the physical crucifixion. He simply writes, **"Then they crucified Him"** (Matthew 27:35). His emphasis was on the unseen world.

We have been given little about the physical description

of Jesus. How tall was He? What were His facial features? The prophet Isaiah described Him as, *"He has no form or comeliness (splendor); and when we see Him, there is no beauty that we should desire Him"* (Isaiah 53:2). The Holy Spirit did not think it was any value for us to know or see the physical appearance of Jesus. In contrast to the lack of a physical description, we have many of His spoken words. Page after page of the Gospel accounts relate the words from the lips of Christ. The emphasis is on "hearing."

The Greek word "akouo," translated *hearing* in our verse, highlights the emphasis of the Scriptures. In Jesus' culture, Greek mythology was strong. Gnosticism was heavily stressed. They proposed that "hearing" could easily lead you astray while "seeing" would not. Although there might be revelation by hearing, the true mystery of God would be known by sight. Even their arts and sculptures depicted religious acts showing that grasping truth comes with vision.

But the Scriptures have a different emphasis. The Old Testament highlights the danger in seeing. Moses came face to face with God in the burning bush. The emphasis on the encounter is not about what Moses saw but what he heard. *"Moreover He said, 'I am the God of your Father – the God of Abraham, the God of Isaac, and the God of Jacob.' And Moses hid his face, for he was afraid to look upon God"* (Exodus 3:6). Even when Moses faced God, the writer's emphasis was on what Moses heard. God said to Moses, *"You cannot see My face; for no man shall see Me, and live"* (Exodus 33:20). Throughout the Old Testament, "seeing God" is a setting for "hearing God." Isaiah said, *"In the year that King Uzziah died, I saw the Lord sitting on a throne, high and lifted up, and the train of His robe filled the temple"* (Isaiah 6:1). The vision as Isaiah described it is not a deception of God but is the setting in which Isaiah hears from God. His mission as a prophet is understood through hearing.

Hearing is a requirement. In our passage there were two

groups of hearers. Luke said, ***"However, many of those who heard the word believed"*** (Acts 4:4), which indicates another group. They also heard the word but did not believe. A quality of hearing present in one group was not present in the other. The element of "hearing" separated from the element of "believing" or "nonbelieving" is impossible in reality. These two elements, "hearing and believing," are so intertwined that they cannot be separated. We must separate them for discussion, but "believing" describes the quality of "hearing."

Jesus' great manifesto of the Kingdom of God was the Sermon on the Mount. The climactic story of the sermon was focused on "hearing" (Matthew 7:24-27). The wise man hears the teachings of Jesus and follows them. The foolish man hears the teachings of Jesus and does not follow them. It seems obvious that what the wise man heard from Jesus is not what the foolish man heard. A quality of hearing happened in the wise man that caused him to respond. The Greek word "poieo," translated ***doing***, in this parable is familiar to us. The word is used for trees "bringing forth" fruit. It points to nature and the inner flow of the being. In other words, the quality of hearing necessary to be wise is a "hearing" that is not just hearing words, ideas, or theology; however, it is an embraced hearing that allows the words to change, produce, and materialize into the fiber of you. You must catch and be caught by what you hear.

Emphasis on Him
(Content)

Our passage reads, ***"However, many of those who heard the word believed"*** (Acts 4:4). The Greek word "logos," translated ***word***, is a direct reference to Jesus in John's prologue (John 1:1). Although the case for the focus must not be based on this fact, it is an interesting fact that Luke includes this word. It requires little research to view the exhortation of Peter on Solomon's Porch (Acts 3:12-26). Jesus, or Christ, is mentioned five times in fifteen verses. Luke uses a pronoun directly referring to Jesus eleven times. Other titles were given to Jesus eight times. This means Jesus is highlighted twenty-four times in fifteen verses. Is there any question that Jesus is the One we are to hear?

The emphasis in the passage is not on just hearing what Jesus says or hearing information about Jesus. "Hearing" involves embracing the person of Jesus. For example, hearing Jesus say, ***"I am the way, the truth, and the life"*** (John 14:6) is not simply data. If I am to hear, I must embrace Him as He is in my life. The only way to correctly hear what Peter said at Solomon's Porch was to embrace Jesus as they heard Him to be! What Peter said in this exhortation was not void of the presence of the resurrected Lord. Contained in the truth preached and taught was the real Jesus. He must be embraced.

When Jesus explained the Parable of the Sower, His emphasis was on "hearing." He began His explanation, ***"Therefore hear the parable of the sower"*** (Matthew 13:18). Then He explained the first type of soil, the wayside. He described the person who, ***"hears the word of the kingdom, and does not understand it, then the wicked one comes and snatches away what was sown in his heart"*** (Matthew 13:19). The intent of sowing the seed was not just to hear but also to understand. The Greek word "suniemi," translated ***understand***, describes embracing the seed. "Sun" means together or together with, and "hiemi" means to send or put. The word means to put things together, comprehend, understand, or perceive. The comprehending activity of the mind is the detonation of "suniemi." It entails assembling individual facts into an organized whole. All the pieces of a puzzle are put together. The mind grasps ideas and sees the proper relationship between them. In the New Testament, this verb is seldom used with a direct object.

The Parable of the Sower is climaxed with the explanation

of the good soil. Three Greek words are used in the explanation, "akuou," "suniemi," and "poieo." ***"But he who received seed on the good ground is he who hears*** (akuou) ***the word and understands*** (suniemi) ***it, who indeed bears*** (poieo) ***fruit and produces; some a hundredfold, some sixty, some thirty"*** (Matthew 13:23). This passage describes one who embraces the Word of the Kingdom. This is not a problem to solve or an intellectual process of figuring it out. Jesus is the Word! In the embrace of His person, understanding happens and "bearing fruit" occurs. Proper hearing cannot happen without the embrace. Jesus is the focus of our hearing.

To hear Jesus is to embrace Him. This may be why the devil's greatest tool against us is distraction. I met a young man who was in a bowling league. I noticed his desk was filled with magazines and books related to bowling. His wall displayed trophies from bowling tournaments. As we spoke, he flexed a rubber ball in his hand to strengthen his bowling grip. He rejected my invitation to church because of his bowling activities. Sunday was out of the question because he participated in bowling tournaments. All he heard, focused on, and embraced was bowling, and bowling had also embraced him. He was mastered, dominated, and consumed by bowling. Bowling was not just information, a game of recreation, or a passing interest. He became a slave to all he heard in bowling.

The same commitment will be true with Jesus as well. Hearing Him involves embracing Him, but He will also embrace you. He will consume your life. He makes Himself the center of everything, and you will not be able to live without Him. If you hear Him and respond, be prepared for all contained in His presence to be yours. His presence becomes the correct lens through which the world is made plain. His presence becomes the platform on which you experience life and produce fruit.

Emphasis on Heeding
(Convinced)

Will you heed what you hear? Jesus took on the responsibility of telling you. He knows your culture, background, and failures. He knows exactly how to talk to you. He will not allow you to miss Him. The only chance of not hearing is that you do not want to listen. Luke highlights this in our passage. *"However, many of those who heard the word believed"* (Acts 4:4). The indication is that more heard the message than responded. Not everyone heeded what he or she heard. The alliance was in that group.

The same plea to heed is made by the writer of the Book of Hebrews. He quotes the Old Testament psalm (Psalms 95:7-11). The first quotation is introduced with the statement, *"Therefore, as the Holy Spirit says"* (Hebrews 3:7). God calls us to listen! That call is clearly understood in the mind of the book's writer. The first statement of each quotation is, *"Today, if you will hear His voice"* (Hebrews 3:7; 15; 4:7). We are to listen now. The voice of God is sounding forth, and there is no hindrance to our hearing. God takes on the responsibility of telling us. The writer's appeal is not that we seek and find the voice of God, or that we interpret God's voice. If God speaks, it will be clear. We will hear, understand, and be responsible for heeding.

If we do not heed, the response is described for us. He says, *"Do not harden your hearts as in the rebellion, in the day of trial in the wilderness, where your fathers tested Me, tried Me"* (Hebrews 3:8-9). In other words, the only way not to hear is to harden your heart. The Greek word "skleruno" is translated **harden** and comes from the root word "skleros," meaning hard. It means to make hard, stiff, or to be stubborn. In the New Testament, this word is applied figuratively to the heart or mind (Acts 19:9; Romans 9:18; Hebrews 3:8, 13, 15; 4:7). In our passage the writer refers to the spiritual heart of man.

Part One: The Announced Resurrection

"Today, if you will hear His voice" (Hebrews 3:7). The main verb, translated ***hear,*** is in the subjunctive mood and is represented as contingent. There is no certainty either way. In other words, you have a choice. God is going to speak. He will speak to you! He has taken on the responsibility of telling you truth. The uncertainty is in your response. Will you respond or will you not? Your response determines what you hear.

Acts 4:4

THOSE WHO BELIEVED

"However, many of those who heard the word believed; and the number of the men came to be about five thousand" (Acts 4:4).

Growth in the Christian movement finds its surge amid persecution not in comfort and ease. Luke gives the details of this story in the first recorded act of persecution against the early Church. When the early Church was a small group of unorganized believers they proposed little threat. They found favor with the people of Jerusalem and the Church's numbers increased substantially (Acts 2:47). Then the apostles began performing miracles and the threat increased. The healing of the lame beggar set the stage for the proclamation of the resurrected Jesus. The leadership of Israel could no longer tolerate the teaching and preaching, **"in Jesus the resurrection from the dead."**

Throughout the history of the persecuted Church, the persecutors did not understand the source of the miracles. To stop the "teaching and preaching," they would have to eliminate the source. The alliance thought the apostles were the source of the miracles, but they were NOT. They were instruments of Jesus, the resurrected Lord! Even the devil did not see the truth of this Source and boldly marched into the plan of God (Acts 2:23). Although he attempted to eliminate the message from the life of the physical Jesus, he thrust Jesus into the eternal

Part One: The Announced Resurrection

realm. Through the fullness of the Spirit, Jesus' life would be revealed and proclaimed forever. Satan and his cohorts could eliminate the messengers, but they could not stop the Message! How frustrating this must have been for the ungodly world.

No wonder Luke cried, "However!" The authority of the temple descended on Peter and John. *"And they laid hands on them, and put them in custody until the next day"* (Acts 4:3). But this did not stop the flow of the resurrected Jesus to the lives of the people. *"Many of those who heard the word believed"* (Acts 4:4). In a previous study, we discussed the grammar of this sentence, and it is important for our consideration in this study. The main verb of the sentence is *"believed"* in the indicative mood, a simple statement of fact. This verb indicates and presents to us the subject of the sentence. The subject is a third-person pronoun (they or those). *"Heard"* is a verb in the participle form and in the nominative causing it to modify the subject. "The hearing ones believed." *"Many"* is an adjective in the nominative also giving content to the main subject. "Many hearing ones believed."

The main statement and focus of this sentence is the response of five thousand men; they *"believed,"* a translation of the Greek verb "pisteuo." "Pistis" is the noun form. The noun and the verb form occur two hundred and forty-three times each in the New Testament. John, in his Gospel account and his three epistles, uses only the verb form. The writers of Colossians, Philemon, 2 Peter and Revelation use only the noun form. The same statements can be expressed either by the verb or the noun. Their use and frequency demonstrate a theological idea, which is our correct relationship to God and the essence of our Christian experience. In the New Testament, "faith" is the central and comprehensive designation for our relationship to God. The act of believing is to entrust our spiritual well being to Christ!

We must answer several questions about our passage.

What Did They Believe?

The early Church believed in the PERSON of Jesus. We define the noun and the verb of faith as "invoking the activity of the Second party!" We create disaster in our lives because we have invoked the activity of the first party, self. We live out of our own resource. Our talent, education, and experiences are the source of our actions. You can hear it in our language: "I am trying," "I am doing my best," and "I am giving it all I have." These are expressions of our dependence on us. We have had faith in ourselves. The call of the Gospel is to invoke Jesus' activity instead of ours. This is faith in Christ.

This kind of faith is unquestionable the setting of our passage (Acts 3). Peter's message was Jesus, the Person. His focus on Jesus began with the miracle and continued to the final recorded sentence. The lame beggar spent his life focusing on the need of money (Acts 3:2), and Peter's focus was on his need of Jesus (Acts 3:6). Jesus was the focus of Peter's life, so he gave the beggar what he had, Jesus (Acts 3:6). He healed the lame beggar in the name of Jesus with the strength and power of the person the name represented (Acts 3:6). As Peter, John, and the healed beggar moved into the temple area, Peter realized the crowd attributed the miracle to him. All concentration was on Peter with the healed beggar holding onto him (Acts 3:11).

Immediately Peter broke into an exhortation about Jesus; the theme being "Jesus is the sole source of this miracle." He gave detail in His description of the resurrected Lord. Jesus was the One glorified by the God of Abraham, Isaac, and Jacob (Acts 3:13). He did not introduce the crowd to Jesus, because they *"delivered up and denied* Jesus *in the presence of Pilate, when he was determined to let Him go"* (Acts 3:13). Jesus was *"the Holy One and the Just,"* the substitute for Barabbas whose release they demanded (Acts 3:14). They killed Jesus, the Prince of life, and He was the one, *"God raised from the dead, of which we are witnesses"* (Acts 3:15).

Just in case anyone was confused, Peter said, *"And His name, through faith in His name, has made this man strong, whom you see and know. Yes the faith which comes through Him has given him this perfect soundness in the presence of you all"* (Acts 3:16). Peter continued to show Jesus as the focus of the prophets' message (Acts 3:22-24). In fact, Jesus is the center of the covenant God made with His people (Acts 3:25).

Peter did not present a new theology or belief system. He presented a Person. This presentation was not a new organization worshipping in a different location. He challenged them to embrace the Person of Jesus. The call was to turn from denial, rejection, and disbelief in Jesus to acceptance, embrace, and belief in Him. "Delivering Him up," murder and crucifixion must become acknowledgment, truth, and relationship. This presentation was not about religious seminars and the development of religious beliefs. Instead, it was about Jesus! The change was not in philosophy, approach to life, or change of opinion; it was not acknowledgment of guilt about the crucifixion, but about embracing the resurrected Jesus.

However, to believe in the PERSON of Jesus, this crowd had to believe in the PURPOSE of Jesus. You cannot separate the purpose of Jesus from His person. When a person believes in Jesus (invokes the activity of the Second party) he or she subjects himself or herself to what Jesus wants to accomplish. The description by Peter of Jesus describes of the purpose of His coming!

Peter gave the image of Jesus as the fulfillment of the covenant God made with the crowd's forefathers. God said to Abraham, *"And in your seed all the families of the earth shall be blessed"* (Acts 3:25). The word *"seed"* is singular, and is a reference to Jesus! Paul clarified this by saying, *"Now to Abraham and his Seed were the promises made. He does not say, 'And to seeds,' as of many, but as of one, 'And to your Seed,' who is Christ'"* (Galatians 3:16). The fulfillment of the covenant is not a religious system. It is Jesus! The purpose of the covenant was for us to experience salvation in its fullest meaning. Peter explained it as, *"To you first, God, having raised up His Servant Jesus, sent Him to bless you, in turning away every one of you from your iniquities"* (Acts 3:26). If you believe in Jesus, you repent (give up a former thought to embrace a new thought). The purpose of repentance is, *"that your sins may be blotted out, so that times of refreshing may come from the presence of the Lord"* (Acts 3:19). Although the removal of sin from our lives is wonderful, the purpose of such is to bring us into relationship with this Person, Jesus.

This relationship has a startling reality for you and me. It is in Jesus that we experience the fulfillment of God's purpose in our lives. Jesus does not tell us this purpose so we can accomplish it; Jesus is the purpose. The purpose is in His nature and the structure of His Person. There is no way to embrace His purpose without embracing Him. Do not focus on His purpose in your life but focus everything on His person!

To believe in the PERSON of Jesus, you must believe in the PURPOSE of Jesus, and to experience the PURPOSE of Jesus, you must believe in the PLAN of Jesus. The details of the plan are rugged and can be discouraging. Peter began his exhortation by presenting Jesus as, *"His Servant Jesus"* (Acts 3:13), and before the alliance interrupted him, his closing statement was, *"His Servant Jesus"* (Acts 3:26). Between these two statements, Peter displayed the details of the plan. As he recalled the prophecies, he revealed the long-range view of the plan (Acts 3:22-24).

The significance of the plan is not only in its details but also in the plan's nature. The crucifixion details are the display of the nature of the Person of Jesus. The details of the denial, murder, and crucifixion for redemption do not surprise those who know the Person of Jesus. He is the display of His Father's nature. The reason for the plan is the nature of the Planner. You cannot believe in the plan (invoke the activity of the Second party) without embracing the nature of the Person. The "purpose" and the "plan" bring us back to the "person." Will you embrace His nature? This embrace is the call to your heart!

When Did They Believe?

"Believe" is the main verb, and it is in the aorist tense. This aorist is a non-tense. It does not focus on the time when the belief happened but focuses on the response of the belief itself. What if belief was not something I do at a particular moment, but it is present in the human heart all the time? Would you be startled to know that God planted belief in the DNA of your spiritual life, and it constantly cries for your response to His call?

You do not have to encourage children to respond in belief. "The current Barna study indicates that nearly half of Americans who accept Jesus Christ as their Savior do so before reaching the age of thirteen (43%), and that two out of three born-again Christians (64%) made that commitment to Christ before their eighteenth birthday. One out of eight born-again people (13%) made their profession of faith while eighteen to twenty-one years old. Less than one out of every four born-again Christians (23%) embraced Christ after their twenty-first birthday." The heart's natural response of a child is to believe. After the experiences of life harden the inner being, we have difficulty responding with faith. This highlights the truth that God planted belief into the nature of each of us.

A study of sociology highlights this truth. The sociologists have not discovered any tribe, race, or culture that does not have an established belief in God! Even people groups isolated from all others maintain a belief in God. Paul relates this in his letter to the Romans. He wrote, ***"Because what may be*** *known of God is manifested in them, for God has shown it to them*" (Romans 1:19). The revelation shown to them is from the creation of the world (Romans 1:20). The revelation manifested in them is the witness of God's Spirit revealing truth. Paul's conclusion based on these facts was that *"they are without excuse"* (Romans 1:20). This conclusion should convince us that the normal response of the human is to believe in God. To not believe, he or she must fight against the nature of his or her system.

What Caused Them to Believe?

Luke is specific about what called these people to belief, *"However, many of those who heard the word believed"* (Acts 4:4). The Greek word, translated *word*, is "logos." We do not want to highlight the content of this word more than it is in this passage, but in light of our previous study of, *"they taught the people and preached in Jesus the resurrection from the dead"* it is proper to mention this Greek word often refers to Jesus (John 1:1).

Even if the Greek word "logos" refers only to the exhortation from Peter's teaching and preaching, it still refers to Jesus. Contained in the teaching of the apostles is the presence of the One to whom they refer. What is this teaching? The Greek word "didasko" had inherent in it the intent to influence the understanding of the person taught. In other words, teaching in this context contains the motive for convincing and changing the perspective of an individual through the truth. Teaching is never the simple act of speaking data or about information. Teaching is about life-changing truth presented to bring change to the one being taught.

In this context we begin to understand the proper view and definition for preaching. Teaching is the informing of truth

Part One: The Announced Resurrection

not merely facts that the learners might assimilate some truth into their lives. Truth involves the interaction of the Living Word being revealed in the Written Word. Preaching is the proclamation of truth not an announcement of information. An individual filled with the Living Word proclaims the Written Word through the flow of the Living Word. Therefore, preaching is in a category far beyond a speech, lecture, or exhortation. In our passage preaching is the apostle filled with the resurrected Lord, proclaiming the reality of the resurrected Lord through the resurrected Lord's power. If the risen Lord is not present, it is a lecture.

Jesus, the resurrected Lord, presented Himself to the crowd gathered at Solomon's Porch. The inner Spirit of Christ in those listening took the outer words of truth to convict the being of the listeners. Everyone could have believed. Everyone should have believed. Belief is a response to the reality of Jesus coming to our lives. This is a moment of belief!

PART 2
ACTS 4:5-12

THE ANALYTICAL RESPONSE

Acts 4:5-12

LET THE CONTEST BEGIN!

And it came to pass, on the next day, that their rulers, elders, and scribes, as well as Annas the high priest, Caiaphas, John, and Alexander, and as many as were of the family of the high priest, were gathered together at Jerusalem. And when they had set them in the midst, they asked, "By what power or by what name have you done this?" Then Peter, filled with the Holy Spirit, said to them, "Rulers of the people and elders of Israel: If we this day are judged for a good deed done to a helpless man, by what means he has been made well, let it be known to you all, and to all the people of Israel, that by the name of Jesus Christ of Nazareth, whom you crucified, whom God raised from the dead, by Him this man stands here before you whole. This is the 'stone which was rejected by you builders, which has become the chief cornerstone.' Nor is there salvation in any other, for there is no other name under heaven given among men by which we must be saved (Acts 4:5-12).

Elijah, the Tishbite, was a prophet of God. Ahab was a King of Israel. ***Ahab did more to provoke the Lord God of Israel to anger than all the kings of Israel who were before him*** (Kings 16:33). God announced, through Elijah, that there would be neither dew nor rain except at His word (1Kings 17:1), and Elijah immediately went into hiding. For months he hid by the Brook Cherith, which flows into the Jordan River. Morning and night the ravens brought him bread and meat, but as God had spoken, the brook became dry from the lack of rain.

The Lord then instructed Elijah to go down to Zarephath where a widow gathered sticks for a fire. Elijah called out to the widow telling her to bring him a little water in a cup and a morsel of bread. She replied quickly that there was no bread. In fact, she was gathering wood to cook the last handful of flour left in the bin, and she had only a little oil in a jar. She and her son would eat this last meal and die. But the prophet assured her that the Lord would provide for them until the rains returned. In obedience, she shared what she had with the prophet. ***The bin of flour was not used up, nor did the jar of oil run dry, according to the word of the Lord which He spoke by Elijah*** (1 Kings 17:16). The widow's son became sick and died. The widow appealed to Elijah, and he cried out to God three times. ***And Elijah said, "See, your son lives!"*** (1 Kings 17:23).

Obadiah was in charge of Ahab's house, and he feared the Lord. Jezebel, Ahab's wife, had massacred the prophets of the Lord, but Obadiah had hidden and cared for one hundred of them in caves. Ahab sent servants into all the surrounding nations hunting for Elijah (1 Kings 18:10). However, no one could find him. One day Ahab came to Obadiah with a plan to search though out the country for water and grass to keep the horses and mules alive. Ahab went one direction and Obadiah went the opposite. Elijah met Obadiah and told him to tell Ahab of his presence. Obadiah was frightened for his life, but Elijah assured him that he was hiding no longer.

In fact, it was time for a contest. The issue must be settled. Elijah proposed a gathering at Mount Carmel. The people of Israel, four hundred and fifty prophets of Baal, and the four hundred prophets of Asherah who ate at Jezebel's table came together. At the proper time, Elijah extended the challenge, ***"How long will you falter between two opinions? If the Lord is God, follow Him; but if Baal, follow him"*** (Kings 1:18:21). Elijah proposed two bulls and two sacrifice altars. The prophets of Baal were to begin first. From morning until noon, they cried out for Baal, the god of lightning, to answer by fire. Elijah mocked them, ***"Cry aloud, for he is a god; either he is meditating, or he is busy, or he is on a journey, or perhaps he is sleeping and must be awakened"*** (1 Kings 18:27). From midday to the time of the evening sacrifice, they increased their intensity. They cut themselves until their blood gushed. ***But there was no voice; no one answered, no one paid attention*** (1 Kings 18:29). Then Elijah called the people of Israel to draw near. He repaired the neglected altar of the Lord. Amid the drought he dug a trench and poured four water pots of water on the burnt sacrifice and on the wood. He did this three times until the water trench was full. ***At the time of the evening sacrifice, Elijah made a simple prayer to God; then the fire of the Lord fell and consumed the burnt sacrifice, and the wood and the stones and the dust, and it licked up the water that was in the trench*** (1 Kings 18:38). The Israelites seized the prophets of Baal and executed them. It began to rain!

The contest was over! Again God revealed Himself; His plan was sovereign. The prophets of Baal had finished. Only one true God exists! All other gods are made by our self-centered wills. The deep internal cry of our souls for worship drives us to the reality of God. However, as we embrace this desire, our self-centeredness will allow us to embrace only a god we can control. This self-centeredness makes us god! We build a religion that caters to our selfish carnal minds, but the "god of self" always ends in defeat and destruction.

This scene is reenacted in our passage. The scene on Mount Carmel took place more than one thousand years prior to our passage. Our culture is different, and our circumstances have changed, but the same contest exists. Let the contest begin!

Part 2: The Analytical Response

The Court
Acts 4:5-6

The apostles came to the temple for the evening hour of prayer and sacrifice at three o'clock. A miracle happened in the life of the begging lame man, who begged at the Gate Beautiful. Most worshippers at the temple knew this man because he had begged at this location for nearly forty years. His crippled life was the stage on which men would see Jesus. Let the contest begin!

The focus of the miracle is Jesus. There have been many miracles, and the forces of evil cannot tolerate them. Religious people always focus on a physical but temporary change in their lives. These changes range from a financial miracle, a new job, a better car, or a parking spot close to the front door of Walmart. This kind of focus is not a problem to the demonic forces, but the healing of the lame beggar became the platform for a focus on Jesus. Peter approached the lame beggar with this proposition, *"Silver and gold I do not have, but what I do have I give you: In the name of Jesus Christ of Nazareth, rise up and walk"* (Acts 3:6). If this beggar had received his miracle, returned to his home, and quietly lived his life, everything would have been all right. But *he, leaping up, stood and walked and entered the temple with them — walking, leaping, and praising God. And all the people saw him walking and praising God* (Acts 3:8-9).

If this healing was demonstrated only in the temple, the demons could have tolerated it. But the healed beggar would not leave Peter and John alone. *Now as the lame man who was healed held on to Peter and John, all the people ran together to them in the porch which is called Solomon's, greatly amazed* (Acts 3:11). That is what the demonic world could not bear. Peter realized the Jewish crowd of thousands thought he was responsible for this miracle. He addressed the crowd, *"Men of Israel, why do you marvel at this? Or why look so intently at us, as though by our own power or godliness we had made this man walk?"* (Acts 3:12). Peter would not stand for one moment of self-aggrandizement. He began to exhort this crowd about Jesus. He did not discuss the Messiah who was to come, but he proclaimed Jesus as the Messiah who had already come. Peter identified Jesus as the one they crucified, murdered, and betrayed for Barabbas. But what shook and irritated the demonic world the most was the proclamation that Jesus' presence was among them now. Jesus was raised from the dead, and they had another chance to embrace Him as this healed beggar had done. Peter confronted all the temple movement with the risen Lord. Five thousand men besides their families had already been captivated by the resurrected Jesus' presence, and this interest was a problem. Let the contest begin!

The alliance marched to capture this moment. ***The priests, the captain of the temple, and the Sadducees came upon them*** (Acts 4:1). But this group, as powerful as they were, was not adequate for this contest. They put Peter and John in jail for the night to engage all the forces necessary. The next morning all necessary forces gathered. Luke lists those there for the side of evil. He began with ***their rulers, elders, and scribes*** (Acts 4:5). This list formed the Sanhedrin, the highest ruling body of Israel. It consisted of seventy-one of the most powerful men in Israel. But even this group was not adequate to represent the forces of evil. ***Annas the high priest, Caiaphas, John, and Alexander, and as many as were of the family of the high priest, were gathered together at Jerusalem*** (Acts 4:6). Every one of importance was included. They were all here. Let the contest begin!

Surely we would not parallel these godly leaders of Israel with the prophets of Baal. Ahab, the king of Israel, allowed a mixture of religious influence to dominate the land. Jehovah was worshipped. Jehovah worshippers maintained all the sacrifices and ceremonies, but they had the additional options of Baal. The Israelites were still singing the songs of Israel and teaching the history of Jehovah's deliverances in their schools. But the statues of Baal were on the mantels of their homes. This divide was the reason for a contest! Elijah called for a housecleaning revival, a time to get in or get out! It was time to get in or get out! Elijah extended the challenge, **"How long will you falter between two opinions? If the Lord is God, follow Him"** (1 Kings 18:21). In other words, we can never do both!

There were no statues of Baal on the mantels of the leaders of Israel's homes, and furthermore they would have been shocked by such a suggestion. After all they studied the Scriptures and observed six hundred and thirteen oral traditions to maintain their godliness. The operation of the temple was at peak efficiency. They were selling more sacrificial lambs, the crowds were large, and the offerings were at an all-time high. What could have been better? They had compromised! They allowed the god of self to mix with their worship of Jehovah. Their man-made applications of the Scriptures, the oral traditions, became more important than the message of God in the Scriptures (Matthew 15:3-6). Their religion became self-produced. Self was promoted by everything they did. Jesus said, **"But all their works they do to be seen by men"** (Matthew 23:5). They had fallen into the worst of idolatry, the worship of self. They used their religious practices for themselves. They did not mind God being God so long as He served them. They wanted a god who brought healing to their bodies, finances to their pockets, and death to their enemies. What they wanted was all about self. Let the contest begin!

The Consideration
Acts 4:7

The alliance asked, **"By what power or by what name have you done this?"** (Acts 4:7). If they thought for one moment that Peter would answer by quoting an incantation or magical formula, they were wrong. Would he present a new mixture of herbs with special procedures of application? No! No! The answer was simple, *"Let it be known to you all, and to all the people of Israel, that by the name of Jesus Christ of Nazareth, whom you crucified, whom God raised from the dead, by Him this man stands here before you whole"* Acts 4:10).

Let the contest begin! The sacrifice altars are erected; our lives are the living sacrifice. By what power or by what name is your life produced? Who is the god who will answer by being the fire of your living? Will the "god of self" take a lame beggar and transform his life? Will self-sufficiency pull your life together and give you spiritual victory? If you do your best, try your hardest, and discipline yourself, will you walk again and live in victory? Perhaps if you make all the right sacrifices, keep all the feast days, and obey the oral traditions, wholeness can be yours. Let the "god of self" answer with fire!

On the other side, there is Jesus! He is not an idea, ceremony, or rule. He is the raised from the dead Jesus of Nazareth. Soak the sacrifice altar with water three times until the trench is full. All incantations, herb mixtures, or meditations to manipulate Him would be more "god of self." Will you completely submit yourself to Him? Will you admit you are inadequate and in helplessness allow Him to be who He is in your life? Jesus does not send the fire; He is the fire. He does not give instructions providing an answer; He is the answer. Jesus does not share techniques of discipline; He is Lord of our lives! Let the contest begin!

The Communication
Acts 4:8-12

Then Peter, filled with the Holy Spirit, said to them... (Acts 4:8). Indeed, the fire would fall. The communication

Part 2: The Analytical Response

of the Spirit of the Resurrected Lord flowed through Peter to communicate the reality of truth. When the demonstration had finished they marveled. They realized that Peter and John were ***uneducated and untrained men***. But they realized that they had been with Jesus (Acts 4:13). The Greek word "esan," translated ***they had been***, is the imperfect tense of "eimi." This "eimi" is the Greek verb translated "I am," a state of being. The imperfect tense expresses an event in the past that has continuing effect and demonstration in the present. In other words, as they had dwelt with Jesus in the past, they were continuing to dwell with Him now. It was the fullness of the Spirit experienced at Pentecost. Jesus came and burned the sacrifice with water in the trench. He is the answer!

The contest experienced by Elijah and the prophets of Baal took place nearly one thousand years before the contest experienced by Peter and the leaders of Israel. But it is the same contest! Here we are nearly two thousand years later. In our lives we experience the same contest. Let the contest begin! The "god of self" with all of its talent, education, and pride demands control. On the other side is a lowly Nazarene named Jesus. Will you trust Him or yourself? Let the contest begin!

I challenge you to view your past and the circumstances of your present. Perhaps as with Elijah it has not rained for a long period and the drought in your life is great. The supply for your spiritual life is just not adequate. The "god of self" has exhausted itself. It cannot produce fire. The best we can do is not enough. Can we recognize that all our self-sufficiency brought us to where we are? How can the "god of self" rescue us when the "god of self" is responsible for where we are? Self-centeredness cannot guide us through the maze of our circumstances because it has produced the maze.

Where is the God who can answer by fire? His name is Jesus! We are called to a new and deep intimacy with Him. He is the answer. With all our religious self-sufficiency, we become the, ***"blind leaders of the blind. And if the blind leads the blind, both will fall into a ditch"*** (Matthew 15:14). We are in the ditch and cannot deliver ourselves.

Let the contest begin*!* ***"How long will you falter between two opinions? If the Lord is God, follow Him; but if Baal, follow him"*** (1 Kings 18:21). If you are adequate for your own living, continue in your adequacy. If you are going to trust Jesus, let your trust be complete. We cannot falter between two options. Either you are a Christian or you are not. Let the contest begin!

Acts 4:5

THE SANHEDRIN

"And it came to pass, on the next day, that their rulers, elders, and scribes" (Acts 4:5).

The Sanhedrin was the most powerful governing and ruling body of Israel. They were responsible for the religious order of all Jews everywhere, but their influence did not often extend beyond Judea. This court governed the temple with all of its various activities and celebrations, and it determined the political affairs of Israel.

Israel was not like other nations. They did not have a man king for the first third of their history. Jehovah was their King! He was the great Provider for all their needs. He gave them quail out of the bush, manna from the sky, and water from a rock. He was not a king who used the nation to meet His needs. He did not need a palace, servants, or financial security. He did not need armies to defeat His enemies. He provided strategy for war, strength in weariness, and land for the families. God delighted in providing for His children.

It was in this context that God provided leadership for the nation. The Israelites feasted on the manna but complained over the lack of meat. Moses felt the responsibility and burden of leading the people. He cried out to Jehovah, ***"I am not able to bear all these people alone, because the burden is too heavy for me"*** (Numbers 11:14). God told Moses to *...select seventy men*

The Sanhedrin | Acts 4:5

of the elders of Israel, whom you know to be the elders of the people and officers over them; bring them to the tabernacle of meeting, that they may stand there with you (Numbers 11:16). God met with them, and He took the Spirit that was on Moses for leadership and extended it to these seventy. They were to bear the burden of the people with Moses. There seemed to be two main responsibilities for this group. They were to know the power of the Spirit for leadership, being able to direct the nation with the mind of God, and they were to focus on the needs of the people.

In the second third of Jewish history, the Israelites demanded a king. God warned them against this type of government and leadership, but they would not listen. During this period, the leadership of the seventy elders seemed to have been set aside. The kings were sovereign. The last third of Jewish history was without kings. The Israelites, while under the leadership of Ezra and Nehemiah returned from Babylonian captivity. Ezra was said to have established the Great Synagogue during this period, which seemed to be the Sanhedrin of Jesus' day. The leadership of this group fell on the priests.

The Roman Empire dominated the world during the days of Jesus. After they conquered a nation, they required only two things, a strong taxation of the people and a requirement to live in peace. Each nation had the right to govern itself, have its own customs, and continue its own religions. Thus, the leadership of Israel fell into the hands of the Sanhedrin under the leadership of the high priest. They must cater to Roman demands while maintaining their culture and beliefs.

Our passage gives us a clear list of those who made up the membership in the Sanhedrin, **rulers, elders, and scribes.** In the Greek text there is an article before each group. It reads *the* **rulers,** *the* **elders, and** *the* **scribes.** The Greek word "archon," translated **rulers,** is used thirty-seven times in the New Testament, but within these many uses, there are three distinctions made. A reference to Christ (Revelation 1:5) is a distinction. References

Part 2: The Analytical Response

to Roman and Jewish governing officials or persons who hold positions of importance are another distinction. References to supra worldly powers (demonic rulers) that, as a rule, exercise lordship against God are the third distinction. As rulers in the Sanhedrin, this group constituted the Jewish officials who have positions of leadership in the community.

The Greek word "presbuteros," translated ***elders***, refers to the lay members of the Jewish Sanhedrin. The phrase most commonly used is "chief priests and the scribes and the elders." Those called ***elders*** as lay members of the Sanhedrin came from wealthy families who theologically followed the example of the Sadducees and the high-priestly nobility.

The Greek word "grammateus," translated ***scribes***, were exegetes, interpreters of Scripture, who established its instructions bindingly for the present. Others were teachers who sought to equip the greatest possible number of pupils with the methods of interpretation and jurists who as trial judges administered the law in practical situations.

As these groups are seen in the unfolding of our story, the heartbreaking reality becomes visible again. Instead of being the extension of divine governing, they become the visible hand of the demonic world (John 8:44). Like Moses, the Spirit of the Lord was to rest on them. The Sanhedrin was to be the extended hand of God to guide and provide for the people, but they became the opposite. Among the many truths proclaimed in this story, the Sanhedrin revealed its true nature. They became perverted in the three main arenas of leadership.

Authority
Acts 4:7

The story opens with the Sanhedrin admitting a new "recognition." We see this in the question, ***"By what power or*** *by what name have you done this?"* (Acts 4:7). The apostles demonstrated something beyond their capacity. The evidence stood before them, the healed beggar. The Greek word "poieo," translated *have done*, is significant. It highlights the creative nature flowing to bring something into being. The Sanhedrin recognized the apostles because ordinary men were not responsible for this miracle. Something was present beyond their ability, knowledge, and training.

Although the Book of Acts is not an instruction manual on church growth or evangelism, it does give us insight into patterns and principles. Continually throughout the growth of the early Church, the Spirit of God followed a pattern. First, God did something so dramatic that everyone was in awe of the occasion. At Pentecost the Spirit spoke through the apostles in fifteen dialectics. It astounded several thousand Jews listening to their own language. Now the Spirit of God flowed through the apostles to amaze more than five thousand Jews who crowded Solomon's Porch. A lame beggar had been a consistent figure at the Gate Beautiful. Everyone knew of who he was! He was healed! After the crowd was amazed, God always had someone on hand to explain the divine source. In each case Peter preached the explanation. Now in our passage, Peter presented to the Sanhedrin the explanation of Jesus again!

If we are going to win our world, there must be something happening that is beyond us. Christianity dare not be a product of our discipline or cultural setting. Our lives must not be a demonstration of our talent, abilities, or wisdom. We must live in the fullness of the Spirit.

What was the response of the Sanhedrin? It was "resistance." The fact that they asked the question verifies suspicion and hesitation. Did they not know what the apostles were going to say? Had not enough miracles been done and enough messages been preached that there was no question about the *name*?

Part 2: The Analytical Response

Maybe they thought the apostles were like themselves, self-sourced. Did they think the explanation would be incantations or magical spells? The apostles did not invade and push back the demonic realm as the sons of the Pharisees did (Matthew 12:27). Each miracle and every sermon focused on Jesus. The apostles were specific about Jesus' description, leaving no question. He is, *"Jesus Christ of Nazareth, whom you crucified, whom God raised from the dead"* (Acts 4:10).

The Sanhedrin was looking for an alternative source, but they were constrained to admit that Jesus was the source. The apostles offered no other source and the healed beggar stood before them. There was no way to explain him away. No different choice to be given as an explanation. If the apostles would attribute the miracle to only some incantation or magic potion, the leaders of Israel would have embraced that. Then they would have allowed the apostles to start a school in the name of this new formula. They could preach this doctrine or magic, and it would be tolerated, but not Jesus. Herein is the resistance!

Suddenly there is a "realization." They were face to face with Jesus again! He would not just go away. They crucified Him, and He rose from the dead. They lied about Him, and He persisted in being the truth. They denied Him, and He continued to reveal His power among them. They adjusted and rationalized, and He created a situation that had no alternative but His presence. They suggested He did not exist in the present, but His presence was felt. They wanted to argue theology and doctrine, and His person pressed them. They could not deny the miracle (Acts 4:14, 16). Maybe they could ignore Him if the proclamation of His name was silenced (Acts 4: 17-18). What other choice did they have?

Appearance
Acts 4:16

A focus on law is a focus on "doing." A focus on "doing" is a focus on "appearance." How it looked became the major issue! The Sanhedrin was driven to an indisputable "recognition." A healed beggar was standing before them. If he were an outsider, one who came from a foreign city, they could explain it away. But this man was born and raised here in Jerusalem. The faithful crowds who came daily to the temple, morning and afternoon, were accustomed to his begging at the Gate Beautiful. He had been there for years (he was more than forty years). Hundreds of people knew his condition. They told everyone that this miracle was real. It became **evident to all who dwell in Jerusalem** that they could not be denied (Acts 4:15).

The Sanhedrin recognized the reality that something happened beyond their explanation. The lame beggar had received a miracle, but it was more than the miracle of a lame man walking; it was Peter and John. The Sanhedrin had encountered Peter and John on other occasions, but something was different about them now. The Sanhedrin came together for a single purpose, the intimidation of Peter and John. This was the Supreme Court of the nation of Israel. They held in their hands the verdict of life and death. This was the group that successfully crucified Jesus. Peter and John were with the most powerful, educated, and wealthy men of Israel. **"Now when they saw the boldness of Peter and John, and perceived that they were uneducated and untrained men, they marveled. And they realized that they had been with Jesus"** (Acts 4:13). How can we explain it?

The Sanhedrin immediately expressed the consistent response of "resistance." Luke records, **"They conferred among themselves"** (Acts 4:15). The Greek word "sumballo," translated **they conferred**, is a combination of "sun," meaning "together," and "ballo," meaning "to cast." It conveys the idea of "more than one" and "throwing out ideas." They turned into themselves, expressed their own reasoning, and used the source of their own wisdom. This self-sourcing drove them to return to the traditions and patterns of their past. Jesus accused them of saying, **"If we had lived in the days of our fathers, we would not have been partakers with them in the blood of the prophets"** (Matthew 23:30). Jesus reminded them that this statement was a confession that they were sons of those who murdered the prophets. They were sent messengers from God; in fact the very Son of God came to them. Although their forefathers were guilty of murdering the prophets, they were guilty of murdering the Messiah sent to redeem them.

The Sanhedrin consulted among themselves and maintained their consistent pattern. They resisted the truth as they had always done! Could they break out of this pattern? Could they go beyond themselves, their patterns, and their traditions and be open to the new revelation of God? Would they resist the shift because of what the people might think? They had a "realization." They were the most powerful ruling body in Israel, and they would have to admit, "We were wrong!" How would that appear?

This admission is the foundation of repentance, "giving up a former thought to embrace a new thought." This was Peter's message to every group to whom he preached, and he did no less to this group. The Sanhedrin was responsible for crucifying Jesus, and they must repent. No salvation is outside Jesus! They had been wrong about Jesus, and they hand to embrace Him now!

Retainment
Acts 4:17

The Sanhedrin refused to repent and quickly come to "recognition." They could not eliminate what was already in

The Sanhedrin | **Acts 4:5**

place, so the best thing to do was maintain their control, their image, and their power. They protected their laws, their temple, and their ceremonies. This protection was a powerful focus on them. Any shift in control would jeopardize their finances and future prosperity. Jesus threatened to disturb all this. If they embraced Jesus, the sacrifices would no longer be needed. They would lose control over people, and the revenue of the temple would be greatly reduced. Let's maintain!

In light of the healed beggar and all those in Jerusalem realizing this miracle, the best they could do was eliminate the witness. They expressed "resistance" to all God proposed through the apostles. The success of the Gospel is not in its programs or buildings, but is in its proclamation. The consistent hammering of one voice after another, speaking His name, breaks the stronghold of evil. They must contain the damage. They determined in their ***hearts that it spreads no further among the people, let us severely threaten them, that from now on they speak to no man in this name*** (Acts 4:17). No one is against miracles. The issue is Jesus! Lame beggars can be delivered and everyone is glad. The problem is Jesus! You have the right to believe and express that belief as you desire. The exception is Jesus! The Sanhedrin would not tolerate Jesus. They would rather have Barabbas, a murderer, than Jesus, a redeemer.

So the Sanhedrin came to a "realization" that it was a message problem, and they must eliminate the expression of the message. ***So they called them and commanded them not to speak at all nor teach in the name of Jesus*** (Acts 4:18). They could speak and teach in any other name but Jesus. But there is no salvation outside Jesus. The lame beggar would not become "perfectly sound" apart from Jesus. Without Jesus there is no hope. We must surrender to Him!

Acts 4:6

THE CONGREGATION

"As well as Annas the high priest, Caiaphas, John, and Alexander, and as many as were of the family of the high priest, were gathered together at Jerusalem" (Acts 4:6).

One of the principles of biblical saturation is "proportion." Because of the limited space and time involved in writing a letter such as the Book of Acts, Luke mentions only what is necessary to fulfill his purpose. He spends two verses highlighting the constituents of those judging Peter and John, making this significant. He begins with **rulers, elders, and scribes.** All Jews would have recognized this group as the Sanhedrin, making the argument that Luke was writing to a much larger audience. However, contained in this group was the wealthy, aristocratic, elite, and highly educated, indicating that there was more involved here than was familiar to the Jews.

Luke then added more detail about this elevated group (Acts 4:6). He begins with **Annas the high priest**, a man commanding influence, and the head of the priestly party in Jerusalem during the time of Christ. He introduced **Caiaphas**, the son-in-law of Annas. Understanding the political system of that hour is important. When the chief members of the priestly group were listed, Annas was always listed first as the high priest. However, in John's account of the Gospel, he called Caiaphas the high priest (John 18:13, 24). Luke indicated in his Gospel account that two priests jointly held the office. *"While Annas and Caiaphas were high priests, the word of God came to John the son of Zacharias in the wilderness"* (Luke 3:2).

The proper understanding is in the political structure of their day. In the Jewish system, when a person became a high priest it was for life. But in the time of our passage, the Romans were ruling the world. They allowed each culture to maintain its own structure and religion but with some control. In the case of Judaism, the Roman authorities had to approve the position of high priest before bribery became a key factor. The priest who could afford the largest bribe acquired and maintained the position. For many years, Annas was that person. His money supply came from the temple's business. The high priest had to approve every lamb before it could be sacrificed. Each Jewish family had to purchase their sacrificial lamb from the outer court of the temple, and the approved lambs were more expensive than the usual market price. Typical currency was not allowed in the temple marketplace; therefore moneychangers were in the outer court to exchange the Jewish money for temple currency. The high priest was in charge of this business enterprise.

Annas held the position of high priest for many years because his bribe appeased the Roman leadership. But because he became so powerful in the Jewish system, Roman authorities decided he should be replaced as high priest. Annas, not to be outdone, furnished the bribe for one of his sons. In fact, five of the sons of Annas were high priests and his son-in-law, Caiaphas. If you remember, when Jesus was captured in the Garden of Gethsemane, He was first taken to Annas, the high priest, for a brief trial. Then He was escorted to Caiaphas, the current high priest (John 18:13). Annas managed to maintain influence and control over the political structure and decisions of Israel. He was arrogant, shrewd, ambitious, and enormously wealthy.

Luke completes the group, *"John, and Alexander, and as many as were of the family of the high priest"* (Acts 4:6). We have nothing in the records to identify John and Alexander, but they had to have influence to be in this list. Many of these men would not have been on duty in Jerusalem for the normal meetings of the Sanhedrin but would have been notified and asked to gather in Jerusalem. The continual flow of miracles, the growth of the early church, and the constant proclamation of, ***"in Jesus the resurrection from the dead"*** demanded the participation and interest of this influential group in its entirety. This group's intention was that the crucifixion of Jesus would resolve this issue, but here it is again.

The common aspect of this group is that they were Sadducees. This meant they were rationalists in religion. They denied the supernatural, and they affirmed the power of the human will. They were opposed and held in contempt everything the Pharisees acclaimed, dismissing the oral traditions of the Pharisees. They did not believe in angels, spirits, or the resurrection (Acts 24:15). They were religious because they believed in God and the Law of Moses, but they denied every miraculous story in the Old Testament. The Sadducees was the group that turned the Hebrew economy into an ethical system. Because they did not believe in the resurrection from the dead, they focused on the comfort and pleasure of their present world. Anything that confronted or threatened this focus received their strongest pressure.

What was happening to the comfortable, materialistic, self-sourced religion of this political/religious group? Peter and John stepped into their world. Jesus, the carpenter, was bad enough, but now there were two Galilean fishermen. These men had never attended any important schools and had none of the necessary degrees. They were **uneducated and untrained men** (Acts 4:13). These two men should have stayed in Galilee. They could have been tolerated there but not in Jerusalem, the citadel of this political/religion.

Peter and John were not just ordinary fishermen with a new

idea. God had yanked their lives out of a materialistic focus to a full-fledged spiritual encounter with Him through Jesus. For three years these men had experienced the Spirit's flow, manifesting the image of God through Jesus, something the Sanhedrin had only heard about. Peter and John lived in the constant spiritual invasion of demonic territory as they walked with Jesus daily. He had given them the same power and spiritual abilities. ***He gave them power over unclean spirits, to cast them out, and to heal all kinds of sickness and all kinds of disease*** (Matthew 10:1). Their fishing business was no longer their life. The spiritual world was now displayed in their physical lives. This facilitated physical changes, but the focus of their lives was the spiritual realm.

The death of Jesus interrupted the disciples' focus. Their physical world came crashing down in powerful ways, blinding their spiritual focus. Suddenly, the death of one man became the end of all they dreamed for the spiritual and the physical. But Jesus would not let them go! Without physical death, how would the physical and spiritual move to the other side of the grave? The message of Jesus was never about the ease and comfort of this world. Jesus calls us to the vision of eternal living where the spiritual overwhelms the physical. The physical truly becomes the platform for the life of the spiritual!

Capture

Luke highlights the transformation that happened in the lives of Peter and John. Although they experienced the unseen world displayed in the life of Jesus, the reality of such a life had not gripped them. They still dreamed a physical kingdom being established in their physical world. They became aware of spiritual reality, but it was not their focus. They participated in and experienced the ministry of the spiritual world in their

Part 2: The Analytical Response

physical world, but it did not become their focus. Then the resurrection of Jesus invaded their world. They spent forty days with Jesus who was still physical, but He dwelt in a new body sourced by the spiritual. They received a vision of something beyond their physical existence. Jesus called them to a life beyond fishing, paying bills, and physical comfort. They began to experience what they could not imagine, and they were captured by the reality beyond their physical shortsightedness.

The eternal realm invaded their physical existence. They interacted with the risen Lord for forty days and received the promise that the Holy Spirit would be given to them. The vision Jesus had for the kingdom became theirs. The Holy Spirit indwelling them increased and deepened what Jesus started. They were no longer in a physical world trying to accomplish spiritual activities. They were filled with the spiritual realm, the Spirit sourcing them, causing their goals and desires to become spiritual. They subjected their physical beings to the spiritual focus of their lives. Instead of the physical wanting to use the spiritual to its advantage, the physical submitted to the spiritual. The disciples began to display the unseen world in their physical lives.

Peter reached out to a lame beggar. No one from the high priestly family had ever expressed any interest in him. He could never enter the temple because of his disability. People with physical disabilities were not worthy to participate in the physical activities of physical worship to God. This man was of no advantage to the physical comfort of the priests whose focus was on materialism and physical advantage. What could a lame beggar contribute to them? But Peter's focus was not physical. He said, ***"Silver and gold I do not have, but what I do have I give you: In the name of Jesus Christ of Nazareth, rise up and walk"*** (Acts 3:6). Do not misunderstand! Peter definitely involved the physical. God physically, through Peter, restored the lame beggar, but it was much more than physical. Begging and collecting coins for physical survival had been the physical focus of this beggar. But he also tried to tap into the spiritual to achieve his physical focus. For some forty years he sat outside the temple, the symbol of the spiritual realm. His encounter with Peter and John changed everything for this beggar both in the physical and spiritual.

These leaders of Israel denied the supernatural world and focused only on the physical. Again Jesus invaded their world with the jarring reality of the spiritual realm. They could not deny the miracle. No other explanation was given except the resurrected Christ. Peter's message to them was focused on the spiritual. Jesus wanted to capture them with spiritual realities.

Choice

How do you and I handle our problems? Do we consider a problem as an invasion of the spiritual in our world? Is the spiritual trying to capture us? In the middle of this invasion, there is a choice!

Peter and John were confronted with this choice. Peter focused on the physical and failed miserably. Jesus had warned Peter that his failure was coming. He told him that he would deny Him three times before the rooster announced the morning dawn (Matthew 26:34). He saw the spiritual realm, but he focused on the physical. It overwhelmed him into denying the spiritual. He had a choice, and he failed. But he was given a second chance. Thank God for second chances! The opposite of this picture is Judas. He betrayed the spiritual for the physical. He had repeated chances as well. He had a choice!

The ***family of the high priest*** had chance after chance. The physical presence of Jesus brought the spiritual reality to them repeatedly. Nicodemus and Joseph of Arimathea were among some of their own leaders who had urged them to consider the

Part 2: The Analytical Response

spiritual reality of Jesus. The soldiers guarding the tomb of Jesus were shaken to the core when the angel rolled the stone away. The bright light of the angel and the emptiness of the tomb brought a spiritual revelation into the midst of their physical world. The soldiers were quick to share this with their leaders (Matthew 28:11). But these leaders continued in their physical focus. Peter and John were the avenues of spiritual reality that thundered into their priestly lives. Here was a miracle they could not deny and were amazed by this powerful witness. These aristocratic leaders came to the reality that *they could say nothing against it* (Acts 4:14). These leaders were given every reason to embrace Jesus, but their focus was so strongly fixed on the physical that they would not waver. They had a choice.

Peter and John returned to the early church. The leaders of Israel wanted to silence and dismiss their spiritual focus, and they threatened them with harm if they ever mentioned the name of Jesus again. Peter reported to the members of the church the threats from the leaders' physical focus. How did the early church respond? They broke into a praise session. *They raised their voice to God with one accord and said: "Lord, You are God, who made heaven and earth and the sea, and all that is in them"* (Acts 4:24). Then they quoted a Psalm from David. *"Why did the nations rage, and the people plot vain things? The kings of the earth took their stand, and the rulers were gathered together against the Lord and against His Christ"* (Acts 4:25-26). They were so filled with the spiritual realm that *they spoke the word of God with boldness* (Acts 4:31). They had a choice.

Common

The same is true for you and me. The Book of Acts does not emphasize personality types, emotional traits, or background influences. Neither spiritual focus nor the physical focus is determined by environment or upbringing, and being a sensitive person has nothing to do with it. Jesus invades our physical life with spiritual realities. He drives us to see the unmistakable truth. If we reject the spiritual focus and miss the fullness of the Spirit, it is a choice we make.

This choice is a common element in every person's life. No one is void of the revelation and invasion of the spiritual world into his or her reality. We are without excuse. This choice is the amazing truth of "prevenient grace." Paul said, *"For the grace of God that brings salvation has appeared to all men, teaching us that, denying ungodliness and worldly lusts, we should live soberly, righteously, and godly in the present age, looking for the blessed hope and glorious appearing of our great God and Savior Jesus Christ, who gave Himself for us, that He might redeem us from every lawless deed and purify for Himself His own special people, zealous for good works"* (Titus 2:11-14). Please read these verses carefully. Do you see the promised invasion of the spiritual world into the physical reality?

In our passage, God comes again to the family of the high priest who has repeatedly decided he desires the physical over the spiritual. Yet God spoke again. He will never leave us alone. He speaks to you. You can see the physical complications as simple physical problems to be solved. You can attempt to get the spiritual realm to help you solve your physical problems, but your focus is still physical. God calls you to something beyond the physical circumstances and comfort of your life. He calls you to intimacy with Him. He wants to flow His world through your physical life. The physical realm is not bad, and it is never dismissed as unimportant. The physical realm is to be the instrument of divine action as He fills you. You have a choice!

Acts 4:7

THE CONFRONTATION

And when they had set them in the midst, they asked, "By what power or by what name have you done this?" (Acts 4:7).

The air of the scene was filled with intensity. Seventy-one powerful members of the Sanhedrin gathered with Annas the high priest, his son-in-law, Caiaphas, John and Alexander, and the members of the family of Annas. According to tradition, they were seated in a semicircle with the president in the center. Law students were probably gathered around, listening to every case, and becoming acquainted with the process of law.

Standing amid these powerful representatives were two apostles with a healed beggar by their side. The two Galileans faced the wealthiest, best educated, and most powerful people in Israel. Peter and John were not used to such company. The accent of their language, their vocabulary, and the accusations against them were each devastating elements to their confidence.

We must never forget that the force behind the persecution in the Book of Acts was the Sadducees, not the Pharisees. This source was an abrupt change from the Gospel accounts of Jesus. The persecution and death of Jesus came from the plotting and anger of the Pharisees. The Sadducees were present and participated in the background of Jesus' persecution, but the Pharisees were primary. The law was the justification for the persecution, but more specifically, the law of the oral traditions.

Jesus consistently violated, dismissed, and preached against their oral traditions.

But the powerful group accusing Peter and John was the Sadducees. They were the aristocratic wealthy of Jerusalem. They denied the supernatural and affirmed only the freedom of human will. They rejected and strongly rebuked the oral traditions of the Pharisees. They were rationalists in religion. They believed in God and the Mosaic Law, but they denied every story in the Old Testament containing the miraculous. They denied the resurrection, laughed at the existence of angels, and ridiculed the idea of spirits. Before them stood the two apostles filled with the Holy Spirit, preached the resurrection of Jesus, and participated in a miracle that was an amazing encounter.

That encounter revolved around a question and set the stage for the decision that the Sanhedrin would make. We superficially make inquiry in our everyday lives. "How are you doing?" is a question for which we really do not want an answer. "Isn't this a beautiful day?" is asked without care. But the setting of our passage is a court of law. They designed this question to gather information by which the court could bring proper judgment to Peter and John, and it seemed the Sanhedrin was not sure what the apostle's offence was. Their question was, ***"By what power or by what name have you done this?"***

There are three assumptions promoting this question, and by asking it the Sadducees revealed their hearts. Getting anyone to ask a question in a large crowd is difficult because a question reveals the level of comprehension, the motive of the person asking, and what is really important in the eyes of the inquirer. In other words, the deep inner heart of the one asking comes to light, true for the members of the Sanhedrin!

Part 2: The Analytical Response

Reality

The question being asked by the Sanhedrin was, ***"By what power or by what name have you done this?"*** (Acts 4:7). The content of our passage indicates they asked this question of Peter and John. The "alliance" consisted of ***"the priests, the captain of the temple, and the Sadducees"*** (Acts 4:1), and they represented the Sanhedrin. They were in charge of the temple during this ***"hour of prayer, the ninth hour"*** (Acts 3:1). Peter and John were the focus of the alliance's disturbance. These leaders were ***"greatly disturbed that they taught the people and preached in Jesus the resurrection from the dead"*** (Acts 4:2). Because the hour was late, the alliance put the apostles in jail for the night. The next morning the court met in force. Peter and John were set in the midst of the court, and the question was addressed to them.

From the details just spoken, we must assume that Peter and John were the instruments through which some unknown power created this miracle. They were not innocent people standing on the sidelines, but were the instigators of this miracle. If someone was to be punished for what had happened, it should be Peter and John. Peter and John took full responsibility for their participation in this miracle. They did not shirk their involvement, and they embraced it with enthusiasm. The right people were on trial.

In the question being asked, the Sanhedrin expressed an attitude toward Peter and John. In the Greek text, the expression is revealed in the word order. The word *you* is a translation of the Greek word "humeis," and it is the last word in the question. **Vincent's New Testament Word Studies** relates *"you"* ends the sentence in the Greek with a contemptuous emphasis, "you people." The Sanhedrin viewed the apostles as Galilean fishermen without status, proper manners, or value. They asked, "How did people like you manage to do such a miracle?"

With the assumption that Peter and John were responsible instruments for the miracle, it was assumed the miracle needed an explanation. In the question, what did they mean by the word *this*? They were not willing to call what happened a miracle at this point. They dismissed Peter and John so they could deliberate. They said, *"What shall we do to these men? For, indeed, that a notable miracle has been done through them is evident to all who dwell in Jerusalem, and we cannot deny it"* (Acts 4:16). This conclusion was the result of *"seeing the man who had been healed standing with them"* (Acts 4:14), and this greatly disturbed the Sanhedrin. The doctrine of the resurrection was a point of contention between the Sadducees and Pharisees, but that was not what this controversy was about. This conflict did not involve temple policy or the reconstruction of a temple room. This conflict was about a changed life! They could not deny this.

This witness in the Book of Acts brought about the evangelization of the world, and in seventy years Christianity became the world's religion. Christianity was not recognized because of the construction of church buildings or the development of schools for educating ministers. The lives of people in the early Church forced everyone to admit a miracle had happened!

Resource

The Sanhedrin assumed a miracle happened. They would not call it a "miracle" but entitled it *"this."* They also assumed that Peter and John participated in and were responsible for this miracle. Let us examine the question again. *"By what power or by what name have you done this?"* (Acts 4:7). The nature of the question assumed there was a power working through and beyond the apostles. Two aspects to the question in the text are,

Part 2: The Analytical Response

"By what power" and *"by what name."* In each case the Greek word "en," translated *by*, means "in"! The heart of the question is not "In what authority?" The question is: "In what manner of power;" "What is the enabling cause; or "What is the element in which it was done?" The question is not "In what name," but "By what manner of name?" In other words, the question is, "What force did you employ to set this man on his feet?" This is a technical question.

The procedure followed by the Sanhedrin is in the instructions given by God to Israel in the Old Testament (Deuteronomy 13:1-5). He gave them guidance to protect them from the influences that would entice them *"from the way in which the Lord your God commanded you to walk. So you shall put away the evil from your midst"* (Deuteronomy 13:5). The instructions were simple. When a prophet or a "dreamer of dreams" appeared to the Israelites and gave them a sign or a wonder (miracle) to entice them to follow and serve other gods, they were to recognize that as a test. The test was from the Lord their God, *"to know whether you love the Lord your God with all your heart and with all your soul"* (Deuteronomy 13:3). The instructions encouraged them to, *"walk after the Lord your God and fear Him, and keep His commandments and obey His voice; you shall serve Him and hold fast to Him"* (Deuteronomy 13:4). Then they were to put to death the prophet or "dreamer of dreams" because he attempted to turn them from their God!

We should applaud the Sanhedrin for following the instruction of God. They called Peter and John before the supreme council because they performed a sign or wonder. Did they think Peter would give them the name of some false god, a magic formula, or an incantation? But Peter puts all this firmly in the hands of their God! Their God raised Jesus from the dead (Acts 4:10). He quoted the Old Testament Psalms that said their God had put the chief cornerstone in place (Acts 4:11; Psalms 118:22). When the Sanhedrin threatened Peter and John, their response was, ***"Whether it is right in the sight of God to listen to you more than to God, you judge"*** (Acts 4:19). The apostles continually talked about what God was doing in and through Jesus, and this talk was a problem for the Sanhedrin.

The Sadducees developed an impersonal religion. They believed in the God of the Old Testament, but He was a belief structure. They adapted and shaped Him in their materialistic life form. Jesus was far from present in their lives. He preached in their streets and lived a lifestyle opposed to their system. They participated in His crucifixion only to have Him continue in the lives of the apostles. We can accept God, but when He becomes Jesus we are disturbed! He indwells us, goes to work with us, enters our entertainment, dictates our language, and affects our relationship with others. If they could have eliminated Jesus from their scene, all would have been well.

Refusal

One other assumption exists. If you slipped into the Sanhedrin and heard the question asked, you might immediately assume the answer is Jesus. Does not everyone know this? The outpouring of the Holy Spirit, the day of Pentecost, happened with all the temple workers present. Peter preached an amazing explanatory sermon in answer to an inquiry of the Jews. His presentation was about Jesus. He told of God raising Jesus from the dead (Acts 2:24, 32), God making Jesus Lord and Christ (Acts 2:36), and God seating Jesus at His right hand, giving Him the fullness of the Promise of the Father (Acts 2:33). The explanation for Pentecost is Jesus. Everything the Father did in Jesus He is doing wonderfully in us!

In the following days and months (we do not know the exact time), the apostles spent all their time teaching and preaching Jesus. The early Church grew in Jerusalem. Did the Sanhedrin

Part 2: The Analytical Response

know what they were preaching? Did they not hear the message of Jesus? *"Then fear came upon every soul, and many wonders and signs were done through the apostles"* (Acts 2:43). Their miracles were done in the name of Jesus, and the Sadducees had to know this. Now Peter and John participated in the healing of the lame beggar (Acts 3). This miracle had nothing new or unusual about it. Jesus was the heart of it. However, this miracle precipitated Peter's opportunity to speak to a crowd in the temple at Solomon's porch. Peter gave an exhortation about Jesus. He began with this fact. *"The God of Abraham, Isaac, and Jacob, the God of our fathers, glorified His Servant Jesus"* (Acts 3:13). Peter called Jesus *"the Holy One and the Just"* (Acts 3:14), and *"the Prince of life, whom God raised from the dead"* (Acts 3:16). Peter lifted up the name of Jesus. *"And His name, through faith in His name, has made this man strong"* (Acts 3:16). He proclaimed that all the prophets of old spoke of Jesus (Acts 3:18, 21-25). His message was that the Trinity God of the Old Testament raised Jesus from the dead and sent Him *"to bless you, in turning away every one of you from your iniquities"* (Acts 3:26).

The resurrection was the event that brought the action of the alliance aggressively against Peter and John. They were *"greatly disturbed that they taught the people and preached in Jesus the resurrection from the dead"* (Acts 4:2). Jesus was the answer to the Sanhedrin's question about the power of the miracle. But why was it necessary for them to even ask? The apostles consistently spoke of Jesus. Jesus was the heart of their answer to everything. Evidently the Sanhedrin could not assume that answer, but how could they miss it?

They refused it! They stubbornly pushed Jesus aside. Regardless of the evidence or the demonstration, they maintained their comfortable, materialistic view. They refused to acknowledge any supernatural miracles, any movement of the spiritual world, and any life after death. They could not seek truth because it would demand life change. They could not entertain the visitation of God on their lives for that would bring them to repentance. The message of Jesus came in full revelation, and they refused.

This refusal is our reality. Jesus has not left us without His witness. His presence is pressing us. The revelation of His Person is all around us! Are we open?

Acts 4:7

LIFE'S QUESTION

And when they had set them in the midst, they asked, "By what power or by what name have you done this?" (Acts 4:7).

I would like you to place yourself in this scene. Perhaps you want to change your name to Peter or John and participate in this trial as if it were your own. There are parallels between what is happening in your daily life and the events of our passage. Life has been good to you in these last months. You have success in ministry. The indwelling Spirit of God coming into you was an awakening unprecedented in experience. You are experiencing miracles; lives are changed before you. The church is growing, and you are one of the key leaders. You have a sense of worth and value as people look to you for leadership and guidance.

Jesus warned us about getting comfortable. In the middle of ministry, He spoke about persecution as if it were certain. He said, *"And you will be hated by all for My name's sake"* (Matthew 10:22). *"It is enough for a disciple that he be like his teacher, and a servant like his master. If they have called the master of the house Beelzebub, how much more will they call those of his household!"* (Matthew 10:25).

Jesus did not submit this truth to us once or twice. He did it repeatedly because it really mattered. As we plunge below the surface of Jesus' teaching, we discover He expressed a joy over persecution. Knowing it presented an opportunity for witness, it was as if He relished its evil thrust. In fact, the greater the persecution is the greater the impact of witness!

Let me remind you of the beauty of the Beatitudes (Matthew 5:3-12). They are the picture of a helpless person (***poor in spirit***) who embraces his helplessness as a grief-stricken soul embraces his grief (***mourn***). This opens the door for the resource of God to envelop him (***comfort***). Out of this embrace, a new creature called the Kingdom of God is born. Flowing from the resource of God through a man's helplessness will be meekness, mercy, fullness, purity, and peace. What a beautiful picture! You would think everyone would rush to embrace this kind of relationship. What is the conclusion of the Spirit-filled life? The last Beatitude is, ***"Blessed are those who are persecuted!"*** (Matthew 5:10). We are to embrace this with rejoicing and exceeding gladness (Matthew 5:12). Persecution becomes the perfect platform for God to display all the attributes of the Kingdom person. Persecution is where God's attributes are exhibited in the sharpest and most vibrate colors.

The writer of the Book of Hebrews chides us for our gripes, complaints, and woes. The writer urges us to look to Jesus. After all, we have not shed any of our blood resisting sin. Jesus is ***the author and finisher of our faith, who for the joy that was set before Him endured the cross, despising the shame, and has sat down at the right hand of the throne of God*** (Hebrews 12:2). Jesus embraced the cross in all its persecution with joy. He does not call us to do something He has not already done!

Peter and John were yanked out of the pulpit before the sermon was completed. They had no chance to bring the crowd to a decision, yet ***many of those who heard the word believed*** (Acts 4:4). The hour in which this occurred was inconvenient. Because it was late, Peter and John spent the night in jail. This holdover gave the leaders of Israel time to notify the most influential people of Jerusalem to attend the trial. The question of the hour expresses the persecution the apostles experienced

Part 2: The Analytical Response

and the attitude of persecution coming from the Sanhedrin. Persecution is not just their scene; it is our reality.

Attitude

Let us begin with the underlying attitude prompted by such treatment. Luke wrote, **"And when they had set them in the midst, they asked"** (Acts 4:7). **When they had set them in the midst** is a participle clause giving content to the main subject **they**. The main verb is **asked** in the middle voice, imperfect tense, and indicative mood. In other words, it is a simple statement of fact originating in the personal preferences of the Sanhedrin. Because they have posed and are now posing the question, it is related to the past, because they have not just started asking the question. Evidently this question has been discussed in the group daily as miracles, preaching, and teaching occurred through the apostles. This query was the first time they officially could confront the apostles with this long-standing question.

The Greek word "punthanomai," translated **asked**, comes from the root word meaning, "to question." Its focus is on finding information by inquiry; it is a matter merely of data. All other motives that might affect the asking are eliminated. It parallels the casual question of "What time is it?" This word differs from the Greek word "erotao," which means a request such as a favor. The Greek word "aiteo," a demand for something deserved or earned, and the Greek word "zeteo," which implies a search for something hidden or lost, are different. "Zeteo" is also different from the Greek word "deomai," which involves the idea of an urgent need.

The Sadducees denied the supernatural and affirmed only the freedom of human will. They were rationalists in religion. They believed in God and the Mosaic Law, but they denied every story in the Old Testament containing the miraculous.

They denied the resurrection from the dead, the existence of angels, and the idea of spirits. So their question was strictly an intellectual query to learn by casual intelligence.

Their asking does not contain seeking, desire for truth, or expansion of spiritual realities. They expressed no concern for the healed beggar. They never searched for an answer to the social problem of the handicapped or the devastation to family life because of financial poverty. They were never excited about what was happening in the early Church, and they never thought it might be the answer to this need. They heard Peter's answer, dismissed the apostles, and discussed what must be done, with no expression of care, love, or compassion for the needs of others. Their approach was strictly rational logic. They had their rules, religious system, and materialistic structure that must not be disturbed.

The result when the heart of Christ is lost is religion without the cross, lacking the bleeding, suffering, and dying of the Savior. A belief system only in the head misses the heart. I hear it expressed often in religious circles, "We have always done it this way!" "They just do not fit with us!" Without a caring heart that knows the cause, people judge and condemn. Where are they hurting? What are the circumstances; what are they experiencing? This attitude knows nothing of the song, *"He looked beyond my faults and saw my need!"* They focus only on the fault; they do not have a caring heart for the needy, a religion without compassion.

No one wants this kind of religion imposed on them, yet we are quite content to readily extend it to others. We are jaded in our approach; we would not call this persecution. If witnessing causes us to lose a job, we call that persecution. If we are shunned from a fellowship group for speaking of Jesus, we call that persecution. Peter and John preached in Jesus the resurrection from the dead, and they were placed in jail; that was persecution. However, if I am a professed Christian, and I avoid my hurting brother, I am persecuting him. Caring only for my traditions to the elimination of others is persecution. Ousting a person from my fellowship because his manners are uncomfortable for me is persecution. Anytime my needs are superior to the needs of others, I am a persecutor. My rationalistic religious approach dictates to me rather than the caring heart of God. Could it be I am a persecutor?

Abasement

Let's go to the other end of our verse. In the Greek text, the word order tells us something of the attitude of the Sanhedrin. We highlighted this truth in previous studies, but it is important to note it again. The word *"you"* is a translation of the Greek word "humeis." The word is the last word in the question. Vincent's New Testament Word Studies relates *"you"* close the sentence in the Greek with a contemptuous emphasis, "you people." One of the consistent elements of persecution is "superiority."

Peter and John were Galileans. They were fishermen doing the menial tasks of caring for their nets, cleaning their fish, and working with their hands. The Sanhedrin referred to them *as uneducated and untrained men* (Acts 4:13). The Sanhedrin consisted of educated, wealthy businessmen who hired people like the apostles to do the dirty jobs they would not do. The members of the Sanhedrin were superior to the apostles in style of living, acquired materialism, educational status, position in the religious and political system, and in the priestly heritage. The Sanhedrin viewed these Galilean fishermen as men with no status, proper manners, or value. They asked, "How did people like you manage to do such a miracle?" They degraded, belittled, and demeaned the apostles.

This kind of superiority breeds persecution. In every scene of persecution, someone expresses an element of superiority.

If superiority is removed, and the humble spirit of bleeding, suffering, and dying for others is expressed, persecution ceases to exist. The only way I can persecute you is to feel superior; that justifies me in my persecution. You walk into my space, and I demean you by ignoring your existence. You are not worthy of my consideration. That ignoring is a form of persecution. I belittle you instead of encouraging, strengthening, and supporting. Belittling is a form of persecution. I exalt myself by standing on you; that is persecution.

Action

The heart of the question revolves around the words *"power"* (dunamis) and *"name"* (onoma). In each case the Greek word "en," translated *by*, means "in." The heart of the question is not "In what authority" but "In what manner of power, what is the enabling cause, or the element in which it was done?" The question is not "In what name" but "By what manner of name?" In other words, "What force did you employ to set this man on his feet?" This query is a technical question.

The Greek word "dunamis" must be seen in light of the Greek word "ischus." "Ischus" is the actual resource; "dunamis" is the action of the resource. Dynamite placed on the shelf of a storage room is "ischus." All the potential for explosion, the moving of mountains, and the uprooting of timber is there. However, none of this potential is happening; there is no action. When the dynamite is planted in the right place and its power is released, "dunamis" takes place.

The question of the Sanhedrin was concerned with the active change in a lame beggar. They could not bring themselves to call it a miracle because they did not believe in the supernatural. In the question they referred to the miracle as *"this."* The restored lame beggar was nothing but a *"this"* to them. Their concern

Part 2: The Analytical Response

was not for him at all but the active force moving to accomplish this through the apostles.

This idea is highlighted in the Greek word "poieo," translated **"have done."** We are forced to consider this word repeatedly in the New Testament, as it is the Greek word expressing trees "bearing" fruit. It refers to the nature flowing and producing through the individual. A person can do their duty, meet their obligations, and discipline their actions. However, this word (poieo) is spontaneous in its action, meaning I cannot help myself, and it is the natural action of the individual's heart. This is the "birthing" of my life! I had no choice on the color of my hair, the height of my body, or the size of my nose. A power (dunamis) in me is "poieo" in my life. This is the question of the Sanhedrin.

A normal, everyday question for every life is the same. What is in you that makes you as you are? Why do you swear, lose your temper, or desire evil? Why do I demean, belittle, feel prejudice, or judge others? Why were the Sanhedrin as they were and the apostles as they were? There was a power flowing through the apostles that the Sanhedrin did not have. Each believed in God Jehovah; each offered sacrificial lambs and observed the accepted feast days. But they were different. I need to answer this question for my life!

This is the primary question of Christianity. Christianity is not a religion of activities, laws, and patterns. If it were possible to reproduce all the right patterns of Christianity, we would still not be Christian. Christianity is defined by what is "poieo" or "birthing" you. The apostles were filled with the Spirit of Jesus. Peter could not help himself as he walked by the lame beggar at the Gate Beautiful. The Spirit of God birthed in him a care for the beggar that demanded the flow of Jesus Christ of Nazareth's explosive power. The Sadducees walked by the same man and felt no compulsion; in fact they felt repulsion.

The Sanhedrin threatened the two apostles and let them

go. The threat was that they were *"not to speak at all nor teach in the name of Jesus"* (Acts 4:18). Here is how they responded. *"Whether it is right in the sight of God to listen to you more than to God, you judge. For we cannot but speak the things which we have seen and heard"* (Acts 4:19-20). The Sanhedrin wanted the name of Jesus silenced; the apostles could not help proclaiming His name. The difference was in them, and God's nature was producing them.

Actualizer

In the question asked by the Sanhedrin is the *"name"* issue. The Greek word is "onoma." The question implies authority; it means to come or to do something in or by the name of someone, using his name. With whom are you connected? An explosive power is flowing (poieo) through the apostles. The Sanhedrin is demanding an identification of the One responsible for this power.

How could they even ask this question? The name of Jesus had been highlighted repeatedly. When the lame beggar received his miracle, Peter called on only one name. *"In the name of Jesus Christ of Nazareth, rise up and walk"* (Acts 3:6). In Peter's exhortation at Solomon's Porch, he identified the name as, *"Jesus, whom you delivered up and denied in the presence of Pilate"* (Acts 3:13). The trial before the Sanhedrin was a result of these leaders **being greatly disturbed that they taught the people and preached in Jesus the resurrection from the dead** (Acts 4:2). Peter was filled with the Holy Spirit and did not hesitate to declare, *"that by the name of Jesus Christ of Nazareth, whom you crucified, whom God raised from the dead, by Him this man stands here before you whole"* (Acts 4:10). In fact, *"Nor is there salvation in any other, for there is no other name under heaven given among men by*

Part 2: The Analytical Response

which we must be saved" (Acts 4:12). There is no possible escape from identifying the exact Person responsible for the explosive power of redemption in the healed beggar!

The issue at hand is Jesus. Our problem is not with doctrine or theology but with the Person of Jesus' embrace. Our need is not reform or adjustment; we must embrace the Person of Jesus. The reason persecution is certain for the Christian is the revelation of the Person of Jesus. To set Jesus aside is to no longer be Christian. To the degree we are not His is the degree we are not Christian. We need a complete urging for Jesus. May our hearts hunger for Him, Jesus!

Acts 4:8-12

THE COMMUNICATION

"Then Peter, filled with the Holy Spirit, said to them, "Rulers of the people and elders of Israel: If we this day are judged for a good deed done to a helpless man, by what means he has been made well, let it be known to you all, and to all the people of Israel, that by the name of Jesus Christ of Nazareth, whom you crucified, whom God raised from the dead, by Him this man stands here before you whole. This is the 'stone which was rejected by you builders, which has become the chief cornerstone.' Nor is there salvation in any other, for there is no other name under heaven given among men by which we must be saved" (Acts 4:8-12).

The theme of the Scriptures is "God is love." We must always evaluate judgment, wrath, and hell in light of God's love. His love is on a different level than our self-centered love, and because of that, it demanded a word with new content. A word from the classical Greek language was adopted into the New Testament. This word was given the content of selfless, self-sacrificing, and self-giving love. This sounds like "cross style" but is "agape" love.

When God's love approaches us before the salvation experience, it is called "prevenient grace." This grace is highly characterized by God's initiative. God's action toward us is motivated and sourced by His love. We did not earn or merit such love. Nothing in us can ever "win" His love. All expressions

Part 2: The Analytical Response

of love toward us come from the nature of God. Nothing we have ever done has been good enough to cause God to love us; nothing we will ever do is bad enough to cause God not to love us. His love is not dependent on us but on Himself! He decided to love us!

There is an amazing illustration of this in our story. The leadership of Israel is responsible for the spiritual welfare of the Jewish people, but they manipulated their religion to benefit themselves. The Pharisees were focused on the Law and their oral traditions, which brought them into conflict with Jesus. Jesus' focus was the Scriptures, and He wanted to bring the Jews back to that. The conflict the Sadducees had with Jesus and the apostles was the threat they felt to their economic welfare. God took the initiative to reach out to this leadership repeatedly. God's attitude was expressed through the words of Jesus. "O Jerusalem, *Jerusalem, the one who kills the prophets and stones those who are sent to her! How often I wanted to gather your children together, as a hen gathers her chicks under her wings, but you were not willing!*" (Matthew 23:37).

You would think after the brutality and complete rejection expressed by these leaders in the crucifixion of Jesus that God would eliminate His love in any expression. But the most elite of the Roman soldiers fainted from fear at the tomb of Christ. An angel descended, and the body of Jesus was gone. They rushed into Jerusalem to report this to the leadership. They *"reported to the chief priests all the things that had happened"* (Matthew 28:11). From the lips of the pagan soldiers came a testimony of Jesus' resurrection. A loving God gave them another witness.

Pentecost gave birth to the early Church. Hundreds of Jerusalem Jews came under the influence of the risen Lord. Again, God gave a witness to the leadership of Israel. Through the presence of Jesus, the apostles demonstrated the power of God in miracles. Our passage occurs in this renewed witness.

The Communication | **Acts 4:8-12**

One miracle out of all miracles affected the leadership of Israel the most. This miracle could not be disputed because the healed beggar, whom was known by many in Jerusalem since his birth, stood in their presence (Acts 4:14). The leaders admitted, ***"For, indeed, that a notable miracle has been done through them is evident to all who dwell in Jerusalem, and we cannot deny it"*** (Acts 4:16). God orchestrated this scene to bring another witness to this aristocratic group. Peter was given a chance to stand before them and account the power and name by which the miracle was done! Jesus will be proclaimed!

Let this truth grip your heart. God often and powerfully demands an audience with you. He manipulates the circumstances of your life to place you in the middle of His love message. You run from His influence only to find He was before you and behind you. You run right into His arms. Continual refusal and resistance is your only way out. But even then He comes after you. Will He not continue until you make your bed in hell?

Cause
Acts 4:8

Luke was specific about the cause of the communication, the Holy Spirit (Acts 4:8). Would God go through all the difficulty to assemble such a gathering and rely on Peter's wisdom? The last time Peter was exposed to the power of this group, he denied Jesus three times before the rooster crowed (Matthew 26:69-75). The selection of the words flowing from Peter's mouth was under the direction of the Holy Spirit.

After months of "on the job training," Jesus decided to send the disciples on an evangelistic tour. He took some of the power in Himself and transferred it to them (Matthew 10:1). In His instructions prior to sending them forth, He said, ***"But when they deliver you up, do not worry about how or what you should*** *speak. For it will be given to you in that hour what you should speak"* (Matthew 10:19).

If God could flow through the disciples to project the languages of fifteen different nationalities, could He not speak to the leaders of Israel through Peter (Acts 2:4)? Jesus said, ***"For out of the abundance of the heart the mouth speaks"*** (Matthew 12:34). Could the Spirit of God dwell in the heart and produce speech? Peter, filled with the Spirit, came before this court, and Jesus flowed through him as he spoke. The leaders were affected by his words. ***"Now when they saw the boldness of Peter and John, and perceived that they were uneducated and untrained men, they marveled"*** (Acts 4:13). Oh, to be filled with the Spirit of Jesus; this is also our calling!

Case
Acts 4:9

The case is not normal because a normal situation is of an evil deed. We are caught; judgment and correction must be appropriated; we are placed before the court and suspected of guilt. The case in our passage is that Peter and John did something right and good. A helpless man was made productive and whole. What is there to judge or punish?

I confess that most of the time, I am guilty of wrong. I enter the court of my own judging, and the court of others finds me guilty. I should have done better. What is difficult is when I am not guilty. I did everything right, but I am being blamed, criticized, and judged. A person who does the crime must do the time. What I find impossible to tolerate is doing the time when there was no crime.

But what if God has a purpose I cannot see? What if He is desperate to communicate the message to the heart of Judaism again and He needs me? God forced the leadership of Israel to acknowledge the miracle, to be astounded by the Spirit of God in the apostles, and to hear the message of Jesus! Would it be difficult to believe this? Every moment of suffering found in the life of the Spirit filled person fulfills a role in the accomplishment of God's plan. He consistently glorifies Himself through the difficulties of our lives?

The disciples asked Jesus, *"Who sinned, this man or his parents, that he was born blind?"* (John 9:2). Jesus strongly protested that it was not because of a wrong deed; the intent of the blindness was a right deed. The purpose of this work was to reveal God in the healed man! Paul and Silas were in the Philippi jail with bleeding backs. Was that the result of a mistake or evil deed? A sovereign God planned to bring redemption to the jailer's household, win a city, and produce an epistle in the New Testament. This must be the perspective through which we see the events of suffering in our lives.

Crucified One
Acts 4:10

The apostles carefully identified Jesus in their witness. They not only proclaimed Jesus as the answer to every situation, but they so completely described Him that no one could be confused about who He was! This is the fourth message of Peter recorded in the Book of Acts. In each message, he identified Jesus as the One crucified and raised from the dead. Peter highlighted the supreme function and purpose of being an apostle as, *"a witness with us of His resurrection"* (Acts 1:22). In each of Peter's three messages addressed to the Jews, he boldly proclaimed Jesus as the One they crucified.

Peter appeared before this court and communicated bleeding, suffering, and dying (cross style) as the heart of the Gospel. The cross was the heart's expression of the court's guilt

Part 2: The Analytical Response

and sin. To Peter and John, the cross style was the heart of what they experienced in the will of God. If God allowed the unfair persecution placed on them to communicate Jesus to these leaders, it would have of necessity the tone of the cross. We must understand this as the core of all ministries. ***"And according to the law almost all things are purified with blood, and without shedding of blood there is no remission"*** (Hebrews 9:22). Jesus used the image of ***"sheep in the midst of wolves"*** (Matthew 10:16) to describe ministry to His disciples. This image was a picture of the ministry of bleeding, suffering, and dying. Redemption happens only as wolves bite sheep. If I am a Spirit-filled sheep, as the wolf bites me, he tastes Jesus! Jesus immediately expanded this in His explanation to speak of persecution in every area (Matthew 10:17-20). But it is the delight of a disciple to be like His Master. ***"It is enough for a disciple that he be like his teacher, and a servant like his master. If they have called the master of the house Beelzebub, how much more will they call those of his household!"*** (Matthew 10:25). Evidently, we must live the cross style if we want to be in Jesus' household.

Peter related the "wholeness" of the healed beggar, who stood before the court directly, to ***"the name of Jesus Christ of Nazareth, whom you crucified, whom God raised from the dead"*** (Acts 4:10). Again, notice the clarity in Jesus' identification of this court's guilt regarding His crucifixion, and then notice God's approval of Jesus when He raised Him from the dead. This verse is a continuation of the previous verse. The idea of these two verses establishes a contrast between the ***good deed done to a helpless man,*** and the "bad deed done by the court." This court was responsible for crucifying Jesus, who is responsible for the ***good deed.*** A good deed was the platform for conviction; Jesus did nothing but good, and we respond by doing nothing but bad. His bleeding, suffering, and dying are a direct response to our sinfulness.

Cornerstone
Acts 4:11

The next verse confirms and describes the reality of this contrast to the Scriptures. *"This is the 'stone which was rejected by you builders, which has become the chief cornerstone'"* (Acts 4:11; Psalms 118:22). The members of the court understood this imagery. God prophesied this through the prophet Isaiah. *"Behold, I lay in Zion a stone for a foundation, a tried stone, a precious cornerstone, a sure foundation; whoever believes will not act hastily"* (Isaiah 28:16).

If this court hoped that Peter would reveal some foreign god or magic incantation as the cause of this miracle, they were greatly disappointed. If Peter tried to lead the people from Jehovah to serve other gods, they would have had a perfect right to stone him to death. However, he did the opposite. The Trinity God selected Jesus. As revealed through the Old Testament, the Trinity God planned, dreamed, and moved to set this *cornerstone* in place as the foundation for all the fulfilled structure of redemption. The members of this court boldly rejected God's selection. In reality, Peter said they should be the ones on trial for leading Israel astray. At the heart of their rejection was the crucifixion of Jesus. The writer of the Book of Hebrews reminded us of what happens to those who reject Jesus and fall away. *"If they fall away, to renew them again to repentance, since they crucify again for themselves the Son of God, and put Him to an open shame"* (Hebrews 6:6). We cannot boldly criticize the members of this court for their materialistic mindset. They adapted their belief system to fulfill their need for power and the comfort of achievement. What have we done? Any level of rejection of Jesus in favor of self-results in renewed crucifixion. We reside in the sandals of Barabbas! If we save ourselves, we must crucify Jesus. If Jesus

Part 2: The Analytical Response

is to live in us, we must be crucified. Crucifixion is inevitable! Someone must die!

Concentration
Acts 4:12

We have to wonder how long Peter's exhortation lasted. Were their additional illustrations from the Old Testament? Did the Sanhedrin react so forcibly he could not continue? The closing statement of Peter's presentation is one of "concentration." ***"Nor is there salvation in any other, for there is no other name under heaven given among men by which we must be saved"*** (Acts 4:12).

It is deeply encouraging that "salvation" is within the grasp of every person. The materialistic wealthy and the penniless homeless can all find salvation's blessing. There is nothing in the statement that would exclude anyone from this reality. There is no list of deeds including or excluding anyone from salvation. Evidently, we are all equally guilty with equal opportunity. Jesus provided for all!

A "singularity" is in this statement, and there is no room for adjustment, toleration of other possibilities, or further investigation. Evidently, God did what He wanted to do regarding salvation by sealing or delivering it to us in Jesus. Our embrace of this single Person will determine our salvation! Peter boldly declared that salvation couldn't be found in any other person. However, he declared to this court the reason for his statement. In their original question (Acts 4:7), they wanted to know about the power and about the name in which this miracle was done. Peter declared it clearly in this statement. ***"Jesus Christ of Nazareth, whom you crucified"*** is the name!

The beauty of this statement is its "simplicity!" Theology and doctrine are not included; arguments of philosophy are pushed aside. There is no educational level expected or learning standard to master. Would you give your life to Jesus? There is no merit system, no required accomplishments, or no expected goodness. Just give your life to Jesus! Nothing is better than Jesus; nothing is worse than not responding to Jesus. Jesus Christ of Nazareth, whom you crucified, is your answer!

Acts 4:8

WHO IS SPEAKING?

Then Peter, filled with the Holy Spirit, said to them, "Rulers of the people and elders of Israel" (Acts 4:8).

Peter was personally impacted by the life of Jesus. The effect did not happen immediately, but progressed over three years. It began when Peter's brother, Andrew, was one of two disciples following John the Baptist. When Andrew first met Jesus, he spent the whole day with him (John 1:39), and he became so excited about Jesus that he wanted to introduce Peter to Him. Peter and Andrew then traveled with Jesus to attend the wedding in Cana of Galilee. After the wedding, Jesus returned to Judea while Peter continued his fishing. Jesus moved His ministry from Judea to Galilee, and Peter began to support Him during His preaching campaigns in Galilee.

Not long after that, Jesus found Peter and other disciples as they returned from an all-night fishing trip. They were discouraged because they had caught nothing. As they cleaned their nets, Jesus requested to use their boat as a platform to preach to the people. At the close of His message, Jesus suggested to Peter that he go fishing again. Peter was weary from being out all night and catching nothing, and his nets were now clean. But Jesus insisted. They responded to Jesus' suggestion and caught so many fish that their nets were breaking (Luke 5:1-11). Peter's faith was stimulated, and he repented, and when they had returned to shore, he and the others forsook all and followed Jesus. Peter had a new focus.

These disciples were still fishing when Jesus found them a fourth time. Jesus called them to follow Him, and He changed them to fishers of men (Matthew 4:19). From that time forth, Peter fully committed to join Jesus in ministry, and he exhibited personal sacrifice to keep his commitment. For the next two and half years, his faith in Christ developed. Jesus imparted to Peter the power to duplicate His ministry and His miracles. One of Peter's greatest moments was his confession, **"You are the Christ, the Son of the living God"** (Matthew 16:16).

Although Peter exhibited belief and loyalty, something about him that caused Jesus concern. His self-sufficiency was visible repeatedly. Peter was in conflict over position (Matthew 18:1), ministry (Luke 9:49), and racial superiority (Luke 9:51-56), and he greatly influenced the other disciples. This self-sourcing nature will eventually drive a person to utter destruction, and it climaxed for Peter in ultimate defeat.

The upper room was a meeting place for Jesus and His disciples; a place Jesus shared His heart. On a trip to the Mount of Olives, Jesus announced some startling news. He warned the disciples that shortly they would be made to stumble because of Him, quoting a Scripture as the basis of His prediction (Matthew 26:31). In his typical self-centeredness, Peter expressed his strong belief that this might be true of the other disciples but not him. Jesus quickly responded that before the rooster crowed in the morning Peter would deny Him three times. Peter was abhorred by Jesus' prediction, and with the rest of the disciples boldly proclaimed they would die before they denied Him (Matthew 26:35).

The scene quickly unfolded throughout the night hours. Three times Peter and two others were asked by Jesus to watch with Him, but their self-sourcing produced only sleep (Matthew 26:40,43,45). Peter and all the disciples forsook Jesus

Part 2: The Analytical Response

and fled when the multitude, ordered by the chief priests and elders of the people, came with swords and clubs to capture Jesus. Peter did follow Jesus at a distance, slipped into the high priest's courtyard, entered the back of the court, and sat with the servants wanting to see the end (Matthew 26:58). A young servant girl came to him and accused him of being one of the disciples of Jesus. He quickly denied it before them all (Matthew 26:70). Being desperate to escape, he went out to the gateway, only to be confronted by another girl who pointed him out to everyone present as a disciple of Jesus. This time Peter denied Jesus with an oath (Matthew 26:72). A short time later his accent betrayed him, and he exploded with curses and swearing in denial that he even knew Jesus. Then the roosted crowed (Matthew 26:74).

Hearing the rooster crow, Peter remembered what Jesus told him. Repentance gripped his heart as he wept bitterly (Matthew 26:75). It was a complete picture of what Peter could produce. His self-sourcing, with his best discipline, could not remain strong in the presence of the servants of the high priest. After all, Peter was not familiar with the aristocratic circles of the leadership of Israel. He was a Galilean fisherman. His educational level, manners, and customs were not on their level. What chance did he have?

The Sanhedrin, family members of the high priest, and other important elders *"were gathered together"* (Acts 4:6-7). If the pressure Peter felt in the courtyard of the high priest caused him to deny Jesus, how would he respond to the added pressure of the Sanhedrin?

Now we come to our passage. ***"And when they had set them in the midst, they asked, 'By what power or by what name have you done this?'"*** (Acts 4:7). Normally Sanhedrin sat in a semicircle so they might see each other. Peter and John probably stood in the center of the semicircle. They faced the most powerful men of Israel, the ones who manipulated the crucifixion of Christ. The air was filled with tension. If Peter were challenged with a fistfight, he would do well. If you want to know where to catch fish in the Sea of Galilee, Peter had the answer. He knew how to maintain his boat in the midst of a fierce storm. Peter was strong and knowledgeable about many things, but standing before the Sanhedrin, he was destined for defeat. He could not compete against this circle of intellectual, highly educated, and aristocratic leaders of Israel. He had no experience in this kind of setting. How will he survive?

The answer comes thundering from the pages of the Scriptures. ***Then Peter, filled with the Holy Spirit, said to them*** (Acts 4:8). **"Peter"** is the subject of the sentence, and the main verb is **"said."** The Greek word "eipen," translated **"said,"** has no special focus. This word is not focused on content (as is "lego") or on the act of speaking (as is "laleo"). This word declares that Peter said something and we should move on to other important matters. The statement describing Peter is what matters. Peter was **"filled with the Holy Spirit."** The Greek word "pletho," translated **"filled,"** is a participle in the passive voice. That means Peter was not responsible for the act of the filling. Peter entered this pressured situation filled with the Spirit, and the Spirit filled Him throughout the confrontation.

State of Existence

Luke used distinctive Greek terms. He uses "pletho" consistently in connection for the filling of the Holy Spirit. However, on occasions of filling he uses "pleroo." These two Greek words can be used interchangeably; it becomes a matter of preference. Because Luke specifically used "pletho" for the coming of the Holy Spirit, he distinguished it to give special content. The idea of placing content into a container until it is filled is within the parameter of this Greek word. It describes a beautiful picture of the person of the Holy Spirit (content) moving into the essence of the being and flesh of a person (container).

In a previous chapter, Luke described this event occurring in a group of one hundred and twenty believers (Acts 2:1-4). Peter was one of those people. He became a container filled with the content of the Holy Spirit. Obviously Luke suggests that Peter entered this new crisis before the Sanhedrin filled with the Spirit of Jesus. He does not suggest an absence of the Holy Spirit and a recurrence of the Pentecost event. Peter was filled with the Holy Spirit at Pentecost and remained filled to experience the active role of ministry in the early Church. The Holy Spirit did not visit him on occasions of special empowerment. In the Old Covenant, there were selected times of the Holy Spirit's filling, and those fillings were task-oriented. This type of filling was not so with Peter's filling. He experienced the New Covenant intimacy and the consistent indwelling of the Holy Spirit.

The indication of the statement is not a psychological filling. In other words it is not simply feelings or even the thinking of Peter. The filling of the Spirit was not the coming of a presence to strengthen him. The person of God came to live in the person of Peter, causing a uniting of their beings into a functioning unit called the Kingdom of God. I struggle to find language to express this merging of two beings. The merging is a fusion of two elements making them one. God and man have united to become the Kingdom of God on Earth.

Our example of this union is Jesus. Peter gave this illustration in his sermon explaining Pentecost (Acts 2:16-47). He proposed that Jesus was the first human being to experience this. The Trinity God proved Pentecost in Jesus. God answered all the questions about the fullness of the Holy Spirit in the life of Jesus. How does a person act when filled with the Spirit? How does a person think when filled with the Spirit? What is the attitude of a person when filled with the Spirit? The answer is always Jesus.

Peter also demonstrated these qualities. At the close of our passage, the Sanhedrin became aware of Jesus' presence. Jesus presented a powerful manifestation of Himself through Peter; the Sanhedrin recognized His influence (Acts 4:13). They could not deny it. The fullness of the Spirit of Jesus makes Jesus known in every situation! Peter dwelt in this state of existence. He was filled with the Spirit of Jesus when he took the lame beggar by the hand and lifted him to his feet (Acts 3:6, 7). He was filled with the Spirit on Solomon's porch as he exhorted the people concerning the truth about Jesus (Acts 3:11). Those were glorious moments of success. Now in the moments of pressure and stress he remained filled with the Spirit. He lived in this state of fullness.

Although you can expect ministry to happen, this is not a state to accomplish ministry or miracles. This is not a state of comfort and ease because we have an enemy; we are at war. This is not a state of convenience because God is unfolding a plan of redemption and evangelism. The fullness of the Spirit is not focused on us, on our desires, or on our comfort. Jesus is Lord! He merges with our helplessness to demonstrate His greatness and accomplish His will. We do not use Him; He uses us. What a privilege!

State of Emerging

This brings us to another expression of Peter being filled with the Spirit. Within the boundaries of the meaning of the Greek word "pletho" is the wonder of accomplishment, completion, or finishing. We see it repeatedly in the Book of Acts. The Holy Spirit already indwells a person. When a need arises, the Spirit moves through the person to fulfill that need. Thus, the Spirit-filled Christian consistently experiences Jesus' Spirit moving through them accomplishing His determined plan.

Part 2: The Analytical Response

The Spirit of God is not idle in the person. God, in His great power, indwells the helpless person. His position as Lord moves this person from situation to situation fulfilling the Divine plan. He not only brings us into the scene of need, but He dynamically flows through us to accomplish the full destiny of the situation. Our location and our accomplishment within the location are a direct result of Him!

This result was plainly visible in Peter's life. He was not responsible for this threatening situation. The pressure of the most powerful men of Israel judged him, a direct result of the Holy Spirit's indwelling of Peter. The Spirit of God rose in and through Peter to touch a lame beggar. The Spirit of God flowed through Peter to exhort the crowd at Solomon's porch. Now the Spirit of God filled Peter again in this new situation to accomplish God's will.

The preceding scenario is the standard pattern for the Spirit-filled believer. Should it not be expected repeatedly? When we react in our helplessness, this attitude is the key that unlocks and releases the filling of the Spirit. The moment we cease to be helpless we squelch the filling of the Spirit. The Spirit of Jesus indwells and flows only through helpless people. Cockiness, pride, and arrogance are characteristics of self-centeredness and are the only deterrent to being possessed by the Spirit.

The Spirit-filled believer will constantly demonstrate the power and person of Jesus. They will consistently love in hateful situations. They will be persistent in the face of rejection. Their lives will portray the wonder of Christ. People will be reminded of Jesus through their lives. Everything we desire in the spiritual realm will naturally belong to us. Our lives will become the expression of the fruit of the Spirit (Galatians 5:22-23).

Peter was filled with the Spirit. He came into the scene of the lame beggar filled with the Spirit; he ministered to the lame beggar filled with the Spirit; he was victorious before the Sanhedrin filled with the Spirit. What a confidence! Here is my commitment. I do not want to experience anything without the direction of the Spirit of God. Jesus was brought into the wilderness to be tempted by the devil (Matthew 4:1). Whether the situation is pleasant or uncomfortable, I want to know I am there by the direction and conveyance of the Spirit of Jesus. I want the Spirit of Jesus to be released through me to dictate every action, every word, and every result in the event. I never want to handle anything in my life out of self-sourcing.

I must embrace Jesus in a new and deeper relationship. Oh, to be filled with the Spirit! May any other filling disappear from my life; may I know Him alone. May Jesus be my all in all, my only focus, and my consistent director. Let every expression of my life become an expression empowered by His presence. Let all ministries be focused on Him rather than on success, stardom, or fame. Let my single goal be the demonstration of His person. *"It is enough for a disciple that he be like his teacher, and a servant like his master. If they have called the master of the house Beelzebub, how much more will they call those of his household!"* (Matthew 10:25). I want to be of His household!

Acts 4:8

FILLED WITH THE HOLY SPIRIT

Then Peter, filled with the Holy Spirit, said to them, "Rulers of the people and elders of Israel" (Acts 4:8).

"The Acts of the Apostles" is what most Bible translators give as the title for The Book of Acts. However, "The Acts of the Holy Spirit" would be much closer to the truth. Although God enjoys using the instrument of humanity to demonstrate His Divine power, He is the source of the action. No one can dispute the consistent action and presence of the Holy Spirit throughout this book!

Luke first highlights the PATERNAL INFLUENCE of the Holy Spirit. His presence gives birth to the New Covenant lifestyle. Although the Holy Spirit was present in the Old Testament for special tasks and ministries, He comes on all flesh in this new hour (Acts 2:17). The first chapter of Acts is filled with the promise of His coming; it is a reminder of what was previously told (Acts 1:4) and is also a preparation for His coming. The early disciples were told to remain in Jerusalem until the hour of new birth occurs (Acts 1:4). The outpouring of the Holy Spirit thunders through the second chapter in manifestation and explanation. The disciples from Galilee spoke in fifteen different languages to several thousand Jews who surrounded them (Acts 2:7-8). The foreign languages were a demonstration declaring a new level of living. Peter would later explain to this crowd what occurred in their presence. What was now going on in the disciples was what happened in Jesus (Acts 2:22). The Spirit of Jesus birthed the New Covenant.

Luke then highlights the PORTRAIT INFLUENCE of the Holy Spirit. The Trinity God gave the Holy Spirit the assignment to reveal Jesus. Jesus told the disciples that the Holy Spirit was coming. ***"But when the Helper comes, whom I shall send to you from the Father, the Spirit of truth who proceeds from the Father, He will testify of Me"*** (John 15:26). ***"He will glorify Me, for He will take of what is Mine and declare it to you"*** (John 16:14). Our lives are the canvas on which the Holy Spirit paints the face of Jesus for the world to see. He will reveal the heart, the mind, and the nature of Jesus, and He will reproduce the life of Christ through us. As Jesus was the visible image of the Father through the power of the Holy Spirit (Colossians 1:15), so we will be the visible image of Jesus who sits at the right hand of the Father! The result of Peter's explanation to the Sanhedrin clearly verifies this reality. The leaders of Israel ***"realized that they had been with Jesus"*** (Acts 4:13). They recognized the influence of Jesus flowing through the apostles because the teachings and miracles demonstrated Him.

Thirdly, Luke highlights the PRODUCTION INFLUENCE of the Holy Spirit. Although this thought is interwoven into all of the above, it is important enough to be separate and distinct. The Holy Spirit is the source of the believer's life! He sources the actions of the believer as gasoline sources the movement of the car. He is the driving force for the focus of the Christian as self-centeredness drives the focus of the unbeliever. The Holy Spirit forms the Christian's life as the potter shapes the vessel. Yet all of these statements leave much to be desired. What is the truth? The depth of truth must be found in the merging, oneness, and intimacy of the believer and the Holy Spirit. The believer consistently surrenders to the Spirit as a hand surrenders to a glove. The hand, the Holy Spirit, produces the action of the glove, the believer's life!

Our passage fits well with the purpose of Luke's writing. This book is about the acts of the Holy Spirit. Here is a sample of what the Spirit of God wants to do in and through our lives. He does not come to intimidate us; he comes to invite us to the fullness of the Holy Spirit. The fullness of the Holy Spirit was proved in Jesus, the Man (Acts 2:22), and now we see it proven in the lives of the apostles. This "indwelling" must be present in our lives! Let us enlarge our search with three aspects of this truth.

State of Existence

"Then Peter, filled with the Holy Spirit, said to them" (Acts 4:8). Luke gives us insight into Peter with this description. We made this point in our previous study, but we need to remind you of this again. *"Peter"* is the subject of the sentence, and the main verb is *"said."* The Greek word "eipen," translated *"said,"* has no special focus. This word is not focused on content (as is "lego"), or on the act of speaking (as is "laleo"). This word declares that Peter said something and we should move on to other important matters. The statement describing Peter is important. Peter is *"filled with the Holy Spirit."* The Greek word "pletho," translated *"filled"* is a participle, in the passive voice. That means Peter is not responsible for the act of the filling. Peter entered this pressured situation filled with the Spirit, and the Spirit filled Him through the confrontation.

Knowing the participle is in the passive voice is important. Peter is not responsible for the act of the filling. The state of the filling cannot be earned or produced by self. Any activity of self to manufacture such a state nullifies the activity of the Spirit. The response enabling the fullness of the Spirit is not a "doing" response but a "receptive" response. The act is not a combination

Filled with the Holy Spirit | Acts 4:8

of Peter's resource and the resource of the Spirit; however, Peter is vital in the activity. Peter is more than an instrument of the Holy Spirit; He responds to the action of the Spirit. Although the Holy Spirit acted on him, Peter cooperated and participated wonderfully in that act!

The verb tense of *"filled"* (pletho) is the aorist. This tense is a focus on the activity of the filling rather than on the time of the filling and is a state of existence for the believer. We do not celebrate a moment in the past, marking the beginning of the Spirit's filling, though we have great memories of His indwelling. This filling is not a rare movement or exceptional empowering for a particular time. The Holy Spirit does not come on us to accomplish a particular task such as preaching, singing or give us victory in persecution. This is the consistent state in which we dwell. We are filled!

Although there is an ebb and flow in our emotional response to the Spirit, He does not change in His indwelling. The "dark night of the soul" is not an absence of His presence; when this period is over, He proves to us that He was abiding even then. When the battle rages, He is present; when we dwell in relaxation, He is present. When spiritual war is at our door, the Spirit of God lives in us. When peace floods our path, the Spirit of Jesus abides. In the hour of acceptance and fame, he embraces us. In the hour of persecution and rejection, we know Him the same. This state of existence does not change but must be the one unchangeable and fundamental reality of our lives!

The reason for its importance is in the structure of the Kingdom person. The Kingdom is not a location we arrive; it is an intimacy in which we dwell. The embrace of the Spirit of Jesus is the essence of our existence. We depend on Him; He is our resource. When God and the Spirit fills man's embrace, the Kingdom person is born. I am not this on my own, and He is not this on His own; it is the "oneness." In other words, if He does not indwell us, we are no longer a Kingdom person. If I am without Jesus for a single moment, I revert to the demonic person I was. I do not need Him every hour; I need Him every second!

This relationship has to be my life's focus. I dare not get distracted from it. This relationship is my salvation. His indwelling is not a benefit to my salvation; He is my salvation. Only in the intimacy of His presence do I exist. As my lungs need breath, so my being must have Him. Christianity is not contained its blessing or about heaven being my home; instead, it is about the fullness of the Spirit of Jesus. Everything fades in the importance of this element, Jesus! No wonder all the sermons in the Book of Acts focus on Jesus and only Jesus. This focus is not a doctrinal presentation or a seminar for self-improvement; it is Jesus embracing and filling us. This filling is the radical change proposed to the Sanhedrin. They have always dealt with legal matters, and they are comfortable with academic thought, but now they were confronted with a person, Jesus and His fullness.

State of Expression

Peter was filled with the Spirit, and this state of existence expressed itself. Our passage (Acts 4:8-12) reveals the expression of Peter's heart, which is the nature and heart of God. The Sanhedrin recognized this new nature. Peter had changed, expressing in a way and on a level that was beyond his norm. The old Peter expressed his self-sourcing. When Jesus said Peter would deny Him, he quickly reported he would die but not deny (Matthew 26, 35). When confronted with the challenge to bleed, suffer, and die, he argued about his claim to hold the superior position in the Kingdom (Matthew 18:1). When rejected by a Samaritan village because he was a disciple, he spoke forth wrath and judgment (Luke 9:54). When confronted with forgiving others, Peter wanted to limit his forgiveness (Matthew 18:21). The self-centered state of Peter's existence always expressed itself!

Filled with the Holy Spirit | **Acts 4:8**

What has happened to Peter? He was filled with the Spirit! This filling was his new state of existence, and the Sanhedrin recognized this radical change. Peter spoke from his culture, knowledge, and experiences, revealing his level of education. He was a Galilean. He did not have training in the wisdom and knowledge of the Jerusalem schools. Before his infilling he could speak long about his fishing skills, and he knew how to fight for the best fishing spots. Something in Peter was different now. His expressions were far beyond his level of knowledge, causing the Sanhedrin to remark about it. *"Now when they saw the boldness of Peter and John, and perceived that they were uneducated and untrained men, they marveled"* (Acts 4:13).

This is the message of the Book of Acts, the New Covenant. God now expresses Himself through the lives of human beings, a radical change in the sourcing of the human life. Man is no longer filled with himself, doing the best he can to accomplish what is in his capacity. God comes in His full nature to live in the believer. We are filled with the Spirit. This nature now expresses itself through us in full resource. The only deterrent to this expression is self.

Jesus is the result of the full expression of God's nature. *"He is the image of the invisible God"* (Colossians 1:15) visible for all to see. God manifests all His qualities through Jesus. Jesus is God's demonstration of how He feels about children, He views women, and how He wants us to treat our enemies. Jesus does not express Himself! *"Most assuredly, I say to you, the Son can do nothing of Himself, but what He sees the Father do; for whatever He does, the Son also does in like manner"* (John 5:19). *"I can of Myself do nothing. As I hear, I judge; and My judgment is righteous, because I do not seek My own will but the will of the Father who sent Me"* (John 5:30).

We will always express the nature that possesses us, but that is not to be our primary concern. We are to be concerned about being filled with the Holy Spirit, and then we will have and express His nature. Jesus expressed this when He gave instructions for ministry. He took the power in Himself and transferred it to His disciples. What was the extent of this resource? How was this resource manifested? ***"But when they deliver you up, do not worry about how or what you should speak. For it will be given to you in that hour what you should speak"*** (Matthew 10:19). We can see this being fulfilled in our passage through the apostles!

State of Expectation

Peter expressed the new normal before the Sanhedrin. Self-centeredness was gone, and He was filled with the Spirit. From Pentecost Day to this hour before the Jerusalem Court, Peter experienced the repeated movement of the Holy Spirit through his life. As he was imprisoned and later brought before the Sanhedrin, he had no hesitation. Why should he? When had the Holy Spirit failed to meet the need of his hour? The same Holy Spirit who enabled the raising of the lame beggar could manifest Himself through Peter before the Sanhedrin. After all, this interrogation was the Holy Spirit's concern, not Peter's. What a beautiful expectation in which to live!

Paul and others developed this idea of expectation in the language of faith. An experience with Jesus is saturated with this faith. ***"For by grace you have been saved through faith, and that not of yourselves; it is the gift of God, not of works, lest anyone should boast"*** (Ephesians 2:8-10). The writer of the Book of Hebrews exploded with the same language and concept. In chapter 11 he gave examples of men and women who lived lives of faith. Although these people had not experienced the New Covenant, they lived in expectation of its coming. The proof of their hope was in their faithfulness to suffering in obedience. The Hebrews writer ends this chapter with, ***"God having provided*** *something better for us, that they should not be made perfect apart from us"* (Hebrews 11:40). The "something better" in the New Covenant is the indwelling Spirit of God. The state of faith in the Old Covenant is the state of faith in the New Covenant.

Peter's faith was evident in his statement to the Sanhedrin. Their power did not intimidate him because of his confidence in Jesus. He boldly proclaimed that Jesus was the source of the lame beggar's healing, the man who stood before them. He proclaimed Jesus as the One, *"whom you crucified, whom God raised from the dead, by Him this man stands here before you whole"* (Acts 4:10). Peter was so sure of Jesus that he declared Him the cornerstone, fulfilling Old Testament prophecy (Acts 4:11). He proclaims Jesus as the only possibility of salvation (Acts 4:12). The Holy Spirit fulfilled His role in Peter by revealing Jesus in Him!

Through our intimacy with the Holy Spirit, we are convinced of Jesus. As the Holy Spirit convinces us, He enables us to invoke the activity of this Second Party (Jesus) in our lives! We will then live in the expectation and confidence *"that all things work together for good to those who love God, to those who are the called according to His purpose"* (Romans 8:28)!

Acts 4:9

JUDGED

"If we this day are judged for a good deed done to a helpless man, by what means he has been made well" (Acts 4:9).

Peter and John stood before THE COURT (Acts 4:5-6). This court was a distinguished group of men, which Luke lists for us. It seems his purpose was to contrast the educated, powerful, wealthy, and aristocratic Sanhedrin with the uneducated and untrained Galileans. There was no contest between these two groups because the Spirit of Jesus made the difference in Peter and John. The court quickly suggested THE CONSIDERATION (Acts 4:7), saying it as a question. **"By what power or by what name have you done this?"** (Acts 4:7). The Sanhedrin revealed their attitude toward Peter and John, expressed by the word order of the Greek text. The word *"you"* is a translation of the Greek word "humeis," the last word in the question. **Vincent's New Testament Word Studies** says the Greek word *"you"* closes the sentence with a contemptuous emphasis, "you people." The Sanhedrin viewed the Galilean fisherman without status, proper manners, and value. They asked, "How did people like you manage to do such a thing as this?"

The question the Sanhedrin asked was vague, referring to the situation as *"this"* rather than acknowledging the miracle. Peter powerfully said THE COMMUNICATION (Acts 4:8-12) with the first verse being "The Cause" (Acts 4:8). Luke forcibly writes that the uneducated and untrained fishermen were adequate for any situation because they had the fullness of the Spirit of Jesus! The source of the lame beggar's walking and the wisdom of the apostles was the Spirit.

As Peter continued to answer their question, he clarified the issue concerning their examination. The Sanhedrin's question was not specific to a miracle; instead, they referred to the event as *"this"* (Acts 4:7). However, after dismissing Peter and John so they could deliberate, they said among themselves, **"What shall we do to these men? For, indeed, that a notable miracle has been done through them is evident to all who dwell in Jerusalem, and we cannot deny it"** (Acts 4:16). This quandary was a result of them **"seeing the man who had been healed standing with them"** (Acts 4:14). This miracle is what disturbed the Sanhedrin. The provocation was not about the doctrine of the resurrection, a constant debate between the Pharisees and Sadducees, or about a temple policy or reconstruction of a temple room. Before them stood a changed life! They could not deny it. The Sanhedrin assumed Peter and John were responsible for the miracle; it was assumed there was a miracle that needed to be explained.

Peter boldly proclaimed the answer to their question. Without hesitation, he assumed *"this"* referred to the miracle experienced by the lame beggar. His opening statement presented "The Case" (Acts 4:9) and "The Crucified One" (Acts 4:10). He then quoted the Old Testament prophecy (Acts 4:11), "The Cornerstone," and climaxed with "The Concentration" (Acts 4:12).

Peter's opening statement was one sentence containing two verses. The first verse contains two dependent clauses introducing a conditional statement. The first clause begins with *"If"* (ei). If what Peter says in these two opening dependent clauses is true, then **"let it be known."** The first dependent clause in Peter's statement is, **"If we this day are judged for a good deed done to a helpless man."** The subject of this dependent

Part 2: The Analytical Response

clause is *"we,"* a translation of the Greek word "hemeis," and is also contained in the ending clauses' verb. Peter made a strong emphasis on the judgment of this court. They were focused on these two apostles not on the healed beggar. The beggar was present with them, as we will discover.

The main verb of the clause is *"are judged,"* a translation of the compound Greek word (anakrinometha). "Ana" is an emphatic emphasis. "Krino" means to examine, judge, or discuss. The word is in the passive voice, meaning the Sanhedrin acted on the apostles, and the indicative mood, a simple statement of fact. In some translations it reads, *"be examined,"* and in the New Testament, this word is confined to the writings of Luke and Paul. They used it frequently, and usually in the sense of judicial investigation, literally or figuratively.

The Greek word "euergesia," translated *"good deed done,"* comes from the root word for benefactor, and is a singular noun. Peter focused the trial on this miracle involving the lame beggar. He did not discuss the resurrection doctrine they taught and preached. He did not wonder about the interruption of the temple schedule. What happened in this *"helpless man,"* was what it was all about. The Greek word "asthenes," translated *"helpless,"* is an adjective meaning "without strength."

In Peter's opening statement, he made his own accusation. The basic idea of the verse is the attitude of the leaders of Israel. In most judicial investigations, there is a certainty of wrongdoing. The court is to decide whether a specific party is guilty of doing this wrong deed. Peter declared to the Sanhedrin that they were judging them not over a wrong deed but a good deed. This judgment was not the design of the court. The leaders of Israel were again doing what they had done repeatedly, considering a good deed to be bad. They took what was good and made it bad. The plan of God, demonstrated in righteousness and displayed by God's nature, was held in contempt. This contempt drove them to arrest the apostles and accuse them, their continual pattern.

The Pharisees caught the disciples picking grain and eating it on the Sabbath (Matthew 12:1-8). Jesus gave them a strong discourse that should have ended this issue. However, they attempted to trap Him in the synagogue. A man with a withered hand was brought to Jesus (Matthew 12:9-13). They knew Jesus would heal him even on the Sabbath, and they go to the conference room to plot the murder of Jesus (Matthew 12:14). While they were there, Jesus embraced the entire multitude and healed them all (Matthew 12:15). Filled with hatred and dismay, the leaders of Israel joined the crowd. Jesus casts out a demon and the crowds began to proclaim Him as the Messiah (Matthew 12:23). This suggestion pushed the leaders of Israel over the edge, and they accused Him of being filled with Beelzebub, the ruler of the demons (Matthew 12:24). Hundreds of lives were changed; revival came among the people. God did a new thing; the Messiah brought redemption. The demonic territory was conquered. The leaders of Israel declared what God did through Jesus as the activity of the devil!

This was not the first time for this sort of accusation. Earlier in Jesus' Galilean ministry, He cast out a demon and a mute man spoke. The crowd was so moved by the power of God that they cried, *"It was never seen like this in Israel!"* (Matthew 9:33). The leaders of Israel immediately responded, *"He casts out demons by the ruler of the demons"* (Matthew 9:34). This attitude was consistently expressed in all the interactions between Jesus and these leaders of Israel. They devalued everything the Spirit accomplished through Him. They turned what was good into evil.

But wait! Is it not necessary to be careful? We must not rush to a conclusion. Just because something might look good on the surface, it could be bad. Is not this at the heart of Satan's temptation? He takes the filth of the world, covers it with glitter, and surrounds it with bright lights. It looks so good. That was the first temptation in the Garden of Eden. *"So when the woman saw that the tree was good for food, that it was pleasant to the eyes, and a tree desirable to make one wise, she took of its fruit and ate"* (Genesis 3:6). We can hardly blame these leaders for being careful.

Perhaps we should hold our court and stand these leaders before us. They appear good and righteous in all their law keeping. They are the best their society can produce. They are the most religious of their day. But is their goodness merely evil in disguise? Did not Jesus use the word "hypocrite" for them repeatedly (Matthew 23)?

How can I tell for sure? What is the final test to determine real righteousness? I do not want to be fooled. Peter gave the Sanhedrin insight into determining what was good and what was bad. Here are his suggestions.

Source

The source of the good deed for which they were being judged was *"the name of Jesus Christ of Nazareth, whom you crucified, whom God raised from the dead, by Him this man stands here before you whole"* (Acts 4:10). This was a significant statement for this group. Peter did not acclaim a new religion with a new god or a new method of worship. The God of Abraham, Isaac, and Jacob planned redemption for mankind from the beginning. The Trinity God prophesied through the prophets about one Man, the Messiah, who would be the avenue of deliverance. Peter continued saying Jesus was the cornerstone intended by God (Acts 4:11).

The method Peter used to communicate this truth was not new. He did it by a contrast. The involvement and interaction of the Sanhedrin with Jesus was one of rejection. They crucified Him! However, God's involvement and interaction with Jesus was one of sourcing. God raised Him from the dead. The Trinity God was sourcing Jesus. Everything that happened, through and because of Jesus, was happening through and because of the Trinity God. When that happens it is "good"!

The test of good and evil is not the act of the deed but the sourcing. The Father sources everything Jesus does. Everything the Father produces is good! This production result is because of His nature. *"Every good gift and every perfect gift is from above, and comes down from the Father of lights, with whom there is no variation or shadow of turning"* (James 1:17). Peter was filled with *"the Father of lights."* Holiness derives from this indwelling nature and determines the quality of the deed.

This indwelling nature is the heart of the New Covenant, which Jesus established through His death and resurrection. His nature living in and through us sources the life called "good." Anything in our life He does not produce is "evil." How it appears is not the deciding element. How pleasant it may feel does not determine its value. Does the indwelling Spirit of Christ source it?

Salvation

The motive of the nature is another determining element between good deeds and evil deeds. How can I tell whether a deed is sourced by God or by the demonic self-centered nature? Hundreds of people passed by the lame beggar. A few of them threw a small offering his way. Perhaps it was to help him, but it also made them feel good about themselves. Peter and John did not have any financial funds to offer, but what they did have they gave to him. The power of Jesus moved through them to redeem the beggar. As noted in other studies, he was given *"perfect soundness"* (Acts 3:16). This statement conveys redemption in every area. All the psychological scars of rejection, begging for a living, and abuse were cleansed; it was not merely a physical healing. He was redeemed through the power of Jesus into the new creature God intended him to be.

Part 2: The Analytical Response

Everything sourced by Jesus is redemptive. There is no selfish motive or hidden strategy. What would Peter and John gain from this miracle? Their ministry was questioned because of it. It opened the door to persecution for the early Church in Jerusalem. They could have easily lost their lives because of this miracle. This miracle was not a proper, valid activity bringing safety and security to their lives. Nor was it a proper, politically correct endeavor. These miracles were an expression of the redemptive nature of God!

What happened to the apostles is contrasted with the members of the Sanhedrin. All their religious activities were done with the motive to be seen by men (Matthew 23:5). They placed their goodness on parade. They proclaimed the commandments of the law but did not observe them (Matthew 23:3). They performed for the prestige of the moment, such as the best places at the feasts and the best seats in the synagogues (Matthew 23:6). They displayed their positions by their titles as they were greeted in the marketplaces (Matthew 23:7). Jesus called all produced by this motive "hypocritical" (Matthew 23:13). It was evil because it was not redemptive but promoted by self-gain. The Spirit of Jesus never sources any activity with this motive.

Secret

How can we determine whether the motive is redemptive? It involves the openness and sincerity of the person. The person sourced by self-centeredness must cover, camouflage, or conceal such a motive. He may not allow even his own heart to embrace the reality of his motive. He lives in deception. But the person sourced by the Spirit is open and transparent. Peter addressed this Sanhedrin, **"Let it be known to you all and to all the people of Israel,"** (Acts 4:10).

Peter did not reveal partial truth; he did not embellish

the truth or detract from it. He did not attempt to appease the Sanhedrin by adjusting the truth to link with this court. The threat of the hour did not cause him to twist the truth to fit what was acceptable to these leaders. Peter pointed out that Jesus is the truth, the One they crucified. In fact, the God of their forefathers raised Him from the dead. Even though they did not believe in the resurrection of the dead, the power of this miracle came from the name of the One risen (Acts 4:10). Jesus is the chief cornerstone that was rejected by their actions (Acts 4:11). Salvation is found only in Jesus (Acts 4:12), a complete disclosure of truth! In this there is no deception, no hidden secrets, and no defilement. Self-centeredness cannot respond in such a manner. Self always needs to adjust the truth to make appearances pleasing to its self-promotion. Self cannot live in truth!

The Sanhedrin was in a terrible dilemma. Peter confronted their deception with truth. Their darkness was exposed with the light. Again God gave them an opportunity to respond to the call of truth. Will we do better than they did? Truth has come to us; let us not live in self-deception.

Acts 4:9

THE HEART OF GOD

"If we this day are judged for a good deed done to a helpless man, by what means he has been made well (Acts 4:9).

Every good story has the element of choice. The drama of the story captures your attention, and your heart pulls you into the dilemma of choosing. A good writer will use his narrative to put his characters into a situation that tests them, requiring a choice. The Scriptures show people in situations demanding moral and spiritual choices. Our world is the battleground where God and the devil fight for the mastery of every person's soul. But that soul has a choice!

The Bible begins with the choice as a condition of human life. Adam and Eve live with a forbidden tree (Genesis 2:17). The devil's temptation put them into a position of choice of loyalty to God or self. This first recorded human choice was the tragic event that caused the fall of humanity. Even after the fall, God did not change the ground rules for human life. He left people with the capacity to choose God or self. Cain chose self and killed his brother, Abel (Genesis 4:8). Cain's choice was birthed from his anger at God for rejecting his sacrificial offering of the fruit of the ground (Genesis 4:3). God selected Noah from all of the earth's population to build an ark because Noah had chosen to be a just man in his generation (Genesis 6:9). God presented Noah the directions for building the ark, and Noah chose to do all that God commanded him (Genesis 6:22). Abraham chose to live by faith and obeyed God (Hebrews 11:8-10). The Scriptures are filled with people who made good and bad choices.

Each of us must view our immediate life's situation, knowing we did not arrive in our present state accidently. We are a result of our choices. You might argue that the choices of others have affected your status in life. Although this is true, it is not the determining element. God has staggering promises for those who choose Him. *"And we know that all things work together for good to those who love God, to those who are the called according to His purpose"* (Romans 8:28).

Now we come to our passage (Acts 4:9). Peter speaks to the issue of being called in to court for the healing of the lame beggar. The Sanhedrin (*their rulers, elders, and scribes*) had not gathered with, *"Annas the high priest, Caiaphas, John and Alexander, and as many as were of the family of the high priest"* for a birthday party. This court was not a social gathering for fellowship. Peter said, *"If we this day are judged for a good deed done to a helpless man, by what means he has been made well"* (Acts 4:9). This gathering was a court of judgment. The Greek word "anakrino," translated *"we are judged,"* implies accusation and authority. Some translations translate it "we are examined," which is far too weak. We must understand it to mean, "called in question, called to account, or required to explain or justify one's choice."

The Sanhedrin and other friends have accused the apostles of doing a bad deed when the healing of the lame beggar was a good deed! What the apostles considered a good deed, the leaders of Israel considered evil. How could each view the same choice so differently? Perhaps the difference was cultural. The social practices of Galilee differed from that of Jerusalem, but the historical background was the same. The prophets of old had spoken to the people of Galilee and the people of Jerusalem, and each group lived by the same Scriptures. Your culture and what you have been taught do not determine your choices, but your choices determine how you view things.

Maybe their personality traits caused their preferences. Their educational experiences, family environment, and financial status would have affected what they believed. The Galileans and the people of Jerusalem made choices in education, family, and finances, and their circumstances in each of these areas influenced their choices. But in every area of life, a fundamental choice gives direction to and shapes that life. What determines this core choice?

It is nature! This was the difficulty between the leaders of Israel and the apostles. Their natures were different, giving them opposite perspectives. Jesus confronted this repeatedly with the leadership of Israel. He expressed it through imagery of birth and fatherhood. He encouraged Nicodemus to be born from above. If he were born of flesh, all his choices would be made from the perspective of the flesh. If he were born of the Spirit of God, his choices would come from the nature of the Spirit (John 3:8). The Pharisees argued that Abraham was their father (John 8:39). This claim could not be true. If Abraham were their father, they would have the nature of Abraham, and they would have made the same choices as Abraham. They argued that God was their Father (John 8:41). If so, they would have loved Jesus because God fathered Jesus. They did not have the nature of God; therefore, their choices were the opposite of God's nature. In fact, they were of their father, the devil (John 8:44). Having the nature of the devil, they chose an alliance with evil desires.

I am amazed at the method of Luke's writing. He belabors the involvement and the description of the healed beggar. This beggar appeared in all the various scenes of the story. He was at the heart of the initial miracle (Acts 3:1-10). Luke described his condition, his daily routine, and the duration of his state. The scene changed to Solomon's Porch, where

The Heart of God | **Acts 4:9**

Peter gave an exhortation as an explanation of the miracle. The healed beggar was at the heart of the message. He was not only present (Acts 3:11), but Peter referred to him in the message (Acts 3:16). When the alliance captured the apostles, evidently they also included this beggar. After a night in jail, the whole group was brought before the Sanhedrin; the healed beggar was there with the apostles. He was the focus in Peter's message (Acts 4:10), and he was the heart of the Sanhedrin's deliberation (Acts 4:14, 16).

Luke attempted to exhaust the Greek language by using at least five different Greek words to describe the change in this beggar's life. The change was a vital part of the contrast between the nature of the leaders of Israel and the nature of the apostles. The Sanhedrin would have easily dismissed any discussion of this miracle and would have advocated silence about Jesus (Acts 4:17). But the miracle could not be hidden; the message could not be silenced.

Luke began with the Greek word "stero" (Acts 3:16), translated *strong*. Its root word means, "to solidify." This word focuses on stable, firm, strong, or strengthened. Luke described the early Church as, ***"strengthened*** (stero) ***in the faith and increased in number daily"*** (Acts 16:5). This Greek word is used only three times in the New Testament. Once it describes the churches, and twice it describes the healed beggar.

Luke adds the Greek word "holokieria," translated ***"this perfect soundness,"*** to describe the miracle (Acts 3:16), and it is used only here in the New Testament. This word focuses on integrity, wholeness, or completeness, and it involves more than mere physical completeness. It involves the mental, emotional, and spiritual aspects of the beggar's life as well.

In our passage (Acts 4:9), Luke uses the Greek word "sozo," translated ***"been made well."*** This Greek word is also translated ***"saved"*** (Acts 4:12), "to save from mortal danger and death," "disease and possession," "guilt (sin) and alienation from God," and "eternal ruin." It is used fifty-four times in the Gospels, fourteen relate to deliverances from disease or demon possession, twenty refer to the rescue of physical life from some impending peril or instant death, and the remaining twenty refer times to spiritual salvation.

Peter continued in his response to the Sanhedrin, referring to the presence of the healed beggar as standing before them *"whole"* (Acts 4:10), a translation of the Greek word "hugies." This word is used eleven times in the New Testament as an adjective referring to physical health, and is used once in Paul's epistles for healthy or sound speech (Titus 2:8). This word comes from a word group that focuses more on rational, intelligent, reliable, and whole. Health implies a proper balance of the whole being, including the spiritual.

Luke referred to the beggar standing with the apostles as, *"healed"* (Acts 4:14). The Greek word used is "therapeuo," meaning "to worship, to adore, or to relieve." It contains the idea of attending, serving, and ministering. The acts of healing are not described as medical procedures within the natural laws but manifestations of the divine Spirit pushing back the demonic forces. In the New Testament, "therapeuo" never refers to someone serving secularly. Paul used it once to denote worship to God (Acts 17:25). He preached in Athens to the philosophers about the sovereignty of God. His point was that the true God is not the product of a small nation or group needing constant service (therapeuo). The service needed by idols is inappropriate to God!

Perhaps one of the words would not be significant, but all of them together give a declaration of the Sanhedrin's inner nature in contrast to the apostles. This nature determined the choices each made. This fact brings us to the consideration of another concept.

The Mystical

In each word Luke used, there was an interweaving of the physical and the spiritual. The apostles did not consider the healing of the lame beggar as the correction only of his crippled condition. Although the physical aspect is present in a surface encounter with the beggar, the Spirit of God brought wholeness to the beggar in every area of his existence. This man was greater than forty years of age (Acts 4:22). His physical condition prompted physical and emotional abuse. The psychological scars of not being like other children who could play, go to school, and work in a fulfilling career must have been enormous. He was blocked from any spiritual involvement of temple worship and connection to the people of God. Because of his disability he was banned from the temple. He would have been treated as one beyond salvation. Although his physical condition was corrected in the miracle, what happens to his crippled spirit? God healed the whole man!

The Sadducees had lost this view. Their concern was the immediate physical condition only of their own state. Although they may have had a slight interest in the physical miracle accomplished, they had no interest, or even awareness, in the spiritual healing in the beggar's inner man. They dismissed the mystical, spiritual world. They viewed the lame beggar at the Gate Beautiful as discarded, unimportant, and of no value. He could make no physical contribution to their world. All their choices sprang from a nature focused on their physical convenience and comfort. Consider how narrow and confining this view is in regard to your life's view! All your decisions are determined by your physical circumstances and desires.

Peter was the opposite. The wonder of the spiritual world had captured him. He was in love with Jesus, the resurrected One. The mystical world was moving through Jesus to bring salvation to every person. He cried, ***"Nor is there salvation in any other, for there is no other name under heaven given among men by which we must be saved"*** (Acts 4:12). Peter did not view his involvement with the lame beggar as giving physical aid and improvement but the correction of the man's complete life. The lame beggar was made whole; he was restored. Peter based his choices not on the physical contribution of a lame beggar but on the spiritual value of this man in light of the mystical world.

It is a clear call to our lives. We must be filled with the Spirit of Jesus, and we must see with His eyes. The value beyond the physical must grip us with new passion. There is something greater than the simple physical circumstances of your setting. In the midst of a physical crisis, you must not allow your physical view to determine your decisions; the physical must not dominate and control your attitude. A movement beyond what you can see is occurring. Will you be in tune with the spiritual realities?

The Maturity

The Sadducees had no concept of the end view. They saw only the immediate, and they were frustrated by the apostles' disturbance of their physical world. They did not see the work of the resurrected Lord making a lame beggar whole. One of the aspects of the Greek words Luke used to describe this healed beggar was completeness. He was not only made complete in every area of his life, but the dream of God for him was also completed. The dream of God for this man was never that he occupied the best begging place at the Gate Beautiful. God's end view was not a healed lame begging man now leaping, running, entering the temple, and working and contributing to society. Only Jesus fully knew the end view for this man, and He raised him to his feet through Peter and John.

The Sadducees' view was limited to the materialism of their

hour. They believed in nothing beyond what they could touch, measure, and control. This view is so strange! Their forefathers were the people of God who lived by faith. The writer of the Book of Hebrews lists them (Hebrews 11). By faith, they saw beyond their circumstances into the completeness God was going to bring to His people. *"And all these, having obtained a good testimony through faith, did not receive the promise, God having provided something better for us, that they should not be made perfect apart from us"* (Hebrews 11:39-40). How had the Sadducees become so shortsighted? Yet here they are again being called to a new view. Their choices are determined by their view.

It is a clear call to our lives! How easy it is to be consumed with the immediate need and circumstances of our lives. What is the end view of God's dream for your life? What is His dream for my life? We must not miss it! Our objectives and goals must not be shortsighted because they will determine our choices! We must be filled with the Spirit of Jesus; it is with the mind of Christ that we will sense His dreams beyond the present circumstances of our lives. Here we will not just endure but rejoice in the adversity taking us to the fulfillment of God's dreams. Allow the pressure of the present mold and shape you into the dream He has for you.

In our passage, the Sadducees considered the movement of God achieving His dream for the lame beggar as an evil deed to be judged. The dream of God for the person of lowest status in Jewish society was great enough to disrupt their immediate lives. God's dreams for us are huge. We must not choose the cheap, immediate, and temporal when the eternally significant is pressing in on us!

Acts 4:10

THE TOTAL MESSAGE

"Let it be known to you all, and to all the people of Israel, that by the name of Jesus Christ of Nazareth, whom you crucified, whom God raised from the dead, by Him this man stands here before you whole" (Acts 4:10).

Any verse with a focus on Jesus is amazing, but this one exceeds them all! This verse embraces the Old Testament message, a single verse revealing the message of the prophets. Peter explained and verified the heart of redemption. He added nothing and set nothing aside. Here is the perfect summary of the grand scheme of God's redemptive heart! What an amazing verse!

If you knew nothing of the Scriptures except this verse, you would know it all. The scene of our passage is earth shaking. The most elite scholars of the Old Testament, the Sanhedrin, were present. But they did not understand the content of this verse. God did not hide this information from them. They handled the sacrifices day after day that testified to this verse. The fixtures of the temple proclaimed to them the truth of this verse. Their forefathers passed on the traditions giving them insight into this verse. But they missed it!

This scenario should be a warning to us. To focus on "tradition" is so easy with our security becoming the familiar. A wife in an abusive marriage will continually endure the familiar abuse rather than risk the insecurity of being alone. The Pharisees and Sadducees adjusted their knowledge of the Old Testament to maintain their personal security and positions. Any truth violating what was familiar to them was discarded. They were maintaining. But when we simply maintain, we do not continue in our present spiritual status. Jesus spoke to this group in parables. His explanation was, *"seeing they do not see, and hearing they do not hear, nor do they understand"* (Matthew 13:13). His promise was that when this condition is *"even what he has will be taken away from him"* (Matthew 13:12). In other words, any attempt to stay where we are produces only slippage and deterioration.

"Theology" can easily become our focus. Regarding the Pharisees and Sadducees, their theology was their approach to the law. They were bound. If they would not listen or consider anything but what they already thought, how would new expanding truth be given to them? In the case of the leadership of Israel, the new truth, which in a sense was opposite of what they had always heard, was now being presented. Peter gave them a fuller revelation of what they had always heard. Jesus was the fulfillment of all the prophecies of the Old Testament. They chose to live in the expectation rather than in the fulfillment. The fulfillment demanded far too many changes in their theology. This can be disastrous for us as well!

The "theatrical" can easily become our focus. The performance becomes more important than the script. For the leadership of Israel, their religion was a performance, and they maintained the ceremonies that brought them financial prosperity. In Jesus, they were confronted with their need of a relationship with God rather than a ceremony to perform. As noted in our previous studies, this confrontation occurred repeatedly. Now again, truth beyond their "tradition, theology, and theatrical activities" was presented to them. It came through the power of the Holy Spirit!

Part 2: The Analytical Response

Trinity God
"God raised from the dead"

A reference to all the Sanhedrin knew from their past was at the heart of Peter's statement. Peter did not present a new and radical religion that demonstrated the power of a new god. All that happened in Jesus unfolded the plan and dreams of the God who spoke to and guided their forefathers, the God to whom they had already pledged their love and loyalty.

The difficulty with our evangelical traditions is that we isolate the term "God" to "God, the Father." When God is mentioned, we do not think of "Jesus" or the "Holy Spirit." Our attention is drawn to "the Father." But this singularity is not the desire or the design of the Old Testament language. In the Hebrew language of the Old Testament, **"God"** is the translation of the Hebrew word "Elohim," which is always plural. Although the word "Trinity" is never used in the Scriptures, it is a theological term referring to this plurality.

When the Septuagint (the Greek translation of the Old Testament) was translated, the Hebrew plural name "Elohim," when used for the true God was replaced by the singular Greek word "Theos," meaning God. "Theoi," meaning gods, was never the replacement. The reason was that at the time the Septuagint translation was made, Greek idolatry was the prevailing superstition. Their gods were intelligent beings separated and distinct. No unity or oneness, only conflict and chaos, was among these many beings. If the translators rendered the name of the true God by the plural "theoi," they would have supported the heathen concept of the disunity and inconsistent desires of their gods. However, by translating the Hebrew "Elohim" as "God (Theos)," they inculcated the unity of God and simultaneously did not deny a plurality of persons in the divine nature. Therefore, in the New Testament and the Septuagint, the Greek word "Theos," translated "God," most often refers to the Old Testament plural name "Elohim" that denotes Trinity God!

This denotation is especially true in our passage. Peter cried to the Sanhedrin the wonder of what the Trinity God of the Old Testament planned in the person of Christ. He limited his focus to the resurrection, but he could have expanded his message to include the incarnation, the miracles, the ascension, and the outpouring of the Holy Spirit. Jesus' birth at Christmas was a direct result of the execution of the Trinity God's careful plan. "Elohim" brought about the birth of Jesus. The careful guarding of Jesus' genealogy bespeaks the involvement of the Trinity God. Matthew writes of the Trinity's provisions to protect Jesus from the most powerful men on Earth (Matthew 2). Nothing would hinder the unfolding of the Trinity God's redemptive plan. Are not the miracles all signs of God's invasion of the demonic possessions and territory? Is not God, Elohim, stomping through history fulfilling His (Their) promises (Acts 2:22)?

The resurrection displayed this truth! Peter repeatedly proclaimed, "God raised Him from the dead" (Acts 2:24, 27, 30, 31, 32; 3:15, 26; 4:10). But forever remember, he referred to God, the Three in One! The Trinity was involved in the resurrection of Jesus from the dead. *"But if the Spirit of Him who raised Jesus from the dead dwells in you, He who raised Christ from the dead will also give life to your mortal bodies through His Spirit who dwells in you"* (Romans 8:11). The Holy Spirit was active in the resurrection, the giving of life. If He achieved this in the death of Jesus, will He now bestow life on us?

Jesus often referred to His involvement in His resurrection from the dead. After He cleansed the temple, the Jews demanded a sign from Him. His answer was, *"Destroy this temple, and in three days I will raise it up"* (John 2:19). The Jews thought this statement was ridiculous. They reported that it had taken forty-six years to build the temple, and Jesus proposed to do it in three days. John carefully explained, *"He was speaking of the temple of His body"* (John 2:21). John also said, *"Therefore, when He had risen from the dead, His disciples remembered that He had said this to them; and they believed the Scriptures and the word which Jesus had said"* (John 2:22).

During a discussion with the Pharisees, Jesus gave illustrations involving sheep and shepherds. Because raising sheep was a strong part of their culture, He thought this would easily be understood. He presented Himself as the good Shepherd, *"the good shepherd gives His life for the sheep"* (John 10:11). He contrasted this with the hireling who flees because he does not care for the sheep. Jesus continued, *"As the Father knows Me even so I know the Father; and I lay down My life for the sheep,"* (John 10:15). *"Therefore My Father loves Me, because I lay down My life that I may take it again. No one takes it from Me, but I lay it down of Myself. I have power to lay it down, and I have power to take it again. This command I have received from My Father"* (John 10:17-18).

Peter referenced God the Father in all of his messages. He and the other apostles could not obey the threats of the Sanhedrin to not speak of Jesus. When these leaders brought Peter before the court and questioned him, he answered, *"We ought to obey God rather than men. The God of our fathers raised up Jesus whom you murdered by hanging on a tree. Him God has exalted to His right hand to be Prince and Savior, to give repentance to Israel and forgiveness of sins"* (Acts 5:29-31).

If the Godhead is involved in this plan, what exactly is the plan?

Tangible God
"Jesus Christ of Nazareth, whom you crucified"

God expressed His plan in Jesus! God wants intimacy. He wants me to love Him with all my being. Jesus revealed this love. The plan of the Trinity God was and is to reestablish the human race on the level Adam first experienced in creation. This reestablishment would take a "second Adam," the beginning of a new species of humanity. Jesus is this Adam! He is the first man to live sourced by the Holy Spirit. He became the visible image of the invisible God. In Him the New Covenant was launched. If the time it took to achieve the plan is any indication of the severity and strength of the plan, it is beyond comprehension.

In every message of Peter, he clearly defined Jesus. He is ***"Jesus Christ of Nazareth, whom you crucified"*** (Acts 4:10). In his previous message at Solomon's Porch, he described Jesus in greater detail. He began his message with a direct reference to the Trinity God, ***"The God of Abraham, Isaac, and Jacob, the God of our fathers"*** (Acts 3:13). This Trinity God had a distinct plan; it was Jesus! The plan of God was fulfilled in the person of Jesus. Jesus was the One they ***"delivered up and denied in the presence of Pilate when he was determined to let Him go"*** (Acts 3:13). Peter continued with greater detail, ***"But you denied the Holy One and the Just, and asked for a murderer to be granted to you and killed the Prince of life"*** (Acts 3:14-15).

The Trinity God focused the redemptive plan in and on Jesus. Understanding that the focus was not on the accomplishment of specific deeds is important. In other words, the plan was not focused on crucifixion. Anyone who could accomplish this task would be acceptable in the plan. The focus of the plan was on the Person of Jesus who would accomplish crucifixion. Jesus must be crucified, and Jesus must be raised from the dead. Although the crucifixion and resurrection had to take place, the focus was not on those accomplishments but on Jesus.

Jesus, the Second Member of the Trinity, was the only plan of the Trinity God. He set aside all He possessed as God; He emptied Himself of all but "love." He became a Man filled with and sourced by the Spirit of God. He entered into the state of helplessness and became dependent on the Spirit of God, the

Part 2: The Analytical Response

original formation of the Kingdom of God. This formation would open the door for birthing a new breed or species of people. They are the children of God! The focus was not on the faithfulness of Jesus, although faithfulness was necessary, nor on His crucifixion and resurrection, although they were essential, it was Jesus! Jesus was the focus of the plan of the Trinity God. No wonder Peter spoke of nothing but Jesus. He went beyond measure to describe Jesus, the focus of God's plan. Peter's presentation to the Sanhedrin was the necessity of embracing Jesus, but they rejected Him in crucifixion. Jesus is the only hope!

I understand how the sourcing of the Holy Spirit could work in Jesus to achieve the plan of God. He was the One who was beloved. He was tempted yet victorious. He pleased the Father. But when I consider myself, I experience the sinking sensation of hopelessness. Jesus could live in wholeness, sourcing, and the fullness of the Spirit, but can I expect that for my life?

Testimony of God
"this man stands here before you"

Yes, this verse is amazing! Peter introduced to the Sanhedrin the Trinity God and revealed this Trinity with a plan. God's plan was Jesus. Then Peter stood before them with the healed beggar. He presented him as **"whole,"** silencing the skeptics. **"And seeing the man who had been healed standing with them, they could say nothing against it"** (Acts 4:14).

What God did in Jesus, He was now doing in and through the beggar. This man was of the lowest "social status." As a beggar, he was considered the lowest among the Jews. God reached into the lowest category of society, the lame beggar, and brought him into wholeness! If this could happen in his life, could it not be true for all of us? The beggar was a man without "strength." Peter could not have possibly encouraged him to use his own strength and ability to gain back his life. He dwelt in helplessness. Therapy, counseling, and hours of self-discipline could not explain the change in this man. He was void of all strength. Jesus was the only explanation.

This man was considered "sinful." He was banned from the temple with all of its salvation benefits, and there was no hope for him. His society considered his physical and spiritual state as a direct result of someone's sin. He endured this state for greater than forty years (Acts 4:22). Consider a lifetime of belittlement, debasing, and rejection. The ridicule and laughter of his peers during childhood had devastated his self-worth. His vocation was limited to begging. Yet, this man stood before them whole. Everything he lacked was now his through Jesus. It was as if he had been born again.

If this man could be restored and know the redeeming plan of God in his life, could it not be true for me? What the Trinity God achieved in Jesus, He now achieved in a lame beggar, and He wants to achieve in me. We can find this all in Jesus. This is the message to the Sanhedrin, is that they must embrace Jesus. The message to our hearts is that we must embrace Jesus. This message is not a theological discussion or a philosophical investigation, but encourages an encounter with Jesus. Could we enter into a deeper love relationship with Him? Can we embrace Him as the sole element in the plan of God for our lives?

Acts 4:10

A POWERFUL NAME

"Let it be known to you all, and to all the people of Israel, that by the name of Jesus Christ of Nazareth, whom you crucified, whom God raised from the dead, by Him this man stands here before you whole" (Acts 4:10).

The element of power drew multitudes to Jesus. If the miracles were removed from the Gospel account, we would not find the multitudes present. The Gospel writers connected the fame of Jesus' ministry with His miracles. ***"Then His fame went throughout all Syria; and they brought to Him all sick people who were afflicted with various diseases and torments, and those who were demon-possessed, epileptics, and paralytics; and He healed them"*** (Matthew 4:24). Matthew emphasized the spread of Jesus' popularity into the foreign land of Syria because of His powerful activities.

The Gospel writers used a variety of words to emphasize, illustrate, and describe this power. The Greek word "teras" is often translated "wonder" (John 4:48). The consistent use of "sign" (semeion) is found throughout the Gospel accounts (John 2:11). One of the most familiar is the Greek word "dunamis," used one hundred and nineteen times in the New Testament. Seven times it is translated "miracle." "Dunamis" is the Greek word referring to "power" (Mark 6:2). These three words are used most frequently. "Megaleios" is translated "great things" or "wonderful works" (Luke 1:49). "Endoxos" is translated "glorious things" (Luke 13:17). The idea of "strange" or "contrary to expectation" is portrayed in "paradoxos" (Luke 5:26). The seventh word is "thaumasios," translated "wonderful thing" (Matthew 21:15).

Although this emphasis on power is definitely connected to the life of Jesus and even the apostles in the early Church, there are consistent warnings given to us about "power." Simon practiced sorcery in a city in Samaria. He claimed to be someone great because of the power he possessed. He became a believer through the preaching of Philip. When Peter and John came to this city Simon saw the power of the Holy Spirit demonstrated in miracles. He offered to buy this power from them (Acts 8:18). Peter immediately warned him of his destruction and he repented. We are not unlike him; we are easily impressed with power.

Paul consistently downplayed the wisdom and power of this world in contrast to the wisdom and power of God. Many scholars think he was a short unimposing man, and his presence would not have impressed us as powerful. He admitted in his own writings that he *"did not come with excellence of speech or of wisdom declaring to you the testimony of God"* (1 Corinthians 2:1). Paul estimated his presence when he said; *"I was with you in weakness, in fear, and in much trembling"* (1 Corinthians 2:3). He described his preaching as *"not with persuasive words of human wisdom, but in demonstration of the Spirit and of power"* (1 Corinthians 2:4).

Paul warned us of the coming of *"the lawless one"* (2 Thessalonians 2:8). His coming would be declared, *"according to the working of Satan, with all power, signs, and lying wonders."* In the Book of Revelation we are told of the coming of *"another beast." "And he exercises all the authority of the first beast in his presence, and causes the earth and those who dwell in it to worship the first beast, whose deadly wound was healed"* (Revelation 13:12). His method for capturing the worship of the

Earth would be through power. ***"He performs great signs, so that he even makes fire come down from heaven on the earth in the sight of men. And he deceives those who dwell on the earth by those signs which he was granted to do in the sight of the beast"*** (Revelation 13:13-14). By the power of these signs, he convinced the people of Earth to make an image to the beast and with power cause him to speak (Revelation 13:15). It is easy to be deceived by the demonstration of power.

This seemed to be the concern the Sanhedrin had about the apostles. The entire focus of this trial centered on power. We must view the key question of the trial, ***"By what power or by what name have you done this?"*** (Acts 4:7). The word order of the question is revealing. The first issue is power, and the second issue is the name sourcing the power. In our passage Peter boldly reversed the order. First, he presented the person, and secondly he revealed the power.

The Person
(Source)

Jesus is the sole explanation for the healing of the lame beggar! Thus, the focus of Peter's answer and the dominant theme of the New Testament is Jesus! Although power is mentioned in various settings, it is always about the Person of Jesus. Just before His ascension, Jesus promised the disciples power. ***"But you shall receive power when the Holy Spirit has come upon you; and you shall be witnesses to Me in Jerusalem, and in all Judea and Samaria, and to the end of the earth"*** (Acts 1:8). Power is never present as a mystical force or influence; it is a Person.

Paul quickly corrected any tendency to think the roles of ministry were by some special anointing, mystical talent, or special endowment. ***"And He Himself gave some to be apostles, some prophets, some evangelists, and some pastors and teachers"***

(Ephesians 4:11). Every role is fulfilled only in intimacy with Jesus. Any thought of ministering apart from Him is ludicrous.

We must consider victory over sin in this manner. Paul wrote, *"I say then: Walk in the Spirit, and you shall not fulfill the lust of the flesh"* (Galatians 5:16). His explanation for this statement was, *"For the flesh lusts against the Spirit, and the Spirit against the flesh; and these are contrary to one another, so that you do not do the things that you wish"* (Galatians 5:17). The secret is not in any special power, discipline, or meditation; it is the Spirit of Jesus! Furthermore he says, *"But the fruit of the Spirit is love, joy, peace, longsuffering, kindness, goodness, faithfulness, gentleness, self-control"* (Galatians 5:22-23). These attributes are not present because of a special force of power; they are present because of the intertwining of Jesus' person with us. Because these attributes are His nature, the way He is, we also demonstrate these qualities because of His presence.

There is no room in the New Testament for the separation of Jesus and spiritual power. This resource is not an anointing, endowment, or gift, but it is Jesus! The standard teaching of the New Testament is consistently simple. There are no steps to take, techniques to develop, or disciplines to acquire. Everything we need is found in intimacy with Jesus. In the fusion of you and Him, your weakness becomes a manifestation of His strength, your foolishness experiences His wisdom, and your inabilities gives way to His abilities. All is found in Him. Everything God wants you to have He placed in Jesus. Your position is in Him alone. He does not give you anything; He is everything. Your need becomes singular; it is Him!

This reality consistently maintains His Lordship in our lives. If we secured the power apart from Him, we would control it. No doubt He would give us instructions on how to use the power, but we would manipulate those instructions and ultimately our self-centeredness would use the power for self. We would become stars accepting the credit from grateful people who connect

Part 2: The Analytical Response

the power to us. Financial gain would become an aspect of the administration of the power. The power would be viewed as a talent or ability we possess because Jesus gave it to us. He does not give us power; He is our power. He does not give us strength; He is our strength. He does not give us happiness; He is our happiness. He does not give us peace; He is our peace. Nothing is outside of Him. My driving passion must be for Him. I must have a single eye!

We must not allow our Christian faith to ever experience a separation from Him. In separation from Him, we become an organization focused on good deeds. Legalism reigns again. Political considerations become dominate. Our own academic wisdom determines our decisions. Talent is bought and sold on the marketplace of performance. We compete, and division thrives. Jesus does not have the source we need; He is the source! Whenever the power of God is moving, He is there to dictate, direct, and oversee its activity. The power is His; He is the power!

The Power
(Strength)

If what we have just discussed is thoroughly experienced and understood, we are enabled to grasp the next expression of Peter in the passage. Peter reversed the order of the Sanhedrin's request. They wanted to know the power used for the miracle and the name of the person from whom the power came (Acts 4:7). Peter's focus was not on power but on Jesus! He began with the declaration of the name, Jesus! Then he began to describe the power involved in changing the life of a lame beggar. The power is the same as contained in **"God raised from the dead."**

This expression is used repeatedly in the New Testament to describe the power of the Spirit of Jesus. The continued emphasis of the power of the cross is unquestionable, but this power is released only in life. Look carefully at how Paul intertwines these ideas. *"That I may know Him and the power of His resurrection, and the fellowship of His sufferings, being conformed to His death"* (Philippians 3:10). In the introduction of his writings to the Romans, Paul said this regarding Jesus, *"and declared to be the Son of God with power according to the Spirit of holiness, by the resurrection from the dead"* (Romans 1:4). The writer of the Book of Hebrews acclaims Jesus as a superior high priest. He parallels Him with the type of priesthood found in Melchizedek. Jesus arose as a high priest, *"who has come, not according to the law of a fleshly commandment, but according to the power of an endless life"* (Hebrews 7:16).

Although these declarations are significant, we must recognize that the focus is not on an event. The resurrection of Jesus did occur. This statement was not an attempt to belittle the historic events of the crucifixion and resurrection. However, the event is significant only because there is life! The power of God is expressed in the life of Jesus. This expression gives new meaning to John's declaration, *"In Him was life and the life was the light of men"* (John 1:4).

Therefore, Peter is precise about the name or person who performed this miracle, Jesus. The Trinity God focused their life in the man called Jesus. Jesus is the manifestation, demonstration, and instrument of this life. We have come full circle in this thinking. The power of God is a person, Jesus! He is not a result of the power, and He is not the one who possesses the power. Jesus is the power of God to salvation. There was no chance for the Sanhedrin to know anything about God without embracing Jesus. This was not an adjustment in theology or philosophy but was an acceptance of Jesus. Therefore, the name in which the miracle was done was Jesus, and the power that did the miracle was Jesus. Jesus is the total focus!

Jesus was not the proposal of a new deity; He was the recognition of the God of their forefathers. Their God was redeeming them despite themselves. Everything He promised in loving redemption He placed in this Person, Jesus. To reject Jesus is to reject the God who raised Him from the dead. To disbelieve in Jesus is to disown the God of the Old Testament who extended Himself to us through Jesus. The Trinity God does no act of redemption outside Jesus. We are face to face with Jesus, the power of God!

The Pattern
(Standard)

The pattern found in the Christian faith is unprecedented in the world. No world religion comes close to the reality of Christianity. The Trinity God fully displays Himself in the person of Jesus. Jesus has been given all authority in heaven and on Earth (Matthew 28:18). He does not have it in the sense of an object of possession; instead, He is in Himself the full power and authority of the Trinity God. As this Trinity God moves through the person of Jesus, He is revealed in life. The revelation is not manifested in destruction of life, but is manifested in the living of life. But we must not consider living life in terms of activities or possessions. A man who was the irrefutable manifestation of the life of Jesus was standing before the Sanhedrin. Yes, it was a demonstration in the fact he was walking, leaping, and praising God. He was lame but now is standing. He was a beggar but will now be a productive part of society. Although all these activities contribute to the demonstration, the reality was found in the man (Acts 4:14).

We do not have any record of the healed beggar speaking any words to the Sanhedrin. He did not preach or perform feats. He simply stood there. He was the witness! The contrast between who he had been for more than forty years and who he was now is the truth of Peter's message to them. They could not adjust the pattern; they could not deny it. They simply rejected it.

Could this be what God wants to do in your life? The Trinity God moves in the person of Jesus to come to your life. He wants to impart to you much more than wisdom, knowledge, or additional understanding. He does not want to move on your life in a limited physical adjustment, a miracle. He does not want to help you with your problems. Improvement of your social and relational circumstances is not His goal. He wants to come to indwell you in the sense of becoming one with you. In other words, it is not a "touch," but it is a "fusion." Could He merge with you through the Spirit of Jesus? You would be the irrefutable revelation of the "name" and "power" of the Trinity God. Jesus is the "name" and "power" indwelling your life!

Acts 4:10-12

THE CONSISTENCY

" Let it be known to you all, and to all the people of Israel, that by the name of Jesus Christ of Nazareth, whom you crucified, whom God raised from the dead, by Him this man stands here before you. This is the stone which was rejected by you builders, which has become the chief cornerstone. Nor is there salvation in any other, for there is no other name under heaven given among men by which we must be saved" (Acts 4:10-12).

Seeking answers is the basic and common element of life, and the core of every area of life. Many jobs are based on problem solving, making people who can provide the answers important people. Research provides answers; therefore, foundations exist to provide money for that research. I need answers for my physical life, but I also need answers for my spiritual life. We consistently try to find spiritual answers in our physical existence. God gave us the physical to point us to the spiritual. However, the spiritual need of our lives is not answered in the materialistic realm. Looking for spiritual needs in a materialistic world has created the wreckage and ruin of human life piled around us. Our attempt to find answers for the spiritual realm in the physical existence has created this destruction.

Trying to find spiritual answers in physical solutions is common in religious circles. Legalism is the result of such an attempt, proposing that physical religious activities will provide spiritual answers. Spiritual answers demonstrate themselves in physical actions, but physical actions will not produce spiritual answers. We try to find spiritual answers in our spiritual disciplines such as Bible reading, tithing, prayer, and fasting. But these disciplines do not give us answers either. They are only a means to bring us to spiritual answers. Our hearts crave something beyond another physical "doing."

The members of the Sanhedrin are a prime example of this thought. They were religious but did not believe in the realm of the Spirit. Their lives were filled with religious activity, but they did not believe in eternal life. They sought answers only in the physical temple, ceremonies, and religious practices. When a physical miracle happened, they looked for the answer in the physical realm. Such was the case with the healed beggar, *"By what power or by what name have you done this?"* They were doing what they always did! They wanted to reduce the supernatural to a physical solution within their control.

The Book of Acts has one theme; the Spirit of Jesus is the answer! In our passage, the SOURCE OF THE ANSWER is plainly stated. **"Then Peter, filled with the Holy Spirit, said to them"** (Acts 4:8). Even the leaders of Israel should have recognized this answer did not come from these apostles (Acts 4:13). There are no answers outside of His Person. When the SPIRIT OF THE ANSWER is an expression of the nature of this Person, there is no surprise. The tone of everything Peter said was an overflow of God's heart! It was redemptive, and Peter continued with the SCORN OF THE ANSWER (Acts 4:9). He mocked them for their attempt to judge and condemn a good deed. They consistently took the goodness of God and contributed it to evil. Despite how they responded, there is the SECURITY OF THE ANSWER (Acts 4:10), and it is in the name of Jesus. Paul pronounced this Name as above every name. At this Name every knee will bow and every tongue will confess Jesus' Lordship (Philippians 2:9-10). A strong aspect of this security

Part 2: The Analytical Response

is the SUFFERING OF THE ANSWER (Acts 4:10). He is the Crucified One! He is not an answer removed from our plight. He joined the battle against sin with great consequences and won, and this is highlighted in the SINFULNESS AGAINST THE ANSWER (Acts 4:10). We actually fought against and crucified our only hope and answer. But not all is lost; there is the SURVIVING OF THE ANSWER (Acts 4:10). God raised Jesus from the dead! This picture is in the STONE OF THE ANSWER (Acts 4:10). This answer is the fulfillment of prophecy. Jesus is THE SAVIOR OF THE ANSWER (Acts 4:11), an exclusive position. What a Savior!

Peter makes three distinct statements (Acts 4:10-12). At first I thought they built on one another. He started with a foundational truth, built a structure on this foundation, and placed a beautiful finish on the presentation. There may be some element of truth to this approach; however, a more realistic approach is to view each statement as the same. In other words he said the same truth each time, but phrased it differently for clarification. Each statement was the declaration of one concept.

Peter's declared concept has three aspects.

Clarifies the ANSWER

The SENSE of each of these statements is immediate. Certainly Peter had a tone in his voice as he spoke to the Sanhedrin. In fact, Luke refers to this immediately after the three statements. *"Now when they saw the boldness of Peter and John"* (Acts 4:13). The Greek word "theoreo," translated *"saw,"* means "to look closely at," suggesting "to gaze, to look with interest and for a purpose." It usually indicates the careful observation of details. The content of what Peter said was no what impressed the Sanhedrin but the spirit, tone, and emphatic way he said it. Peter was filled with the Holy Spirit and spoke the mind of God. He did not suggest, call them to consider, or even offer an alternative idea. His tone was definite, compelling, authoritative, and without hesitation. The Sanhedrin could not misunderstand the intent of these apostles, Peter and John.

This sense is present in each bold statement. He unreservedly proclaimed the name of Jesus as the explanation for the healing of the lame beggar (Acts 4:10). In quoting the Old Testament prophecy, Peter forcibly clarifies who is the Chief Cornerstone (Acts 4:11). Jesus is the only possibility for salvation (Acts 4:12). Peter had been with Jesus for three years of ministry. He had doubted and denied that he knew Jesus before the resurrection, but after the resurrection he spent forty days with the resurrected Lord (Acts 1). There was no question in Peter's mind about the risen Jesus. Pentecost came to his life (Acts 2:1-4). He was surer that Jesus indwelt him now than he was about being physically present with Him for the previous three years. Peter lived in the flow of this presence in teaching, preaching, and miracles. He boldly proclaimed Jesus.

There is an obvious SINGULARITY to these statements. We will speak of this repeatedly. The heart of each statement is the focus on Jesus, the answer! If the discussion is the miracle received by the lame beggar, the explanation is Jesus. The explanation is not the doctrine of Jesus, the concept of Jesus, nor the power of Jesus; instead, it is Jesus! How could Peter give any other testimony? He reached out with his right hand to pull the lame beggar to his feet. He cried out in faith, ***"In the name of Jesus Christ of Nazareth, rise up and walk"*** (Acts 3:6). When he was confronted at Solomon's Porch with the possibility of personal credit for this miracle, Peter was appalled. With great power of persuasion, he pointed the crowd to Jesus. There was no room for Jesus plus other powers, methods, and beliefs. It was simply Jesus.

If the discussion is the prophecy of the Old Testament and the building of the house of Israel, there is one chief cornerstone, and it is Jesus. Any rejection of this one stone will result in the collapse of the house. The weight of the structure rests on Him. Everything finds its place because of Him. No other combination of additional stones can supplant this single Stone. Jesus is the answer!

If the discussion is the salvation of the world, there is One remaining choice. Jesus is the answer. If you seek salvation you, must seek Him. Peter's bold statement is, *"Nor is there salvation in any other"* (Acts 4:12). The impact of the statement pinpoints the location of all salvation. Salvation is not something Jesus provides for us; He does not give it to us apart from Himself. We cannot enjoy it because we visit Him often. He is not our weekly shot or pill to get us through a difficult week. Salvation is in Him. He is our salvation!

When we see through the eyes of Jesus, what is the SCOPE for this salvation? Peter began with a focus on a single man. The beggar was not the kind of man who impressed the Sanhedrin. He was not from their social status, their educational level, or their leadership circle. The focus on this beggar was a direct statement of Jesus' heart. There was no advantage, hidden agenda, or political maneuverings connected to this miracle. God's heart was focused on meeting the need of one unworthy person.

The concern of God was for the Jews, the builders of the house. The Sanhedrin, presently listening to Peter's exhortation, received in abundance the mercies of God. In all their stubbornness, self-centeredness, and arrogance, God brought them the Answer! In Peter's exhortation from Solomon's Porch, he declared, *"To you first, God, having raised up His Servant Jesus, sent Him to bless you, in turning away everyone of you from your iniquities"* (Acts 3:26).

The heart of God is after all men. This powerful name of Jesus has been given among men for salvation (Acts 4:12). God's intent was to save everyone from the lowest lame beggar to the highest members of the Sanhedrin. God intends salvation for everyone in the person of Jesus! No one is left out. Jesus is the Savior for all mankind! Jesus was the answer for this lame beggar, and for the nation of Israel, and He is the answer for all men.

Clarifies the ACCUSATION

Accusation is a negative projection of finger pointing and demeaning, and is often harmful. However, we must understand the SENSE of Peter's accusation in light of God's heart. Peter was bold in his pronouncement of the truth. He said, *"whom you crucified"* and *"which was rejected by you builders"* (Acts 4:10-11). The enormity of what the Sanhedrin did must be seen in light of what God was doing in Jesus.

Peter allowed the truth's strength to bring the condemnation to their hearts. He simply proclaimed the fact of their participation in the crucifixion. He did not elaborate on the punishment they would receive. He did not threaten or attempt to scare them. When the Sanhedrin decided to threaten the disciples, they commanded them never to speak in Jesus' name again. The apostles thought they were obligated to speak what God placed on them. *"For we cannot but speak the things which we have seen and heard"* (Acts 4:20). This was not an expression of a rebellious heart but honesty declared.

The SINGULARITY of Peter's accusation is somewhat startling. According to him everyone is guilty of the same thing! He did not address their participation in ceremonies, observances of the laws, or devotion to temple worship. The oral traditions of the Pharisees did not seem to be an issue. The doctrinal differences about their belief in the resurrection of the dead were not mentioned. He did not address their lack of belief in the afterlife, spirit world, or angels. Materialism was also not Peter's concern. The rejection of Jesus was the guilt of all. This problem was a relational and singular matter. They are not in proper relationship with Jesus. All other issues that may be considered sin were simply by-products of this one issue. The correction of all other issues would not reduce the amount of guilt; our guilt is singular!

The SCOPE of his accusation is clear. It included everyone. In his opening statement, Peter said, **"Let it be known to you all, and to all the people of Israel"** (Acts 4:10). Then he progressed through the list of those who were guilty. Our self-centeredness tends to shift the responsibility for wrongdoing to someone or something other than us. But Peter would not allow this. He began by addressing **"*you*"** (Acts 4:10). The **"*builders*"** were equally guilty (Acts 4:11). In fact, all mankind must embrace their guilt for salvation includes them (Acts 4:12). You rejected Jesus; the builders rejected Jesus; men rejected Jesus.

Clarifies the APPLICATION

The exciting news is that there is an answer, and it is Jesus. The SENSE of this application or answer is positive. There are no conditions surrounding it. As strong as Peter's message was in the guilt of all mankind, he was even stronger in the salvation of all mankind. If there were requirements or prerequisites for being included in salvation, not everyone would be included. But Peter boldly announced the presence of salvation for all.

He did not propose that all would be saved regardless. The amazing truth is that salvation for each person is already accomplished and located in Jesus. It is yours! Do you or do you not want to participate in Jesus? This is your choice. Therefore, the tone of Peter's voice must have been to the point of yelling. How exciting to exclaim to all mankind that salvation is theirs.

The SINGULARITY of salvation focuses on Jesus. Are we repeating what we have already said several times? But it is the heart of the passage. Jesus equals salvation; salvation equals Jesus. They are the same! Outside of Jesus there is no salvation, but in Jesus there is nothing but salvation. This makes the singular element of salvation Jesus! You must understand that this statement is coming from the heart of Peter, a Jew. He had spent a lifetime under the domination of the Old Testament law and more specifically the oral traditions of the Pharisees. He will be forced to apply what he spoke to the Jerusalem council to the issue of the Gentiles. He will participate in the special introduction of the New Covenant to Cornelius and Gentile friends (Acts 10-11). Is salvation found in Jesus plus Jewish laws? Is salvation found partially in Jesus but must be completed by specific disciplines and religious activities? The answer is firmly and confidently "no." Salvation is found only in Jesus!

The SCOPE of salvation finds no limits. Jesus is not partial salvation, and He is not salvation for people morally correct. No wonder Peter began with the healed beggar. As he spoke of salvation, he pointed to ***"this man stands here before you whole"*** (Acts 4:10). This man was a disgrace to his Jewish heritage. He or his parents had disobeyed God and were being punished for their sin. This man had never been allowed in the temple to participate in the means of salvation. He was eliminated from all hope. Then he found Jesus. In Jesus there was no problem; there was no condition beyond His reach. The self-righteous builders responsible for the building can find their salvation in only Jesus. The key and the strength to their structure must be Jesus. There is no salvation in any other (Acts 4:12). Do not spend your time looking. Come to Jesus!

Acts 4:10-12

THE ATTITUDE INVOLVED

"Let it be known to you all, and to all the people of Israel, that by the name of Jesus Christ of Nazareth, whom you crucified, whom God raised from the dead, by Him this man stands here before you whole. This is the stone which was rejected by you builders, which has become the chief cornerstone. Nor is there salvation in any other, for there is no other name under heaven given among men by which we must be saved" (Acts 4:10-12).

Peter took one thought and expressed it three ways, giving these verses unity. The one thought is focused on Jesus and our interaction with Him, making it impossible to miss this truth. In this sense Peter expressed the Scriptures. Hearing people criticize preachers by saying, "You are a funnel preacher" is common. It does not matter where you start; you always end at the same place." Peter fits this description. In fact, there are three recorded messages by Peter in the Book of Acts, and each follows the same pattern highlighted in these three verses.

Peter aggressively wove the Old Testament prophecies into his presentation. He made no attempt to suggest Jesus was a new thought, setting aside what God intended in the Old Covenant. Jesus of Nazareth is the fulfillment of God's dream. There has never been any other plan. The Israelites participated in the plan of God throughout their history. Now the Sanhedrin, listening to Peter, must realize the plan that God always had for them.

The Attitude Involved | Acts 4:10-12

It finds its fulfillment in Jesus.

Peter began with a "practical approach." ***"Let it be known to you all, and to all the people of Israel, that by the name of Jesus Christ of Nazareth, whom you crucified, whom God raised from the dead, by Him this man stands here before you whole"*** (Acts 4:10). Peter did not propose a theory, theology, or doctrine. The man who had been lame was standing before them as a demonstration to the power in the name of Jesus. This demonstration was not a mystical vision or dream but was the practical reality of life changed by the power of Christ. Based on this practical demonstration, the Sanhedrin must understand Jesus is the chief cornerstone of all God wants to build (Acts 4:11). In fact, there is no other possibility. Salvation is in Jesus who goes to the core of a person's existence (Acts 4:12). Jesus' salvation touches the total life.

Peter continued with a "prophetic approach." ***"This is the stone which was rejected by you builders, which has become the chief cornerstone"*** (Acts 4:11). The prophecies foretold the Scriptures. They were not fairy tales or myths, but prophecy revealed the practical approach. God planned with long-range precision to fulfill His dream. This fulfillment is Jesus. Throughout the Old Testament stories there was a mystical involvement of God among His people, but it was always practical. All the laws of God affected the daily routine and practical lives of the Israelites. The laws regarding food were for their health. Even the strange strategies of war were practical and produced astounding victory over the enemies of Israel. However, all the immediate practical involvements of God in their lives were a part of the long-range practical plan. The problem with the Sanhedrin was that they missed the long-range plan of God. Peter would not excuse them for this but consistently reminded them of their straying! Jesus called them back to the prophecies of the prophets. Peter was doing the same.

Peter continued with the "particular approach." ***"Nor***

Part 2: The Analytical Response

is there salvation in any other, for there is no other name under heaven given among men by which we must be saved" (Acts 4:12). Not many details were there to confuse or consider. God's plan is Jesus with no additions or secondary ideas. God had no substitutes, replacements, or alternatives in mind. He did not plan many roads to the same location but designed the only Way! He did not give many truths to consider but established the only Truth! His intention was not to have many doors to enter, but entrance is made through the only Door! He did not want many shepherds giving guidance but designated the only Shepherd! We do not have many names to consider; we have only the name of Jesus!

At the heart of Peter's statements are several contrasts with a focus on attitudes. In each statement Peter emphasized the difference between the attitudes of the leaders of Israel and the attitude of God. The attitude the leaders had toward Jesus was the opposite of God's attitude. Their attitude destroyed the practical, prophetic, and particular involvement of God in their lives. But it was not too late; God gave them another witness in the healed beggar.

The first descriptive attitude that Peter highlighted was SPIRITUAL MURDER (Acts 4:10). He identified Jesus as *"Jesus Christ of Nazareth, whom you crucified."* Crucifixion was the cruelest method of execution in history. The lingering torturous method normally took two and one-half days to achieve death. The battle to stay alive during this time was mixed with the desire to die, and the public watching it added to the torture. Crucifixion was punishment for the most severe crimes against the government, but the problem with the crucifixion of Jesus was that He was not guilty of any crime. All Roman officials from Herod to Pilate cleared Him. Pilate declared, *"I have found no fault in this Man concerning those things of which you accuse Him"* (Luke 23:14).

Peter highlighted the attitude of the Sanhedrin. Jesus did

nothing but good deeds, which the Sanhedrin considered bad. A lame beggar was healed by the power of this same Jesus, but they thought it was bad. Their opinion shaped their attitude, and it was their "Continual Attitude." They could not blame circumstances, culture, or misunderstanding because this attitude did not come and go but was always present as a driving force in the lives of the Sanhedrin. In the Greek grammar, the verb translated *"crucified"* is in the aorist tense. In the English grammar there is nothing like it. Normally it is translated into the past tense; however, the full intent of this tense is to focus on the action of the verb without regard to the time element. What the Sanhedrin expressed in the crucifixion of Jesus in the past was now being expressed again toward the movement of Jesus in the life of the lame beggar. Nothing had changed!

The writer of Hebrews gives powerful expression to this truth. He speaks of those babyish in their attitude toward Jesus, continuing in this state year after year. The consequence is sad; they will fall away, and it will be impossible, **"to renew them again to repentance, since they crucify again for themselves the Son of God, and put Him to an open shame"** (Hebrews 6:6). The Greek word "palin," translated *"again,"* promotes the idea of oscillatory repetition. The Greek word "anastauroo," in the present tense, translated *"crucify,"* promotes the idea of "re-crucify" or "crucify afresh." The present tense is an occurrence happening now with continuous action. The writer was not speaking of a physical crucifixion but the living attitude of crucifixion or spiritual murder living in our lives.

The Sanhedrin had a "Combative Attitude." Jesus met a need in the Jewish society. Hundreds of people were doing better spiritually and physically than they had ever done. A change for the good was occurring in the Jewish culture, a move toward righteousness. Why could not the leaders of Israel leave Jesus alone? The apostles continued to do miracles; what was the harm? In fact, this was proposed by a member of

Part 2: The Analytical Response

the council, ***"a Pharisee named Gamaliel, a teacher of the law held in respect by all the people"*** (Acts 5:34), gave an example of Theudas, a man who created a following of around four hundred people. He claimed to be a great leader but ended up slain and everyone scattered (Acts 5:36). He gave another illustration of Judas of Galilee (Acts 5:37). Why not allow the same thing to happen to these apostles?

But the Sanhedrin could not! Deep in the heart of their self-centeredness was a survival nature that fought against everything that threatened their desires. Jesus could not be tolerated either in presence or in message. The manifestation of His presence irritated their core of selfishness. Carnal self-centeredness must fight against Jesus until He is silenced. No neutrality or toleration is present, but a declaration of war is!

This Sanhedrin had a "Compulsive Attitude." At the heart of their declaration of war was anger. They did not have only an outside activity of crucifixion. Self-centeredness exploded in their fits of aggression driven by their inward rage. Jesus equated this anger with spiritual murder (Matthew 5:21- 22). What murder is to the physical world, anger is to the spiritual world. The oral traditions of Jesus' day accepted anger but would not tolerate murder. The Kingdom of God will not tolerate nor allow either. The members of the Sanhedrin killed Jesus in the spiritual realm long before they saw Him physically on the cross. Even in the moment of our passage they are spiritually murdering the apostles while they do not have the courage to actually bring them to physical death.

The Sanhedrin could not help themselves. Not lacking free will, they made choices that brought them to this place. A compulsion overwhelmed them and drove them to self-protection, a dangerous place to dwell. It concluded in their crucifixion of Jesus repeatedly. No one is exempt from crucifying Christ. We can argue that we were not present two thousand years ago. Yet the attitude present in the Sanhedrin then is present now in our lives. This attitude is at the heart of the Gospel and must come to death!

Peter contrasted the attitude of the Sanhedrin with God's attitude toward Jesus *"whom God raised from the dead"* (Acts 4:10). The Trinity God dramatically reversed all the Sanhedrin's expression of anger when He raised Jesus from the dead. The Sanhedrin and God were not in agreement. This disagreement should push us to recognize the need of examining our lives. Does God need to reverse all our actions and intents?

Peter moved to a second description of this attitude as he related a prophecy of the Old Testament. **"This is the stone which was rejected by you builders, which has become the chief cornerstone"** (Acts 4:11). This description is SCORNFUL MOCKERY. *"Builders"* were the members of the Sanhedrin. Their attitude was *"rejected,"* a translation of the Greek word "exouthenethes." It means, "to bring to naught, to despise, to treat with scorn, reject, low opinion of, or to treat cheap." The descriptive term most striking for my life is "to treat cheap." The Sanhedrin did not value Jesus. His ministry did not matter; His teachings were of no value; His miracles were inconsequential. His life was easily tossed aside for what they did consider valuable, their comfort and power.

They had a "Continual Attitude" and did not waver in their estimate of Jesus' value. This meeting of the Sanhedrin resulted in their threatening the apostles to never speak of Jesus again. Jesus was so valueless to them that they felt no loss in never again hearing His name. To feel this way about Jesus is to feel this way about much of mankind. The healed beggar was of no consequence to them and had no value in their sight. He could continue to beg at the Gate Beautiful, and it would not bother them. He did not register on their awareness list. He did not exist in their world. Their attitude toward Jesus extended to every area of their lives. When you

Part 2: The Analytical Response

and I are so focused on ourselves that others and their needs do not affect us, it is sad.

We can devalue a person by simply ignoring them. They do not matter so they do not exist. But we cannot do this to Jesus. If we do, we create a "Combative Attitude." God determines that every person through prevenient grace will be confronted with the value of Jesus. This confrontation produces a battle within your value system. When your wisdom takes priority over His, you have demeaned and belittled Him. When I cling to my will instead of His will, I reject His designs for my life as valueless. When my comfort and expectations are more important to me than His plan for my life, I have treated Him as cheap. How easily we disregard His presence. We ignore His probing in our lives. A little white stick of poison I place in my mouth and draw smoke from becomes more important to my life than His redemptive power. My sexual satisfaction becomes more important than His dream of home, children, and love. How easily I disregard His opinion and desire for my life. He does not matter!

This personal preference above His is a "Compulsive Attitude." With my mind, I know better. I shout the value of His presence because I know the theology of His redemption. But something in me drives me to treat Him as if He does not matter. This attitude was present in the Sanhedrin. The irrefutable truth was standing before them in the man no longer a lame beggar. But it does not matter to them. The veil in the temple can be ripped, the rocks can split, and the earth may quake but it does not matter (Matthew 27:51). We will continue in our self-centeredness; we will hire a seamstress to repair the veil, and we will clean the broken rocks.

The compulsion attitude is contrasted with God's opinion of Jesus. He made Him ***"the Chief Cornerstone."*** We must take sides with Him against ourselves. He is the only one who can deliver us. Our value system is wrong; we are selling ourselves for the rubbish of our selfishness. May God have mercy on us!

The Attitude Involved | Acts 4:10-12

The third statement of this prevailing attitude is the SELECTIVE MEMBERS. Peter said it this way, *"Nor is there salvation in any other, for there is no other name under heaven given among men by which we must be saved"* (Acts 4:12). Peter took the attitudes of the previous statements and drew them together into a negative statement. *"Nor"* is a translation of the Greek word "ouk," often translated "not." This is a "Continual Attitude." This particular negative is an absolute negative expressing an independent attitude and is a statement of absolute reality. It is not dependent on anyone's opinion but is an expression of the way it really is! It is the bold statement of this sentence, which begins the expression. In other words, this is not the present condition but will change in the future. Jesus is the only way to salvation. This is the way it has always been and will remain so. Those who maintain the previous attitude of spiritual murder and scornful mockery will not experience salvation in any degree.

It is a "Combative Attitude." These two conditions stand at opposite ends of the spectrum. They are in constant conflict. There will be no peace agreement, and compromises will not be made. Neither attitude is willing to adjust for the other. Self-centeredness will never cease its crucifixions, and the merge of a person with Jesus cannot happen while we are self-centered. There can never be half and half in the Kingdom life. Jesus calls for surrender. The wonder of His life living through us can never be experienced as long as we demand to live our life. He will never tolerate us living our lives for Him because it is not the attitude of God.

This self-reliance will demand a total change in our "Compulsive Attitude." If neither side will relent, there must be a radical change in one's attitude. This change is what Jesus died and rose again to produce in the life of the believer. God's attitude can become our attitude. The self-centered, murderous, rejecting attitude can never change the attitude of God, but

Part 2: The Analytical Response

God can change the attitude of self-centeredness. The Trinity God focuses all redemption in Jesus. He is the answer for every life, and there is no other resource or solution. Jesus is God's provision for us. Let us embrace Him!

Acts 4:10-12

THE ACTION RESPONSE

> " Let it be known to you all, and to all the people of Israel, that by the name of Jesus Christ of Nazareth, whom you crucified, whom God raised from the dead, by Him this man stands here before you. This is the stone, which was rejected by you builders, which has become the chief cornerstone. Nor is there salvation in any other, for there is no other name under heaven given among men by which we must be saved" (Acts 4:10-12).

Peter gave three bold statements to the Sanhedrin. He was not wordy in his approach, and he did not give the historical background of God's plan because they already knew those details. He did not describe the symbolism of the ceremonies or temple facilities. Peter gave the bare truth they needed, Jesus! Each statement repeats the truth of the preceding statement. He gave these statements in a different language and perspective from ours. We list these as "the practical approach," "the prophetic approach," and "the particular approach."

In our previous study, we discovered a series of contrasts in each statement. Peter contrasts the attitude of the Sanhedrin with the attitude of the Trinity God toward Jesus. According to "The New Oxford American Dictionary," the meaning of attitude is "a settled way of thinking or feeling about someone or something, typically one that is reflected in a person's behavior." In other words it is normal practice that one's attitude will reveal

Part 2: The Analytical Response

itself in action. It is acceptable to presume that my feelings and thinking about a situation or thing will be the source of my action toward that situation or thing. Actions are sourced by attitude. If you want to change the actions of your life, you must change your attitude.

Sometimes we recognize our wrong attitude and make an adjustment. Or we discover what we thought was true about a situation is not, and this discovery changes our attitude. However, this change of attitude was not what Peter expressed in our passage. The members of the Sanhedrin had an attitude at the core of their lives. This attitude was expressed in the crucifixion of Jesus, and now we see it in their resistance to the apostles. Information did not source their attitudes. Something significant dwelt in their hearts. They had a "settled way of thinking." The Bible calls it "the carnal nature," a selfish, self-centered manner that infiltrates every area and expression of life.

This attitude of the carnal nature dominated and determined the lives of the Sadducees. They rejected all spiritual and supernatural activities. They disbelieved any miracle of God in the Old Testament. They did not accept the existence of angels, spirits, or demons. Their focus was on materialistic comfort and wealth, and they thought there was no life after death, no resurrection. The attitude of their self-centered carnality formed their theological view. Their practices of the temple ceremonies and sacrifices said they believed in the Messiah, but their lifestyles revealed their true belief. Jesus had to confront their carnality, and because we have this carnality, He confronts us as well. The Sadducees' responded by crucifying Jesus, but now He confronts them again through the apostles.

Peter highlighted a contrast between the actions that resulted from the attitude of the Sanhedrin and the actions from the attitude of the Trinity God.

Peter began with the contrast in THE ACTION OF CRUCIFIXION (Acts 4:10). The dramatic boldness of Peter and John impressed the Sanhedrin (Acts 4:13). They were not affected by Peter's message but by the strength of his presentation. After all, they had the power of life and death for Peter and John. The apostles were far beneath the members of the Sanhedrin in social status, finances, education, and religious training. Who was Peter to give correction to these leaders of Israel?

Peter boldly began with, **"Jesus Christ of Nazareth, whom you crucified."** He did not need to give details for it was all present in the minds of these members. The self-centered carnal attitude was so strong in the hearts of each member of the Sanhedrin that it drove them to plot murder. They did not get caught up in the moment and act in ways contrary to their typical patterns. They premeditated murder. They schemed, manipulated, and directed the activities, meeting to plan the event. They blackmailed Pilate to achieve their goal. They could not excuse or reject the responsibility of their actions.

As we view the verses after Peter's presentation, the Sanhedrin made no attempt to deny their part in the crucifixion (Acts 4:13-22). They gave no rationalization to lighten their guilt, ignoring the issue. Their goal was to eliminate any talk or thought about Jesus. They did not want to hear His name mentioned again. This elimination was and had always been their approach. They would not embrace truth. If we never hear the name of Jesus, does the reality of sin cease? If we never again hear His name preached, does this eliminate our guilt? If the self-centered carnal attitude of the members of the Sanhedrin was the cause of the most hideous crime in history, does it not speak to the evil of this nature? The One who is Light blaringly reveals the darkness of our inner lives! We cannot tolerate or ignore it. It drives us to crucifixion. Jesus must be eliminated; His name must never be spoken again.

In the first century AD, crucifixion was one of the strongest forms of deterrent against insurrection or political uprising in the Roman provinces. Most crucifixions were connected to an

Part 2: The Analytical Response

action against the present rule and authority. It was no different with Jesus in the physical world of His day and in the spiritual world of our hour. Self-ruling and Christ-ruling cannot exist side by side. Someone must be crucified. The Sanhedrin could not continue in their self-rule and permit the name of Jesus to be proclaimed. They crucified His person; they must now crucify His name. This scene is reenacted in our lives.

What we do to Jesus to save ourselves is directly contrasted with what He did for us. An attitude of self-centered carnality expressed itself in the crucifixion. Similarly the attitude of God's nature is clearly defined in His action toward us. Peter highlighted it in, **"this man stands before you whole"** (Acts 4:10). Nothing shouts the selfless nature of God like this miracle. If Jesus extended a miracle to the Rich Young Ruler, our self-nature has some understanding to the reason. He was a person of means, talent, and power. His future could benefit the Kingdom of God. If Jesus did a miracle for Nicodemus, we would not be surprised. Nicodemus' influence, as a teacher of the teachers, could assure Jesus' status among the influential people of Jerusalem. This influence would be a huge step forward to building the Kingdom.

However, the resource of God focused on a beggar had no advantage. One who had the psychological scars from forty years of begging would have no value. He had developed no talent, gained no position of power, and could contribute no meaningful leadership. What was the point in giving him a miracle? The answer to this question is the crux of the issue. The redemptive heart of God is the answer! The cross style of bleeding, suffering, and dying has no angle, hidden strategy, or selfish motive. The attitude of Jesus is always one of redemption.

Notice that Peter was an instrument expressing God's heart. Perhaps we should say it stronger. Peter became God's heart. He was, **"filled with the Spirit"** (Acts 4:8). Peter's being and the Spirit of Jesus became a new creature. In Peter's helplessness, the Spirit of Jesus merged with Peter, and he entered into the mind of Christ. He was a partaker of the divine nature (2 Peter 1:4). He became the hand reaching out to the lame beggar. He gave the lame beggar hope in Jesus. What did Peter gain from this confrontation as he defended the miracle of a healed beggar? Nothing resulted but persecution and further threats. But Peter had the mind of Christ, expressed the nature of Jesus, and changed his world with his actions.

This call is for us as well. Oh, to become the expression of Christ's heart. Do not allow the self-centered carnal mind to adjust and manipulate your soul into a false mixture of Jesus and self. How easy it is to embrace Christianity for our benefit. You have a plan for your life, and you are quick to ask God to help you achieve it. What if God, the Creator, has the plan for your life? You may not have any consciousness of this plan. Will you surrender to Him so He can achieve His plan in and through you, or will you crucify Him again?

Another action, which results from an attitude expressed in this concept, is THE ACTION OF CONDESCENSION (Acts 4:11). When the carnal mind dominates, condescension happens. The Sanhedrin considered themselves experts on the Scriptures. Peter quoted the sacred Scriptures, a prophecy familiar to this group. He highlighted this attitude in light of their participation in God's plan. They were not outsiders who lacked understanding of God's plan. They were a people birthed to construct the building into which the world would be invited. Redemption flowed from this building to every person. The prophecy called them *"you builders."* They got to read the blueprints. The revelation of God's heart came to them repeatedly. The tragedy was in the pattern established in their forefathers. Although they denied the fact, they became like them (Matthew 23:30).

In Peter's previous message, he admonished the Jewish crowd, **"To you first, God, having raised up His Servant Jesus, sent Him to bless you, in turning away every one of you from** *your iniquities"* (Acts 3:26). In our investigation of this passage, we discovered God did not love them more than the others of the world. They did not have special talents or abilities that caused God to choose them over others. God's loving heart for every person forced Him to begin with someone. He formed an entire nation of people designed to be the **"builders."** What a privilege that would be!

But this verse displays a tragic picture. The Greek words used in the text leave us somewhat confused. A combination of two Greek words, "kephale" and "gonia," are translated **"chief cornerstone."** The first Greek word, "kephale," is a feminine noun placing it in the abstract. It refers to the head, top, or whatever is uppermost in relationship to something. "Gonia" is also a feminine noun referring to an angle or corner. Two approaches are made in this word's translation. Some understand this to be a reference to the stone that held the walls together, the **"cornerstone."** Others think it as the final stone in the building placed over the entrance, a kind of "keystone."

However you visualize this, the most important stone of the building was rejected. It may relate to an incident connected with the building of the temple. The first stone that came down from the quarry was complicated, and the builders could not find a place for it so it was dragged into a corner of the building area and in time covered with debris. When the building was completed, there was no cornerstone until someone remembered the rejected stone. They uncovered this rejected stone; it was the perfect shape and size!

The builders were not mean, evil, or demon possessed. They simply found no value in the stone. It did not fit into the building they were constructing. They had nothing against the stone; it might be fine elsewhere but not in their building. At various times Jesus pleaded with the leaders of Israel but to no avail. According to the Old Testament tradition, witnesses were important to validate truth. Jesus presented a list of witnesses

The Action Response | Acts 4:10-12

proclaiming His significance. It did not seem to matter to them. Jesus confronted them, ***"How can you believe, who receive honor from one another, and do not seek the honor that comes from the only God?"*** (John 5:44). The Greek word translated *"honor"* is "doxa," and is often translated "glory." The basic word refers to perspective or viewpoint with the flavor of what one values. Jesus is the stone that had no value to them.

I cringe to think of how often I have treated Jesus as one without value. I did not give Him consideration because my opinion was of greater value to me. His value was treated far beneath my physical comfort; He was not as important to me as my materialism. My favorite ball team was placed far above Jesus in importance. I sold myself for things that did not matter and flung the one thing that mattered aside as valueless. I sacrificed for the temporal and wasted the eternal. I am as guilty as these members of the Sanhedrin.

My devaluation of Jesus is contrasted with God's value system. The Trinity God placed Jesus as redemption's core for all humanity. The building rests on Him. No one can take His place. Without Him there is no building! He is so valuable to the Trinity God that He raised Him from the dead. In other words the Trinity would not allow anything or anyone to obstruct the achievement of God's plan fulfilled in Jesus. Jesus is the focus of the Trinity!

Luke describes a third act in the final statement of this concept (Acts 4:12) resulting from the attitude of those involved. This act is not as pronounced as the previous two, but it is present as THE ACTION OF THE CYNICAL (Acts 4:12). The final statement Peter makes begins with the word *"Nor,"* a translation of two Greek words, "kai" and "ouk." "Kai" is a coordinating conjunction that links this statement with the previous verses. "Ouk" is an absolute negative, not dependent on or an expression of the opinion of anyone but it is a statement of reality. Salvation is nowhere outside of Jesus; this is simply the way it is!

Although it is not stated, it is concluded that non-salvation is outside of Jesus. This conclusion is the choice of the cynical person. The possibility of this choice is amazing. Why would anyone choose destruction and defeat when they could choose salvation? The answer focuses on Jesus. If *"salvation"* is the sole issue, everyone will choose correctly. But when *"salvation"* is Jesus, the focus moves to this Person. The issue is longer *"salvation"* but is Jesus! No one rejects *"salvation;"* they reject Jesus.

Jesus is a Person. That fact is what makes this so difficult. If salvation was a system, we could manipulate it, we could fit into it, and we could adjust it. The Pharisees proved this in Jesus' day. They adjusted the Old Testament religious system. However, a relationship with a Person who is Lord cannot be adjusted or manipulated. If salvation is a belief structure, we can give mental assent and still have other opinions. We are skilled at this, embracing a belief while simultaneously tolerating actions contrary to that belief. But salvation is not a belief structure; it is a Person. If salvation is a series of activities, we can learn and accomplish the pattern. However, this gives us freedom to maintain our lifestyles and adjust the religious activities around our schedule. But salvation is a Person, Jesus! Therefore, we embrace non-salvation.

Luke contrasts this with the Trinity's response to Jesus. The focus of the verse is the gracious, extravagant gift of God. *"For there is no other name under heaven GIVEN among men by which we must be saved"* (Acts 4:12). Peter boldly said the opinion and purpose of God, *"For there is no other name."* Listen to the singularity of this statement, which is an absolute focus on the Person of Jesus as the only means for salvation. The statement *"under heaven"* proclaims the completeness of salvation in Jesus. In other words, there is no need to look elsewhere. There is no place, no region, no realm, or spiritual existence where salvation will be found outside of Jesus. Salvation is *"given"* as a gracious, extravagant gift of God. The entire resource of God's person comes together in Jesus. Here is the movement of His powerful hand. Even the statement *"among men"* brings us to this conclusion. There is no salvation anywhere among the realm of humanity outside of Jesus. *"We must"* is a translation of the Greek word "dei." As a divine necessity, the sovereign hand of Almighty God backs it up.

Mankind crucified, rejected, and chose non-salvation; the Trinity God embraces Jesus. It is time to love and embrace Jesus.

Acts 4:10-12

THE AGENTS

" Let it be known to you all, and to all the people of Israel, that by the name of Jesus Christ of Nazareth, whom you crucified, whom God raised from the dead, by Him this man stands here before you. This is the stone, which was rejected by you builders, which has become the chief cornerstone. Nor is there salvation in any other, for there is no other name under heaven given among men by which we must be saved" (Acts 4:10-12).

Peter gives the Sanhedrin the heart of the Gospel in three statements. Each statement is identical in concept and links to the other two. In other words, Peter proclaimed the truth three ways with each focused on Jesus. He identified Him as ***"Jesus Christ of Nazareth,"*** leaving no confusion about this Person. The identity of Jesus must be made known to the Sanhedrin, ***"whom you crucified, whom God raised from the dead."*** Everything Peter said to them related to this one Person. Christianity cannot be defined or understood outside of Jesus. A Christian is "a Christ in." When Christ is removed, Christianity ceases to exist.

Peter's first statement was focused on the PRESENT (Acts 4:10). The members of the Sanhedrin sat in a semicircle with Peter, John, and the healed beggar standing amid them. The atmosphere was filled with tension. The Sanhedrin had dealt with Jesus for years. The focus of their previous months had been on eliminating Jesus, but now He confronts them again. Jesus will not go away! His influence and presence stands before them as a lame beggar made whole. Jesus is not a problem of the past; He is not someone to consider sometime or an agenda for the future. They were not dealing with His "second coming" at the end of the world. They were compelled by His presence now!

A strong fact in the present is the reality of the PAST (Acts 4:11). The problem of the past did not negate what was now; instead, it highlighted and intensified the present. Peter proclaimed a familiar, often quoted Old Testament prophecy regarding the redemptive plan that Jesus fulfilled in their hour. The Trinity God was constructing a building of redemption. The final stone of the building was secured, and the building was complete in Jesus. The dream of the past was now the reality of the present. This was a new day! How could the Sanhedrin miss Jesus!

In my experience, Jesus has bombarded my past with the reality of His truth. His present confrontation in my life is a product of His continual revelation through the past. Paul said this is true for all of us (Romans 1:19-20). God has consistently and persistently spoken in my past. If I reject Him in the present, I also reject all that He has revealed in my past. To deny Jesus in the present is to deny my past. The guilt of such denial hangs heavy in my reality.

Peter's next statement of POTENTIAL keeps us from complete despair (Acts 4:12). Despite our sin, Jesus completes the building, faithfully overcoming our obstacles and resistance. His salvation is in place for everyone. Peter confronted the Sanhedrin with their offer of salvation in Jesus. Our Savior will not allow us to miss salvation. If we do not walk in victory, it is because we reject Him as He persistently confronts our lives. We cannot reject Jesus' offer of salvation because of ignorance or by accident. To reject Jesus we must reenact the stubborn, blatant, act of the Sanhedrin.

Peter's presentation to the Sanhedrin was in the form of a contrast. He contrasted how the Trinity God felt about Jesus with the response of the Sanhedrin. The Sanhedrin crucified Him; the Trinity God raised Him from the dead. As builders, the Sanhedrin rejected Him; the Trinity God selected Him as the cornerstone. The Sanhedrin said no to salvation in Jesus; the Trinity God placed salvation in Jesus alone. What a vivid contrast!

Peter had several elements in this contrast. The ATTITUDE of God was much different from that of the Sanhedrin. God's attitude was acceptance. ***"This is My beloved Son, in whom I am well pleased. Hear Him!"*** (Matthew 17:5). The Sanhedrin's attitude was rejection, ***"So they called them and commanded them not to speak at all nor teach in the name of Jesus"*** (Acts 4:18).

The second was a contrast of ACTION. God and the Sanhedrin each were dominated by their attitudes, causing them to act in different ways. The Sanhedrin had to crucify Jesus, and the Trinity God had to raise Him from the dead. The core attitude of each demanded their specific response. The builders (Sanhedrin) could not tolerate Jesus because they saw no value in Him. The Trinity God made Him the cornerstone on which the building rested.

AGENT is the third aspect in the contrast. This aspect requires a more detailed explanation.

The Agents of Crucifixion
Acts 4:10

The English dictionary defines agent as "a person acting on behalf of another." For example, a travel agent acts on behalf of someone who wants to travel. If his client is going by air, the agent's responsibility is to find the lowest price with the best flight connections. The agent is not going to travel; he is acting on behalf of his client. With this representation in mind, we come to our passage, *"let it be known to you all, and to all the people of Israel, that by the name of Jesus Christ of Nazareth, whom you crucified, whom God raised from the dead, by Him this man stands here before you whole"* (Acts 4:10).

The second person, plural, pronoun *"you,"* a translation of the Greek word "humin" is used three times in this verse. This word focuses on the Sanhedrin. He did not refer to their forefathers who had been guilty of the attitude of murder toward the prophets. The Gentile population was filled with the evils of the world, but Peter did not consider them. He addressed the Sanhedrin whose members represented all of Israel. By an act of their will, they made the decisions that caused Jesus' crucifixion, and they were responsible for crucifying Jesus. The weight of the guilt and responsibility rests on them.

Peter did know that the members of the Sanhedrin were mere agents of the crucifixion. Thus far in the Book of Acts, Peter has proposed a truth. An interaction of good and evil is working through these agents. The Sanhedrin and the Trinity God each desiring Jesus' crucifixion is a mystery! The difference is in their motives. Good and evil are extreme opposites. Evil is motivating the Sanhedrin while perfect love is motivating God. Although they are used as an agent, it does not eliminate their responsibility. The Sanhedrin was guilty of crucifying Jesus as Peter said.

Listen to Peter's statement from his first sermon, *"Him, being delivered by the determined purpose and foreknowledge of God, you have taken by lawless hands, having crucified, and put to death"* (Acts 2:23). God used the wickedness of man to source his redemption, and this is the ironic element in the history of the world. The writer of the Book of Hebrews said, *"Inasmuch then as the children have partaken of flesh and blood, He Himself likewise shared in the same, that through death He might destroy him who had the power of death, that is, the devil"* (Hebrews 2:14). God takes death and turns it back on the source of death; therefore, death destroys itself!

Do you remember the interaction of Jesus with the leaders of Israel? They claimed Abraham and God as their father. They criticized Jesus for not knowing His father. When they made their accusations, Jesus said, ***"You are of your father the devil, and the desires of your father you want to do. He was a murderer from the beginning and does not stand in the truth, because there is no truth in him"*** (John 8:44). The nature of self-centered carnality that motivates the devil was the nature that possessed the leaders of Israel. Although they may not have been demon possessed, they were possessed by the demonic nature. They wanted to crucify Christ because they were agents of the devil's desires.

This desire is the expression of all sin. We have fallen into the same trap? Any expression of self-will, self-sufficiency, or self-centeredness is a manifestation of our link with the demonic world, proposing the elimination of Jesus' name (Acts 4:17). We become an agent! The contrast to agents of the devil is the thrust of Peter's call to the Sanhedrin. Pentecost could happen in their lives. They could experience all that is known in "salvation". They could be agents of Jesus' life, and there is no salvation outside of His person.

The Agents of Construction
Acts 4:11

The Old Testament prophecy, so familiar to the Sanhedrin, placed them in the position of "builders." Rather than trembling at the responsibility of such a position, they exerted their authority and selfishly displayed their power. Instead of following the blueprints of God, they designed the building for their own profit. This prophecy was a contrast between the material God wanted in the finished building and the material these builders desired. The end result was that they ceased to be "agents of construction" and became "agents of destruction."

God's plan cannot be destroyed. He will take what these builders did and work His will regardless. Through His omniscience His redemptive heart cannot be stopped. God placed the stone counted as valueless and tossed aside by the builders as the cornerstone. The building of redemption was secure and destruction took place in the lives of the builders.

After declaring Himself King of Israel on Palm Sunday, Jesus went to the temple to cleanse it. The following day He returned to the temple and began to teach, standing amid the debris of His cleansing. Hearing of His return these leaders rushed to interrupt Him. They asked Him by whose authority did He cleanse the temple (Matthew 21:23). He did not answer their question but asked them a question instead, which they refused to answer.

Therefore, Jesus answered them in parables. Jesus told several stories about their response. An owner of a vineyard had two sons. He requested that each help him in the vineyard. The first son refused, but the second responded with glad acceptance. The son who refused soon repented and joined his father in the work. The second son who accepted never came to the vineyard (Matthew 21:28-32). This parable is the story of these builders who do not work in the Father's vineyard.

In the second story an owner leased his vineyard to some vinedressers. At harvest time, they refused to make the lease payment. They beat, stone, and killed the servants the owner sent to receive the payment. Finally, the owner sent his Son, and they killed Him as well. This is the parable of the builders rejecting the stone given them for the building. The end result was their destruction (Matthew 21:33-46). Jesus applied this parable to this crowd, and He quoted the prophecy found in our passage (Psalms 118:22-23). He said the Kingdom would be taken from them and given to another nation.

This runs parallel to our lives. We can participate in redemption building. We can be agents of construction if we are in intimacy with Jesus. He is the heart of the construction. Remove Him and there is nothing but destruction. Regardless of the sincerity of your activities or the skills of your training, there is nothing but destruction without Jesus. The best of man's wisdom becomes absolute foolishness without Him. All righteousness is but filthy rags and every ministry is self-serving without Him. Truth does not exist outside of Jesus. To be adequate constructors we must have Him!

The Agents of Conversion
Acts 4:12

Were the leaders of Israel bad people? Compared to a pagan world, they were shining stars. They had a singleness of dedication to one God, Jehovah, and there were occasions in their history where they risked their lives because of their commitment to traditional beliefs. The one instruction of Peter to this group focused on Jesus. The discussion was about their embrace of Him. They were to be agents for conversion, but they suggested other means besides Jesus. This was their problem!

Peter's proposition is narrow in focus, has no adjustment, is intolerant to everything but Jesus, and troubles many. When we promote the offering of sacrificial lambs instead of Jesus, we cease to be agents of conversion and become agents of diversion. When the temple ceremonies are more important than Jesus, we have become instruments of misdirection ending in chaos. Our theology can deter others and us from Him. When our programs become our focus, we cease to point to Him. Any addition to Jesus destroys the heart of conversion

When Jesus becomes an example to follow instead of

a Savior to embrace, we are damned. If Jesus becomes a theology to believe instead of one to love, we are lost. Jesus, the idea, must submit to Jesus, the person. He must be alive in our lives. When Jesus becomes an organization to maintain, we have cursed our society with another false doctrine. If religion becomes the participation in sacraments, we are of all men most miserable. Conversion is found only in Him; there is *"no other name."* Will you or will you not be His? He will crowd out all other loves. He alone is my Rescuer! He is my Savior!

Acts 4:10-12

IN HIS NAME

"Let it be known to you all, and to all the people of Israel, that by the name of Jesus Christ of Nazareth, whom you crucified, whom God raised from the dead, by Him this man stands here before you. This is the stone, which was rejected by you builders, which has become the chief cornerstone. Nor is there salvation in any other, for there is no other name under heaven given among men by which we must be saved" (Acts 4:10-12).

Peter amazingly summarizes the Gospel in three statements. If we knew nothing about the Gospel except these statements, we would know it all. He pushed aside all minor issues and clearly revealed the heart of Christianity, a focus on Jesus. In other words, we do not have "information to learn" but "Jesus to embrace." Peter does not confront with the "requirement of performance" but the "reality of the Person."

We are two thousand years removed from the event of our passage, and this can cause us to miss what is important. In our removal state, we seem to consider Jesus an idea, theology, or doctrine. Seeing Jesus in these ways violates everything Peter proposed. If we remain in the scene, Peter confronts us with the Person of Jesus, **"whom you crucified"** (Acts 4:10). He is **"Jesus Christ of Nazareth, whom you crucified"** (Acts 4:10). In fact, to make it more specific, He is **"Jesus Christ of Nazareth, whom you crucified, whom God raised from the dead"** (Acts 4:10).

This confrontation was dramatic for the Sanhedrin, who had indeed participated in the crucifixion of Jesus. Their guilt was not only theological, but it focused on a rejection of the Person. Sin for them was not telling a few lies, harboring hurt feelings, or breaking religious laws. Their sin was focused on the Person of Jesus Christ. If they were to repent, it would require them to reverse their feelings about Jesus. They would have to move from calling Him a false Messiah and embrace Him as their Messiah. Jesus' teachings violated their oral traditions, and if they accepted Him, they would have to adopt His teachings into their lives.

This acceptance is also true for our lives. We may not have violated religious practices or broke some of the Ten Commandments, but we have rejected and crucified Jesus as our Savior. Even we who have accepted the Christian belief system and believe in Jesus have refused to give Him the position of King in our relationship with Him. Thus, we have never become the Kingdom. Jesus calls us to embrace Him just as He also called the Sanhedrin. In other words, our salvation is focused on and determined by our relationship with Jesus.

Most of us would say we have accepted Jesus as our Savior. But accepting Jesus as our Savior is beyond saying a few words or making a public confession at church. The problem in our passage is accepting Jesus as our Messiah in the same manner and depth in which we crucified Him. We were not just witnesses or casual observers of His crucifixion, but we aggressively yelled, threatened, plotted, and instigated His removal from our lives. Many of us have never come to terms with this level of our guilt. If we yelled against Him, we must begin to yell for Him. If we threatened Him, we must now allow Him to embrace us. If we removed Him from our lives, we must now allow Him to bring our lives under His control.

It is time in our passage to consider Peter's continual reference to the *"name,"* a translation of "onoma." The Greek word "onoma" is used two hundred and thirty times in the New Testament. In the Gospel of Luke and the Book of Acts, Luke used "onoma" ninety-four times. In a scan of the messages preached in the early church, the name of Jesus was cited repeatedly. When the lame beggar was healed at the Gate Beautiful, the miracle began with Peter's words, *"In the name of Jesus Christ of Nazareth, rise up and walk"* (Acts 3:6). When Peter explained the miracle to the crowd, he said, *"And His name, through faith in His name, has made this man strong, whom you see and know"* (Acts 3:16). The question of the Sanhedrin was, *"By what power or by what name have you done this?"* (Acts 4:7). Peter boldly proclaimed, *"that by the name of Jesus Christ of Nazareth, whom you crucified, whom God raised from the dead, by Him this man stands here before you whole"* (Acts 4:10).

Understanding the elements using the word "name" in the New Testament may help us. Let us look at those together.

Name - Character
Who He Is

A name communicates something essential or a characteristic about the bearer (Matthew 1:23, 25). That name becomes an expression of the nature and heart of the person. We see this in Jacob's encounter with God. Jacob had not seen his brother, Esau, for years after he cheated him out of his birthright. Now Esau was coming with four hundred men to meet Jacob. Jacob was afraid and made preparations to appease his brother, sending Esau gifts and extending his friendship. Jacob took his family across the river Jabbok. *"Then Jacob was left alone; and a Man wrestled with him until the breaking of day"* (Genesis 32:24). Was this *"Man"* an angel or maybe Jesus? In his desperation, Jacob would not let the Man escape. Finally, the Man asked Jacob to say his name. The name Jacob means, "liar, trickster, or cheater," what Jacob had been all his life. Then the Man said, *"Your name shall no longer be called Jacob, but Israel; for you have struggled with God and with men, and have prevailed"* (Genesis 32:28). "Israel" means, "a prince of God." Jacob's nature was changed, changing his name.

Matthew illustrated this truth in the Christmas story. In the first Christmas narrative he stated a prophesy from Isaiah about Jesus. *"Behold, the virgin shall be with child, and bear a Son, and they shall call His name Immanuel, which is translated, God with us"* (Matthew 1:23). His name characterizes who He is! His name is not just a label or a means to identify Him, but it gives a description of His nature. This would be the name given to Jesus from the people. In other words, this is how they saw Him; He is *"God with us."* But allow me to relate to you how God sees Jesus. *"And she will bring forth a Son, and you shall call His name Jesus, for He will save His people from their sins"* (Matthew 1:21). *"Jesus"* means "Yahweh is salvation." Jesus' heart and nature contained the redemptive concern. All the redemptive love of God is revealed in Jesus.

This redemptive love is significant in our passage. Peter declared to the Sanhedrin that the source of the miracle was the loving nature of Jesus. This nature of Jesus holds the structure of the building together. Jesus' character and nature provides salvation to every man, and no salvation is found outside the nature of His Person! Death, resurrection and ascension were expressions of the uniqueness of the character and nature of His Person. The cross was the visible expression of His nature, and this is where we find salvation. When we embrace Jesus, we are saved. When we have Him and He has us, we are saved. There is no salvation apart from Jesus!

Satan's deception is his greatest attempt to sidetrack us from Jesus! He does not care about what dominates our attention or interest as long as it is not Jesus. Drugs, pornography, hatred, bitterness, hurts, church, ministry, rules, and doctrine are all possible substitutes for Jesus. Religious ceremonies can become more valuable than Jesus. Demonic deception can cause us to miss Jesus. We need to allow Jesus to be our focus, speak only of Him and nothing else, and highlight Jesus alone.

Name - Calling
What He Does

Using the *"name"* in our passage has a second element. When God gives a specific name to a person, He chooses them. Why would He invest in the details of that person's name unless He is specifically linked to them? When God gives a name, He does so with purpose, and that name makes a statement.

God specifically selected the name of Jesus. ***"And she will bring forth a Son, and you shall call His name Jesus, for He will save His people from their sins"*** (Matthew 1:21). The angel of the Lord delivered this message to Joseph amid his moral dilemma. The name **"Jesus"** was given to the newborn King, highlighting the purpose He would fulfill in the redemptive plan of the Trinity God. His name revealed the task and focus of His high calling.

The name "Jesus" is used one thousand two hundred and seventy-three times in the New Testament. Each use is linked to His redemptive role. His call to redemptive love permeates the use of His name and the context in which it is found. ***"Saving His people from their sins"*** is ingrained in Jesus' nature. He has no other activities or interests. Even in the worst of circumstances, He is focused on forgiveness (Luke 23:34). The worst of His circumstances were brought by the task related to His name.

In Peter's first statement (Acts 4:10), he proclaims the name of Jesus as the source of healing for the lame beggar. The beggar's wholeness does not result from a chant, magic words, or a secret password. He was healed in the nature and character of the Person named Jesus, whose nature has one effect on humanity, redemption. Jesus is light, and darkness cannot tolerate Him. Jesus is love, and hatred cannot stand His presence. Miracles are not His activities but are the natural result of His presence! When Jesus is present, sin cowers and is repressed while relationships bloom and expand.

The significance of the name is highlighted repeatedly in the Book of Revelation. Jesus spoke of it about us. To the church of Pergamos, Jesus said, *"He who has an ear, let him hear what the Spirit says to the churches. To him who overcomes I will give some of the hidden manna to eat. And I will give him a white stone, and on the stone a new name written which no one knows except him who receives it"* (Revelation 2:17). This thought is difficult to comprehend. Jesus wants a relationship with us that will change our nature. This change demands a new name to identify who we are and will focus His destiny for our lives.

To the church in Sardis, Jesus said, *"I know your works, that you have a name that you are alive, but you are dead"* (Revelation 3:1). Their name proclaimed their false character. Their name told of their destiny but their works were not completed before God (Revelation 3:2). If our name does not match our character or the calling on our lives, it will be blotted from the Book of Life, and Jesus will not confess it before the Father (Revelation 3:5). None of this is true about Jesus. His name is His character and His calling.

Name - Connection
Whom He Knows

This idea thunders to a natural conclusion in our passage. The name of Jesus is connected to His character. If we know His name, we know His nature. For any person to embrace the name of Jesus without embracing His nature is impossible. The name of Jesus is connected to His calling. If we know the name of Jesus, we know His nature, and we are embraced by His calling. We cannot know Jesus without being rescued from sin. The core of Jesus' calling is the heart of His nature, His name.

Because there is such a close connection between the name of Jesus and His Person, if you know Jesus' name, you know His Person. Luke makes this explicit in our passage. The Sanhedrin wanted to know who was responsible for the miracle in the lame beggar, who stood before them. Both the physical and spiritual change in the beggar's life emanated from the name of Jesus. The miracle did not come because the beggar chanted Jesus' name but because he embraced the Person of Jesus, causing Jesus' nature to envelop this man. The purpose and focus of this nature brought the healed beggar life, health, emotional stability, and wholeness. This is the only result possible in knowing Jesus' name because to know His name you must know His Person.

What if the healed beggar, filled with the character and nature of Jesus (His name), continued to beg at the Gate Beautiful? What if he never entered the temple in celebration and praise? Suppose he chose to live in the desperation and hopelessness of being crippled. That choice cannot be! He could not take the name of Jesus without embracing the Person of Jesus, bringing the manifestation of Jesus' character into his life.

That is why Peter made this bold statement, **"Let it be known to you all, and to all the people of Israel, that by the name of Jesus Christ of Nazareth, whom you crucified, whom God raised from the dead, by Him this man stands here before you whole"** (Acts 4:10). The nature and character of Jesus filled this lame beggar, resulting in his wholeness. What else would you expect? When I am in His character and nature, I am complete. This completion is the location of victory in my life.

This name **"is the stone which was rejected by you builders, which has become the chief cornerstone"** (Acts 4:11). Jesus' character and nature holds the building together. Take His name away and you destroy the building. No structure in life can stand outside His presence. Building in any other name is a house of cards like the parable of the building of the wise man and the foolish man (Matthew 7:24-27). His name (character and nature) is a rock foundation, and there is no stability outside of Jesus.

It can be said another way, ***"Nor is there salvation in any other, for there is no other name under heaven given among men by which we must be saved"*** (Acts 4:12). You cannot duplicate or substitute this Person! His character, His nature, is salvation. I must be found in this Person, He must be found in me, or all is lost. Peter used words such as ***"under heaven"*** and ***"among men."*** Salvation, the wholeness shown in the lame beggar, is isolated to being enveloped by this Person. Jesus is our only message! Jesus is our only hope!

Acts 4:10-12

BY

"Let it be known to you all, and to all the people of Israel, that by the name of Jesus Christ of Nazareth, whom you crucified, whom God raised from the dead, by Him this man stands here before you. This is the stone, which was rejected by you builders, which has become the chief cornerstone. Nor is there salvation in any other, for there is no other name under heaven given among men by which we must be saved" (Acts 4:10-12).

Translation from one language to another is difficult. It involves interpretation, and you cannot translate word for word. There are standards by which all translations are governed. Even when translators recognize these standards, they cannot always express them in the translations. For instance, a Greek word may be used in different situations with various nuances; therefore, it needs several English words with the context determining the selection of each word. But the root meaning of the Greek word must be present despite different uses of the word.

The Greek word "homologeo" is used in the New Testament for confessing one's sins (1 John 1:9). "Homologeo" is also used for praising God and giving Him thanks (Hebrews 13:15), and for acknowledgement or affirmation (Acts 23:9). This use of "homologeo" may be correct in the context of each translation, but the basic meaning must be maintained and understood. The word means "to say the same thing," coming from two root words, "homos" meaning "the same" and "lego" meaning "to speak." In confessing my sins, I agree with God about His opinion of my guilt. In praising Him, I agree with His worthiness of praise. In each case, the application is different but the meaning of the word is maintained.

The Greek word "eido" is another example. "Eido" is one of the four Greek words translated "know;" also translated "behold," "look," "perceive," "see," "know," and "understand." Before Jesus died He made an appointment to meet the disciples in Galilee after His resurrection (Matthew 26:32, 28:10). *"When they saw* (eido) *Him, they worshiped Him; but some doubted"* (Matthew 28:17). Because there is no doubt the disciples saw the resurrected Jesus with their physical eyes, the translators used "saw." However, the primary meaning of "to perceive" or "understand" must not be lost; therefore, seeing the resurrected Jesus was much more than a physical sighting.

This translation problem happens in our passage with the Greek word "en," translated *"by."* Peter said, *"Let it be known to you all, and to all the people of Israel, that by* (en) *the name of Jesus Christ of Nazareth, whom you crucified, whom God raised from the dead, by* (en) *Him this man stands here before you whole"* (Acts 4:10). He continues, *"Nor is there salvation in* (en) *any other, for there is no other name under heaven given among men by* (en) *which we must be saved"* (Acts 4:12). Peter uses the Greek word "en" four times in these two statements. The nuance of each use is instrumentality; thus it is translated *"by"* in three instances. In other words, Jesus is the instrument through which the lame beggar was made whole and by which we are saved. No Christian would argue with this translation.

But this translation does not indicate or include the primary meaning of the Greek word "en." "En" is a primary preposition denoting; a fixed position in a place, time, or state; focuses on a relation of rest; and is contrasted with two other words for moving or changing location. These contrasting words are "from" (apo or ek) and "into" (eis). Our Greek word "en" by implication in specific contexts may indicate instrumentality, but the primary meaning should not be lost. In our passage, Jesus is the instrument for wholeness in the lame beggar's life, and He is our only means of salvation. But the method or function by which He achieves this is the primary meaning of the word. Wholeness and salvation are in His person. When I am in Jesus I experience "these things" because "these things" are who Jesus is! We find wholeness or salvation in the Person of Jesus Christ, the fixed position. Wholeness and salvation do not exist outside Jesus.

Our passage holds a depth of truth, which we must look at carefully.

The Residence of Salvation

We begin with a restating of the principle of translation. A Greek word may be used in different situations with various nuances, but it must always be understood in light of its primary meaning. Peter made three statements at the heart of his communication. He declared that the miracle of the lame beggar happened *"by the name of Jesus Christ of Nazareth,"* and it is *"by Him."* Regarding the rest of mankind, no one else *"under heaven given among men by which we must be saved"* exists.

Peter plainly said that Jesus was the instrument of salvation. We should have no difficulty comprehending that Jesus is the tool, implement, means, method, agency, cause, channel, medium, or vehicle for salvation. He is the person (object or device) who produces salvation. A musical instrument is the object or device producing musical sounds; Jesus is salvation's instrument for producing the song of salvation. We can derive this understanding from Peter's declaration.

But this does not give Peter's intent. The primary meaning

of the Greek word "en," translated *"by,"* denotes a fixed position in place, time, or state. In other words, the fixed state or place of salvation is in Jesus. He does not deliver salvation to our door, as we would get pizza. While we enjoy our salvation, Jesus delivers salvation to others. That means salvation comes "through Him" but is not "in Him." Peter boldly declared that salvation is in Jesus alone!

There may be no English word that captures both ideas, salvation coming "through Him" and "in Him." Translating the verse completely means both ideas of method and state of existence must be given. The Amplified New Testament says it best,

"Let it be known and understood by all of you, and by the whole house of Israel, that in the name and through the power and authority of Jesus Christ of Nazareth, Whom you crucified, [but] Whom God raised from the dead, in Him and by means of Him this man is standing here before you well and sound in body" (Acts 4:10).

Perhaps we need to consider the use of the word *"inside."* Peter said, **"That by** (inside) **the name of Jesus Christ of Nazareth, whom you crucified, whom God raised from the dead, by** (inside) **Him this man stands here before you whole"** (Acts 4:10). The wholeness of the lame beggar does not come from a deed Jesus did. Instead, Jesus took the lame beggar within Himself, and the lame beggar found his wholeness as he dwelt in the Person of Jesus. He is inside Jesus!

Paul had much to say about this subject. **"Blessed be the God and Father of our Lord Jesus Christ, who has blessed us with every spiritual blessing in the heavenly places in Christ, just as He chose us in Him before the foundation of the world, that we should be holy and without blame before Him in love, having predestined us to adoption as sons by Jesus Christ to Himself, according to the good pleasure of His will, to the praise of the glory of His grace, by which He made us accepted in the**

Beloved" (Ephesians 1:3-6). He uses the word "en" seven times, but this is only the beginning. I encourage you to read the Book of Ephesians and underline every "in" and "with," because "en" is sometimes translated "with."

I am not sure we can understand what the depth of being "in Jesus" means. Jesus surrounds me, is the boundary in which I live and have my being, and is the atmosphere of my existence. His aroma is all I breathe, and nothing can touch me that does not come through Him. All is well! No sin can live in Jesus; therefore, I am assured of victory over sin in His presence. All that is true about Jesus touches and affects my life. His peace is my peace; He is all that allures me; He is the thrill of my life! I rest in Him, not perform for Him. He is my dwelling place for now and eternity. I am "in Christ!"

Concentrating on and being in Jesus, I have a singular purpose and focus for life. I am in Him, and nothing can separate us. *"For I am persuaded that neither death nor life, nor angels nor principalities nor powers, nor things present nor things to come, nor height nor depth, nor any other created thing, shall be able to separate us from the love of God which is in* (en) *Christ Jesus our Lord"* (Romans 8:38-39). Jesus sources my confidence for the adversities of life. Let us run to His arms and stay there!

The Resource of Salvation

Salvation, in the full use of the word, is inside Jesus. He is my dwelling place. Because Jesus is salvation, how does this affect my life? If He does not give me salvation because He is salvation, how does this work practically? Referring to the healed beggar, Peter said, *"This man stands here before you whole"* (Acts 4:10). The Greek word "paristemi," translated *"stands here,"* shares the same problem as "en." "Paristemi" is used forty-one times in the New Testament, has a variety of meanings, each determined by its context. In our passage Peter says the healed beggar is present in the courtroom, and everyone can see he is a healed man. But the primary meaning of this Greek word comes from a combination of two Greek words, "para" meaning "near or beside," and "histemi" meaning "standing or rising."

We could interpret "paristemi" to mean that the healed beggar is standing in the presence of the Sanhedrin. However, the next Greek word "enopion," translated *"before,"* has the idea of "in the face of." ***Stands here*** is connected to ***"by Him."*** This whole man, once a lame beggar, now stands in Jesus in the presence of the Sanhedrin. He was not given wholeness to use as he desired, but he has been strengthened and completed because of the presence of Jesus. "In Jesus" resource flows in the beggar. He derives continuous wholeness from Jesus as he is "in Jesus."

The presence of Jesus gave the lame beggar his wholeness. What was present in Jesus was now present in the beggar. The deriving wholeness principle applies to every area of Christian living. We can never claim holiness and righteousness as ours, but we derive these qualities from the presence of Christ in us. All our righteousness is as filthy rags (Isaiah 64:6). Moses was commanded to remove his shoes because the ground around the burning bush was holy. How can mountainous ground be sacred and holy? The day before was not holy, tomorrow would not be holy, but today is holy. The presence of the Lord was on it; the ground derived holiness from God's presence.

All that was present in Jesus was now flowing in and through the healed beggar. He was "inside Jesus." He lacked physical and spiritual resource, making him an example. He had not reformed his life. If he were removed from being "in Jesus" he would be at the Gate Beautiful begging again. The full potential of life was staggering. In the Ephesians passage, Paul gives a list of the spiritual blessings we experience by being "in Jesus" (Ephesians 1). We are holy and without blame; we are adopted as sons and accepted. We experience redemption and forgiveness of sins, discovering the mysteries of His will. The list continues with glowing detail!

We can never attain this by performance or discipline. We must cease any thought of our rights or self-expression. Jesus is enough; Jesus is all we need. Christianity is not what we do for Him; Christianity is always what He does through us! I am not a contributor or a receiver. He gives me life! My responsibility is the continuous demonstration of the wholeness from Jesus so generously and consistently flowing in my life. The only deterrent is for self to contribute instead of receive. The moment we exhibit pride of ownership we hinder the resource of His presence. I derive from Him by clinging to all He gives. He is my sole resource, giving me all He is! What a privilege!

The Resurrection of Salvation

Everything we have just discussed Peter expressed. He attached all the results of being "in Jesus" to the resurrection. He was specific in describing the One in whom the healed beggar experienced new life. *"Jesus Christ of Nazareth, whom you crucified, whom God raised from the dead."* The miracle received by the lame beggar was not what instigated the arrest of the apostles because they had been used in many miracles.

"The Sadducees came upon them, being greatly disturbed that they taught the people and preached in Jesus the resurrection from the dead" (Acts 4:1-2). The arrest of the apostles was instigated because *"they preached in Jesus the resurrection from the dead."*

We are again faced with the problem of translating into English. The Greek word usually translated *"in"* is translated *"by"* in this passage; other translations use "through." Again we have the idea of instrument, but we cannot lose sight of the word's primary meaning. The resurrection came through Jesus;

however, it was not an event He experienced but the state of His existence. We find salvation "in Him" only, so the resurrection of life is "in Him" only. There is no resurrection or life unless we are inside Jesus.

The Sanhedrin was not against life or salvation. They were against Jesus. They could discuss salvation from a variety of viewpoints and depart as friends, but Jesus being salvation was their difficulty. Resurrection of life was a philosophy they debated, but when the resurrection was placed inside Jesus, their tempers ignited, they expressed anger, and they crucified Jesus. The resurrected life is only inside Jesus, and Jesus was their problem. The Trinity God placed Jesus in this state, and everyone who dwells in resurrected life dwells in Him.

Peter made this statement about life and salvation, **"nor is there salvation in** (en) **any other"** (Acts 4:10). Again, "en" is the idea of instrument and the primary meaning of a "fixed state." Peter went on to say, **"for there is no other name under heaven given among men by** (en) **which we must be saved"** (Acts 4:12). Jesus is the instrument of all salvation, but the means of the instrument is a state in which we dwell. It is JESUS!

This truth is simple. I do not have to understand or intellectually master any level of theology. I do not have to perform masterful feats to achieve. I need to embrace Jesus. Why is this so difficult for us? Let us give our lives to Jesus!

Acts 4:12

SALVATION

"Nor is there salvation in any other, for there is no other name under heaven given among men by which we must be saved" (Acts 4:12).

Salvation is the story from the beginning of the Old Testament to the end of the New Testament! This story is not about judgment, condemnation, or God seeking revenge for the betrayal of sin. We all can quote, **"For God so loved the world that He gave His only begotten Son, that whoever believes in Him should not perish but have everlasting life"** (John 3:16). The verse that follows is also significant, giving content to the love and motive for God sending Jesus. **"For God did not send his Son into the world to condemn the world, but that the world through Him might be saved"** (John 3:17). The Greek word "gar," translated *"for,"* expresses the reason for the preceding verse. If the Scriptures, from the Messianic promise (Genesis 3:15) to the final call (Revelation 22:17), are about Jesus, then the Scriptures are about salvation.

In previous studies we have examined the idea of salvation in the context of the New Testament. In our passage, both the noun and verb forms are used. The Greek verb form (sozo) occurs fifty-four times in the Gospels. Fourteen times it relates to deliverance from disease or demon possession (Matthew 9:21-22; Mark 3:4; 5:23, 28, 34; 6:56; 10:52; Luke 6:9; 8:36, 48, 50;

17:19; 18:42; John 11:12). Twenty times the inference is to the rescue of physical life from impending peril or instant death (Matthew 8:25; 14:30; 16:25; 27:40, 42, 49; Mark 8:35; 15:30-31; Luke 9:24, 56; 23:35, 37, 39; John 12:27). The remaining twenty times, the reference is to spiritual salvation (Matthew 1:21; 10:22; 19:25; 24:13, 22; Mark 8:35; 10:26; 13:13, 20; 16:16; Luke 7:50; 8:12; 9:24; 13:23; 18:26; 19:10; John 3:17; 10:9; 12:47).

The Greek noun form (soteria) is well represented in the New Testament, but we must understand the primary meaning of the word from its use in the Old Testament. "Salvation" represents several Hebrew words, referring to "help, deliverance, or salvation" by God's deliverance through people or circumstances. This word signifies God's activity in the larger sense but does not overlook His individual deeds. In other words, when Jesus heals a person, that healing is not limited to the correction of physical disability. The healing always is intended for long-term liberation from evil powers and the final Day of Judgment. Peter had this in mind in our passage. He spoke of salvation happening in the healed beggar who stands before the court; however, we must understand the broader view of salvation for the healed beggar and the Sanhedrin. Salvation is a present state that will explode to an eternal state, so powerfully linked that they cannot be separated. We can correctly say that we dwell in the eternal state of salvation when we are in the present state of salvation because what we believe and anticipate in the eternal realm, we experience in the present. John consistently said that "we have" eternal life (John 3:16; 11:25, 26; 17:3). Salvation is present tense!

Sin is the hindrance to salvation. We must not rest in the narrow definition of sin, which is more than an incorrect act that can be forgiven. A halfhearted, "I am sorry," cannot eliminate the twisted nature of the heart focused on self, revealing this nature. Salvation's focus is to eliminate the nature and its demonstrations. Before Jesus was born, an angel of the Lord appeared to Joseph and proclaimed, *"And you shall call His name Jesus, for He will save His people from their sins"* (Matthew 1:21). This was the mission statement for what the Trinity God would achieve in Christ.

Any attempt of man to adjust this salvation is heresy of the biblical message. To excuse sin in any form degrades the redemption in Jesus. We cannot embrace a salvation that tolerates sin. Salvation's strength is the strength of Jesus to fulfill the will of the Trinity God. God's focus is the elimination of sin, delivering us from all that separates us from Him and restoring us to wholeness. Luke uses every Greek word he can find to describe the activity of salvation in the healing of the lame beggar. He presents the healed beggar in *"perfect soundness in the presence of you all"* (Acts 3:16). The Holy Spirit authored the Scriptures but each writer expressed the Scriptures through his personality. Luke used his profession as a doctor to detail his special insight and interest, declaring to the world the wholeness of the healed beggar. Salvation is complete in Jesus!

Salvation is a Person
"Nor is there salvation in any other"

Salvation is in the person of Jesus. Salvation is not something Jesus does for or to you, but He is salvation in you. Salvation is in the boundaries of His person. The state of salvation is you dwelling in His person. Outside the Person of Jesus there is no salvation, and we cannot experience any aspect of salvation apart from Jesus.

In approaching this concept, I know my understanding of salvation comes from my experience with Jesus. How do we explain that "salvation is a Person" to someone who has never intimately known Jesus? That explanation would be like explaining the taste of a decadent dessert to someone who has

Salvation | **Acts 4:12**

never tasted that dessert. They can use only your explanation and their previous taste sensations to decide what are the flavors and textures of this dessert, missing what it really tastes like.

Salvation is a "relationship" with the Person of Jesus. You cannot attain it through your performance, achievements, or merits. Salvation is not in ceremonies, spiritual disciplines, or rituals, and you can never find it in organizational structure, membership, or position in the church. Salvation is only in relationship with Jesus. You may have experienced "the new birth" in the past but not know Jesus in the present. You may have knelt at the altar in repentance, but if you do not have intimacy with Jesus, you do not have salvation. Salvation is yours only when you have relationship with Jesus.

A person who does not have relationship with Jesus may misinterpret salvation. Our lives are filled with many relationships on various levels. We can have a friend who lives hundreds of miles from us, but we continue that relationship without constant contact. Can this be true of Jesus and salvation? I may have had a conversion experience as a child but have strayed from my relationship with Jesus. I believe in Him but my relationship with Him is long distance. Does that mean I have salvation?

Peter clarifies this in his message to the Sanhedrin, declaring the relationship of salvation causes "relocation." In other words, we cannot have a long-distance relationship with Jesus. Every saved person is "in" Jesus Christ, which we discovered in our previous study. The Greek word "en," translated ***"by"*** three times and translated ***"in"*** once, holds the key to "in Jesus," expressing the instrumentality of salvation. Jesus is the instrument through which I receive salvation, but the primary meaning of the word must be maintained, "inside." When I am "in" Jesus, He is the instrument of my salvation, and a long distance relationship is impossible. Salvation is mine only when I am "in" Him!

The image of the prophecy quoted by Peter verifies this truth (Acts 4:11). The Trinity God constructs a building of salvation. The Chief Cornerstone is Jesus, and He holds the building together, containing the building in Him. When I dwell in the building of His Person, I dwell in salvation. He became man, allowing mankind to be the material of the building, and redemption comes through humanity as well as God, bringing us full circle! Salvation is God and man in intimacy, becoming the "resource" of salvation. When Jesus dwells in me, He is the source of salvation; I derive salvation from His nature. Darkness cannot exist in light, and hate cannot exist in love. When I am in Jesus and He is in me, His nature becomes my nature. That oneness is salvation! Salvation is a Person, Jesus!

Salvation is a Provision
"for there is no other name under heaven given (didomi) among men"

Jesus is the Trinity God's gift to us. Salvation is a gift of God to us! The Scriptures that propose this truth are too numerous to print in this limited space. *"For the wages of sin is death, but the gift of God is eternal life in Christ Jesus our Lord"* (Romans 6:23). *"For God so loved the world that He gave* (didomi) *His only begotten Son, that whoever believes in Him should not perish but have everlasting life"* (John 3:16).

The Greek word "didomi," translated "give" or "gift," is the most common expression for the procedure whereby a subject transfers something to someone or something making it available to the recipient. Jesus is the gift (John 3:16). Peter echoes (Acts 4:12) "salvation" is a gift from God to all mankind, a high priority in the Scriptures. *"For by grace you have been saved through faith, and that not of yourselves; it is the gift of God, not of works, lest anyone should boast"* (Ephesians 2:8-9). From God's first thought of redemption to the final words of Jesus, *"It is finished"* (John 19:30), God took the initiative for salvation. The Scriptures never allow any thought of additional or complementary works added to Jesus, our salvation. Jesus is the gift!

I am saved only in Jesus, because He is salvation and He is given to me. I must live within the boundaries of my relationship with His presence, excluding everything that is not of His nature. Speaking in loving tones to his children, the beloved apostle John said, ***"This is the message which we have heard from Him and declare to you, that God is light and in Him is no darkness at all. If we say that we have fellowship with Him, and walk in darkness, we lie and do not practice the truth"*** (1 John 1:5-6). To focus on darkness, define it, and abstain from it does not constitute salvation. Darkness cannot abide in light; therefore, when I live in Jesus, the Light, darkness is gone. Salvation is not my performance, keeping the rules, or my spiritual discipline. Salvation is relationship with Jesus and having His nature. He gives me victory, purity, love, and wisdom, and as I dwell in the resourcing of His nature, His nature becomes mine with all spiritual blessings (Ephesians 1:3-14).

Salvation is the impact of our passage (Acts 4:10-12). Peter boldly declared the crucifixion of Jesus and reminded the Sanhedrin of their guilt. But the Trinity God gifted us with the resurrection of Jesus (Acts 4:10). The builders rejected Jesus, the chief cornerstone of the building, but the Trinity God restored Jesus (Acts 4:11). Men claiming salvation have many names, but there is only one ***"name under heaven given among men by which we must be saved"*** (Acts 4:12). The Trinity God poured all His resource into Jesus, the one avenue of salvation. There is no backup plan and no provision for another means to salvation because Jesus is adequate. God has given a single gift to your heart. There is no greater gift, no other gift is needed, and additional resources cannot enrich this gift. Jesus is enough! He is the gift of salvation!

Part 2: The Analytical Response

Salvation is a Passion
"by which we must (dei) be saved"

Luke uses one important word in our last verse (Acts 4:12), which the casual reader might ignore. When you understand the background of this word, the passage explodes. The Greek word is "dei," translated *"must."* "Dei" suggests need, is necessary, has need of, or is inevitable in the nature of things. It designates an unconditional necessity in the New Testament. The sentences containing this verb are absolute, unquestioned, and have a deterministic character. They are understood as divine decrees.

In other words, salvation is only in Jesus! Because the Trinity God decreed it to be so, it is so! This fact cannot be debated, argued, or supplemented. Salvation in Jesus is the passion and inevitable expression of the Trinity's heart. In discussing the mercies of God fundamental to salvation, Paul asks, *"For who has known the mind of the Lord? Or who has become His counselor? Or what has first given to Him and it shall be repaid to him?"* (Romans 11:34-35). The question is ridiculous! No one advised God or obligated Him to provide salvation. The mercies of God that reach our lives in salvation come from the passionate heart of God who could do nothing else.

Jesus is the visible image of the invisible God (Colossians 1:15). *"No one has seen God at any time. The only begotten Son, who is in the bosom of the Father, He has declared Him"* (John 1:18). Driven by His heart's passion, the Trinity God reached inside Himself, pulled out His heart and placed it on our streets. His name is Jesus! He is the passion of God's heart, salvation! God never hopes we do not respond so He can judge us. He is not angry with us, nor is He waiting to catch us doing something wrong. The biblical view says God focuses His resource on us because He is passionate about redemption.

Peter's message to the Sanhedrin contains no condemnation.

The lack of condemnation is remarkable because he is bold about their rejection of Jesus. He gives no warning of judgment to come but gives a clear call to listen to God's heart. The message of the Gospel is that Jesus is the heart of salvation. The divine *"must"* continually calls us to Him. God can never leave us alone. His amazing grace is without fear. If this grace does not win us, what will? Let His love bring you to a new level of relationship!

Acts 4:12

EXCLUSIVE

"Nor is there salvation in any other, for there is no other name under heaven given among men by which we must be saved" (Acts 4:12).

Peter had a single idea he wanted to tell the Sanhedrin. He carried a consistent theme in the three verses with numerous supporting themes, but we must not lose sight of his central idea. This theme is the exclusiveness of Jesus. Salvation is only in Jesus! Our salvation is the exclusive state of dwelling in Him!

You can discard the grammar details, the uniqueness of the Greek words, and the modifying phrases, but you must understand the theme of these three verses (Acts 4:10-12). Everyone reading these verses, from the experienced Greek student to the casual Bible reader, will be equally convinced. Though you may not agree with the proposal of exclusiveness, you must agree it is Peter's proposal. He does not hide it, and he does not reserve it for those who diligently search the passage. Everyone who touches these verses discovers the truth of exclusiveness.

Christianity is not for those who want diversity, many choices, and unlimited toleration. If you prefer philosophy, doctrine, and mental exercise, you will not embrace salvation because it is only in the person of Jesus. If your pride demands salvation achieved by brilliant performance and strict discipline, you will miss it because it is only in intimate relationship with Jesus. If you want salvation in the future, insurance against pending doom, and assurance for a rainy day, you will not want the indwelt Jesus in this present moment. If you are looking for an experience rather than a relationship, you will not find this salvation. If relief from emotional guilt is your focus, then you will not be pleased with Jesus' claim on your life.

Peter proposed Jesus as the exclusive state of salvation. We are saved only as we dwell in Jesus, and He in us. Constrains of love bind us to Him in relationship. Pleasing Him becomes our passion, not obligation to keep the rules. We set aside serving Him for the delight of participation in His desires. Love prevails, duty is tossed aside, and we become addicted to discovering Jesus. We burn as a flaming torch in His presence. He is salvation!

Salvation is the intent of our passage. The details of this passage provide a foundation for this unshakable truth, and Peter said it so well that it does not need to be proven. Some will not accept this truth or get distracted from it, but everyone must agree that salvation is the presented idea. As we investigate the details of our passage, we will see the strength of this truth. Jesus is salvation, and it is only in Him!

Exclusively Exclusive

We will divide our passage into two independent clauses for clarity. Peter's first statement is, ***"Nor is there salvation in any other"*** (Acts 4:12). Peter focused on Jesus, supporting the exclusive nature of his statement. "Nor" is a translation of two Greek words. The first is the conjunction "kai," most often translated "and," connecting our clause to the previous two statements, and the second is the word "ouk," a negative (not). In the Greek "me" is also translated "not," but the difference between the two words is important. "Me" is a dependent negative, expressing the opinion of the person speaking but may not be truth for everyone. "Ouk" is an independent negative, expressing reality aside from the opinion or perspective of the person speaking. In our passage, Peter expressed the reality of the situation and not his opinion.

In the Greek Peter's emphasis begins the sentence. Peter expressed salvation in Jesus in the negative and highlighted the inadequacy of other means of salvation. Salvation aside from Jesus only is an absolute NOT, eliminating any possibility of it being "mostly," ninety-nine percent," or "most likely." Peter's statement drew a line saying salvation is in Jesus, and it cannot be found elsewhere.

Peter's emphasis of salvation being only in Jesus only would be adequate for most people but not Peter. Not satisfied, he includes another negative in this clause. This negative is the Greek word "oudeis," translated *"any,"* primarily meaning "not even one." "Oudeis" comes from two Greek words, "ouk" a negative (not), and "heis" the primary number one. Peter boldly declared that salvation is in Jesus and is never found in "not even one."

The New Testament writers use "oudeis" repeatedly to boldly proclaim man's exclusive experience of salvation. Paul wrote, *"Therefore I make known to you that no one* (oudeis) *speaking by the Spirit of God calls Jesus accursed, and no one* (oudeis) *can say that Jesus is Lord except by the Holy Spirit"* (1 Corinthians 12:3). The writer of Hebrews said it this way, *"Holiness, without which no one* (oudeis) *will see the Lord"* (Hebrews 12:14).

"Oudeis" designates exclusivity of a matter or group of people. Jesus was engaged in a debate with Jewish leaders and told them the only one true is the one who seeks the Father. He said, *"Did not Moses give you the law, yet none* (oudeis) *of you keeps the law?"* (John 7:19). Not one Jewish leader could hold claim to achieving the law of God. Jesus was in the upper room with His disciples preparing them for His departure when He told them, *"But now I go away to Him who sent Me, and none* (oudeis) *of you asks Me, 'Where are you going?'"* (John 16:5). Not even one disciple could focus on Jesus and His destination because they were focusing on themselves and their sorrow filled hearts (John 16:6).

Peter used these negatives, "ouk" and "oudeis" in our passage. Each word presents the case, but that was not enough for Peter in his address to the Sanhedrin about Jesus. Instead, he combined both words in a short, bold, and unmistakable statement, *"Nor* (ouk) *is there salvation in any* (oudeis) *other"* (Acts 4:12). These two negatives used together make an emphatic negation that cannot be questioned. Peter left no room for adjustment and allows no one to leave wondering about salvation being in Jesus. Peter's use of these two negatives identifies the "exclusively exclusive" nature of salvation in Jesus!

Why does this not drive us to a single focus? Jesus is our only hope! All our efforts and attempts are futile, and trying to attain salvation in any other way is a waste of our lives. Let us concentrate all our time, energy, and intent on running to Jesus. We have only one message because we have only one Savior. The light of Jesus gives us the ability to see clearly and recognize the enemy's deception. The bright glitter of self-salvation will pale in the brilliance of the Light! Trust in Jesus!

Exceptionally Exclusive

Peter chose to focus further on this emphatic negative, no salvation in any "other." "Other" is a translation of the Greek word "allos," a specific expression referring to others of the same kind. "Allos" is contrasted with the Greek word "heteros," which is qualitative but different in kind. For instance, if I to speak about picking an apple, I might say that I chose "another" apple.

Part 2: The Analytical Response

I did not pick an orange or a different kind of fruit but picked another apple of the same kind. "Allos is the word in our passage.

Jesus spent much time in the upper room with His disciples during His last days on Earth, and He spoke about the New Covenant, the fullness of the Spirit (John 14, 15, and 16). He told them, *"And I will pray the Father, and He will give you another* (allos) *Helper, that He may abide with you forever"* (John 14:16). The Holy Spirit is the Spirit of Jesus not another kind of Jesus. The Spirit of Jesus thinks as Jesus, has the same style of Jesus, and approaches me the same as Jesus. He wanted the disciples to know that the Spirit would give them the same kind of help that He gave them because the Spirit and Jesus are the same. The Spirit sourced Jesus.

In our passage Peter presented the uniqueness of salvation in Jesus, saying that there is no salvation "in any other." Jesus is the only kind of salvation. Any other proposal of salvation would be of a different kind, not sourced by Jesus. Jesus who is salvation is unique making salvation unique. Jesus stands alone, can be compared to no other, and is in a category by Himself.

Where is a god who compares to our God? The Trinity God sourced redemption when one member leaped from His throne of power and authority to become a helpless baby in Mary's womb. Where is His equal? Who matched His sacrifice of emptying Himself of all that He had as God to become a helpless man? He was not wealthy, and He did not replace Caesar in his rule. He was born in a stable, not a palace, with shepherds witnessing His birth. He lived on Earth as a peasant without political power or recognition. He died as a criminal on a cross. Where is there another of this kind?

If by chance someone produced a kind of salvation, it would never be on the level of Jesus' salvation, conquering death, defeating sin, and extending His hand to us. Where is there another savior of this kind? Jesus is unique! Biblical accounts ring with this truth. Paul said, *"He promised before through His prophets in the Holy Scriptures, concerning His Son Jesus Christ the Lord, who was born of the seed of David according to the flesh, and declared to be the Son of God with power according to the Spirit of holiness, by the resurrection from the dead"* (Romans 1:2-4). Jesus is the long-range plan that the Trinity God proclaimed through the prophets of the Old Testament. The Trinity God produced Jesus in His humanity, fulfilled the promise of His lineage through King David, and declared His power of salvation when they raised Him from the dead. Where is there a savior of this equal?

The Trinity God uniquely designed Jesus for salvation. No one else meets the qualifications to be the Savior, the only chance we have. Hallelujah, what a Savior! Outside Jesus there is no one else. Peter persisted to make Jesus and His uniqueness known to the Sanhedrin. They crucified Jesus, but God raised Him from the dead. The lame beggar stood before the Sanhedrin whole because of Jesus' power. Jesus is the Trinity God's answer to the strength and stability of the house of redemption. They rejected Jesus but God chose Him to be the chief cornerstone (Acts 4:11). Salvation is not in any other because there is no one else in His category; He is unique (Acts 4:12).

Experientially Exclusive

Peter uses a second independent clause in the original text with the Greek word "oude," translated *"no,"* a combination of two Greek words, "ouk" and "de." "Ouk" is the independent negative, and "de" is the contrasting conjunction "but." He takes the strength of the negative in the first statement and brings it into the second statement. In the first statement, he applies it to something of the same kind (allos). Jesus is in a category all His own, and no one else claims to be a savior of His kind. In all other categories, the negative must apply to every savior. *"For*

there is no (oude) ***other*** (heteros) ***name under heaven given among men by which we must be saved"*** (Acts 4:10).

"Heteros" is a parallel term to the Greek word "allos," translated ***"other"*** in the first clause. "Allos" is another of the same kind, and "heteros" is another of a different kind. Although there is no one else of the same kind as Jesus, there is equally no salvation in any other kind, and Peter covered all possibilities from which salvation might emerge. Because there is none like Jesus, there is no salvation in anyone like Him, He is the only Source of salvation.

Peter continued with ***"under heaven."*** In the Greek language, this refers to subjection or influence, which in human terms is "everything" or all human experience. There is no salvation anywhere else. Philosophies of men cannot produce salvation, and life's major issues are never solved by academic knowledge and scientific pursuit. Salvation comes through only Jesus, not talent, abilities, materialism, or comfort. Discipline and self-denial contribute to our pride, produce emptiness, and cater to our bitterness. There is no salvation in any of our striving. Where can we go ***"under heaven"*** in human experience to find salvation? Jesus is the only one!

Peter reveals his intent in the last phrase of our final verse, ***"by which we must be saved"*** (Acts 4:12). The Greek word "sozo," translated "be saved," is an infinitive. ***"To be saved"*** is a good translation. The Greek word "en," translated ***"in,"*** introduces this prepositional phrase, carrying the meaning of instrument but keeping the primary meaning of being "inside" Jesus. The Greek word "hos," translated ***"which,"*** refers to ***"name."*** This is a direct reference to Jesus! The Greek word "dei," translated ***"must,"*** is a strong word, speaking to absolute necessity determined by the hand of God.

Therefore, a person has to be "in His name" to be saved! Because there is no other name, we must be "in Jesus" to be saved. Jesus is the exclusive source and state of salvation, and we must of necessity be "in Him" to receive salvation, an experiential exclusiveness. We only experience salvation when we are "in Him." As a fish cannot survive outside of water, so we cannot survive outside the Person of Jesus. To be "in Him" is parallel to "Him in," embracing, enveloping, and submerging our lives in His presence. We must be surrounded inside and out by oxygen to live, and to live in the state of salvation we must be "in Him" and "Him in."

PART THREE
ACTS 4:13-22

THE ABSOLUTE RATIFICATION

Acts 4:13-22

THEY SAW

Now when they saw the boldness of Peter and John, and perceived that they were uneducated and untrained men, they marveled. And they realized that they had been with Jesus. And seeing the man who had been healed standing with them, they could say nothing against it. But when they had commanded them to go aside out of the council, they conferred among themselves, saying, "What shall we do to these men? For, indeed, that a notable miracle has been done through them is evident to all who dwell in Jerusalem, and we cannot deny it. But so that it spreads no further among the people, let us severely threaten them, that from now on they speak to no man in this name." So they called them and commanded them not to speak at all nor teach in the name of Jesus. But Peter and John answered and said to them, "Whether it is right in the sight of God to listen to you more than to God, you judge. For we cannot but speak the things which we have seen and heard." So when they had further threatened them, they let them go, finding no way of punishing them, because of the people, since they all glorified God for what had been done. For the man was over forty years old on whom this miracle of healing had been performed (Acts 4:13-22).

"The Alliance" consisted of **"the priests, the captain of the temple, and the Sadducees"** (Acts 4:1). These were the influential members present in the temple. As we come to our passage, we enter the scene of the busiest time of the day for temple activity, ***"the hour of prayer, the ninth hour"*** (Acts 3:1), three in the afternoon. A crowd gathered to see the lame beggar whom God had healed through Peter, and they were witnesses to Peter's strong exhortation. This well-known beggar sat begging at the Gate Beautiful for most of his adult life (Acts 3:2), and he was more than forty years old (Acts 4:22). The Holy Spirit through Peter reached into this beggar's life and made him whole. He entered the temple for the first time, ***"walking, leaping, and praising God"*** (Acts 3:8), an event that attracted and astonished this crowd.

Peter's exhortation was Spirit-filled and focused on Jesus whom Peter acclaimed as the source of the beggar's miracle. In the crowd were people responsible for the crucifixion of Jesus whom God raised from the dead. These were the same people who denied the Messiah, Jesus, and preferred to release a murderer instead (Acts 3:14). These folks could not deny their participation in such a mockery as Peter re-counted Jesus' trial scene before Pilate. Not wanting this to continue, the temple "alliance" came to force a stop to this gathering and arrested Peter and John.

The members the Sanhedrin had dismissed for the day causing the apostles to spend the night in prison awaiting trial the following morning. This extra time allowed other influential people to join the Sanhedrin to hear the case (Acts 4:6). Their issue was clear and concise, ***"By what power or by what name have you done this?"*** (Acts 4:7). These court members knew the answer yet were amazed at the boldness of Peter (Acts 4:13). Peter answered without hesitation or compromise, announcing that the source of the beggar's miracle was Jesus. ***"Let it be known to you all, and to all the people of Israel, that by the name of Jesus Christ of Nazareth, whom you crucified, whom God raised from the dead, by Him this man stands here before you whole"*** (Acts 4:10). Peter did not cower under their pressure or authority; he proclaimed Jesus as the only possibility of salvation (Acts 4:12).

These powerful men of Israel found themselves in a dilemma, for indeed they had crucified Jesus. Their actions toward the Messiah were messy and unfortunate but necessary to maintain their traditions. They hoped it was all behind them and was forgotten by everyone lost in the busyness of their lives. But these apostles kept refueling the issue; the miracles only complicate it more. The leaders of Israel must stop this!

This is the context of our passage (Acts 4:13-22). The idea of this passage demonstrates prevenient grace. Another word for "grace" is "love." We cannot overstate the love of God because words can never adequately describe it. The depth of this love has never been fathomed because it is inexhaustible. Hurt can never shrink it, and its immensity opens it to immeasurable suffering. The quality of God's love is so pure that it never mixes with self-love or self-survival. His love is consistent and is an unending source. His nature is enormous and so dominated by His love that He maintains an exploding pressure of loving embrace that bombards everyone. He exerts His love on our lives, maintaining the same intensity and pressure, and it never varies! When I am bad, He loves me, and when I am good, He loves me. Whether good or bad, He loves me the same. I can experience His love because I am not the source of it; He is! Nothing I have done or ever will do will cause Him to love me; therefore, nothing I have ever done or will ever do will cause Him NOT to love me!

This love, in its "prevenient" state, amazes the hardest heart. "Prevenient" means "going before." God loves us before we can love Him in return. We do not cultivate the love of God. We do not seek and find or search and discover. He takes the initiative, which His love demands. He finds us in our sin and rebellion and conquers us with His love. We are incapable of seeking Him because we are bound by depravity, blinded by darkness, and corrupted in our thinking. We can know Him only when He reveals Himself to us, see Him only when He enlightens us, and experience His embrace only when He releases us!

Our passage tells us that the Sanhedrin is not the Jewish crowd that the apostles could manipulate. These Jewish leaders were the instigators. They plotted and planned the execution of Jesus. These leaders had to know because God had revealed Himself through the Scriptures, and they were the experts of the prophets' messages. Did these leaders not receive the announcement of Jesus' birth by angelic hosts, humble shepherds, and the wise men from the East? They were impacted and exposed to three years of Jesus' ministry. Yet they crucified Him. Is not that enough? I would have eliminated them from my list! Enough is enough! Yet the love of God pressured them repeatedly through the resurrection of Jesus. The Roman soldiers who guarded the tomb gave them a convincing witness that the body of Jesus was gone, but these leaders of Israel rejected rather than accepted this truth. You would think this would cause God to withdraw His love. I would have walked away and never returned. But the love of God can never do that!

God had something special just for this hardened group. Jesus passed this lame beggar at the Gate Beautiful repeatedly. But his changed life was reserved for continued pressure of God's love on these rebellious leaders. God selected **"uneducated and untrained men"** through which to express His love. The forty-year-old healed beggar was an irrefutable demonstration of God's love (Acts 4:14). The response of all Jerusalem gave validation to **"we cannot deny it"** (Acts 4:16). Peter's answer to their threat brought them face-to-face with the speaking God (Acts 4:19).

The pressure of God's love felt by these leaders of Israel is also present in our lives. God consistently backs us into a corner, probes our lives, and brings us to a place of decision. We cannot escape! His love confronts us consistently, at every turn and event. He removes from us the value of all previous commitments and traditions. His love is persistent. The cry of the Psalmist rings in our ears. ***"Where can I go from Your Spirit? Or where can I flee from Your presence? If I ascend into heaven, You are there; if I make my bed in hell, behold, You are there. If I take the wings of the morning, and dwell in the uttermost parts of the sea, even there Your hand shall lead me, and Your right hand shall hold me. If I say, 'Surely the darkness shall fall on me,' even the night shall be light about me; indeed, the darkness shall not hide from You, but the night shines as the day; the darkness and the light are both alike to You"*** (Psalms 139 7-12).

This passage describes the consistent pressure of His love on your life. He manipulates every circumstance to confront us. We cannot escape the love of God. We can reject it, but we cannot eliminate it. Our rejection must be continuous, or we will be consumed with Him because His love is continuous! The moment we become open He is there with His pressing love; He never leaves us! What God did in the lives of these leaders of Israel, He does in our lives. It is the same pressuring love.

Isolated

One of the strong aspects of God's love is stated in our passage. The leaders of Israel were resisting the person of Jesus. He confronted them daily. The prophets consistently reminded their forefathers of the coming Messiah. The four hundred years of silence between the Old and New Testaments brought them to submission to the Roman Empire. They were stripped of their dignity and freedom. Everything they had was in jeopardy, and they needed the Messiah! Three years of ministry through Jesus focused them on Him. Their lives were consumed with their plotting for His crucifixion. His resurrection continued

Part Three: The Absolute Ratification

the avalanche of His person in their lives. Now Peter and John were waving His revelation in their faces again. Jesus would not go away!

The issue in our passage is not religious structure. The disciples were not being judged for dinner meetings, house churches, or miracles. Helping the poor and needy in Jerusalem was not a discussion at their trial. The issue was isolated to, ***"let us severely threaten them, that from now on they speak to no man in this name"*** (Acts 4:17). Making this decision, ***"they called them and commanded them not to speak at all nor teach in the name of Jesus"*** (Acts 4:18). The apostles could teach morals, Jewish law, and feast days, but they were not to teach about Jesus. Their practices could include religious activities, miracles, and house churches, but they were never to speak of Jesus. Nothing they did was objectionable except their speaking of Jesus!

To threaten the disciples, the council said they were ***"not to speak at all nor teach in*** (epi) ***the name of Jesus"*** (Acts 4:18). From this point on, they were not to speak to any man "***in*** (epi) ***the name***" (Acts 4:17). The Greek word "epi" is used in a variety of ways but always has the intent of superimposing. "Epi" is used for an item placed on the table (Luke 22:21), or Jesus walking on the water (John 6:19). This was not about teaching data or information about Jesus or referring to His name. The disciples were consistently imposing the Spirit of Jesus on every situation. They did not teach the lame beggar about the life of Jesus; they imposed on the man the person of Jesus that resulted in a miracle. The doctrine of Peter and John was not the problem; they had a problem person of Jesus. If the person of Jesus ceases to flow and minister through our lives, we will become a harmless religious organization acceptable to the Sanhedrin.

They Saw | **Acts 4:13-22**

Irrefutable

We give an irrefutable witness when we express the presence of Jesus in our daily lives. People may choose to reject that witness, but they cannot deny it! Jesus' presence in our lives brings clarity and erases disorder and confusion. That explains the response of the Sanhedrin to Peter, John, and the healed beggar. Peter and John's clarity and confidence was irrefutable, and that shook the leaders of Israel. When the apostles stood in the presence of the Sanhedrin, they were out of their element, but the presence of Jesus made the difference (Acts 4:13). The miracle of the lame beggar was equally irrefutable. He stood with the apostles as a whole man, and the leaders of Israel *"could say nothing against it"* (Acts 4:14). As the Sanhedrin talked among themselves, they said, *"What shall we do to these men? For, indeed, that a notable miracle has been done through them is evident to all who dwell in Jerusalem, and we cannot deny it"* (Acts 4:16). Peter, John, and the healed beggar declared the person of Jesus was responsible for the miracle, and the members of the Sanhedrin could not dispute these results.

The Book of Acts expresses the heart of evangelism. These new Christians did not grow because of spectacular leadership, programs, or entertainment. They did not display their talents to catch the attention of the needy crowd. Jesus flowed through their lives and duplicated His life again. Through their living these men demonstrated everything they taught about Jesus, and that was irrefutable!

The disciples' demonstration of Jesus crowded the leaders of Israel to decision and forced them to act. They could not ignore what happened among them. They could not hide the presence of Jesus, treat it as insignificant, or ridicule it. They could reject the truth, but they could not deny His presence. The Sanhedrin had to deal with this revelation repeatedly; it is the same for you and me. The fullness of Jesus' Spirit must merge with me to produce irrefutable evidence of His presence. Religious activities are not enough, and participation in the church organization is not convincing. There are good people in religious and civic organizations, but their lives do not convince people of Jesus. The presence of Jesus in my life is what gives irrefutable evidence to my world!

When Peter and John were threatened by the Sanhedrin not to speak the name of Jesus they said, ***"Whether it is right in the sight of God to listen to you more than to God, you judge. For we cannot but speak the things which we have seen and heard"*** (Acts 4:19-20). The phrase, ***"which we have seen and heard,"*** speaks of the disciples interaction with Jesus during the previous three years. That interaction climaxed in living with Jesus' resurrected presence for forty days (Acts 1:3). Then they were filled with His Spirit at Pentecost, giving irrefutable evidence that they had merged with Jesus. They did not learn this from a textbook or in a seminary classroom. They began to live in Jesus!

Importance

There is a contrast in the outcome of the decisions made by the people in our text. The Holy Spirit again brings an irrefutable witness into the lives of the leaders of Israel. They have come face to face with Jesus once more. They cannot deny Him, but they can reject Him. Where will this take them? What will be their destiny? The apostles are again confronted with life threatening decisions. Will they bow to the authority of the Sanhedrin, or will they follow Jesus? They cannot deny Him, but they can reject Him. Where will this take them? What will be their destiny?

The future of each group flows from their decisions in this moment. The directions of their lives and their families are in the balance. The future of the Jewish nation is determined by this confrontation. We are privileged to view their history and know the outcome. In a matter of a few decades the nation of Israel disappeared. Everything they fought to protect and save was lost! Oh! What have we done to ourselves?

It can be no different for us. I do not know the future; I know only there is no salvation in that future without Jesus in my present. I have no choice regarding the confrontation of His presence in my life. He comes! I did not ask Him! I did not merit His irrefutable presence. Out of His love for me, He comes. I do not have a choice about my future. I cannot shape or control it. The only choice I have is this moment and the embrace of His presence. This will determine everything for me.

Acts 4:13

AM I IGNORANT?

"Now when they saw the boldness of Peter and John, and perceived that they were uneducated and untrained men, they marveled. And they realized that they had been with Jesus"
(Acts 4:13).

Do ignorant people irritate you? Ignorant people do not know they are ignorant. They give unreasonable opinions on subjects they do not understand. They do not know the proper procedures and make unnecessary mistakes for others to correct. Were the disciples in this category? The leaders of Israel perceived them as ***"uneducated and untrained men"*** (Acts 4:13).

The Greek word "agrammatos," translated **uneducated**, is also translated "unlearned, ordinary, and unschooled." "Agrammatos" is used only in this New Testament passage. It corresponds to our English word "illiterate." We are not concerned with the authenticity of this statement. Even though the leaders of Israel might have perceived Peter and John to be illiterate, that is not in our discussion of this passage.

Would you agree with the leaders of Israel's opinion of the disciples? They lived in Galilee, eighty to one hundred miles north of Jerusalem. They lived on the exterior of influential Judaism, and they experienced many foreign influences and philosophies. They were ignorant of the confrontational battles of the Sanhedrin to keep their Jewish traditions and theology pure.

These disciples had never attended the schools in Jerusalem, had never wrestled with the issues of Jewish theology, and did not know its depth.

There were practical aspects to maintaining the temple because of the many practices and operations. The disciples knew little about such requirements to keep things in proper motion. The number of priests representing supported families was astounding. The disciples were ignorant about the scheduling of hundreds of duties and tasks done on a daily basis.

These disciples were unaware of what it was to protect the Jewish way of life in the face of the Roman Empire. They sat around the nightly campfire criticizing the politics of the hour but had never sat on a committee with the Roman representatives. The Jews were without a king and were living under the pressure of being a conquered people. They were overwhelmed while trying to maintain their Jewish lifestyle under such conditions. What did these disciples know about such difficulties? They were ignorant.

These disciples were ignorant of the stress and pressure of being born and raised in the high cultural class of Judah. Those born into that culture were burdened with tremendous responsibility. The seventy men who formed the Sanhedrin governed the welfare of all people in the Jewish faith. Protecting the foundation of the Jewish culture from eroding and undermining influences was a staggering responsibility. These peasant disciples knew nothing of such things. They were ignorant.

All the things we have mentioned thus far were true of the disciples, yet there was one thing of which they were not ignorant. They knew Jesus! The Sanhedrin became painfully aware of this fact. **"And they realized that they had been with Jesus"** (Acts 4:13). The Greek word "epiginosko" is translated **"they realized."** Out of the four Greek words translated "know" in the New Testament, "epiginosko" is the strongest. "Ginosko" is an

Part Three: The Absolute Ratification

expanding knowledge involving experience and relationship. It is the word used for the most intimate relationship in marriage. In our passage, the prefix "epi" is attached to "ginosko," intensifying the basic use of this word. This word is not knowledge from data or information, and it meant much more than these leaders becoming aware that Peter and John were two of the twelve disciples who were with Jesus for three years. The Sanhedrin interacted with Peter and John and witnessed the influence Jesus had on these disciples.

The verb **"realized"** is in the imperfect tense, giving a sense of continual and progressive deepening of this awareness. It began with the boldness and clarity of Peter and John about Jesus and continued as these leaders interacted with the disciples. These disciples may have been ignorant about many things, but they were not ignorant about Jesus. Their insight and discernment about Jesus was mind changing. This insight became alarming knowledge for the Sanhedrin as they debated the fate of Peter, John, and the healed beggar.

Perhaps the ignorance was in the Sanhedrin. They were ignorant about the fullness of Jesus' presence filling and transforming lives. They were ignorant of the working of redemption that took place through the cross, and they were certainly ignorant about Jesus' resurrection. They did not spend forty days with Jesus in His resurrection presence as the disciples had. They did not hear and embrace the challenge to win the world. They did not experience the fullness of the Spirit of Jesus indwelling and sourcing their lives and bringing revelation to their minds. So who were the ignorant ones in our passage?

Our world is in the same state of ignorance. How do we negotiate the pressures of foreign influence? What is the solution for the decline of morals in our society? I am ignorant about the depth of these pressures. I am not in the political arena wrestling with resolving practical matters. I sit on the sidelines and criticize in my ignorance. But I do know Jesus! I know His mind and heart! The spiritual concepts of the Word of God in which all answers are found are within my grasp! I fear the Sanhedrin of our day does not know what I know.

There are patterns revealed in our passage that always dominate those who are ignorant about the spiritual reality of Jesus.

Pretense

Ignorance always chooses pretense. The dilemma of the Sanhedrin's ignorance exists in the presence of the lame beggar. When the miracle happened, *"the lame man who was healed held on to Peter and John"* (Acts 3:11). Then *"the priests, the captain of the temple, and the Sadducees came upon them"* (Acts 4:1). The miracle did not concern these leaders as much as the preaching *"in Jesus the resurrection from the dead"* (Acts 4:2). They arrested Peter and John and put them in jail for the night. The Scriptures do not specifically tell us if the healed beggar went to jail with them. However, when they were brought to court the next day, the healed beggar was present.

As the court hearing for Peter and John took place, *"the man who had been healed standing with them, they could say nothing against it"* (Acts 4:14). In order to discuss this matter privately, the Sanhedrin dismissed the disciples. These leaders of Israel had a problem. *"What shall we do to these men? For, indeed, that a notable miracle has been done through them is evident to all who dwell in Jerusalem, and we cannot deny it"* (Acts 4:16).

It is here in our passage that these leaders reveal their pattern of ignorance. They cannot deny Jesus' responsibility for the healing, but they will not accept it! Their solution is to treat it as if it did not happen, and they threatened the disciples never to speak in the name of Jesus again. Their solution was to silence the message, ignore the miracle, and pretend that it never happened.

The Sanhedrin's solution to the healing shows the pattern of ignorance. Herod Antipas went to Rome on business. On this trip he visited his brother, Philip, had an adulterous affair with his brother's wife, and seduced her to come live with him. At the heart of Perea's throne was a scandalous sin. John the Baptist did most of his preaching in this territory, and he could not ignore this sin. It became the topic of his sermons repeatedly. Luke wrote, ***"But Herod the tetrarch, being rebuked by him concerning Herodias, his brother Philip's wife, and for all the evils which Herod had done, also added this, above all, that he shut John up in prison"*** (Luke 3:19-20). Herod had done terrible things of which adultery was not the least. But Luke says that putting John in prison goes beyond all of his other sins. He silenced the voice of God and pretended everything was all right.

A paramount truth of the Scriptures is the faithfulness of God to communicate His truth to us. He will not allow us to miss His will. He consistently speaks and reveals His truth to our lives. Jesus is the faithful "hound of heaven" who will not leave us alone. The only possibility for going astray is to silence His voice. We pretend! What would happen in your life if from this point on you always listened to the guiding voice of Jesus? Although there might be painful changes in your life, He will bring you into the fullness of His plan. Your life will expand into the person He created you to be? This is a call to respond to the leadership of Christ's Spirit in your life. Do not pretend!

Preserve

Ignorance will always choose to preserve. The leaders of Israel found themselves in a difficult position. Jerusalem

Am I Ignorant? | Acts 4:13

maintained a population of two hundred and fifty thousand people. The temple was in Jerusalem, the citadel of all religious activities for the Jewish people. What happened in Jerusalem set the standard for all Judaism, and the Sanhedrin was responsible for this! However, they were in a dilemma because *"a notable miracle"* had taken place. If that miracle had happened in a small town in Galilee, there would never have been an issue. But *"it is evident to all who dwell in Jerusalem"* that the lame man, now more than forty years of age, who had begged at the Gate Beautiful since childhood, was standing before them a whole man. Everyone knew him and was speaking of this miracle. The leaders of Israel *"cannot deny it."*

The problem was that this miracle promoted the message of the disciples that Jesus was responsible. The Sanhedrin's major issue with Jesus was His resurrection from the dead. If these leaders embrace Jesus, it will be impossible to maintain the Jewish structure, as they have always known it. They must reject Jesus to continue the temple schedule, maintain the daily sacrifices, and live in the material comfort it provides. *"But so that it spreads no further among the people, let us severely threaten them, that from now on they speak to no man in this name"* (Acts 4:17). They must maintain their ignorance about Jesus to preserve their present manner of living.

Preserving our present manner of living is also true about us. We would rather live in deception than change. The leaders of Israel faced problems in their nation that affected their daily lives, needing answers and changes to happen. God had brought the solution for which their nation was born to their doorstep. The promised Messiah, the fulfillment of their destiny, was birthed in their presence. They crucified this fulfillment, yet God afforded them another opportunity. What will they do with this continued yet new revelation? If they embrace Jesus now, they would be confessing they were wrong in crucifying Him. Such a confession would change everything in Israel. They would rather live in deception than change. They decided to remain ignorant to preserve their present state.

Jesus comes to our lives again. What will we do? Will we put John the Baptist in prison and silence the voice of God? Will we threaten the disciples and never hear the name of Jesus again. Will we adjust our theology to fit the way we want to live? Will we live excusing ourselves by blaming everyone else? Despite truth and knowledge of His presence on every hand, will we remain ignorant to preserve the way we are? We must not fall into this trap! Jesus said, *"The lamp of the body is the eye. If therefore your eye is good, your whole body will be full of light. But if your eye is bad, your whole body will be full of darkness. If therefore the light that is in you is darkness, how great is that darkness!"* (Matthew 6:22-23).

Perplexity

Ignorance always results in perplexity. The leaders of Israel sent the disciples outside the council and conferred among themselves. They said, *"So when they had further threatened them, they let them go, finding no way of punishing them, because of the people, since they all glorified God for what had been done"* (Acts 4:21). The leaders of Israel were filled with confusion and did not know what to do. If "Jesus is the Answer," anything outside of intimacy with Him is confusion and perplexity. How will Israel solve the rising tide of unrest and dissatisfaction with Roman domination? Jerusalem will be destroyed in a matter of a few years (70AD); could that have been avoided? Was Israel's answer Jesus?

Luke's contrast between the leaders of Israel and the disciples in the Book of Acts is unmistakable. Jesus expressed such a strong evidence of confidence and security through the disciples that the leaders of Israel marveled (Acts 4:13). However, this expression did not exempt the disciples from suffering and difficulties because they quickly entered days of persecution. The apostles spent time in jail (Acts 5:18). Stephen was stoned to death (Acts 7:59). ***"At that time a great persecution arose against the church which was at Jerusalem; and they were all scattered throughout the regions of Judea and Samaria, except the apostles"*** (Acts 8:1). Herod the king killed James with the sword (Acts 12:1). Peter was kept in prison (Acts 12:5). Yet, in the midst of all this difficulty, God's divine plan unfolded. Those persecuted walked in praise and confidence. They lived in security in unsecure circumstances because of Jesus! The leaders of Israel were filled with uncertainty and perplexity. They did not know what to do. Outside Jesus they had no plan. Their nation would cease to exist in just a few years.

Ignorance pretends to preserve its selfish ways. Ignorance is filled with perplexity because there is no security or plan. Life is bigger than we can comprehend. We do not know what to do. We were not created to be independent. Jesus consistently calls us to Himself. If we will embrace our ignorance, He will fill us with His wisdom. Jesus has a plan! In fact, Jesus is the plan! We must not live in the chaos of our ignorance. Jesus is the answer!

Acts 4:13

A SPIRITUAL MIND

"Now when they saw the boldness of Peter and John, and perceived that they were uneducated and untrained men, they marveled. And they realized that they had been with Jesus"
(Acts 4:13).

Fear is a shadow hovering over a discussion we need to have! At the heart of this fear is a concern about misunderstanding. It is easy to miss the central issue of our discussion, but I ask you to please stay focused! Our verse (Acts 4:13) highlights a fundamental contrast consistent in the New Testament. Attempting to clarify the contrast, let us state it as follows: man's thoughts sourced by his intellect is contrasted with man's thoughts sourced by his merger with the Divine Mind! Are the actions and decisions of my life determined by the best my mind can reason, along with the corporate thinking of generations before me, or are they the result of intimate consultation with Jesus? Are the deciding conclusions of my life a product of education, philosophy, or tradition? Are they a product of an intimate relationship with the mind of Christ?

This contrast between man's thoughts sourced by his intellect and man's thoughts sourced by his merger with the Divine Mind is highlighted in our passage (Acts 4:13). The leaders of Israel saw Peter and John as **"uneducated and untrained men."** However, Peter and John spoke with boldness of knowledge and the confidence of wisdom. Then the leaders of Israel realized *"that they had been with Jesus."* The contrast is between "educated and learned" and *"been with Jesus."* Our discussion is not an attempt to demean or belittle education because that is not the discussion in this passage. Nor are we elevating ignorance or lack of knowledge because that is not in our passage either.

The Sanhedrin tried to digest a powerful message delivered by Peter (Acts 4:8-12). Luke is specific in acknowledging that Peter was filled with the Holy Spirit. The source of Peter's logic and reasoning was beyond the intellectual training and schooling available. An interaction between the mind of Christ through the Spirit of Peter's heart and mind resulted in an understanding beyond the knowledge and tradition of the present culture. The members of the Sanhedrin knew nothing of this interaction. When they heard the message of Peter, they could not determine the source of his understanding because he appeared *"uneducated and untrained."* The single observation was *"they* (the apostles) *had been with Jesus."* Peter's presentation reminded them of Jesus because He had the same interaction with the Spirit of God's mind.

This contrast between man's thoughts sourced by his intellect and man's thoughts sourced by his merger with the Divine Mind is presented repeatedly in the Scriptures. In Paul's first letter to the Church at Corinth, he declared the *"message of the cross is foolish"* (1 Corinthians 1:18). It is only foolish to those who are perishing, regardless of how brilliant their intellect, because redemption through the cross does not make sense. However, those who *"are being saved"* understand the cross through merger with the Spirit of Jesus' mind. The saved ones experience the cross in their lives as *"the power of God."* Paul presented this as a fulfillment of Old Testament prophecy. *"I will destroy the wisdom of the wise, and bring to nothing the understanding of the prudent"* (1 Corinthians 1:19). Paul explained the reason for God's actions. ***"The world through wisdom did not know God"*** (1 Corinthians 1:21). Man's inventive, creative, and productive thinking did not enable him to know God. When man is left to the understanding of his reasoning, he cannot think his way to redemption. The foolishness of God that crucified Christ for redemption is wiser than the intellect of men. So the cross is a stumbling block to the Jew and foolishness to the Greek. The intellect of man is contrasted with the element of the mind of Christ!

In another epistle to the same church, Paul said, ***"Not that we are sufficient of ourselves to think of anything as being from ourselves, but our sufficiency is from God"*** (2 Corinthians 3:5). To illustrate this sufficiency, Paul contrasts *"the letter"* with *"the Spirit."* *"The letter"* is what is written and comprehended by the intellect of man and all education and scholarship can produce. *"The Spirit"* is the material viewed through the mind of man merged with the mind of the Spirit. Education and training without the Spirit of God *"kills"* (2 Corinthians 3:6). The Spirit of Christ merged with the intellect of man "gives life."

Allow the Spirit of Jesus to think with you on the significance of this truth. Schools who promote intellectual education without the fullness of the Spirit produce death. Encouraging your child to learn what man surmises in his thinking produces death also. Academic education without the Spirit of God creates destruction. Life is only in the revelation and knowledge of the Spirit of Jesus!

Context of Conflict

This contrast between man's thoughts sourced by his intellect and man's thoughts sourced by his merger with the Divine Mind produces CONFLICT. The context of our passage (Acts 4:13) is conflict. The members of the Sanhedrin are the scholars of their day. These experts of the Law and the prophets were judging Peter and John. These leaders experienced a lifetime of study and interaction with the Scriptures, spending hours debating the knowledge and truth of the passages. The scribes had levels of achievement with specific books isolated to those scribes of the highest levels. They were the only ones capable of interpreting and understanding the content.

Peter, an ***"uneducated and untrained"*** man, had the audacity to stand before these scholars and give religious instruction. The idea of Peter's boldness produced conflict. What could this fisherman possibly know that would instruct a scribe who had access to material beyond Peter's qualifications? No idea he proposed would be worth consideration. His boldness in teaching and preaching offended those academically superior with conflict as the natural result.

Why did God do this? He gave knowledge and wisdom to men who were academically inferior. When they presented truth to those who were intellectually superior, it was offensive. God had to know that would be the result. Why would He persist in such a method? If a person was captured by the boundaries of his own knowledge, how could you give him truth beyond those boundaries? A self-centered person's intellect thinks only what he can imagine, and he will never comprehend the spiritual beyond the limit of his academic pursuit. The presence of conflict bespeaks the self-centeredness of his mind. Education and learning is not the problem; education and learning without the mind of Christ is the problem. The problem is in the self-centeredness of the mind, which causes an uneducated person to be as self-centered as the educated. The wonder of what Jesus wants to teach us is beyond description. Will we be open to His instruction?

Jesus was faced with a conflict in His ministry. His strategy was to win the three largest cities of Galilee and include the leadership of Israel. All three cities, Chorazin, Bethsaida, and

Capernaum, had rejected His teaching (Matthew 11:20-24). The leaders of Israel wanted to kill Him. Jesus, through the Spirit, understood the plan of the Father. In a moment of praise, He said, ***"I thank You, Father, Lord of heaven and earth, that You have hidden these things from the wise and prudent and have revealed them to babes"*** (Matthew 11:25). Jesus refers to these leaders of Israel as the ***"wise and prudent"*** because they were again rejecting the instruction of the Spirit (Acts 4:13). They were educated, experts in the Law and the prophets, but all that God did in Jesus was hidden from them because they would not go beyond the boundaries of their intellect. They were locked in the cage of their self-centered understanding while God was revealing His truth to ***"babes."*** It is a presentation of our contrast again. The self-centered intellectual thinkers are contrasted with those who know nothing. Infants are those whose minds are open to truth, and they think beyond the boundaries of what they know. Again we see the contrast between man's thoughts sourced by his intellect and man's thoughts sourced by his merger with the Divine Mind amid conflict.

I know this to be true in my life. In the midst of the Spirit's revelation, I must surrender to Jesus my reasonable thinking, my experience and computed knowledge, and my education. The conflict is between what I think and what He wants to reveal to me. Will I allow the merging of my mind with His? The conflict in our passage is the conflict of my life, which is suggested in the question, ***"By what power or by what name have you done this?"*** (Acts 4:7). Will I reject any power or name apart from my knowledge? Will I allow Jesus to teach me His truth?

Condition of Consequence

This conflict between man's thoughts sourced by his intellect and man's thoughts sourced by his merger with the

A Spiritual Mind | **Acts 4:13**

Divine Mind results in CONSEQUENCES. Our passage is not the beginning but is in the middle years of conflict resulting from the revelation of God's heart. The members of the Sanhedrin lived their lives in the awareness of their call. They were chosen by God to bring redemption to the world, living in the Old Testament fulfillment of the revelation. They saw the Messiah about whom their forefathers spoke. They were so opinionated in their academic system any adjustment by the revelation from God's mind could not be tolerated. The intolerance was not a superficial dismissal of knowledge but the crucifixion of the unmistakable revelations of God's heart and mind. God raised Jesus from the dead, directed witnesses to these leaders, and offered them another chance after they crucified Jesus. Then revelation comes to them again through the witness of ***"uneducated and untrained men."*** An undeniable and notable miracle stands before them in the healed beggar.

In the midst of the contrast we find a conflict. The leaders of Israel lived their lives operating from the knowledge of their own reasoning. Their academic pursuit was adjusted to fit their self-centered lifestyle. But now ***"uneducated and untrained men"*** who have the mind of Christ are bringing revelation again without neutrality. They could not maintain what had been. In their rejection of the truth beyond their box of knowledge they launched the first stage of persecution against the church. Their representatives followed the Apostle Paul through his missionary journeys. Ultimately that resulted in the death of one of the most powerful writers of the New Testament.

The consequences were not only what they did to the church and the spread of the Gospel but also what they did to themselves. Because these consequences were so extreme, we are stunned in their reality. In forty years, Jerusalem was totally destroyed. All of their academic knowledge and debated theology was gone. Their nation ceased to exist. They missed the opportunity to know the mind of God. They chose to live

Part Three: The Absolute Ratification

in the small box of their thinking; they sourced their reasoning and it fell short!

However, on the other side of the contrast there were also consequences. Peter and John knew increasing boldness after being threatened to keep silent. Demonstrations of Christ's power affected thousands of lives. They were placed in prison only to be delivered by an angel of the Lord in the night hour! The Sanhedrin met and sent to have the apostles brought from prison only to discover they were not there, but they were at the temple preaching the revelation of Jesus' mind (Acts 5:22). In seventy years the whole world embraced Christianity.

You must remember that this is not a demeaning or belittling of education or knowledge. It is a call for us to go beyond a self-centered, self-sourced thinking of our time and merge with the mind of Christ. Can we be moved from the prison of our opinions and see truth through Jesus' eyes? We find it easy to embrace all the philosophy and psychology of our day and adjust our decisions according to what seems right in our culture. The consequences for our families and communities are just as severe as they were for the Sanhedrin. The box of our academic mind sets a prison in which we will rot. The revelation of Jesus is on us! Will we be open to Him?

Confession of Christ

Our verse is about man's thoughts sourced by his intellect contrasted with man's thoughts sourced by his merger with the Divine Mind! This contrast is always found in the midst of conflict, sometimes in the heart of a person but is always in the culture surrounding it. If you reject the mind of Christ, the consequences are severe and a strong warning is required. But one last element in the contrast is always true. Jesus is present. He is not an academic Jesus, information about Jesus, or a belief system concerning Jesus. He is the present person of Jesus. The revelation of Jesus to the academic thinking of man is not a superior academic thought or more profound truth. The revelation is Jesus Himself!

This revelation is strangely revealed in our passage! The apostles mystify the legalistic Sanhedrin, members oriented to an academic religion. The passage says, *"they marveled."* The Greek word is "thaumazo," having to do with a wonder, the idea of astonishment and admiration. The Sanhedrin searched for an academic explanation for the bold, reasonable, and forceful message of the apostles because Peter and John impressed them. The explanation could not be found in their education or training. Finally they were forced to recognize the influence of Jesus! In fact, He became the only explanation. If Jesus were removed from these Galileans, they would be fishermen without religious influence. But Jesus was present!

The person whose mind and heart is sourced by his own intellect finds his value in this intellectual superiority. But the person whose mind and heart is sourced by Jesus finds his value in Jesus' presence. How easy it is to be impressed with our own intellect. Our clever remarks, our knowledge of a specialized subject, or our ability to instruct others becomes the goal of our self-sourced intellect. What will the mind of Christ create in us? Will we impress those around us with how clever we are, or will they see Jesus? Will our brilliant thoughts be acclaimed, or will Jesus be applauded? Perhaps this is the test of whether we are sourced by our intellect or Jesus living in us!

Acts 4:13

WITH JESUS

"Now when they saw the boldness of Peter and John, and perceived that they were uneducated and untrained men, they marveled. And they realized that they had been with Jesus"
(Acts 4:13).

Peer pressure influences our lives, causing people to act out of character and participate in unbelievable activities. However, peer pressure must be included in our surrender to God. Concern with how others see us is encouraged in the Scriptures. In the Sermon on the Mount, Jesus insisted we would function in the world as salt and light (Matthew 5:13-16). **"Let your light so shine before men, that they may see your good works and glorify your Father in heaven"** (Matthew 5:16). How others see us is important!

The passage for our study is about how the Sanhedrin viewed Peter and John (Acts 4:13). The apostles were not bowing to the peer pressure of these leaders. The leaders of Israel were, however, being moved by what they saw demonstrated in the lives of the apostles. Miracles came, went, and were soon forgotten, but the miracle of the lame beggar was not what worried the Sanhedrin even though they could not deny it (Acts 4:16). Theology can be argued and easily dismissed, so it was not the theology of the apostles that worried the Sanhedrin either. Neither were they concerned about philosophies because they were personal and could be adjusted in the mind. The pressure the Sanhedrin felt from the apostles was about Jesus. *"And they realized they had been with Jesus."* The apostles brought the Sanhedrin face to face with Jesus again!

This statement in the Greek contains an undercurrent of strength that our English translation does not communicate. *"They realized"* is a translation of the Greek word "epiginosko." "Ginosko" is one of four Greek words that give us various ideas of "knowing." The word is a relational term, knowledge coming through an experience with what you know and is used for the most intimate relationship in marriage (Matthew 1:25). The word is a "knowing" that is unfolding and growing, and it moves toward completeness. "Epi" means "upon" and is a prefix suggesting intensity.

Paul spoke about becoming a man and putting away childish things. He said, *"For now we see in a mirror, dimly, but then face to face. Now I know in part, but then I shall know* (ginosko) *just as I also am known* (epiginosko)*"* (1 Corinthians 13:12). He described his experience with Jesus in the present as "ginosko," a relationship of intimacy through the fullness of Jesus' Spirit. But this relationship was as *"we see in a mirror, dimly."* The future relationship in heaven will be "epiginosko." What will it be like? In our passage (Acts 4:13), the Sanhedrin interacted with the apostles. As this experience progressed, they became aware that Jesus was influencing these apostles. This awareness exploded in their minds, and they could not dismiss it. Luke described this as "epiginosko," an intensified knowledge.

"And they realized that they had been with Jesus." The preposition *"with"* is a translation of the Greek word "sun" and is a primary preposition denoting union, with, or together. You must not read into the use of this word more than what the writer intended though there is something significant about it. "Sun" points to a closer relationship than two other words Luke could have used, "para," also a primary preposition meaning

Part Three: The Absolute Ratification

"near, beside, or in proximity to something," and "meta," also a primary preposition, denoting "accompaniment, amid, or among." Luke said this relationship was something beyond the Sanhedrin remembering the apostles being seen with Jesus, attending services with Him in the synagogue, or standing in the Garden of Gethsemane with Him. "Sun" relates the idea of partnership with Jesus. The Sanhedrin did not grasp the idea that the apostles were filled with the nature and Spirit of Jesus and were seeing Jesus demonstrated through the Acts of the Apostles. But Luke insists the Sanhedrin came to a moment of knowledge when they understood and became intensely aware of Jesus as they interacted with Peter and John. Luke used the strongest preposition available (sun) to describe the interaction of Jesus in and through these apostles.

How did the Sanhedrin see the apostles? What did they experience throughout this interaction with them? *"And they realized that they had been with Jesus"* (Acts 4:13). What does this mean?

Conversation

The most significant part of this encounter between the apostles and the Sanhedrin was Peter and John's constant reference to Jesus. The Sanhedrin had become aware of the connection between Jesus and the apostles because Peter and John could not keep still about Jesus. They kept crying His name! The Sanhedrin entered this court scene aware of the apostle's emphasis on Jesus. *"Now as they spoke to the people, the priests, the captain of the temple, and the Sadducees came upon them, being greatly disturbed that they taught the people and preached in Jesus the resurrection from the dead"* (Acts 4:2). The issue was not a matter of theological differences. The issue was Jesus! The Pharisees and Sadducees differed in their belief about the resurrection, but they agreed that so much talk about Jesus could not be tolerated. What greatly disturbed them was the constant emphasis on Jesus.

Now the apostles stood before the Sanhedrin in a more intimate encounter. This encounter was not a preaching session, but a confrontational examination. The central question was raised, **"By what power or by what name have you done this?"** (Acts 4:7). Peter's answer is recorded in five verses where the name "Jesus" or the pronoun referring to His name is used five times. Two other references are made to Him from the prophetic quotation, **"stone"** and **"chief cornerstone."**

"They saw the boldness of Peter and John." The Sanhedrin was impacted by the consistent reference to Jesus and by the attitude of the apostles. This attitude was more impressive because **"they were uneducated and untrained men."** The Greek word "theoreo," translated **"they saw,"** is a specific word used for "seeing" and focuses on "looking closely at or to gaze." "Theoreo" highlights the emphasis of being a spectator. This seeing was not a passing glance or a casual observance. The Sanhedrin was thoroughly impacted by how Peter delivered his exhortation.

Peter's attitude was one of **"boldness."** The Greek word is "parrhesia," referring to the manner of speaking in frankness or speaking as one feels or thinks without a cocky or arrogant attitude. Two pictures of Peter are contrasted, one before the resurrection and one after the resurrection. Peter was intimidated by a servant girl in the courtyard during Jesus' trial at Caiaphas' Palace and denied he ever knew Jesus. In our passage he stands before seventy of the most powerful men of Israel and speaks his heart without fear. "Parrhesia" is the idea of confidence and assurance filtering throughout Peter's speaking. Peter had been with Jesus for forty days in His resurrection appearance (Acts 1:3), being convinced of the reality of that resurrection. Pentecost flooded his life with the Spirit of Jesus (Acts 2:1-4). Ministering in Jerusalem, he witnessed the power of Jesus changing lives. It had just happened in the lame beggar! Peter was not being argumentative. His heart was filled with Jesus, and he had to express that! He could not keep still. When threatened not to speak or teach in the name of Jesus, he said, ***"Whether it is right in the sight of God to listen to you more than to God, you judge. For we cannot but speak the things which we have seen and heard"*** (Acts 4:19-20). Peter's exhortation was not a product of a new career or sales technique. He was radically convinced!

How does this translate into your life? This exhortation is not a scolding for not witnessing to others, as we should, but a call to examine our intimacy with Jesus. How convinced are we? Does His presence burn in our hearts? Is Jesus such a reality in our lives that His name comes up in all discussions? How can we be filled with Him and keep still about Him? Are we listening more to what the world's promotions than we are to Jesus? The apostles said, ***"For we cannot but speak the things which we have seen and heard"*** (Acts 4:20). Is He what we see and hear? Is He the topic of our conversation?

This promotion is not an issue of technique or method, but it is a heart issue. The question is not, "Do you or do you not witness?" We must ask, "Why don't you?" How can we be silent? I want my life to burst forth with Jesus. I want Him to be in every conversation. I want every encounter with every person I meet be an encounter with Jesus. It must be so!

Characteristics

"And they realized that they had been with Jesus" (Acts 4:13). Another aspect of this statement must have been on the minds of the Sanhedrin. They were content to push from their minds all encounters and conflicts they had with Jesus. There were numerous embarrassing moments in those encounters. This Galilean, Peter, without formal education,

forcibly revealed truth they could not refute. The members of the court began to see the similarities between Jesus and His disciples. These leaders of Israel were amazed when Jesus taught openly in the temple during the Feast of the Tabernacles. **"And the Jews marveled, saying, "How does this Man know letters, having never studied?"** (John 7:15).

Jesus' questionable birth was a constant irritation to the leaders of Israel (John 8:41). They were not a product of fornication because Abraham was their father. How could anyone with such a questionable background propose to know truth? Jesus should know His place! Jesus' proposals were so radical to these leaders that their only possible explanation was that He was demon possessed (John 8:48; 10:21). The Old Testament pattern was the death of such people. These leaders spent much of their time plotting how they could kill Jesus.

All the characteristics they recognized in Jesus were now being manifested in His apostles. Everything that bothered them about Jesus was bothering them through His disciples as if Jesus was back in another physical form. Miracles were done; truth was stated; uneducated people claimed to know God. All the old irritations they felt toward Jesus now flowed again toward the apostles. Suddenly, the issue shifts from these apostles to Jesus. He just will not go away!

The leaders of Israel threatened the disciples because of their connection with Jesus, which validated their problem. They do not care about anything the disciples were doing except that Jesus was sourcing them. This sourcing was their complaint about the message of the resurrection. The Alliance forcibly moved into the crowd to silence Peter during his exhortation. Luke said that the leaders of Israel were not disturbed about the resurrection specifically, but they captured the apostles because they were, **"being greatly disturbed that they taught the people and preached *in Jesus* the resurrection from the dead"** (Acts 4:2). There was always a continuing debate about the resurrection

Part Three: The Absolute Ratification

between the Pharisees and Sadducees, which they could tolerate, but what the apostles were doing was different. Now their threat was in direct connection to preaching in Jesus' name. *"So they called them and commanded them not to speak at all nor teach in the name of Jesus"* (Acts 4:18). The leaders of Israel had no problem with the apostles' teaching, healing, or their compassionate ministry, but they had to eliminate Jesus!

The devil has only one plan concerning your life. He wants to eliminate Jesus. Your religion, worship, ceremonies, good deeds, and prayer do not concern him. The issue is Jesus! He does not want you focused on Jesus. You can do all the religious activities you want as long as you do not involve Jesus. You can sing, but do not sing about Jesus. You can testify as long as it is not about Jesus. You can promote the church but don't speak the name of Jesus. The only thing the devil fears is a person consumed and in love with Jesus. You can be of low rank, *"uneducated and untrained,"* but if Jesus is involved, the devil will tremble. What is your relationship with Jesus?

Confusion

The leaders of Israel did not understand what we know. *"And they realized that they had been with Jesus"* (Acts 4:13). They did not understand that Jesus was present in the court, not in a ghostly or spiritual sense, but that Peter was filled with the nature and person of Jesus! They did not understand Pentecost.

The leaders of Israel recognized all parties. They saw Peter and John, but they were reminded of Jesus. Peter and John, unique individuals, were present. God created every person as a self. In the theological language of "death to self," we may leave the impression that surrender to Jesus means self no longer exists. That impression is wrong! God created you as a "self," unlike anyone else. Your uniqueness has a purpose. God does not want to deliver you from being yourself but wants to merge with you, enhancing your uniqueness. God wants you to be all He intended you to be. The merger between you and Jesus gives "self" the sourcing for the complete expression of who you are! Jesus was right! He said, *"For whoever desires to save his life will lose it, but whoever loses his life for My sake will find it"* (Matthew 16:25). When a person sources self (*"desires to save his life"*), his expression of self is twisted, meager, and inferior (*"will lose it"*). When a person merges with Jesus (*"loses his life for My sake"*), his expression of self is fulfilled, enhanced, and complete (*"will find it"*).

Therefore, self (your uniqueness) is not eliminated but fully seen. However, Jesus is also fully seen in His uniqueness through your "self." The phrase "less of me and more of Him" becomes improper in light of this concept. The reality of Christianity is a union of all of me with all of Him. We are united in an expression of the unique person I am created to be! Jesus referred to this as, *"I have come that they may have life, and that they may have it more abundantly"* (John 10:10). The nature and Spirit of God indwelt Jesus and was now indwelling the apostles. The Sanhedrin witnessed this Spirit through Jesus and now through the apostles. This multiplication surely frustrated the devil! To eliminate Jesus he must eliminate everyone in whom Jesus dwells. The demonic glee rejoicing over the removal of Jesus at the crucifixion soon turned to stress. Pentecost produced another one hundred and twenty of the same type of people. It exploded through the generations. We have the opportunity to participate in the same.

Acts 4:13

THE GREAT COMMISSION

"Now when they saw the boldness of Peter and John, and perceived that they were uneducated and untrained men, they marveled. And they realized that they had been with Jesus"
(Acts 4:13).

Matthew climaxed his Gospel account with The Great Commission (Matthew 28:16-20). ***"Go therefore and make disciples of all the nations, baptizing them in the name of the Father and of the Son and of the Holy Spirit, teaching them to observe all things that I have commanded you"*** (Matthew 28:19-20). Jesus' command was not to ***"go"*** but to ***"make disciples."*** We assume that all Christians will go. If you are not going, you have a spiritual problem. How are we to make disciples? What are the methods and techniques for making disciples? "Making disciples" is contained in "being a disciple." The Spirit-sourced person will consistently shape those around him; he is teaching by the influence of His life. Jesus did not give us a curriculum or syllabus to follow; He never suggested techniques or methods. Jesus gave us Jesus!

Luke, the apostle, wrote the Book of Luke and the Book of Acts at the same simultaneously. They were volume one and volume two with a single purpose forming one book. As this book was read in the early church, volume one was recognized as a Gospel account. Therefore, it was joined to the other Gospel

The Great Commission | Acts 4:13

accounts to give us the four Gospels. But volume two was viewed as valuable and needed, providing the necessary bridge between the life of Jesus (Gospel accounts) and the epistles (established churches). The Book of Acts is the incredible account of the early Church's growth. Christianity expanded from a handful of disciples to a world religion. Men and women who never traveled more than one hundred miles from their birthplaces became world evangelists. How did this happen? The Book of Acts is their story.

Evangelism seminars promoting church growth inevitably highlight the Book of Acts. It became the blueprint for the establishment of the Church. Those interested in church growth carefully studied this writing to discover the techniques for evangelism. Our cry became, "We must be like the early Church!" However, there is a fallacy in this approach. The techniques and methods of the early church were necessary for their culture. They did not have Christian schools, the New Testament, Christian literature, and the structured church. They did not have printing presses or the media level of communication. They were limited in their travel so their methods were designed for their cultural setting not ours. We do not study the Book of Acts to find methods and techniques for evangelism.

However, eternal principles and biblical patterns are presented to us in the Book of Acts. These principles shape our methods but should not determine them. Methods are not sacred, but biblical principles are! Luke established the biblical pattern in our passage (Acts 4:13). The early Christians duplicated it repeatedly throughout the evangelism of the early church, forming a progression. The Sanhedrin saw (SEEING) the boldness of Peter and John, perceived (SEIZING) that they were uneducated and untrained men, marveled (SURPRISING) at what they could to say and do, and realized (SENSING) that they had been with Jesus!

Part Three: The Absolute Ratification

Seeing

In our passage the beginning of the progression is *"they saw,"* translated from Greek word "theoreo." Vine's Expository Dictionary of New Testament Words lists eleven Greek words for the verb "see," each highlighting one aspect or emphasis of "seeing." "Theoreo" denotes the participation as a spectator, a person who carefully examines, inspects, or checks the details of an event or object. This word points to the action of the person seeing and is frequently translated in some translations "to behold!" The Greek words "blepo" and "horao" are used for the physical act of seeing. Mary Magdalene declared to Peter and John the news that Jesus' body was absent from the tomb. Peter and John immediately ran to see, with John entering the empty tomb first. John *"saw (blepo) the linen cloths lying there"* (John 20:5). Then Peter *"went into the tomb; and he saw (theoreo) the linen cloths lying there, and the handkerchief that had been around His head, not lying with the linen cloths, but folded together in a place by itself"* (John 20:6-7). Our Greek word "theoreo" expresses a closer examination.

In our passage the Sanhedrin was not just glancing at the apostles, but they were spectators examining closely the attitude expressed in Peter's explanation. *"Now when they saw (theoreo) the boldness of Peter and John"* (Acts 4:13). *"Saw"* is the verb in the present tense, meaning it is not occurring only now but continues, which establishes the foundation for the rest of the event recorded in our passage. As the Sanhedrin continued to observe the apostles, they had a growing awareness that something was different about these men.

This encounter was the beginning of evangelism. Something has to happen to capture the observation of a person. In this case it was the healing of the lame beggar accompanied by the preaching of Peter. This created the court scene where the observation was made. The Spirit of Jesus sourced the recurring observations, which occurred repeatedly throughout the Book of Acts. Some events were miracles and some were sufferings through persecution, but all included interactions with others.

The people around us must observe our Christianity. Jesus is consistently sourcing circumstances in our lives for others' observation. Is this the purpose for your job? How tragic to spend most of your time just to make money. A higher purpose would be to display Jesus in your life on the job. Could this be your reason for involvement in recreational activities? The driving force is not "fun" but the opportunity to display Jesus! Could it be there are no involvements in your life that do not include this driving passion? Even the activities necessary for the survival of life present the opportunities of interaction with others for Christ. Our lives are continually on center stage for the visualization of the Spirit of Jesus who has no days off and no vacations. Jesus calls us to an intimacy with His Spirit to display His person. What a privilege!

Seizing

Luke added to the Sanhedrin's response when he said, **"and perceived that they were uneducated and untrained men"** (Acts 4:13). The first step of "SEEING" leads to further involvement in others' observation. After observing the courage of Peter and John, the Sanhedrin became acutely aware of the apostles' lack of proper education. Luke used the Greek word "katalambano," translated **"perceived."** "Katalambano" originally portrayed the meaning "to seize on or lay hold of."

"Katalambano" appears in the New Testament in different phrases of this original sense. Paul desired, **"that Christ may dwell in your hearts through faith; that you, being rooted and grounded in love, may be able to comprehend** (katalambano) *with all the saints what is the width and length and depth and height — to know the love of Christ"* (Ephesians 3:17-19). In speaking of his passion, Paul wrote, *"Not that I have already attained, or am already perfected; but I press on, that I may lay hold of* (katalambano) *that for which Christ Jesus has also laid hold* (katalambano) *of me"* (Philippians 3:12).

The father of a demon-possessed son described his situation to Jesus. *"Teacher, I brought You my son, who has a mute spirit. And wherever it seizes* (katalambano) *him, it throws him down; he foams at the mouth, gnashes his teeth, and becomes rigid"* (Mark 9:17-18). Jesus used this term for *"darkness overtake* (katalambano) *you"* (John 12:35). Luke used "katalambano" other times in the Book of Acts for "comprehending, grasping mentally" as he did in our passage. Peter proclaimed, *"In truth I perceive that God shows no partiality"* (Acts 10:34). King Festus said this about Paul, *"But when I found that he had committed nothing deserving of death, and that he himself had appealed to Augustus, I decided to send him"* (Acts 25:25).

Using "katalambano" in our passage highlights the progression of intensity and involvement with the apostles. Luke wrote the main verb of this sentence (marveled) in the imperfect tense to depict the continuing effect of this involvement. The boldness and courage of Peter and John sourced by the Holy Spirit caused the Sanhedrin to investigate further into the lives of the apostles. They had not discovered the source was Jesus. However, the first steps were taken, drawing the Sanhedrin into the reality of this truth!

Through our daily involvement with others, we display courage and boldness as a pattern that demands their attention. With renewed intensity they discover our courage and boldness are not caused by temperament, talent, or training. We capture their attention, causing their deeper investigation. For more than a year, we had two large pictures hanging on the sidewall of our church sanctuary. They were removed almost six months ago, and not a single person has asked me about them. Why? Our people never really saw them, because they were unimportant to them. The pictures were seen, yet they unseen. You drive down the road and see road sign after road sign but forget them. Why? They are unimportant to you. The Spirit of Jesus must possess your life to display a movement of His presence through you that will initially cause your world to engage your life. We must have a deepening of this engagement with those around us until they investigate who we are.

Surprising

"They marveled" is the main verb of the first sentence, a translation of the Greek word "thaumazo." Initially in our passage we find the Greek word "thaumazo," translated *"they saw"* and related by its root to "theoreo." "Thaumazo" denotes the amazement awakened by sight, often translated "be amazed or to be astonished" and has several nuances depending on its context. "Thaumazo" can refer to a bewildered, questioning astonishment (Luke 24:12; John 3:7) or surprise (Mark 15:44; Luke 1:63). This Greek word can also include fear (Luke 8:25) or a joyful (Luke 24:41) or impressed (Matthew 9:33) astonishment, and sometimes its meaning can include reverence or adoration (Revelation 13:3; 2 Thessalonians 1:10).

"Thaumazo" is used most often in Luke's Gospel. From the birth of Jesus (Luke 2:18, 33) to His resurrection (Luke 24:12, 41), His life and work evoked astonishment. The people of Nazareth were astonished at His preaching (Luke 4:22). His individual miracles consistently evoked astonishment (Luke 8:25; 11:14). In Luke "astonishment" is positively interpreted as "an awesome sense of astonishment at the Divine," manifested by Jesus and continued into the Book of Acts.

However, we must note that this astonishment is not

identical with authentic faith (Luke 4:22; 9:43). Astonishing others with our embrace of Jesus is a necessary step in the pattern expressed in the Book of Acts but does not guarantee the outcome of them embracing Jesus. The Sanhedrin continued to reject Jesus even though they were astonished at the miracle. Not everyone may embrace Jesus, but everyone has to come to an awareness of His presence. God will bring everyone to the crossroads of a decision about Jesus.

I must be filled with Jesus; He must flow through my life and engage my world. I must draw those around me into a deeper investigation of Jesus' activity in my life. I must astonish them by what Jesus does in, through, and upon me! This was suggested by the opening question of this court; ***"By what power or by what name have you done this?"*** (Acts 4:7). The Sanhedrin assumed the apostles controlled the instruments and symbols of authority and power. They were shocked when the power seemed to be flowing from men as lowly as Peter and John. Peter could speak before this assembly of powerful men through the sourcing of the Holy Spirit (Acts 4:8).

The progression ending in astonishment was not a result of Peter's training, education, or talent. The Sanhedrin was astonished because the Spirit of God demonstrated Himself through the weakness or lack in Peter. Astonishment because of our skill, cleverness, and ability does not bring men to salvation. What speaks to the heart of a person is the movement of God through our weakness, which is the core of this biblical pattern. Evangelism occurred in the Book of Acts only because God demonstrated Himself through the weakness of His servants.

We discovered God's demonstration of Himself through our weakness in the evangelism at Pentecost (Acts 2:5-11) when three thousand men accepted Jesus. God spoke through the Galilean disciples in fifteen different dialects unknown to them, amazing the crowd. God demonstrated Himself through the weakness of the disciples not through their strengths, and He did it again in our passage, astonishing everyone with the miracle given to the lame beggar. Peter assumed no credit for the miracles; he was weak. God placed Peter in the position of speaking boldly to the most educated men of his culture. Peter was weak, and the Sanhedrin was astonished.

This must be the pattern for our lives. If we are sourced by our abilities, our world will see only us. God must constantly source us. We must embrace our helplessness that Jesus' life might be demonstrated. The Christian Gospel revolves around this truth. We define faith as: invoking the activity of the second party. I must always say, "I can't but He can!" Christianity is a life lived beyond our abilities. When this happens, our world will closely examine our lives, seize with comprehension that something is occurring beyond our ability, and be surprised enough that they will begin to investigate.

Sensing

The goal of this process is in the climax! A person sees something in a Christian's life that brings them face-to-face with the person of Jesus. *"And they realized that they had been with Jesus"* (Acts 4:7). In our last study, we discussed the Greek word "epiginosko." "Ginosko" is one of four Greek words used to communicate various ideas of "knowing." "Ginosko" is a relational term, knowledge that comes through relationship with what you know, and is used for the most intimate relationship in marriage (Matthew 1:25). This word denotes an unfolding and growing knowledge, moving toward a complete knowledge. "Epi" means "upon" and as a prefix suggests intensity.

Paul wrote of putting away childish things when becoming a man. He said, *"For now we see in a mirror, dimly, but then face to face. Now I know* (ginosko) *in part, but then I shall know* (epiginosko) *just as I also am known* (epiginosko)*"*

Part Three: The Absolute Ratification

(1 Corinthians 13:12). He described his experience with Jesus in the present as "ginosko," a relationship of intimacy through the fullness of the Spirit of Jesus. However, this relationship is as ***"we see in a mirror, dimly."*** The future relationship in heaven will be "epiginosko." What will it be like? In our passage (Acts 4:13) the Sanhedrin experienced interaction with the apostles. As their experience progressed, they became aware of one fact. Jesus influenced these apostles. This awareness exploded in their minds, and they could not dismiss it. Luke described this as "epiginosko," an intensified knowledge.

"Epiginosko" does not remove freewill; it does leave us without excuse. The Sanhedrin recognized the truth and will be held accountable for their decision. When Jesus is displayed in and through our lives, our world is brought to an encounter with Him, experiencing Jesus as He is. This experience is not as previous ones through theology, doctrine, or concept but in the reality of His presence. His presence is our goal. Others around us are most likely to accept Him as they experience Him in us! We must not scar or diminish His demonstration. We must live in the fullness of the Spirit!

The Sanhedrin saw (SEEING) the boldness of Peter and John, perceived (SEIZING) that they were uneducated and untrained men, marveled (SURPRISING) at what they could say and do, and realized (SENSING) that they had been with Jesus!

Acts 4:14

THE ANNEX

"And seeing the man who had been healed standing with them, they could say nothing against it" (Acts 4:14).

What a story! The beginning of persecution was in the early Church, and the Holy Spirit was right in the middle. He was not just present in His omnipresence, but He indwelt Peter, the Apostle. An unmistakable boldness erupted through Peter as the Holy Spirit sourced him. A convincing truth flowed through these untrained and uneducated fishermen. The educated men of that day "marveled" (Acts 4:13). Peter did not use this new Source, but the new Source used Peter. In other words, Peter was not displayed, glorified, or accredited as the source, but He was a demonstration, a stage or platform where the New Source could be visualized. These educated leaders of Israel were forced to see Jesus, the Source, in the arena of the uneducated fishermen. ***"And they realized that they had been with Jesus"*** (Acts 4:13).

In the next verse (Acts 4:14), Luke writes of the distinct instruction about the leaders of Israel's realization. This realization cannot be set aside and easily forgotten because it influenced the positive and negative decisions to be made. The verse begins with ***"And"*** (Acts 4:14) and is a translation of the second word in the Greek text. The Greek word is "te." "But" is a contrast of two ideas, while "and" is a link of two equal ideas.

Part Three: The Absolute Ratification

"Te" is used differently than "but" or "and." "Te" presents the idea of annexing; it demands a previous idea on which we can add and build. Everything in our verse is a direct result of the Sanhedrin's realization that the apostles had been with Jesus. The leaders of Israel's awareness of Jesus becomes the foundation on which we will annex this additional thought.

Jesus is the main building of life with all other additions established and related to Him is the biblical pattern for life! The architectural structure, brick formation, and attractiveness are in this addition. No one can say, "It does not fit." The Christmas story validates this truth. Why is Jesus, the Savior of the world, born in a smelly stable among lowly shepherds and from a peasant mother? This scene is an annex coming from the heart of God. At the core of the Triune God is holiness. The Christmas scene is an expression of the state of God's heart. He never thinks about Himself but is always redemptive. He is a bleeding, suffering, and dying Messiah! Palm Sunday validates this truth. The crowds proclaimed His fame, and He was extremely popular. Jesus rode into this scene on a donkey, a symbol of service, but it was an occasion of the highest acclaim. He did not come as a conquering Lord but as a humble Redeemer! His entrance was a fitting annex to the heart of God.

This humility of heart and action is the call of the Book of Acts. We must be filled with God's heart, the Spirit of Jesus. We are the annex to all the Triune God has done in and through Jesus. We will sing in Philippi jails, embrace the defiled Gentile, and pour out our lives for others. Listen to the description of the early church in Jerusalem. ***"Now the multitude of those who believed were of one heart and one soul; neither did anyone say that any of the things he possessed was his own, but they had all things in common"*** (Acts 4:32). This description is a fitting annex constructed by the heart of God!

The Miracle

Our passage begins with a description of the annex present in the courtroom of the Sanhedrin. *"And seeing the man who had been healed"* (Acts 4:14), who was *"over forty years old"* (Acts 4:22), and was previously excluded from all religious temple involvement was now for the first time in the temple. He was poor, disgraced, and nonessential to the function of Jewish culture. From his begging place he had observed Jesus entering the temple. Peter, John, and the other apostles passed him daily. But God destined this man for this hour. He was an annex to the heart of God! The power and person of Jesus was demonstrated through the setting of a beggar.

The miracle was unquestionable! *"They could say nothing against it"* (Acts 4:14). The members of the Sanhedrin said to each other, *"What shall we do to these men? For, indeed, that a notable miracle has been done through them is evident to all who dwell in Jerusalem, and we cannot deny it"* (Acts 4:16). They concluded they could do nothing to the apostles. *"So when they had further threatened them, they let them go, finding no way of punishing them, because of the people, since they all glorified God for what had been done"* (Acts 4:21). There was no question a miracle had happened!

A careful study of the Book of Acts reveals God consistently intervened in human existence to do something so radical it is called "a miracle." Luke described it when he wrote, *"Then fear came upon every soul, and many wonders and signs were done through the apostles"* (Acts 2:43). When the Sanhedrin's threat was related to the early Church, the believers broke into a praise session. *"Now, Lord, look on their threats, and grant to Your servants that with all boldness they may speak Your word, by stretching out Your hand to heal, and that signs and wonders may be done through the name of Your holy Servant Jesus"*

Part Three: The Absolute Ratification

(Acts 4:29-30). The early Church expected and experienced miracles, an annex to the heart of God!

Some people of the modern day want to confine miracles to the early Church, but biblically that is impossible. Paul said, ***"And God has appointed these in the church: first apostles, second prophets, third teachers, after that miracles, then gifts of healings, helps, administrations, varieties of tongues"*** (1 Corinthians 12:23). He followed that by asking a series of questions that proclaimed their answers. ***"Are all apostles? Are all prophets? Are all teachers? Are all workers of miracles? Do all have gifts of healings? Do all speak with tongues? Do all interpret?"*** (1 Corinthians 12:29-30). Then he wrote a chapter on what all can and must experience. We all can know love (1 Corinthians 13).

Miracles happen when God expresses His heart! It was true in Paul's day and it is true today. God's power has not waned. However, Paul emphasized that while miracles are immediate demonstrations of God's heart, the important thing is His love, "the heart of God." If we see only miracles, we miss the truth of the annex!

The truth of our passage (Acts 4:14) is that the healed beggar was standing in the presence of the Sanhedrin. They could not deny him. His miracle was woven into the fiber of the encounter presented in chapters three and four. No one denied the miracle, but it was not the focus. It was the stage for the action of the verse, the annex to the real building. The focus was an addition to the real issue, highlighting the significance. Jesus is the focus! If Jesus is removed, the miracle ceases to exist. Jesus, the source of the miracle, gives the healing its significance.

Why do we not emphasize miracles? Do we not believe in miracles? Absolutely, I believe God can and does heal. I believe I live in the consistent intervention of God in my physical world! I believe miracles occur when I am not even aware. God interacts with my physical world to protect and deliver when it is not apparent to me. The miracle is not the focus; Jesus is the focus! Anything that distracts me from Jesus quickly becomes sin. When miracles capture my attention, self-centeredness demands recognition. Jesus spoke of this in His closing of the Sermon on the Mount. ***"Many will say to Me in that day, 'Lord, Lord, have we not prophesied in Your name, cast out demons in Your name, and done many wonders in Your name?' And then I will declare to them, 'I never knew you; depart from Me, you who practice lawlessness!'"*** (Matthew 7:22-23). A miracle focused on self is declared ***"lawlessness,"*** and is an attempt to manipulate God. If we can tell God what to do, we think we are greater than God. The focus is not on the miracle. The focus of the miracle is on Jesus!

The Motive

Now we come to our second consideration. The Sanhedrin was negative. Luke wrote, ***"They could say nothing against it"*** (Acts 4:14). This tells us that they wanted to say something against it, referring to the miracle received by the lame beggar. The leaders of Israel would have loved to refute the miracle, discrediting the apostles and their message. But by their admission, they conceded, ***"For, indeed, that a notable miracle has been done through them is evident to all who dwell in Jerusalem, and we cannot deny it"*** (Acts 4:16). However, the miracle was a secondary issue for these leaders. Their central issue was Jesus. They were not denying the miracle but denying Jesus. They did not care what miracles took place so long as those miracles were not acclaimed in the name of Jesus, but the miracle was sourced by Jesus, making no way to separate it from Him. If you removed Jesus from the scene, there would not have been a miracle. Without the miracle, Jesus would not be proclaimed.

Part Three: The Absolute Ratification

Here lies the problem with miracles. If Jesus passed out miracles, I would get in line. Who does not want to be well, have financial wealth, or be saved from a physical disaster? However, Jesus accomplishes a miracle for a purpose, never casually, "just for the fun of it," or on a whim. Miracles always ring with a purpose! A miracle accomplishes something for a reason.

The unfolding drama of the healed beggar fills two chapters. The drama is not a story recalling a miracle, and the focus is not on the healed beggar. We are never told his name, and there is no mention of a community wide celebration of his healing. We never learn of the future success of the healed man's life. The purpose of the miracle does not seem centered on him. God did something bigger than one man as the miracle became the instrument for a spiritual demonstration in the temple. This disruption sets the stage for the beginning persecution of the church in Jerusalem. As the persecution escalated, the Jewish Christians scattered into the surrounding countries. Evangelism happened, and Christianity was no longer a Jewish sect confined to Jerusalem. The Great Commission (Matthew 28:16-10) was achieved. This miracle had a purpose!

If I want a miracle from Jesus, am I willing to bow under the authority of His purpose? When He does a miracle it always involves "purpose." However, there is another possibility. If He does not grant a miracle, that denial also has a purpose. Am I attached to the miracle or the purpose? If I am determined to possess my miracle with no regard to the purpose, I become miracle focused rather than Jesus focused.

If we understand the heart of Jesus, we understand the miracle. His presence is to indwell, flow, and live through every miracle. There is never a miracle outside of Jesus' presence. If He restores my life, He will be involved in my living. If He works a miracle in my finances, He will be involved in how I spend my money. He is like the leaven in the bread, beginning in one section and permeating the whole loaf. He heals me physically and wants to engage my attitude. You cannot isolate His presence to the physical miracle.

Paul captured this truth in his view of the cross. He said, *"Or do you not know that your body is the temple of the Holy Spirit who is in you, whom you have from God, and you are not your own? For you were bought at a price; therefore glorify God in your body and in your spirit, which are God's"* (1 Corinthians 6:19-20). Does the miracle of the cross redeem us from death and set us free? Does this miracle involve Jesus' purchase of you *"at a price"* so that *"you are not your own?"* You are now His!

The Management

Luke describes this encounter with overbearing language. *"And seeing the man who had been healed standing with them, they could say nothing against it"* (Acts 4:14). The direct emphasis on *"standing"* is undeniable, though it was not necessary. It points to the reliability of the miracle. There is no question about the existence of the miracle or Jesus' involvement. Remember that Luke is annexing this statement. *"And they realized that they had been with Jesus"* (Acts 4:13).

As the story progresses, the Sanhedrin's realization of Jesus involvement in the miracle becomes evident. They had no desire to limit the number of miracles, and they did not want to manage or control these events. The miracles did not concern them, and they did not seem to be anxious about the growth of the early Church. A variety of religious sects were in and around Jerusalem, much like the various denominations in our community. Adding one more Jewish sect to the list was not an issue for these leaders. The Sanhedrin did not care about the popularity of the early Church. The focus of their concern was Jesus! They wanted to end all emphasis of His involvement.

Part Three: The Absolute Ratification

They did not want the disciples to ever speak in the name of Jesus. They wanted Him eliminated. They did want to manage the focus on Jesus!

Managing the focus on Jesus has been true in my Christian life from the beginning. As a teenager, I gave my life to Christ and experienced only defeat. I was caught in the typical up and down of Christian life. I was; then I was not. One day in desperation, I left school on my lunch break and made my way to our church across the street. Without emotions or tears, I pleaded with Jesus and challenged Him. Either His presence in my life would become real or I was going to look elsewhere for the answers. God began something incredible in me that day. Over time I realized that Jesus was my answer. My answer is not the idea of Jesus, the theology of Jesus, or the church of Jesus but the Person of Jesus! When I focus on Jesus, I have victory. The answer is in Jesus as He continually interacts and is involved in my life. I must maintain a God-awareness in my life always. This awareness is not about miracles, the gifts of the Spirit, church activities, or biblical knowledge. This is about Jesus. I must be His!

Acts 4:15

REJECTION

"But when they had commanded them to go aside out of the council, they conferred among themselves" (Acts 4:15).

Peter and John are in a tense situation! These two uneducated and untrained apostles stand before the most educated men of their day. These Galilean fishermen were with the directors of the schools, the protectors of religious purity, and controllers of worship. With great boldness, Peter and John spoke their hearts. **"For we cannot but speak the things which we have seen and heard"** (Acts 4:20). But they revealed much more than information or data; Jesus was present with them. The same Spirit of God that flowed through Jesus now flowed through these apostles. What the Sanhedrin experienced in their confrontations with Jesus, they were experiencing again with these disciples! **"And they realized that they had been with Jesus"** (Acts 4:13).

The reality of Jesus is the main building on which Luke wants to put an annex. The second word in the Greek text is "te" (Acts 4:14), translated **"and."** Luke uses it differently than "but," a contrast of two ideas, and he uses it differently than "and," a link between two equal ideas. "Te" presents the idea of annexing, demanding a previous idea to add or build on. The main building is Jesus, and the miracle of the lame beggar is annexed to Him. The miracle is never the main building.

Part Three: The Absolute Ratification

However, there is another part to this annex, the contrast *"but"* (Acts 4:15). It suggests two distinct contrasts, each valid and presenting the same conclusion. One contrast is a larger setting than the Sanhedrin and these two apostles. After they were threatened, *"they went to their own companions and reported all that the chief priests and elders had said to them"* (Acts 4:23). We assume this to be the assembling of the early Church believers in Jerusalem. The apostles reported to these believers the threats made by the Sanhedrin about them speaking in Jesus' name. On hearing these threats, the believers immediately began to pray together in *"one accord"* (Acts 4:24). They quoted psalms to each other, not asking for deliverance from the threats, but desiring to be overcome with boldness to proclaim the name of Jesus with increased miracles (Acts 4:29-30). As they prayed, *"they were all filled with the Holy Spirit, and they spoke the word of God with boldness"* (Acts 4:31). The contrast in the annex is that the members of the Sanhedrin rejected and threatened, but the early Church embraced and participated in Jesus' name.

But there is another contrast in the annex, Jesus (the main building) and the miracle (the annex). Luke emphasizes the use of *"standing"* in the previous verse, pointing to the validity of the miracle. Two facts are undeniable; they are the miracle and the source of the miracle. The leaders of Israel *"could say nothing against it"* (Acts 4:14). They made an admission in their own words. *"For, indeed, that a notable miracle has been done through them is evident to all who dwell in Jerusalem, and we cannot deny it"* (Acts 4:16). Their issue was not the miracle; their issue was with Jesus, the source of the miracle. They demanded that Jesus no longer be preached or acclaimed by Peter and John. The apostles could do all the miracles they wanted, but they were to leave Jesus out of the equation. In contrast with the rejection of the Sanhedrin was the acceptance of the apostles. They spoke what they *"have seen and heard."*

They could stop doing miracles, but they could never give up Jesus.

We must carefully examine our verse. *"But when they had commanded them to go aside out of the council, they conferred among themselves"* (Acts 4:15). The leaders of Israel could do nothing about the miracle; it was undeniable. However, they could not tolerate Jesus (the main building). In the Sanhedrin's hearts, and therefore in their actions, they rejected Jesus! Luke gives us elements of their rejection.

Strength of the Rejection

Luke wrote, *"They had commanded them to go aside out of the council"* (Acts 4:15). The Sanhedrin members faced a dilemma. They could not deny the miracle, but they were not going to embrace Jesus. They needed to discuss this among themselves. They ordered the disciple outside the court gathering so they could discuss their situation, and Jesus would not have a place or input in this discussion.

"When they had commanded" is translated from the Greek word "keleuo," used twenty-five times in the New Testament and comes from the primary word "kello," meaning, "to urge on." You can find it used seven times in Matthew's Gospel and eighteen times in the Gospel of Luke. "Keleuo" is always followed by an infinitive, a verb that acts like an adverb giving content to the main verb and always has the same subject as the main verb. In our verse the infinitive is *"to go aside,"* a translation of the Greek word "aperchomai." The accusative or direct object of the infinitive is *"them."* The Sanhedrin desires a closed discussion among their membership, ordering the apostles *"to go aside"* so they will not have input in their discussion.

The Greek word "keleuo" means "to order or command." We see the strength of this order or command in the context of

Part Three: The Absolute Ratification

our passage. These leaders of Israel were rulers in the temple. They marched with force at Solomon's Porch to interrupt Peter's exhortation on the resurrection of Jesus. They captured Peter and John and put them in jail, and on the following day the apostles were on trial for their lives. The Sanhedrin demanded an answer to their question regarding the miracle. Nothing about this context that indicates leniency. This order or command would be enforced by the Sanhedrin and obeyed by the apostles.

This confrontation was a strong rejection by the leaders of Israel. How did they get to this place? They had traveled a long road. The Gospel accounts record their story of rejection. How many times did Jesus interact with them? How many times did the truth penetrate their hearts, bringing them to anger? The leaders of Israel's outrage climaxed with the crucifixion of Jesus. The soldiers rushed from the empty tomb to give an account of the resurrection, but the Pharisees pushed it aside to embrace a lie! Now they were given another opportunity to embrace Jesus through the miracle of the lame beggar. The message of Jesus was preached in Jerusalem and the miracle underscored its validity. However, the leaders of Israel pushed aside the message outside their counsel. Jesus would not have input in their discussion!

These leaders were faithful in worship, church attendance, the hour of prayer, the Scriptures, and the giving of sacrificial offerings, but none of this mattered. What mattered was receiving Jesus through openness, receptivity, desire, and embrace. We must not mistake our faithfulness in devotions, prayer or worship for response, availability, and passion. Do not allow your heart to arrive in the position of rejection! The rejection of the leaders of Israel should convince us to be completely open. The rejection of truth on any level brings us to this destiny. No religious activity can replace of our heart response to Jesus!

Separation of Rejection

Luke wrote that the Sanhedrin *"conferred among themselves"* (Acts 4:15). "Sumballo" is the Greek word translated *"conferred."* "Sum" is the prefix meaning, "to get together," and the main word is "ballo" meaning, "to cast." In the context of our passage, "sumballo" refers to speaking together or conversing. It is a picture of a group of people gathering to discuss an issue or make a decision. The focus of our verse is regarding those not wanted in the discussion. The apostles had been forced to stay outside the room while the Sanhedrin dominated the discussion.

Peter and John were not among the "elite," "the in group." ***"Uneducated and untrained men"*** were not welcome in the Sanhedrin's discussion because their teaching *"greatly disturbed"* this leadership group. Those who taught *"in Jesus the resurrection from the dead"* were considered offensive and therefore not included in the discussion. The apostles were Jewish but they were from a remote section of the country. Galilee was eighty to one hundred miles from Jerusalem. Galilee was an area where men were sometimes involved in non-Jewish influences. The Sanhedrin had to protect the temple, the citadel of Jewish truth, from outside influences of the rougher, lower educated people.

Those who *"had been with Jesus"* would not be welcome in this discussion. The Sanhedrin would not hinder the apostles from teaching the resurrection but teaching *"in Jesus the resurrection from the dead"* would not be allowed. Although the Sanhedrin might not have known, Luke revealed the secret of it all, *"Then Peter, filled with the Holy Spirit, said to them"* (Acts 4:8). The Sanhedrin was not disturbed that the apostles had a past association with Jesus or that they were teaching the doctrine of the resurrection. The Spirit of Jesus flowed through the lives of the apostles, and the Sanhedrin separated themselves from any contact or input from that Spirit.

Part Three: The Absolute Ratification

We need to be practical in our discussion of this passage. These leaders did not deliberately think about Jesus or His Spirit and keep the apostles out of the meeting. But there is a principle of separation dominating the Sanhedrin's decisions and actions. They continually resisted the influence of Jesus on their lives throughout exposure to His ministry. They consistently resisted Jesus' teachings and sought to kill Him throughout His ministry (John 7:1; 30, 44).

After the resurrection of Jesus, the soldiers rushed into Jerusalem from the empty grave to tell all that had happened. Matthew wrote, **"When they had assembled with the elders and consulted together"** (Matthew 28:12). The Greek word "sumboulion," translated "consulted together," presents the idea of a closed group coming together for input and decision. They turned inward to themselves for the decision. They wanted no input from the facts of the resurrection; they did not want the experience of the soldiers to influence them.

Think about what this might do to every decision we might make! If we turn inward to what we have always known, we will decide to do what we have always done. We will never grow or change in our lives. The members of the Sanhedrin placed the apostles outside their group. They did not want the input of anyone who had been with Jesus; they did not want the advice of those filled with the Spirit. They turned into themselves to decide what to do, and their decision was determined by what they had always thought and done.

How would God get through to a group limited by their thoughts? He gave signs, made wonders happen, presented them astonishing miracles they could not deny. Uneducated apostles spoke wisely with boldness in forcing the issue, yet nothing prevailed. These leaders of Israel turned inward and remained in their closed box. What if God wanted to do something new in your life? How would He reveal Himself to you? How would He break you out of your routine patterns? How would He disturb your life? It is easy to approach every decision with the same reasoning we have always had. We consistently experience the same results invariably because we turn inward. Could the present patterns of your life be the intervention of Jesus in your life? Will you allow Him to have input in your living? Now is a moment to be open, receptive, and responsive. We consistently *"crucify again"* for ourselves *"the Son of God, and put Him to an open shame"* (Hebrews 6:6).

Solution of the Rejection

There is an ironic conclusion in the Sanhedrin's final decision. They did not know what to do! In a private meeting, they asked, *"What shall we do to these men?"* (Acts 4:16). On the one hand, a notable miracle was done through the apostles. The miracle was evident to all who dwelt in Jerusalem and even this group could not deny it. On the other hand, this emphasis on Jesus could not be allowed to continue. In order to threaten the apostles, the Sanhedrin allowed them to return. However, the apostles immediately had input into the decision made by the Sanhedrin. Peter and John said, *"Whether it is right in the sight of God to listen to you more than to God, you judge. For we cannot but speak the things which we have seen and heard"* (Acts 4:19-20). The closed-minded leaders did not allow this input to affect them. They threatened them again and could find no way to punish them because all the people were glorifying God for Jesus' miracle through Peter and John.

We could almost feel sorry for the members of the Sanhedrin in their dilemma. They have no solution in themselves and yet they refuse to be open and receptive to the truth from the disciples. This left them in a hopeless situation with nothing but destruction in their future. We know their future. In thirty to forty years, their organization was eliminated and their

Part Three: The Absolute Ratification

nation ceased to exist. They turned within themselves, within the limitations of their strength and self-sourcing, and they had no solution!

The above narrative is the story of our lives. We may respond by saying we are open to the input of others, go to counselors who help us work through our problems, seek the input of friends and family who know our situation, but in the end we exist in the closed box of our humanistic self-centeredness. The dilemma confronting our lives is simple. Our self-sourcing turns to self and considers the input of Jesus as threatening. We explain away miracles, rationalize and dismiss truth, and allow deception to color the path we should travel.

What would Jesus need to do to awaken your heart to Him? But I say to you, "He has already done it!" Paul admonished us, ***"Or do you despise the riches of His goodness, forbearance, and longsuffering, not knowing that the goodness of God leads you to repentance? But in accordance with your hardness and your impenitent heart you are treasuring up for yourself wrath in the day of wrath and revelation of the righteous judgment of God"*** (Romans 2:4-5). His goodness has come in abundance to our lives. As He came to the leaders of Israel, He comes to us. Please respond!

Acts 4:16

CAN I REALLY CHOOSE?

"What shall we do to these men? For, indeed, that a notable miracle has been done through them is evident to all who dwell in Jerusalem, and we cannot deny it" (Acts 4:16).

Many religious circles heavily debate the matter of freewill. However, when we approach the Scriptures, we are confronted with the element of choice in every story. Moses' challenge before the people of Israel was one of the most forceful. His time in leadership had ended. In a final call, he reminded Israel of all they had gone through together. The covenant of God was still before them. ***"I call heaven and earth as witnesses today against you, that I have set before you life and death, blessing and cursing; therefore choose life, that both you and your descendants may live"*** (Deuteronomy 30:19). Joshua called Israel to the same decision. In Shechem, he gathered all the tribes of Israel and challenged them. ***"Choose for yourselves this day whom you will serve, whether the gods which your fathers served that were on the other side of the River, or the gods of the Amorites, in whose land you dwell. But as for me and my house, we will serve the Lord"*** (Joshua 24:15).

Elijah, the prophet, had a similar situation. King Ahab called Elijah, ***"O troubler of Israel"*** (1 Kings 18:17). Elijah challenged King Ahab to gather all Israel on Mount Carmel. He insisted the four hundred and fifty prophets of Baal, and the four hundred prophets of Asherah, who ate at Jezebel's table, should be there. At that gathering, Elijah, a single prophet, presented the challenge. *"How long will you falter between two opinions? If the Lord is God, follow Him; but if Baal, follow him"* (1 Kings 18:21). Israel had to choose! All of us must understand that we face the same dilemma of choice!

The word "choose" in the Scriptures is used in the majority of cases to refer to God's choice rather than human choice. In the Book of Acts, there are five distinct references to God's choices and no references to human choice (Acts 1:2, 24; 9:15; 10:41; 22:14). Paul consistently used this word regarding God's choices. In making a list of "spiritual blessings" God placed in Jesus, Paul said, *"just as He chose us in Him before the foundation of the world"* (Ephesians 1:4). In Colossians Paul highlighted God's choice regarding us. *"To them God willed to make known what are the riches of the glory of this mystery among the Gentiles: which is Christ in you, the hope of glory"* (Colossians 1:27).

God's character is a consistent element in all His choices. God always chooses according to who He is. The determining factor about God's choices is His inner nature. Paul said, *"If we are faithless, He remains faithful; He cannot deny Himself"* (2 Timothy 2:13). God cannot be or choose anything outside of His inner nature. If *"God is love"* (1 John 4:8, 16), nothing God chooses to do will be mean-spirited, vindictive, or wrong. God cannot act in any way that is inconsistent with His inner nature! Despite how His actions may seem to you, the inner nature of God, holy and love, causes His actions. That is why we can always trust Him. We must trust God because He is the only certain and secure thing in our lives.

God's choices arise from His inner nature, are always consistent with who He is, and are based on His divinely chosen plan. God does not discover love in His inner nature and therefore make random choices to express that love. God's choices are purposeful rather than arbitrary, not a random collection of chosen acts or decisions that have no inner goodness, grace, or love. God weaves His eternal design into the daily activities of our lives determining the final history of our world. Paul said, ***"Having made known to us the mystery of His will, according to His good pleasure which He purposed in Himself, that in the dispensation of the fullness of the times He might gather together in one all things in Christ, both which are in heaven and which are on earth — in Him. In Him also we have obtained an inheritance, being predestined according to the purpose of Him who works all things according to the counsel of His will"*** (Ephesians 1:9-11).

How do God's choices relate to you and I? If God's choices arise from His inner nature and are always consistent with who He is, the same is true for those who are made in His image. What blessing and responsibility is ours. God planted the responsibility of choice in the creation of our person! We follow the pattern of God, adhering to the plan He set forth, and choosing according to our inner nature. Two word groups in the Greek language of the New Testament highlight this fact. One is the word group "boulee," meaning "the inner volitional purposes or desires." "Boulema" relates to the mentally directed intentions of a choice. "Bolemai" has to do with a deliberated and free decision of the will. A second word group is "theloo," which refers to the desires, wishes, or will of the person. "Theleema" relates to the will or the intention. Interestingly, that the word group of "thelo" is used two hundred and seven times, while the word group of "boulee" is used thirty-seven times. Although we may logically think of the pros and cons to our decision (boulee), more often than not we will decide based on the influence of how we feel or what we want (thelo). We go to the auto dealership because we want a new car. We allow the car salesman to convince our minds why we should buy his car. The salesman helps us fulfill our desire.

Joseph faced a staggering dilemma. He discovered Mary was with child. How he felt and what he desired (theloo) conflicted with the facts his mind (boulee) needed to process and decide. He logically could not wed Mary because that would be an admission of participation in her sin. However, he desired to protect her because he was *"not wanting* (theloo) *to make her a public example"* (Matthew 1:19). Joseph made the best choice in line with his intention. The moment he received more information from the angel, Joseph responded according to his desire (theloo), his inner nature.

In every area of human life, Jesus is the example of a person living in complete compliance with God's will, but there is never a diminishing freedom of personal choice. How could Jesus live in such consistent obedience? His decisions were a result of the inner nature of His Father. As with the Trinity God, Jesus' choices were determined by His inner nature. Even in the most difficult of decisions, Jesus demonstrated this. Jesus came to the moments when the destiny of His life was no longer something to discuss but something to experience. The last hours of His life were upon Him. He was alone; even the core group of His disciples fell asleep. No one was watching with Him. He did not pray a superficial prayer. *"And being in agony, He prayed more earnestly. Then His sweat became like great drops of blood falling down to the ground"* (Luke 22:44). Jesus prayed three times, and the Scriptures indicate that each prayer session was at least one hour.

The focus of Jesus' prayer was revealed as He cried, *"Father, if it is Your will* (boulomai), *take this cup away from Me; nevertheless not My will* (thelema*), but Yours, be done"* (Luke 22:42). The deliberate and free choice (boulomai) of the Father took precedence over the desires and wishes (thelema) of Jesus. In other words, Jesus was so merged and yielded to the nature of the Father that the Father's desire took precedence over His own. He lived out of His Father's nature! Our choices are not determined by comfort, ease, or safety; they are determined by the nature that controls us.

Every time the Sanhedrin faced a choice, they responded from their nature! They did not try to protect their religious heritage, their theology, or even their temple tradition, but they made their choice about Jesus from the inner nature that possessed them. They chose Barabbas and crucified Jesus! What was the logic of that choice? It was not a choice of logic but a choice of nature. When the soldiers confronted them with Jesus' resurrection, they were again forced to a choice. Would they lie, deny, and reject or would they yield, surrender, and embrace? They responded from their nature.

God invaded their scene repeatedly to bring them to a choice. The apostles stood before them proposing the reality of Jesus and His resurrection. The healed beggar became the logical evidence of the reality of Jesus' presence. The leaders of Israel rejected the chief cornerstone. There was no salvation outside of this Person of Jesus. Now God confronted these leaders again, and He did so through uneducated and untrained men. God used the uneducated to confront the highly educated with the truth of Jesus!

The Sanhedrin commanded the apostles be removed from their group. They would not accept any input from Jesus or His followers regarding their choice. The moment they were alone they raised a significant question, **"What shall we do to these men?"** (Acts 4:16). The prevenient grace of God invaded their lives again in a remarkable manner. By His grace and mercy, God drove them to a choice. The problem was that they did not understand the choice. They believed their choice was about the punishment they should inflict on the apostles. They wanted to stone them to death and be done with them, but they feared the people. What was the proper punishment they should declare?

The question these leaders of Israel asked did not include the choice of releasing the apostles with encouragement to witness for Jesus, and there was no way they would consider becoming disciples' of Christ. They had already chosen to reject Jesus and were now choosing how to punish His apostles. In reality they had made their choice, and their decision came from their nature. In every encounter with Jesus or the truth about Him, their self-centered demonic nature decided to reject. How they would punish the apostles was a mute question because rejection had already been decided by their nature.

The Greek word "poieo" is translated *"do"* in the question, a direct reference to an internal flow of nature producing results. This Greek word is used for trees bearing fruit. **"What shall we do to these men?"** (Acts 4:16). They did not realize what they were asking? "What does our inner nature desire to do to these men?" In other words, it was already decided what they would do. Perhaps they had not decided the details or method of their actions, but their intent was beyond their choice. They could respond only from their nature. As God must respond from His nature, so the Sanhedrin must respond from their nature.

Does this mean that they did not have a choice? They had a choice but not in the area of intent. Their nature did not allow any variance or adjustment to its decision. This fixed intent was true for every area of living in the members of the Sanhedrin. Each choice was an expression of their self-centered nature. That nature permeated their finances, religion, worship, and their relationships with God and all people. They were dominated by their self-centered nature, and this was the deciding factor that cast their votes.

What does this mean? Is freewill a hoax, an illusion? All the choices we make daily are decided by our nature. Is that why the husband cannot refrain from abusing his wife though he says he is sorry? Is that why the drug addict cannot resist taking drugs? Is that why we seem to be mastered by our faults, pride, and hatred? We are mastered by our natures and all our so-called choices are dominated and controlled by it. We have no choice! We are slaves to our natures!

However, we must not be confused! There is freewill and choice. I can choose my nature! My nature may dictate my life decisions, but I can choose my nature. I have a choice about the nature that will dominate my life's direction. Paul said, *"Do you not know that to whom you present yourselves slaves to obey, you are that one's slaves whom you obey, whether of sin leading to death, or of obedience leading to righteousness? But God be thanked that though you were slaves of sin, yet you obeyed from the heart that form of doctrine to which you were delivered. And having been set free from sin, you became slaves of righteousness"* (Romans 6:16-18).

You are either a slave to sin (nature) or a slave to righteousness (nature). In either condition you are a slave. You have no choice about the result of your nature, but you can choose whether your nature will be self-centered or righteous. A logical conclusion is that if I am a slave to sin nature, I will never be allowed to choose the nature of righteousness. But God intervenes in my life by prevenient grace, the grace of God that comes to give us a moment of choice. You and I can in those moments respond to divine movement in our hearts. God will deliver us! Here is Paul's admonition. *"And do not present your members as instruments of unrighteousness to sin, but present yourselves to God as being alive from the dead, and your members as instruments of righteousness to God"* (Romans 6:13).

Jesus gave the Sanhedrin another prevenient grace moment of choice. They could continue to be slaves to their self-centered natures, but they would not have a choice on how they would deal with the apostles. Or they could seize the moment, break with their self-centered natures, and receive the nature of Christ, making all their decisions different because of their change of nature.

Part Three: The Absolute Ratification

The choice of your life is what nature will you choose. Your nature determines your intent (theloo) and your intent determines your inner desires (bolemai). We need struggle no longer with desires, wishes, or intent. We must come face to face with our nature. Here is the choice, the real choice, Jesus or self!

Acts 4:16

SPIRITUAL EYES

"What shall we do to these men? For, indeed, that a notable miracle has been done through them is evident to all who dwell in Jerusalem, and we cannot deny it" (Acts 4:16).

An amazing Old Testament story illustrates the concept of our passage. When God translated Elijah into heaven, the mantle of Elijah fell on the prophet Elisha. Elisha's ministry began to be known for many miracles in Israel. The King of Syria decided to war against Israel. In his private chambers, the Syrian King told his servants where he would establish his military headquarters and camp. God revealed this information to Elisha and warned him of the King's chosen location. The Israelites avoided the territory and thus thwarted the plans of the Syrian King. The King of Syria supposed one of his servants had betrayed him but was quickly informed, **"Elisha, the prophet who is in Israel, tells the king of Israel the words that you speak in your bedroom"** (2 Kings 6:12). The King sent his men to investigate the location of the prophet. When he discovered the town in which Elisha lived, **"he sent horses and chariots and a great army there, and they came by night and surrounded the city"** (2 Kings 6:14).

Elisha's servant arose early that morning and found an army had surrounded them. He ran to Elisha greatly frightened. Elisha said to him, **"Do not fear, for those who are with us are more**

Part Three: The Absolute Ratification

than those who are with them" (2 Kings 6:16). The servant did not understand because they did not have an army. *"And Elisha prayed, and said, 'Lord, I pray, open his eyes that he may see'"* (2 Kings 6:17). The Lord answered Elisha's prayer, and the young servant immediately saw that the mountain was full of horses and chariots of fire.

What we see in the physical is not the complete story. We live in fear, form our conclusions, and surrender our lives to the enemy when horses and chariots of fire surround us. Our enemy is outnumbered and already defeated, but we are blinded to this reality. Paul said, *"But even if our gospel is veiled, it is veiled to those who are perishing, whose minds the god of this age has blinded, who do not believe, lest the light of the gospel of the glory of Christ, who is the image of God, should shine on them"* (2 Corinthians 4:3-4). For those living in defeat, my heart cries, "Oh, if you could only see the victory that surrounds you through Jesus!" If God could open their eyes!

Jesus showed the same concern throughout His ministry. After He battled with the leaders of Israel for an entire Sabbath day, He began to preach in parables because of their blindness. When His disciples questioned Him about this change in preaching style, He said, *"Therefore I speak to them in parables, because seeing they do not see, and hearing they do not hear, nor do they understand"* (Matthew 13:13). He was not trying to hide the truth but to reveal it. How could He get spiritually blind individuals to see what surrounded them?

Spiritual blindness of the Pharisees is the truth of our passage. This is the same group who now formed the Sanhedrin. They did not see the horses and chariots of fire that surrounded Jesus, and now they did not see them surrounding Peter, John, and the healed beggar. Peter was filled with the Holy Spirit (Acts 4:8), and the Spirit of Jesus revealed Himself through Peter's presentation. How could the Sanhedrin miss it? They recognized the influence of Jesus in and through these apostles. The miracle of the lame beggar was undeniable. Horses and chariots of fire surrounded them, but they did not see!

They removed the apostles from their midst, eliminating all spiritual influence from their presence. They asked, ***"What shall we do to these men? For, indeed, that a notable miracle has been done through them is evident to all who dwell in Jerusalem, and we cannot deny it"*** (Acts 4:16). The Greek word "gnostos," translated *"notable,"* is an adjective modifying the main subject, *"miracle,"* and is worth investigation. "Gnostos" is the basic word referring to knowledge, data, or information, is one of four Greek words for "know." All Jerusalem embraced the miracle on this level. The news spread like wildfire as everyone talked about it on the streets. The Sanhedrin knew about the miracle because the healed beggar stood before them. They could not deny it, but they did not know the miracle.

They did not "ginosko" (know) the miracle. The power working at the heart of the miracle did not penetrate their lives. They did not embrace this healed man and enter into the joy of God's touch on his life. The Sanhedrin observed the change in the beggar's life, but they did not experience it. They did not "oideo" (know) the miracle. They did not perceive the Spirit of Jesus moving in his life. The details of transformation that brought wholeness to this beggar's life did not embrace them. They observed a miracle as one would observe a car accident in passing on the highway.

Our lives are full of the same casual observance. God distinctly moves in our midst; we observe, note, and acknowledge the event. We "gnostos" God's presence, but we do not see beyond the data. We argue theology but do not experience the God of theology. We come to church to observe the ceremonies of our God but do not encounter the God of our ceremonies. We participate in the rhythm of the worship songs about Jesus but do not experience the Jesus of whom we sing. We acknowledge the miracle but do not see. What are we not seeing?

Part Three: The Absolute Ratification

The Focus

The Greek word "semeion," translated ***"miracle,"*** is a sign, meaning "an object or act that points to a spiritual reality." The focus of a miracle is never to be on the miracle, but it is to point to something beyond. The ministry of Jesus was filled with "signs" pointing to His Father. For instance, Jesus multiplied the fish and bread to feed more than five thousand men (John 6:1-14). The following day this crowd crossed the sea to find Him. Jesus explained to them why they had searched for Him. ***"Most assuredly, I say to you, you seek Me, not because you saw the signs, but because you ate of the loaves and were filled"*** (John 6:26). Their motive was to get another free meal from Jesus. They did not see (oideo) the miracle, sign. They did not go beyond the physical satisfaction of free food to embrace Jesus. The purpose of the miracle was to reveal Jesus to them. Jesus compared them to their forefathers who received manna from God. They never went beyond the physical bread in the wilderness. The Sanhedrin missed the focus of the miracle, which was to bring them to complete trust in Jesus.

The Sanhedrin observed the miracle of the lame beggar but refused to go beyond the data. The purpose of the miracle was to bring them to an intimate encounter with Jesus. Let us view the progression. The miracle prompted Peter's exhortation, which brought five thousand men to salvation. The declaration of ***"in Jesus the resurrection from the dead"*** (Acts 4:2) so disturbed the Sanhedrin that they arrested the apostles, giving everyone the opportunity for further insight into the purpose of the miracle. Peter, filled with the Spirit, clearly presented Jesus to them (Acts 4:8-12). The miracle was a sign pointing them to Jesus, the focus!

I am humbled as I consider my life. The miracles Jesus has poured on my life are as the sands of the seashore. I treat them as coincidences. I take them for granted. I view them as I hurry to seek my selfish desires. What would Jesus need to do to bring me to Himself? What other miracle would He need to perform? I have received my fair share! I need to focus on what all these blessings of God in my life highlight. How easy it is to criticize the self-centered Sanhedrin when I am as guilty! If every touch of God in my life equaled an inch of spiritual growth, I would be a giant in the faith!

Miracles are everywhere. The fact that the Bible, the Word of God, still exists today is many miracles combined. One evening after a revival service a woman from the congregation informed me of her devotions. She said she was awake at three in the morning studying Bible trivia. Everything she said told me she had focused on data, trivia, and knowledge but did not encounter Jesus. She spent her time investigating side issues and missed the Lover of her soul! The miracle of the Scriptures was a miss for her. Every touch of God on your life is to bring you to Him! Paul described the miracle of nature in this same manner. The wonder of the creation around us is to bring us to Jesus (Romans 1:19-20). The scientists who know the most about the structure of our world should be the greatest of Christians among us. Paul ended his statement with **"so that they are without excuse."**

Once again, God confronted the Sanhedrin with a miracle they could not deny. The miracle came through the uneducated and untrained apostles. Peter and John claimed it was Jesus! The leaders of Israel were forced again to decide about Jesus. It was a miracle with a focus.

The Fullness

The leaders of Israel dismissed the completeness involved in this miracle. They sat in a semicircle with Peter, John, and

Part Three: The Absolute Ratification

the healed beggar standing where all could see them. What did they observe? They saw a once crippled man now standing and walking. They missed the spiritual change that happened in this man's life. The miracle was not a mere correction of bone structure, but a complete healing physically, emotionally, and spiritually.

In Luke's account, he used five Greek words to describe this miracle's fullness. He began with the Greek word "stero," translated *"strong"* (Acts 3:16). The root word means, "to solidify." This word focuses on stable, firm, strong, or strengthened and is used only three times in the New Testament. Once it describes the churches, and twice it describes the healed beggar.

Luke added the Greek word "holokieria" to his description of the miracle (Acts 3:16), translated *"this perfect soundness,"* that focused on integrity, wholeness, and completeness. This is the only time "holokieria" is used in the New Testament. It involves more than mere physical completeness but involves the mental, emotional, and spiritual aspects of the beggar's life.

Luke used the Greek word "sozo" (Acts 4:9), translated *"been made well."* This same Greek word is used again regarding all mankind and is translated, *"saved"* (Acts 4:12), and highlights "to save from mortal danger and death," "disease and possession," "guilt (sin) and alienation from God," and "eternal ruin." The word is used fifty-four times in the Gospels of which fourteen relate to deliverance from disease or demon possession, twenty refer to the rescue of physical life from some impending peril or instant death, and the remaining twenty times to spiritual salvation.

In his response to the Sanhedrin, Peter continued to refer to the presence of the healed beggar standing before them *"whole"* (Acts 4:10). The Greek word "hugies," translated "whole," is used eleven times in the New Testament as an adjective referring to physical health. This word comes from a word group that focuses on rational, intelligent, reliable, and whole. Health implies a proper balance of the whole being, which includes the spiritual.

Luke also called the beggar standing with the apostles *"healed"* (Acts 4:14), a translation of the Greek word "therapeuo," meaning "to worship, to adore, or to relieve." It suggests the idea of attending, serving, and ministering. The acts of healing are not described as medical procedures in the natural laws but rather as manifestations of the divine Spirit pushing back the demonic forces. In the New Testament, "therapeuo" never refers to someone serving secularly.

How could the Sanhedrin have missed it? They did not embrace this miracle or the healed beggar who received the miracle. If they had interacted with him, would they have discovered the depth of Jesus now present in his life? Could they have observed the transformation in this man's purpose and destiny of life? So long as we touch only the physical surface, we will never know the fullness of what God wants to do in the inner heart. The solution to our physical needs seems more important to us than the depth of our spiritual need. We rejoice the physical aspect of the miracle more than the eternal, spiritual alteration in the soul. Our FOCUS misses the FULLNESS!

The Frustration

The Sanhedrin did not see the long-range consequences of their blindness. In their limited vision, their only action was to threaten the disciples *"not to speak at all nor teach in the name of Jesus"* (Acts 4:18). But Jesus was the heart of the miracle. This miracle was a gigantic finger pointing to Jesus. These leaders of Israel were not concerned about the miracle, only the purpose of the miracle. Therefore, their rejection was not about miracles but about purpose, Jesus!

I think it would be significant if we could hear the

testimony of the Sanhedrin's members now. That testimony would probably compare to the *"certain rich man who was clothed in purple and fine linen and fared sumptuously every day"* (Luke 16:19). A beggar lay at the gate of a rich man. Both the beggar and the rich man died and entered their final resting place, the rich man in hell, and Lazarus, the beggar, went to Abraham's bosom. The rich man cried for some meager intervention from Lazarus but that was impossible. The rich man pleaded for someone to be sent to witness to his five brothers. But Moses and the prophets had already given them the truth. Jesus concluded the matter by saying, *"If they do not hear Moses and the prophets, neither will they be persuaded though one rise from the dead"* (Luke 16:31).

The Sanhedrin did not realize that they frustrated the purpose for which God had chosen them. Their rejection of Jesus was the rejection of their destiny. They brought damnation on their nation, which was eliminated a few years later. If they only understood what was offered to them in Jesus!

We can reject the same truth in our lives. What more could Jesus do to communicate to us? The revelation of His reality comes to us repeatedly. This revelation is a call to respond. We must respond to Him to the same degree He reveals His truth to us. All the miracles of our lives point us to Jesus. Let us embrace Him!

Acts 4:17

ALL ABOUT THE HEART

> *"But so that it spreads no further among the people, let us severely threaten them, that from now on they speak to no man in this name"* (Acts 4:17).

The Greek word "kardiognoosta" is an impactive word used only twice in the New Testament, each time in the Book of Acts (Acts 1:24; 15:8), spoken by Peter and attributed to God. "Kardiognoosta" is a combination of two Greek words, "kardio" meaning "the heart," and "gnoosta" meaning "the state of knowing because of relationship and experience." "Gnoosta" is the Greek word "ginosko," giving us a distinct picture of affection and embrace. This word signifies "to be taking in knowledge, to come to know, recognize, understand," or "to understand completely." "Gnoosta" frequently indicates a relation between the person "knowing" and the object known, presenting us with the idea that what is "known" is of value or importance to the one who knows and therefore the establishment of the relationship. This is the word used as a verb to convey the thought of connection or union, as between husband and wife. Matthew wrote about Joseph, **"And did not know** (ginosko) **her till she had brought forth her firstborn Son"** (Matthew 1:25).

When we take this idea of "knowing" and place the word "kardia" as a prefix, we have a knowledge experienced deep in the heart, making a powerful statement. The Old Testament Scripture says, *"the life of the flesh is in the blood"* (Leviticus 17:11). The heart is the source of life. "Kardia" is never used in the New Testament for the physical organ but always refers to the spiritual core of man's being. "Kardiognoosta" can be translated "heart-knower" and is attributed to only God!

Jesus demonstrated this "heart-knower" in His ministry. He consistently proposed God's concern for the heart, and in the Sermon on the Mount He highlighted the heart. The twisted "tradition of the elders" continually focused on surface, physical activities, but Jesus pointed to the attitude and inner motive of the heart. Jesus clarified the defilement of human life, *"Not what goes into the mouth defiles a man; but what comes out of the mouth, this defiles a man"* (Matthew 15:11). He quoted Old Testament prophecies, *"These people draw near to Me with their mouth, and honor Me with their lips, but their heart is far from Me"* (Matthew 15:8). Jesus used the imagery of the "cup and dish." *"For you cleanse the outside of the cup and dish, but inside they are full of extortion and self-indulgence"* (Matthew 23:25). Jesus gave us the imagery of "white-washed tombs." *"For you are like whitewashed tombs which indeed appear beautiful outwardly, but inside are full of dead men's bones and all uncleanness"* (Matthew 23:27). If anyone is to be faithful to the ministry of Jesus, he must concentrate on the heart-condition. What is the heart like?

The apostles maintained the concern about the heart in their ministry to the early Church. As the lame beggar received healing of his physical condition, God also transformed his spiritual heart. The healed beggar remained connected to Peter and John even when they were put in jail and brought to trial (Acts 4:14). The healed beggar contributed to the influence and presence of Jesus sensed by the Sanhedrin. Jesus confronted these leaders of Israel again with the issue of the heart. However, they refused this focus on the heart and continued their obsession with the physical aspects of life.

The heart can never be eliminated from the equation. When these leaders of Israel focused on the physical they revealed their hearts. Even when man denies his heart, He exposes his heart because it is impossible to eliminate the heart or its expressions from your life. What you and I are in our hearts is revealed in our living! We can see this clearly in our passage.

Heart' Concern
"But"

Our passage (Acts 4:17) comes at the close of the private conversation held by the Sanhedrin. The members heard Peter's explanation and became deeply aware of Jesus' presence. They could not discredit the miracle because the healed beggar stood before them. They were dumbfounded. They finally called for a private conversation among themselves. They eliminated any influence or message from Jesus through the apostles. **"When they had commanded them to go aside out of the council, they conferred among themselves"** (Acts 4:15).

In this closed, self-focused discussion, the Sanhedrin decided their next action against the apostles. First, they noted that there was nothing they could do about the miracle. They could not erase or discredit it because the healed beggar stood before them. Everyone in Jerusalem was talking about it, trapping the Sanhedrin into an admission that a miracle had happened.

The concluding statement of these leaders of Israel begins with **"but."** This word is neither a translation of "de" (but) that expresses contrast nor a translation of "kai" (and) that links two equal ideas. The word is a translation of the Greek word "alla," "on the contrary." "Alla" indicates the difference with or contrast to what precedes. As the Sanhedrin began their discussion, they asked, **"What shall we do to these men?"** (Acts 4:16). They declared their chief dilemma, a miracle they could not deny. It

Part Three: The Absolute Ratification

was a notable miracle with which everyone in Jerusalem was now familiar. They admitted, ***"And we cannot deny it"*** (Acts 4:16).

The first word in our passage (Acts 4:17) is the Greek word "alla." The Sanhedrin could not deny that a notable miracle was done, but their response was astounding. WE DO NOT CARE. We do not care about the evidence that is standing before us. We will not allow it to sway or influence our hearts. From the core and source of our lives, we have decided. The evidence does not sway us! We choose to ignore it and maintain our heart's concern. We want stronger and more compelling evidence of a miracle.

WE DO NOT CARE what the prophet's spoke. Peter can quote the writings of King David, but we do not care. We will not apply the prophecy of the Psalms (Acts 4:11; Psalm 118:22). Our heart's concern will determine how we translate and interpret every prophecy of the Old Testament. We choose not to come with an open mind and heart to allow the Word of God to shape and determine our hearts. We have our agenda, dictated by our hearts, and we do not care about the prophecies.

WE DO NOT CARE! Maybe we sinned when we crucified Jesus. Others can repent, but we will not. We will protect our heart's concern. We will continue to fight for the elimination of everything connected to the name of Jesus. Though we witnessed the presence of Jesus flowing through Peter and John, it will not detour us. We will calm our emotions, conquer our fears, and sear our conscience for maintaining our self-centered heart's concern. If we are wrong, we do not care.

WE DO NOT CARE what the consequences might be. Although we may set in motion the loss of our nation in forty years, our temple is destroyed, and Jerusalem becomes a plowed field, we must cling to our self-centered heart's concern. We must protect and maintain our pride. We will not be moved. Our decisions may damage others, but we do not care. We will not change what drives us from our heart's concern.

WE DO NOT CARE about truth! We will shape what

we believe from the dictation of our heart's concern. If Jesus is truth, then we will choose the lie. The Roman soldiers may burst through our door declaring Jesus' resurrection from the dead, but we will pay them to tell the lie that the disciples stole His body. We know that did not happen, and the soldiers know it as well, but we do not care about the truth. We care only about our heart's concern. We are driven, controlled, and dominated by what is in our hearts.

The attitude of the Pharisees is in sharp contrast to the response of those who heard Peter's sermon at Pentecost. As the truth flowed from Peter, powered by the Holy Spirit, **"they were cut to the heart, and said to Peter and the rest of the apostles, 'Men and brethren, what shall we do?'"** (Acts 2:37). This truth changed lives, and those who received that truth embraced Jesus. The wrong became right. Maybe we should care! What if that caring leads our hearts to seek truth and reality? Is Jesus calling us to a new heart? It is time for our self-centered heart's concern to yield to the loving heart of Jesus. Our self-centeredness deceives and twists us to care for wrong things! Maybe we need to care about what concerns us, change what is false and destructive, and allow Jesus to change our "heart's concern."

Heart's Concentration
"so that"

The Greek word "iva," translated **"so that,"** is used as a marker in the statement, denoting purpose, aim, and goal. "Iva" can be translated "in order that." The rest of the verse gives the purpose, aim, or goal of maintaining and protecting the "heart's concern." Because we do not care about anything except our heart's concern, we do not care what we have to do to achieve that concern.

In the "Heart's Concern," we went to some length to declare

that the leaders of Israel did not care. We may have said it loud enough to leave you thinking they did not care about anything. Because their heart's concern was so strong, they cared about nothing else. That concern governed their approach to all areas of life, religious observations (Matthew 23:3-4), dress code (Matthew 23:5), and relationships with others (Matthew 23:6-7). They were controlled by their heart's concern for self. Their prayer life and compassionate ministries were shaped by self-centeredness (Matthew 23:14). Their evangelism determined their heart's concern (Matthew 23:15), their honesty and integrity of character exposed their self-love (Matthew 23:16-22), and their self-concern dictated their giving to the church (Matthew 23:23-24). Their self-centeredness caused them to focus on externals and ignore the inner being (Matthew 23:25-28). Their "heart's concern" governed their "heart's concentration." They were focused on themselves.

Have you noted the concerns of those around you? Some are concerned about fashion and how they look while others have a passion for expensive automobiles. Sports or fishing, hunting, and guns obsess some people. Job opportunities and climbing the corporate ladder is the concentration of many. There are always people focused on religion like the legalistic Christian whose concern is the law, or those focused on the answers to prayer, always looking for a miracle. The numbers of people in their sanctuaries is of utmost importance to some. Is it wrong to have a concentration to one's heart concern? Absolutely not! In fact, it is necessary to have a heart's concern. That concern is the nature of who we are! Our heart's concentration should so dominate our lives that we will do anything necessary to ensure its achievement. Regardless of what form our concentration takes, it is either self-centered or Jesus-centered.

The single threat to our heart's concentration on self is Jesus! The moment Jesus touches our life, He threatens the core concentration of our heart. We have to eliminate Jesus *"so that"* we can maintain our self-centered heart's concern. Jesus bombarded the leaders of Israel for three years. They argued with Him, tried to trick and embarrass Him, plotted His murder, and bribed the necessary people to bring about His death. They accepted Barabbas, a violent criminal, as their choice to free at the feast rather than Jesus. To cover the resurrection of Christ, they embraced a lie. Now here they are again! What must they do *"so that"* Jesus is eliminated?

Heart's Conclusion
"speak"

How strong or severe is the determination of this heart's concentration? Self-centeredness will not tolerate the presence of Jesus. You can adopt and adapt everything else but not Jesus. Self-centeredness can accept and use other religions but not Jesus. I can embrace rules and contribute to my pride but not Jesus. Materialistic things can supply my self-centeredness but not Jesus. Self-centeredness must eliminate Jesus!

The Greek word "laleo," translated "speak," focuses on the act of speaking. "Laleo" is contrasted with "lego," which has to do with what we speak. Therefore, in our passage the leaders of Israel proposed any act of speaking that does not contain Jesus was acceptable. Speaking about Jesus would not be tolerated.

The doctrine of the resurrection could be argued between the Pharisees and the Sadducees with fervor, and they were not disturbed. What disturbed them was, **"that they taught the people and preached in Jesus the resurrection from the dead"** (Acts 4:2). This teaching was unacceptable. Spreading the news of miracles was of no consequence, but miracles in the name of Jesus had to cease. The Sanhedrin had little interest in the proposed messiahs and schemes of salvation being taught by many, but they had no tolerance for, **"Nor is there salvation in**

Part Three: The Absolute Ratification

any other, for there is no other name under heaven given among men by which we must be saved" (Acts 4:12).

The one deterrent to victorious Christianity is our distraction from Jesus, the heart of Satan's master plan. Everything he flashes before us is to allure us from Jesus. His one endeavor is to eliminate Jesus from your life. He will allow you to embrace every form of self-centered attractions to cloud the face of Jesus. He does not care how wicked or religious you become so long as it is not Jesus. He even uses our problems to side track us from Jesus.

Christianity is intimacy with Jesus. He wants to merge with your life to form a new creature that is indestructible. The Spirit-filled and Spirit-focused person thwarts the forces of hell. The issue of every hour is what position Jesus has in your life. How is your relationship with Him? Is your heart's concern filled with a heart concentration on Jesus? This is the "heart's conclusion!"

Acts 4:17

SUPERIMPOSING

"But so that it spreads no further among the people, let us severely threaten them, that from now on they speak to no man in this name" (Acts 4:17).

We all have experiences that influence our lives. I was impacted in my early days of ministry by an experience that has become an illustration I use often. A couple came to our church for help with their wedding. We were excited about affecting their lives with Jesus as they established their new home. After weeks of planning and involvement, we united them in a beautiful marriage ceremony. However, we were disappointed when they did not attend church after their honeymoon and made no attempt to remain in fellowship. Finally, I went to call on them.

The new husband greeted me with excitement. He grabbed me by the arm and ushered me into a special room in their home. His face expressed joy and enthusiasm as he introduced me to something important in his life. He proudly pointed to a shelf lined with bowling trophies as he gave me details of the victories that earned him these magnificent prizes. In two hours he had covered only half of them. He was squeezing and releasing a rubber ball in his hand as he talked. I interrupted him to ask about the ball. He explained that he was strengthening his bowling hand. When I quizzed him about the open books and materials on his desk, he informed me that he was studying bowling techniques. I expressed my concern that they had not been to church since their honeymoon. He informed me that church did not fit into his bowling schedule because the tournaments were on the weekends, and he had to practice his bowling throughout the week. When I asked about his work, he said it was just a job to support his bowling. His deepest desire was to be a professional bowler.

This young man was not bad, but he superimposed bowling on every aspect of his life. His schedule, plans, mental involvement, learning, physical body, and all of his interest were about bowling. Bowling, although not evil, was the most important thing in his life. He had superimposed bowling on the totality of his existence and was completely dedicated to this sport.

In another example from my early days in ministry, I spent some time with a young father from our farming community. He drove grain-filled trucks from the fields to be unloaded at a mill several hours away. I accompanied him on one of these trips. As we waited to unload the grain, we overheard a conversation between two men shoveling the excess grain that had fallen during the previous unloading. You would think these men would be tired after a day of difficult work, but one man told the other that when he left work he spent his night with prostitutes. Cursing under his breath, all his sentences were related to sexual activity.

What an evil man! He took his God-created body appetite and superimposed it on every aspect of his life. His language, thought process, job, schedule, physical life, sense of pleasure, and attitude were all about sexuality. He dedicated himself to one thing.

I had no problem labeling him evil, but how does he differ from the bowler? The young man, dedicated to bowling, certainly was more acceptable in respect to family values, social structure, and morals. Most of us would be comfortable spending an evening bowling with him. The men in our examples have definite differences, but they are not different in the spiritual realm. The Bible teaches that when we superimpose anything other than Jesus upon our lives, we sin. Therefore, sin is not determined by the activity of a deed but by the relationship of that deed to Jesus. That is a narrow view. If these deeds are not of Jesus, even the best deeds, including religious activities, can be sin.

Your response to this might be, "I am not dominated by one thing. I would never superimpose my hobby or selfish desires upon my life." But will you look at this in the spiritual realm? Your inner nature superimposes itself in every area of your living. You might brag that bowling, sexuality, money, career, or achievement of your goals are not superimposed upon your life, but is it possible that your nature influences every area?

The influence of your nature on your life is the biblical case! We see this truth depicted in the account of man's fall. After man sinned, he experienced the full consequences of his sin. **"And they heard the sound of the Lord God walking in the garden in the cool of the day, and Adam and his wife hid themselves from the presence of the Lord God among the trees of the garden"** (Genesis 3:8). God called out to Adam. When Adam finally revealed himself he said, **"I heard Your voice in the garden, and I was afraid because I was naked; and I hid myself"** (Genesis 3:10). God responded, **"Who told you that you were naked? Have you eaten from the tree of which I commanded you that you should not eat?"** (Genesis 3:11).

God commanded Adam and Eve to not eat of one tree in the Garden. He did not randomly select a fruit tree and mark it off limits to tempt them. The issue of man's sin was not his disobedience. Whatever was involved in this tree would change man's nature and therefore his perspective. When Adam and Eve ate of the tree, they felt guilt for the first time and hid themselves, not because of their disobedience but because their perspective had changed. They were no longer the same in their nature. God created man with a nature dependent on Him. This dependence enabled a merger, oneness, and interaction between God and man. When man sinned, he no longer saw with the eyes of God but saw through his own eyes. Man's nature was no longer God dependent but had become independent. Sin superimposed itself upon every area of man's life, and his nature became sinful and self-centered, even in his sexuality. Man's nature dominates, influences, and controls every action, decision, and involvement. When as Christians we embrace a nature change, we move from self-sourced to God-sourced.

Our passage demonstrates and contrasts the difference between a God-sourced nature and a self-sourced nature. The self-sourced nature can be seen in the extreme irritation of the Sanhedrin. Peter and John consistently superimposed Jesus upon every situation of life. The Sanhedrin discussed the healing event and agreed, ***"But so that it spreads no further among the people, let us severely threaten them, that from now on they speak to no man in this name"*** (Acts 4:17). The Sanhedrin's objection was not about the apostles' teaching, preaching, or miracles. Their objection was that they superimposed Jesus upon all of life. The preposition "in" is not the Greek word "en" that would indicate a fixed position. "Epi" expresses the basic idea of "upon"! Jesus sourced the apostles' lives, influencing and superimposing Himself upon every aspect of their lives. Peter referred to Jesus in every conversation. When he was asked about the miracle of the lame beggar, he took no credit for himself but highlighted Jesus. The heart of Peter's preaching was Jesus! He taught only Jesus. Peter superimposed Jesus upon his entire life! This was the problem raised by the Sanhedrin.

The idea of miracles presents the SUPERNATURAL area of life. Every miracle has two aspects, the wonder and the sign. The "wonder" comes because God intervenes in the natural course of our world and alters it. We are astonished! The "sign" is the miracle acting like a billboard pointing to Someone beyond the intervention. If a person were privileged to be an instrument for the Divine flow of God's power in daily circumstances, why would he not assume credit for it? Such a person would have to be special in his relationship with God, special in his gifting from God, and special in administering this power to such needy people. Although he might not be the source of the miracle's power, he is the instrument of the power. This deserves recognition.

Peter said, *"Let it be known to you all, and to all the people of Israel, that by the name of Jesus Christ of Nazareth, whom you crucified, whom God raised from the dead, by Him this man stands here before you whole"* (Acts 4:10). Where does Peter claim recognition for this miracle? Would not a self-centered nature manipulate God's power for self-advantage and fame? Would not a self-centered person superimpose his standing upon the miracle? How could he resist taking some credit for self-advantage? Yet, there is not a hint of self-focus in Peter's proclamation.

How can a person superimpose Jesus upon every accomplishment of his life? He would have to be cleansed of all self-centeredness and embrace his helplessness in a consistent surrender. At every moment he would need to be conscious of his dependence upon Jesus. He could not separate his dependence in his religious moments from his secular circumstances. He would have to live in the complete superimposing of Jesus upon all aspects of his living.

Self-centered people are greatly irritated by the superimposing of Jesus upon all life's activities. Self-centered people use God for their self-centered ends; they "con" Him for self-advantage, self-comfort, and self-appeasement. Self-centeredness is spontaneous in them; they cannot help themselves. Peter was *"filled with the Holy Spirit"* (Acts 4:8), which caused the disturbance with the Sanhedrin. They could

Part Three: The Absolute Ratification

not deny the miracle of the lame beggar (Acts 4:16), but they do not care about it. They cannot accept Jesus superimposed upon the miracle. The Sanhedrin does not have a problem with miracles in general so long as the apostles cease to impose Jesus upon the miracle.

The apostles were always superimposing Jesus upon SALVATION, which was worse in the eyes of the Sanhedrin. No one is against being saved. Everyone has a sense of guilt and a desperate need to be rescued. This is a fundamental need of all world religions. On one of our mission trips, my wife and I were standing in the shadows of a religious temple in the busy city of Taipei, Taiwan. We witnessed the consistent rush of people from the local streets seeking some kind of salvation. The temple had three main sections, one containing a statue of Confucius, the second a statue of Buddha, and the third a statue of Jesus Christ. Various items were available to be used to present your need to one of the gods represented by the statues. Candles were available to light to call attention to a personal need. They could purchase fake money and burn it at the feet of at least one statue. To request direction from one of the gods, the people could purchase a cluster of sticks to be dropped at the feet of each statue. Depending on how the sticks landed a person received future decision-making. The drive of the human life is to find salvation!

In my responsibility as assistant chaplain in our local county jail, I am amazed at the reasons inmates request a Bible. Many of these men and women have never read or studied the Bible. But in the desperation of their incarceration, they seek some manner of deliverance, some answer to the failure of their lives, or some guidance to a better way. Can a person find salvation in the success of their career, the achievement of helping others, keeping religious laws, the immorality of self-centered living, their alcohol or drug addiction, or the hours of their prayer life?

How would a self-centered life achieve salvation? Would

it not focus on self-achievement? Would not laws and religious activities be at the heart? The Sanhedrin lived their lives in such a self-centered approach. How could they tolerate Peter's statement, *"Nor is there salvation in any other, for there is no other name under heaven given among men by which we must be saved"* (Acts 4:12)? Peter left no room for any addition to the person of Jesus in regard to salvation! Salvation is found only in Jesus. Not in Jesus plus good works; not in Jesus plus religious activities; not in Jesus plus laws. It is just in Jesus! Peter superimposed Jesus upon salvation.

A person filled with a self-centered nature can never feel comfortable with such a narrow view. Self-centered people may admit that Jesus is involved, that His death is important, but they have to play a role in their salvation. They think they have to do something that contributes to and increases their salvation. They must receive credit for their repentance. In their minds it is Jesus plus their repentance that saves them! Then they can brag about how they finally came to their senses and mustered the courage to come to Jesus. But Peter indicated that we do not come to Jesus; Jesus comes to us. Salvation is exclusive to the action of Jesus. We receive His grace!

The apostles also superimposed Jesus upon the SEERS, the prophets of old. Peter and John claimed everything that happened in Jesus' life was a fulfillment of Old Testament prophecies, proposing Jesus as the message of the prophets. To the crowd gathered at Solomon's Porch, Peter said, *"But those things which God foretold by the mouth of all His prophets, that the Christ would suffer, He has thus fulfilled"* (Acts 3:18).

The Old Testament prophets had a sense of disconnection as they addressed the need for social reform in their period of history. We can learn from their prophecies how God dealt with nations, instructed through the law, and established patterns of worship. This is good information for us to know, but it does not affect our daily living. Peter implied that everything the prophets wrote pointed to Jesus, and every page of the Old Testament declared His coming. In the same way Peter confronted the Sanhedrin with the prophets of old, the crucified Jesus confronts us now in the fullness of the Holy Spirit. Peter superimposed Jesus upon the message of the Old Testament. This superimposing can be very disconcerting to the self-centered person.

We have enough problems adapting to the requirements of religion without imposing Jesus as a companion in living. To have God in church is one thing and to have Him in the marketplace is another. If Jesus lives in the human being, will he ever have a moment to call his own? Jesus will influence and dominate that life. If I desire this type of influence for my life, the only possibility for me is to let the message of the prophets be fulfilled in me. I must superimpose Jesus upon my life.

The worst thing for the Sanhedrin was that the apostles superimposed Jesus upon the SOVEREIGN God. Peter and John believed everything God did was centered in Jesus. Their source of connection was again the prophets. Peter boldly accused the Sanhedrin of rejecting the stone that God selected to be the chief cornerstone of redemption's structure (Acts 4:11). Peter explained this on Solomon's Porch when he said, **"The God of Abraham, Isaac, and Jacob, the God of our fathers, glorified His Servant Jesus, whom you delivered up and denied in the presence of Pilate, when he was determined to let Him go"** (Acts 3:13).

Does the sovereign God have only one plan, one idea, and one desire? Is His solution only in the revelation of Jesus? Does this mean to deny Jesus is to deny everything God wants to do in my life? Do I face only one decision, what will I do with Jesus? Will I allow His Person to envelop my life, His presence to influence every aspect of my living, and His wisdom guide every decision of my will? My relationship to Jesus is the only issue of Christianity!

Acts 4:18

ELIMINATE

"So they called them and commanded them not to speak at all nor teach in the name of Jesus" (Acts 4:18).

"There is no middle ground with Jesus." That is the concept I want to share with you as we begin our study. My goal is to establish a foundation of truth from the Scriptures, the platform from which the Holy Spirit can do His deep work in our lives. Only He can produce a response from our hearts. We can never be lukewarm with Jesus. Our involvement with Him is never casual.

Why were the leaders of Israel motivated to eliminate Jesus? He had involved Himself in the lives of their people and reduced their suffering. Although He healed masses of people, these leaders sought to crucify Him. Matthew wrote of Jesus' power and fame as He ministered in Galilee. ***"Then His fame went throughout all Syria"*** (Matthew 4:24), a foreign country bordering Palestine. ***"Great multitudes followed Him — from Galilee, and from Decapolis, Jerusalem, Judea, and beyond the Jordan"*** (Matthew 4:25). Jesus' fame was widespread, and the crowds plotted to make Him their king (John 6:15).

The Pharisees had difficulty with Jesus because their focus was on the law, the traditions of the elders. In their minds their Jewish lifestyle was protected by their six hundred and thirteen oral traditions. Jesus was disturbing the core of their establishment, their basic patterns of life. The sacrificial system gave them control over the people politically, financially and spiritually. Jesus came with the New Covenant. If the New Covenant superseded the Old Covenant, their present position of leadership would be gone. Although Jesus' ministry brought many benefits, these Pharisees felt the traditions that they held dear were severely threatened. They had to eliminate Jesus!

The Pharisees moved to put radical measures in place! The crucifixion was extreme, but Jesus was undermining their essence of Jewish control. Although miracles and compassionate ministries were valuable, the Pharisees felt their enforcement of the religious and political system made Judaism great. The leaders of Israel asked for the release of the **"*notorious prisoner called Barabbas*"** (Matthew 27:16), which they considered a small compromise compared with the goal of saving Judaism. They made a choice between Jesus and everything they cherished!

Do you see that the heart of the issue has not changed? The leaders of Israel, especially the Sadducees, faced the same pressure. Although Jesus and the early Church found favor with the populace of Jerusalem, there was a fundamental threat to the core of the religious and political system of the Jews. Even though these threats were factors in the elimination of Jesus' name, there is something more basic, my life! If Jesus is the Messiah, and there is no salvation outside of Him, then everything else is wrong. In every message, Peter proposed Jesus as the One they crucified. They chose Barabbas over Jesus; they killed the Prince of life. To embrace Jesus meant a complete change in their thought process. If Jesus indwells me, I will not be in charge of my life. Jesus would be Lord, and my self-centeredness repels even the thought of that. Jesus and self-sovereignty cannot dwell in the same life. Jesus must be eliminated; He must be crucified.

However, in our culture we are much more advanced and sophisticated. We would never be so cruel that we would crucify

Jesus. Such treatment would be distasteful to our educated and refined view, but in the spiritual realm the elimination is the same. Society simply cannot tolerate Jesus. The writer of the Book of Hebrews said, *"they crucify again for themselves the Son of God, and put Him to an open shame"* (Hebrews 6:6).

The lack of tolerating Jesus is the truth in our passage. The leaders of Israel had participated in the physical crucifixion of Jesus. They voted on the committee; they pressured Pilate; they manipulated every circumstance to eliminate Jesus. Now they were doing the same to Peter and John. They did not use nails or bring blood, but the intent was the same. Jesus' name must never be spoken again. They wanted His name eliminated, crucifying Him again in the spiritual realm.

Not tolerating Jesus is also true in our lives! We sit in the crowd and hear the same message. God's sovereign control challenges our self-centeredness. He comes to us as Lord, and we choose to be our own Lord. We have to eliminate someone; someone has to die. If I do not die to my self-centeredness, then I crucify Jesus again.

The details of our passage are specific. Let us look at them together.

Personal

The power of Jesus moves through Peter to heal the lame beggar. That creates a stir in the temple because everyone is familiar with this man. Peter confronts the crowd with a message about Jesus and five thousand men respond (Acts 4:2). The leaders of Israel capture Peter, John, and the healed beggar and bring them before the Sanhedrin the following day. Peter again declares the message of Jesus, confronting these powerful men of Israel with the Jesus they crucified. These leaders must decide again what they will do with Jesus. They cannot continue to live for themselves and at the same time accept Jesus; they must eliminate Him.

The apostles are taken outside the court, and the leaders of Israel turn inward to decide. They cannot deny that a miracle has happened. However, they cannot tolerate Jesus. *"So they called them and commanded them not to speak at all nor teach in the name of Jesus"* (Acts 4:18). The Greek word "me," translated *"not"* is personal.

There are two basic Greek words that present the negative. One is the Greek word "ouk," a negative regarded as universal truth and is undisputable. In other words, "ouk" expresses direct and full negation independently; therefore, it is objective. But in our passage the Greek word "me" implies a conditional and hypothetical negation and is subjective.

The Sanhedrin turned inward to their self-centeredness. Their conclusions were a result of their selfish desires and thoughts. They did not express a universal truth or propose biblical truth. They did not act as prophets of God repeating truth from the Divine. They gave their opinion. Their decision was that to control their world the name of Jesus could never be spoken again.

The Scriptures are clear in declaring our involvement in the crucifixion of Jesus. Paul discovered this in his life and applied it to our lives. Because my self-centeredness crucified Christ, I must either be crucified with Jesus or continue to crucify Him. Listen to Paul's cry in Galatians. *"But God forbid that I should boast except in the cross of our Lord Jesus Christ, by whom the world has been crucified to me, and I to the world"* (Galatians 6:14). *"I have been crucified with Christ; it is no longer I who live, but Christ lives in me; and the life which I now live in the flesh I live by faith in the Son of God, who loved me and gave Himself for me"* (Galatians 2:20).

This knowledge brings me to a crossroads. My sin produced a physical cross in a physical world. Now that this has happened,

Jesus confronts my spiritual world with the fact that I will either continue to crucify Him, or I will join Him in His death. Only one person can reign in my life, Jesus or me; therefore, someone has to die so someone else can live. I have a personal decision. I cannot maintain my self-sovereignty and embrace Jesus. Unless I embrace Him, I must eliminate Him.

Percentage

Surrendering my life to Jesus' is so radical. Why can't I just love Jesus more? I haven't given Jesus all my life, but I am willing to give Him some of it. I am willing to surrender enough of my life to Jesus to receive the benefits of the Christian faith. If Jesus will allow me to live my life the way I want now, I will give Him my eternity. That seems like the best alternative to me. Do we not realize that giving Jesus a part of us is not possible in Christianity? Jesus' nature demands my all and nothing less.

"So they called them and commanded them not to speak at all nor teach in the name of Jesus" (Acts 4:18). The Greek word "phtheggomai," translated *"speak,"* is an unusual word used only three times in the New Testament. Luke uses this word only in our passage, and Peter uses the word twice in his second epistle (2 Peter 2:16, 18). Peter, while speaking of false prophets, gave the illustration of Balaam from the Old Testament. God used a dumb donkey to speak (phtheggomai) with a man's voice to communicate to Balaam. Peter described the false prophets as speaking (phtheggomai) with swelling words of emptiness. Now Luke uses "phtheggomai" as the command from the Sanhedrin. Peter and John were *"not to speak* (phtheggomai) *at all nor teach in the name of Jesus."*

Luke could have used two other Greek words. "Lego" refers to the content of speaking. Why did he not use "lego"? The members of the Sanhedrin were concerned about the content of

Part Three: The Absolute Ratification

the apostles' message and its focus on Jesus. "Lalo" refers to the act of speaking. The leaders of Israel did not want the people to be affected by what the apostles were saying. Everything Peter and John said contained the name of Jesus. But Luke did not use either "lego" or "lalo."

This Greek word "phtheggomai" refers to speaking or uttering a sound, but it also has a tone of "absolute" in its meaning. In other words, "phtheggomai" refers to a clear and unmistakable communication, and in our passage it is negative. The Sanhedrin demanded in every way that the name of Jesus never be mentioned again. These leaders did not want the name of Jesus "to ever pass through the lips of the disciples." Therefore, Luke used the Greek word "phtheggomai," and he strengthened its meaning with the word "katholou," translated *"at all."* "Katholou" means "whole, entirely, or completely." Our passage is the only place this Greek word is used in the New Testament."

Self-centered men made demands on the apostles. They demanded the elimination of Jesus' name from their vocabulary. Peter used Jesus' name when he took the lame beggar by the right hand and lifted him to his feet. He cried, **"In the name of Jesus Christ of Nazareth, rise up and walk"** (Acts 3:6). Pete also used this word for the resurrection from the dead. **"They taught the people and preached in Jesus the resurrection from the dead"** (Acts 4:2). The issue for the capture and now the interrogation of the apostles was, **"By what power or by what name have you done this?"** (Acts 4:7). Peter's answer was unmistakable. **"By the name of Jesus Christ of Nazareth, whom you crucified, whom God raised from the dead, by Him this man stands here before you whole"** (Acts 4:10). In fact, Peter declared, **"Nor is there salvation in any other, for there is no other name under heaven given among men by which we must be saved"** (Acts 4:12).

If Christianity was a religion, we might participate in degrees. Some would be more dedicated than others. If

Christianity were ceremonies, a person might participate more or less than others in such ceremonies and still qualify. If it is an organization called "church," people might join but not be faithful to the services. But Christianity is Jesus? You are either His or you are not; there are no percentages. Either you are in the light or in the dark; there is no gray. You must eliminate Jesus or embrace Him fully.

Power

Why is it that we must either eliminate Jesus or embrace Him? The answer resides in the power of His person. This power source is what concerned the Sanhedrin. ***"By what power or by what name have you done this?"*** (Acts 4:7). They recognized the power that produced the miracle of the lame beggar was contained in the name of Jesus! ***"So they called them and commanded them not to speak at all nor teach in the name of Jesus"*** (Acts 4:18). They repeated the previous verse, ***"that from now on they speak to no man in this name"*** (Acts 4:17). They highlighted the power of this statement recognizing the absolute power of the name of Jesus.

Although the power of Jesus' name was unquestionable, the vehicle of this power was in the superimposing, ***"in** (epi) **the name."*** From the previous verse, we learned that "epi" presents the idea of "upon." Peter and John consistently superimposed Jesus upon every situation. They were under the influence of His person. Everything about them from their attitudes, actions and purposes fell under the control of Jesus. Everything the Sanhedrin experienced from Jesus before the crucifixion, they were now encountering in the apostles. How could that be? The Spirit and nature of Jesus was superimposed, merged, and influenced upon every aspect of these apostles' lives. Jesus was not present in one compartment of their lives only. They did not partition Him off

Part Three: The Absolute Ratification

in the religious section of their living, restraining His access to all other aspects of their lives. Jesus dominated, invaded, and determined every arena of their existence. They superimposed Him upon their total living.

If you do not find completeness in Jesus, you must eliminate Him from your existence. The nature of a relationship with Jesus means He superimposes Himself upon your life. You cannot partially involve Him in your living. He does not visit with you or set up appointments to meet with you. He is not a counselor you visit or a guest in your home. The lame beggar did not receive only a healing from Jesus; Jesus invaded his life and worked a miracle in him. We face a decision. We will either belong to Jesus or we will not belong to Him. He will be Lord of all, or He will not be Lord at all. There is no half way, partial, or maybe involved in a relationship with Jesus. He will superimpose Himself upon every area of our lives, or we will not speak of Him at all. It is our choice!

Acts 4:19

DISCERNMENT

"But Peter and John answered and said to them, 'Whether it is right in the sight of God to listen to you more than to God, you judge'" (Acts 4:19).

Peter was *"filled with the Holy Spirit"* (Acts 4:8). This fact is highlighted in our study-verse and the verse that follows. This statement gave insight beyond Peter's wisdom and understanding. This statement was logical, but it also clarified the spiritual condition of the leaders of Israel. Peter forced these leaders to recognize that their traditions violated God's requirements.

The phrase, **"But Peter and John answered and said to them"** has the same sentence structure and wordage used when the devil tempted Jesus in the wilderness (Matthew 4:1-11). Jesus was in an extreme spiritual war with the devil for forty days and nights, leaving Him exhausted and hungry. He had not eaten during the forty days, and when He finally tried to relax, His body screamed from physical hunger. It must have been overwhelming. The devil leaped to the occasion with a piercing temptation. Jesus could have easily taken His Divine power and transformed the stones into bread. Eating is not a sin; bread is not unrighteous. What would have been the harm?

"But He answered and said, 'It is written, 'Man shall not live by bread alone, but by every word that proceeds from the mouth of God'" (Matthew 4:4). Matthew presents a contrast between Jesus and the devil. He uses the Greek conjunction (de), translated "but." The devil tempted Jesus to violate the sourcing of the Father in His life. He called Him to a reversal of the incarnation and asked Him to reject what He just experienced in the baptism, the fullness of the Spirit. Jesus knew the presence of the Father, *"descending like a dove and alighting upon Him"* (Matthew 3:16). The Father empowered Jesus with the Spirit and added to their intimacy. This empowerment was not for a task or mission. The oneness between God and man happened in this Man, the beginning of the New Covenant! The devil refused and still refuses to live dependent on God. He asked Jesus to join him in self-sourcing. This was the heart of the devil's temptation of Jesus.

"He answered and said." "Answered" is a verb in the participle form, in the nominative case, making it an adjective that modifies the subject of the sentence. This is a specific Greek word beginning with the prefix "apo," which means "from," and the root word "krino," meaning "to separate, discern, or judge." This answer is not to speak or make a statement but to respond in relationship or reference to the preceding circumstance. This is an answer not lightly suggested but one that is done with discretion and discernment, receiving further strength due to the article attached to it. "The answering" is a more likely translation. Therefore, the subject of the sentence is the act of Jesus' carefully listening to the mind of the Father who sourced Him as He expressed the "answer." What is the Father's opinion? Jesus will not let any action come from His life not sourced by the Father! The devil pressed Jesus with a physical temptation. Jesus did not respond until He ran back to the arms of His Father and evaluated and discerned the Father's heart. He knew He could not trust His hunger drive. He was overwhelmed with His physical need and could not properly evaluate it in the moment. Was there a trick in all this? How could Jesus tell? He must know the mind and heart of His Father!

When we are self-sourced, we respond quickly and react without discernment. We do not see the complete picture; there are dynamics happening beyond a physical need. The Spirit-sourced person must know the heart of the Spirit. What are the thoughts of the Spirit?

In our passage the verb of the sentence is *"said."* The same Greek word, "eipen," used for the speaking of the tempter in the preceding verse (Matthew 4:3) and is the same Greek word translated *"said"* in our verse. Two other Greek words can be used for *"said,"* "laleo," the act of speaking, and "lego," which concentrates on the content being spoken. The Greek word "eipen" is insignificant in our passage. We are encouraged to ignore its use and move to the statement the devil made. That statement is what matters! The devil suggested that Jesus should reverse the incarnation and not be a man sourced by the Spirit. Jesus set aside all He had as God in the incarnation. He could take back what He had as God and source Himself. Jesus refused to make a snap decision, relapsed into the arms of His Father, and cried for His wisdom and counsel. He evaluated the circumstance with the Father. His decision was either to trust the Father's provision for His life or live out of Himself?

Peter's situation copied Jesus' temptation, and every temptation follows this pattern. The language and grammar are the same, beginning with the contrast, *"but."* Would Peter join the Sanhedrin in self-sourcing, or amid their threat would he trust the Spirit of Jesus filling him? The Sanhedrin put the apostles outside and *"conferred among themselves"* (Acts 4:15). They did not want the insight, evaluation, or discernment from Jesus! What was the response of Peter and John? They responded by running to the wisdom of Jesus' Spirit to guide them.

Every temptation contains this element of decision. Will I run to the wisdom of *"Christ in you"* (Colossians 1:27), or will I source myself? The circumstances of your temptations will differ from time to time. Sometimes your temptations

Part Three: The Absolute Ratification

come through your physical drives and other times through persecution. But the temptation is always the same. Will I listen to Jesus or myself? Peter highlighted this in his statement to the Sanhedrin. *"Whether it is right in the sight of God to listen to you more than to God, you judge. For we cannot but speak the things which we have seen and heard"* (Acts 4:19-20).

There is a contrast of LISTENING! Peter's statement contrasts the idea of "listening to God" or "listening to the Sanhedrin." He used the Greek word "akouo," often translated "to hear" and is sometimes expanded to include more than physical hearing. It takes on the meaning of understanding and responding positively. Jesus explained His shift to preaching in parables to, *"hearing* (akouo) *they do not hear* (akouo)*, nor do they understand"* (Matthew 13:13). "Akouo" is the root word Paul used to describe the response of children to their parents. *"Children, obey* (hupoakouo) *your parents in the Lord, for this is right"* (Ephesians 6:1). The prefix "hupo" presents the idea of "under." "Akouo" is the response of one subordinate. Every translation I have found translates this word in Ephesians as "obey." Simply keeping the rules of your parents is not enough, but Paul encouraged children to listen, come under the influence, or permit their lives to be shaped by their parents. This is in the content of "akouo."

The Sanhedrin lived in reverence to the reality of Jehovah. The strength of their belief in God had kept them from wavering in their loyalty for four hundred years. They experienced tension and endured many disturbances during Pilate's reign over Judea. Pilate sent a military unit of Roman soldiers to Jerusalem, causing a revolt among these leaders of Israel. These leaders revolted because the military used standards that displayed the image of the emperor. The image offended to the Jews because of their unwavering commitment to one God; there must be no graven images in their Holy City.

Peter proposed a major question to this group. What did

they recommend the apostles do now? Should they listen to the Sanhedrin and their commandment or listen to the sovereign God in which the Sanhedrin believed? The apostles wanted to know who should influence their lives? Were they to obey God or the Sanhedrin? We live with the same dilemma. Who are we going to allow as the influential force governing our lives? Will our immediate circumstance have control over us, bending to what is comfortable to us? Will we allow those with a selfish agenda to dictate our decision? To whom will we listen? There will always be a Sanhedrin or other worldly power waiting to control us. But Jesus whispers in the background. We must make a choice!

SPEAKING is also a contrast. God is speaking! We must answer a question about this issue quickly. Jesus has not left us alone to our reason, designs, and efforts. It seems as if Jesus abandoned us for moments in history and our personal past. But that is false! The difficulty seems to be the blindness or deafness of the human spirit to recognize God's voice.

Elijah knew victory in Israel. Fire from the hand of God demonstrated His power and presence. The fire consumed the sacrifice, the altar of stone, and the water. The prophets of Baal were slaughtered; evil was defeated. Could the movement of God in the human life be more evident? Ahab, the King of Israel, told Jezebel about the Divine intervention. She sent a messenger to Elijah with a report. ***"So let the gods do to me, and more also, if I do not make your life as the life of one of them by tomorrow about this time"*** (1 Kings 19:2). Elijah ran for his life into the wilderness, sat down under a broom tree, and prayed that he might die. He went to sleep, and an angel touched him and told him to rise and eat. He looked, and there was a cake baking on the coals and a jar of water nearby. After Elijah ate, he slept again. Again an angel touched him and told him to eat. On the strength of this food he traveled forty days and nights to Horeb, the mountain of God. He went into a cave and slept. God spoke to Him. ***"What are you doing here, Elijah?"*** (1 Kings 19:9). Elijah told God how dedicated he was and how he was alone because all the others prophets had been killed. He lamented that even his life was threatened.

God told Elijah that he should go out and stand on the mountain before the Lord. A wind tore into the mountain and broke the rocks in pieces, but God was not in the wind. An earthquake followed the strong wind, but God was not in the earthquake either. Then the mountain was swept by fire, but God was not in the fire. However, after the fire came a still small voice, the voice of God! We, the people of the New Covenant, should understand this far beyond Elijah of the Old Covenant. In the intimacy of the indwelt Spirit of Jesus, would we not live in the moment-by-moment instruction and guidance of His Spirit?

The Sanhedrin's of the world will always yell at us through the wind, earthquakes, and fire. The clamor and noise of the immediate crisis demands our attention. We are moved to adjust to what is comfortable for the moment. This crisis is a call to wait, run to the arms of Jesus, and evaluate by merging with His mind!

We cannot refute the logic of such a suggestion. Even the Sanhedrin would admit we should listen to the speaking of God rather than the demands of their counsel. The problem is discerning His voice. Would you consider that there are not many voices speaking to us? The only other voice besides God, despite the form it takes, is the voice of self. Self is so deceptive it often seems to be the voice of God. Self is the voice of logic because it often makes sense amid the circumstances. Self will always speak with the tradition of religion, like the case of the Sanhedrin.

The deterrent to self-deception is a determined openness to Jesus. If you want to hear His voice regardless of the circumstances, He will speak. He is not silent. He knows your language, experiences, and level of understanding. He will not speak in ways you cannot understand. Jesus has committed

Discernment | Acts 4:19

Himself to communicate to you. You cannot miss His will, unless you want to. We must do as Jesus, Peter, and John did. We must close off the noise of the circumstances and run back to the arms of Jesus. He will embrace us in evaluating and discerning the needed response for our moment. He is speaking!

The SUPPLY has a contrast. Peter and John told the Sanhedrin that they *"cannot but speak the things which we have seen and heard"* (Acts 4:20). In other words, they reacted to the threat of their religious authority. They responded to the moment-by-moment movement of God in their lives. They lived with Jesus for three years. Yes, they argued with Him and miscalculated His call, but after the resurrection they acquired new understanding. In the fullness of the indwelt Spirit of Jesus at Pentecost, they had new revelation. All the teaching and purpose of Jesus from the previous three years became clear to them. They understood the Scriptures in light of Jesus' presence.

The Sanhedrin did not have a spiritual connection with God. They responded from the self-centeredness of their own thinking. They adjusted their religious experiences *"to be seen by men"* (Matthew 23:5). Their interpretation of Scriptures was made from their logic dictated by their selfishness. The Sanhedrin could also say, we *"cannot but speak the things which we have seen and heard"* (Acts 4:20). These leaders of Israel only had one view. They lived out of the things they had seen and heard from their relational connection with self. On the other hand, the apostles lived out of their relational connection with Jesus. The things they had seen and heard determined the words they spoke. The Sanhedrin and the apostles were trapped in their relational connection.

However, God again intervened in the narrow world of the leaders of Israel. Prevenient grace bombarded their closed lives. The call came from the heart of God to their hearts; moments of spiritual clarity were granted to them. But note their response. They quickly placed the apostles outside the council so they could confer among themselves. They refused these moments when God broke in on their closed relational connection with themselves. This left them without excuse.

How often have you said, "I am just this way"! The undercurrent of this statement is that we cannot do anything about it. We are also dominated by our relational connection with ourselves and must express ourselves as we have seen and heard. Our platform of operation is one of self-centeredness. We cannot do anything about it.

But that is the message of this passage. God is not satisfied to leave you there. He consistently breaks through your world. "Healed beggars" intersect your schedule. Messages from the apostles bombard your ears. You recognize another possibility of "seeing and hearing." How will you respond?

Acts 4:19

WHAT IS RIGHT

"But Peter and John answered and said to them, 'Whether it is right in the sight of God to listen to you more than to God, you judge'" (Acts 4:19).

"I am doing my best!" This is a statement we here daily from people around us. Every counseling session begins with each party proclaiming they are doing their best. The scribes and the Pharisees considered their accomplishments through the law of God and the traditions of the elders as the best they could do. How can we expect any more from our fellowman? If we require more than a person's best, we smother them in discouragement and defeat. Many religious movements require too much from their followers, setting a standard beyond a person's capabilities. And on the opposite side we can reduce the standards and expect too little, which produces a lack of commitment and laziness.

Jesus confronted this issue at the beginning of the Sermon on the Mount. He presented the standard for the Kingdom of Heaven. ***"For I say to you, that unless your righteousness exceeds the righteousness of the scribes and Pharisees, you will by no means enter the kingdom of heaven"*** (Matthew 5:20). The standard of righteousness for the scribes and Pharisees was "do your best," and requiring anything beyond "your best" was ridiculous. No one can accomplish more than their best, unless there is an infusion of additional power and presence beyond the person. If this infusion happened, the standard of "my best" would become insignificant. This is the call to be filled with Jesus! Would this take me to a new level?

"Doing your best" was the conflicting issue between the apostles and the Sanhedrin. The lame beggar's miracle of wholeness bespeaks the impartation of power beyond a human being doing "his best." The Sanhedrin admitted this when they questioned the apostles, ***"By what power or by what name have you done this?"*** (Acts 4:7). They acknowledged that the apostles were an instrument to something or someone beyond themselves. The Sanhedrin readily admitted, ***"that a notable miracle has been done through them"*** (Acts 4:16). What upset the Sanhedrin was that the apostles insisted that Jesus was that someone! Peter and John had not done their best; they were filled with the Spirit of Jesus.

When a person refuses the infusion of Jesus' Spirit, there are limits for living. One of our boundaries for living becomes our knowledge, and we cannot go beyond our understanding. We "do the best we can." This was never the intent of God for one made in His image. We were created to be an expression of His best. All the qualities of His nature are to be the expression of our living. The Kingdom of God cannot accept anything less.

Jesus expressed this through six illustrations in His Sermon on the Mount. He contrasted the best the scribes and Pharisees could do with the actions of the person filled with the Spirit of Christ. The scribes and Pharisees considered the best they could do was to not murder, but the Kingdom calls Christians not to be angry (Matthew 5:21-26). The scribes and Pharisees considered their sexuality a simple body drive to be curbed. The best they could do was not commit adultery with their neighbor's wife. Jesus enables the Christian to express the heart of God through their sexuality, because the heart of God changes our view concerning of sexuality (Matthew 5:27-30). The scribes and Pharisees considered their best was giving their wife a certificate of divorce when they wanted to embrace someone else. The mind of Christ is concerned with what a husband "causes" in his wife (Matthew 5:31-32). The best for the scribes and Pharisees was telling the truth only when they had to; Jesus advocated integrity and full-time honesty (Matthew 5:33-37). The scribes and Pharisees saw their best as doing to others what others did to them; Jesus expressed the redemptive heart of God that never lived for self (Matthew 5:38-42). The best for the scribes and Pharisees was to love their neighbor and hate their enemy. Jesus died for those considered His enemies (Matthew 5:43-48). The best we can produce through our discipline and strength will never match merging with His Spirit! Why would we hesitate to surrender the core of our lives to Jesus? The fullness of who God intended us to be is found in this merger!

This surrender is the challenge Peter and John proposed to the Sanhedrin. They said, *"Whether it is right in the sight of God to listen to you more than to God, you judge"* (Acts 4:19).

Sight

The Greek word "ei," translated *"whether,"* is a conditional conjunction, often translated "if." In Peter's statement it established two distinct conditions demanding the judgment of the Sanhedrin. The first condition is "if it is right in the sight of God to listen to you." The second condition is "if it is right in the sight of God to listen to Jesus."

The phrase *"in the sight"* is a translation of the Greek word "enopion." This word is a compound word containing "en" and "ops." "En" is our English word "in." The two movement terms in English and Greek are "from" and "into." "In (en)" is a fixed position without movement. "Ops" is the face or area around the eye. Therefore, our lives are in a fixed position before the sight, face, or presence of God. Everything about us is seen and

Part Three: The Absolute Ratification

known by the Trinity, the arena for man's every action. What we say, how we say it, and when we say it, are done in His sight. You and I have the freedom of choice. We can live as we will, but you and I will do it in His sight because there is no privacy from Him.

One of the strong characteristics of man's self-centered nature is privacy. Self-centeredness wants no supervision regarding the normal aspects of life. After all, we have a right to our privacy. We want no one entering our property, no solicitation, or even a pastoral call. What I do behind the closed doors of my house is my business. The phrase "what's done in Vegas stays in Vegas" has been expanded to many arenas of our lives. It is the human heart's expression and desire to experience places and times in absolute privacy.

It is understandable and acceptable that God would have some input into our lives, but with a limit! Limitless involvement is the problem we have with His position as Lord, King of Kings. If He is King as the president who lives in Washington, DC, we have no difficulty because that supervision is over areas of interest that we are not capable of controlling. I need someone to handle the interaction with the nations of the world, the road system, taxation, and many other problems. I do not have the time or the interest to deal with those issues. I am willing for the president to handle those matters, but I do not want his interference in personal matters. I know Jesus loves me. I am willing to relinquish control of my eternal destiny, evangelization the world, and control of the church. But I have desires and involvements that are private matters. His involvement in those things is not necessary.

David, the psalmist, was deeply aware of the consistent and penetrating sight of God on his life. Listen to his words,

> *"O Lord, You have searched me and known me.*
> *You know my sitting down and my rising up;*

You understand my thought afar off.
You comprehend my path and my lying down,
And are acquainted with all my ways.
For there is not a word on my tongue,
But behold, O Lord, You know it altogether.
Psalm 139:1-4

"Where can I go from Your Spirit?
Or where can I flee from Your presence?
If I ascend into heaven, You are there;
If I make my bed in hell, behold, You are there.
If I take the wings of the morning,
And dwell in the uttermost parts of the sea,
Even there Your hand shall lead me,
And Your right hand shall hold me.
If I say, 'Surely the darkness shall fall on me,'
Even the night shall be light about me;
Indeed, the darkness shall not hide from You,
But the night shines as the day;
The darkness and the light are both alike to You."
Psalm 139:7-12

We have no privacy from His Spirit. This is true for the Christian and for the non-Christian. Everything we do is in His sight! The difference between the Christian and the non-Christian is not in His knowledge of the circumstance, but in His involvement. Everything is done in the sight of God for the non-Christian. But the Spirit of Jesus indwells the Christian. Jesus is not only aware of what the Christian is doing but He participates in it. We have no activities on our own. There is no service rendered apart from His involvement. He is the source and power of life's expression of the believer.

Part Three: The Absolute Ratification

Standard

Everyone has an opinion about what they see. Two individuals can witness the same event and each has a different account of its details. A person's understanding is determined by their inner perspective or nature. God's inner nature determines how He evaluates what He sees. God is love (1 John 4:8, 16). God is holy (Leviticus 11:44). Every detail is dominated by the view of God's redemptive nature. He never sees or evaluates with selfish anger or impatience. The last public proclamation of Jesus is recorded in Matthew's Gospel (Matthew 23). He gives "seven woes" to the scribes and Pharisees in their absence, warning His disciples to not be like the Pharisees. Jesus interacted with the scribes and Pharisees for three years. He discerned their inner motive through the eyes of His Father. He was not scolding them when He cried, ***"How often I wanted to gather your children together, as a hen gathers her chicks under her wings, but you were not willing! See! Your house is left to you desolate"*** (Matthew 23:37-38). Jesus was not angry; He was not punishing. He was judging and evaluating all their acts and rejections through the standard of the God's redemptive heart.

God's discernment has strong ramifications for our lives. When we are filled with our self-centered natures, how will we evaluate what we see? Our evaluations will be determined by the effect it has on us. No consideration is given to the context of hurt, distress, or pain for the person we encounter. Nothing but judgment, belittlement, and demeaning comes from our view. But what about the person who is filled with the mind of Christ? Listen to Jesus words from the cross. ***"Father, forgive them for they do not know what they do"*** (Luke 23:34). That is an expression of how the Father sees things through the eyes of Jesus!

In our passage, Peter appealed to this "sight." He challenged the Sanhedrin to allow their threats to be placed *"in the sight of God."* To know truth they needed to remove their decisions and thoughts from the dominance of self-rule and move to the heart of God. To arrive at and maintain their conclusion, they placed the apostles outside the counsel (Acts 4:15). Without input or influence from the apostles, Jesus, or the Father, the Sanhedrin could threaten the apostles to eliminate the name of Jesus. Elimination of Jesus' name cannot be done when we seek the face of God, and it is the challenge for our lives. Although nothing can be done that He does not see, it is vastly different to open our lives to His perspective. Once the Sanhedrin placed the apostles outside the counsel, *"they conferred among themselves"* (Acts 4:15). Although God saw all this, He was not consulted or brought into the discussion. Our lives are all being lived *"in the sight of God,"* but are we consulting Him? Have we conferred among only ourselves? If so, we never live beyond our decisions, strengths, and desires. The standard becomes our limited abilities. We can live in His sight, and He can be our standard. The destiny and resource of His person can be ours as well as His limits.

Insecurity plagues our lives. Fear gnaws at the soul of man bringing him into bondage. Even "the best we can do" does not remove this haunting sensation; we are limited. There are too many variables beyond our control. We were not created to be the god of our lives. Our security is in Jesus and only Him.

Selection

Here is the most disturbing part. *"You judge."* This is the translation of the Greek word "krino." It means to discern, evaluate, or judge. This is the root word used at the beginning of our verse, *"But Peter and John answered* (apokrino)." Peter

Part Three: The Absolute Ratification

and John challenged the Sanhedrin to do what they had done. The Sanhedrin must select, but it will not be done in ignorance or in privacy. They must come into the full sight of God and decide. What is the significance of this? Their decision to threaten the apostles was done in an attempt of privacy without the sight of God. Now they must decide to listen to themselves in the context of God's influence while they are in the full blaring sight of God. They cannot hide.

Ultimately we all come to this place of living in the sight of God. The prevenient grace of God continually injects His influence, "His sight" calls us. How gracious He is! He will not leave us alone. In the bondage of their self-centeredness, the Sanhedrin will again push the pressing presence of God aside. God was pulling them to go beyond themselves but they would not. They listened to themselves rather than to God.

You and I can choose *"in the sight of God."* Are we listening to ourselves, or are we listening to God? Data or information is not the key. We do not come to a counselor to get advice or are not called to follow a friend's advice. This is a call to reverse our self-governing attitude to embrace Jesus, whom we crucified, whom then God raised from the dead. This is moving from private interpretation of our needs to embrace everything *"in the sight of God."* We must move from "doing our best" to the fulfillment of "His unlimited best" in and through our lives. Logically this shift makes total sense; yet, self-centeredness fights to maintain its control. ***"You judge!"***

Acts 4:20

A KNOWING BELIEF

"For we cannot but speak the things which we have seen and heard" (Acts 4:20).

The Greek word "pistis" is a noun most often translated "faith." The Greek word "pisteuo" is a verb most often translated "believe." The noun and the verb occur two hundred and forty-three times each in the New Testament. John used neither word in his second and third epistles. He used only the verb in his Gospel account and the first epistle, and in the Book of Revelation he used only the noun. Paul used the noun form only in Colossians and Philemon. Peter used this noun form only in his second epistle. Because the verb and the noun can express the same meaning, these two words are treated as the same.

The ways these two Greek words are frequently used demonstrate that this is a central theological concept of the New Testament. These words represent the correct relationship to God and ultimately the essence of Christianity. The Gospel (good news) focuses on believing in or having faith in Jesus! All other subjects are shaped by this basic proposition. Therefore, a key element in every decision in Christianity is about faith in Jesus.

Faith in Jesus is the fundamental premise of Peter's three messages delivered thus far in the Book of Acts. His beginning message was an explanation of Pentecost (Acts 2:14+). Three to five thousand Jews wanted to know what one hundred and

Part Three: The Absolute Ratification

twenty disciples of Jesus had experienced. The outpouring of the Spirit was explained in terms of Jesus. Jesus came in response to the plan of the Trinity God. Filled with the Spirit of God, Jesus demonstrated the nature of God in His life. Though the Jews were responsible for crucifying Jesus, God delivered Jesus to redemptive death and raised Him from the dead. Jesus was raised to sit at the right hand of the Father where He received the promise of the Spirit. This promise was poured out on the believers, and the New Covenant came into place! Those hearing this message *"were cut to the heart"* (Acts 2:37). They cried for instruction on how to respond. The issue was clear. They must believe in Jesus! In their disbelief they crucified Jesus; now in their belief they must embrace Him.

Peter's second message was delivered at Solomon's Porch (Acts 3:12+). The healing of a lame beggar brought a crowd of five to ten thousand people into the temple. As they marveled over the miracle, Peter accredited the miracle exclusively to Jesus. Jesus was the One they crucified, denied, and exchanged for a murderer. Peter declared, *"And His name, through faith in His name, has made this man strong, whom you see and know. Yes, the faith which comes through Him has given him this perfect soundness in the presence of you all"* (Acts 3:16). Though the leaders of Israel interrupted this gathering and placed Peter and John in jail, five thousand *"of those who heard the word believed"* (Acts 4:4). In disbelief they crucified and denied Jesus, but now they believed!

The Sanhedrin was not satisfied. They had Peter, John and the healed beggar brought before them. They demanded to know, *"By what power or by what name have you done this?"* Peter told them it was in the name of Jesus. Jesus was the One they crucified, but God raised Him from the dead. There was no chance of salvation outside of embracing Jesus. They must change their minds about Jesus. They crucified Him through disbelief; they must now embrace Him through faith! But this was the dilemma; they would not believe. The evidence was everywhere; God gave many demonstrations. They cannot deny the miracle, but they will not embrace Jesus through faith. In fact, they do the opposite. *"So they called them and commanded them not to speak at all nor teach in the name of Jesus"* (Acts 4:18).

The demand of the Sanhedrin that the apostles were never again to preach in the name of Jesus presented a huge problem. Peter and John believed in Jesus. What were they to do? *"Whether it is right in the sight of God to listen to you more than to God, you judge"* (Acts 4:19). They asked the Sanhedrin to put themselves in their position and judge. Should they do what the Sanhedrin commanded, or should they respond and obey the One in whom they believed? Before the Sanhedrin could answer, Peter declared, *"For we cannot but speak the things which we have seen and heard"* (Acts 4:20).

Procedure of Belief

One such moment was the occasion of Jesus' question, *"But who do you say that I am?"* (Matthew 16:15). Peter gave an expression of faith that truly impressed Jesus, *"You are the Christ, the Son of the living God"* (Matthew 16:16). Jesus congratulated Peter because He recognized that Peter connected with the mind of His Father. The expression was a significant statement of belief, but though Peter's answer was right, his belief was flawed. Belief is much more than the declaration of a concept. Belief is an issue of what you know in the heart of your being. As great as this belief statement was, it did not cause Peter to be faithful at the crucifixion of Jesus. This belief enabled him to return in confession and repentance, but it was not adequate for victory.

Multitudes of people struggle with this dilemma. They declare their faith in Jesus, but they deny Him in their moments of temptation. They quote the theology of who Jesus is, the Christ, the Son of the living God, but it does not carry them through to faithfulness. "I want to be His," they cry. They know the function and patterns of religious activities, but they cannot maintain victory. They do not doubt His reality, but Jesus is not real to them. They believe without knowing!

What a statement Peter makes to the Sanhedrin! After Pentecost, Peter moved from thinking to knowing it was true. That knowledge enabled him to speak strongly to the Sanhedrin. His belief system changed because he spent forty days and nights with the resurrected Lord. He rose in the middle of the night to be sure Jesus was still there. He ate with the resurrected Jesus. They traveled together; Jesus taught him. Luke said it was ***infallible proofs*** (Acts 1:3). At the close of these forty days, Peter watched the ascension of Jesus. As He ascended, Jesus promised to send His Spirit to fill them. They must tarry in Jerusalem. The embracing of Jesus in the fullness of His Spirit took Peter to a new level of belief. He experienced intimacy with Jesus beyond the physical connection he knew as a disciple. Merging with the heart, mind, and nature of Jesus gave Him new perspective. Peter lived in the power and resource of Jesus' Spirit. He now knew victory over temptation. Signs and wonders, such as the healing of the lame beggar, began to flow from him as he lived in this fullness. Wisdom and knowledge became his as the mind of Christ merged with his mind. His belief in the past became "knowing" in the present. He did not relate to the Sanhedrin the traditions of his past, the typical learning from the synagogue, or information he gathered by experience. He knew Jesus! Faith became knowing! No wonder he cried, **"For we cannot but speak the things which we have seen and heard"** (Acts 4:20). Peter did not speak what he hoped was true or what he believed might be true. He proclaimed to the Sanhedrin and to his world what had become reality in his life. Belief became knowing!

The Greek words "pisteuo" and "ginosko" are related in the Scriptures. "Ginosko" is one of four Greek words for "knowing," and it is a relational term having to do with experience. The knowledge continually increases with experience. The association of these two words indicates that the structure of faith includes an element of recognition and knowledge. Knowledge is not a stage beyond faith, but is rather a structural element of faith.

The Jews wanted to stone Jesus. Listen to His instruction to them. ***"If I do not do the works of My Father, do not believe Me; but if I do, though you do not believe Me, believe the works, that you may know and believe that the Father is in Me, and I in Him"*** (John 10:37-38). Jesus challenged them to embrace the power of God flowing in His works. They believed in the reality of a Messiah. Could they know the presence of the Father in the works and belief in Jesus, and allow the Messiah to grip their hearts?

In His "High Priestly Prayer," Jesus prayed, ***"For I have given to them the words which You have given Me; and they have received them, and have known surely that I came forth from You; and they have believed that You sent Me"*** (John 17:8). The disciples believed in Jesus, and their belief was linked with all He had said and done with them. Their belief about Jesus became belief in Jesus through that interaction. They knew!

In John's first epistle, he presents God as love. He challenges us to love each other as God loves us. This can happen only when we are indwelt with God's nature, love. Because of this embrace or experience, ***"we have known and believed the love that God has for us. God is love, and he who abides in love abides in God, and God in him"*** (1 John 4:16). Although we think God loves us, we must come to the reality of that knowledge. He does love us; we know this because of our interaction with Him, and abiding in Him and Him in us.

The Scriptures are specific about the process of believing and knowing. We do not know and then believe. Peter said, ***"But***

also for this very reason, giving all diligence, add to your faith virtue, to virtue knowledge" (2 Peter 1:5). Do not be confused. Our comprehension, figuring it out, or understanding is not what creates faith. Our belief opens the door to experientially embracing Jesus and knowing Him. We must not demand knowledge first; it always follows faith. Jesus told us, ***"If anyone wills to do His will, he shall know concerning the doctrine"*** (John 7:17). If you believe and allow that belief to create desires in you, Jesus will certainly give you the knowledge of Himself!

Peter and the members of the Sanhedrin believed in a coming Messiah. However, Peter's faith interacted with Jesus, and He now knows. In the midst of the Sanhedrin's threats, Peter could only ***"speak the things which we have seen and heard"*** (Acts 4:20). Many of us rank with the members of the Sanhedrin; we have a belief system. We have been raised in the church and a culture that teaches Jesus. However, we do not know; our belief has not become knowledge. We believe He is love, but we live in fear. We believe He saves, but we are insecure and anxious. We believe He intervenes in the lives of His people, but we struggle daily to survive. We believe, but we do not know!

Particularity of Belief

The particularity of belief is that we know Jesus! Knowing Jesus was at the heart of Peter's statement to the Sanhedrin. ***"For we cannot but speak the things which we have seen and heard"*** (Acts 4:20). What is it that they ***"have seen and heard"***? It is Jesus! Jesus encountered the disciples, and they became fishers of men. Jesus took the power in Him and transferred it to the disciples, sending them out to minister in His name. Each miracle was a new revelation of the flow of His Spirit. Even the tragedy of Peter's denial, a denial of his belief, was focused on Jesus. His denial was not a theological denial but a denial of the person of Jesus. The knowledge added to faith in the resurrection was an interaction with the resurrected Jesus, not a seminar on eternal life. Peter's belief took on the knowledge of the eternal world through Jesus. The fullness of the Spirit descended on Peter, and Peter merged with the Spirit of Jesus. People were impacted when Jesus stood beside Peter as his master. But Jesus sourcing Peter's existence was mind blowing.

In our passage, Peter was threatened by the Sanhedrin to eliminate the name of Jesus from his vocabulary. This demand was not about changing his philosophy of life or altering his theological position but was about what he had *"seen and heard."* This silencing was not about a religious belief taught by his parents or about the Jewish culture in which he lived but was about the living Christ encountering and filling him. How could Peter possibly deny the name of Jesus ever again? His faith had become knowing.

As we study the Book of Acts, we discover the state of those who won the world to Christ. How did Stephen see *"Jesus standing at the right hand of God"*? (Acts 7:55). He could see because he was *"full of the Holy Spirit"* (Acts 7:55). Stephen's belief had the quality of knowing, and the Spirit of Jesus gave him sight beyond ordinary ability. How did Paul and Silas sing and experience an earthquake in the Philippi jail (Acts 16:25)? The belief system of a doctrine can never reach this level. Paul and Silas embraced Jesus in the midst of their daily lives extending change to a slave girl. They did not confront the *"spirit of divination"* in her as an attempt of deliverance. They did not wonder whether they were able. Their belief had moved into knowing. All the way through the Book of Acts, we are brought back to embracing Jesus in daily experience, knowing Him in intimacy.

This knowing has to be a proven truth in our lives as well! Faith will not take on the quality of knowing except as it focuses on interaction, relationship, and oneness with Jesus.

Part Three: The Absolute Ratification

Jesus is the point of belief! Correct theology, legal observances, or denominational standing is not the point. "Knowing" takes place only with Jesus!

Power of Belief

Peter had a tone in his statement. ***"For we cannot but speak the things which we have seen and heard"*** (Acts 4:20). Two Greek words are in the translation of ***"we cannot."*** The Greek word "ouk" is an absolute, independent negative, not dependent on the opinion of the speaker. "Ouk" is an indisputable, self-evident negative. The verb "dunamai" focuses not on the resource itself but on the action of the resource. It has to do with "being able to do." This is not a matter of choice. In other words, Peter was not saying that we choose not to keep silent but to speak what we have seen and heard. He said that he and John do not have a choice in the matter.

Peter's faith was not that which he possessed, rather it possessed him. He was captured by his faith. His faith was not a simple creed that he stubbornly resisted changing, but it was saturated with knowing. He had seen and heard; it had captured him, and he could not deny it. Belief that becomes knowing cannot compromise. When we say that our circumstances overtake us and cause us to compromise, we admit our faith has not become knowing. We have not interacted with Jesus, experienced His presence, and become convinced of His greatness. Let us embrace Him!

Acts 4:21

WHERE IS THE DEVIL?

"So when they had further threatened them, they let them go, finding no way of punishing them, because of the people, since they all glorified God for what had been done" (Acts 4:21).

We live our lives in the physical realm. Do not be defensive! The problems consuming our time and energy all seem focused on the physical. Mechanical problems, health issues, schedules, and obligations all exist in the physical world. Who has time for anything else? There may be a spiritual realm, but it receives the leftovers of my physical involvements. The physical realm dominates my thinking, which causes me to view the spiritual world as physical. I should make more time for church activities. I do need to spend more time in physical prayer, and I need to do the physical activity of devotions and Bible reading. Somehow the doing of my physical activities overcomes my spiritual involvement.

All my religious activities show a deficiency in my understanding. None of us lack spiritual involvement. We display our spiritual lives through our physical activities, which do not depend on our awareness. Our religious actions are involuntary and spontaneous. In other words, we display our spiritual lives in our attitudes and perspectives, influencing and controlling every activity in the physical. The spiritual realm determines the dynamics in our relationships. There is no lack of spiritual involvement; we just do not take note of it.

Focusing on the physical realm is a tragedy; it is backwards. Our focus should be on nurturing and fostering the spiritual realm. If we focus the energy and attention of our physical circumstances on our spiritual lives, we would quickly become people of God! If we would feed our spiritual lives equivalent to the way we feed our physical lives, our spiritual lives would not be anemic. Obviously both the spiritual and the physical are important; however, we must engage our spiritual lives because the spiritual demonstrates itself in the physical and controls our activities.

There is a remarkable concept in our passage; it is the parallel between what happened to Peter and John and what is happening in our lives. The blaring details of the unfolding story were in the physical. The lame beggar struggled for more than forty years with his disability. The best he could accomplish in his physical world was to beg. His physical world received a change called a miracle. This set into motion the physical activities of the leaders of Israel. The apostles spent a physical night in a physical jail. They physically stood before the seventy most powerful men of Israel. The physical results were the physical threats regarding the physical speaking of the name of Jesus. In the physical world, there was a simple solution. If they ceased to physically speak and teach in Jesus' name, their physical problem would be solved.

We all experience this pressure. Our problems easily produce a physical action. A better job, a bigger home, a newer car, or a different church will solve the problem. Peter experienced Pentecost and was filled with the Spirit (Acts 4:8). The issue for him was not a physical solution. He raised the question, **"Whether it is right in the sight of God to listen to you more than to God, you judge. For we cannot but speak the things which we have seen and heard"** (Acts 4:19, 20). Peter contrasted the physical answer of the Sanhedrin against the spiritual insight from God. What Peter and John had seen and heard was vastly different from the Sanhedrin's view. Although everything Peter and John saw and heard happened in the physical realm, it was a physical demonstration of the spiritual realm. The resurrection of Jesus from the dead and the infilling of the Spirit of Jesus were beyond physical activities. The issue now was not physical but spiritual. To deny the spiritual realities of all they experienced in Jesus was utterly impossible!

I propose that in your life the concept of this passage is the same as the situation of Peter and John.

Prime Mover

The significant player in this miracle is not the lame beggar. We are never given his name. We do not know what happened to him or what his role was in the early Church. The focus was the beginning of persecution and its escalation. The Church was driven out of Jerusalem and quickly expanded into the Gentile world. The leaders of Israel continued to express their demonic nature. Their self-centeredness was again face to face with the Lordship of Jesus. The devil battled the spread of Jesus and His message. Is the devil the prime mover?

At the same time, the hand of a sovereign God is moving! The Trinity God unfolded a plan that scattered the early Church and facilitated the redemption of the world. Christianity would have remained a small Jewish sect in Jerusalem. The early Church was clustered in Jerusalem, participating in the temple worship, and evangelizing the Jewish population. Persecution began with this miracle and scattered the early Church into the Gentile world. Is Jesus the Prime Mover?

The same dynamic was experienced in the crucifixion of Jesus. The Trinity God, the Prime Mover, used the sinful rebellion of mankind to facilitate the world's redemption. Or was

Part Three: The Absolute Ratification

the devil the prime mover? Did he enter into Judas (Luke 22:3) to instigate a plan ending in crucifixion? Was Jesus brought to death *"by the determined purpose and foreknowledge of God"* or was He *"taken by lawless hands, have crucified, and put to death"* (Acts 2:23)? The obvious answer is in the interaction of God's sovereignty and the demonic rebellion of Satan. A war occurred in the spiritual world that displayed itself in our physical existence. The leaders of Israel were again allowing their spiritual allegiance to dictate their physical actions. Everything flowing from the lives of the apostles was recognized as coming from Jesus. What the leaders hated about Jesus they were now experiencing from the apostles. The spiritual lives of the leaders demanded an elimination of Jesus through the radical method of crucifixion. Their spiritual conditions required a physical response to the ministry of the apostles. They must eliminate the name of Jesus from the speaking and teaching of the apostles.

We seem to advocate that demonic activity is the cause of every flat tire or difficulty in our lives, but would you recognize that your response to such difficulties comes from the spiritual world? Our responses to our physical circumstances are a direct result of our spiritual condition. Our spiritual nature determines our physical response and reveals itself in our physical actions. The members of the Sanhedrin were filled with the demonic nature of self-centeredness. Their response toward this miracle and the message of the apostles was a result of this self-centered nature. Peter and John were filled with the Spirit of Jesus. Their involvement and focus on this physical situation was a direct result of God's nature. Therefore, the conflict demonstrated in this story was not a physical battle to be solved by physical methods; it was a spiritual war. The prime mover for the members of the Sanhedrin was their demonic self-centeredness; the prime mover for the apostles was the Spirit of Jesus.

Prime Matter

The primary issue of this conflict is Jesus! This is most significant. We have discovered repeatedly that the primary matter is Jesus, and the focus of the conflict in this drama is Jesus. From the start of the conflict to this final threatening, Jesus is the issue. *"The priests, the captain of the temple, and the Sadducees"* rushed to Solomon's Porch to disband the gathering of the crowd who witnessed the miracle wrought by Jesus through the apostles (Acts 4:1). Luke is clear about what upset this group and caused their physical response, *"being greatly disturbed that they taught the people and preached in Jesus the resurrection from the dead"* (Acts 4:2). The resurrection from the dead was debated consistently between the Pharisees and the Sadducees. No one was upset about this debate. The difficulty was with the apostles' discussion of the resurrection of Jesus!

The miracle witnessed in the lame beggar was not the problem. The favor of the early Church among the populace of Jerusalem was not a frustration. The issue was Jesus. Peter declared, *"that by the name of Jesus Christ of Nazareth, whom you crucified, whom God raised from the dead, by Him this man stands here before you whole"* (Acts 4:10). Peter declared Jesus as the fulfillment of prophecy. Jesus was the stone that they rejected but God chose (Acts 4:11). Peter presented Jesus as the only means to salvation. All other means for being saved was set aside in light of Jesus (Acts 4:12). No wonder the members of the Sanhedrin were focused on the elimination of Jesus. They had Him crucified, and this should have ended the matter. Now, the apostles constantly talked about Him. They must be silenced. The prime matter is Jesus.

It is important to notice that the prime matter is not just a physical Jesus. It is the Spiritual Jesus displayed Himself in the physical. He did that in the incarnation and was crucified, eliminating Him from our physical world. Now Jesus displayed Himself in the physical world through these apostles. The Sanhedrin sensed the same pressure of Jesus through the apostles. They were filled with the Spirit of Jesus. He was the Prime Matter! The members of the Sanhedrin just could not get rid of Jesus.

The prime matter is not just a spiritual Jesus. We can tolerate the sovereign God of the universes so long as He stays in the galaxies. We can tolerate the Great Spirit of the Sky if he makes few demands, has few rules, and requires some ceremonial worship. But Jesus is far beyond any of this! God of the spiritual realm became a physical man. He invaded our physical realm! He did not come with a new set of rules but with a new kind of relationship. He not only wants to invade our physical world, but He wants to indwell our physical flesh, invading our physical world through our spiritual world. He wants to merge with us in such intimacy that our physical lives become an expression of Him.

Do you grasp how extreme this is? If Jesus would dwell in the spiritual section of our existence, we could tolerate Him. We will worship Him on special occasions and even keep some physical rules necessary to appease Him. But when He invades my spiritual world to control my physical world, I am left without self-centered freedom. When we allow Jesus to dwell in our spiritual realm, we are stripped of self-control and are dominated by Spirit-control. Our rights bend under the influence of the rightness of His Lordship. He no longer becomes a religious figure to be worshipped; He becomes Lord of my life, spiritually and physically. He is the Prime Matter!

Prime Mastery

A key phrase in our verse comes to full declaration at this section of our study is, *"because of the people, since they all glorified God for what had been done"* (Acts 4:21). The prime mover in the hearts of the Sanhedrin was their self-centeredness, the demonic nature. That demonic nature warred against the Prime Mover of their forefathers, the redemptive Trinity God. This war focused on the Prime Matter, Jesus. There were no other issues other than Jesus. Self-centeredness cannot tolerate the ruling of Jesus in the spiritual realm as He masters the physical realm. He must be eliminated. The leaders of Israel wanted to physically eliminate the apostles as they did the physical Jesus, but they were hindered.

What is so powerful that it can block the demonic forces' physical demonstration of power in the spiritual realm? There was a group of people who **"glorified God for what has been done."** The Greek word translated **"glorified God"** is "doxazo." The undercurrent of this word is always the idea of "perspective." In other words, one always honors or praises what is worthy in their opinion or perspective. This Greek word means, "to express an opinion, to influence one's opinion about another so as to enhance the latter's reputation, praise, honor, or extol."

The exaltation of Jesus happening among the people blocked and hindered the self-centered demonic nature of the Sanhedrin and kept them from punishing the apostles. Everyone talked about the power of God demonstrated in the healed beggar. The name of Jesus was glorified, honored, and extolled. The leaders of Israel desired and sought to find a way to eliminate the influence of Jesus in the physical realm, but they could do nothing in the physical realm because of the spiritual realm's influence. Although the people of Jerusalem were physically praising, it was the interaction of the spiritual flowing into the physical. It was not the physical activity that hindered, but the spiritual hearts of men and women captured by the wonder of Jesus moving in their midst.

You and I have physical circumstances needing answers or change. For change to happen, the first step is that we recognize

Part Three: The Absolute Ratification

the "prime mover." There is a spiritual nature that dictates all our physical actions and circumstances. We participate in a spiritual war not only in our society but also in our personal lives. We must come to grips with the inner prime mover of our lives. Are we filled with the demonic nature of self-centeredness, or are we filled with the Spirit of Jesus? Once we determine that, we must recognize the "prime matter." The issue is Jesus, His Spirit and His physical person. The issue is not that we adjust our responses, discipline our body drives, or increase our religious activities. The issue is His Lordship in our spiritual lives. Will I be filled with Him and allow all my physical activities to be generated from His Spirit?

Once I decide, I am a vessel, an avenue, through which Jesus can be glorified. My perspective for every physical circumstance will be seen through His eyes. He will determine my physical expressions in all my physical circumstances, and that will generate the victory power in my life! Even crucifixion cannot defeat me! Death itself cannot hold me! The way to victory is in the Spirit of Jesus manifesting Himself in my physical life!

Acts 4:21

PUNISHING

> *"So when they had further threatened them, they let them go, finding no way of punishing them, because of the people, since they all glorified God for what had been done" (Acts 4:21).*

A particular attitude, a natural offspring of the state of self-centeredness needs our investigation. Self-centeredness or self-sovereignty is the nature of sin called in the Scriptures, "carnal" (1 Corinthians 3:4), "the carnal mind" (Romans 8:7), "the flesh" (Galatians 5:17), and "the old man" (Romans 6:6). This "carnal" nature permeates our relationships and is the driving force in how we respond to others. The spontaneous and natural expression of the sinful nature is self-centeredness. The "carnal" is the direct opposite of the mind of Christ!

If you have any spiritual sensitivity, you will be abhorred when you discover this attitude in your life. We cannot tolerate "carnality" in our lives, yet we are powerless to eliminate it. "Carnality" is so powerful and controlling that we become slaves to its dictates. "Carnality" will drive us to actions of which we never dreamed we were capable. We have given "carnality" dominion over us; we are now slaves to this sinful nature.

The attitude of "carnality" is at the heart of our passage and the story forming its context. ***"So"*** is a translation of the Greek word "de," and it is the opening word in our English translations. In the Greek text "de" is the second word and is

Part Three: The Absolute Ratification

used as a contrast, "but." The contrast in our passage is between the attitude expressed by the leaders of Israel and the attitude of Peter and John in their stated response. Luke contrasted self-sourcing with Spirit-sourcing! The Sanhedrin threatened the apostles not to speak or teach in the name of Jesus (Acts 4:18). Peter and John were not rebellious, belligerent, or threatening. In a sense they threw up their hands and pleaded with these leaders, "We do not know what to do." They knew they were not on the theological level of the scribes and Sadducees, men who knew much more about the business operation of the temple. But Peter and John had experienced truth! Their lives were not changed by organization, philosophy, or theology; they had encountered the living Christ. *"In Jesus the resurrection from the dead"* was their reality. They lived with the resurrected Jesus for forty days, and they watched Him ascend into Heaven. At Pentecost His Spirit returned to them in the upper room and filled them. How could they keep still about this truth? This truth was the hope and destiny of Israel and the world! Please consider this truth!

The Spirit-filled Peter demonstrated a Spirit-sourced attitude in each of his discourses in the preceding chapters. Peter identified Jesus as the One they crucified but God raised from the dead. However, Peter's delivery never had a threatening tone but a plea to the reality of truth. He presented a message of hope to those who chose Barabbas instead of Jesus. Jesus again confronted the leaders of Israel! They killed the Prince of Life (Acts 3:15), but He was still alive. Jesus gave the Sanhedrin another opportunity!

Our passage shows a contrast of those who *"had further threatened them"* with those who *"glorified God for what had been done."* The contrast is the difference between demeaning someone and encouraging them. Punishment is contrasted with redemption, deep in the character and nature of a person.

The operative word in our passage is "punishing." It is

a translation of the Greek word "kolazo," used twice in the New Testament. The intent of this word is to cause one to suffer, to injure, or to penalize. Peter used this expression regarding the doom of the false teachers. He described them as *"presumptuous, self-willed."* They were *"like natural brute beasts made to be caught and destroyed, speak evil of the things they do not understand, and will utterly perish in their own corruption, and will receive the wages of unrighteousness, as those who count it pleasure to carouse in the daytime"* (2 Peter 2:12-13). Peter explained that the Lord knows how to deliver us out of temptations. However, He reserved unjust false prophets under, *"punishment* (kolazo) *for the day of judgment"* (2 Peter 2:9). He did not say what the Lord was going to do to them, but God allowed them to stay in the state that would bring suffering. They would experience the consequences of their state. "Punishing" never describes the actions of God; it is not His design or desire for anyone. "Punishment" does not dwell in the motives of God's heart!

In our passage, Luke contrasts the leaders of Israel with Spirit-filled Peter and John. The leaders wanted to punish, cause to suffer, and penalize the apostles but found it impossible to do. On the other hand, the apostles offered the revelation of Jesus to rescue and save. The motive of the Sanhedrin's self-sourcing was opposite of the motive of the Apostles' Spirit-sourcing. It was a contrast of self-sourcing and Spirit sourcing.

Vindictive

One aspect of the contrast is the vindictive motive. The dictionary describes this motive as a "strong and unreasonable passion for revenge," not a focus on revenge. This passion is strongly indicated at the beginning of the Sanhedrin's involvement. In other words, this passion continually appeared in the response of the Sanhedrin.

Part Three: The Absolute Ratification

"The priests, the captain of the temple, and the Sadducees came upon them, being greatly disturbed that they taught the people and preached in Jesus the resurrection from the dead" (Acts 4:1-2). The Greek word "ephistemi," translated *"came upon,"* appears twenty-one times in the New Testament, and seventeen times are in the writings of Luke. "Ephistemi" is a compound word; "epi" means "by, near, or upon" and "histemi" means "to stand." The word can be used in a positive sense, but also in a violent and threatening sense. The strength of the word must be translated in light of its context. In our passage the disciples were violently placed in jail and threatened the next day by these leaders. Thus, *"came upon"* is a violent, attacking action revealing the vindictive nature of their passion.

Another indicator of their violent motive toward the apostles is the Greek participle "diaponeo," translated *"being greatly disturbed"* (Acts 4:2). The participle is an adjective modifying the subject, a nominative and compound word. "Dia" means "through;" "poneo" means "to labor." However, the root word of "poneo" is "ponos" meaning "toil with the idea of pain." One of the translations says, "vexed through and through." These leaders are weary or grieved at the continuation of the teaching and preaching of the apostles. One of the Greek lexicons defines "diaponeo" as "to be very angry."

The leaders of Israel reveal their vindictive attitude when they recognize Jesus' connection with the apostles, *"And they realized that they had been with Jesus"* (Acts 4:13). Everything that irritated them about Jesus was now being witnessed in the apostles. For nearly three years, these leaders battled the influence and presence of Jesus. Even though Jesus moved His ministry from the region of Judea (Jerusalem) into Galilee, He was still a threat to them. At various times they sent special delegates to spy, trap, and undermine the ministry of Jesus (Matthew 15:1), climaxing in the crucifixion of Jesus! What else could they do? They had to eliminate Jesus! Months had passed since Jesus' crucifixion; Jesus should have been forgotten and His followers scattered. But once again the Sanhedrin experienced the same vexation with the disciples that they knew with Jesus, as if He was present again!

Why will we not allow the Spirit of God to investigate our spirits? I am spiritual enough to recognize I must embrace Jesus, and I would never have participated with the Pharisees in crucifying Jesus. A vindictive spirit against Jesus is just not acceptable. However, now this same spirit appears against the disciples of Jesus. What they did to the physical person of Jesus, they continued to do toward others.

In fact, Jesus gave us this truth in a warning! He told the Parables of the Judgment (Matthew 25). **"When the Son of Man comes in His glory, and all the holy angels with Him, then He will sit on the throne of His glory"** (Matthew 25:31). He described the process of judgment as dividing the sheep from the goats. It takes little discernment to distinguish sheep from goats. However, Jesus said the difference is not in physical appearance, but in the attitude toward others. Jesus declared to the sheep, **"I was hungry and you gave Me food; I was thirsty and you gave Me drink; I was a stranger and you took Me in; I was naked and you clothed Me; I was sick and you visited Me; I was in prison and you came to Me"** (Matthew 25:35-36). He said the goats were opposite. Jesus did not stress physical activities but the attitude of the heart. His conclusion was that whatever attitude we have toward others is the attitude we have toward Him!

It would be good for us to analyze our relationships would be good. We often welcome the elimination of a relationship rather than the opportunity of ministry in that relationship because it causes us discomfort and suffering. We may experience an attitude of punishment, demeaning, and injury to bring the revelation of Jesus to us. Who wants to be stoned that Jesus might be revealed to an angry heart? Stephen, the first martyr, **"knelt** *down and cried out with a loud voice, 'Lord, do not charge them with this sin'"* (Acts 7:60). This was Stephen's response when they, *"ran at him with one accord; and they cast him out of the city and stoned him"* (Acts 7:57-58). This is the heart of our passage! Will I have the vindictive attitude of self-centeredness or the attitude and nature of the Spirit of Jesus?

Vengeance

A "vindictive" spirit is an inner attitude. "Vengeance" is the result of the "vindictive" attitude, a punishment inflicted on a person. This attitude is the frustration expressed throughout our passage. The Sanhedrin wanted to eliminate the influence of the apostles concerning Jesus. The difficulty was the miracle of the healed beggar. This beggar sat at the Gate Beautiful for years (he was more than forty years old). Hundreds of consistent worshippers at the temple knew him and his condition. The healed beggar's miracle could not be hidden. Even the Sanhedrin admitted, *"For, indeed, that a notable miracle has been done through them is evident to all who dwell in Jerusalem, and we cannot deny it"* (Acts 4:16).

The Sanhedrin must have been highly frustrated. The only expression they could show of their self-centered vindictive attitude was to *"threaten them."* They therefore decided to, *"severely threaten them"* (Acts 4:17). After the Sanhedrin's threat, Peter gave insight into the spiritual issue of the occasion (Acts 4:19). Peter asked, "To whom should we listen?" The Sanhedrin's message had always been to listen to God. Should the apostles heed the vindictive and vengeful response of the Sanhedrin, or should they listen to the caring, ministering, and redemptive nature of God?

At this time, the Sanhedrin limited their vengeance to threats. But what was limited now would be expanded. *"They were filled with indignation, and laid their hands on the apostles and put them in the common prison"* (Acts 5:17-18). The problem with vengeance is that God keeps intervening. The angel of the Lord opened the jail doors and told them to go to the temple and preach the Word of life (Acts 5:19-20). The vengeful spirit of the Sanhedrin must have been frustrated when they discovered those they thought they silenced by imprisonment returned to preach again. Then they beat and threatened the apostles (Acts 5:40). But soon the crowd of Jews was so angered by the message that they martyred Stephen. **"They cried out with a loud voice, stopped their ears, and ran at him with one accord; and they cast him out of the city and stoned him"** (Acts 7:57-58). Then Saul began to persecute the church (Acts 8), and later James, the apostle, was killed (Acts 12:2).

When a person with a self-centered heart is confronted It is important to note that they will be vindictive and vengeful. Although that person may be hindered in expression, he or she will find a way to give physical action to their spirit of self-centeredness. In our passage the Sanhedrin found *"no way of punishing them."* But this did not remain true. The issue was not a moment in time. A moment in time becomes the past, and it can be forgotten. But this issue is an attitude of self-centeredness that continues to grow and fester in the sinful nature of the heart. We will find a way to express our desires! The same is true for those who *"glorified God for what had been done."* They could not be silenced. As they scattered from the persecution in Jerusalem, they gave witness to Jesus causing a worldwide movement (Acts 8:1-2).

Villain

According to the dictionary, a villain is a person or thing responsible for specified trouble, harm, or damage. The seventy members of the Sanhedrin constituted the most powerful, religious, and righteous men of the world. They represented all that God wanted to do throughout the Old Testament. Yet, their self-centered carnal nature became a vindictive and revengeful attitude. We must see them as "villains." Their intent was "punishment."

Again, I want to forcibly say punishment is not the heart of God! He is never a villain; *"God is love"* (1 John 4:8). The nature of God is redemptive; it is impossible for God to be a villain. His activities are determined by, *"For God so loved the world that He gave His only begotten Son"* (John 3:16). He does not think of punishment but of redemption. He is never vindictive and vengeful, but there are consequences for sin. *"For the wages of sin is death, but the gift of God is eternal life in Christ Jesus our Lord"* (Romans 6:23).

Therefore, the Christian cannot be a "villain!" We receive the nature of God. As Christ was the visible image of the invisible Father, so are we! Every action, expression, and attitude of our being becomes redemptive. Our intent is always one of service. Jesus taught His disciples, *"And whoever desires to be first among you, let him be your slave – just as the Son of Man did not come to be served, but to serve, and to give His life a ransom for many"* (Matthew 20:27-28). This is not an action to learn or a discipline to master; it is a nature at the heart of the person. Self-centered carnality is vindictive and revengeful; Spirit-centeredness is redemptive and loving. Are you filled with yourself or with Him?

Acts 4:22

FORTY YEARS OLD

"For the man was over forty years old on whom this miracle of healing had been performed" (Acts 4:22).

This is the final verse in our current study, and the central character of the story dominates chapters three and four of the Book of Acts. The lame beggar and his miracle of healing will not appear in the pages of this book again. The story his healing created will continue in the next paragraph as the early Church meets and responds to the ensuing persecution. We will see God's power demonstrated in His people as they face great opposition. However, none of the details include the healed beggar.

Our verse begins with the word *"for,"* the Greek word "gar" and the second word in the Greek text. The first Greek word is "etos," translated *"years old."* The focus of this verse is the healed beggar's age. "Gar" is an explanatory or causative word, connecting us to the preceding verse. Luke, in this brief paragraph, repeatedly emphasized the impossibility of denying the miracle. As the members of the Sanhedrin interrogated the apostles, *"they realized that they had been with Jesus"* (Acts 4:13). Everything that irritated the Sanhedrin about Jesus now irritated them about the apostles. These leaders of Israel now faced a huge quandary. *"And seeing the man who had been healed standing with them, they could say nothing against it"* (Acts 4:14). Their response was to place the apostles outside the room so they could confer among themselves. They did not want Peter and John or the Spirit of Jesus in them to have input in their discussion. Even in this private conversation, they admitted, *"a notable miracle has been done through them is evident to all who dwell in Jerusalem, and we cannot deny it"* (Acts 4:16).

The miracle of the lame beggar was real, and the Sanhedrin could not deny it. This was the dilemma that brought them to the conclusion that they could not punish Peter and John because the miracle was real. The best they could do was to threaten the apostles. *"So when they had further threatened them, they let them go, finding no way of punishing them, because of the people, since they all glorified God for what had been done"* (Acts 4:21). Now we come to our passage. *"For the man was over forty years old on whom the miracle of healing had been performed"* (Acts 4:22). The word *"for"* (gar) introduces the cause or reason the people glorified God. The age of the man is given as the explanation for the irrefutable miracle. There had been many other miracles accomplished through the apostles (Acts 2:43), but none of those miracles had the impact of this one. Luke gave the age of the man as the basis for the impact on Jerusalem.

This last verse (Acts 4:22) should be coupled with the first and second verses of the story (Acts 3:1-2). Peter and John went to the temple at the hour of prayer, three in the afternoon, the most popular hour because it involved sacrifices. There were probably twenty to twenty-five thousand people present in the temple. Luke wrote, *"And a certain man lame from his mother's womb was carried, whom they laid daily at the gate of the temple which is called Beautiful, to ask alms from those who entered the temple"* (Acts 3:2). He began begging daily as a child, which was the custom. Perhaps he begged at the Gate Beautiful for forty years. He was a fixture, a common element, begging at the most popular entrance to the temple. Everyone knew him! Many older people who had sympathized with the parent's heartbreak at this abnormal birth would have related his story to those younger. Some people supported him regularly. Everyone knew his healing was a genuine miracle wrought by the power of Jesus! All the people glorified God for this miracle because of its authenticity and widespread knowledge. Luke related the extent of their praise based on the age of this healed man. This man in a crippled state was exposed to all Jerusalem for more than forty years! He had been healed!

Emphasis

The story of the lame beggar and his healing miracle dominates two chapters of the Book of Acts. The story begins with his healing and his participation develops throughout. Luke used all the Greek words he could find to describe the completeness of the healing. The healing was a miracle that was physical, spiritual, mental and emotional. When Peter gave his exhortation on Solomon's Porch, the healed beggar was hanging on him. He was the main object of the exhibit. When Peter and John spent the night in jail, the healed beggar was with them. The next morning the healed beggar stood with Peter and John before the Sanhedrin, who discussed how to punish these apostles. This healed beggar dominated much of that discussion.

Even though the healed beggar is important to this story, we are never given his name. We know nothing of his family, and we are left to assume the conditions of his childhood. We are told he was more than forty, but we do not have any record of his future involvement in ministry. Why is this? Although this man participated in the story, he is not the focus. The focus of these two chapters is not on this man, but on the persecution of the early Church. This story begins the strong persecution of the Christians that will scatter them throughout the world.

Part Three: The Absolute Ratification

Most Christians of this period were Jews. They were clustered in Jerusalem and continued to go to the temple daily. They followed the Jewish requirements and sacrifices. Jesus was a fulfillment of everything foretold in the Old Testament. Christianity did not separate them from Judaism; it was the fulfillment of Judaism. If this had remained, Christianity would have become a Jewish sect with many others. Christians would have been tolerated like Judaism but with an additional flavor. The Pharisees had their approach to the Old Testament; the Sadducees had their interpretation of the Scriptures; now the world had the addition of Christianity

Persecution brought a radical change to Christianity! The apostles continued to preach and were returned to jail. Stephen was martyred. Saul was at the stoning of Stephen, giving his consent (Acts 8:1). ***"As for Saul, he made havoc of the church, entering every house, and dragging off men and women, committing them to prison"*** (Acts 8:3). Amid this persecution the church at Jerusalem began to scatter (Acts 8:1). This scattering eliminated the clustering of Jewish Christians and created world evangelism. Within seventy years, Christianity was recognized as the world's religion. It all started with the miracle of the lame beggar!

God had a plan! The people questioned God about the persecution. Why would God allow this to happen to them? It appeared to them as a terrible turn of events. Although God did not cause the persecution, He certainly utilized it just as He did the cross. The healing of the lame beggar was at the foundation of this worldwide movement.

Therefore, the focus of the miracle was not on the healed beggar; it was on the plan of God. Was the plan of God more important than the person participating in the plan? Usually, we focus on the person; if we personalize it, we focus on ourselves. We are the most important! God loves us; He sent His Son for us. Every time God exerted His power in the Old Testament, He did it for us! Jesus came to seek and to save the lost; He wants to redeem us. We are the objects of His desire! Although all this is true, do not lose sight of the plan. God has a plan; everything He wants for us is in His plan. For instance, the supreme desire of God for our lives is not happiness; it is His plan. In His plan we find happiness. God desperately wants us to experience abundant life. In His plan we are fulfilled. God wants us to live in power and victory, and it is only in His plan that victory and power are ours. The focus is not on us experiencing these things, but on the plan.

The plan is Jesus! His plan is not in the accomplishment of great feats or the building of organizational structures but in intimacy with His person! A lame beggar experienced Jesus! In this plan persecution existed, and it was the catalyst for the redemption of the world. You and I are not the plan; may we give our lives to the plan? When we focus on what we need, want, and desire, we miss Him! We desperately want Jesus to accomplish miracles in our lives because we think we are what really matters. He wants to accomplish His plan in our lives by giving us miracles. But the miracles will never be experienced without the purpose of the plan. We must belong to Jesus!

Extent

The reference to the age of the healed beggar seems to be significant, and our verse is dedicated to it. We do not know his name but we know his age. We do not know the exact time between Pentecost Day and this miracle. How long had the early Church been flourishing in Jerusalem? Perhaps six months, or it could have possibly been a year. Regardless of your conclusion, it is reasonable to think that Jesus walked by this lame man as he begged at the Gate Beautiful. Each time Jesus came to Jerusalem for the feast of the Passover, He undoubtedly passed this man.

Part Three: The Absolute Ratification

Many times the Scriptures relates that Jesus healed a multitude of people. He never neglected anyone, but He did not heal this lame beggar. To suggest that Jesus may have encountered this lame beggar many times is reasonable, but He did not heal him then.

We could make this observation in regard to Peter and John. They did many signs and wonders during these days of the fullness of the Holy Spirit, but they did not encounter this man. They walked by him daily as they entered the temple, but there is no indication they developed a friendship with him, that they were praying for him, or they ever spoke to him.

Why on this day did the apostles approach this beggar? Certainly this day was not the first time the beggar asked alms of Peter and John (Acts 3:3). Why did the apostles focus on this man (Acts 3:4)? The beggar did not ask for a miracle; he asked for money. Peter was relentless in his treatment of this man. He reported there was no money to give, but he did have a supply of something far better. He boldly offered Jesus! At this point Peter grabbed the beggar by the right hand, yanked him to his feet, and immediately the miracle happened. No report of faith flowed from the beggar. This day was the appointed time for the lame beggar's miracle; it was as if God waited until this day!

Was the duration of the forty years necessary for the plan of God? Although God did not cause this man to be crippled, was His purpose to allow this man to dwell in this condition with all its consequences until this moment? Was the plan to wait the forty years necessary for this stir to happen in Jerusalem? Did the timing of this miracle relate directly to the scattering of the Church and the redemption of the world found in the heart of God? Did God's divine plan need a lame beggar more than forty to receive a miracle?

Amid personal situations and pressures, we demand immediate relief. We do not see the larger picture of God's will relating to the world. How does my immediate circumstance affect people I do not know? This is a question the lame beggar could have legitimately asked? Paul and Silas must have wondered what their bloody backs, their hands in stocks, and bars imprisoning them had to do with God's plans for their lives. John the Baptist, in a dungeon cell with his life being threatened, wondered if Jesus was really the Christ (Matthew 11:2-3). Does God want me to endure forty years of scorn, physical handicap, and poverty to bring about His redemptive plan?

Will I be captured by something greater than my personal needs? Will my prayer life go beyond the immediate difficulties of my life to engulf the dreams of God?

Envelope

We are not attempting to play down the significance of the lame beggar's miracle. A radical change took place in his life physically and spiritually. Until his miracle, his fellow Jews considered this man's life unworthy of spiritual redemption. He could not worship in the temple, offer sacrifices for his sins, or give thank offerings. For more than forty years, this beggar could not find redemption. Suddenly he moved from Judaism, which restricted him from God, to a New Covenant that embraced him in the fullness of the Spirit! His personal life became fulfilled in the presence of the Spirit of Jesus.

Simultaneously, the plan of God's heart moved forward to fulfillment. The beggar filled the role for which God destined him. The beggar's involvement fulfilled God's plan, and God's plan fulfilled the healed beggar. Could it be that they enveloped each other? There was no need to choose between them. God, the Creator, designed and created us to find our fulfillment in the completeness of His plan for our lives.

This design is why self-centeredness, the heart of sin, never brings fulfillment to your life. Self-centeredness is

Part Three: The Absolute Ratification

always destructive and always dissatisfying. Fulfillment is not in accomplishment of our desires but in experiencing the destiny Jesus planned for us. Our self-centered attempts at happiness are so worthless. We struggle, try, and exert all our energy to reach some level of comfort and peace. All these self-centered efforts work in reverse. What we think brings peace brings only restlessness. What seems to give happiness gives only misery. What we consider victory is really defeat!

We are exactly like the lame beggar. Our healing is only in the fulfillment of God's plan. When Jesus envelops us, we move from self-seeking to Jesus-seeking. The answer to every need of my life is in Jesus. As it was with the healed beggar, my answer is not in frantic attempts but responsive to the movement of Jesus in my life. Abandonment to His presence is my only need. Just be His!

PART 4
ACTS 4:23-31

THE ABSOLUTE REIGN

Acts 4:23-31

GOD IS SOVEREIGN

"And being let go, they went to their own companions and reported all that the chief priests and elders had said to them. So when they heard that, they raised their voice to God with one accord and said: 'Lord, You are God, who made heaven and earth and the sea, and all that is in them, who by the mouth of Your servant David have said:
'Why did the nations rage, And the people plot vain things? The kings of the earth took their stand, And the rulers were gathered together Against the Lord and against His Christ.'
For truly against Your holy Servant Jesus, whom You anointed, both Herod and Pontius Pilate, with the Gentiles and the people of Israel, were gathered together to do whatever Your hand and Your purpose determined before to be done. Now, Lord, look on their threats, and grant to Your servants that with all boldness they may speak Your word, by stretching out Your hand to heal, and that signs and wonders may be done through the name of Your holy Servant Jesus.' And when they had prayed, the place where they were assembled together was shaken; and they were all filled with the Holy Spirit, and they spoke the word of God with boldness" (Acts 4:23-31).

All Christians believe in the theological premise that God is sovereign. The sovereign God has power and might of dominion over His creatures, to determine or dispose them as

He desires. The strangest sources have acknowledged God's sovereignty. God worked through Daniel to move the wicked King Nebuchadnezzar. The king broke out in praise, saying, *"All the inhabitants of the earth are reputed as nothing; He does according to His will in the army of heaven and among the inhabitants of the earth. No one can restrain His hand or say to Him, 'What have you done'"* (Daniel 4:35)? Although the musings of this pagan king in the Old Testament may not impress you, listen to the theological presentation of a New Testament writer, *"In Him, also we have obtained an inheritance being predestined according to the purpose of Him who works all things according to the counsel of His will"* (Ephesians 1:11). God is sovereign!

This theological premise may seem as an argument for the classroom, but it is a realistic concept for daily life. Your attitudes, destiny, and relationships are determined by your position on the sovereignty of God. When you falsely elevate your position of sovereignty, you diminish the power of God. If you do not allow God to be sovereign in your life, you fill His rightful place with yourself. God's sovereignty for you is determined by your surrender to His sovereign will. This position of sovereignty is the concept of our passage (Acts 4:23-31).

The Situation
(Acts 4:23)

The sovereignty of God is not an abstract, theoretical concept. We discover its reality in the circumstances of daily life. A group of disciples was captured by the resurrection of Jesus. They spent 40 days with Him as He taught them about the Kingdom of God (Acts 1:3). Beside such training they experienced the promise of the Father and the filling of the Holy Spirit (Acts 2:1-4). The presence of God merged with the life of man and shook the world at its core. This merger was and is the fulfillment of the dream of God through an Old Testament and the life of Christ. What Jesus revealed in life was now demonstrated in the lives of believers.

These new believers revealed their new reality throughout Jerusalem. Thousands of people experienced the Spirit of Jesus in their lives. The early Church thrived as they worshipped together, received biblical training, and witnessed miracles. These converted Jews were continually in the temple observing the Jewish traditions. They were, *"praising God and having favor with all the people"* (Acts 2:47). Then it happened! The plan of the Sovereign God clashing with the rebellious, demonic, and humanistic self-wills of the leaders of Israel was inevitable. The same self-will that demanded the crucifixion of Jesus would not allow the apostles to proclaim the resurrection of Jesus.

However, the conflict is never beyond the sovereignty of God. God's *"determined purpose and foreknowledge"* (Acts 2:23) had a plan. A lame beggar, more than 40 years of age (Acts 4:22) begged daily at the Gate Beautiful (Acts 3:2). To assume Jesus had passed by this beggar is logical; Peter and the other disciples must have seen him on their visits to the temple. But what was the difference on the day of the beggar's healing? Peter and John walked by the beggar on this day, and Jesus healed him. This movement of God caused the beginning of persecution for the early Church. These Jewish Christians were forced to scatter throughout the world and evangelism was the result. Our God is so sovereign that circumstances designed by the enemy to hinder Christianity become the stepping-stones to achieve His will.

Peter stood on Solomon's Porch with the healed beggar hanging on him to announce that Jesus sourced this miracle (Acts 3:11). The leaders of the temple were disturbed that Peter *"preached in Jesus the resurrection from the dead"* (Acts 4:2). These leaders captured Peter and John and put them in jail until the next day. The Sanhedrin and others confronted Peter, John, and the healed beggar. Their issue was Jesus! The miracle was evident, and the Sanhedrin could not deny it (Acts 4:14, 16), but they could not tolerate the promotion of Jesus. They threatened the apostles severely saying they would never again tolerate their use of Jesus' name! If they crucified Jesus, what would they do to those who promoted His name?

"And being let go, they went to their own companions and reported all that the chief priests and elders had said to them" (Acts 4:23). Our paragraph of study begins with this statement. Luke linked two facts about Peter, John, and, we assume, the healed beggar. The three were dismissed, released, or sent away (apoluo); they went to the members of the early Church. They were not released on Monday and waited until Sunday to report to the Church, but they went immediately. The early Church feared and prayed for the lives of the apostles; this was the pattern of the future (Acts 12:5). Luke is specific about the extent of their report to the Church. They *"reported all."* The Greek word translated *"all"* is not the typical word "pas." Luke used "hosos," which means a duplication of the experience. The apostles and the healed beggar gave an account with all the details of their experience, leaving the early Church with the understanding that the threat made to Peter and John was also made to them. They were under the same penalty. This threat was no light matter; it was a threat to their belief system and life pattern.

Amid life's disturbing circumstances, how do we cope? How do we react to the announcement that we have cancer? When the results of sin press you, whether they are self-inflicted or from others, what is your response? When someone asks me about the ministry of our church, my common response is, "It is messy." We are always in the middle of a mess. Although we are afforded opportunity in ministry, we are always pressed with the demonic forces of evil. Paul painted this picture of ministry, *"We are hard-pressed on every side, yet not crushed; we are perplexed, but not in despair; persecuted, but not forsaken;*

struck down, but not destroyed – always carrying about in the body the dying of the Lord Jesus, that the life of Jesus also may be manifested in our body" (2 Corinthians 4:8-10). What was the response of the early Church?

The Sovereignty
(Acts 4:24-30)

The early Church responded to the miracle of the healed beggar and to the threat of the Sanhedrin in the same way. Most of our passage records that response. I would love to have been among this group. The power of God's presence must have been overwhelming. Anyone who experienced the corporate link of Jesus' Spirit moving through these men and women of faith had to be changed forever. Did that link parallel the experience of the Israelites at the dedication of Solomon's temple (2 Chronicles 7)? The people of the early Church praised and proclaimed adoration for their God. They found security in His presence, which overshadowed the threats of the Sanhedrin making them insignificant.

Jesus experienced the same pattern. He focused His ministry in Galilee, affecting the major cities of Chorizan, Bethsaida, and Capernaum where He performed most of His miracles (Matthew 11:20). He wanted to win these three cities and the leaders of Israel to His cause but neither happened. The three cities concentrated on their commercial success and had little time for Jesus. The leaders of Israel were busy plotting how to kill Him. How did Jesus respond to this failure and rejection? He responded with praise to His Father (Matthew 11:25). His response was an example followed by the early church as recorded in our passage.

The content and focus of praise in response to hardship by Jesus and the early church was the same. God is sovereign!

Part 4: The Absolute Reign

When Jesus met crisis in His ministry, He responded, *"I thank You, Father, Lord of heaven and earth, that You have hidden these things from the wise and prudent and have revealed them to babes"* (Matthew 11:25). Jesus and the early Church knew that the sovereign Father was Lord over everything happening in heaven and in Earth. Listen to the praise of Peter and John in their crisis, *"Lord, You are God, who made heaven and earth and the sea, and all that is in them"* (Acts 4:24). In each case praise to the Father was the response to life threatening circumstances.

Jesus and the apostles erupted in spontaneous praise when confronted with opposition to the plan of God. They had not been instructed to respond in such a manner. They had never been told that praise would overshadow the evil circumstances around them, nor had they attended a seminar on the effects of praise to God. Their praise amid of turmoil was an expression of their faith and absolute confidence in God's sovereignty. Where can you and I find security in an insecure world? How can we face circumstances over which we have no control? The pressure and stress of bombarding evil on the human spirit is crushing. How can we maintain victory? All is lost if Jesus is not sovereign!

Our passage reveals three issues in this focus on sovereignty. The first is "creation," (Acts 4:24-26). There is a contrast in the praise. The early Church quoted a passage from the Old Testament, one of David's psalms, painting the picture of kings and nations warring against God and His plan. God created the heaven, the Earth, and the sea and everything in them, and the apostles contrasted the Creator with His creation. Does this seem ridiculous to you? Paul expanded this idea when he said, *"For by Him all things were created that are in heaven and that are on earth, visible and invisible, whether throne or dominions or principalities or powers. All things were created through Him and for Him"* (Colossians 1:16). The Sovereign Creator not only created everything, but He planned a destiny for every individual thing He created. All things are created *"for Him,"* which places everything happening in my life in the middle of His plan.

The Creator is in charge! We can rest in confidence that He has sovereign control over the circumstances of His creation. Things are not out of control. Movements containing solutions that we know nothing about are in action. Admit your helplessness and embrace His sovereignty. The Creator is adequate for your situation. If necessary, He can create newness in your chaos. Trust Him!

A second issue in the early Church's focus on sovereignty was "crucifixion." Listen to the way they proclaimed this truth, **"Herod and Pontius Pilate, with the Gentiles and the people of Israel, were gathered together to do whatever Your hand and Your purpose determined before to be done"** (Acts 4:27-28). The crucifixion of Jesus was a direct result of the plan of the sovereign God carried out by the leaders of Israel, the people of Israel, and the Gentiles. They, knowingly or unknowingly, participated in the sovereign God's plan to redeem the world through Christ.

This redemption adds a new dimension to the truth of God's sovereignty. God is sovereign because He is the creator. He can create circumstances amid my difficulty. In addition, His sovereign position enables Him to take the evil created from my failures or the evil thrust on me from others and redeem it. He brings those circumstances into His plan and makes it a benefit to all involved. He is redemptive; He can redeem all things. He is sovereign; He can bring all redeemed things into His *"purpose determined before to be done."*

Now we come to the third issue of sovereignty, "confession" (Acts 4:29-30). A desperate plea arose from the early Church to their sovereign God. Is there any question that their sovereign God knew their situation? Did He not know about the threats of the Sanhedrin? Was there any additional information that they needed to share with Him? In His sovereignty, God not only knew their threats, but He knew the actions needed for their future. He determined the fulfillment of the plan in which these threats would benefit. Therefore, the plea of the early Church was for the continued flow of God's Spirit through them. They did not want the circumstance created by the threats of the Sanhedrin to determine their ministry. The early Church wanted the sovereign plan of God to continually be fulfilled in them at any cost!

We must respond to God's sovereignty in the same way. Do we have unpleasant circumstances? Are we amid a spiritual war with physical and spiritual consequences? Are we not threatened? But none of the circumstances should dictate our response. We are to look beyond the difficulties of the moment to the sovereignty of God. He is in charge and has a *"purpose determined before to be done."* Our empowerment by the Holy Spirit is not to keep us safe; the purpose is His *"purpose determined."* He does not come to give us happiness; He comes to give us destiny!

The Solution
(Acts 4:31)

The openness and surrender of the early Church brought immediate results from the sovereign God. The believers' interaction with the sovereign God was relational. Luke wrote, *"And when they had prayed"* (Acts 4:31). The Greek word "deomai," translated *"when they had prayed,"* is often translated "beg." It expresses the act of making one's need known, to beseech, to ask. After embracing the reality of God's sovereignty, they embraced the reality of their own helplessness. *"The place where they were assembled together was shaken"* by His presence (Acts 4:31). Intimate relationship was expressed in the interaction of God and His believers.

"They were all filled with the Holy Spirit" (Acts 4:31). They

received the filling of the Holy Spirit at Pentecost, and He moved into their new situation. ***"They spoke the word of God with boldness"*** (Acts 4:31). The Spirit of God refreshed them in His presence; the result was an answer to their prayer. ***"Now, Lord, look on their threats, and grant to Your servants that with all boldness they may speak Your word"*** (Acts 4:29). The believers thought like Jesus, were filled with Jesus, and proclaimed Jesus. What a relationship!

This relationship was founded on the awareness of God's sovereignty. In this awareness threats were seen with a proper perspective. No difficulty was overwhelming. Stress was not necessary. Despair was not present. Circumstances held no power to capture or hinder. Freedom was their experience. He is a sovereign God!

Acts 4:23

I NEED YOU

"And being let go, they went to their own companions and reported all that the chief priests and elders had said to them" (Acts 4:23).

The Book of Acts is most often titled "The Acts of the Apostles." However, this violates the premise of the book, because The Book of Acts is really "The Acts of the Holy Spirit." Neither title gives the complete story. Perhaps the title would be better lengthened to "The Acts of the Holy Spirit through the Apostles." The Book of Acts is a report of the merger between God and man in the New Covenant. God and man act in unison. The Kingdom person expresses himself as a new creature. The oneness of God and man can be seen amid life's difficulties. If a person hopes that his difficulties will be eliminated in this union, that hope is soon lost. This new relationship with God brings additional troubles.

The lame beggar was healed. You would think everyone would rejoice at his good fortune. The problem was not in the healing but in the source of the healing. The apostles said Jesus was responsible for the healing, which created difficulty. The leaders of Israel could not ignore the apostles' proclamation of Jesus. Peter's statements were narrow and specific. **"Nor is there salvation in any other, for there is no other name under heaven given among men by which we must be saved"** (Acts 4:12). He identified Jesus as the healer. He said, **"by the name of Jesus**

Christ of Nazareth, whom you crucified, whom God raised from the dead, by Him this man stands here before you whole" (Acts 4:10). There was no room to adjust this statement. No one could misunderstand what Peter said.

The most powerful ruling group in Israel, the ones who crucified Christ, now threatened Peter and John. This group told the apostles they could continue to participate in the Jewish temple ceremonies, and they did not need to deny their friends and associates. They were still approved to hold religious gatherings and suppers. They were, however, to refrain from one thing, **"from now on they speak to no man in this name"** (Acts 4:17). All preaching and teaching in the name of Jesus was to cease (Acts 4:18). This was no light threat. They would not be fined; their lives were at risk. What were they to do? How were they to handle their problems? How were they to respond amid difficulties?

Contrast

Luke's opening word in our English translation is *"and"* (Acts 4:23). *"And"* is the second word in the Greek text, a translation of the Greek word "de," and it remains dominant. The primary meaning of this word is "but," and Luke used this word to present his contrast, comparing two boldly different situations. The Sanhedrin wanted to add strength to their decision, so they called additional people for support (Acts 4:6). The atmosphere was tense; this group had experienced the crucifixion of Jesus. He was dead and buried. They had moved past His death, but everyone was speaking about Jesus as if He was still there! The talk of His resurrection backed up by His miracles fueled the frustration and irritation of these leaders.

The Sanhedrin also experienced the pressure of the Jerusalem crowds. The miracle of healing happened in a remote section among a small crowd. The lame beggar was at the Gate Beautiful, the main entrance to the temple, where he had begged from childhood (Acts 3:2) for more than 40 years (Acts 4:22). The healing created a huge stir in Jerusalem because everyone knew the beggar and his situation (Acts 4:16). Therefore, the Sanhedrin was hindered from doing all they would have liked to the apostles (Acts 4:21), leaving them frustrated and annoyed. They were negative, impatient, exasperated, angry, and intolerant of even the mention of the name of Jesus.

In direct contrast with the Sanhedrin, the apostles and members of the early Church gathered in a different atmosphere. Peter was relaxed and secure in his relationship with Jesus. He said, ***"For we cannot but speak the things which we have seen and heard"*** (Acts 4:20). The apostles had in them the reality of Jesus! They could not deny the certainty of His resurrection. They had no question about the embrace of the Spirit of Jesus. The evidence of the miracle was indisputable. Even amid the upheaval, they were calm.

When Peter and John reported the threats to the members of the early Church, they responded in praise. They knew exactly what to do. They had experienced the sovereignty of God in the face of death. They saw Jesus die, yet He lived. Miracles occurred repeatedly. Changed lives were on every hand. The prayers of the early Church were filled with a positive confidence. They asked for continued boldness to proclaim His name. There was no question about what needed to be done. They boldly spoke the name of Jesus everywhere! The movement of His presence continued to flow through them without hesitation.

Where do you and I fit in this picture? Are we narrow, negative, shut down? Surely, we would not stand against proclaiming of the name of Jesus. Although we would not threaten those who speak His name, are we among those who boldly proclaim it? We would not resist miracles, but are we the means through which the miracle of changed lives can happen?

We may not form the court that condemns the Church; but are we in the group that causes life in the Church, throbbing with His presence? If everyone in the Church is like you, how vibrant will the Church be? If everyone sings like you sing, comes like you come, proclaims Jesus like you proclaim Him, or dwells in His presence like you dwell, what kind of Church will we have?

We can no longer be the crowd on the street or the people in the temple. We have been dragged into the court of the Sanhedrin. Do we sit in the judgment seats condemning, or are we released to join the atmosphere of the early Church? The lines are clear. This is about us!

Compelling

We can see in Luke's "contrast" a compelling, forcing something to happen. In the original language the first word of the text is "apoluo," a word we know from other studies. "Apo" means "from"; "luo" means to "release or loose." It appears 66 times in the New Testament in the active and the passive voice, but only in the Gospels, the Book of Acts, and once in Hebrews. This word projects the idea of "releasing or setting free" and is often used in a strong sense, carrying with it the idea of repelling or forcing a departure.

Jesus was teaching in the synagogue on the Sabbath. A woman with a spirit of infirmity for 18 years was bent over and unable to walk straight. Jesus approached her, laid His hands on her, and said to her, **"Woman, you are loosed from** (apolou) **your infirmity"** (Luke 13:12). In the context of this word is the sense of struggle, battle, or resistance. Jesus stepped into the bondage, forcibly repelled the infirmity, and the woman was released or separated from her illness.

Jesus also told a story of forgiveness. A king wanted to settle accounts with his servants. A servant owed the king ten thousand talents ($2,370,000), which he could not pay. The king commanded the man to be sold, with his wife, with his children, and everything he owned. The servant expressed such repentance and desperation that the king had mercy on him. **"Then the master of that servant was moved with compassion, released** (apoluo) **him, and forgave him the debt"** (Matthew 18:27). The act of releasing is amid trauma. The desperation of what would happen to the servant, his family, and the loss accrued by the king presented the struggle in which the debt was repelled from the situation. The servant was released from the obligation!

There are two accounts in the Book of Matthew where Jesus' message on divorce includes the word "apoluo." The translation of the word is not "divorce" but "separate." Jesus said, **"Furthermore it has been said, 'Whoever divorces** (apoluo) **his wife, let him give her a certificate of divorce'"** (Matthew 5:31; also see Matthew 19:7). A man's separation from his wife leading to a divorce sets the context for this word. Arguments, conflicts, and emotional upsets surround separation in a marriage. The tension and discomfort become so strong it compels a person to leave. The departure is not casual but is disruptive and forceful.

Although "apoluo" can be used in a casual manner, our context demands the stronger interpretation. Luke reported the attitude of the leaders of Israel as violent during Peter and John's arrest. They **"came upon them, being greatly disturbed that they taught the people and preached in Jesus the resurrection from the dead"** (Acts 4:1-2). The fact that **"they laid hands on them, and put them in custody until the next day"** was not a calming act (Acts 4:3). Their anger caused them to want to punish the apostles, but the crowds prohibited them (Acts 4:21). Now the apostles and probably the healed beggar were **"being let go"** (Acts 4:23). They were thrust forth, repelled from, or kicked out with anger!

Do you identify with the apostles and their situation? We may not have been captured, judged, or condemned by the religious court, but we know the pressure of being repelled. Crisis circumstances thrust us into directions we would not ordinarily go. We become experts in areas we have no interest except in crisis moments. Conflict can enter our lives and push us into things we have never experienced. Those experiences occur in our marriages, jobs, and social relationships. Like the apostles, it is beyond our control.

The issue is not will this happen in my life. It will happen; we will be thrust out and repelled. The issue is how we respond to this new circumstance. The way we respond is the focus of our passage. When thrust forth to whom will we go? Where will you and I be found? In whom will we confide?

Companions

In the "contrast" there is a "compelling." In the "compelling" there are "companions." *"And being let go, they went to their own companions and reported all that the chief priests and elders had said to them"* (Acts 4:23). The Greek word "apaggello," translated *"reported,"* is an interesting word. This compound word means "a messenger who announces" and consists of "apo," meaning "from," and "aggello," meaning "to proclaim." However, included in the word is the idea of details, then it is followed by the Greek word "hoso," translated *"all that."* This means it is a reduplication of the event. So, the apostles gave a detailed account of all the interaction they had with the Sanhedrin.

The Greek word "idious," translated *"their own companions,"* is equally interesting. "Idious" refers to what is properly one's own, a private person not public. "Idious" is private, particular, and individual, as opposed to "demosios," which commonly means "public, open, and komos." The Jewish leaders became upset with Jesus and persecuted Him, seeking to kill Him. The leaders reasoning, *"He not only broke the Sabbath,*

but also said that God was His (idious) ***Father"*** (John 5:18).

In writing about the first recorded board meeting of the early Church, Luke gave insight into Judas. The disciples had to replace Judas who had killed himself. The early Church realized that the sin of Judas was not his betrayal of Jesus for the 30 pieces of silver, or the fact that he stole from the treasury. God had created Judas for the office of apostleship. However, Judas refused this office and decided to create his own. Luke wrote, ***"Judas by transgression fell, that he might go to his own*** (idious) ***place"*** (Acts 1:25).

When Peter, John, and the healed beggar were thrust or repelled out, where did they go? They were in the middle of conflict, possible punishment, and had been threatened. Their circumstances had thrust them forth, and they went to their companions. Where else could they have gone? They went to those who loved them, those with whom they could share, and those who would pray for them. They did not go back to the temple to speak with the priests; they went to their own! That was true of Judas as well. Even in death where would he have gone? He went to his own.

This passage leaves us with several concerns. Who is your own? You have difficulty and are thrust out from your circumstances. To whom will you go? Is Jesus your own? These apostles were thrust into praise focused on the sovereignty of God. They were flung to the side by their difficulties, and praise was where they landed. Nothing was so big in their life that it could overshadow their relationship with Jesus. In fact, their relationship with Jesus got them into this difficulty, and their relationship with Him saw them through their difficulty. In life or in death, this is where they found themselves, because He was their own.

Our relationship with others provides another application. Am I the person others gravitate to, as they are repelled forth from their difficulties? Think of the opportunities this affords us. Everyone we meet finishes being thrust forth from his or her difficulties. Do they feel safe with us? Have we developed a close enough relationship with others that they can report all that their difficulties are doing to them? Is our church a haven for those hurting? When hurting people are thrust forth from difficulties, are we those who condemn, judge, and ridicule, or are we the place of understanding, comfort, and love?

The story of the prodigal son (Luke 15:11) who could leave the pigpen and return home because of the Father is a good illustration. He knew the love of the Father. The Father threw a party, killed the fatted calf, and restored him. He went home despite the older brother who condemned, criticized, and would not forgive. We will have difficulties. To whom will we go?

Acts 4:24

ONENESS IN AKOUO

"So when they heard that, they raised their voice to God with one accord and said: 'Lord, you are God, who made heaven and earth and sea, and all that is in them" (Acts 4:24).

Can you imagine coming to Sunday morning worship and finding the speaker has just been released from Wilson County Jail? He shares the experience of his jail time and court orders. You are left with the viewpoint that the political structure of your day has an intolerable attitude toward Jesus Christ. Jesus may be your hope and Savior, and you believe in Him with your whole heart, but those in power over your culture and lifestyle are against even the mention of His name! In fact, the powers that be inform you that any further teaching in Jesus' name will initiate strong punishment and possible death. How will you respond?

Although this has not happened in our Sunday morning worship, we do know the pressure of such resistance in our culture. Because of this pressure, it is easy for us to keep silent and our silence comes under the guise of not offending. Are we strong in our profession of Jesus? May I establish a relationship with another person and keep the name of Jesus absent from that relationship? Does everyone with whom I associate need to be pressed with Jesus? How may I be filled with Jesus and not affect those whose hands I shake?

"For we cannot but speak the things which we have seen

and heard" (Acts 4:20). This is the premise Peter proposed to the Sanhedrin. How could they deny the revelation of 40 days in His resurrection presence? How could they ignore the indwelt Spirit of Jesus radically changing their existence? How could they dispute the signs and wonders they experienced through the growth of the early Church in Jerusalem? Jesus was dominant in their lives; He became their life! To deny Jesus was to deny what they had become. If I reject Jesus, I revert to the devil I once was! What will we do with our culture's pressure to be silent about Jesus?

Luke's first contrast was between the threats of the Sanhedrin and the freedom of the apostles to return to the members of the early Church (Acts 4:23). Then he established another contrast. In this study, Luke begins our verse with the English word *"so,"* making a second contrast. (Acts 4:24). *"So"* is a translation of the Greek word "de," primarily meaning "but." This second contrast is between all the reported threats from the Sanhedrin and the response of the body of Christ. Now the dilemma was expanded to include the early Church and required a response. Business as usual was not an option. A decision had to be made.

The early Church responded in unity. **"So when they heard that, they raised their voice to God with one accord"** (Acts 4:24). This was an unusual response, but it was not their first show of unity (Acts 1:14; 2:46). The phrase, **"with one accord,"** is a translation of the Greek word "homothumadon." "Homo" means, "same place and time." "Thumos" refers to "passion," and has to do with "as if heavy breathing." This combination of two words is expressive and signifies that all their minds, affections, desires, and wishes, were concentrated on one object. Everyone's focus had the same end in view. They had one desire. No person was uninterested, unconcerned, or lukewarm; all were in earnest. This kind of unity gives the Holy Spirit divine action in our world, a powerful platform!

We have nothing to indicate that the members of the early

Church were without differences. *"One accord"* does not mean the people involved agree about something. People of *"one accord"* unite in their passion for one purpose, concentrating on one concern. They had varying likes and dislikes, but in our passage they had an overwhelming passion for Jesus. We have learned from our previous studies they were captivated by the resurrected Lord. He had shared the dreams of the Kingdom of God with them for 40 days (Acts 1:3). Jesus was so large in their vision nothing else seemed to matter. Their love for Him overtook all other concerns, not eliminating those concerns but certainly diminishing them.

We could make a case for unity in the Sanhedrin. Peter and John's preaching about Jesus brought a new crisis to the lives of these leaders. People seemed to come together against an enemy, and the Sanhedrin had a common foe in Jesus. They were united in their passion to end the preaching in Jesus' name. But there was a vast difference between the *"one accord"* of the Sanhedrin and *"one accord"* of the early Church.

What did the Sanhedrin hear, and what did the early Church hear? That was the difference in the *"one accord."* According to our verse, the early Church focused their praise on the sovereignty of God because of what they heard. Luke wrote, *"So when they heard* (akouo) *that, they raised their voice to God with one accord"* (Acts 4:24). *"They heard"* is a direct reference to, *"reported all that the chief priests and elders had said to them"* (Acts 4:23). The Greek word "apaggello," translated *"reported,"* comes from two Greek words, "apo," meaning "from" and "aggello," meaning "to proclaim." "Apaggello" means a messenger who announces but also includes the idea of details. "Apaggello" is followed by the Greek word "hoso," translated *"all that,"* meaning a duplication of the event. So, the apostles gave a detailed account of the interaction they had with the Sanhedrin; however, we have only what the Holy Spirit saw fit to share with us through Luke.

Oneness in Akouo | Acts 4:24

The Sanhedrin reacted to the powerful statements of Peter (Acts 4:8-12). He named Jesus the only source of this miracle and salvation. The Sanhedrin *"saw the boldness of Peter and John, and perceived that they were uneducated and untrained men"* (Acts 4:13). They marveled at this and recognized that they were under the influence of Jesus.

The emphasis of the Sanhedrin's discussion was on their inability to deny the miracle. *"What shall we do to these men? For, indeed, that a notable miracle has been done through them is evident to all who dwell in Jerusalem, and we cannot deny it"* (Acts 4:16). Luke wrote, *"And seeing the man who had been healed standing with them, they could say nothing against it"* (Acts 4:14).

The Sanhedrin could not deny the miracle, which Luke suggested would limit their punishment of Peter and John. *"So when they had further threatened them, they let them go, finding no way of punishing them, because of the people, since they all glorified God for what had been done"* (Acts 4:21). This gives us insight into the perspective of the Sanhedrin. They were not glorifying God for what had been done. They were disappointed with the limited punishment they could extend to the apostles. The phrase, *"they had further threatened"* is a translation of "prosapeileo." This compound word is a combination of "pros," meaning "in addition," and "apeileo," meaning "to threaten." They added threat after threat. This is contrasted with the quote from the Sanhedrin, *"But so that it spreads no further among the people, let us severely threaten them"* (Acts 4:17). The phrase, *"let us severely threaten"* is a translation of two Greek words. *"Severely"* is translated from the Greek word "apeile," and *"threaten"* is a translation from "apeileo." These two words are a form of the same word, making this a double statement, *"threaten, threaten."*

As the early Church heard the details of the miracle and the response of the Sanhedrin, what did they hear? What they heard was determined by their focus on Jesus, and that focus caused their unity. What the Trinity God did in Christ captured and mastered the early Church. They saw everything through the lens of Jesus.

Presence

The Sanhedrin wanted to know who was responsible for healing the lame beggar. Peter gave the credit to Jesus. The response of the Sanhedrin was, ***"they marveled"*** (Acts 4:13), a translation of the Greek word "thaumazo." It is used 43 times in the New Testament with 30 of those in the Gospel accounts. It speaks of an amazement awakened by sight, which is why it is used so often in the Gospels. The signs and wonders of Jesus were shocking the people and causing them to wonder.

Now the amazement of the Jewish people happened to the Sanhedrin! They were mystified by the boldness and certainty of Peter, an uneducated fisherman, as he spoke about Jesus. This untrained man should have cowered in their presence because he was far beneath their level of education and knowledge. They recognized this inferiority was the way they felt about Jesus, and what they hated in Jesus was standing before them in a man called Peter. They demeaned and belittled Peter and John. These apostles should have known their place in light of the Sanhedrin's authority. Who did they think they were?

But the early Church did not respond to the criticism of the Sanhedrin; they praised the sovereign God. The lame beggar's miracle forced the Sanhedrin to recognize the authority in the lives of Peter and John higher than position or education. The Trinity God executed His plan though the Sanhedrin wanted to eliminate Jesus again. He had explained this to His disciples before His crucifixion. ***"If the world hates you, you know that it hated Me before it hated you"*** (John 15:18). ***"A disciple is not*** *above his teacher, nor a servant above his master. It is enough for the disciple that he be like his teacher, and a servant like his master"* (Matthew 10:24-25). The thrill of their lives was to be like Jesus! *"When they heard that, they raised their voice to God with one accord."* They praised! They were blessed! In the Sermon on the Mount Jesus told them, *"Blessed are you when they revile and persecute you, and say all kinds of evil against you falsely for My sake. Rejoice and be exceedingly glad"* (Matthew 5:11-12).

This was the repeated response among the believers. Stephen, the first martyr, while suffering extreme persecution said, *"Look! I see the heavens opened and the Son of Man standing at the right hand of God!"* (Acts 7:56). This response so infuriated his persecutors that they took him outside the city and stoned him to death. Stephen called on God saying, *"Lord Jesus, receive my spirit." Then he knelt down and cried out with a loud voice, "Lord, do not charge them with this sin." And when he had said this, he fell asleep"* (Acts 7:59-60).

These early Christians were so captured by Jesus that all other circumstance grew dim in light of their merge with Him. Can Jesus be in your life without this event? Does this mean the proper involvement of Jesus in me will produce an intimacy with Him that makes everything else minor in significance?

Positive

The Sadducees made up half the Sanhedrin, and they did not believe in the supernatural. They rejected the idea of angels, the resurrection of the dead, and miracles. Yet they were confronted with this miracle of the lame beggar. They said, *"For, indeed, that a notable miracle has been done through them is evident to all who dwell in Jerusalem, and we cannot deny it"* (Acts 4:16). The Trinity God moved through the Spirit of Jesus, and the Sanhedrin was forced to see it. Yet having seen it, they would not embrace it! They chose to live in deception rather than change.

What did the persecution and threats of the Sanhedrin's deception produce in the early Church? They broke into praise! They saw God as bigger than the persecution. They did not focus on the threats; they focused on the sovereignty of God who is bigger than the threats. Their God was sovereign; He used those threats to complete His plan! How did they know this? They knew because He did this in Jesus. *"For truly against Your holy Servant Jesus, whom You anointed, both Herod and Pontius Pilate, with the Gentiles and the people of Israel, were gathered together to do whatever Your hand and Your purpose determined before to be done"* (Acts 4:27-28).

Can you imagine the merger of His presence and your life? Can you imagine such intimacy with Him that adverse circumstances become the stage of rejoicing? Adverse circumstances are the means by which God accomplishes His plan for your world, and you are privileged to be a part of it! We become a people who live above our circumstances, pressures, and obstacles; we see His hand moving through them! Even when we do not know the details of His plan, our confidence is in Him and not in our knowledge of the plan!

Position

The attitude of the Sanhedrin was one of authority. The *"priests, the captain of the temple, and the Sadducees"* who instigated this event (Acts 4:1). They formed the temple police who were in charge. Now two uneducated and untrained apostles confronted the most powerful court of Israel. A lowly beggar stood with them, so reduced in rank that he had never been allowed into the temple. The Sanhedrin invited other powerful, high-ranking individuals to join their interrogation (Acts 4:5-6). The question of the Sanhedrin was one of authority, *"By what power or by what name have you done this?"* (Acts 4:7). Power and authority determined the punishment for these apostles. The Sanhedrin dared not do all they would want because the people glorified God for the miracle (Acts 4:21). If they did, they would lose power and authority in the eyes of the people.

Do you see the irony in this? Amid the authority and power of the Sanhedrin, they admitted they were powerless. As these men of authority conferred, they said, *"What shall we do to these men?"* (Acts 4:16). They admitted this situation was beyond them. They released Peter and John only to put them back in jail later. When the Sanhedrin sent for them, they were not there because an angel of the Lord had opened the jail doors (Acts 5:19). These leaders found the apostles in the temple teaching and preaching Jesus, proving the obvious; the Sanhedrin was not in charge.

The early Church had readily embraced the fact that they were not it charge. They rejoiced in lack of authority. Their praise was to a sovereign God who *"made heaven and earth and the sea, and all that is in them"* (Acts 4:24). All gentiles and Jews are under God's authority. Even amid their free will, they participated in His *"purpose determined before to be done"* (Acts 4:28). God is sovereign! God is in charge!

God's sovereignty is why Jesus insisted, **"Therefore I say to you, do not worry about your life"** (Matthew 6:25). There is no room for stress, anxiety, depression, or worry in your relationship with Jesus. These are symptoms of the self-centeredness that refuses to yield control. A lifestyle of praise to the sovereign God who merges with us to fulfill His plan in and through our lives is needed now!

Acts 4:24

ONENESS IN ADMIRATION

"So when they heard that, they raised their voice to God with one accord and said: 'Lord, you are God, who made heaven and earth and sea, and all that is in them" (Acts 4:24).

This verse describes the response of the early Church to the threats of the Sanhedrin. The early Church had many things for which to praise. Their lives had been filled with the fullness of Christ's Spirit. The healed beggar stood in their midst, a living testimony of God's movement. The new Christians of this movement were affecting the city of Jerusalem. The apostles **"reported all that the chief priests and elders had said to them"** (Acts 4:23). Things had been going well for the early Church, but now they were confronted with a blockade. They all lived with the memory of Jesus' crucifixion! Now the Sanhedrin threatened the early Church, and it was not a minor disagreement that could be resolved with proper compromises.

Luke began our verse with the Greek word "de." The primary meaning of this word is "but," expressing a contrast, and it is the second word in the Greek text. While the early Church received this discouraging news, they responded in a positive manner. In spite of the Sanhedrin's threats, they worshipped and praised the Lord who is God concluding in a prayer for His continued movement in their midst.

The structure of the rest of the verse is of keen interest

to us. Luke presented a participle, which is a verb that serves as an adjective. This participle is the Greek word "akouo," translated, *"when they heard that." "They"* becomes the subject of the sentence, which refers to those who heard the report from the apostles. But the subject is "they, the hearing ones" not just *"they." "Raised"* (airo) and *"said"* (epo) become the compound verb of the sentence. However, the key factor of the statement is "homothumadon," which is translated *"with one accord."* This word is an adverb and gives content to all the verbs of the sentence. In other words, they were in one accord in their hearing, in raising their voices, and in what they said! Therefore, they had "Oneness in Akouo," "Oneness in Admiration," and "Oneness in Articulation." This gives us a structure for our study.

In our previous study, we discussed "Oneness in Akouo." "Homothumadon" is the Greek word translated *"with one accord."* "Homo" means, "same place and time," and "thumos" refers to passion, "as if heavy breathing." The combination of these two words is expressive, emphasizing all are passionately focused on the same thing. They had only one desire. The believers were united in what they heard from the report of the apostles. Because they heard in unity, they expressed themselves in unity. Intimacy with Jesus produced a passion within them that they had to express. We want to carefully examine this inner passion!

"They raised their voice to God." This is "Oneness in Admiration." "Homothumadon" is an adverb giving content to the main verb *"raised."* It explains the spirit and passion that motivated their actions. What was this passion? It was "worship!" Other words describing worship are reverence, veneration, adoration, glorification, exaltation, and honor. These are all inner feelings or attitudes. Our statement is not focused on how they expressed themselves; that investigation will follow at a later time. What caused them to raise their voices to God? They all

felt, sensed, or experienced the same inner attitude. They were ***"with one accord."***

How do we measure "worship?" Is the worshipper with two hands raised expressing more that the worshipper who raises one hand? Does the person standing worship better than the people who are seated? The outward expression of worship must be released to each person's preference. Our concern is not the outward expression but the inner presence of worship. Should there not be definite times in the believer when inner love, gratitude, and adoration burn with passion? The "dark night of the soul" is experienced at times. Perhaps praise and worship is given but not felt. But this is not the norm! Should not the believer, even in the midst of threats, be consumed with the greatness of our God?

Creation

The first burning passion the early Church expressed was for creation. They cried, ***"Lord, You are God, who made heaven and earth and the sea, and all that is in them"*** (Acts 4:24). They were certainly not the first to express the greatness of our Creator. This is a continual theme of the Psalms. Carefully consider a psalm entitled "The Sovereignty of the Lord in Creation and History."

> *"By the word of the Lord the heavens were made,*
> *And all the host of them by the breath of His mouth.*
> *He gathers the waters of the sea together as a heap;*
> *He lays up the deep in storehouses.*
> *Let all the earth fear the Lord;*
> *Let all the inhabitants of the world stand in awe of Him.*
> *For He spoke, and it was done;*
> *He commanded, and it stood fast"* (Psalms 33:6-9).

The New Testament is equally dominated by this same theme. Paul could hardly contain his worship as he wrote, *"For by Him* (Jesus) *all things were created that are in heaven and that are on earth, visible and invisible, whether thrones or dominions or principalities or powers. All things were created through Him and for Him. And He is before all things, and in Him all things consist"* (Colossians 1:16-17).

Some claim that they can better worship God amid His creation rather than in a church building on Sunday morning. Something can be said about the grandeur of the mountains or the wonder of a sunset; however, to become enamored by created things may cause us to miss the Creator. The moment that happens we become idolaters. Paul described the pagan worshipers as, *"Professing to be wise, they became fools, and changed the glory of the incorruptible God into an image made like corruptible man – and birds and four-footed animals and creeping things,"* (Romans 1:22-23). They *"worshiped and served the creature rather than the Creator, who is blessed forever. Amen"* (Romans 1:25). Unless the creation reveals His Person, the creation becomes an idol.

The early Church witnessed a multitude of signs and wonders, and now the healed beggar stood in their midst. In their hour of threat the early Church prayed, *"grant to Your servants that with all boldness they may speak Your word, by stretching out Your hand to heal, and that signs and wonders may be done through the name of Your holy Servant Jesus"* (Acts 4:29, 30). It would have been easy for them to focus on the miracles. They could have worshipped miracles rather than Jesus. Could their inside passion be stimulated and focused on blessings instead of the One blessing? Signs and wonders could become an idol replacing Jesus!

Jesus gave great provision to the early Church. They *"had all things in common, and sold their possessions and goods, and divided them among all, as anyone had need"* (Acts 2:44, 45).

Could the early Church have become so focused on the solutions of their needs that they missed the Provider? Jesus alone must become the sole focus of our worship! If every material and spiritual blessing is in Jesus, He must be what stirs the inner passion of worship.

Concentration

Our verse has a focus or concentration! *"So when they heard that, they raised their voice to God"* (Acts 4:24). The Greek word "pros," translated *"to,"* is a preposition of direction, a key understanding, which must be grasped. This reality moves worship from a ceremony or emotional feeling into the embrace of a Person. The Apostle Paul expresses the concept consistently in his epistles. The Greek word "en" is our English word "in." "Into" and "from" are movement terms for changing locations. But "in" refers to a fixed position! Paul expressed the reality of *"Christ in you, the hope of glory"* (Colossians 1:27). He also gave expression to our position in Christ. *"Even when we were dead in trespasses, made us alive together with Christ (by grace you have been saved), and raised us up together, and made us sit together in the heavenly places in Christ Jesus"* (Ephesians 2:5, 6).

This dual action is the heart of worship. While we see a beautiful sunset and experience emotional feelings of awe and wonder, it is not Biblical worship. A person approaches worship only when their feelings become aware of the Creator and Source of the sunset. However, the awareness must not be data or knowledge that a superior power created the sunset; it is the embrace of the Creator of the sunset who lives within. In worship I experience His presence. In the experience of this intimacy with Him, I begin to express an attitude of submission and honor only God can source. In a sense, God who lives within me and is sourcing my life begins to express worship back to Him through me! Both of these spiritual actions must happen in order for worship to be Biblical! Christ in you reveals the greatness of His reality; He enables you to give expression to that greatness in worship.

Consecration

Most of the present-day church would be content to end our discussion here and now. We would simply bask in the greatness of His presence for these moments and return to our normal lives unaffected and with no interference. However, the early Church could not be satisfied with indifference. Their worship quickly turned into a request. They cried out, ***"Lord, look on their threats, and grant to Your servants that will all boldness they may speak Your word"*** (Acts 4:29). They understood the seriousness of the Sanhedrin's threats. They visualized how their ability to speak His word could be hampered. They cried for boldness that only Christ indwelling them could source. But they understood He would not simply give them boldness to speak His word but would need to demonstrate that boldness through them ***"by stretching out Your hand to heal, and that signs and wonders may be done through the name of Your holy Servant Jesus"*** (Acts 4:30).

The early Church embraced the heart of worship. Worship at its core is the surrender of my being to the revelation of the One living in me. The worshiper becomes aware of the presence of the Spirit of Jesus within and responds by surrendering themselves to the flow of the ministry of the Spirit through them. If both aspects of worship do not take place, worship is degraded to ceremony or cheap emotionalism. Therefore, worship can never be isolated to moments in a church service. Worship must be the life style of the believer.

Part 4: The Absolute Reign

The story is told of a monk who experienced a special moment in the presence of Christ. It was his hour of prayer; Jesus was especially real to him, and He sensed the presence of Christ more than ever before. During these moments of worship, he became aware of ministry obligations. It was drawing close to the time when he must serve the meal to the poor, but He did not want to leave the warmth of Jesus' presence to minister to the needy. Finally, he slipped out of the prayer time to serve. After all was finished, he rushed back to the place of prayer afraid the presence of Christ would be gone. To his amazement he discovered the presence of Christ was greater than when he left. He exclaimed to Jesus, "Oh, I thought you would be gone because I left." Jesus explained, "No, my son, if you had not gone, I would not have stayed."

Experiencing a special moment of Jesus' presence is refreshing and stimulating. But ultimately that emotional experience means nothing without the demonstration of that Presence in ministry to my world. Perhaps the test of His presence experienced in a moment is the experience of His presence in the daily ministry in my world. Entertainment Christianity has produced an atmosphere of emotional stimuli giving us the sense of His presence. But it falls short of real worship when there is no surrender. It quickly becomes a false security giving the appearance that we live in Him, but He does not live in us because we are not His!

Confirmation

The certainty of what the early Church knew about God was in the Scriptures. Therefore, the worship of the early Church was rooted and founded in the Scriptures. Amid the threats against their lives, they ran back to the Scriptures. They cried out to God; they knew Him as the Creator of the **"heaven and earth** *and the sea, and all that is in them"* (Acts 4:24). He is sovereign. He is not just the Creator to them, but He is speaking to them! They proceeded to quote David, the psalmist (Acts 4:25-26). According to them, this quoted Psalm was not sourced or spoken by David, but was spoken by God who simply used *"the mouth of Your servant David"* (Acts 4:25).

The confirmation of their worship was not visions, trances, or dreams. It was not the expression of any particular gift of the Spirit. Their confirmation was the Scriptures. In fact, their prayer and desire were that *"with all boldness they may speak Your word."* God spoke the Psalm they quoted through the mouth of David, making this Scripture the word of God. Their desire that they might speak the word of God with boldness would refer to the Scriptures. Since the New Testament had not been written at this time, they referred to the Old Testament.

Should the content of our worship be the Scriptures? Our songs, praises, and testimonies should be focused on the Living Word flowing through the Written Word. But if worship is not concentrated in a building during a particular time, should not the content of our daily lifestyle of worship be the Scriptures? Should we not be saturating moment by moment in His presence through His Word? Is this the lifestyle of worship?

Acts 4:24

ONENESS IN ARTICULATION

"So when they heard that, they raised their voice to God with one accord and said: 'Lord, you are God, who made heaven and earth and sea, and all that is in them" (Acts 4:24).

The clarity of a theological belief is never revealed in an argument or discovered in a classroom setting. You cannot portray the depth of your convictions in a sermon or Sunday school lesson. The reality of your belief is revealed in the crisis moments of your life when you spontaneously gush forth with physical and verbal expressions. That kind of expression is what is happening in our passage; the early Church felt persecution for the first time. The Sanhedrin wanted to do much more to the apostles and the early Church than merely threaten them; however, the miracle of the lame beggar's healing was well known. All the people of Jerusalem **"glorified God for what had been done"** (Acts 4:21).

The persecution of the apostles naturally extended to the members of the early Church. As the apostles reported the details of the Sanhedrin's threats, the spontaneous response of the early Church revealed their convictions. The dominant feature that infiltrated all they believed was "unity." We discovered the Greek word "homothumadon," translated **"with one accord,"** is an adverb. "Homo" means "same place and time," and "thumos" refers to "passion," "as if heavy breathing." "Homothumadon" modifies all the verbs in this opening statement (Acts 4:24) and relates to their hearing, **"So when they heard that,"** they worshipped, **"they raised their voice to God."** They gave expression **"and said."** The early Church began to speak with one voice in response to the report of the apostles.

The early Church began to express a united opinion about God, knowing they had a connection between God and themselves. The link between them and God was strong, leaving us to think they were filled and merged with Him. God's thought became their thought. What was true for God, they embraced as true for themselves. Their desperate desire was for this reality to be known in their world.

The early Church broke forth in the quotation of a great messianic Psalm (Psalms 2), describing the heart of the Trinity God's redemptive act in Jesus! David, the psalmist, described the evil rage of the world's nations against the Divine plan, a rebellion **"against the Lord and against His Christ"** (Acts 4:26). Prophetic fulfillment revealed Herod and Pontius Pilate with the Gentiles and the Israelite nation warring against the Divine **"purpose determined before to be done"** (Acts 4:28). The early Church viewed themselves as a fulfillment of this continued prophecy. The threats they felt were not against them but **"against the Lord and against His Christ."** They participated in the drama of fulfilled prophecy. What happened to them happened to Jesus, and what happened to Jesus happened to them. They were linked not only with His plan but with Him through the fulfillment of Christ's Spirit.

In oneness the early Church articulated this link! Their oneness was not in a common cause or fellowship. They were one in Christ. It was not just a cause or a fellowship; it was Jesus! Jesus is the cause; Jesus is the fellowship. We must understand this! Because they were filled with the nature of God, they became one with Him in the enterprise of redemption. All the difficulties and battles involved in such an enterprise were gladly endured because of oneness with His Person. In merging with Him, they merged with His vision. As each individual lived in this merger, they found themselves one with each other. This merger extended even to their physical needs, *"Nor was there anyone among them who lacked; for all who were possessors of lands or houses sold them, and brought the proceeds of the things that were sold, and laid them at the apostles' feet; and they distributed to each as anyone had need"* (Acts 4:34-35).

The early Church began to express the desire of the Trinity God. The way Jesus approached suffering (Matthew 26:36+) became their approach to suffering. The attitude Jesus expressed in persecution (Luke 23:34) became their attitude toward persecution. Jesus always expressed the nature of the Trinity, and now the early Church expressed the Trinity's nature. They were linked with the nature of God. They were in the same circumstances and felt the same way, moving them to "oneness in articulation." Luke expressed this in the simple Greek word "epo," translated, *"said,"* generally used for "saying or speaking" followed with the accusative (direct object) of what was said. What is important in our verse is that Luke gave us the content of the speaking. They were one in the hearing; they were one in raising their voice to God. These two elements give us the picture of *"said."* All the passion (heavy breathing) of oneness was focused on Christ causing oneness in "akouo" (hearing) and in "admiration" (worship). This was the atmosphere of what they said.

Creative Speaking

Several elements are in the content of their praise expression. Listen closely to the unison voice of the early Church. *"Lord, You are God, who made heaven and earth and the sea, and all that is in them"* (Acts 4:24). The first word in the Greek text is translated *"Lord,"* a Greek vocative designating the person being addressed, and is used to emphatically or with heightened emotion designate the person being addressed. *"Lord"* is a master or one with supreme authority. This person becomes the subject of the sentence. The verb is understood as "eimi," a verb of being. The Greek verb "poieo," translated *"made,"* becomes a predicate noun, giving content to and is equal to the subject.

The early Church amid threats focused on the sovereign Lord and His creative nature! We have often explained the word "poieo," doing distinctly tied to whatever flows from one's nature. The word is doing but not simply in the sense of activity, duty, or discipline. It is doing with artistry, flow, or to bear. Trees do not do fruit; they bear (poieo) fruit! This type of doing is the reality of God's nature. We know that He is good because everything flowing from His nature is good. He has manifested Himself to us and in us through all that He created (Romans 1:19- 20). God is love: it is His nature (1 John 4:8). The love (nature) of God is demonstrated toward us; we know that He absolutely loves us. He sent His only begotten Son into our world so we might live through Him (1 John 4:9). He loved us (nature) and sent His Son to be our Redeemer because of our sins (1 John 4:10). The nature of God always creates according to the desire and delight of that nature. If the speaking of God is the method of creation, then God speaks according to His nature.

The early Church was in one accord with the nature of God; therefore, the early Church spoke and created the same design and expressed the same desire as God. The reason they said the same thing was because they had the same nature, God's nature. As you listen to the testimony of these early Christians, they had the same tone as what God said,

> *"I will declare the decree:*
> *The Lord said to Me,*
> *'You are My son,*
> *Today I have begotten You.*

Part 4: The Absolute Reign

> *Ask of Me, and I will give You*
> *The nations for Your inheritance,*
> *And the ends of the earth for Your possession.*
> *You shall break them with a rod of iron;*
> *You shall dash them to pieces like a potter's vessel'"*
> *(Psalms 2:7-9).*

This Psalm is an expression of God's nature and His creative plan. Listen to the expression of the nature of God merged with the early Church, **"Now, Lord, look on their threats, and grant to Your servants that with all boldness they may speak Your word, by stretching out Your hand to heal, and that signs and wonders may be done through the name of Your holy Servant Jesus"** (Acts 4:29, 30). The same tone is produced by the same nature. Even amid threats from the most powerful men of Israel, there is the nature of God, His plan empowered by the sovereignty of His being, and His calling on us.

The unity of the early Church was in their expression of God's nature. They expressed the nature of God because they were filled with Him. Unity was not in joining the same organization; it was not a result of the challenge of a new cause. Unity was birthed from the inner being, the nature. We must become one with God in nature to become one with each other. We find unity in Him; division is an expression of not knowing Him. His desire, purpose, and plan become our focus!

Contractual Speaking

Luke gave us additional insight into the expression of unity in the early Church. After hearing the full report of the apostles concerning the present threats of the Sanhedrin, they, with one accord, were moved with passionate worship. They focused on the sovereignty of God who created all things. But the foundation of their worship was found in the Scriptures. They began to quote a Messianic Psalm (Psalms 2), a psalm that paralleled their present situation. The nations were raging and the people were plotting vain things (Acts 4:25; Psalms 2:1). The authorities of this world gathered for the battle (Acts 4:26; Psalms 2:2). These authorities fought *"against the Lord and against His Christ"* (Acts 4:26; Psalms 2:2).

The early Church understood this battle was fulfilled in Herod, Pontius Pilate with the Gentiles, and the people of Israel. The crucifixion and suffering of Jesus were fresh in their minds. Yet, through all the conflict, God was sovereign. Even the suffering of Christ inflicted on Him through the battle was dominated by the sovereign **"hand and Your purpose determined before to be done"** (Acts 4:28). No less was true in the lives of the early Church as they faced the present threats of the Sanhedrin. The early Church saw what was happening in their lives in light of what had happened in the life of Christ.

From where did this Messianic Psalm originate? David, the psalmist, wrote it but He did not speak it. The early Church believed this psalm was spoken by God, but through the mouth of David (Acts 4:25). Therefore, the nature of God spoke the words of God. Dwelling in the core of the early Church was this nature of God. This nature spoke the words of God with the attitude of God. Later Stephen, the first martyr of the early Church revealed God's nature while he was stoned. **"Then he knelt down and cried out with a loud voice, 'Lord, do not charge them with this sin'"** (Acts 7:60). We heard this same intent from the crucified Christ (Luke 23:34). The nature of God is speaking through the mouth of a man.

Two aspects to the unity of the early Church exist. They were in union with the nature of God, giving them the power to speak the words of God. They were in unity with each other because of their unity with the nature of God. Therefore, they spoke the words of God. In threatening moments are you and

I in oneness with the Spirit of God? The answer will be revealed in whether we speak the words of God. If we mimic the words of God in moments of ease, the testing of threats will soon come. The words of God come from the nature of God that gives us the mind of God. This mimicking is not a call to increased discipline or self-control but is a call to deeper unity and merger with His heart. View your life in the threatening moments for the revelation of your mind. Are you united with Him?

Consecrated Speaking

Because the early Church was united with Christ, they were united. In this oneness God enabled them to speak His words. In fact, it became their one desire, and it was amazing! Their prayers were not for God to remove the threats or eliminate the persecution of the Sanhedrin. What a dramatic change this was from the days of early discipleship when the disciples traveled with Jesus toward Jerusalem. They were rejected when they entered a village of the Samaritans, planning to stay the night. Their immediate response was ***"Lord, do You want us to command fire to come down from heaven and consume them, just as Elijah did"*** (Luke 9:54)? They did not know the mind of Christ. They were not even embarrassed by their carnal desires. Jesus rebuked them with great insight, ***"You do not know what manner of spirit you are of. For the Son of Man did not come to destroy men's lives but to save them"*** (Luke 9:55-56). If you do not have the mind of Christ, whose mind do you have? The nature of Jesus did not indwell them; therefore, His intentions were not theirs.

The early Church was filled with the nature of Christ. Their supreme desire was not to escape difficulty. They did not cry for personal safety or demand release from their difficulties. They desired God to look at the threats and match the degree of those threats with the degree of boldness they needed to continue speaking His word (Acts 4:29). This word was not to be spoken in a well-organized seminar or in the safety of the local church sanctuary. This word was to be declared as the demonstration of God's Spirit moving through them in the power of Jesus' name. In other words, they desired the indwelling Spirit of Christ to show the power of the name they were not to mention. No secondary plan or hidden means was to be. The word of God was to be spoken in boldness, which would manifest itself in visible results because of Jesus' name.

Evidently, the early Church was as convinced of Jesus' reality as were the apostles. They were not fighting against the unfair threats of the leaders of Israel. They did not seem to care about the filth of the jail in which they dwelt for one night. They said nothing about the unfair criticisms of the Sanhedrin because of their lack of education. The power of Jesus' name must be recognized and maintained. Despite the consequences they desired the manifestation of His name.

Unison with the nature of Christ brought about unison in the speaking of His name, their one focus and consecration. He captured them without distractions. They consecrated themselves saying, **"Your purpose determined before to be done."** The need of this hour is for the same merging and oneness with Christ and therefore with each other.

Acts 4:24

MASTER / DESPOT

"So when they heard that, they raised their voice to God with one accord and said: 'Lord, you are God, who made heaven and earth and sea, and all that is in them" (Acts 4:24).

Jesus is the expression of the God's heart. **"He is the image of the invisible God"** (Colossians 1:15). When I think about God, I think about Jesus. When the Holy Spirit is mentioned, I immediately refer to the Spirit of Jesus. Jesus is the doorway to my understanding of God. In heaven, I will see only Jesus, for He is the only member of the Godhead with a physical body. Jesus shapes my perception of God.

Who is Jesus? He is referred to repeatedly in the Scriptures as God (John 1:1; Isaiah 9:6; Hebrews 1:8-9). Any attempt to consider Him less than God or a creation of God is against the Scriptures. But the wonder of wonders is the incarnation! God became man. A tremendous submission had to occur for this to transpire. Jesus, who is God, surrendered His omnipresence to be conceived in His mother's womb. He limited Himself to the boundaries of His flesh. Jesus, who is God, surrendered His omniscience. Everything He knew as God was set aside when He became a babe who knew nothing. Luke wrote, **"And Jesus increased in wisdom and stature, and in favor with God and men"** (Luke 2:52). Jesus, who is God, surrendered His omnipotence. He became a helpless babe in His mother's arms. He was not only helpless physically, but He fulfilled the requirement of the first Beatitude (Matthew 5:3). He became ***"poor in spirit."*** He became a helpless man filled with the Spirit of God. A helpless man merged with the Spirit of God became the first Kingdom Person!

Jesus fulfilled the Law and the prophets (Matthew 5:17). Everything God intended in the Law and the prophets was clearly revealed and accomplished in the life of Jesus. Jesus gives us clear understanding of the Old Testament. He determines our perception of God. The truth of God being holy becomes visible in Jesus. God is love; God's love is revealed beyond question in Jesus. We revel in this; it is the theme of the party; it pulls from us worship that never grows old or stale. We are in love with Jesus. Jesus said, ***"I am gentle and lowly in heart, and you will find rest for your souls. For My yoke is easy and My burden is light"*** (Matthew 11:29-30). The Scriptures give us imagery to remind us of our intimate relationship and merger with Him. He is our Bridegroom, and we are His bride (Ephesians 5). We experience oneness in His love. We are the branches, and He is the vine (John 15). We live in the flow of life from His being. He is the good Shepherd, and we are His sheep (Matthew 18:12-14). We are safe in His arms. We are baptized into the fullness of His being. We are submerged in Him.

You and I can be and should be captured by this reality. We do not belittle the love connection between Jesus and the believer. However, in light of God's love there is something important we may forget. Jesus is the absolute sovereign Lord! The early Church did not forget His sovereignty. They cried, ***"Lord, You are God, who made heaven and earth and the sea, and all that is in them"*** (Acts 4:24). The Greek word "despotes," translated *"Lord,"* is not the typical word. "Kurios" is used 7 hundred and 17 times in the New Testament and is usually translated "Lord" or "Master." "Despotes" is used only 10 times in the New Testament describing a man's relationship with his slaves, while "kurios" refers to his relationship with his wife and children. When they spoke to or of the master, they gave him this title of honor.

The distinction between "despotes" and "kurios" suggest the issue of moral limitations. "Kurios" implies an authority that owns these limitations. The implication is that Lord (kurios) has an authority that includes a consideration of good for the one over whom the sovereignty is exercised. However, "despotes" exercises a more unrestricted power and absolute domination, confessing no such limitations or restraints. When someone addresses another as ***"Lord"*** (despotes), it contains an emphasis of submission that "kurios" does not have. This word is used for Jesus in two passages. ***"Therefore if anyone cleanses himself from the latter, he will be a vessel for honor, sanctified and useful for the Master*** (despotes)*"* (2 Timothy 2:21); ***"But there were also false prophets among the people, even as there will be false teachers among you, who will secretly bring in destructive heresies, even denying the Lord*** (despotes) ***who bought them, and bring on themselves swift destruction"*** (2 Peter 2:1).

The early Church experienced an intimate, loving relationship with the fullness of Jesus' Spirit, yet they did not lose sight of His position as ***"Lord"*** (despotes). He was not the Grandfather of the sky whom they could easily manipulate. He was not Santa Claus who continued to give gifts to naughty children. God is a "gentle giant," but He is still a giant! Although freewill is in the structure of man's design, it is true that man will ***"do whatever Your hand and Your purpose determined before to be done"*** (Acts 4:28). God's sovereignty is secure and absolute. He is in charge!

In light of this fact, the early Church approached the threats of the Sanhedrin with a question,

Why did the nations rage,
And the people plot vain things?
The kings of the earth took their stand,

> *And the rulers were gathered together*
> *Against the Lord* (kurios) *and against His Christ*
> (Acts 4:25-26).

Who did the Sanhedrin think they were in light of the sovereign God? The nations raged against the Lord God Almighty in great folly. Did they not know that they plotted in vain? How would you describe this foolish conflict? Is it not like a four-year-old child trying to conquer his father? Is it not a person whose life is destroyed by the cancer of sin? In weakness and bedridden helplessness, he attempts to dethrone the powerful one. Are we not helpless and decayed by our sin? Would not our attempted stand against the Lord and His Christ be laughable if it were not so tragic? In our fallen state, we continually think we know better than God. We resist His input in our lives. We who were never intended to be anything but helpless attempt to be God! How foolish is our attempt?

Originator

The early Church rested in the sovereignty of Jesus. He is sovereign in origination. *"Lord, You are God, who made heaven and earth and the sea, and all that is in them"* (Acts 4:24). In our culture the masters are those who invent and can see with a vision. This vision enables them to take what is, re-create it, and go beyond what we who are ordinary can imagine. That ability is amazing. But our Sovereign Christ is not an inventor. He does not adjust what is already present into a working model for His glory. God speaks the idea in His mind into existence. Out of nothing He brings everything. He is sovereign in creation!

His creation is our means to measure His sovereignty. We say He is greater than the world. Although this is true, we measure with the world's measuring rod. God is greater than the universes, but this is a comparison of His greatness to the measurement of the universes. God is greater than the world or the universes. We simply choose the greatest thing we know and compare God with it. But these are all created entities. How great is God really? We have no measurement!

Is it not enough to know that our sovereign Lord created you and me? Out of nothing, He brought us into being. Listen to the psalmist's understanding of this,

For you formed my inward parts;
You covered me in my mother's womb.
I will praise You, for I am fearfully and wonderfully made;
Marvelous are Your works,
And that my soul knows very well.
My frame was not hidden from You,
When I was made in secret,
And skillfully wrought in the lowest parts of the earth.
Your eyes saw my substance, being yet unformed.
And in Your book they all were written,
The days fashioned for me,
When as yet there were none of them
(Psalms 139:13-16).

Are there any words more powerful to describe God's involvement in the creation of our being prior to our existence? Are you and I not the product of His dream and the result of His powerful hands?

The early Church understood the involvement of the Sovereign Creator. God creates but we do not. We are not to create because that role belongs to God. Amid threats, persecution, and serious life issue, who is the creator? Who is it that creates solutions for those He created with a purpose from the beginning? The Hebrew author invites us to enter *"a rest for the people of God. For he who has entered His rest has himself also ceased from his works as God did from His"* (Hebrews 4:9-10). What were the works of God from which He rested? He rested from creating. We are to rest from creating solutions to our problems, answers for our questions, and provisions for our needs. He is the Sovereign Creator. We live without stress and worry when we rest in His sovereignty! Embrace His plan and *"purpose determined before to be done."*

Owner

"Lord, You are God, who made heaven and earth and the sea, and all that is in them" (Acts 4:24). The reality of God as the "Originator" places Him as "Owner." He is the Owner in all the parables Jesus told. He is the Owner of the field in which the good seed was planted, and an enemy came at night and planted tares (Matthew 13:24-25). He is the Owner of the mustard seed sown in His field and that grew into a large tree (Matthew 13:31). He is the Owner of the leaven and the three measures of meal (Matthew 13:33). He is the Owner of 100 sheep from which one strayed (Matthew 18:12). He is the king from which a servant stole 10,000 talents (Matthew 18:23). He is the Owner of the vineyard who hired servants at various hours throughout the day and paid them all the same at the end (Matthew 20:1). He is the Owner of the vineyard who leased it to greedy vinedressers (Matthew 21:33). He is the King who arranged for the marriage of His Son (Matthew 22:2). His sovereignty shouts His ownership!

As a child, I learned many stories of ownership. With the help of his father, a young boy made a toy sailboat. Carefully carving its shape, painting its structure, and placing the sails, the sailboat was ready to launch. The wind caught the sails, and the boat began sailing the lake. The boy was thrilled. Each day he took his boat to the lake; he carefully attached a string so as not to lose it. But one day the string broke. To his discouragement he lost his boat. He searched the shores of the lake but could not find his boat. One day he walked past the pawnshop and discovered his boat in the window. With delight, he marched into the shop to declare his ownership. A fisherman found the boat and sold it to the pawnshop. The boy would have to pay money to reclaim the boat he built. To acquire the funds, he worked at every odd job he could find. Finally, the day came when he could purchase his boat. Coming from the pawnshop he was heard to say to his boat, "You are mine twice! First, I made you. Second, I bought you back." Do we not belong to our Sovereign God twice?

"Why did the nations rage, and the people plot vain things?" (Acts 4:25). Is it not because they did not recognize God's ownership? Our raging reveals our stress, anxiety, and worry. Ownership is the issue! Ownership brings responsibility, and responsibility causes stress. I do not stress over checking the oil in a rented car. I simply do not care because it is not my car. I have concern and will certainly place your children on my prayer list, but I do not pray all night for them. They are not my children. It is my financial bills that worry me; it is my life that gives me concern.

The early Church knew the threats of the chief priests and elders. Their immediate response was to praise. The praise was not a positive approach to a bad situation. They recognized the ownership of their Sovereign God. They did not own the circumstances caused by the filling of His Spirit; He did. They were not responsible for the solution; He was. They did not cause the miracle instigating this persecution; He did. They are not the ones with a plan; He is! This is the core issue of surrender. It seems we place surrender in the context of things, items, or specific issues rather than in ownership. Surrender to Jesus means I give up ownership. Nothing is mine! Paul cried, **"Or do you not know that your body is the temple of the Holy Spirit who is in you, whom you have from God, and you are not your own?"** (1 Corinthians 6:19).

Order

"Lord, You are God, who made heaven and earth and the sea, and all that is in them" (Acts 4:24). Remember the Greek word translated *"Lord"* is "despotes." It means one who exercises unrestricted power and absolute domination. It is the basis of our English word "despot" meaning, "a ruler or other person who holds absolute power, typically one who exercises it in a cruel or oppressive way." God occupying this position is frightening. God is sovereign; therefore, we become mere objects of His whims and desires. This would explain, *"Why did the nations rage, and the people plot vain things?"* Although all our efforts may be futile against such power, we must do something against such a tyrant.

However, the key when dealing with "despot" is found in the Greek word "poieo," translated *"made."* The creation, "poieo," by our Sovereign God is a display and result of His nature. The Greek word "poieo" is used for trees bearing fruit. It involves the expression of the inner nature. If God is mean, vindictive, or cruel, we must protest His authority. If God is love and always redemptive, we can safely surrender to Him. In fact, it is a privilege. Paul was strong concerning this truth, *"For since the creation of the world His invisible attributes are clearly seen, being understood by the things that are made, even His eternal power and Godhead, so that they are without excuse"* (Romans 1:20).

Although the power of our Sovereign God is seen in His creation, it also displays His loving nature. Remember, *"God is love. In this the love of God was manifested toward us, that God has sent His only begotten Son into the world, that we might live through Him"* (1 John 4:8-9). *"For God so loved the world that He gave His only begotten Son, that whoever believes in Him should not perish but have everlasting life"* (John 3:16). If

Part 4: The Absolute Reign

I were to quote all the Scripture verses stating this fact, I would quote the entire Bible. Jesus is the manifestation of the nature of the Trinity God. He, the Sovereign Creator, the Owner of all things, became the created One who was owned. He revealed the throbbing heart of the Trinity God. Our Sovereign God is exactly like Jesus. Jesus is the full revelation of God. If so, you can trust Him. His plan is secure, and His plan is love! He is the bleeding, suffering, and dying One who never thinks about Himself. He constantly works for your betterment. Therefore, ***"Why did the nations rage, and the people plot vain things?"*** That attitude is foolishness. In fighting against our Sovereign loving God, we are fighting against ourselves. We hang onto our own destruction. Amid every circumstance we must do exactly as the early Church did! We must submit in praise and joy to the sovereign plan. Things are not out of control; it is time for submission!

Acts 4:25

OUR SOVEREIGN SPEAKS

Who by the mouth of Your servant David have said: "Why did the nations rage, and the people plot vain things?" (Acts 4:25).

The Book of Acts is far more than a historical account of the early Church's development. Acts gives us important information about the churches planted by Paul on his missionary journeys. Luke explains the theological issues of the Jewish requirements for the Gentile converts. He highlights the unprecedented movement of God's Spirit repeatedly. The reader of the book is allowed to see the unfolding plan of God revealed through the daily circumstances of the early believers' lives and the overall thrust of evangelism throughout the world. The message is to us! This purpose and movement did not end within the time bracket of this book; it continues into our lives.

One of the benefits of the Book of Acts is the revelation of the early Church's beliefs. We are exposed to their approach to daily circumstances, crisis moments, and expectations. The basic focus on unshakable principles is highlighted in the book. Although the book consists of a series of historical accounts, these stories reveal the thinking of the early believers. For instance, how did they view the Scriptures, the Old Testament? What role did the Scriptures play in their decisions? What did they think about the Scriptures' authenticity? Did they take the stories of the Old Testament literally?

Part 4: The Absolute Reign

Luke presents the answers to these questions in our passage. The Sanhedrin threatened Peter and John. The threat was *"not to speak at all nor teach in the name of Jesus"* (Acts 4:18). If the apostles obeyed this command, Christianity would cease. The focus of their faith, teaching, and inner desires were on Jesus. To eliminate Jesus would be to eliminate Christianity. When they were released they returned to the early Church members and gave a full account. When these members understood the threats, they broke into rejoicing and praise. Their attention was immediately turned toward the Scriptures (Acts 4:25-26), a Psalm (2:1-2) by David, which they acknowledged. However, in Luke's introduction to the Psalm, we receive insight into how they viewed the Scriptures. He wrote, *"who by the mouth of Your servant David have said:"* (Acts 4:25).

There seems to be three radical suggestions in the statement. "Inspiration" is the first suggestion. They did not consider David the source of the Psalm. He was not the author of these words or the originator of the thoughts. God spoke this Psalm, not David. This was not an isolated suggestion in the Book of Acts. During the first recorded business meeting of the early Church, Peter quoted two Psalms. He introduced these with this statement, *"Men and brethren, this Scripture had to be fulfilled, which the Holy Spirit spoke before by the mouth of David concerning Judas"* (Acts 1:16). Peter believed that God spoke the Old Testament. During Paul's house arrest in Rome, he invited the Jews to spend the day. He revealed Jesus to them through the Old Testament. Some believed in Jesus, but others did not. Paul sent them off with a parting word, *"The Holy Spirit spoke rightly through Isaiah the prophet to our fathers, saying"* (Acts 28:25). He quoted the prophet Isaiah (6:9-10). This basic idea is found repeatedly in the Scriptures.

"Instrument" is the second suggestion. God used the personalities of David and Isaiah to present these passages to us, but the early Church believed Isaiah and David were instruments;

our sovereign God was the source of the words. The writings of David and Isaiah reflected two personalities, styles, and manners. This fact does not reduce the reality that God used the instrument of man to deliver His message!

The third suggestion is "instruction." The early Church believed that the Scriptures, sourced by God and spoken through men, were Divine instruction to all. How would you engage the Scriptures if you believed this? You actually have a document that is a personal message from God to you! When you read it, God's lips part and He speaks directly to you. To believe this makes the Scriptures the single source of your instruction. You then live in its truths and saturate in its precepts.

The Sovereignty
of God

We need to embrace the reality of our passage. In our previous studies, we realized the strength of the early Church's belief. They were unmovable in their commitment to the sovereignty of God. Their beginning response to the crisis threats of the Sanhedrin was, **"Lord, You are God, who made heaven and earth and the sea, and all that is in them"** (Acts 4:24). They believed God was sovereign based on His creation of everything! It was because of the Scriptures! They believed Jesus' crucifixion was a result of this sovereignty. Although the high-ranking authorities of the Gentile world gathered with the people of Israel, they performed **"whatever Your hand and Your purpose determined before to be done"** (Acts 4:28). How did they know this? They knew this because it was a fulfillment of the Scriptures!

Although I believe the previous paragraph, there is another side to this reality. Although the sovereignty of God was embraced because the early Church believed the Scriptures, they believed the Scriptures because they embraced a sovereign God. They did not do an academic study of the Scriptures and decide God was sovereign. They did not research the background of the Scriptures and conclude its inspiration. The early Church was filled with the Holy Spirit, the Author of the Scriptures. This Author told the truth contained in the Scriptures and revealed all said within. They communicated with the Author who spoke the Scriptures to them. The Scriptures became an organism through the life of our sovereign God.

If a sovereign God speaks the story of the early Church through the Scriptures, perhaps He speaks our story through the same Scriptures. On hearing the reported threats of the Sanhedrin, the early Church immediately turned to the Scriptures proclaiming a sovereign God. Their confidence was not in a document but in a sovereign Person who spoke to them through the Scriptures. Their confidence was not in a sovereign person of their design but in the sovereign God revealed through the Scriptures. Our sovereign God reveals Himself through the Scriptures and does not deviate from them!

The Scriptures set the pattern for our lives. We must saturate in His presence through saturation in His Word. This saturation is how we will know Him. He speaks to us through the Scriptures. If we experience His presence aside from His Word, we do not know who He is. If we only have a document speaking about Him, we simply have data and information; we become legalistic and argumentative. We must know Him in His presence and allow Him to speak to us through His Word.

We must understand our circumstances through this interaction. Are not the crises of our circumstances under His control? Is He not sovereign? Has He revealed His sovereignty to us through His Word? May we boldly confront our world because of His revelation in us? May we break into praise and quote the Scriptures that our sovereign God **"by the mouth of Your servant David"** has spoken to us? Is panic, worry, and stress a result of the lack of this interaction of the sovereign Lord and the sovereign Word in my life?

The Servanthood
of man

It is a mystery! The sovereign God, who needs nothing, placed Himself in the position of the limited expression of *"the mouth of Your servant David;"* it is a mystery! The Greek word translated *"servant"* is not "doulos," a person in bondage to his master, instead it is the Greek word "pais." "Pais" is used 24 times in the New Testament but only in the writings of Matthew and Luke. The word is a collective term for all members of a household subordinate to the master of the house. It emphasizes the idea of descent but gives special prominence to age, denoting a young child. "Pais" is used often as in our passage, "a servant of the Lord." The focus is on an attendant who participates in the will of a superior, often translated "child" (Matthew 17:18; 21:15; Luke 2:43; 9:42).

The early Church responded to the threats of the Sanhedrin and referred to Jesus as the "pais" of the sovereign God. The phrase, *"Your holy servant (pais) Jesus"* is used twice (Acts 4:27, 30). Therefore, the concept of bondage does not relate to Jesus or to David. The focus is on the subordinate, immature, or inferior status of man's being to the sovereign God. The merger between God and man is a mystery. Why would God limit Himself to our personalities? Why would He hide *"these things from the wise and prudent and have revealed them to babes"* (Matthew 11:25)?

The answer to this mystery lies in the link of His sovereignty and our creation. The concept of sovereignty screams of purpose and plan. Sovereignty does not act out of pressure or necessity. Who is able to force our sovereign God? Paul gave expression to this reality! Our relationship to Him is one of sons. We are "pais." He predestined us as sons, *"by Jesus Christ to Himself, according to the good pleasure of His will, to the praise of the glory of His grace, by which He made us accepted in the Beloved"* (Ephesians 1:5-6). We received the *"riches of His grace."* These riches came to us in abundance through His *"wisdom and prudence."* He is sovereign, and we are "pais." He makes *"known to us the mystery of His will, according to His good pleasure which He purpose in Himself"* (Ephesians 1:9). Sovereignty acts out of superior wisdom and righteous pleasure.

Our creation as "pais" is essential to the fulfillment of His *"purpose determined before to be done,"* but it is not proper to think of all mankind (although every person is included). The destiny in the plan of our sovereign God is individually focused. This individual focus bespeaks the reality of the merger between sovereign God and the person. The uniqueness of each person in timing of birth, personality characteristics, and experiences cannot be accidental. God is sovereign. Has He not uniquely created the person for merger? Is this merger not focused on giving unique expression of whom God is?

In our passage the word of God is expressed through *"the mouth of Your servant David."* This expression was different than the expression through Isaiah. In other words, the speaking of God through these men in the Scriptures was not the sovereign God using them as mouthpieces. No one could give the same expression David gave. The sovereign God merged with David and used the unique qualities of his life to express the mind of God. No one else was capable of this expression but David. Yet, David was incapable without the merger of the sovereign God.

You must apply this to your life! You are a creation of the sovereign God. You are significant in the expression of what He wants to say. The uniqueness of your personhood is so manifold it cannot be adequately described. Those of us observing you recognize only surface qualities of what our sovereign God has masterfully carved in you. You have talents, abilities, and potentials present that need to be developed. Each of these is under the guidance of His sovereign hand, although some things about us may not be totally developed until eternity. Are we not "pais?" We have not yet arrived or are completed; we are the unfolding, developing expression of God's speaking in and through our lives. What a privilege!

Sequence
of use

A sequence is suggested in our passage; it is the pattern of God's involvement in our lives. It starts with **"Lord"** (Acts 4:24). The New King James translation adds the phrase, **"You are God"** (Acts 4:24). In the Greek text, these words are not there. The translator attempts to adequately treat the word **"Lord"** (despotes). As described in previous studies, it is not the typical word (kurios) for "lord." "Despotes" describes a man's relationship with his slaves, while "kurios" refers to his relationship with his wife and children. The distinction between these two Greek words suggests moral limitations. "Kurios" implies an authority that owns these limitations. "Despotes" exercises a more unrestricted power and absolute dominance, confessing no such limitations or restraints.

God, absolute Lord, created you. By the nature of sovereignty, this bespeaks purpose and design. He created you with destiny. In the comparison of His creation, each person is unique. We are children (pais) who are a part of the same family yet uniquely different. All these features are understood in the context of His sovereignty. Destiny is woven throughout the sovereign plan.

This Creator merged with David and spoke His word through him. The words coming from David were considered the sovereign God's words. The words contained the flavor and expression of David, but they did not belong to him; they were the words of God. David was considered a "pais" of the sovereign God. The words of God to be truly expressed needed the personality of David; however, the personality of David was not the source of the words. God designed the uniqueness of David to help shape what He wanted to say.

What a marvelous mystery for our lives. God's desire is to merge with us! In fact, it is necessary for the true expression of what He wants to say. He designed in the creation of your being a uniqueness that when merged with Him expresses the truth about Him. It cannot be done without you; yet, it cannot be done by you. The sovereign God has limited His sovereignty to your free will. He risks the expression of His own being, the fulfillment of His own pleasure to your surrender.

However, you will never know your full purpose without His expression through you. The only possible experience of your potential is in God's expression through you. The merger between God and man is a mystery. Although we do not understand everything about it, we do understand something about it. Will we respond to what we know?

Acts 4:25-26

SNORTING HORSES

> *"Who by the mouth of Your servant David have said: 'Why did the nations rage, and the people plot vain things? The kings of the earth took their stand, and the rulers were gathered together against the Lord and against His Christ'" (Acts 4:25-26).*

The Book of Acts gives us the history of the early Church. We glean from its pages the thought process of these Christians from the beginning. Although the culture and times of the early Church are vastly different from ours, the biblical principles and concepts remain the same.

"Scriptures"

How did the early Church view the Scriptures? From our previous study, we know they believed that God is the Author of the Scriptures. They quoted a Psalm, which they considered spoken by God through the mouth of David. They stood firm in the knowledge that God wrote the Scriptures.

Our passage is a quotation of Psalms 2, and is the eighth quotation of an Old Testament passage in the first four chapters of the Book of Acts, an average of twice in each chapter. This highlights the importance of the "Scriptures" in their lives. As in our passage, they related every event in their lives to the

Scriptures. The Scriptures were the final authority and formed their view of life.

"Synthesis"

The lifestyle of the early Church and the Scriptures was a "synthesis." The Scriptures determined their attitude, controlled their decisions, and decided the ultimate meaning of every event. Because they believed God spoke the Scriptures, they believed no event was outside His sovereign control as viewed through the Scriptures. The Scriptures were the revelation of God's spoken voice. They were neither a book of advice nor a list of rules for life. They were the expression of the indwelling Spirit of Jesus.

"Supervision"

The sovereign control for their responses and choices was God's voice through the Scriptures. The "supervision" for their every move was the Scriptures. A spontaneous response to this crisis moment (Acts 4:23) for the early Church was to quote the Scriptures. They understood their past and present in light of the Scriptures, and their identity within the framework of history was found in the Scriptures. They responded according to the Scriptures.

Their quotation is the first of four sections found in the second Psalm. The history of the Psalm is unknown. According to the early Church, God through David sourced it, a Messianic Psalm. The Psalm has four sections each containing three verses. There appears to be a different speaker for each section giving us different perspectives.

"Protestors"

It begins with the "protestors" as recorded in our passage (Psalms 2:1-3; Acts 4:25-26). The two opening lines of the Psalms state the same truth about the same group of people. It asks without expecting an answer. The Greek word "phruasso," translated *"rage,"* is an expression of senseless noise. It refers to a snorting horse. The rider of the horse is in charge with the bit and the bridle despite the horse's snorting. The noise making is simply *"vain things,"* a translation of the Greek word "keno," which means empty.

The most powerful men of the world taking a stand or uniting together explain this "empty snorting," however, it means nothing because they unite against the sovereign Lord and against the redeeming Messiah belonging to the sovereign One. Can you imagine superman holding at bay a skinny teenager wildly flinging his arms to destroy him? Can you imagine a three year old yelling and hitting his father in an attempt to get what he wants? The empty snorting of creatures of a sovereign God coming against Him who is almighty far exceeds these images!

The "empty snorting" is not simply a noise of irritation. A casual or indifferent sin does not exist. We are not a people who ignore God and want to do our thing. We are not merely irritated when He interferes in our lives, and we go our way in our concerns. The statement of the early Church does not include the final statement of the Psalmist who records what they say,

> *"Let us break Their bonds in pieces*
> *And cast away Their cords from us"*
> (Psalms 2:3).

There is nothing casual in these statements. We see the rebellion of the creature against his Creator. Each statement refers to the control of God over the life of man. All sin is contained within the boundaries of this rebellion. We are at war with Divine control. We were created to be dependent on God; any attempt to be independent is an act of war against His sovereignty.

"Planner"

The next section in this Psalm records the speaking of the "Planner" describing God in His sovereignty.
"He who sits in the heavens shall laugh;
The Lord shall hold them in derision.
Then He shall speak to them in His wrath,
And distress them in His deep displeasure"
(Psalms 2:4-5).

We must understand this section in light of the God's revelation in Jesus. The attitude of God toward His creation is not stimulated by His sovereignty alone. His sovereignty establishes a plan and executes it. The Trinity, as represented through the Father, said,
"Yet I have set My King
On My holy hill of Zion"
(Psalms 2:6).

The sovereign plan is focused on Jesus. The Hebrew word "nacak," translated *"set,"* means to pour out. It contains the idea of "anointing," which corresponds to the idea of the King. As we will see in the next section of the Psalm, Jesus, the Son, is the Anointed One. He is the King of the Kingdom of God. The Kingdom in the New Covenant is a merger between the helplessness of man and the sovereign power of God. When these two unite, a new creature is created. The rebellion of man is against this plan, the ruling of Jesus as King in my life!

The words that God *"shall laugh," "hold them in derision,"* and *"speak to them in His wrath"* must be interpreted through Jesus. *"Laugh"* and *"derision"* are associated with mocking. *"Wrath"* (aph) comes from the idea of one's nose or nostrils. It portrays the idea of passion or burning. In light of Jesus, all this suggests the moving passion of God's love coupled with complete awareness that rebellion is futile. The picture of Jesus weeping over Jerusalem (Matthew 23:37-39) shows this. We have no comprehension of the deep agony our omniscient God experiences over the foolish rebellion of His creation. His plan in Christ for our lives is fulfilling and complete. We must ask again, *"Why do the nations rage and the people plot a vain thing?"* (Psalms 2:1, Acts 4:25).

"Plan"

We must understand the "Planner" in light of the "Plan" (Psalms 2:7-9). The speaker in these three verses changes from the Trinity God represented by the Father to the Trinity God represented by the Son. The promises given to the Son from the Father (Trinity) are listed.

> *"I will declare the decree:*
> *The Lord has said to Me,*
> *'You are My Son,*
> *Today have I begotten You'"*
> (Psalms 2:7).

The Father generates the life of the Son. Jesus is the first Son, the only Begotten One. Many sourced by the same generating life (Hebrews 2:10-11) will follow. Jesus established and He exists as the plan of God for the Kingdom person. The merging life of God in the Man, Jesus, is to merge with all those who will embrace their helplessness. The fullness of life in Him will also be theirs. Why are they raging against the sovereign sourcing of life?

Part 4: The Absolute Reign

The Sovereign God made a promise to His Creation.
"Ask of me, and I will give You
The nations for Your inheritance,
And the ends of the earth for Your possession"
(Psalms 2:8).

No rebellious people will establish a dominion outside God. Everything will be under His rule and belong to Him. Only those merged with Him will *"inherit the earth"* (Matthew 5:5). This will happen because all rebellious people will be destroyed.
"You shall break them with a rod of iron;
"You shall dash them to pieces like a potter's vessel"
(Psalms 2:9).

The early Church understood this to be fulfilled in Jesus. The *"nations rage"* is directly related to *"Herod and Pontius Pilate, with the Gentiles and the people of Israel, were gathered together"* (Acts 4:27). All the power of a rebellious world came together to achieve the crucifixion and elimination of Jesus. But here is how the early Church described the crucifixion, *"to do whatever Your hand and Your purpose determined before to be done"* (Acts 4:28). In other words, the "protestors" can rage all they want and enlist their greatest power, but the "Planner" (Trinity God represented by the Father), who has a "Plan" (Trinity God as represented by the Son), is sovereign. Even their protesting plays into the hands of His "Plan." His sovereignty is so great that they smashed themselves on the plan they tried to defeat. He does not need to war against them; He does not need to destroy them. They destroy themselves in their rebellion.

"Paraclete"

Then comes the final section of our Psalm (Psalms 2:10-12). The speaker is the Trinity God represented by the Holy Spirit. He gives a call to carefully consider truth.

"Now therefore, be wise, O kings;
Be instructed, you judges of the earth"
(Psalms 2:10).

They are to be wise (sakhal), to act with insight. They are to have a teachable a spirit. They are to recognize the sovereignty of the "Planner" and understand the wonder of His "Plan." They are to merge with His presence and allow Him to shape them into His image. Come to Him in rebellion and you are destroyed. Come to Him in submission and you are shaped into the fullness of life.

God admonishes,

"Serve the Lord with fear'
And rejoice with trembling.
Kiss the Son, lest He be angry,
And you perish in the way,
When His wrath is kindled but a little.
Blessed are all those who put their trust in Him"
(Psalms 2:11-12).

This is a beautiful picture of submission and merging to the full life provided by the "Plan." We are to *"serve"* (abad) Him, which means to be enslaved to Him. But in the lack of resource and the state of helplessness, why would we not avail ourselves of all He dreams for us? We are to *"kiss* (hashag) **the Son."** This presents the idea of being fastened or fixed to Him and of merging in the most intimate way.

The early Church understood this prophecy to be fulfilled

in their lives and an instruction to them for their moment of persecution. The plan of their sovereign God is Jesus, the Person. Even rebellion against Him is still in the scope of His sovereignty. Herod and Pilate gathering with the people of Israel fulfilled only the plan of sovereign God. So, what did they gain from their rebellion? The *"nations rage"* was nothing but the snorting of a horse and an empty thing. They recognize the threats of the Sanhedrin as mere noise in light of the sovereignty of God. There is no need to panic or despair; they must *"kiss the Son"*!

In their moments of threat, the early Church understood the Scriptures were instructing them and gave direction to their circumstances. Whatever your crisis or pressure, this applies to you!

Snorting Horses

The same demonic force manifested in the crucifixion of Jesus was now displayed in the beginning persecution of the early Church. Did the apostles think the world would readily accept the message of Jesus, the Resurrected One? The resistance that caused His crucifixion would be unleashed on anyone who proposed victory through His presence. Did the apostles return to their companions shocked by this resistance? Did they consider this a "new" resistance?

What did you think would happen in your life as you surrender to Jesus? Have the demonic forces that claim you for defeat and destruction fallen asleep? Are they not working with renewed effort in this closing age? Every obstacle under the dominion of the evil one will be planted in your path. Financial difficulty, home conflicts, church upsets, physical health, family issues, and job difficulties will all become a platform for the enemy's distraction.

We must respond exactly as the early Church! Any demonic concoction of any circumstance pressuring you to turn to self-sufficiency is simply a snorting horse. Any threat that would cause you to hesitate or question His sovereignty and resource is an empty thing. God is moving in ways far beyond what you see in the physical world.

Snuggle with the Son

You must respond as instructed in the Psalms (Psalms 2). We are instructed to **"be wise," "be instructed," "serve the Lord," "rejoice with trembling,"** and **"kiss the Son"** (Psalms 2:10-12). If you will live in wisdom, you will merge with the Son. He is the plan of God for all fulfillment; you are included in the plan. Will you surrender to His instruction, because He is the truth? Therefore, you will not master truth as data or information, but you will be mastered by Truth as you are filled with Him. Will you serve the Lord? But what could you possibly do that He would need done? Only in becoming one with Him will you find value in any activity, because the activity must be sourced by His power. You must rejoice! But rejoicing is worthwhile only when it is experienced with trembling. You see His greatness; you are overwhelmed with His majesty. No problem or pressure creates such stress that He is overshadowed. The threats of the Sanhedrin are swallowed in the wonder of His presence. You rejoice with trembling at His greatness. This manner of surrender allows you to **"kiss the Son."**

Does the old statement, "love conquers all," apply here? In His embrace all tension is removed; worry must flee. You are His bride and the Bridegroom is magnificent. His provisions are extravagant. His protection is complete. You are safe in His arms. Please **"kiss the Son."**

Sovereignty of God

God is the sovereign One. Any attempt to provide for Him is a reproach to His greatness. Any thought of instructing Him is unthinkable arrogance. One moment of worry reveals self-centeredness, self-dependence, and self-sufficiency. Is He not sovereign? Will my belief about Him be determined by my circumstances or by His embrace and oneness in my life? I must ***"kiss the Son."*** Here is my dwelling place.

Acts 4:25-26

KISS THE SON

"Who by the mouth of Your servant David have said: 'Why did the nations rage, and the people plot vain things? The kings of the earth took their stand, and the rulers were gathered together against the Lord and against His Christ'" (Acts 4:25-26).

"Kiss the Son lest He be angry, And you perish in the way, When His wrath is kindled but a little. Blessed are all those who put their trust in Him" (Psalms 2:12).

Jesus is **"gentle and lowly in heart"** (Matthew 11:29), and there is no record of Him ever harming anyone, even those who persecuted Him. Yet, He was divisive, causing disagreement or hostility between people. His pattern was to engage the multitudes **"and He healed them all"** (Matthew 12:15). However, He consistently divided His crowd. This division cannot be accredited just to the Jewish culture of His hour because in our culture and present hour Jesus is not tolerated. The United States is a tolerant nation, supporting any influence in our schools but not allowing Jesus. We embrace "in God we trust" but not Jesus. There is something about Him that will not permit indifference. You cannot simply walk away and ignore Him.

The leaders of Israel faced Jesus again. What they thought was settled in His crucifixion was alive and well in His resurrection. His return appearance through the apostles became unbearable in the miracle received by the lame beggar (Acts 3:1-10). The Sanhedrin threatened Peter and John never to speak in the name of Jesus. The High Court had to eliminate Jesus again. When Peter and John were released from jail, they returned to the members of the early Church. After giving a full report of the threats, the early Church erupted with praise. The basis of their praise was the sovereignty of God (Acts 4:24). Their expression of this truth is through the Scriptures. They quoted the words of God spoken through the mouth of David (Acts 4:25-26; Psalms 2).

Psalms 2 is in a progression. It contains four sections, each with three verses. The first two verses of the first section are quoted in our passage. However, to assume that they quoted the entire Psalm is reasonable. There appears to be a different speaker proclaiming each section. Let me review these speakers with you.

Protesters
"Snorting Horses"
Psalms 2:1-3

The first three verses focus on the rebellion of the world's people against the sovereignty of God, who insist on overthrowing the authority of God. The early Church understood this to be fulfilled in the gathering of **"Herod and Pontius Pilate, with the Gentiles and the people of Israel"** (Acts 4:27). In arrogance these Jewish leaders crucified Jesus, not realizing they were doing **"whatever Your hand and Your purpose determined before to be done"** (Acts 4:28). They were simply "snorting horses," making senseless noise against the sovereign God.

Planner
"Trinity God represented by the Father"
Psalms 2:4-6

All the nation's senseless noise does not affect the plan of our God! God is pictured as laughing and speaking in wrath. All this must be viewed in light of God's plan, Jesus. His laugh and wrath are in the context of His love and redemption in Jesus. His laughter and His wrath are an expression of His passion to redeem. He is not angry; He is not a god who has lost his temper. He has not turned from redemption to destruction. The "snorting horses" have not altered His desire or plan!

Plan
"Trinity God represented by the Son"
Psalms 2:7-9

The Son was begotten! The sovereign God decreed it! Jesus will inherit the nations. No rebellious people will be outside His dominion. Even those who rebel cooperate with the plan of the sovereign God. The rebellious will find they destroy themselves on the plan they try to defeat. Their rebellion is their demise.

Paraclete
"Trinity God represented by the Holy Spirit"
Psalms 2:10-12

In the last section we viewed the mind of the Trinity in the context of the New Covenant. The Old Covenant is a prophecy of the intimacy and merger experienced in the fullness of the Spirit. In the Old Testament setting, David never experienced the New Covenant. He saw everything through the context of the law. He grasped the reality of promises from Jehovah God, but he understood these promises in the context of the Old Testament. He knew the promises had meaning for the future, but he could not grasp that reality. His expression of these promises, although inspired by the Holy Spirit, was shaped in his culture and limited to the vocabulary of his understanding. God gave insight and revelation to what David could not express. As we dwell in the fullness of the Spirit's revelation we are able to understand better what God said through the mouth of David.

God through David expressed the merger of God and man in the phrase, **"Kiss the Son"** (Psalms 2:12). **"Kiss"** is a translation of the Hebrew word "nashaq" and the Greek word (in the Septuagint) "draxasthe." The Hebrew verb means "to kiss, to touch lightly." The word rarely has romantic implications (Proverbs 7:13; Song of Solomon 1:2). Often, along with tears and embraces, kisses expressed the dearness of relationships between friends and family, especially at a farewell (Ruth 1:9,14; 1 Samuel 20:41; 1 Kings 19:20); or a reunion (Genesis 45:15; cf. Romans 16:16; 1 Peter 5:14). Kisses also expressed acceptance of a person (Genesis 45:15; 2 Samuel 14:33), and even the mutual acceptance or harmony of moral qualities (Psalms 85:10). They also were associated with giving blessings (Genesis 27:27; 2 Samuel 19:39). Kisses sometimes expressed the worship of idols (1 Kings 19:18; Hosea 13:2), and now in our passage the worship of the Messiah (Psalms 2:12; cf. Psalms 2:7; Hebrews 1:5).

The main word for "worship" in the New Testament Greek language is "proskuneo," a combination of "pros," meaning "from or movement" and "kuneo," meaning "to kiss and adore." The ancient Oriental (especially Persian) mode of salutation between people of equal ranks was to kiss each other on the lips; when the difference of rank was slight, they kissed on the cheek; when one was much inferior, he fell on his knees and touched his forehead to the ground or prostrated himself while simultaneously throwing kisses toward the superior. This latter mode of salutation is expressed by the Greek word "proskuneo" (Matthew 28:17).

"Kiss the Son" is an expression of the merger of my helplessness and Jesus' powerful person. When my inferiority mergers with His superiority, the new creature of the Kingdom is formed, the New Covenant. This merger is the purpose of my creation. Why are the nations raging against such a merger? In this last section, the Holy Spirit calls us to a union with the Son!

Determination
Kiss the Son

He cries out to us, ***"Now therefore, be wise, O kings;"*** (Psalms 2:10). The Hebrew word "sakal," translated ***"wise,"*** means circumspect, hence intelligent. This verb means to act with insight, to be prudent, to give insight, to teach, to prosper, to consider, to ponder, to understand, to act prudently, to act with devotion. Kissing the Son is not about being foolish, thoughtless, or unintelligent. The nations of the Earth are raging; they are snorting horses. This makes no sense in light of the God's sovereignty. We would be wise to take action to bend the mind with a determined will to experience the fullness of relationship with the Son.

The plea of God through the prophet Isaiah was to "reason together."

"Come now, and let us reason together,"
Says the Lord,
"Though your sins are like scarlet,
They shall be as white as snow;
Though they are red like crimson,
They shall be as wool.

Part 4: The Absolute Reign

> *If you are willing and obedient,*
> *You shall eat the good of the land;*
> *But if you refuse and rebel,*
> *You shall be devoured by the sword";*
> *For the mouth of the Lord has spoken*
> *(Isaiah 1:18-20).*

Discipline
Kissing the Son

The Holy Spirit calls us, **"Be instructed, you judges of the earth"** (Psalms 2:10). The Hebrew word "yacar," translated **"Be instructed,"** is a verb that means to discipline, to chasten, to instruct, to teach, to punish. "Yacar" is used with two general thrusts of meaning, chastening or instructing, merged often in its use. Human beings are sometimes used in the instructing, but God is the ultimate source of true instruction and chastening. According to the Hebrew writer, discipline through instruction is a sign of being sons (Hebrews 12:7). Human fathers discipline their sons **"as seem best to them, but He for our profit, that we may be partakers of His holiness"** (Hebrews 12:10). Kissing the Son is not for pleasure; it is merging with His being to be shaped by His nature, though sometimes painful but rewarding in the knowledge of His person!

Deliver
Kissing the Son

The Spirit commands, **"Serve the Lord with fear"** (Psalms 2:11). The Hebrew word "abad," translated **"serve,"** can be focused on things, others, or God, but it is never focused on "self." The Greek word "doulos" is used in the Septuagint. Paul referred to himself consistently as a "doulos" of Jesus (Romans 1:1; Galatians 1:10; Philippians 1:1). This service rendered is always outside of and beyond self. The Holy Spirit proposes a love relationship with the Son. We are to *"Kiss the Son."* The enslavement is love slavery not bond slavery!

This service is to be accomplished in the context of *"fear,"* a translation of the Hebrew word "yirah." This word, which presents the context of abstraction, is a feminine noun referring to a positive quality and usually about God. Therefore, our service is never duty, obligation, or force. We are in love with the Son; service is a privilege, delight, and desire. Self-benefits are forgotten; pleasing Him is our passion. Our selfish desires are lost in the amazement of His being. We are captured by His greatness.

Dance
Kissing the Son

"And rejoice with trembling" (Psalms 2:11) is the urging of the Spirit. "Giyl" is the Hebrew word for *"rejoice."* Its primitive root word means to "spin around" or "dance." It describes a person so filled with emotion that they give physical response in rejoicing *"with trembling"* (readah), a reference to shuddering in the presence of the Lord (Exodus 15:15).

The Holy Spirit gives us a picture of the New Covenant, an intimate merging with the Spirit of Jesus. It operates in the context of our physical, emotion, and spiritual beings immersed in His presence and control. His thinking captures our minds. His instruction disciplines our life expression with a focus on others. This thrilling merger envelopes us, and we dance with delight in being involved! We are kissing the Son.

There is a further question to consider in our passage. What if I do not *"Kiss the Son"*? What if there is no merger? I simply do not delight in my life being used by Him for others, my mind thinking His thoughts, and my existence being determined by Him. What is the result of this state?

> *"Kiss the Son, lest He be angry,*
> *And you perish in the way,*
> *When His wrath is kindled but a little.*
> *Blessed are all those who put their trust in Him"*
> (Psalms 2:12).

This passage must be seen through the lens of the New Covenant. Although it is expressed through the language of David, who knew only the Old Covenant, the Holy Spirit is speaking. The Hebrew word "anaph," translated *"angry,"* is used for "heavy breathing." It highlights an emotional response and is used only about God's response. We dare not impose our style of anger on Him. He does not get mad because we do not obey His commands. However, God does have an emotional response to our disobedience and rebellion. There is an upset and disturbance in the emotional heart of God about our condition. He is dismayed; this is not in the sense of not knowing what to do. In the New Covenant view, this upset caused Him to send His Son (1 John 4:9, 10; John 3:16, 17). God's upset causes Him to act on our behalf.

This response comes because we *"perish in the way"* (Psalms 2:12). The Hebrew word "abad," translated *"perish,"* means "to wander, to perish, to be lost." God does not indicate that He is the cause, but He is the Observer of what happens in our lives because of not "kissing the Son." God begins to experience *"wrath."* The Hebrew word is "aph," means the same as anger with an additional emphasis on the face. "Aph" is heavy breathing through the nose indicating an upset in the emotions of the person. This is not "a losing your temper" kind of wrath.

It describes an emotional disturbance in a heart of love, because God is love. God is distraught over what is happening in our lives. When we do not *"kiss the Son,"* He sees the long-range view of our lives. He experiences the beginning from the end of our destruction. His heart cannot tolerate it. He acts on our behalf in Jesus! So why would the nations snort like horses? Why would anyone choose to go his or her own way? Please *"Kiss the Son."*

Acts 4:27

HOLY INCARNATE JESUS

"For truly against Your holy Servant Jesus, whom You anointed, both Herod and Pontius Pilate, with the Gentiles and the people of Israel were gathered together" (Acts 4:27).

When asked about the topic of an upcoming sermon, my answer is always "Jesus," which brings laughter as if it is a joke. But truthfully, I am dead serious. If I am going to be true to the Bible and its message, what else can I preach? Although there may be subordinate topics such as faith, holiness, grace, and many others, no adequate discussion can be without Jesus, the heart and object of all.

Any expositional study of the Scriptures reveals Jesus as the core of each passage. We discover this in the Book of Acts. At the first recorded business meeting (Acts 1:15-26), Judas was replaced. The requirement for replacing Judas was the candidate must have experienced the life of Jesus from His baptism by John until His ascension (Acts 1:21-22). The sole purpose of the apostle was to **"become a witness with us of His resurrection"** (Acts 1:22). This person could not testify about Jesus' resurrected life unless he had thoroughly known His earthly life. It required a focus on Jesus.

Pentecost was man being indwelt by the Holy Spirit. You would think all the sermons after such an event would be about the Holy Spirit, but all sermons after Pentecost were about Jesus.

Holy Incarnate Jesus | Acts 4:27

The fullness of the Holy Spirit produced a people who talked about Jesus. The theme of every message, the cause of every miracle, and the heart of persecution was Jesus. Before His crucifixion Jesus said, *"However, when He, the Spirit of truth, has come, He will guide you into all truth; for He will not speak on His own authority, but whatever He hears He will speak; and He will tell you things to come. He will glorify Me, for He will take of what is Mine and declare it to you"* (John 16:13-14).

In the context of our passage, Peter's explanation for the lame beggar's miracle and salvation was Jesus. When asked who sourced the miracle, Peter's answer was, *"Jesus Christ of Nazareth, whom you crucified, whom God raised from the dead"* (Acts 4:10). Peter proposed that the only possibility of salvation was Jesus (Acts 4:12).

We have repeatedly highlighted the heart of persecution in our passage is Jesus, not theology, church order, or ceremonies. Jesus is the issue. The threat from the Sanhedrin was focused on *"not to speak at all nor teach in the name of Jesus"* (Acts 4:18). The Sanhedrin's concern was not miracles, the resurrection, or church gatherings; it was Jesus. Luke wrote that the leaders were *"greatly disturbed that they taught the people and preached in Jesus the resurrection from the dead"* (Acts 4:2).

In the context of our passage, the Early Church quoted Psalm 2. It depicts the rage of the nations, the kings taking a stand, and the rulers gathering (Acts 4:25-26). The early Church equated Herod and Pontius Pilate as the nations. Herod represented the Kings, and Pontius Pilate represented the rulers. The people of Israel and the Gentiles gathered against Jesus. Luke said the purpose of their gathering was *"to do whatever Your hand and Your purpose determined before to be done"* (Acts 4:28). The raging of the nations against Jesus was the determined purpose of the Trinity God. Nothing but Jesus is going on in the plan of God, and He is the fulfillment of the unfolding plan in the Old Testament. Jesus is the focus of everything God planned for the

Part 4: The Absolute Reign

New Covenant. God's plan is Jesus and more Jesus!

What is the significance of Jesus? What places Jesus in a superior and focused position? Why is all the rebellion of evil aimed at Him? Why are all the hopes of saving the world contained in His Person? Why Jesus? Who is Jesus?

He is *"Your holy Servant Jesus!"*

Incarnation
"Your"

In our passage *"Your"* refers to the sovereign Trinity God. In their great praise session, the early Church addressed the Trinity God, *"Lord, You are God, who made heaven and earth and the sea, and all that is in them"* (Acts 4:24). This is God who is assumed in the beginning of all things (Genesis 1:1). This was their Holy Account, the Scriptures, given them by Moses. He is referred to as "Elihom," the Hebrew word for "God." The word is always plural. The Trinity God is Creator of all things. He is also the source of the Scriptures, *"who by the mouth of Your servant David have said"* (Acts 4:25). He reveals Himself and His Divine plan through the Scriptures.

The early Church believed the Trinity God was sovereign with a plan about redemption through Jesus. His sovereignty extended to every circumstance concerning Jesus. No king, ruler, nation, or even the people of Israel could gather and accomplish anything outside the plan of God (Acts 4:27-28). The supreme desire of the early Church was to participate in this plan. They understood there would be suffering involved in Jesus' fulfillment of the plan. They knew this suffering would be in their lives as they participated in the plan. But the involvement and intimacy of being at the heart of the Trinity's movement overshadowed any threat of suffering.

The impact of our passage is that Jesus belongs to this

Trinity God. Jesus is *"Your"* holy Servant. This presents to us the "incarnation." Because Jesus belongs to God, such a reality indicates a difference between them. If Jesus is the same as God, then He is not ***"Your holy Servant."*** The "incarnation" bespeaks this difference and is a truth that demands careful thought and discussion without prejudice.

"Incarnation" means, "to assume flesh." The Trinity God is persons not merely functions. Although the three persons of the Trinity express three different functions, it is not the functions that make them a trinity. The Trinity is three personalities equally one. One of these persons is Jesus. We must declare without hesitation, "Jesus is God." All the attributes of God are in Jesus. He is not one-third God; He is fully God. Never is He not God. In the moments of the world's creation, He is seen as God (Colossians 1:16). Throughout the Old Testament, the awareness of His presence as God was felt (Daniel 3:25). Jesus did not give up being God in order to become man. The "incarnation" is God assuming flesh. Every step Jesus took in the flesh was a step of God. The incarnation is essential for the plan of redemption. If Jesus is not God, His death was simply the death of another nice guy. How does it redeem me?

Although this fact must never be lost, an amazing addition took place in the "incarnation." Jesus, who is God, took on the existence of humanity. He did not take on flesh as a costume; He was not a fake man. God merged with man for the sake of man merging with God. This merger established a new breed or species of human. No human had ever been like this since the fall of Adam. Jesus became the first one of this New Covenant humanities.

The marvel of this new addition to God was the required surrender. For God to be man, He had to surrender everything that made Him different from man. All of God's attributes had to be set aside. Omnipresence, omniscience, and omnipotence could not be present in the framework of a man. God became a helpless babe in a woman's womb. In His birth He could not care for Himself. Although He was God, the man Jesus had no knowledge but had to learn. Eventually He merged with God, becoming the first Kingdom person. Jesus was a man filled with God, relied totally on God, and always lived through God's sourcing. This sourcing was the dream of God for humanity, a helpless man filled with the Spirit of God. God merges with man so that man might merge with God. This merger is redemption!

Therefore, Jesus is *"Your"* holy Servant! Although He is God, He became man apart from God. Although He is God, He belongs to God. Although He is God, He is filled with God. Although He is God, He is totally dependent on God. Although He is God, He has become other than God. Carefully consider the sacrifice involved in this surrender. Although the physical suffering on a cross would be extreme for any man, the sacrifice of becoming a man was far beyond physical pain. Jesus surrendered all the comfort, knowledge, and position of His sovereignty. He became one of us, a helpless man. This change was not a temporary sacrifice or surrender. He did not experience this for thirty years and return to what He was as God. His attachment to humanity is eternal. He was resurrected as a man, ascended as a man, sits at the right hand of the Father as a man, and will return as a man. He is King of the Kingdom as a man. He became *"Your"* holy Servant forever.

Incapable
"holy Servant"

The Greek word "pais" is translated *"Servant"* in our passage, the way it is translated often in the New Testament but may be misleading. The focus of the word is a boy or girl child whose age can range from infancy to full-grown youth.

This highlights everything we have said so far in this study. Jesus, who is God, leaped into an additional position other than God. Because He was not conceived as an ordinary human being, how would you describe it? One who had prior existence entered into the womb of Mary and was born. *"And the Word became flesh and dwelt among us, and we beheld His glory, the glory as of the only begotten of the Father, full of grace and truth"* (John 1:14)

However, in the New King James Version they did not call Jesus a "child" but a *"Servant,"* with the probable reason being the period. Our passage speaks of the crucifixion. Jesus was not a child. He was a full-grown man making the shift in emphasis an interpretation of the passage rather than a translation. Although *"Servant"* bespeaks a subordinate position, it does not have the same thrust of "child." Could this be an attempt to propose that Jesus was helpless? As a man He had the same helplessness as a child. As a babe in His mother's arms, so He is in the arms of the Trinity God. As He had no knowledge as a babe, so He knows only the mind of His Father.

Is this statement a reminder? Jesus never stepped outside the boundaries of dependence on the Father. He refused to operate out of Himself. Even with education, development of skills, and the mastery of manhood, He remained dependent. Was this the secret to His victory, His amazing wisdom, His calm in stressful situations, His ability to give abundant forgiveness, His unwavering focus on His mission, His miracles, His conquering position in spiritual warfare, and even His resurrection from the dead?

We discover two amazing truths as we see how the early Church viewed Jesus. Something happened in Jesus that set Him apart from His position as God. Although He certainly is God, there is something happening in and through Him that is other than being God. He merges with man that He might merge with God. The core of this difference is found in helplessness. Even in His manhood at the crucifixion, He fulfilled His plea to the disciples, *"Assuredly, I say to you, unless you are converted and become as little children, you will by no means enter the Kingdom of heaven"* (Matthew 18:3). He remained a child in helplessness. He described this to His disciples when He said, *"Therefore whoever humbles himself as this little child is the greatest in the kingdom of heaven"* (Matthew 18:4). How could He be King of the Kingdom without being the helpless child?

Incorporation
"Jesus"

There are three statements in our passage that become one focus in Jesus. In the quotation from Psalms, Jesus is called *"Christ"* (Acts 4:26), the Greek word "Christos" from "chrio," meaning *"You anointed."* Jesus is identified as the anointed Christ. The fact Jesus is called "Your *holy* Servant" is significant. *"Holy"* is the Greek word "hagios," a word focused on purity or blameless but in the sense of being separated and consecrated. In other words, behind the incarnation of Jesus, and His merging with man, there is a definite plan. He is set aside to accomplish this plan. He is anointed, selected, and ordained to fulfill the dream of the Trinity. What is His dream? God merging with humanity that humanity might merge with God.

God became other than He is. His dream was to incorporate man into Himself. Incorporation means inclusion of something as part of a whole. The Trinity God split Himself down the middle, risked everything He is, and opened Himself to suffering and loss. It was to incorporate us into His heart. He has made provision for and invited us into His nature. He did not invite us to become omnipresent, omniscient, or omnipotent; He has those attributes. He invites us to become a part of who He is!

God invites us to become everything Jesus is. The same merger God has with Jesus, He wants to have with us. In fact, we become *"Your holy Servant."* Jesus merged with God for a specific task; we merge with God for a specific task. Our task is a different task from Jesus' yet is an aspect of the same desire. His demonstration in and through us will be different from Jesus, but it will have tones of the same desire. As Jesus was created in the flesh and became a specific man for this task, we are created for our specific task.

The fulfillment of God's dream is contingent on the merger. The early Church discovered in the moment of threat their merger with the sovereign God was the stabilization for the continued achievement of His plan. They saw it accomplished in Jesus. The resurrection was after the crucifixion. Sin did its worst, but its worst created its defeat. This will be true in our lives also.

We are not to focus on problem solving or how to survive. Our focus is to be on our merger with Jesus. Our incorporation with His Person includes us in the whole. You and I do not want to miss Jesus!

Acts 4:27-28

DECLARATION OF THE CASE

"For truly against Your holy Servant Jesus, whom You anointed, both Herod and Pontius Pilate, with the Gentiles and the people of Israel were gathered together to do whatever Your hand and Your purpose determined before to be done" (Acts 4:27-28).

There are startling elements in our passage. The decisive surrender of the early Church members to the will of God in their persecution is challenging. They demonstrated by their commitment the difference between the righteousness of the scribes and Pharisees and the righteousness of the Kingdom person (Matthew 5:20). The leaders of Israel were self-focused to the extent they were not open to the truth that threatened their selfishness; they feared the crowds and could not react to the apostles as they wanted. The early Church was fearless and completely willing to risk their lives. They had already died to self-centeredness, so as a fantastic contrast, physical death was not a threat.

The early Church was absolute in their belief in the sovereignty of God, which enabled their stability. Our passage is their bold statement of declaration! The first verse reveals the cumulative power and might of the worldly forces, and Herod represents the kings of the Earth. Pontius Pilate represents the rulers of the Earth. The Roman Empire working to conquer the world is presented in its power, the force of the Gentile world.

Also, the people of Israel displayed their strength and desire. In other words, there was no ruling force in the world, not united in crucifying Christ.

The Greek word "sunago" is the compound verb of "sun" (from) and "ago" (to lead together) with no technical meaning but combines a verb and a preposition. This word expresses **"were gathered together"** in the passive voice and presenting the worldly authorities being acted on by something beyond themselves. Something occurred that assembled this crowd. The first impression would be that the crucifixion of Christ brought them together. Although this may be true, Luke's statement verifies it was the sovereignty of God assembling them.

This idea of God's sovereignty is essential and extensive in its scope, and it will require several studies even to suggest its truth. We will repeat several elements in our reviews because they apply to each facet of the study. The sovereignty of God is the power and might of dominion over His creatures, to dispose and determine them as He desires. His sovereignty is because there is nothing or no one higher in power and existence than God, which is frightening and threatening to accept. Despite our response to God's sovereignty, it is a reality. Our denial does not change the fact of its existence.

We must consistently highlight God's nature. His sovereignty and all the power constituted in its context, is dominated and controlled by His nature. God is Holy (Leviticus 11:44), and **"God is love"** (1 John 4:8, 16). These two facts are the same. God can't respond outside His nature of love. The biblical term for God's love is "agape." It is selfless, self-sacrificing, and self-giving love. He never thinks about Himself, but only for the one, He loves. His sovereignty is under the control of this love and means He is always acting on our behalf.

From a biblical view, we can never place our response of hatred, anger, wrath, or temper on God. Even though there may be situations in which it seems that God is not acting in love, He assures us of His love. The earthly father does not always appear to love in the understanding of his immature four-year-old son. The lack is in the son's maturity, not the father's love. So, it is with God! Once we thoroughly establish and understand God's selfless love, we can move on to discuss God's sovereignty. The early Church reached this understanding. They perceived the suffering of Jesus as the act of a sovereign, loving Father! With this understanding, we are ready to discuss the sovereignty of God.

Complete

God's sovereignty is complete! This truth applies to every aspect of God's existence. God's sovereignty is in His wisdom. The blessing of God rested on the reign of King Solomon. God presented himself to Solomon, *"Ask! What shall I give you?"* (2 Chronicles 1:7). Solomon remembered the blessings and promises of God given to his father, King David. He immediately cried to God, *"Now give me wisdom and knowledge, that I may go out and come in before this people; for who can judge this great people of Yours?"* (2 Chronicles 1:10). Solomon became the wisest man in the world. The One who can give wisdom is the One who has it. God is sovereign in wisdom. *"Where is the wise? Where is the scribe? Where is the disputer of this age? Has not God made foolish the wisdom of this world?"* (1 Corinthians 1:20).

"Oh, the depth of the riches both of the wisdom and knowledge of God! How unsearchable are His judgments and His ways past finding out!
For who has known the mind of the Lord?
Or who has become His counselor?
Or who has first given to Him

And it shall be repaid to Him?
For of Him and through Him
and to Him are all things,
to whom be glory forever. Amen"
(Romans 11:33-36).

God's sovereignty is in His power! Even the idea of His sovereignty reflects that power. The psalmist cried, *"Twice I have heard this: that power belongs to God"* (Psalm 62:11). He continued, *"Great is our Lord, and mighty in power; His understanding is infinite"* (Psalm 147:5). Remember Paul's statement, *"For since the creation of the world His invisible attributes are seen, being understood by the things that are made, even His eternal power and Godhead, so that they are without excuse"* (Romans 1:20).

God's sovereignty is present in His existence. From the beginning of creation, He is assumed (Genesis 1:1). *"The eternal God is your refuge, and underneath are the everlasting arms"* (Deuteronomy 33:27). *"Known to God from eternity are all His works"* (Acts 15:18). *"Now to the King eternal, immortal, invisible, to God who alone is wise, be honor and glory forever and ever. Amen"* (1 Timothy 1:17). What more could He add?

The sovereignty of God is dominant in His love! We have already learned that God's sovereignty is dominated by His nature, *"God is love"* (1 John 4:8, 16). Is His sovereignty an attribute He possesses, and His nature is who He is? Is love an attribute He has and His sovereignty who He is? The incarnation clarifies these questions! Jesus set aside all the qualities He possessed as God to become a helpless babe (Philippians 2:5-21). However, He did not give up who He is! One of the attributes He surrendered was His sovereignty; however, He continued to possess the nature of God, which is love, meaning the nature of God owns His sovereignty and dictates its actions and responses. His nature of love dominates the absoluteness of God. Nothing you do causes God to love you; therefore, nothing you will do can cause Him not to love you. He loves you because of who He is.

We must understand the significance of this! All the resources contained in the meaning of sovereignty flows through and empowers this loving nature. The sovereignty of God is the power and might of dominion over His creatures, to dispose and determine them as He desires. Therefore, His desire, love, is enabled by such authority. Nothing can stop the love expression of God's nature. The sin of humanity, the rebellion of an evil heart, or the disbelief of wickedness does not hinder the sovereign love of God. We are loved regardless of what we think or how we respond to Him.

The conclusion of such an understanding should drive us to a positive response. God's sovereignty includes things good and evil. Because His sovereignty empowers His nature of love, He equally allows good and bad circumstances by His sovereignty. We can easily understand God being sovereign in good things. When something beneficial to what we want occurs, we are quick to count it a blessing from God and utter, "Thank you, Lord." It is harder for us to comprehend how we can know sovereign love in suffering circumstances.

The free will of man points to God's limit of His sovereignty regarding our choices; therefore, all circumstances are under the control of His sovereignty while they may not be caused by it. God may not have created your circumstances, but He allows them. God's sovereign love works within the situation for good regardless of how it seems, which was the view of the early Church. The crucifixion of Jesus was fresh in their minds. Herod represented the Kings of the world; Pontius Pilate represented the rulers of the world. The Gentiles and the people of Israel represented the world. They gathered to inflict suffering and death on the only Man in the world who did not deserve it. Where was the sovereign love of God found in such circumstances? Is the crucifixion a product of evil or righteousness unto salvation? Is it the result of hatred or the love of a sovereign God? We know the answer! God is sovereign over good and bad circumstances. *"And we know that all things work together for good to those who love God, to those who are the called according to His purpose"* (Romans 8:28). Can you imagine merging with a sovereign God who takes every evil thing determined to destroy your life and empowers it for your good?

Conversion

Conversion lies in the sovereignty of God. If God merges with you and every circumstance meant for evil is transformed into your benefit, what is the focus? The advantage is redemption! Let me repeat the heart of agape love; it is self-giving, self-sacrifice, and never thinks about itself. God does not focus on winning, getting His way, or protecting Himself. God always pours out His life to provide salvation. God does not approach a circumstance with intent to destroy, put down, or eliminate. Every circumstance is bathed in redemption and empowered by His sovereignty.

This result is the message of our passage. God did not come to the gathering of evil men to stop them from their evil plans. Jesus understood this as He approached the cross. Pilate in irritation, said to Jesus, *"Are You not speaking to me? Do You not know that I have the power to crucify You, and power to release You?"* Jesus answered, *"You could have no power at all against Me unless it had been given you from above"* (John 19:10-11). Jesus knew the Father elevated evil men to the position of decision, thus allowing their participation in the redemptive plan for the world. What would evil men advanced to authority decide? Willingly, they would choose precisely to do what the sovereign God knew they would. All their evil plotting was under the control and empowerment of the sovereign redemptive love of God.

Peter did not understand this, but Jesus did. Peter resisted the arrest of Jesus in the Garden of Gethsemane by drawing a sword. Jesus said Peter, *"Put your sword in its place, for all who take the sword will perish by the sword. Or do you think that I cannot now pray to My Father, and He will provide Me with more than twelve legions of angels"* (Matthew 26:52)? There is no lack of power available; God is sovereign. But God's sovereignty is controlled by His redemptive love.

What would happen if this sovereign God lived in you? Could He take every evil plan initiated by a wicked world and make it a redemptive force? Could the core of what appears to us to be bad be a surprising good that we will eventually see? If God merges with you, can you express the redemptive attitude of God's heart toward those focused on evil for you? Is this why Jesus forgave from a cross (Luke 23:34)? Is this why Stephen, the first martyr, could forgive those who stoned him (Acts 7:60)? Far too often, we take up the sword; we throw the stones back at those who stone us. Do we not understand the sovereign love of God that merges with us?

Cross

The sovereign God always focused on redemption embraces suffering. At its core is crucifixion! God's nature, agape love, is empowered by His sovereignty. This love is selfless, self-sacrificing, and never thinks about self. The single-core focus of such love is redemption. God provides redemption, but of necessity, it will always embrace a cross. Although Peter did not understand this in the Garden of Gethsemane, he realized it at Pentecost. In his explanation of Pentecost, he preached, *"Him, being delivered by the determined purpose and foreknowledge of God, you have taken by lawless hands, have crucified, and put to death"* (Acts 2:23). The sovereignty of God placed Jesus in the hands of lawless men, precisely knew what they would do.

Self-less love is not a new or recent response from the heart of God. Adam sinned; God sacrificed an animal for clothing, uttered the first Messianic promise, and provided a means for redemption. This process is repeated again and again throughout the Old Testament. It culminates in the crucifixion of Jesus. Its truth rings throughout the epistles and overshadows your life as well!

God does not invite us to merge with His sovereignty, making us omniscient, omnipresent, or omnipotent, elements of only God's life. The Trinity God opened His heart to us! He invites us to join Him in His nature. God empowers His nature of love by His sovereignty, which ultimately involves a cross. But there is never suffering without purpose and plan. His love empowers His sovereignty, which brings us to crucifixion.

Jesus began the Sermon on the Mount with the Beatitudes (Matthew 5:3-12). They are beautiful in truth. They speak of humility, comfort, meekness, filling, mercy, purity, and peace. The climax of this truth is not a warning of persecution, but a proposal of certainty. The account of those gone before us provides the consistency of a cross, *"for so they persecuted the prophets who were before you"* (Matthew 5:12). In preparing His disciples for ministry, Jesus used the imagery of sending them forth, *"as sheep amid wolves"* (Matthew 10:16). Jesus filled His discourse on ministry with the awareness of the persecution. After all, *"a disciple is not above his teacher, nor a servant above his master"* (Matthew 10:24). Paul expressed his deep desire when he said, *"That I may know Him and the power of His resurrection, and the fellowship of His sufferings, being conformed to His death"* (Philippians 3:10).

In merging with the nature of God, I find my life in His

Part 4: The Absolute Reign

dying. The sovereignty of God presents death and life in good and bad circumstances. I must lose my life to the redemptive plan of God for my time. Everything negative will become positive in light of His love, which is empowered by His sovereignty when I have merged with His nature!

Acts 4:27-28

DILEMMA OF THE CASE: HIS SUFFERING

"For truly against Your holy Servant Jesus, whom You anointed, both Herod and Pontius Pilate, with the Gentiles and the people of Israel were gathered together to do whatever Your hand and Your purpose determined before to be done" (Acts 4:27-28).

The "Why?" questions in the Old Testament are impossible to enumerate. The Psalmist questioned God. ***"Why do You stand afar off, O Lord? Why do You hide in times of trouble?"*** (Psalms 10:1). Jeremiah cried out to God in great distress. ***"Why does the way of the wicked prosper? Why are those happy who deal so treacherously?"*** (Jeremiah 12:1). The age-old question is, "Why do the righteous suffer?" Why do the godliest people get cancer? Saint Teresa died in her early twenties after spending most of her life in bed with suffering. How can that be? Why do bad things happen to good people?

An author with a brilliant theological mind wrote four Old Testament books (1 & 2 Samuel and 1 & 2 Kings). His goal was to present a theological understanding of the relationship between God's will and events happening in Israel, not the history of a chosen people. He established the premise of "punishment and reward." When the kings regularly and openly transgressed the Law of God, circumstances did not go well for Israel. Punishment for disobedience was proved repeatedly in these books.

The Book of First Samuel opens with Eli, the old priest. He had two sons who were wicked priests. Because of their wickedness, the Philistines attacked Israel, defeated them in battle, and captured the Ark of the Covenant, the symbol of God's presence (1 Samuel 4:10-11). So, the premise holds; when a person disobeys God, the result is destruction, which also was true for the Philistines. When the Philistines had the Ark of the Covenant, they had God's presence dwelling in their land. However, because of their wickedness, God's presence brought misery, not blessing. They voluntarily returned the Ark of the Covenant to Israel (1 Samuel 5).

We see the premise of "punishment" through the reigns of King Saul and King David. Each time these men disobeyed God significant destruction followed. Finally, God split the Kingdom of Israel between the northern ten tribes (Israel) and the southern two (Judah). The story goes from bad to worse. The kings of the North and South disobeyed God. They let the high places of the pagan cults remain, and they did not observe the laws forbidding intermarriage. These kings got progressively more disobedient, proving the premise repeatedly as destruction came to their nation.

No one has ever proved the premise of "reward." Obedience to God should result in blessings and goodness, but we never see a king who obeyed to prove the premise of "reward." However, when we think all is lost, a king appears to test the premise of "punishment and reward." His name is Josiah! ***"Now before him there was no king like him, who turned to the Lord with all his heart, with all his soul, and with all his might, according to all the Law of Moses; nor after him did any arise like him"*** (2 Kings 23:25). Josiah's obedience was a great moment; the blessings of God should flow, and Judah should prosper. The beginning of the next verse is ***"Nevertheless"*** (2 Kings 23:26), a "NO" in the eternal moment. The Pharaoh of Egypt killed Josiah in a battle. Josiah's son became king, reigning in wickedness, and Judah ended in Babylonian captivity, placing a kink in the theological premise. Disobedience creates chaos, but obedience should produce prosperity. How can we explain this?

Admittedly the premise of "reward for obedience" will be proved in the New Testament. Has there ever been one like Jesus? His ministry began with the voice of His Father. ***"This is My beloved Son, in whom I am well pleased"*** (Matthew 3:17). The Father repeated this at the Mount of Transfiguration (Matthew 17:5). Has ever the power of God been demonstrated in such a Man? His miracles were evidence of this power! Surely Jesus will prove the premise when a person is obedient, prosperity, and well-being result.

"Oops!" What is Jesus doing on a cross? Why is He crying out to God, ***"My God, My God, why have You forsaken Me?"*** (Matthew 27:46). Does God forsake people who do right? Maybe the premise is wrong! Our passage has a dilemma. If God is sovereign, will He not protect the good people and punish the bad people? Why would a sovereign God allow His people to suffer? The sovereignty of God is the power and might of dominion over His creatures, to determine and dispose of them as He desires. God is sovereign because there is nothing or no one higher in power and existence than Him. Therefore, why would a good God allow suffering? I can easily see that He does not cause suffering, but why would He allow it? God could prevent every bad thing from happening to me. Why would He not do this?

The answer is in Jesus! The early Church understood their present situation as an extension of Jesus' crucifixion. In uniting and identifying with Jesus, they embraced His suffering. In the last words of Christ, He uttered the statement, ***"It is finished!"*** (John 19:30), referring to the establishment of the Kingdom of God's New Covenant. The early Church viewed all suffering in this battle as an extension of Christ's sufferings. Paul cried, *"that I may know Him and the power of His resurrection, and the fellowship of His sufferings, being conformed to His death"* (Philippians 3:10). Could this be what Paul described? *"I now rejoice in my sufferings for you, and fill up in my flesh what is lacking in the afflictions of Christ, for the sake of His body, which is the church"* (Colossians 1:24). Remember these words, *"For as the sufferings of Christ abound in us, so our consolation also abounds through Christ"* (2 Corinthians 1:5). Paul instructed Timothy, *"Therefore do not be ashamed of the testimony of our Lord, nor of me His prisoner, but share with me in the sufferings for the gospel according to the power of God"* (2 Timothy 1:8). If the sovereign plan of the Trinity God predetermined that Jesus should suffer, why would you and I be exempt? We will now investigate this concept!

Superimposed Suffering

The human arena has various types of suffering. The pain or discomfort endured may be the same in all suffering, but the central issue is the source of the suffering. It has to do with the question, "Why?" When the purpose of suffering accomplishes something, we find it easier to endure. A mother endures the suffering of childbirth with a sense of joy; she gladly does it again. Suffering in the life of the believer is different from the suffering in the life of a nonbeliever. Although there is pleasure in sin for a season, suffering will come. Sin is always destructive and produces suffering. However, it is redemptive when a sinless person suffers for one who has sinned. There is never redemption until one who has not participated in sin bears the suffering of another's sin, the message of our passage. The world gathered, superimposing the suffering of their sin on Jesus, the One who had never sinned. The Trinity predetermined this!

Our text begins with *"For truly"* (Acts 4:27). In the Greek text, "synago," translated *"were gathered together,"* is the first word and the main verb in the verse. The fourth Greek word "aletheia," is translated *"truly."* It expresses the idea of truth or conformity to reality, actuality. In other words, Luke communicated the fact of the case. Although it may not seem this way to some, in the essence of truth, it is reality!

The Greek word "epi," translated *"against,"* expresses the underlying meaning of "upon," taking several forms in the New Testament. Our passage reveals the idea of "superimposing." These two verses present the conflict of our world. *"Herod"* represents all the kings of the world. *"Pontius Pilate"* represents the rulers of the world. *"The Gentiles"* represent the world domination of the Roman Empire. *"The people of Israel"* represent the Jewish nation. Together, they represent the evil of all generations. They are the instruments of demonic forces under the direction and domination of Satan. What have they gathered to do? They have come to superimpose their selfish desires and independence on the plan of God, establishing the platform of suffering in the life of the believer. The demonic realm is superimposing the thinking, hopes, and strategies of a self-centered mind on the selfless, self-sacrificing, never think about yourself thought pattern of God.

Christianity is merging with Jesus; we think as He thinks. We become an expression of His mind in a world determined to live for itself, which results in suffering. Throughout Jesus' instruction to His disciples, He established a pattern of consistency, drawing them into a consciousness of inevitable suffering. He began the Sermon on the Mount with the premise of Christianity. We are *"poor in spirit"* (Matthew 5:3). We are to live conscious of our helplessness, allowing God's nature to merge with us, and we become the Kingdom person, receiving benefits from this merger: meekness, fulfillment, mercy, purity, and peace. The last Beatitude is stunning. *"Blessed are those who are persecuted for righteousness' sake"* (Matthew 5:10).

Part 4: The Absolute Reign

Perhaps Jesus is warning us of what might happen in our lives. But He continues by making it a certainty: ***"Blessed are you when they revile and persecute you, and say all kinds of evil against you falsely for My sake"*** (Matthew 5:11).

Jesus wanted to duplicate His ministry through the disciples. He gave them instructions for ministry, which included a strong warning about suffering. ***"But beware of men, for they will deliver you up"*** (Matthew 10:17). ***"You will be brought before governors and kings for My sake"*** (Matthew 10:18). ***"When they deliver you up, do not worry"*** (Matthew 10:19). ***"When they persecute you in this city, flee to another"*** (Matthew 10:17-23). He continued, ***"A disciple is not above his teacher, nor a servant above his master. It is enough for a disciple that he be like his teacher, and a servant like his master. If they have called the master of the house Beelzebub, how much more will they call those of his household!"*** (Matthew 10:24-25). ***"Do not think that I came to bring peace on earth. I did not come to bring peace but a sword"*** (Matthew 10:34). The suffering of believers is without question.

The wonder of it all is the victory contained in the suffering. Jesus acquired our flesh and blood for suffering. Through this death, He destroyed ***"him who had the power of death, that is, the devil, and release those who through fear of death were all their lifetime subject to bondage"*** (Hebrews 2:14-15). The suffering inflicted on the believer from the self-centered evil of the world is the weapon that destroys them!

The early Church understood that the evil world imposed suffering and death on Jesus, but it was a direct result of the predetermined plan of God. The destruction they imposed became the redemption of the world and destroyed the forces of evil. The early Church understood their participation in this pattern, redemption through suffering. Christianity was not a means to escape suffering, but they were to embrace it for a purpose. Christianity is not a way out but a way in. We participate in the predetermined plan of God to redeem a world. Will we join Him in His death?

Sourcing or Suffering

Luke said the world was united in the crucifixion of Jesus; they were *"gathered together."* The Greek word for *"gathered together"* is the main verb of the sentence in the passive voice. The sovereign Almighty God acted in this group to crucify Jesus. Then, Luke explains the purpose of their gathering. They *"were gathered together to do"* (Acts 4:27, 28). The Greek word "poieo" is translated *"to do."* We discuss it often in our studies. It is not doing something out of duty or habit; it is a doing that flows from the nature of the individuals involved. Trees "poieo" (bare) fruit as an effortless result of their nature. This verb is an infinitive focusing on purpose.

The Trinity God elevated the leaders of the nations to a place of authority and choice. God did not eliminate their freewill; He did not make them robots. God knew these evil, self-centered men would act according to their nature. He allowed them authority and position, enabling them to act out the desires of their nature. They would not be able to tolerate Jesus because of their nature, demanding His removal. They used their authority and power to achieve what they wanted. God predetermined they should gather to crucify Jesus. The proposal was, *"whatever Your hand and Your purpose determined before to be done"* (Acts 4:28).

Jesus, a helpless man, was filled with the nature of God; He is the visible image of the invisible Father. His willingness to embrace redemptive suffering expresses the nature of the Father. He called His disciples to join Him in this style of the cross, the nature of God. When we merge with Jesus, we become an expression of this nature. Our nature, merged with the nature of God, is in direct conflict with the demonic nature of self-centeredness. This merger will inevitably produce conflict, resulting in suffering, when God exposes the demonic nature to His divine nature. We must conclude that the suffering of Christ and the sufferings of all believers is a fulfillment of God's plan and spills forth from the nature of God.

The self-centered, demonic nature is natural, automatic, and predictable. That evil nature has our world and will "do" (poieo) whatever it desires. The nature of God is also natural, automatic, and predictable, and it will "do" (poieo) whatever it wants. The "doing" (poieo) of these two natures are in direct contradiction to each other. Each nature is predictable. It was easy for the Pharisees to structure situations to trap Jesus. They knew what He would "do" (poieo). On the Sabbath, Jesus entered the synagogue; a man with a withered hand was present. The Pharisees hovered and *"watched Him closely, whether He would heal on the Sabbath, that they might find an accusation against Him"* (Luke 6:7). Why would the Pharisees suspect Jesus and watch Him closely? They had enough experiences with Jesus to know how He would respond. *"But He knew their thoughts, and said to the man who had the withered hand, 'Arise and stand here'"* (Luke 6:8). Was Jesus a mind reader, or did He know the nature of the Pharisees? He knew what their natures would produce (poieo). These two natures naturally produce conflict that results in suffering.

We are Kingdom people. Can we merge with Jesus and not enter into the conflict? Oneness with God's nature produces the pattern of Jesus in *"to do whatever Your hand and Your purpose determined before to be done."* The early Church recognized this. They rejoiced in experiencing the suffering of Christ!

Specification of Suffering

We must view this concept of suffering through the sovereignty of God. Nothing catches God off guard; nothing surprises Him! He never asks the question, "What will I do now?" In our passage, the powers of the world were elevated to a position of authority by His sovereignty. In His sovereignty, God allowed these powers to assemble, knowing what they would do. They would *"do whatever Your hand and Your purpose determined before to be done"* (Acts 4:28). Therefore, God knew the suffering of Christ before His crucifixion.

Understanding God's sovereignty working through His plan produced such statements as, *"Looking unto Jesus, the author and finisher of our faith, who for the joy that was set before Him endured the cross, despising the shame, and has sat down at the right hand of the throne of God"* (Hebrews 12:2). The joy was not in the suffering event, but in what the suffering would produce. The suffering was within the parameters of the sovereignty of God!

When we embrace the reality of suffering, we apply God's sovereignty to our lives. Woe to us if we become people who remain self-centered and self-focused. We expect God to eliminate suffering from our lives. We hope He gives us a parking place close to the front doors of Walmart. We want health without sickness, financial security without sacrifice, and the elimination of our enemies without redemption. God becomes the protector of "our" sovereign plan. Our plan would not include suffering, which automatically eliminates redemption.

When you and I merge with God's nature, we will inevitably experience conflict with our self-centered world. This conflict will produce suffering. This suffering is a crucial involvement with the nature of God and His plan for the world's redemption through Christ. To be an expression of the sovereign Trinity's

Part 4: The Absolute Reign

nature is a privilege, which without failure, fosters conflict, suffering, and redemption. Will you embrace the suffering in your battles for the joy set before you?

Acts 4:28

DILEMMA OF THE STATEMENT: FREEWILL

"To do whatever Your hand and Your purpose determined before to be done" (Acts 4:28).

The sovereignty of God is a controversy, dividing the church in its application. All theologians believe in the sovereignty of God, so this is not an issue. If God were not sovereign, He would not be God. The difficulty is in what this means concerning His involvement in my life. If God is sovereign and has a plan for my life, how does that sovereignty affect my living? Do I have a choice, or am I a puppet on a string fulfilling the dream of God for my life? Am I a prisoner trapped in the clutches of One greater than I am? If so, God is another word for fate!

Some propose that the sovereignty of God negates the freewill of man. God is absolutely responsible for everything that happens in my life. God predestines humanity. Your choice does not determine your salvation; God's sovereignty determines the destiny of every man. Judas was predestined by God to betray Jesus; God predestined Saul of Tarsus to receive the blinding light of Jesus' presence on the Damascus Road; God predestined John to exile on Patmos. The sovereignty of God determines everything. God will save some while damning others. Whatever will be, will be!

Some propose the opposite by saying that God set things in motion, and although God is sovereign, He has no interest in me. I am entirely on my own without intervention from Him. The variables beyond my understanding consistently work in my life, causing chaos. I must not confuse these chaotic circumstances with God, for He is not involved. He left us to master our fate and determine our destiny. God is sovereign but is uninterested in my life.

If we become obsessed with the few verses proposing the idea of predestination, we quickly experience problems. We are soon confused when we see any idea mentioned in the Scripture outside the reality of the whole Scriptures. For instance, if sovereign, God determines the salvation of every person without their choice, and Adam and Eve were victims of His sovereignty. God, who cannot sin, became the Author and Creator of sin. God, who created man, caused His creation to experience sin. Immediately He went to great lengths over a long period and with a significant sacrifice to Himself to eliminate and save from sin. Have we the right to ask, "Why did not God simply stop sin initially and eliminate such sacrifice?" He became the cause of the mess that demanded His sacrifice.

Using "predestination" in the New Testament is limited. The Greek word "proorizo," meaning "predestination," has a variety of translations in the New Testament. In our passage, the translation is *"determined"* (Acts 4:28). Paul's use of this word, when translated *"ordained"* is concerned with God's wisdom (1 Corinthians 2:7). Four other times Paul uses this word, translated *"predestined"* (Romans 8:29, 30; Ephesians 1:5, 11). Six times in the New Testament, predestination refers to events and people God foreordained before all time or before their concrete historical time.

A careful examination of these verses reveals a consistent fact. When predestination does not regard a particular person, there is no mention of a name. When people are involved in

Dilemma of the Statement:Freewill | Acts 4:28

predestination, they are always a group or category of people. In other words, those who qualify by meeting specific requirements form the group. For instance, Paul declared, *"having predestined us to adoption as sons by Jesus Christ to Himself, according to the good pleasure of His will"* (Ephesians 1:5). A category of people became sons of God! Who are they? The premise of the passage refers to those who are *"in Him." "Spiritual blessings"* are *"in Him." "Chose us"* is *"in Him." "Holy and without blame"* is *"in Him."* The groups of people *"in Him"* are predestined to become sons of God. Paul expands this thought into the wonder of an *"inheritance"* (Ephesians 1:11), for those *"in Him."*

Paul declared this truth to the Romans! *"For whom He foreknew, He also predestined to be conformed to the image of His Son, that He might be the firstborn among many brethren. Moreover whom He predestined, these He also called; whom He called, these He also justified; and whom He justified, these He also glorified"* (Romans 8:29-30). The Greek word "proginosko," translated *"foreknew,"* focuses on the most intimate knowledge. This group of people is *"conformed to the image of His Son," "called," "justified,"* and *"glorified."* All these qualities are in those He knows; how could He know them without these qualities?

Paul said this predestination applied to *"wisdom," "the hidden wisdom which God ordained* (predestined) *before the ages, for our glory"* (1 Corinthians 2:7). Paul said what we experience now in Jesus was planned by God before time. Paul called the Gospel we preach *"a mystery."* None of the rulers of this age understand this mystery. However, it was present in the wisdom of God before this age began! The sovereignty of God-ordained its truth. Therefore, sovereignty is the strength of God's wisdom. God established truths!

Now we come to our passage (Acts 4:27-28). God brought the evil world together to carry out His predestined plan. God turned evil on itself, causing its destruction. Evil did its worst to Jesus only to discover the worst became His best. Defeat designed to eliminate produced victory. Death conquered, but life triumphed. Evil participated in the destruction of itself, and God predetermined it in His sovereign wisdom! God is sovereign!

The Problem

Understanding God's sovereignty is not tricky. If God were not sovereign, He would not be God. Humanity never tolerates a weak and insufficient God. All the children of Israel with the prophets met at "Mount Carmel" (1 Kings 18), the mount of contest. The sovereign God must answer by fire. A time comes in everyone's life when they set Santa Claus aside, and the tooth fairy no longer visits. If God is sovereign, He must prove it! We will not tolerate a God who cannot intervene in our lives.

The sovereignty of God is necessary and acceptable, but the problem is "absolute" sovereignty. We have learned that "absolute power brings absolute corruption." Surely there are limitations to God's sovereignty. If God does not draw the lines, we will draw them for Him. If God has "absolute" sovereignty, will we not consistently confront Him with the question, "why?" The tragedies of life will cause men to hurl accusations at the sovereign God.

We will find those who say that although God is sovereign, He does not cause everything. We sidestep the real question, which pushes that question further back, causing another confrontation. Because if God did not cause it, and He is absolutely sovereign, He certainly allowed it. Does this not carry with it the same responsibility? If God is sovereign over every event in my life, could He not cause cancer or prevent it? Either way, is He not responsible for cancer? So, God, "Why do I have cancer?" Everyone experiences something in his or her life that raises the question, "Why?" When confronting God with such a question, is He consistently silent concerning the issue? He covers His sovereign guilt with the proposal that we must believe. I am to trust Him amid my crisis regardless of the consequence.

All man's accusations lead back to this dilemma. Terrible sin and evil are in the world. We are at war with demonic forces. But if God is absolutely sovereign, why is the devil not immediately defeated and the terrible destruction of evil eliminated? Why does God allow this to go on repeatedly? So, the grandfather's sin flows into the father's sin that flows into the son's sin. What chance does the younger generation have? Where is a sovereign God amid such chaos, and how can I believe God is absolutely good in His sovereignty? All I experience is evil, heartache, and death? I am not sovereign in power and unquestionably not sovereign in righteousness; however, I cannot stand this in my world. How can God, sovereign in power and in righteousness, tolerate it?

If we want to push the issue, we must ask this question? Why would a sovereign God let a puny person like me challenge His integrity? Why would He allow masses of us to stand with our fists in the air in defiance of His sovereignty? It is the cry of our passage,

> *"Why did the nations rage,*
> *And the people plot vain things?*
> *The kings of the earth took their stand,*
> *And the rulers were gathered together*
> *Against the Lord and His Christ"*
> (Acts 4:25-26).

The Provision

The answer is not that complicated! The answer is in the granting of "freewill." God gives us freedom of choice. If such a reality is true, does this not negate His sovereignty? How can God grant freewill to humanity and simultaneously maintain

His sovereignty? Again, is there not a simple answer? If God is absolutely sovereign, does He not have the right to limit that sovereignty by granting freewill to humanity? This limitation would validate His sovereignty. Who is greater in sovereignty? Is it the person in control and must have his way? Or is it the person in control but limits that control to allow others freedom of choice? The reality of God giving us freewill declares to us His absoluteness sovereignty.

The results of this limitation highlight the greatness of this truth! Because God is sovereign in wisdom, He understands the ramifications of giving humanity freewill. Our sovereign God did not regret His decision after experiencing the results of the limitation. "Freewill" opened the door of possibility to a new realm, "rebellion." We do not create a new realm of rebellion, in the same manner, God's sovereignty created freewill. Sovereignty creates something from nothing. "Sin" takes what God already created and twists it based on an attitude of rebellion. Ironically, the basis of the rebellion is sovereignty. The sovereignty of God giving the freedom of choice becomes the focus of rebellion. Man wants to be sovereign! He does not desire to be absolutely sovereign as God is, but he does want to reign over his universe. In other words, it is self-sovereignty!

Therefore, my ultimate and only choice of God's granted freewill in my life is between who will be sovereign, God, or self? If we choose to live in personal absolute self-sovereignty, we will experience the illusion of that sovereignty. There are dozens of variables flowing into our lives over which we have no control. We did not choose them, and we cannot eliminate them. We are not in control and are not sovereign. But it does not matter to us; we continue to live in the illusion that we are "Lord" of our life. A man created to be nothing more than a man decides to be a god! He is incapable of such a role; his consistent failures scream this reality. God gives us freewill to choose Him as absolute sovereign in our lives. God created us to be dependent, not independent. Jesus is Lord; we are not. The chaos of our distress is in this dilemma.

The Proof

No one dominated by self-centered sovereignty would choose to grant freewill and create the possibility of such chaos. If God were absolutely sovereign in wisdom and power, why would He give man a freewill? Why would He grant such liberty with the knowledge of the sacrifice and personal suffering it requires? God's sovereignty allows man's freewill, concluding the matter!!!

Self-centered sovereignty does not dominate God. ***"God is love"*** (1 John 4:8, 16). Self-centered sovereignty weighs the odds. What benefits will we get in granting humanity freewill? The risk is too high, and the benefits are too small, a human nature focused on self will not enter such an endeavor. But God's nature is love; it is "agape" love, selfless, self-sacrificing, and self-giving. God's nature demands that He grant freewill, regardless of the risk.

The absolute sovereignty and power of Almighty God do not control His nature of love. God's nature of love controls His absolute sovereignty and power. He does not leverage His power to protect His love; He leverages His love to administer His power. Everything in the character of God is dominated and demonstrated through His nature. The love of God must be the first thought. Any deviation from this is blasphemy on the nature of God. It makes the sovereignty of God an instrument of self-centeredness.

Yes, all the kings of the earth represented by ***"Herod,"*** joined with ***"Pontius Pilate,"*** who represented all the world's rulers. All the Gentile nations and the Jewish nation participated in the gathering. They came to do what their nature commanded them ***"to do"*** (Acts 4:27, 28). The sovereign God gave them

Part 4: The Absolute Reign

freewill to choose according to their nature. He allowed them to rise in authority, knowing how they would respond to Jesus. Their self-centered, false sovereignty demanded the elimination of Jesus; Jesus is a threat to all self-focused sovereignty.

The absolute sovereign God allowed self-centered sovereign man to expose the worst of his nature. But amid the destruction of self-centered sovereignty, love won! God's love was the only thing that survived. In the act of crucifixion and destruction, self-centeredness was embraced and brought to death. The nature of God conquered and generated life.

So here we are again! We are back at the beginning, where Adam found himself in the Garden of Eden. God granted man the freewill to choose! Our choice is simple; we must choose self-centered sovereignty or the sovereignty of God because we cannot serve two masters. Will we continue in our illusion of self-sovereignty, or will we allow Jesus to be who He is, Lord of our lives?

Acts 4:27-28

DETERMINATION OF THE PLAN

"For truly against Your holy Servant Jesus, whom You anointed, both Herod and Pontius Pilate, with the Gentiles and the people of Israel were gathered together to do whatever Your hand and Your purpose determined before to be done" (Acts 4:27-28).

The time has come to submerge ourselves in the context of our passage. The miracle of the lame beggar startled all Jerusalem (Acts 4:16). This man was more than 40 years old and had spent most of his life begging at the Gate Beautiful (Acts 4:22). Jesus used Peter and John to heal this beggar, authenticating the miracle, as the bystanders witnessed the event. ***"So he, leaping up, stood and walked and entered the temple with them - walking, leaping, and praising God"*** (Acts 3:8). The apostles were not responsible for this miracle; it was beyond their capabilities. The growing crowd around Solomon's Porch accredited the miracle to Peter and John. ***"So when Peter saw it, he responded to the people: 'Men of Israel, why do you marvel at this? Or why look so intently at us, as though by our own power or godliness we had made this man walk?"*** (Acts 4:12). He delivered a message to this multitude with a focus on Jesus. Five thousand men converted to Christ (Acts 4:4). Peter and John realized they could not save anyone. God moved this great crowd!

Many miracles occurred through the ministry of the early Church. However, this miracle shook Jerusalem as none other.

The Sadducees realized the message, *"in Jesus the resurrection from the dead,"* captured the hearts of the people (Acts 4:2). The Sanhedrin gathered and interrogated Peter and John. The focus on Jesus was strong in the discussion, forcing the Sanhedrin to act. They threatened the apostles to never again speak in the name of Jesus. Peter and John knew Jesus was their source, and there was never a chance the Sanhedrin could silence them in proclaiming the name of Jesus. Then the persecution of the early Church began.

The two verses of our passage record the response of the early Church, a crisis moment threatening the lives of these early Christians. Herod represented all the Kings; Pontius Pilate represented all the rulers. The Gentiles and people of Israel represented the world in those gathered to carry out a single act, *"to do whatever Your hand and Your purpose determined before to be done"* (Acts 4:28).

A significant comparison arises from this statement. The pivotal word is the Greek word "hosos," translated *"whatever,"* an interesting word pertaining to the extent of space or time, the same extent as another extent of the same order. Whatever happened in one arena is compared to the same strength and enthusiasm in another arena, instructing about size or space. For instance, it describes the holy Jerusalem, *"The city is laid out as a square; its length is as great as* (hosos) *its breadth"* (Revelation 21:16). Everything true about the length of the holy city was also true about its breadth. *"And Jesus took the loaves, and when He had given thanks He distributed them to the disciples, and the disciples to those sitting down; and likewise of the fish, as much as* (hosos) *they wanted"* (John 6:11). The number of loaves and fish was equal to the hunger of the crowd. "Hosos" is used to identify groups of people. *"And when the men of that place recognized Him, they sent out into all that surrounding region, brought to Him all who were sick, and begged Him that they might only touch the hem of His garment.*

And as many as (hosos) *touched it were made perfectly well"* (Matthew 14:35-36). A group of sick people touched the hem of His garment; the group touching the hem of His garment was equal to the group healed by Jesus.

Now we will apply this concept to our passage. The world represented by *"Herod and Pontius Pilate, with the Gentiles and the people of Israel were gathered together to do"* (Acts 4:27-28). Whatever the result of their action in size, quantity or amount, and identifying people groups would be equal to, *"Your hand and Your purpose determined before to be done"* (Acts 4:28). Those who have gathered will accomplish the dreams and plans of our sovereign God to its fullest extent.

Can you see the contradiction in the statement? Rebellious humanity in all its self-centered expressions fulfilled the will of our sovereign God. When humanity expresses its determination, the result is that we accomplish the determined purpose of our sovereign God. The crucifixion of Jesus is the focus of our passage. God birthed the dream of redemption in His loving heart. The first Messianic promise states it clearly. In speaking to the devil, God said,

> *"And I will put enmity*
> *Between you and the woman,*
> *And between your seed and her Seed;*
> *He shall bruise your head,*
> *And you shall bruise His heel"*
> (Genesis 3:15).

The willful actions of wicked men completed the desires of our sovereign God.

This truth was declared earlier. The Pentecost event stirred the crowd. The Holy Spirit moved on Peter to bring clarity to the meaning of the event. The body of His message began with an explanation of Jesus becoming a man. Jesus did not do anything He did because He was God; Jesus did everything He did because He was a man sourced by God. He was a manifestation of everything flowing from the nature and heart of God. In the demonstration of this visible image, Peter described the crucifixion of Jesus. ***"Him, being delivered by the determined purpose and foreknowledge of God, you have taken by lawless hands, have crucified, and put to death"*** (Acts 2:23). Everything contained in the wicked plot to crucify Jesus brought the plan of God to fulfillment; it was ***"the determined purpose and foreknowledge of God,"*** which was not an isolated idea of the early Church. What Peter said at Pentecost is now illustrated and embraced in the response of the early Church to life-threatening persecution.

In our passage, there were those who ***"were gathered together."*** The Greek word "sunago" is translated ***"were gathered together"*** and is the main verb in the indicative tense. The subjects of the sentence are ***"Herod"*** and ***"Pontius Pilate,"*** each in the nominative. The Gentiles and the people of Israel are with these leaders. The main verb ***"were gathered together"*** is in the passive voice, meaning that the Kings and rulers, along with world's members, were not responsible for the action of this verb. Something or someone was acting on them. The sovereign God manipulated the circumstances to draw them together ***"to do,"*** a translation of the Greek word "poieo." This verb is an infinitive in the active voice, meaning they are responsible for the action produced from their gathering. A sovereign God linked the world and its leaders together where they would act out of their nature and do what their self-centered hearts demanded. Their self-centeredness crucified Jesus, which was what ***"Your hand and Your purpose determined before to be done."***

Here is a concise statement to relay this idea. "God's sovereignty, controlled by His nature, conceived an irrevocable plan that includes your life." There are four main thrusts of this concept.

Attribute of Sovereignty

The attribute of sovereignty does not need much discussion. God is sovereign. We have already discovered the strength of this truth. However, I am not sure this truth grips our lives in daily activities. Sovereignty describes God's power and might over His creatures to dispose and determine them as He desires. We have made attempts to define and measure this sovereignty. How powerful is our God? Because He is beyond anything that we know, there is no way to see the extent of His greatness. He is greater than the universes. But we do not know how much greater!

The word *"Lord"* in our passage is a proclamation. It is the Greek word "despostes" from which we get the English word "despot" used only ten times in the New Testament. "Kurios" is the common Greek word for "lord," used 717 times, and is an authority that includes a consideration of the good for the one over whom it is exercised. Children would honor their father and call him "lord." But "despotes" is used for a master over slaves with absolute authority and requires a submission beyond normal. It is impossible to overstate God's sovereignty! We begin to experience His sovereignty in creation. *"Lord, You are God, who made heaven and earth and the sea, and all that is in them"* (Acts 4:24). We see His sovereignty in the completeness of creation! We must also see His sovereignty in the scope of the Scriptures. *"Lord, You are God, who made heaven and earth and the sea, and all that is in them, who by the mouth of Your servant David have said"* (Acts 4:24-25). The Scriptures demonstrate the sovereignty of God in content and context.

Attitude of Sovereignty

Overwhelming evidence that forces us to believe in the sovereignty of God surrounds us. To conclude a supreme being is above everything is logical. If you were to take all the individual letters in the writings of Shakespeare and throw them into the air, what are the chances these letters would fall into the right order to form his writings? Can any reasonable person think creation just fell together? The majestic plan of creation is far beyond happen chance. There was a Mastermind.

The next step in our concept is God's nature, which controls His sovereignty. Although everyone seems to believe in a sovereign God, there is some argument about what kind of God He is! However, while this may be a question in the theological world, this is not an issue in the Scriptures. **"God is love"** (1 John 4:8, 16). We have highlighted this in previous studies, and it must remain so. His love is not sentimental; He does not have a "soft-spot" for us. His love is not romantic; something about us has attracted Him to us. He does not generate His love by self-centeredness; He loves us even when we do not contribute to Him. His love is redemptive!

The core of redemptive love is "never think about yourself." Outside of God's presence, we can never experience such love. God's love is not something He has, but instead, God's love has Him! It is His nature! He cannot help Himself. His sovereignty with all His power is dominated and controlled by redemption. God cannot do anything but be redemptive. This redemptive love is the total, absolute, eternal focus of His nature, and He never changes.

The proof of this eternal love is Jesus. The historical Jesus was the *"image of the invisible God"* (Colossians 1:15). Jesus demonstrated everything that God is. The single focus of action, attitude, and atmosphere of Jesus' life was redemptive. We must see everything in the Old Testament through the image of God, as seen in Jesus! God's power is His sovereignty, and He focuses on redemption, which was the belief of the early Church. If the circumstances of life seem destructive and full of discomfort, we must not interpret them by self-centeredness. We must see those circumstances in light of the sovereign God's redemptive heart. ***"And we know that all things work together for good to those who love God, to those who are the called according to His purpose"*** (Romans 8:28). The Apostle Paul said this amid his discussion of "predestination," the sovereignty of God. This statement is valid only if God is sovereign, and God is love!

Aim of Sovereignty

We are looking at the four aspects of the concise statement: "God's sovereignty, controlled by His nature, conceived an irrevocable plan that includes your life." The aim of sovereignty declares the plan that flows from the sovereignty of God controlled by His nature. Love is so dominant in God's nature that He cannot be idle regarding the object of His love. This nature of love drives Him to action. Can you visualize the nature of God flowing from Him, producing a fog of love that surrounds Him? He does not reflect this light; this light naturally flows from its source, His heart. God's heart is powerful, and it demands action.

Observe carefully! This action is not flippant, emotional, or impulsive, but instead is God's well-thought-out plan of redemption. This plan is highlighted in the first Messianic promise (Genesis 3:15) and is exposed throughout hundreds of years in the Old Testament. The prophets continually spoke of this plan. God developed the people of Israel through Abraham and gave the law in light of the plan. This plan was ***"before the foundation of the world"*** (Ephesians 1:4). Although God may have initiated the plan in the creation of man, the redemptive heart of God was already planning for man's redemption.

The plan of redemption is the marvel of our passage. Who can comprehend its depth? The kings, rulers, and people of the world **"were gathered together."** They were acted on and brought together by the sovereign God who had a plan. He raised them to a place of prominence and gave them a platform to express their choice. They did what God knew they would do, His plan. The plan in the Old Testamen revealed 332 verbal predictive prophecies. They were not general predictions but specific in detail. The scourging, the piercing of His hands, one of His own betraying Him, the crown of thorns, no broken bones, the price of 30 pieces of silver, vinegar offered as a drink, the piercing of His side, His grave among the rich, and the mockery of the crowd were all in the plan. These prophecies were a mere expression of the planned details coming from the heart of God for redemption.

Accomplishment of Sovereignty

Although all these details and more were accomplished, the focus of God's plan is you? Not "you" in the plural sense, but "you" in the singular sense. There are specific details in the plan focused exclusively on you. The sovereignty of God, under the control of His redemptive heart, expresses a plan. All the details declare that God did not create you and then produce a plan. His plan for you was not an afterthought, not a plan for all mankind, but is a plan specifically for you. In other words, God did not create you then try to give you some meaningful purpose. God has a specific plan in place. He is sovereign and redemptive, and He created you out of His plan.

Your unique existence declares this truth. Your fingerprints differ from anyone else, and no other human being matches your DNA. Your appearance and personality are yours alone, expressing your uniqueness. God based His plan on His sovereign redemption. He created you as a unique individual to fulfill a role in this sovereign redemptive plan. You do not have to be a willing participant, but you will participate in the plan.

Your attitude will determine the destiny of your life as you participate in the plan. If you rebel against His plan, you rebel against yourself. You will destroy yourself if you do not submit to His sovereign redemption. You and I will accomplish God's purpose, but the attitude of the accomplishment will mean our salvation or destruction.

In His sovereignty, God knows you better than you know yourself. He knows what you need far beyond your comprehension. He understands the context of your life and knows what to allow and disallow. What should be your proper response? You must radically, without question, submit to Him, because He always acts for your best. You find fulfillment only in His fulfilled plan. You must be His!

Acts 4:29

CRISIS MANAGEMENT

"Now, Lord, look on their threats, and grant to Your servants that with all boldness they may speak Your word" (Acts 4:29).

It is an hour of crisis! It is not a financial crisis, an argument, or environmental disaster but a crisis that threatens life's existence. Will I live or die? The "survival mode" kicks in to protect and save. When you feel as if you are falling, your hands automatically reach out to cushion the fall. When you receive a threat on your life, do you not immediately do what is necessary to live? The act of protecting yourself is entirely natural.

The early Church experienced surprising acceptance in Jerusalem, but there came one miracle or one message too many. The believers proclaimed Jesus with force, and His presence was commanding, changing lives. The focus was on the transformation of the lame beggar known by all. He became a living testimony of the resurrected Jesus. The Sanhedrin would not tolerate such a demonstration; they threatened the early Church, *"that from now on they speak to no man in this name"* (Acts 4:17). Their threats may seem insignificant, except they crucified Jesus not many months before. The memory of those troubled times lingered in the hearts of the early Church.

However, the early Church was confident and secure. *"And they continued steadfastly in the apostles' doctrine and fellowship, in the breaking of bread, and in prayers"* (Acts 2:42).

Crisis Management | **Acts 4:29**

Their security was not in their theological training. Their sense of safety was not in the strong fellowship of many Christians in Jerusalem. Even being together spiritually in times of prayer was not the foundation of their confidence. God's sovereignty captured them. Jesus is *"Lord"* (despotes) (Acts 4:24), and He has the absolute authority over all creation. He is not just the Creator of all things but reigns in authority, and all created things are under His dictates.

God's sovereignty should have produced fear except for one fact! God is "agape" love. We can trust Him! Are these just words? How do we know who He is? We know His voice as He speaks to us! The revelation of His nature comes to us through His Word, the Scriptures (Acts 4:25). Not only does the sovereign God of love indwell us, but He also reveals who He is through the Scriptures. The intertwining of these two realities brings confidence to human life. We are safe in every crisis. The early Church not only believed this, but they demonstrated that faith amid the threats on their lives.

Listen to their response, *"**Now, Lord, look on their threats, and grant to Your servants that with all boldness they may speak Your word, by stretching out Your hand to heal, and that signs and wonders may be done through the name of Your holy Servant Jesus**"* (Acts 4:29-30). They did not respond with a plea for protection, safety, or revenge. No one asked for deliverance from their circumstances; instead, they asked for empowerment in their circumstances. The ministry of Jesus so captured them that they cried out for that ministry to continue and increase! Let's look closely at the details.

Link

The beginning statement reveals the thought pattern of the early Church. The first three words in the Greek text are small but significant, "kai ta nun." The Greek word "nun" is translated *"now"* in most English versions. The first Greek word, "kai," is translated "and." The second Greek word, "ta," is translated "the." Many English translations say, *"And now."* The article "the" focuses us on the present *"now"* of the early Church.

This transitional statement moves us from the circumstances described in the two previous verses to the immediate threat the early Church received. We discovered in these verses that Herod, the King, and Pontius Pilate, the ruler, represented all those in the world. The world, with all the Gentiles and the Jewish nation, gathered together. It is clear from the grammar structure of the verse that the sovereign God caused this gathering. Those gathered did not initiate this gathering, but God moved them into place. What was the purpose of this movement? God elevated them to a position of authority so they would do what their self-centered nature commanded. They crucified Christ! But this was precise *"whatever Your hand and Your purpose determined before to be done"* (Acts 4:28).

God fulfilled His sovereign will through the crucifixion of Jesus, which linked with the threat to the early Church. They saw their threat as an extension of Jesus. The battle they fought was the same battle Jesus fought; it was not two different wars but the same spiritual war. The ministry of Jesus was now their ministry, or was He continuing to minister through them? The world's response to the ministry of Jesus soon reached them. Every early Church member linked with Jesus; His experience was now theirs.

Indeed, the early Church remembered the times Jesus told them this truth. When He was ready to duplicate His ministry through His disciples, He gave them instruction before sending them out. Jesus informed them, *"A disciple is not above his teacher, nor a servant above his master. It is enough for a disciple that he be like his teacher and a servant like his master. If they have called the master of the house Beelzebub, how much more will they call those of his household"* (Matthew 10:24-25)! In the upper room before His crucifixion, Jesus said, *"Remember the word that I said to you, 'A servant is not greater than his master.' If they persecuted Me, they will also persecute you. If they kept My word, they will keep yours also"* (John 15:20). Jesus proposed a link between His experience and theirs.

The boldness of the early Church caused them to respond as Jesus did in persecution. That was because they were linked. The sovereign God manifested this plan in Jesus and was now flowing His plan through them. The disciples were an extension of the life, ministry, and suffering of Jesus. The opportunity of such suffering thrilled them. How could a disciple, a servant, ask for anything more?

We can apply this truth to our lives. The crucifixion was more than two thousand years ago. We did not participate in the event or have nightmares of its impact. Yet are we not in the same battle? Are we not filled with His Spirit? Can we expect a different response from our world? Paul described it as, *"For we do not wrestle against flesh and blood, but against principalities, against powers, against the rulers of the darkness of this age, against spiritual hosts of wickedness in the heavenly places"* (Ephesians 6:12).

We must not join the spoiled generation focusing on themselves, creating a god who eliminates their suffering and grants to them their self-centered heart's desires. How tragic to develop a spoiled generation of Christians who are so anemic and soft they cannot respond to a call to the mission field. They could not endure difficulties or make the sacrifices necessary to experience God's will for their lives. They never make their way to a Philippi jail, experience the earthquake of God, and see the salvation of the jailer. They cannot endure a bleeding back amid their circumstance.

Only when God's Divine movement through our lives

produces dangerous circumstances can we experience the calm known in linking with Jesus. So long as we dwell in our self-centeredness, we tremble in fear and uncertainty. Our insecurity is a call to be filled with Him! We must **"know Him and the power of His resurrection, and the fellowship of His sufferings, being conformed to His death"** (Philippians 3:10). We must carry **"about in the body the dying of the Lord Jesus, that the life of Jesus also may be manifested in our body. For we who live are always delivered to death for Jesus' sake, that the life of Jesus also may be manifested in our mortal flesh. So then death is working in us, but life in you"** (2 Corinthians 4:10-12).

Look

Luke begins our statement with this phrase "kai ta nun," presenting a link between the circumstances of the early Church and the crucifixion of Jesus. The next word in the Greek text is the subject "Kurios," translated **"Lord."** This beginning is a contrast to the way their response started. **"So when they heard that, they raised their voice to God with one accord and said: 'Lord** (despotes), **You are God, who made heaven and earth and the sea, and all that is in them'"** (Acts 4:24). The Greek word "despotes" is translated **"Lord"** in this verse. "Kurios," translated "Lord," is used 717 times in the New Testament; "despotes" is used ten times. "Despotes" is one who has absolute authority without regard to those under him. "Kurios" is often used in the context of family. The father will be called "kurios" as a term of honor and respect. The early Church recognized the position of Jesus as "Despotes." His sovereignty was beyond reproach. But they also knew His attitude controlling that authority. He is "Kurios" because we are His children.

"Look," and **"grant"** are the main verbs in the sentence. Each is in the imperative, meaning they are commands. The force of the early Church's desire relates to us in this imperative. Usually, the command comes from self-centeredness but not in this case. They did not ask for deliverance from their persecution; they did not ask for safety from discomfort. They recognized that the *"purpose determined before to be done"* by the sovereign, *"Your hand,"* was the crucifixion of Jesus. The Trinity God was responsible for gathering together the forces of the world and elevating them to a place of authority. The world would do what their self-centered will determined to do, which carried out God's plan. It involved suffering! The early Church saw their hour of persecution connected to the suffering of Jesus on the cross. They were not asking for deliverance from that suffering. They requested that they might continue to proclaim the name of Jesus boldly. They desired the same signs and wonders that verified what they declared concerning His name!

The Greek word translated *"look"* is "epeidon." "Epi" is the prefix, meaning "upon." "Eido" is the main word, meaning "to look." "Eido" does not portray the idea of a "glance" or "to notice," but is a call to focus on something or someone then respond accordingly. However, not only is "epi" (upon) the prefix of this verb, it is a separate word in the same phrase, making a double emphasis on the statement. They were commanding the sovereign Trinity to focus *"on their threats."* The Greek word translated *"threats"* is "apeile," a declaration of intent to inflict harm on another. The early Church cried out for the sovereign Trinity God to view the threats they received with the same intensity and focus that the Trinity had toward Jesus' crucifixion. As the Trinity was involved in redemption through Jesus' suffering, so the Trinity had to be involved in the suffering of the early Church that redemption might result.

What if the crisis of your life as the over-extension of your credit card stopped? What if the mess of your life was no longer produced from your unsatisfied selfish-desires and wants? Can we cease to experience crisis moments resulting from our willful disobedience, which always brings destruction? Could we join Jesus in His suffering? Can we participate in the dying of the Lord Jesus so that His life is manifested through us, creating chaos in an ungodly world (2 Corinthians 4:10-11)? When we bear the suffering of this chaos, we flow the redemption of Jesus to our world. It is always those with bleeding backs who sing in Philippi jails and bring redemption to jailers! Are we such a people?

Liberate

The early Church declared the truth in their request. A second main verb in the passage is ***"grant,"*** a translation of the Greek word "didomi." "Didomi" is the ninth most frequently used verb in the New Testament and is used in a variety of ways. Yet, it still has a significant focus in our verse. We use this word in the sense of "to endow," with an attitude connected with this giving or endowing, which means to give of one's own accord with goodwill. The early Church did not pressure or bargain with God for what they wanted. Self-centeredness did not drive their request, and we must see it in light of their declaration of God's sovereignty. The suffering of Jesus in crucifixion was accomplished by, ***"Your hand and Your purpose determined before to be done"*** (Acts 4:28). Based on this, they asked God to grant to them what He gave to Jesus. The Trinity God, who enabled Jesus to complete the ***"purpose determined before to be done,"*** must bestow upon the early Church the same blessing. They linked their present threats with the sufferings of Christ.

An essential additional fact is about the early Church's request. They were not asking for permission from God to continue to speak in boldness and produce miracles. They did not see themselves capable of the necessary ministry, even if

God approved their request. They understood how inadequate they were in the face of these threats on their lives. They cried for God to enable them to continue with the same boldness and miracles that produced their crisis circumstances. As God flowed through them in ministry, creating this crisis, may He continue to flow through them within their crisis!

We have to marvel at their view. Fear and uncertainty were present, and they did not know how the events would affect their future lives. But all of this was overshadowed by God's sovereignty. What God did through the sufferings of Christ He would do again through them, which was the focus of their prayer. They did not pray for deliverance from the threats or look for an escape. They did not express revenge in their prayers or desire the destruction of their persecutors. They experienced the movement of God through their lives, which changed those around them. Miracles happened, physically and spiritually. Redemption came to Jerusalem, and the early Church grew. In boldness, they proclaimed their living Christ, which God validated with healings, signs, and wonders. They demanded a continuation of this boldness and validation now amid their persecution.

Therefore, the pattern of our passage is clear. The early Church lived in the fullness of the Spirit of Jesus. He manifested Himself in redemptive ways throughout their lives. Because of this revelation through them, they encountered crisis circumstances, persecution in this case. Their immediate response was to continue with Jesus' manifestation in the crisis just as they did before the crisis. Far too often, I have a mess in my life that is not a product of His presence. I cry out for deliverance from that crisis and a manifestation of His Spirit anew in my life. In my expression of self-centered living, I produce my conflict. Then I want Jesus to remove the consequence of such a production, not the life of a Spirit-filled believer. Jesus must fill me, manifest His life through me, and allow His presence to change my world.

Part 4: The Absolute Reign

He will not eliminate conflict or crisis, but it will be conflict produced by the flow of His Spirit through me. Then I can cease to cry out for deliverance and desire only the continued flow of His Spirit through my life.

Acts 4:29

PRAYING TO CONTINUE

"Now, Lord, look on their threats, and grant to Your servants that with all boldness they may speak Your word" (Acts 4:29).

Prayer was a continual element in the life of the early Church. Prayer was not their tradition or religious activity, but God birthed prayer out of the New Covenant merger with Him! The Greek word "proseuche," translated **prayer** in the noun form, is used thirty-seven times in the New Testament, with nine of those are in the Book of Acts. The verb form of "proseuche" is used sixteen times in the Book of Acts. As we go through this book, we see that the early Church was always in a state of prayer.

In the Book of Acts, prayer began before Pentecost. For not many days, the early Church waited for the outpouring of the Holy Spirit. **"These all continued with one accord in prayer and supplication, with the women and Mary the mother of Jesus, and with His brothers** (Acts 1:14). Again, "proseuche," the Greek word for **"prayer"** as a noun, is used thirty-seven times in the New Testament but only eight in the Gospel accounts. A close investigation of those verses reveals they are always related to Jesus.

What is more surprising is the verb form of "proseuche" is used forty-seven times in the Gospel accounts. Each time it refers to what Jesus did or is used in the words of Jesus. We never see the disciples in the act of prayer. In the Book of Acts, we have the first biblical record of the disciples praying other than the Jewish hours of prayer, morning and evening. But something happened in the Book of Acts above the tradition of prayer and should be titled something else. The interconnectedness and communication they experienced with God were far beyond any previous prayer time.

For the first time, the disciples participated in what Jesus taught them. Jesus ascended to the right hand of the Father, and they now prayed in His name. Opening before them was a new era of communication between God and man. Were they aware as they prayed that Jesus went behind the veil of the Holy tabernacle not made with hands to make intercession for them (Hebrews 7:25)?

Can you imagine the amazement of the angels? They often rejoiced over the prayers of a repentant sinner, but now they were hearing prayers authorized and accredited by the name of the only begotten of the Father. They were prayers based on the name, which had recently become *"a name which is above every name"* (Philippians 2:9). Can you imagine the joy of that first prayer in the name of Christ? Something new happened! Unique access and interaction were between heaven and earth. Something happened that was impossible before the new High Priest arrived.

What exactly did the disciples pray, and how long did this prayer last? Did they sacrifice to pray, and was it vital to the experience for which God was preparing them? We need to look at the three essential words for prayer, as listed by Timothy. These words will give us the best picture of the distinction between the ideas suggested in prayer. **"Therefore I exhort first of all that supplications, prayers, intercessions, and giving of thanks be made for all men"** (1 Timothy 2:1). The Greek word "deeseis," translated *"supplications,"* is the statement of petition and focuses on the expression of a need. This word is possibly used in relationship not only to God but also to your fellowman.

"Prayers," the Greek word "proseuche," is used exclusively toward God, and no one or anything else. "Proseuche" is a word of a sacred character and has the idea of devotion and fellowship. Then the Greek word "enteuxeis," translated *"intercessions,"* is the heart expressed to God with childlike confidence.

In our passage, the focus on their activity was not "intercessions" nor "prayers" but "supplications," which is the context of our passage (Acts 4:23-31). Luke acknowledged the early Church's response to the threats as a prayer of supplication. He does this at the end of the passage and gives us the results of the answered prayer. *"And when they had prayed (deomai), the place where they were assembled together was shaken; and they were all filled with the Holy Spirit, and they spoke the word of God with boldness"* (Acts 4:31).

Three elements of their prayer may be a guide for us in making requests.

Acknowledge

The early Church began their request with an acknowledgment of who God is! *"Lord, You are God, who made heaven and earth and the sea and all that is in them"* (Acts 4:24). The overall concept of this paragraph (Acts 4:23-31) is the sovereignty of God. We continually talk about it because it is in every verse and was the basis of their request. God is the Creator of all things, meaning He is greater than the measuring rod of what we know in creation. God is outside the realm of our ability to measure. How big and significant is He? There is absolutely nothing to which we can compare Him.

Let me remind you that the early Church called Him, *"Lord"* (Despotes). The Greek word "Kurios," translated *"Lord,"* is not normal. In their language, "Despotes" describes a person who has absolute authority and is responsible to no one! Every aspect of God's creation comes under His supreme authority, including the circumstances that faced the early Church.

Jesus made an appointment with His disciples before His crucifixion. He told them to meet Him in Galilee after His resurrection. Coming from the Passover Feast on their way to Gethsemane, Jesus said to them, *"But after I have been raised, I will go before you to Galilee"* (Matthew 26:32). Mary Magdalene and the other Mary encountered the angel of the Lord as he descended and rolled the stone away. Jesus invited them to inspect the empty tomb. The angel sent them to share this information with the disciples but added, *"and indeed He is going before you to Galilee; there you will see Him. Behold I have told you"* (Matthew 28:7). As they ran in obedience to the angel's instructions, the Resurrected Lord appeared to them. His message was, *"Do not be afraid. Go and tell My brethren to go to Galilee, and there they will see Me"* (Matthew 28:10).

Finally, the hour arrived; the disciples were at the mountain for this appointed meeting. Jesus appeared, and they worshipped Him. *"And Jesus came and spoke to them, 'All authority has been given to Me in heaven and on earth'"* (Matthew 28:18). The Greek word "exousia," translated *"authority,"* is not the same as "dunamis," often translated "power" or "mighty deeds." "Dunamis" is explosive by nature, but "exousai" is permission, right, or liberty to do something. *"Authority"* (exousia) contains "power" (dunamis). Still, it focuses on "having the right." Jesus told His disciples the Father had given them the right to decide over all things contained in heaven and on earth. Nothing could come to the disciples' lives unless it first passed through Jesus. He dictates all circumstances, and the Father gave Him sovereign authority! Jesus' position is King of the Kingdom.

The early Church was deeply aware of this reality, and it was the attitude of their prayer. Every prayer was a prayer of praise and worship and never a selfish demand or bargaining. Prayer can never be a "con." The recognition of who Jesus is eliminates such attitudes. Anything outside this recognition is considered "sin!" Every deed of sin, at its conception, is a refusal to recognize God's position as sovereign. We must not eliminate just such acts, but we must reject the attitude that produces them. I must live in the awareness of who He is!

Paul talked about this state in the lives of the world's pagans. He declared God reveals His wrath from heaven, a source beyond us. We have no control over it. The ungodliness and unrighteousness of men receive such wrath (Romans 1:18). Paul described such a condition as the revelation of God's sovereignty! Contained in the creation of all things, God expressed His sovereignty. His eternal power and Godhead are in every heartbeat of life, leaving us all without excuse (Romans 1:19). How do we respond to this knowledge of His sovereignty? *"Because, although they knew God, they did not glorify Him as God, nor were thankful, but became futile in their thoughts, and their foolish hearts were darkened. Professing to be wise, they became fools, and changed the glory of the incorruptible God into an image made like corruptible man - and birds and four-footed animals and creeping things"* (Romans 1:21-23). The one created knew the sovereignty of the Creator but refused to acknowledge it. The created one made the creation sovereign instead of the Creator and called it "wise."

Can you imagine the sovereign God giving us the right to do as we please? We dishonored Him and ourselves. We *"exchanged the truth of God for the lie, and worshiped and served the creature rather than the Creator, who is blessed forever. Amen"* (Romans 1:25). Paul gave a long list of evil actions, which result from a debased mind that refuses to acknowledge what it knows, the sovereignty of God (Romans 1:29-32). The issue is not these terrible acts but the refusal to embrace what is known by everything created; God is sovereign.

Part 4: The Absolute Reign

Alignment

The Scriptural belief of the early Church was that God is sovereign. This belief dominated their prayers. Because God is sovereign, the early Church believed they could align their lives and their requests with whatever God desired. If we did this, we would always pray in the will of God and receive answers to our prayers. Prayer becomes an expression of submission rather than a manipulation to acquire personal desires.

We learned there are two main verbs in our verse, *"look"* and *"grant."* These verbs are the heart of the early Church's request. Each verb is an imperative, a command. The early Church made demands of God based on their circumstances. However, their belief that God is sovereign determined their demands. Because God is sovereign and His nature is orderly, He must have a plan. The demands of the early Church were within the boundaries of His sovereign will. They demanded that He view the threats of the Sanhedrin and allow them to continue the ministry in which He placed them. They boldly spoke His name, producing persecution. They desired the strength to continue speaking with the same boldness. Miracles occurred to verify their claims; they wished to continue speaking with this verification.

The early Church prayed during their first recorded business meeting with this emphasis of trust in their sovereign God's plan. They had to replace Judas, who hanged himself. When they established the requirements for the replacement, they discovered only two qualifying candidates in their group. Because this was before Pentecost, they relied on the Old Testament strategy for finding God's will. They cast lots and offered a prayer. *"You, O Lord, who know the hearts of all, show which of these two You have chosen to take part in this ministry and apostleship from which Judas by transgression fell, that he might go to his own place"* (Acts 1:24- 25).

The word *"show"* demonstrates the emphasis of the prayer and is in the imperative mood, a command (mood). The boldness of these disciples making demands of the Lord is startling. **"Lord, who knows the hearts of all,"** was their recognition of God's sovereignty. Because the knowledge of God is complete, He knows which disciple the disciples should choose to replace Judas. The Greek word "anadeixon," translated *"show,"* gives us the motivation for their boldness. They were not cocky or demanding their rights. Their confidence in God's sovereignty caused their boldness to demand.

The Greek word "anadeixon" is two words put together. The basic word is "deiknumi," which means to show or to exhibit. However, they added the prefix "ana" to this basic word, sometimes translated "up." Thus, what they demanded and boldly requested was much more than to show or reveal. "Anadeixon" means to lift anything on high and exhibit it for all to behold, to show accurately and clearly, and to disclose anything hidden. They requested with a desire that God would lift on high, and would openly exhibit the one He had chosen. Their boldness was not in getting what they wanted, but they were bold in learning what God had already decided. They focused their prayer on discovering the decision God already made! They aligned their desires with God's.

These believers boldly demanded that God carry out His plan, which was the pattern of the early Church. They did not manipulate God for their desires or comfort. They were desperate to participate in what their sovereign God was doing, even if it meant persecution. Without hesitation, they were available.

Availability

The early Church expressed its availability for the continuation of His plan. They did not ask for a change of plans

Part 4: The Absolute Reign

because of the threat. In their prayer, they identified themselves as *"Your servants."* Their prayer was, ***"Now, Lord, look on their threats, and grant to Your servants that with all boldness they may speak Your word"*** (Acts 4:29). The subject of the verse is *"Lord."* The two main verbs are *"look"* and *"grant."* They requested that God grant them *"boldness." "Your servants"* becomes the indirect object receiving the action of *"Lord."*

"Servants" is a translation of the Greek word "doulos." The sense of the word is "a person legally owned by someone else and whose livelihood and purpose is determined by their master." In other words, the members of the early Church did not focus on a career, and they attended church on Sunday. They did not have a variety of interests, with one being the church. They certainly had jobs, families, and benefits, but their one demanding and controlling focus was being "slaves" of Jesus! Wherever Jesus called them, and whatever purpose He had, they were available. They had no concern about the high risk of their involvement and were available for whatever consequence came with it. And remember the crucifixion of Jesus was fresh in their memories.

The early Church prayed to request, *"They may speak Your word."* The Greek word "laleo," translated *"they may speak,"* does not focus on the content but on the act of speaking. They did not pray for correct theology in their speech; they did not want new teaching about Jesus. Sometimes we are so concerned about what we might say that we do not speak at all. The threat to the early Church was not to talk about the name of Jesus, but they continued to speak His name boldly.

This Greek word "laleo" is in the active voice. The subject is responsible for the action of the verb. The early Church realized they were responsible for actively speaking the name of Jesus. They requested from the sovereign God *"that with all boldness,"* they would speak His name, but the speaking must come from the action of their own will.

This study is a call to investigate your prayer life. Do you desire God to grant you the same boldness and ministry the early Church requested? Do you have the same focus they did? Are you willing to bear the consequences of such a ministry, including the persecution?

Acts 4:29-30

MOMENTUM

"Now, Lord, look on their threats, and grant to Your servants that with all boldness they may speak Your word, by stretching out Your hand to heal, and that signs and wonders may be done through the name of Your holy servant Jesus" (Acts 4:29-30).

Momentum is defined as the mass in motion and is a subject to be considered when studying physics. All objects have mass, so if an object is moving, then it has momentum. Therefore, momentum is determined by how much and how fast "stuff" is moving. How much "stuff" is moving is called "mass." How fast this mass is moving in a given direction is called "velocity." The symbol for "mass" is "m," and "v" is the symbol for "velocity." The symbol selected for "momentum" is "p." Therefore, "p" (momentum) is equal to "m" (mass) multiplied by "v" (velocity). The equation is $p = m \times v$. Mass that is not in motion has a momentum of zero.

"Force" is the central issue of momentum. Momentum begins when there is a force strong enough to propel the mass into motion. However, if this force does not continue the momentum gradually reduces. You can push a tire into motion. It will roll on its own for a while but will lose momentum and stop. The force must overcome the resistance to maintain momentum.

The early Church (mass) was moving at a rapid rate

(velocity), daily gaining momentum! Jesus explained the force causing this momentum to the disciples. At the close of His forty-day resurrection appearance, He gathered them for final instruction before His ascension. He reminded them of the ***"Promise of the Father"*** (Acts 1:4) and told them the Holy Spirit would baptize them soon (Acts 1:5)! The Spirit of Jesus would be the force-producing their momentum. Jesus explained, ***"But you shall receive power when the Holy Spirit has come upon you; and you shall be witnesses to Me in Jerusalem, and in all Judea and Samaria, and to the end of the earth"*** (Acts 1:8).

Indeed, the force of Jesus' Spirit came upon them. ***"And they were all filled with the Holy Spirit"*** (Acts 2:4). Peter, moved by the force of the Spirit of Christ, proclaimed his explanation of the event to the watching crowd (Acts 2:14). ***"Then those who gladly received his word were baptized; and that day about three thousand souls were added to them"*** (Acts 2:41). Their momentum increased!

In describing the early Church, Luke made a point concerning their momentum. He said, ***"And they continued steadfastly in the apostles' doctrine and fellowship, in the breaking of bread, and in prayers"*** (Acts 2:42). In this same description, he added, ***"So continuing daily with one accord in the temple, and breaking bread from house to house, they ate their food with gladness and simplicity of heart, praising God and having favor with all the people. And the Lord added to the church daily those who were being saved"*** (Acts 2:46-47). In each statement, Luke emphasized, ***"continued steadfastly"*** and ***"continued daily,"*** each a translation of the Greek word "proskartereo." The sense of this word is "to persevere in some activity." Each use of this verb is in the present tense, which expresses the present moment with continuous action. The mass of the early Church increased, and the velocity continued. The momentum of the early Church did not decline but increased!

In this increasing momentum, God healed the lame beggar (Acts 3:7). Luke reported this miracle because of its impact on the momentum. The beggar was more than forty years of age and had been begging for most of those years (Acts 4:22). This miracle created a massive stir throughout Jerusalem (Acts 4:16, 21), producing an occasion for Peter to urge the crowd concerning Jesus. Five thousand men believed! The momentum increased even more!

The velocity of the momentum compelled the Sanhedrin's involvement. They were concerned about the force behind this momentum. They asked, **"By what power or by what name have you done this?"** (Acts 4:7). Luke wrote that from the beginning, the force behind the momentum moved upon Peter. **"Then Peter, filled with the Holy Spirit, said to them"** (Acts 4:8). The momentum so radically flowed through Peter that the Sanhedrin was affected. The Scripture says, **"they marveled"** (Acts 4:13). In fact, **"they realized that they had been with Jesus"** (Acts 4:13). The Sanhedrin realized there was only one way to stop this momentum. They must eliminate Jesus, the force! Thus, they threatened, **"that from now on they speak to no man in this name"** (Acts 4:17).

When released, the apostles returned to the early Church to report all the details of the threat. Luke said, **"they raised their voice to God with one accord and said"** (Acts 4:24). The nature of their words proclaimed praise and worship. They focused on the sovereignty of God in the crucifixion of Jesus, viewing their persecution as an extension of Jesus' crucifixion. However, as their praise continued, it became evident they were praying. **"Now, Lord, look on their threats, and grant to Your servants that with all boldness they may speak Your word, by stretching out Your hand to heal, and that signs and wonders may be done through the name of Your holy Servant Jesus"** (Acts 4:29-30). Luke called this a prayer (Acts 4:31).

The focus of their prayer is amazing! The principal concept

of our verse and study is in this focus. They prayed that the momentum they experienced in the past God would maintain in the present and future. Later, while Peter was in prison, *"constant prayer was offered to God for him by the church"* (Acts 12:5). Is it possible this focus was in their prayers for Peter? While we may not say all the prayers offered for the early Church in persecution had this focus, it is logical. Can the power of Jesus' Spirit that brought them to the present momentum maintain them in boldness and power despite hindering threats? Their concern was not for safety but continued momentum!

Present

There are three infinitive verbs in our two verses. *"Now, Lord, look on their threats, and grant to Your servants that with all boldness they may speak Your word, by stretching out Your hand to heal, and that signs and wonders may be done through the name of Your holy Servant Jesus"* (Acts 4:29-30). These three infinitive verbs are: *"may speak"* (laleo), *"stretching"* (ekteino), and *"may be done"* (ginomai). An infinitive always expresses the purpose and still has the same subject as the main verb, revealing the use of that verb. In our sentence, there are two main verbs, *"look"* and *"grant."* The subject is *"Lord."* The purpose of the Lord looking and granting was that the early Church might continue to speak His word with boldness, might be an extension of His hand in healing, and might be used as instruments for the manifestation of signs and wonders. All three of the infinitive verbs are in the present tense. The early Church prayed the momentum of the past to be manifested in the present and continue in the future. They realized the Lord was the force behind this momentum. The resistance of the Sanhedrin could reduce the Church's momentum until it was lost. The Lord must be the

One to override this resistance and cause their momentum to continue.

This prayer of the early Church is astounding. They prayed their experience in the past would continue in the present and future. No one can remain in what has not already been. It is more likely that what is present now in your life will continue. We establish patterns for living; the momentum of those patterns continues and even increases. The leaders of Israel operated according to this principle. Their self-centered resistance to Jesus gained momentum and climaxed in His crucifixion. Their self-beneficial patterns were well established; Jesus was a constant threat to those traditions. Their momentum of resistance against Jesus was still in full force. Just as they threatened His life, they were now threatening His name. In the events of the future, they manifested an increase in their resistance to Jesus.

We ask you to sift through your prayer focus. I have well established my patterns of living with strong momentum. I do not want God to make adjustments in those patterns. However, many of my patterns produce consequences that are uncomfortable for me, which causes me to demand that God change the results of my choices but not change my habits. I consistently beg God to remove those unbearable consequences. I want God to let me continue in my self-centered patterns but relieve me of their results. Can this be the reason I receive so few answers to my prayers?

The immensely important aspect of this principle is the eternal view! The direction we travel in the present has enough momentum to bring us into eternal focus. The established patterns in our present lives will not disappear at death. Often, we consider the death of our Savior. All the things we do not like about ourselves will suddenly disappear at death. But death is not the Savior; Jesus is the Savior! He not only wanted to save me then, but He wants to save me now! Each of us increases in momentum as we travel through life. We become more and more set in our patterns; we find it more and more difficult to change, as our patterns seem to increase. The call is to be like the early Church. Jesus is central in the past; Jesus is fundamental in the present; Jesus will increasingly become central in the future! If what I am now is what I will continue to be in the future, perhaps it is time for a change.

Problem

Let's review our equation "$p = m \times v$." Mass is represented by "m." Velocity is symbolized by "v." Momentum (p) is equal to mass multiplied by velocity. Velocity is the speed by which the mass travels. The typical automobile has a mass of 4,000 pounds. If it is traveling at 60 miles per hour, the momentum is 240,000 thousand miles per hour. The car must continue a speed of 60 miles per hour to maintain this momentum. The engine of the car provides the force for the momentum, but there are other forces to consider. We often experience a headwind as we travel west. The force of the engine causing speed at 60 miles per hour now produces 50 miles per hour. We lose momentum unless we increase the force to compensate for the resistance. When we go down the mountainside, our speed increases even with the same force. However, ascending the mountain, our speed is reduced with the same force because of the resistance.

For an extended period, the early Church increased in momentum, growing consistently. ***"So continuing daily with one accord in the temple, and breaking bread from house to house, they ate their food with gladness and simplicity of heart, praising God and having favor with all the people. And the Lord added to the church daily those who were being saved"*** (Acts 2:47). The Lord was the force energizing their momentum. There seemed to be little resistance.

Then the early Church came to a vast mountain, which they

must climb; there is a strong headwind, which is typical. We do not live in a vacuum. We must increase the force behind our momentum to maintain and expand our intimacy with Jesus. The early Church faced life-threatening resistance. Everyone in the early Church was keenly aware of Jesus' death. They knew the ability of the Sanhedrin, but this became the key to their momentum. God took the worst the Sanhedrin could do and used it for the best His redemptive heart could do! The resistance from the Sanhedrin added only to the velocity of what God wanted to accomplish. Instead of being a hindrance, their action fulfilled *"the purpose determined before to be done."* God proved His sovereignty in Jesus and continued it in the lives of those in the early Church. They saw these present threats as linked to Jesus' crucifixion. Their prayer was for God to do now what He did then.

God is so sovereign that every temptation, obstacle, or resistance to my spiritual connection can be an asset. C T Studd, a great missionary of the past, proposed an idea. He said it does not matter how much the pressure; it only matters where the pressure lies. If the pressure never gets between you and Jesus, the greater the pressure, the more you are pressed to Him! Temptations only drive me to Jesus because I cannot make it on my own. I must seek Him. My trials only focus me on Jesus, and I cannot survive one moment without Him. The evil resistance and threats of my world only bring me closer to Jesus. I must have Him! Jesus increases the force of His presence and the intensity of my focus on Him; He maintains my momentum!

Propelling

When we stand back and view this passage from afar, we are startled by what we see! Beginning with verse 37, we cannot miss the prayer of the early Church as they faced persecution.

"For truly against YOUR (sou) *holy Servant Jesus, whom You anointed, both Herod and Pontius Pilate, with the Gentiles and the people of Israel, were gathered together to do whatever YOUR* (sou) *hand and YOUR* (sou) *purpose determined before to be done. Now, Lord, look on their threats, and grant to YOUR* (sou) *servants that with all boldness they may speak YOUR* (sou) *word, by stretching out YOUR* (sou) *hand to heal, and that signs and wonders may be done through the name of YOUR* (sou) *holy Servant Jesus"* (Acts 4:27-30).

You will notice the Greek word "sou," translated *"Your,"* a total of seven times in four verses, one time in verse twenty-seven, twice in verse twenty-eight, twice in verse twenty-nine, and twice in verse thirty. The firm belief of the early Church in the sovereignty of God is unquestionable. He is totally in charge. Does not everything belong to and come under the authority of His sovereignty? He not only gave birth to the momentum of the early Church through the resurrection of Jesus, but He also became the inner force maintaining the momentum through the fullness of the Holy Spirit at Pentecost. Were not all of the miracles done by His power? Did the mind of Christ not impart the wisdom of the apostles' teaching? Is it not His plan? In the face of resistance and life-threatening persecution, was He not the one who propelled them into an accelerated momentum?

We must continually remind ourselves of this concept. Jesus is not only the Savior who only brings us salvation; He is the essence of salvation operating within us. He does not give us salvation and then departs for us to use what He provided. Jesus is the provision and substance of salvation within us. He does not launch us in the direction of godly living then departs for the obstacles of life to reduce our momentum. He is the force within us refreshing and empowering us to maintain and increase our momentum. The early Church saw Jesus as a single source and power for the continuation of the ministry they experienced. They prayed that what they experienced before would not be reduced in light of the new obstacle of threats and persecution.

Will it be any different for us? Although there may not be a Sanhedrin in our lives, are there not obstacles? Does not the demonic force of our world always pull on us, attempting to reduce our momentum? Is not the enemy still using conflicts in relationships, misunderstandings in conversations, and wrong impressions of motives trying to reduce our speed? We must come back to Jesus! He is the only force enabling the continued momentum of our Christian experience. The early Church did not rely on committee meetings, instruction of the elders, individual worship sessions, entertainment specials, education, motivational speakers, or any other thing. They counted on Jesus and only Jesus! Jesus is our only chance!

Acts 4:29-30

MY DESPERATE DESIRE

"Now, Lord, look on their threats, and grant to Your servants that with all boldness they may speak Your word, by stretching out Your hand to heal, and that signs and wonders may be done through the name of Your holy servant Jesus" (Acts 4:29-30).

What a day it must have been! The message spread throughout the early Church. In the middle of an excellent preaching service, the Sanhedrin captured Peter and John. They detained the apostles in jail for the night and put them on trial before the most powerful men of Israel. These leaders of Israel were responsible for the death of Jesus. Was the early Church already gathered for prayer when Peter and John were released? They must have been very anxious for the full report of their present dilemma.

The early Church's response to the report is even more startling. The threats of the Sanhedrin drove them to a state of praise. Praise can only happen when you recognize your God is greater than the problem you face, which seems to be the consistent approach throughout the Book of Acts. Each time the early Church faced a threat, they responded in praise to God, who is greater than the danger! If we view our problem as greater than our God, that problem drives us to dismay and depression.

These new Christians viewed God as **"Lord"** (Acts 4:24), a translation of the Greek word "despotes," not the standard

Greek word used to describe a relationship with Jesus. He is a "Despot." Their God is one of power beyond which there is none other! They based it on CREATION - "You made!" ***"Lord, You are God, who made heaven and earth and the sea, and all that is in them"*** (Acts 4:24). God's sovereignty rests on the subordination of everything in the world and creation to the Creator! They see their dilemma in light of His sovereign position. God is greater than His creation, but we do not know how much more significant. We do not have anything by which to compare Him! He is immeasurable! Therefore, He is greater than my distress!

The early Church based their praise on COMMUNICATION - "You spoke." Their sovereign God was not silent; ***"Lord, You are God, ... who by the mouth of Your servant David have said"*** (Acts 4:25). You would think this sovereign God was far removed from His creation. What interests Him in what He created? What contribution could anything God made offer Him? He, the sovereign God, desperately wants to communicate with us! We discovered God's desire to communicate in the passage that the early Church quoted (Psalms 2). The Trinity gave voice to their love for us. Although the creation rebelled against the sovereign Creator, the Father cried out in demonstrable love through His Son (Psalms 2:4-6). The Son cried out in absolute surrender to the promises of the Father (Psalms 2:7-9). His soul agonized over the destructive rebellion of the created world. The Holy Spirit took the heart of the Father and the Son and placed their instruction in the soul of man (Psalms 2:10-12). Creation heard the voice of God from within the structure of their created being, a call to ***"Kiss the Son!"***

The early Church based their praise on CONCLUSION - "You decided." What does the speaking of the sovereign Trinity contain? The sovereign Trinity possesses a plan. God did not create and later invent a strategy. He is so sovereign in His wisdom and knowledge that His plan in creation encompassed the rebellion of His creation. No aspect of creation is outside His sovereignty. His plan is simple yet sophisticated and startling yet assumed when you know the heart nature of God. His plan is Jesus! In His sovereignty, God gathered together all the nations and powers of the world. It was His action! He elevated them to a place of authority to do what their rebellious, self-centered nature would demand. The leaders of Israel decided, *"to do whatever Your hand and Your purpose determined before to be done"* (Acts 4:28). They crucified Jesus!

The early Church understood their present experience linked to Jesus' crucifixion. Their lives merged with His could not possibly escape the discomfort and suffering of His death. But the sovereign Trinity planned for Jesus' death and the early Church. The Trinity raised Jesus from the dead. What would this Trinity do for the early Church? There is safety in this sovereign plan! The security the Sanhedrin experienced in their self-appointed power was only temporary. In a few years, Jerusalem would fall; they would lose everything. The leaders of Israel rejected the sovereign plan causing their destruction. But the early Church was confident in the plan of their sovereign God!

The next section of the early Church's praise session entered into an intense prayer meeting. The prayer meeting began with *"Now, Lord"* (Acts 4:29). The opening three words in the Greek text are "kai ta nyn." Our translation says, *"Now."* The Greek word "kai" is continuative conjunction connecting two events. In their praise, the early Church recognized that God's sovereign hand brought about His sovereign purpose, which was the crucifixion of Jesus. Although it was fresh in their memories, it was an event in the past. The Greek word "ta" is the article "the." The Greek word "nyn" is the sense of "this present moment." Their focused prayer moved from what was in the crucifixion of Jesus to what was in the present. They must now apply their present crisis to the full awareness of God's sovereignty expressed in Jesus' death and resurrection.

The overall concept of the early Church's prayer was a desperate desire for CONTINUATION. The three infinitive verbs, giving purpose to the two main verbs, are in the present tense, pointing to continuous action, not a cry to begin speaking in boldness, experiencing the hand of God, or appearances of signs and wonders. They desperately desired to continue in these things. We cannot speak in boldness in the crisis hour unless we have been speaking when there was no crisis. Do not expect the mighty hand of God to move in your crisis moment unless His hand has been moving in the daily routine of your life. Should signs and wonders be experienced in the threatening moments if they have not been occurring in daily ministry? Dependence on His sovereignty does not develop in the crisis moments but the daily walk of Christian experience.

The early Church selected three crucial things as essential when the Sanhedrin threatened them. Notice they mentioned nothing about safety, deliverance, protection, or the destruction of their enemy. They had no self-focused plan. They fell back on the redemptive plan of their sovereign God with no regard for their comfort. They embraced the suffering of Christ as it applied to their lives, desiring what was initiated in Jesus to continue now in them. They wanted crucifixion with Christ! The way the early Church referred to themselves highlights this truth. They were **"*Your servants.*"** They saw themselves concerning the sovereign God as "slaves," the Greek word "doulos." It refers to a person who is legally owned by another; the owner determines their entire livelihood and purpose. Therefore, they prayed not for their comfort but the fulfillment of His plan.

Speaking

The first request of the early Church focused on communication, which took priority over all other involvements.

They asked the sovereign God to *"look"* and *"grant"* for their communication, corresponding with the threat of the Sanhedrin. The focus of the threat was, *"that from now on they speak to no one in this name"* (Acts 4:17). *"So they called them in and commanded them not to speak at all nor teach in the name of Jesus"* (Acts 4:18). They did not care about the miracles, suppers, church meetings, or any demonstrations. The Sanhedrin's problem was that these Christians were speaking the name of Jesus! The early Church agreed with the Sanhedrin that speaking was the issue! The one thing the early Church had to continue was the communication of Jesus' wonder.

However, these Christians did not want just to speak, but to speak *"with all boldness."* The Greek word "meta," translated *"with,"* is used as a preposition of manner, expressing either method or style. The Greek word "pas," translated *"all,"* constitutes the full quantity or extent, focusing on "completeness." *"Boldness"* was their desire. This word is used three times in this chapter (Acts 4:13, 29, 31), and a compound word composed of "pas" (all) and "rhesis" (the act of speaking). The idea of *"boldness,"* followed by "laleo" (*"they may speak"*), is a double emphasis of their desire. Again, the focus is not on happiness, joy, healing, miracles, demonstrations of gifts, or ceremonies but on "speaking."

The Greek word translated *"they may speak"* is "laleo," a Greek word used to focus exclusively on the act of speaking. Content of the message is an issue, and the early Church's statement guards the content by adding, *"Your word."* But the main concern in their prayer regarded their continual delivery of the message. What they had been speaking, they wanted to continue speaking in boldness! Could this be the failure of our day? Are we distracted from the person of Jesus? He, who was our first love, has become secondary. We did not become corrupt or evil, but we became filled with theology and doctrine. Programs and ministerial careers became our passion: organizational obligations and business overrun us. We cease to be His slave, a person legally owned by another, and whose livelihood and purpose are owner determined. The moment we are distracted from Jesus, the sourcing of His Spirit ceases in us. We rely on education, skills, and experience. Could this be the defeat of our day? If the determining feature of a Christian were how much you speak of Jesus, would you be a Christian? What percentage of your conversation is about Him?

Although the primary concern of the early Church was to continue to speak boldly regardless of the threats, they were also guarding the content of what they said. They added the phrase, *"Your word,"* a translation of the Greek words "sou logos." In their prayer, the content would be *"Your purpose determined before to be done"* (Acts 4:28). Twice in this prayer, they referred to *"Your holy Servant Jesus"* (Acts 4:27, 30). In the Psalms, they quoted a reference to *"His Christ"* (Acts 4:26), and in this context, they refer to Jesus as *"whom You anointed"* (Acts 4:27). Is not all this an expression of Peter's discourse to the Sanhedrin (Acts 4:8-12)? *"Your word"* cannot be understood outside of the context of Jesus! *"And the Word became flesh and dwelt among us, and we beheld His glory, the glory as of the only begotten of the Father, full of grace and truth"* (John 1:14). Peter's message was an explanation of power for transformed living as in the lame beggar. This power is the person of Jesus (Acts 4:10). He is the cornerstone of life's structure and wholeness even though the leaders of Israel rejected Him (Acts 4:11). The core of salvation is only in Jesus, and outside of Him, man is lost (Acts 4:12). Jesus is the only message!

Stretching

There is an assumption that flows forth from the proclamation of Jesus' name. The early Church continued their prayer by saying, *"by stretching out Your hand to heal, and that signs and wonders may be done through the name of Your holy Servant Jesus"* (Acts 4:30). They did not want the healings, signs, and wonders as much as the speaking. Miracles were an assumption of what would happen if the momentum of His name's proclamation continued. In other words, these things are not the focus or the concern and are not highlighted, craved, or elevated. They do not take center stage of the spoken message and do not consume our energy or efforts when Jesus is our focus. But when He is involved, expect transformed lives!

Our verse begins with the phrase, *"by stretching out,"* translated from the Greek words "en to ekteino." The Greek word "ekteino" is the main word with a prefix. It begins with "ek," meaning "out." The main word is "teino," meaning "to stretch." In the context of our verse, it refers to the hand. This idea is introduced by "en," and can be used as an instrument and translated as "by." However, the translation must always have the flavor of the original and principal meaning of the word. This meaning is "in" as in a fixed resting position. Therefore, the early Church cried out that they might continue to experience boldness as they "remain in," "fixed in," or "rest in" the movement of His hand. In other words, the movement is not in them but in their sovereign God as they rest in Him. They are not moving in action but are resting in His activity.

We must not miss this emphasis! Our response and responsibility are singular, a focus on Jesus' person. His name and only His name must possess our lives. Side issues must never dominate our attention. We are **"Your slaves."** My focus on Jesus results in Him extending His hand into my world. The action is His not mine! The results are His, not mine! Remember, a slave is one legally owned by another and whose livelihood and purpose the owner determines. Am I doing miracles of healing? That is not the question to ask. Am I focused on Him? That is the question. We can quickly become miracle-centered instead of Christ-centered. Miracle-centered people become self-focused because it is easy for spiritual pride to develop rather than being **"Your slave."** A person's healing in my shadow is not my concern (Acts 5:15). Their healing is not under my control. I am **"Your slave."**

Signs

This same truth extends to **"that signs and wonders may be done through the name of Your holy Servant Jesus"** (Acts 4:30). The Greek word "semeion," translated **"signs,"** and the Greek word "teras," translated "wonders," are a phrase. This phrase is used more than 30 times in the Book of Acts. At first, I thought they might refer to two miracle styles. On investigation, it seems these two items are different elements of the same miracle. **"Wonders"** points to the astonishing aspect of a miracle. "Teras" derives from "tereo," meaning "to keep, or watch," marking an event, because of its extraordinary character will be observed and kept in one's memory. We regard the miracle as startling, imposing, or surprising. In other words, it is the astonishing element of the miracle that amazes those experiencing it. **"Signs"** (semeion) refer to the miracle's spiritual end or purpose, leading to something out of and beyond the event. Signs are like a giant finger pointing to the grace and power of God. Therefore, the miracle should not capture our attention; we should be astonished as we view the sovereignty of God involved in the miracle.

The content of this prayer of the early Church was a desire to continue to highlight and proclaim Jesus. The Sanhedrin threatened the early Church never to speak His name again; they prayed for a continued boldness to proclaim His name and greatness. The Sanhedrin assumed this proclamation would be accompanied by miracles, which would strengthen the Church's testimony of His greatness. In the text, healings, signs, and wonders were not the Sanhedrin's concern. The early Church desired to continue in the same pattern the Spirit of God had led them, which caused the threats. In other words, they wanted to remain in the same ministry pattern.

In the passage, the early Church's concern was not about the continuation of miracles, healings, or signs and wonders. Their interest was about the proclamation of His name. If we become focused on signs and wonders, we will not be able to maintain in the hour of pressure or crisis. The single defeating trap of the devil is to get us to focus on the performance instead of Christ. He wants to get us sidetracked, and he will use anything, even good things, to eliminate our concentration on Jesus. How often has a ministry, gifts of the Spirit, positions in the church, or relational conflicts consumed our attention? We must come back to Him. There is nothing else to proclaim!

We must join the early Church in one passion! Our sovereign God is bringing about a plan of redemption found only in Jesus. Our "fixed" position is in Christ. Nothing will sidetrack us; we remain fixed in this one focus. All "signs and wonders" are **"through the name of Your holy Servant Jesus."** We will speak only His name! Our only concern is to remain in His name. Jesus' name threatens evil forces. Let us maintain a passion for His name, His person!

Acts 4:30

JESUS IN SOVEREIGNTY

"By stretching out Your hand to heal, and that signs and wonders may be done through the name of Your holy servant Jesus" (Acts 4:30).

The early Church responded to the threat of persecution with a total reliance on the sovereignty of God! Every verse in the overall passage gives reference to God's sovereignty. When they heard the Sanhedrin's threat, the early Church broke out in praise and worship. The core of their response was, **"Lord, You are God, who made heaven and earth and the sea, and all that is in them"** (Acts 4:24). The Greek word "despostes," translated **"Lord,"** is not the official word. It is a reference to a "despot," God is a tyrant. He has absolute power and authority. There is nothing outside His control.

The early Church considered the crucifixion of Jesus a direct result of God's sovereignty. It was not a tragedy or a mistake. It was the fulfillment of **"Your hand and Your purpose determined before to be done"** (Acts 4:28). The nations of the earth are viewed as instruments in the hand of God to accomplish His predetermined plan. If this were true for Jesus, would it not be valid for the **"servants"** of the sovereign God (Acts 4:29)?

The early Church considered themselves to be an extension of Jesus' crucifixion. The Sanhedrin's threats of persecution were a continuation of Jesus' experience. These believers linked with

Jesus in person, plan, and purpose, and God filled them with the Spirit and nature of Jesus. The intimacy they knew with Jesus was the resource for all of their living. This intimacy produced the miracle healing of the lame beggar. That miracle stimulated the beginning of the Sanhedrin's threats and was linked with and connected to Jesus. Multitudes of converted people in Jerusalem resulted from the presence of Jesus flowing through the early Church. Jesus was an intimate part of their lives, and they mentioned His name in all of their conversations, linking with Him in all activities. The threat they received from the Sanhedrin focused on this link.

There are other words to help us understand this link between Jesus and the early Church. "Identification" aligns with linkage. It is the association or connection of one thing with another having to do with "identity." Who I am is now linked with who Jesus is! There is a person in our town that I see every week. I have never forgotten his name. It is Elvis! He looks like Elvis; he acts like Elvis; he sings like Elvis. He has shaped his life in the image of Elvis. It is his identity. Think of this regarding Jesus! He is not a dead singer from the past but is alive in our lives. His Spirit births His life in and through us. We now think as He thinks; we love as He loves; we express His desires. We are one with Jesus!

The early Church understood that their identity was related to the cross. They were now living the cross style of Jesus. Jesus poured His life out, never thinking of Himself. He lived a selfless life, ultimately bringing Him to the cross. The early Church embraced Jesus and the cross and was empowered by Him. He was the Author of the cross style! Paul expressed it best when he said, *"I have been crucified with Christ; it is no longer I who live, but Christ lives in me; and the life which I now live in the flesh I live by faith in the Son of God, who loved me and gave Himself for me"* (Galatians 2:20). Paul so identified with Jesus that the death of Christ became his. Paul said he was *"always carrying about in the body the dying of the Lord Jesus, that the life of Jesus also may be manifested in our body. For we who live are always delivered to death for Jesus' sake, that the life of Jesus also may be manifested in our mortal flesh. So then death is working in us, but life in you"* (2 Corinthians 4:10-12).

This link between Jesus and us is so secure that whatever is happening in Jesus is happening in us. We merge with Him, and His life is ours. The early Church did not see themselves as babied, pampered, or indulged by Jesus. His crucifixion would continue through them. They would never be greater than their Master. Their references to Christ were amazing. They called Him, *"Your holy Servant Jesus"* (Acts 4:27, 30). We must understand how they viewed Jesus in His redemptive role. They saw Him as the One *"whom You anointed"* (Acts 4:27). They quoted the Old Testament Psalms, *"Against the Lord and against His Christ"* (Acts 4:26). These statements contain the sovereignty of God and the futility of man's sinful effort. Each statement also includes the submission of Jesus to the will of God's sovereignty. No one can miss the overarching plan of God in Jesus as He anoints Jesus. This picture of Jesus was vital in the early Church's victory over persecution.

The view of the early Church was unique. We need to try to organize and systematically comprehend that view.

Position
"Servant"

In our passage, the Greek word "pais" means "Servant." This translation may be a little misleading when compared to how the early Church referred to themselves. They prayed, *"Now, Lord, look on their threats, and grant to Your servants that with all boldness they may speak Your word"* (Acts 4:29). The Greek word translated *"servants"* is "doulos." It bespeaks a person who is legally owned by someone else and whose entire livelihood and purpose is master determined. However, "pais" is often translated "child," the primary focus of a boy or girl whose age can range from infancy to full-grown youth.

Living a life determined by the Master highlights everything we understand about the incarnate Jesus. Jesus is God, who chose to leap into a role other than God. Because His conception was not as a normal human being, how would you describe His birth? One who had prior existence entered the womb of Mary and was born. The best description we could find is, ***"And the Word became flesh and dwelt among us, and we beheld His glory, the glory as of the only begotten of the Father, full of grace and truth"*** (John 1:14).

However, the translators (in the NKJV) did not call Jesus a "child" but a ***"Servant."*** The reason for this may be the time involved. Our focus is a statement about the crucifixion. Jesus was not a child; He was a full-grown man. This shift in emphasis becomes an interpretation of the passage rather than a translation. Although "servant" bespeaks a subordinate position, it does not have the same thrust of "child." Could this be an attempt to propose to us that Jesus was helpless consistently? As a man, He had the same helplessness as a child. As a babe in His mother's arms, so Jesus is in the arms of the Trinity God. As Jesus did not know as a babe, so now He knows only the mind of His Father.

This statement is a reminder! Jesus never stepped outside the boundaries of dependency on the Father. He refused to operate out of Himself. Even in His education, development of skills, and mastery of manhood, He remained dependent. Was this the secret to His consistent victory, His fantastic wisdom, His calmness in stressful situations, His ability to give abundant forgiveness, His unwavering focus on His mission, His miracles, His conquering position in spiritual warfare, and even His resurrection from the dead?

Carefully listen again as the early Church refers to Jesus. They called Him *"Your holy Servant Jesus"* (Acts 4:27, 30). They saw Him as the One *"whom You anointed"* (Acts 4:27). They quoted the Old Testament Psalms, *"Against the Lord and against His Christ"* (Acts 4:26). In each statement, they viewed Jesus in relationship to the sovereign God. Jesus, who is the sovereign God, stepped into a submissive role to become a man. It was not His role to pick or choose the events of His life; He was submissive to the sovereign, redemptive God. In His helplessness, Jesus lived in faith. He lived out of the knowledge that God was sovereign, and He submitted to that sovereignty. The early Church fully recognized this truth!

The early Church knew just as this was true for Jesus, so this must be true for them. They did not consider themselves *"Servant"* (pais); they were *"servant"* (doulos). Understand these words in terms of the attitude expressed through the early Church. Jesus, in the boundaries of the Trinity God, experienced a submission to the sovereignty and purpose of the Trinity. The early Church considered themselves "slaves" of Jesus. Many Scriptures call us "sons of God" (John 1:12, 13; Galatians 4:6, 7; Romans 8:14); however, *"servants"* expresses their attitude in the context of His sovereignty. We are even called brothers of Christ (Hebrews 2:11). However, in light of His sovereignty, the early Church focused on their submissive role. The sovereign Trinity commissioned one of its members, and Jesus submitted to the sovereignty of the Trinity. God achieved His sovereign plan through the rebellious will of the nations of the earth. They *"were gathered together to do whatever Your hand and Your purpose determined before to be done"* (Acts 4:27-28). The early Church linked in submission with the One who is submissive to the sovereign Trinity. They viewed the present persecution as an extension of His activity. The calling of Jesus became their calling; His mission was their mission. Their purpose was the same as Jesus' purpose. There was no difference.

Is this not our calling as well? We must not allow self-centered carnality to invade our perspective. Christianity is not about what I can get from Jesus. Are there benefits from being His? Do I get to go to heaven? The answer is, "Yes!" However, this is not involved in our submission to Christ. We are linked with His person, submitted to His mind, and captured by His desires. Whatever possesses Him possesses us.

Personhood
"Holy"

Now we come us to Jesus' personhood. If Jesus fills us, does not His character, who He is, become who we are? The early Church expressed it as *"holy."* It is a translation of the Greek word "hagios," a common root (hag) with "hagnos," which means chaste or pure. Its fundamental idea is separation, consecration, and devotion to the service of God, and sharing in God's purity and abstaining from earth's defilement. There are two fundamental aspects to be considered, purity and consecration. These two are intimately intertwined, each contributes and produces the other.

Purity is definitely at the core of *"holy,"* pointing to the morally pure, upright, and blameless in heart and life. There is a completeness to it that is spoken of as "perfect" or "without blemish" (Romans 12:1). Jesus was certainly in this category, and we assume that all who profess the Christian name are also. This is the basis of the name "saint" (hagioi) (Acts 9:13, 32, 41; 26:10; Romans 1:7; 8:27; 1 Thessalonians 3:13). Consecration, being set apart from common to a sacred use, is also at the core of the word. Jesus was certainly in this category. He was not just holy in activities, but the intent of His heart did not know evil, making Him available for the mission of redemption. Therefore, the early Church summarized His qualification to be the Redeemer of the world with the simple term, *"holy."*

Paul said that sin came into the world through one man. ***"Therefore, just as through one man sin entered the world, and death through sin, and thus death spread to all men because all sinned"*** (Romans 5:12). There must be another man who knew no sin to reverse this process. But it would not be accomplished like the one man through whom sin entered the world. Adam became possessed with sin and simply birthed it into every man. This new man would need to be ***"holy"*** and open to the plan of the sovereign Trinity. Because He had no sin, He could carry the sins of others, bringing suffering, which is the platform for redemption. Because all have sinned, where is such a man? The sovereign God became that man, Jesus! Jesus is the accomplishment of the redemptive dreams of God and why the nations of the world ***"were gathered together to do whatever Your hand and Your purpose determined before to be done"*** (Acts 4:27-28).

The essential ingredient for redemption is "holiness." This man, called to pay the price for sin, must be ***"Your holy servant Jesus."*** Holiness encounters sin, erects a cross, and redemption takes place. There is no redemption without the bleeding, suffering, and dying of a cross. Hate does not redeem hate; it accelerates it. Holy love is the only chance to redeem hate. Meanness does not redeem meanness; it only accelerates it. The kindness of "never thinking about yourself" reaches into wickedness and transforms it. Darkness never turns darkness; light must penetrate the darkness.

The early Church realized they were an extension of this "holiness." Jesus came to dwell within them. What He did on the cross was now extended into their circumstances. The circumstances were not merely events to endure or occasions to overlook; they were redemptive acts. The holiness indwelling their lives was the platform for redemptive suffering. They were the light being used by Jesus to transform the darkness.

Purpose
"Anointed"

The early Church said, *"For truly against Your holy Servant Jesus, whom You anointed"* (Acts 4:27). The Greek word "chrio," translated *"anointed,"* is used in the sense of appointment. It signifies to anoint with oil to exemplify assigning a duty or role. In this same regard, they called Jesus *"Christ"* in the quotation of the Old Testament. The evil of the world was *"Against the Lord and against His Christ"* (Acts 4:26; Psalms 2:2). The Greek word translated Christ is "Christos." It comes from the Greek word "chrio," meaning the anointed one.

The sovereign Trinity appointed Jesus as the extended redemptive power of the Trinity. He is the one who will be the *"holy,"* one capable of becoming the platform for redemptive suffering. Jesus encountered sin on its most profound level, defeated it at the core, and completed His mission! It is the mission established by the sovereign love of God. To accomplish this task, our sovereign God *"gathered together"* the forces of evil in the world. They *"were gathered together to do whatever Your hand and Your purpose determined before to be done"* (Acts 4:27-28). Their freewill acted according to their self-centered natures. They brought suffering to "the anointed One," what the sovereign Trinity God purposed. It was the only possibility of redemption for the world.

The early Church saw themselves as an extension of this purpose. The sovereign God did not anoint them or appoint them to a cross, but He filled them with Jesus. Jesus would continue the application of His calling through them. He commissioned them to go into all the nations and immerse everyone in Him (Matthew 28:18-20). They were to be witnesses (Acts 1:8). However, they were not merely relating a story or historical event. They were a renewal of the redemptive act of suffering. It was their purpose. They did not create opportunities for suffering, but Jesus living in and through them confronted their world. He is **"*holy!*"** This confrontation always creates conflict and always creates an opportunity for redemptive suffering.

Now, Jesus turns to us! Are we to be any different than the disciples? The same Spirit fills us! We receive the same holy calling and commission! Jesus living in and through us will confront our world. He is **"*holy.*"** This confrontation always creates conflict and always creates an opportunity for redemptive suffering. Will we embrace Him in the fullness of who He is in our lives?

Acts 4:31

THE PLACE

> *"And when they had prayed, the place where they were assembled together was shaken; and they were all filled with the Holy Spirit, and they spoke the word of God with boldness"* (Acts 4:31).

"And when they had prayed," is the opening statement of our English translation, which is the same in the Greek text. It is in the aorist tense, establishing the tense as the "non-tense." Luke focused on their act of praying, and what follows is the result of their prayer. He does not tell us how they completed their prayer, but he says they experienced the shaking of their physical world by the presence of God! Could it be we only experience the acts of God when in the intimacy of oneness with Him? Is the wonder of Christian experience the possibility of living moment-by-moment in this intimacy? Could we be the instruments for shaking the foundation of our world? But to be such an instrument, we must be in the midst of prayer!

We have emphasized the content of their prayer in previous studies, but a reminder of its focus is needed. One issue of their prayer was "resistance." They knew the strength of their opposition. The Sanhedrin was the most powerful ruling body in their culture, and this group was making threats against them. The early Church did not separate from Judaism. All Christians at this time were Jews. They continued to worship at the temple and conducted themselves within the boundaries of Jewish traditions. A sovereign God set in place the activities that would change this, but not at present. Within the confines of their society, they found themselves in violation. However, their prayer reveals the threat was much larger than their culture. They faced a worldwide opposition. They quoted the Old Testament Psalms, which spoke of *"the nations rage"* and *"the kings of the earth"* (Acts 4:25, 26; Psalms 2:1-2). They realized the world was in opposition to Christ. *"Herod"* represented all the kings of the world. *"Pontius Pilate"* represented all of the rulers of the world, and equally represented *"the Gentiles"* with *"the people of Israel"* (Acts 4:27). They prayed, *"Now, Lord, look on their threats"* (Acts 4:29), referring to all included in this list. A small group of people in an isolated part of the world stood against the desires and forces of their known world. They were confident in the sovereignty of God who would act upon their world *"to do whatever Your hand and Your purpose determined before to be done."* These isolated Christians were to be the instruments to shake their world. It only happened because they dwelt in prayer. Prayer was not merely an activity for them; prayer was living in the intimacy of His presence.

The focus of intimacy between these Christians and God was not elimination but "recurrence." They never asked God to deliver them from the Sanhedrin's threats or that He would eliminate those who threatened them. Their prayer focused on the continued redemption of their world! They wanted the boldness they knew following the resurrection of Jesus to remain in their present moment of threats. They wanted the same movement of God to continue in their persecution. God did not remove from them the power of the Spirit that produced their evangelism. It is easy to focus on what happens to us rather than on the redemption of others. The moment our problems overshadow the salvation of others, the threats have fulfilled their purpose. We are robbed of the power of Jesus' name regardless of how loud we proclaim Him.

These Christians had a third focus in their prayer. They knew the "routine" of Jesus' Spirit moving through them, and they desperately wanted to maintain that. They did not want the method or source of their present ministry to change. It was ***"through the name of Your holy Servant Jesus"*** (Acts 4:30). But speaking in the name of Jesus was the focus of their persecution. They did not ask God to adjust their method; they did not want to shift to another name or technique. They did not ask God to grant an alternative means for the same results. They were in love with Jesus and would not depart from His embrace, His name! They refused to be distracted. Jesus captured them!

Everything Luke described in the focus of their prayer was physical and spiritual! The early Church recognized the physical resistance of the world against what they had physically experienced through the physical Jesus, whom God physically crucified and physically raised from the dead. They cried out for a continuation of all the physical miracles, signs, and wonders, which would change the physical lives of many. They realized the source of the real ministry was through Jesus, who was physically alive and present! But it was equally valid that the focus of their prayer was spiritual! There was a demonic movement in the spiritual realm that stimulated the physical threat to their lives. This threat was not a physical issue but a spiritual resistance to the purpose and will of God. The early Church did not want mere physical miracles. They wanted the reality of Jesus' Spirit that changed the lives of people. The issue was not the physical elimination of Jesus' name but was the acknowledgment of Jesus' person raised from the dead and alive in the eternal spiritual realm. They were desperate for the spiritual realm to continue to impact their physical reality.

"And when they had prayed, the place where they were assembled together was shaken" (Acts 4:31). After Luke wrote that they continued their communication in the spiritual realm, he highlighted a physical location, *"the place."* There is a definite article related to *"place,"* which is the subject of the sentence. The place of assembling together *"was shaken."* The spiritual realm demonstrated itself in physical reality. Luke again declared the undeniable connection between the physical and spiritual realms. The physical realm is a platform for the display of spiritual truth.

We need to investigate this reality in greater detail.

Integration

The underlying Greek word "saleuo," translated *"was shaken,"* means to move or cause to move back and forth. Luke combined the spiritual intensity of the early Church's prayer with the physical shaking of their location. Before we become enamored with the physical shaking, and seek this manifestation, listen to his explanation of this physical occurrence. ***"And they were all filled with the Holy Spirit, and they spoke the word of God with boldness"*** (Acts 4:31). When these Christians aligned their persecuted lives with the sovereign God, their prayer allowed a physical event in their location. What exactly does this mean? It means that God moved within them with renewed strength, encouragement, and power, enabling them to continue to speak His word with boldness just as they had been doing. Their intimacy with God in the spiritual realm manifested itself in the physical realm, which is always the case!

Luke repeated this truth when He wrote of an event in the city of Philippi. He used the "saleou" connection to the earthquake that happened in the Philippi jail at midnight. Paul and Silas, under great persecution, were placed in this jail. ***"But at midnight Paul and Silas were praying and singing hymns to God, and the prisoners were listening to them"*** (Acts 16:25). The singing of Paul and Silas was equivalent to the prayer of the early Church. The spiritual realm erupted with a purpose in the physical world, a tangible demonstration of power and might. *"The foundations of the prison were shaken* (saleuo), *and immediately all the doors were opened and everyone's chains were loosed"* (Acts 16:26). There is a significant link between the spiritual and the physical. The purpose of the shaking was not to get Paul and Silas out of prison. The shaking was for a radical change in the spiritual realm for the Philippi jailor and his family. The spiritual was manifested in the physical, altering the spiritual.

Sin always integrates the spiritual with the physical, both a positive and a negative. Rebellion against God, never isolated to the spiritual realm, always manifests in the physical. Likewise, a deed of sin in the physical is always combined and sourced by the spiritual. For instance, hate dwells in the heart and is spiritual, a rage deep in the inner spirit. May I propose the issue: "Why do you hate?" The answer will inevitably involve physical activity as well as consequences. A past physical activity resulted in a physical effect that excused the spiritual condition of hate in the inner heart. No one accidentally commits adultery. No one *"praying and singing hymns to God"* awakened to realize they were in a physical adulterous situation. Lust and adultery already exist for some time in the spiritual life of a person before it finally erupts in the physical and shocks everyone.

Luke's premise in the Book of Acts begins with this concept. He described the establishment of the New Covenant with physical imagery. The Spirit of Jesus filling the believer is the height of spiritual experience in the spiritual realm. But when this spiritual reality occurred, *"there came a sound from heaven, as of a rushing mighty wind, and it filled the whole house where they were sitting. Then there appeared to them divided tongues, as of fire, and one sat upon each of them"* (Acts 2:2-3). Immediately we become enamored with the physical manifestations. We want and seek those tangible results. But what do they mean? Luke tells us, ***"They were all filled with the Holy Spirit"*** (Acts 2:4). The spiritual realm manifested itself in the physical circumstances of life! There is never a spiritual movement of God that does not link itself with physical life. The spiritual integrates with the physical; no one can separate them.

The gifts of the Spirit testify of this integration by their very existence. If the gifts of the Spirit exist, it is because a Spirit is sourcing them. The nature of the Spirit proposes a spiritual involvement with the unseen realm. This hidden world interacts with the physical realm in a physical manifestation where the spiritual world integrates with the physical world. Therefore, no one can receive the filling of the Spirit without spiritual gifts flowing naturally from their physical life.

Instigation

Once we understand the interaction between the spiritual and physical, our concern changes. Intimacy with Jesus means I do not have a choice about this integration. Oneness with Jesus means my physical life will be affected. Paul consistently highlights a theological term of this concept in his writings. The term is antinomianism; "aniti" means "against" and "nomos" means law. This theological term proposes that Christians are not responsible for obeying the moral law of Scripture. Some suggest the free grace of God relieved the believer from any moral obligation. In other words, what Jesus provided for us in salvation only applies to the spiritual realm of my life, and we can discard it in the physical realm. There is no link between the spiritual and physical. It leads to the conclusion that my physical life is inherently evil, but God covers my spiritual life by His grace in salvation. Therefore, the two are not linked or integrated. ***"What shall we say then? Shall we continue in sin*** *that grace may abound? Certainly not! How shall we who died to sin live any longer in it?"* (Romans 6:1-2).

Because the spiritual and physical life are integrated with and deeply affected by each other, which one produces the other? Does my physical life instigate my spiritual life, or does my spiritual life prompt my physical life? It is the spiritual life that manifests itself in the physical realm. You do not move from the physical into the spiritual; instead, the opposite is true. I do not correct my physical activity and find that it makes my spiritual life right. *"I say then: Walk in the Spirit, and you shall not fulfill the lust of the flesh"* (Galatians 5:16).

Our passage makes the spiritual manifestation in the physical evidence. The early Church knew oneness with Jesus in the spiritual; this oneness expressed itself in the physical. They were filled with the Holy Spirit and continued to speak the word of God with boldness. "Intimacy" with Jesus must be our focus; we must not focus on the "shaking." Oneness with the Spirit of God is our goal, not being bold in the physical. God does not call us to accomplish both but to focus on one. We can never measure our spiritual success by physical manifestations because the spiritual realm is where we experience oneness with divine purpose. The Divine purpose produces the Divine will for our lives in the physical realm.

The early Church understood this through the life of Jesus. The oneness of Jesus and His Father manifested itself in the physical realm by the accomplishing *"whatever Your hand and Your purpose determined before to be done"* (Acts 4:28). The cross-dismayed the apostles. They could not reconcile the connection between God and the Messiah with bleeding, suffering, and dying. It was the wrong physical manifestation. But this is the situation in our passage. The threats of the Sanhedrin faced the early Church. Were they not in oneness with the Spirit of Jesus? But they understood that unity with the Spirit always manifested itself in redemption in the physical. They did not pray for deliverance; they prayed for redemption.

Our focus must be on the Spirit flowing redemption to the physical environment, not on the physical manifestation of the gifts of the Spirit. We may not receive the gift that is applauded by all and gives us a position in the church body. We may not have a gift that others admire. God might call me to hang on a cross in shame before my world. Will I allow Jesus, whom I embrace, to source my physical life to accomplish His design and desire?

Inescapable

What are my choices? I have no choice in the integration of the spiritual and physical. My spiritual life, good or bad, righteous or evil, will be manifested in my physical world. The spiritual and physical are not separated! My focus on the physical, materialistic world can envelope all my thoughts, time, and physical energy. Still, the spiritual realm of my life displays itself in my physical world.

You and I have no choice in instigating the spiritual within the realm of the physical. Your physical world takes the shape of your spiritual life. Good or bad, righteous or evil, we display our spiritual and influence those around us. There is no way to block the pressure of our spiritual presence in our world. We can develop a belief system that rejects the involvement, but it does not change reality. We can try to make all sins secret so that no one knows, but it does not change the truth. It is not a matter of choice. ***"Do not be deceived, God is not mocked; for whatever a man sows, that he will also reap. For he who sows to his flesh will of the flesh reap corruption, but he who sows to the Spirit will of the Spirit reap everlasting life"*** (Galatians 6:7- 8).

We have no choice concerning reaping what we sow, but we can choose what we will sow! We will manifest our spiritual lives and influence our physical world, so we must determine our spiritual lives. According to our passage, the spiritual world will shake our physical lives; but we can decide that this shaking will result in being filled with the Spirit of Jesus. The self-centered Sanhedrin found their world shaken. Their nation, as well as all their self-power, was destroyed. The early Church rejoiced in intimacy with the Spirit of Jesus and continued to experience the proclamation of God's word with boldness! How about you?

Acts 4:31

FILLED AGAIN

"And when they had prayed, the place where they were assembled together was shaken; and they were all filled with the Holy Spirit, and they spoke the word of God with boldness"
(Acts 4:31).

The resistance against Jesus' ministry seemed to center in Jerusalem, and Jesus insisted the disciples tarry there. The crowds were massive, and the miracles flowed in Galilee. The fame of Jesus spread throughout that region. The most natural thing was to flee Jerusalem; it seemed to be the source of their difficulty. The crucifixion happened in Jerusalem; it was the location of rebellion. However, it also became the seat of power and ministry. God birthed Pentecost in Jerusalem. What an event! The power of the Holy Spirit filled the disciples, launching the New Covenant. The heart of the occasion was, **"And they were all filled with the Holy Spirit and began to speak with other tongues, as the Spirit gave them utterance"** (Acts 2:4).

Following Pentecost, the signs and wonders filled the Scriptures. Miracles gave testimony of God's presence in and among the early Church. The Church grew as the Spirit of Jesus sourced them (Acts 2:46-47). Then a miracle at the Gate Beautiful created an unprecedented stir in Jerusalem (Acts 3:1-10), establishing a platform for the proclamation of the power of Jesus' Spirit among them. It was the final issue that

Filled Again | Acts 4:31

launched the persecution of the early Church. The Sanhedrin had Peter and John dragged before them and interrogated about the source of the lame beggar's healing. The Spirit filled Peter (Acts 4:8). The evidence of the sourcing of the Holy Spirit impacted these powerful men of Israel. They wanted to destroy these Christians but feared the crowds who rejoiced over the miracle. The Sanhedrin threatened the apostles never to speak in the name of Jesus again.

After receiving the Sanhedrin's threat, the apostles returned to the early Church to give a full report. The early Church responded with a prayer filled with praise, worship, and confidence. In the course of this prayer, **"they were all filled with the Holy Spirit, and they spoke the word of God with boldness"** (Acts 4:31). This reoccurrence of the Holy Spirit's filling is a theme that continues throughout the Book of Acts. It became the reason for the world's evangelization. The basis of all miracles, signs, and wonders is in the Holy Spirit's filling, not education and training (Acts 4:13). There was no mention of talent, personality types, or organizational structure. The role of each person became insignificant compared to the filling of the Holy Spirit. Success or failure, life, and death depended on the Spirit's filling.

The Pentecost event was the beginning. **"And they were all filled with the Holy Spirit"** (Acts 2:4). It continued with Peter's interrogation by the Sanhedrin: **"Then Peter, filled with the Holy Spirit, said to them"** (Acts 4:8). The early Church experienced it again: **"and they were all filled with the Holy Spirit"** (Acts 4:31). There are some interesting parallels in these three occurrences. On the day of Pentecost, there was a great **"sound from heaven, as of a rushing mighty wind"** (Acts 4:2), followed by the appearance of **"divided tongues, as of fire"** (Acts 4:3). These imageries are from the Old Testament's depiction of God's movement. When the Sanhedrin interrogated Peter, the filling of the Holy Spirit surrounded the miracle healing of the well-known lame beggar. The leaders of Israel noted, *"that a notable miracle has been done through them is evident to all who dwell in Jerusalem, and we cannot deny it"* (Acts 4:16). As the early Church responded to the threats of persecution, *"the place where they were assembled together was shaken"* (Acts 4:31). The physical and the spiritual worked together, each strongly affected by the "filling of the Holy Spirit."

There are apparent similarities in the context of the spiritual realm displaying itself in the physical realm. We will take a look at those similarities.

Concern Aspect

Prayer is at the heart of two of these situations. The disciples experienced the crucifixion of Jesus. Their failure to stay faithful to Him in that problematic hour surely haunted them. They knew the forgiveness of His presence during the forty-day resurrection appearance of Jesus (Acts 1:3). They sensed that He believed in them, which gave them confidence. He did not scold or judge them; He forgave and embraced them. In this atmosphere of belonging, Jesus proposed to them anew the Kingdom of God. The Kingdom was to be a uniting of what they were with the coming Spirit of Christ. They would merge with God and then be adequate for the call of the "Great Commission" (Matthew 28:16-20).

Jesus instructed them, *"not to depart from Jerusalem, but to wait for the Promise of the Father, 'which,' He said, 'you have heard from Me, for John truly baptized with water, but you shall be baptized with the Holy Spirit not many days from now'"* (Acts 1:4-5). They only needed to wait in Jerusalem for seven days, and the promise would be theirs! What did they do during those seven days of waiting? Luke wrote, *"that they were continually in the temple praising and blessing God. Amen"*

(Luke 24:53). In expanding the content of that explanation, he said, ***"These all continued with one accord in prayer and supplication"*** (Acts 1:14), filled with confidence, not anxiety. They were not worried but were seeking. They expressed an attitude of faith and certainty in the promise of Jesus and were eager to receive it!

Although we do not have the details regarding Peter and John's interrogation before the Sanhedrin, the Scriptures indicate they continued with this same confident attitude. We assume they were in prayer before they appeared before the Sanhedrin. ***"And they laid hands on them, and put them in custody until the next day for it was already evening"*** (Acts 4:3). Knowing something of what they were facing the next day, how did they spend their night? The attitude that caused the Sanhedrin to marvel was their boldness (Acts 4:13). It was not that the apostles were cocky, but they had a confident security that could not be shaken by imprisonment or threats from the seventy most powerful men of Israel. During the night hours as they thought of the coming day, they were open and seeking the steady movement of God through them to the men of the Sanhedrin. No doubt, they expressed the confidence coming from the continued movement of God they had experienced in ministry since Pentecost. The resurrected Lord made promises to them and kept them all! They knew the flow of the Spirit through their lives for miracles, signs, and wonders, transforming life after life. They must have cried out, "Lord, do it again before the Sanhedrin!"

Peter made a presentation before the Sanhedrin. His merger with Jesus allowed him to express love and confidence, filling the atmosphere with the reality of Jesus. This reality was demonstrated through Peter as he proclaimed the resurrected Lord, gaining assurance that could not be shaken by the threats of man. Peter's proclamation came from his heart of openness and oneness with Jesus.

Our passage parallels the concern of God moving through man, linking prayer with, *"they were filled with the Holy Spirit."* The early Church focused a desperate desire that what they experienced in the movement of God's Spirit would continue! They did not ask for an escape from persecution; they were not worried about suffering; they did not focus on protection. They hungered for the full revelation of Jesus' person in and through their lives. The grammar of the statement indicates the early Church experienced the filling of the Holy Spirit because they had a desperate hunger and desire! Is this the condition of the soil in which God plants the seed of His presence? Why didn't the members of the Sanhedrin know the Holy Spirit's filling as Peter did? When God poured out the Holy Spirit at Pentecost, why didn't the crowd surrounding the disciples find themselves filled?

In every situation where the renewed filling of the Holy Spirit occurred, there was desperate seeking for His coming, which is intense instruction for us. But we must go beyond desperately wanting Him. The motive is never selfish. Although in all three situations, they were in prayer, the content of their prayer was not self-centered. They consistently aligned their lives, desires, and focus on the Divine plan. What does God want to do in your situation? The redemptive heart of God filled their prayers! The answer to the prayers of the early Church brought further persecution to their lives. They prayed for boldness to continue speaking His word as they had been. They had no thought for their safety or comfort even when persecuted. Their cry was for the continued evangelization of their world. Could this be our problem?

Causing Aspect

Another aspect is that the Holy Spirit sourced each filling and renewed filling. The early Church called upon the sovereign

God to do what they knew they could not do, and they were direct and desperate in their asking. There is no indication that they called on God to act in a certain way or meet a specific need. The focus of each seems to be the wonder of God sourcing their lives and accomplishing His desires in them.

Can you imagine the overwhelming anticipation the disciples must have felt before Pentecost? They saw Jesus' teachings throughout His three-year ministry from a new perspective. The discourse Jesus delivered to them in the upper room before His death suddenly came alive (John 14, 15, and 16). The teaching on the Kingdom of God from the resurrected Lord reminded them of everything He had previously taught them. They focused on a new and intimate relationship with Jesus from within rather than without. He convinced them His Spirit would indwell them and source them for the divine task. They would be adequate because of Him. They remembered His final words before He ascended. ***"But you shall receive power when the Holy Spirit has come upon you; and you shall be witnesses to Me in Jerusalem, and in all Judea and Samaria, and to the end of the earth"*** (Acts 1:8). Jesus emphasized a new source to accomplish the ordained task.

The awareness of his need gripped Peter as he stood before the Sanhedrin. How could he give a message to these seventy men whose minds were closed to Jesus? When had Peter ever been adequate to debate, convince, or argue with these scribes, Pharisees, and Sadducees? He recognized as they did that he was uneducated and untrained (Acts 4:13). His use of language, his past experiences, and his present talents were simply not on their level. He should have cowered before them. But there came a new filling of the Holy Spirit, which sourced him for this unique circumstance.

The Sanhedrin's interrogation was a sourcing issue. They asked, ***"By what power or by what name have you done this?"*** (Acts 4:7). Peter knew the answer. He hated it that the crowd on Solomon's Porch acknowledged him as the source of the miracle (Acts 3:11). Peter did not take the credit for the lame beggar's healing, but embraced his helplessness and merged with the Spirit of Jesus. In answering their question, he acclaimed nothing but Jesus!

Now the early Church was faced with the threats of the Sanhedrin. They immediately relaxed in God's sovereignty. God is Lord (Despotes), the Creator of all things. He herded the world into position and gave them the authority to do as their self-centeredness desired. They fulfilled His plan by crucifying Christ for the redemption of the world. The early Church considered their situation an extension to the sufferings of Christ. What a privilege! Jesus sourced by the Holy Spirit experienced redemptive suffering. The early Church must continue to be sourced by the Holy Spirit to know redemptive suffering. It was the Spirit who sourced boldness and birthed miracles among them before these threats. The Spirit must continue to empower them.

The early Church established a pattern. In all three events, they experienced the desperate concern and openness for the fulfillment of God's plan in their lives. They knew the only possibility for this plan's fulfillment was the sourcing of the Spirit of Jesus. We cannot expect it to be different for us. The plan of God may surround each person's life with confusion and difficulty. How will we persevere? The Holy Spirit must source us. We must live in constant awareness of our helplessness that He may merge with us in power.

Crisis Aspect

The life of the early Church consistently revealed a crisis pattern. God, in His sovereignty, brings us into uncomfortable situations only to source us with the necessary ingredients for victory within the context of the crisis. He always meets the need of the hour: He designs the solution for the circumstance. The answer is still HIM! He fills us!

Each of the three situations has a crisis aspect. Before Pentecost, the disciples *"were continually in the temple praising and blessing God"* (Luke 24:53). They did not hide in the upper room. They were so convinced of Jesus' resurrection that passion drove them to proclaim it. They boldly expressed Jesus' resurrection to the leadership of Israel. Pentecost so disturbed the crowd in the temple that they began to ask questions. Luke showed the reaction of the crowd five different times in nine verses (Acts 2:5-13). He used four different words to give an adequate description: *"confused, amazed, marveled,* and *perplexed."* It was in the midst of this crisis that Peter was filled with the Spirit and gave an explanation to the crisis; three thousand Jews converted to Jesus!

Peter went beyond confusion and questioning to experience a crisis. He stood before seventy of the most powerful men of Israel. They were responsible for crucifying Jesus; what will they do with him? Peter was never adequate for such a moment. His reaction in times past was to fly off the handle, lose his temper, or grab a sword. How could he possibly minister to this educated group? The Holy Spirit merged with Peter, filling him anew for this crisis. God flooded Peter's mind with truth; God revealed Peter's passion-filled heart; God penetrated Peter's words with power. God spoke through Peter to this group. The Spirit filled Peter to meet the need of the hour.

The crisis now engulfed the early Church. The threat was real. The early Church's heart of concern and desperation caused them to cry out to the only adequate source, sovereign God. They were again filled with the Holy Spirit. The Spirit of Jesus indwelt, permeated, and used them again for this crisis moment. He repeatedly moved through them to meet the need of the hour as they surrendered to Him.

Part 4: The Absolute Reign

Crisis moments face us daily; some are more significant threats than others. However, is there any crisis for which we are adequate in light of God's call? If we are merged and filled with His Spirit, will He not permeate our lives for the new crisis? Will He not flow in and through us to meet the need of our hour? This merger with Jesus is the only way to live!

Acts 4:31

A FILLED SPEAKING

"And when they had prayed, the place where they were assembled together was shaken; and they were all filled with the Holy Spirit, and they spoke the word of God with boldness" (Acts 4:31).

The fact that God filled the early Church believers with the Holy Spirit is biblical. Jesus made it known to all that the Father sourced His life and ministry. ***"The words that I speak to you I do not speak on My own authority; but the Father who dwells in Me does the works"*** (John 14:10). Jesus made clear the content of this indwelling. ***"Believe Me that I am in the Father and the Father in Me, or else believe Me for the sake of the works themselves"*** (John 14:11). He emphasized this teaching to His disciples. ***"And I will pray the Father, and He will give you another Helper, that He may abide with you forever - the Spirit of truth, whom the world cannot receive, because it neither sees Him nor knows Him; but you know Him, for He dwells with you and will be in you. I will not leave you orphans; I will come to you"*** (John 14:16-18). This verse gives us a beautiful picture of the "filling of the Holy Spirit."

In the shadow of the ascension, Jesus gave instructions to His disciples. ***"He commanded them not to depart from Jerusalem, but to wait for the Promise of the Father, 'which,' He said, 'you have heard from Me; for John truly baptized***

with water, but you shall be baptized with the Holy Spirit not many days from now'" (Acts 1:4, 5). Jesus described the fullness of the Spirit! He contrasted the "physical with the spiritual." The baptism of John was a physical experience we remember. Every aspect of its activity was physical. The water, location, baptizer, and effect on the physical person were all evidence of the nature of the baptism. However, the baptism of the Spirit of Jesus focused on the spiritual realm. The baptism of the Holy Spirit will immerse the nature of man with the nature of God. An internal weaving of the Spirit of God will take place with the spirit of man, becoming the new source of the physical activities of man.

Jesus also contrasted the "past with the subsequent." His statement reflected on John the Baptist, who dwelt in the memories of history. He was the best the Old Covenant could offer humanity. However, in just a few days, Jesus proposed a new day was upon them. The New Covenant fulfilled the dream of the old. It is the new level of intimacy with God. Jesus also compared the "protocol with saturation." The baptism of John the Baptist accomplished the proper ceremony related to Old Testament law. The fullness of the Holy Spirit is a saturation of man and God in a new relationship, the focus of the Book of Acts.

There are Bible scholars who propose the "filling of the Holy Spirit" was an empowering of the disciples to accomplish a task on various occasions. There is no denying this as an aspect of the filling. Our sovereign God has a plan! He will empower His people to accomplish His plan, another part of Jesus' instructions to His disciples before His ascension. ***"But you shall receive power when the Holy Spirit has come upon you; and you shall be witnesses to Me in Jerusalem, and in all Judea, and Samaria, and to the end of the earth"*** (Acts 1:8). However, filling a person for an individual task only makes the Old and New Covenant the same. God filled men in the Old Covenant to accomplish a task. Many of the judges and prophets, as well as John the

Baptist, were filled with the Holy Spirit. The New Covenant is far beyond man being an instrument used by God; God births man into a new creature by His indwelling nature.

There are three illustrations given by Luke in the first four chapters of Acts describing the "filling of the Holy Spirit." Peter proposed the initial outpouring of the Holy Spirit on the Day of Pentecost as a fulfillment of Joel's prophecy (Acts 2:17-21). This description of the event is not seen as God using man to accomplish a task but the ushering in of a new relationship. There is a strong emphasis on *"all flesh."* God will bring everyone into a new relationship with Himself through the filling of the Holy Spirit. When Peter stood before the Sanhedrin, the issue concerned the power used to accomplish a task, the healing of the lame beggar. In explaining this resource, Peter presented Jesus, the only possible way to salvation. The issue is not doing a task but a relationship with God. In our present study, the problem was the same. Although they prayed for the continued demonstration of Jesus through signs and wonders, the issue was that they wanted to continue to "be" what they had been! They knew that unity with Jesus that must continue, taking precedence over threats and personal comfort. Jesus had become their life. Let's examine this in light of our passage.

Imperative

The prayer of the early Church began with their focus on the sovereignty of God. They addressed Him as *"Lord"* (Despotes) (Acts 4:24). God is a despot, absolute authority not influenced by anyone or anything, based on the measurement of all His creation. It is also seen in the wonder of the Scriptures because He spoke them. As we move into the heart of the prayer, they address God as *"Lord"* (Acts 4:29). However, the Greek word changes to "Kyrios." We see the position of Lord in the context of family. It is relational and is influenced by what is good for others. God is the One who is the subject of their prayer. There are two main verbs, *"look"* and *"grant,"* and both are in the imperative, demand or command from the early Church to the One who was filling them. It was not a self-centered demand but expressed the urgency and desperation of their desires.

They expressed their desire in *"that with all boldness they may speak Your word"* (Acts 4:29). When their prayer was answered, *"they were all filled with the Holy Spirit, and they spoke the word of God with boldness"* (Acts 4:31). The idea of speaking is paramount in the filling of the Holy Spirit. The early Church not only experienced the speaking but also recognized it. It was an essential ingredient to the growth of the early Church. As Jesus urged His disciples to wait in Jerusalem for the Promise of the Father, He stated the results of this Promise. *"You shall be witnesses to Me in Jerusalem, and in all Judea and Samaria, and to the end of the earth"* (Acts 1:8). Communication and the filling of the Holy Spirit are intimately linked together.

Communication was essential in Luke's description of Pentecost. He described the coming of the Holy Spirit. *"And suddenly there came a sound from heaven, as of a rushing mighty wind, and it filled the whole house where they were sitting"* (Acts 2:2). The Greek word "echos," translated *"sound,"* is our English word "echo." This communication comes *"from heaven."* The Greek word "ek" is translated *"from."* It highlights the movement of communication coming from heaven internally. It was not an outside or superficial issue, but an expression of God's heart. God communicated the depth of His nature to us. Because this is an echo, we become the expression of this communication. We reveal God's heart to our world as we reflect His communication. Luke continued to emphasize the importance of the fullness of the Holy Spirit. *"And they were all filled with the Holy Spirit and began to speak with other tongues, as the Spirit gave them utterance"* (Acts 2:4).

God communicates truth, not data or information! It is a communication of "truth." Jesus is the truth. The function of the Holy Spirit is to reveal the truth to the believer. ***"However, when He, the Spirit of truth, has come, He will guide you into all truth"*** (John 16:13). The moment the believer knows the truth, he or she expresses truth through his or her life. The Spirit of Jesus permeated Peter in a crisis moment before the Sanhedrin. The Spirit spoke through Peter to proclaim the truth of Jesus (Acts 4:8). Data and information did not impact the Sanhedrin, but the Spirit of truth did. They experienced the boldness of Peter and John and sensed Jesus in the proclamation (Acts 4:13). In each of these three illustrations, the result was "speaking." On the Day of Pentecost, "speaking" became a paramount issue. Not only was there a communication from heaven (Acts 2:2), but also the believers ***"were all filled with the Holy Spirit and began to speak with other tongues, as the Spirit gave them utterance"*** (Acts 2:4). Numerous Jews had been living in exile from the days of the Old Testament. They came to Jerusalem each year for the religious feast days. Present in this group were fifteen different nationalities (Acts 2:9-11). When God filled the believers with the Spirit, they began to speak in the various languages of those nationalities. It so amazed this crowd that Luke used four different words to describe it (***confused, amazed, marveled, perplexed***). The believers were not preaching or giving instructions but were expressing ***"the wonderful works of God"*** (Acts 2:11), astonishing the crowd that questioned the activity. Peter, being filled with the Spirit, answered the questions by preaching (Acts 2:14-39).

God filled Peter with the Holy Spirit before the Sanhedrin, and it resulted in communication (Acts 4:8-12). He presented a powerful statement of Jesus and the Sanhedrin's response to Him. The impact of the message caused them to issue their threats. ***"So they called them and commanded them not to speak at all nor teach in the name of Jesus"*** (Acts 4:18). When the early

Church received the report of the threats, their one desire was *"grant to Your servants that with all boldness they may speak Your word"* (Acts 4:29). God answered their prayer! *"They were all filled with the Holy Spirit, and they spoke the word of God with boldness"* (Acts 4:31).

Perhaps we have been silent for too long! Or maybe we are not silent but have filled the air with many sound waves. The difficulty is content; we have not spoken His word.

Initiative

Now we come to the initiative that presents a strange twist in our discussion. If the primary concern is no longer the speaking, but the content of the speaking, why does Luke use the word "laleo," which is translated *"they spoke"*? There are two crucial words in the Greek language for speaking, "laleo" and "lego." "Laleo" is a focus on the act of speaking; "lego" is a focus on the content. Indeed, Luke focused on the content of their speaking; it is the *"word of God."* However, he begins by focusing on the fact they were speaking. This verb is in the imperfect tense, meaning it is an action that occurred in the past and continues into the present with no assessment of the action's completion. In other words, what they spoke in the past caused the threats in the present. They wanted the heart of their prayer to have the same courage and boldness of the past. God answered their prayer.

Luke connected the filling of the Holy Spirit with the act of speaking. The connection is the Greek word "kai" and is a "superordinate conjunction. "Kai" is defined as a word that casts the clause it heads into a superordinate relationship to some other (subordinated) clause. A superordinate clause is a grammatical construction related to, but more prominent than another clause, meaning a superordinate clause is the more critical (superior) of the two subordinate clauses." Therefore, Luke highlighted the act of continuing to speak as an excellent display of the renewed filling of the Holy Spirit. The source of speaking is the Holy Spirit. If Luke gave the details or content of the speaking, we would be impressed with their knowledge, education, and talent to communicate. They simply spoke by the power of the Holy Spirit and displayed boldness.

This filling of the Holy Spirit is a duplicate of the other two previously recorded fillings. Peter was filled with the Holy Spirit as he addressed the interrogation question of the Sanhedrin. His answer was beyond him as the Spirit sourced it. The Sanhedrin recognized his boldness and the presence of Jesus in what he spoke. They compared what they heard with the educational level of the apostles. *"They marveled"* (Acts 4:13).

The disciples who experienced the Day of Pentecost followed the same pattern. There was little emphasis on what they said, but much emphasis on the sourcing of the Holy Spirit. The Jews of the exile were astounded at what they heard. It was not the content, but the fact that the disciples spoke in various languages of the crowd. They cried, *"And how is it that we hear, each in our own language in which we were born?"* (Acts 2:8).

The need of this hour is not that we have profound speeches or talented performances. We need the Spirit of Jesus to source the act of our speaking. No amount of argument can fill the need. Greater displays of philosophical understanding will not suffice. The mind of Jesus supplied through the sourcing of the Holy Spirit is a single need. It was the prayer of the early Church, and they received an answer to their prayer.

Issue

Before Luke closed this description of the early Church, he gave us the content of what they spoke! *"They spoke the word of*

God with boldness (Acts 4:31). The subject must always be the ***"word of God."*** As you might guess, the Greek word translated ***"word"*** is "logos." It is difficult to separate the meaning of this word from the person of Jesus. The threats focused on speaking about Jesus; their prayer was that they continue to speak about Jesus with boldness.

We must make a distinction between speaking data and information about Jesus and speaking Jesus. They did not give a historical outline of Jesus' life or repeat the facts they had heard about Jesus. Because Jesus' Spirit sourced the early Church, they were speaking about Jesus. There was something beyond words, ideas, or concepts, and this was not a doctrinal presentation. The early Church believers were talking about Jesus, and as they spoke, those hearing saw and felt the presence of Jesus.

The Sanhedrin felt the essence of Jesus in their encounter with Peter. What disturbed the leaders of Israel about the miracle of the lame beggar and Peter's preaching was that he ***"taught the people and preached in Jesus the resurrection from the dead"*** (Acts 4:2). The Sadducees and Pharisees continually argued about the resurrection. The Sadducees did not believe in the resurrection from the dead, but the Pharisees did. It was an ongoing debate, which they did not find disturbing, but the apostles speaking about the resurrection angered them. The problem was the presence of Jesus in the resurrection. If He was not there, it was a philosophical debate affecting no one. As the apostles preached the resurrection, the resurrected Lord came in His Spirit to transform the lives of those listening. When Peter proclaimed the power and name by which God accomplished the miracle, ***"they realized they had been with Jesus"*** (Acts 4:13).

Understanding the essence of Jesus in those who are speaking about Him removes our speaking about Jesus from sermon construction, devotional speeches, and debates. Jesus' presence must dominate all of our speech. He must continually flow from our lips. Our lives must be a speech about Him. There is no question! Our lives are a speech about something. We consistently proclaim something to our world. The Spirit of Jesus must source us to proclaim the message of Jesus in the presence of Jesus! Let us never waver from this!

PART 5
ACTS 4:32-37

THE AGREED RESOLVE

Acts 4:32-37

A COMMON THING

"Now the multitude of those who believed were of one heart and one soul; neither did anyone say that any of the things he possessed was his own, but they had all things in common. And with great power the apostles gave witness to the resurrection of the Lord Jesus. And great grace was upon them all. Nor was there anyone among them who lacked; for all who were possessors of lands or houses sold them, and brought the proceeds of the things that were sold, and laid them at the apostles' feet; and they distributed to each as anyone had need. And Joses, who was also named Barnabas by the apostles (which is translated Son of Encouragement), a Levite of the country of Cyprus, having land, sold it, and brought the money and laid it at the apostles' feet." (Acts 4:32-37).

The Apostle Luke authored both the Gospel of Luke and the Book of Acts. In the Gospel of Luke, he gave an account of Jesus' life. He did not intend for the Gospel of Luke to be a separate book from The Book of Acts but presented them as volume one and volume two of one writing. As Luke's gospel circulated in the early Church, the other gospels were eagerly received. Everyone recognized volume one of Luke's account as a gospel; they separated it from the Book of Acts and made it a book on its own, which is essential because of the theme. Luke did not intend to present two writings with different themes. What he wanted to communicate with his gospel account (volume one), he also wanted to communicate with the Book of Acts (volume two). It becomes evident that the central concept is the indwelling of God's life in the human being, which lifestyle demonstrates! Jesus is a Spirit-sourced man in the gospel account, and through Him, the gospel spread into the lives of the disciples in the Book of Acts.

However, another subordinate theme, "materialism," also flows through both volumes. Luke often presents the subject of money and its binding quality in our lives. He makes it evident in his writing that money is not a blessing from God, but is a curse or an obstacle to your spiritual success. If you are to become the godly person desired by God, you must make your way over the barricade of materialism. Materialism will trap, entangle, and control you! *"No servant can serve two masters; for either he will hate the one and love the other, or else he will be loyal to the one and despise the other. You cannot serve God and mammon"* (Luke 16:13).

This theme of materialism is dominant in the parables. A Pharisee invited Jesus to eat in his home. During the meal, a *"woman in the city who was a sinner"* crashed the party. She stood behind Jesus weeping. She washed His feet with her tears and wiped them with her hair; she kissed His feet and anointed them with the alabaster flask of fragrant oil. How could a godly man have intimate contact with this sinful woman? Jesus responded with the "Parable of the Debtors" (Luke 7:41-43). One man owed a creditor 500 denarii, and another man owed 50 denarii. The creditor forgave both men for their debt. Jesus asked, *"Tell me, therefore, which of them will love him more?"* Jesus presented forgiveness of sin in the context of materialism.

On another occasion, a lawyer tried to test Jesus by quizzing Him about the necessary activities to gain eternal life. Jesus pointed him to the summary of the law in the Old Testament, loving God with your whole being and your neighbor as yourself.

But the lawyer, wanting to justify himself, asked Jesus, *"And who is my neighbor?"* Jesus shared the "Parable of the Good Samaritan" (Luke 10:29-37), placing materialism at the center of every action in the story. The parable starts with a person robbed of his materialism; it continues with the priest and Levite not willing to get involved because of the expense. But a Samaritan who should have hated the injured Jew gets financially involved.

In another instance, a man from the crowd asked Jesus to tell his brother to divide the inheritance with him. Jesus answered that it was not His business to do so, but He told the "Parable of the Rich Fool" (Luke 12:16-21). The rich man had plenty; he built more barns and stored more goods. *"And I will say to my soul, 'Soul, you have many goods laid up for many years; take your ease; eat, drink, and be merry.' But God said to him, 'Fool!' This night your soul will be required of you; then whose will those things be which you have provided?'"* (Luke 12:19-20).

The "Parable of the Unjust Steward" is strange (Luke 16:1-8). A steward stole from his master, and the master told him to get ready for an accounting. The steward realized he was in trouble, so he called all the people who owed the master and reduced their debit. He did this so they would help him when the master put him out. Jesus commended this man. He was shrewd in his financial dealings. If you are not wise in your materialism, how can you be trusted with real riches?

When the Pharisees heard the "Parable of the Unjust Steward," they derided Jesus because they were lovers of money. He then told them the "Parable of the Rich Man and Lazarus (Luke 16:19-31). There was a rich man who had the best of everything, and a beggar named Lazarus, covered with sores, laid at his gate. Lazarus desired only to eat the crumbs from the rich man's table. The beggar died and went to the bosom of Abraham while the rich man died and went to Hades. On the other side of death, they had reversed roles. When the rich man cried out to Abraham, he was told, *"Son, remember that in your lifetime you received your good things, and likewise Lazarus evil things, but now he is comforted and you are tormented"* (Luke 16:25).

On another day, as Jesus neared Jerusalem, He told the "Parable of the Minas" (Luke 19:11-27). A master departed to a far country, leaving ten servants in charge of his goods. He gave each ten minas and instructed them to do business until he returned. Upon his return, each servant came before the master to provide an account of his earnings. Each had doubled the amount except one who kept his money in a handkerchief and showed no gain from it. This parable asks, "How do you handle your finances?"

Except for one, all the above parables are exclusively Luke's. He also wrote the story of the Rich Young Ruler, whose life was gripped by money. His materialism trapped him, and he was unable to release his possessions to embrace Jesus. Here again, we see Luke describing money not as a blessing but as a curse. We must climb over the top of materialism because it is a barricade to spiritual success. The evil of materialism is a strong theme throughout the Gospel, according to Luke, and the same theme continues in the Book of Acts. The outpouring of the Holy Spirit ushered the believer into a new dimension of intimacy with the mind of Christ! God merges His nature with the believer. How does this affect the realm of finances in the Kingdom person?

After Pentecost, the outpouring of the Holy Spirit, 3,000 souls were added to the church (Acts 2:41). Luke reported the effect of this on their materialism. *"Now all who believed were together, and had all things in common, and sold their possessions and goods, and divided them among all, as anyone had need"* (Acts 2:44-45). This was no small feat among 3,000 people, but the church continued to grow. Undoubtedly, as the church doubled and tripled, this practice was lost, but repeatedly in this book, Luke presents the effect of God's nature on the materialistic view of the believers.

Connection

Luke connects the movement of God in the early Church with the physical, materialistic response of the believers. Why would Luke make this an essential theme of his writings? How important should it be to us? Each report on the generosity of the early Church connects to the strong movement of the Holy Spirit. For instance, Luke writes, *"Then fear came upon every soul, and many wonders and signs were done through the apostles"* (Acts 2:43). In the following two verses, he proclaims the unity and generosity of the church. They *"sold their possessions and goods, and divided them among all, as anyone had need"* (Acts 2:45).

In chapter three of Acts, Luke highlights the healing of the lame beggar, setting the stage for the next two chapters. This miracle significantly demonstrated the power of God. Peter grabbed the lame beggar by the right hand, yanked him to his feet as he cried, *"In the name of Jesus Christ of Nazareth, rise up and walk"* (Acts 3:6). Immediately the bones in the man's feet and ankles were strengthened. He began to leap, walk, and praise God! In describing this man in the following verse, Luke gives us insight into the extent of the miracle. God healed the beggar completely, making him mentally, emotionally, spiritually, and physically whole!

The lame beggar, over forty years of age, was a fixture in Jerusalem at the Gate Beautiful (Acts 4:22). Everyone knew him. The multitude of temple worshippers passed by him, looked at him with pity, yet supported him. This miracle impacted thousands in the temple. Everyone in Jerusalem was talking about the grace of God granted to a lame beggar (Acts 4:16). It so impacted the leaders of Israel that they had to get involved. This miracle instigated the persecution of the early Church, causing the believers to rely on the sovereignty of God. They prayed not to be saved from persecution but to continue in the same power of ministry that brought them to persecution, remaining in the same boldness as before.

Luke said, "As great as the miracle was among the early Church, let me tell you of an equal miracle." He relates the attitude of the early Church to materialism. No one thought of his possessions as his own; they had all things in common (Acts 4:32). No one among them lacked (Acts 4:34). Luke gives the example of the man nicked name by the apostles as Barnabas. He was an encourager. He sold his land and laid the money at the apostle's feet (Acts 4:36). What a miracle! The miracle in Barnabas' life was equal to the miracle in the life of the lame beggar! The only explanation is the Divine movement of the Holy Spirit! Luke connects the power of the Spirit of Jesus moving on the people of the early Church with their response to materialism!

Combination

Luke proposed that the attitude of the early Church toward materialism connected to the presence of Jesus in their lives. He also established an effective combination between their attitude and the power of Jesus in them. These new Christians had all things in common, and they expressed a powerful witness (Acts 4:33). The victory they had over materialism was evident in their relationship with the Lord Jesus and the grace they received from Him. It was as if their witness to Jesus' power created their victory over materialism. Our attitude toward materialism should combine with our witness of Jesus' resurrection!

How does the power of God fill the believer, and he does not express it in his security? If a person's security is in materialism, would that not affect God filling him with the Spirit of Christ? When people receive the mind of Christ, a shift takes place in the way they think about material things. Luke begins this paragraph with an emphasis on the oneness of heart and soul existing in the early Church. The content of this oneness is so strong that no one looked on his possessions as his own. They had all things in common. Then Luke adds, *"And with great power the apostles gave witness to the resurrection of the Lord Jesus. And great grace was upon them all"* (Acts 4:33). The word beginning the English translation is *"and,"* translated from the Greek word "kai." This word generally combines ideas, which follow directly and necessarily from what precedes. The view of the early Church towards their possessions was in combination with the powerful witness given of the resurrected Jesus.

We discover the combination of the physical and spiritual in the Book of Acts. The early Church's convincing mannerisms and eyewitness accounts were not the power of their testimony. The power was in the presence of the resurrected Lord! As they spoke of Jesus' resurrection, Jesus penetrated the lives of those listening. The people felt His presence. Luke linked their powerful witness with their attitude toward materialism, forcing all to consider the combination of the physical and the spiritual. The principle is secure. When the physical yields to the spiritual, there is a movement in the spiritual world that demonstrates itself in the physical world, changing both worlds forever. If our security is in the physical, that blocks how people see us in the spiritual.

However, in our English translation of this verse (Acts 4:33), *"and"* appears again, a translation of the Greek word "te." "Kai" is used to couple ideas, which follows directly and necessarily from what precedes. Although "te" is generally employed when subjoined with something, which does not directly and necessarily follow. "Kai" connects and "te" annexes. Luke presents the main building as the attitude of the early Church concerning materialism, allowing the Spirit of Jesus to reveal His resurrection presence. But added or annexed to this is, *"And*

great grace was upon them all." The early Church's attitude about their possessions created an atmosphere where Jesus filled their witness with the power. They experienced the blessing of God's grace because of their attitude about their possessions. Therefore, it flows both ways. Our attitude towards materialism affects God's movement on others, but also the movement of God on our lives.

Confirmation

Lest any should think that the question of materialism is a small issue, Luke moved from the positive account of Barnabas' generosity (Acts 4:36-37) to the chilling tale of Ananias and Sapphira (Acts 5:1-11). These stories confirm the radical nature of materialism and its effect on our lives and others. The love of material things is the cause of much self-deceit. There seems to be something quite natural about the lies of Ananias and Sapphira. Have you thought about the many ways we rationalize and excuse our covetousness and greed? "I'm not all that well off," we say. "I have all I can do just to make ends meet." "I worked hard for this and deserve it."

Materialism, along with self-deceit, relates directly to physical insecurity. We focus on the physical instead of the spiritual power released within our merger with Jesus. Martin Luther once called security the ultimate idol. Over and over again, we demonstrate that we are willing to exchange anything for a taste of security. We sacrifice our family, our health, our church, and even truth to get a slight advantage in materialism. "Well," one might say, "it hasn't killed me yet!" But it will! Materialism is of such significance that the early Church recognized this self-deceit about security and confronted it most radically. People consistently ask me about this story and the severity of it. What is the depth of truth in the deaths of Ananias and Sapphira?

The issue of most questions is, "Why was God so severe toward the actions of Ananias and Sapphira?" Perhaps that is not the question that we should ask! Maybe the question should be, "Why do we think what occurred to Ananias and Sapphira was severe?" Is it because we have not been struck dead? Are we admitting our self-deceit concerning our dependency on materialism? Are we looking at the long-suffering of God towards our self-denial? We consistently praise Him for His physical provisions and equally complain when we do not have physical comfort. We even develop a gospel of truth that holds financial and material gain as the epitome of spiritual blessing. What is wrong with us? Maybe we have maintained physical breathing by the grace of God, but we have died in the most crucial area of our lives!

Is Luke right in stating the words of Jesus? *"No servant can serve two masters, for either he will hate the one and love the other, or else he will be loyal to the one and despise the other. You cannot serve God and mammon"* (Luke 16:13). Do we find our security in materialism or Christ?

Acts 4:32

A BELIEVING CHURCH

"Now the multitude of those who believed were of one heart and one soul; neither did anyone say that any of the things he possessed was his own, but they had all things in common" (Acts 4:32).

"Now" is a translation of the Greek word "de" and begins the English translation of our verse. It is a particle standing after one or two words in a clause. It is strictly adversative, but more frequently denotes transition or conversion. In other words, it serves to introduce something else, whether opposed to what precedes or simply continuative or explanatory. The preceding passage, which is the healing of the lame beggar, becomes our focus. Due to the healing of the lame beggar, the Sanhedrin launched the beginning of persecution, threatening Peter and John **"not to speak at all nor teach in the name of Jesus"** (Acts 4:18).

When the early Church heard this threat, they broke into praise and prayer. They focused on the sovereignty of God with no selfishness in their prayer. They were not asking for protection or deliverance. They had only one desire! They wanted the fullness of the Spirit of Jesus to continue, which resulted in the proclamation of His name supported by signs and wonders. Their prayer caused the threat of persecution. God answered their request, **"the place where they were assembled together** *was shaken; and they were filled with the Holy Spirit, and they spoke the word of God with boldness"* (Acts 4:31).

In a new paragraph, Luke described the condition of the early Church, which was a result of their openness and the filling of the Holy Spirit. Their openness and infilling created unity, conquered materialism, and provided for the needs of every person. *"Now the multitude of those who believed were of one heart and one soul; neither did anyone say that any of the things he possessed was his own, but they had all things in common"* (Acts 4:32).

The main verb in the opening sentence is a verb of "being" (eimi), an imperfect indicative verb. It describes a state of being that occurred in the past with no assessment of the state being completed. In other words, it continues into the present. It is a state of *"one heart and one soul!"* This statement is a predicate nominative that renames the subject. Luke described the subject as *"the multitude of those who believed."* A group of people who believe is the same as a group of people who have the same heart and soul.

What did this group believe that united them as having one heart and soul? They believed in Jesus. They believed in a sovereign plan contained in the Person of Jesus, demonstrated in His death and resurrection, and expressed through His Spirit filling them. Many of this group, especially the apostles, spent forty days with the resurrected Jesus! They were not quoting a doctrine they learned in school. They were not accepting a message proposed by the latest fad of their culture. The person of Jesus had captured them. Jesus taught them about this new Kingdom during those forty days. They believed Jesus was alive, and God fulfilled His plan in Him. They had nothing else on the agenda but Jesus. They focused on the reality of His person. This is what united them! He was their sole message. Luke said, *"And with great power the apostles gave witness to the resurrection of the Lord Jesus"* (Acts 4:33).

The early Church continually raised the issue of Jesus! What was this crowd's relationship with Jesus? Peter called them to repent, and Jesus was the issue of that repentance. They had crucified Him; they must now embrace Him. Jesus was the issue of baptism. Their baptism was a demonstration of how wrong they had been about Jesus (Acts 2:38). They received the gift of the Holy Spirit through their embrace of Jesus. Their belief revolved around Him. What is your relationship with Jesus?

Luke reported what this belief caused in the lives of the early Church. This belief allowed Jesus to shape them into His body. They became the church, a living organism.

Organism

These new Christians became the early Church, a group with one soul and the same heart. They were no longer individuals who believed in various doctrines. The dictionary defines an "organism" as a whole with interdependent parts, likened to a living being. The apostle Paul's favorite phrase was "the body of Christ." His epistles to Ephesus and Corinth highlight this picture. *"And He put all things under His feet, and gave Him to be head over all things to the church, which is His Body, the fullness of Him who fills all in all"* (Ephesians 1:22-23). Paul described this in amazing language, *"For as the body is one and has many members, but all the members of that one body, being many, are one body, so also is Christ. For by one Spirit we were all baptized into one body - whether Jews or Greeks, whether slaves or free - and have all been made to drink into one Spirit. For in fact the body is not one member but many"* (1 Corinthians 12:12-14).

Luke describes the birth and growth of the church as Christ's body. As Luke illustrates this oneness, he uses the word "church" for the first time (Acts 5:11). It is a translation of the

Greek word "ekklesia." Its original meaning was an assembly called together. "Ek" means "from" or "out of." "Klosis" is rooted in "kaleo." It means "to call." During Luke's time, people used the word for a body of citizens called together to discuss the affairs of a local community or the state. In the Septuagint, the Greek translation of the Old Testament, "ekklesia" is the word translating the Hebrew word for an assembly of the people of Israel. It is the "called out and called together ones."

We must always remember that Jesus is the One who calls us. We are to come to Him alone, finding our place in and through Him. A. W. Tozer described this with the illustration of one hundred pianos all tuned to the same tuning fork. Every piano tuned to the same tuning fork would be tuned to each other. All one hundred pianos sounded precisely the same (in one accord with one heart and one soul) not because they were tuned to each other, but because they were tuned to a standard to which each surrendered. The early Church had one heart and one soul not because they attempted to be one with each other, but because they were one with Jesus!

The unity the early Church knew in Jesus is described as **"one heart and one soul."** The Greek word "kardia," translated heart, is never used in the New Testament for the physical organ of the body. It is the seat and the center of human life. All the desires, feelings, affections, passions, and impulses are located in and come from the heart, the "place" a person encounters God in a positive or negative sense. It is here in the heart that the spiritual life has its firm foundation, and a person's conduct is determined, often focused on intellectual activity. God spoke through Solomon, *"For as he thinks in his heart, so is he"* (Proverbs 23:7).

In Jewish belief, the *"soul"* is the seat of the will. It is a translation of the Greek word "psyche." "Psyche" refers to the immaterial part of a person, the actuating cause of life. The linking of the *"heart"* and the *"soul"* is the entire being of the person. The members of the early Church thought and wanted the same things. They functioned as if they were one person, a living "organism."

The reality of unity only happened as each person merged with Jesus. As Jesus filled each person, he or she experienced the mind of Christ. Jesus filled each with His nature, bringing unity that could not be manufactured by any other means. Although the uniqueness of each person is present and necessary, they function as one! Each one contributes to the same purpose and desire. What a testimony to the world; unity exceeds physical healing! Our focus is not on unity; it is on Jesus. If we concentrate on unity, we will divide on "how" to be unified. Methodology brings division. If we focus on unity, we develop ways of measurement. Some will think we are united, but others disagree, which results in division. Some declare the presence of "a spirit of division," although others deny such a presence. **"One heart and one soul"** only exists when each person entirely focuses on Jesus.

The early Church knew this oneness in the context of **"the multitude of those who believed."** The Greek word "pisteuo" is translated **"who believed,"** focused on Jesus. It is His name they are not to speak; the threat of the Sanhedrin concerned Jesus. But the early Church was so convinced of the reality of His presence they could not cease. Jesus captured them! Many of them experienced His resurrection appearances, but all of them knew His resurrection presence. The life of Jesus birthed these believers into the living organism of His body.

Orchestration

Luke gives us abundant evidence of how the life of Jesus demonstrated itself in the physical realm through miracles, signs, and wonders. When the Sanhedrin issued threats on

A Believing Church | Acts 4:32

the early Church, this body of believers prayed, *"Now, Lord, look on their threats, and grant to Your servants that with all boldness they may speak Your word, by stretching out Your hand to heal, and that signs and wonders may be done through the name of Your holy Servant Jesus"* (Acts 4:29-30). The physical demonstration of miracles, signs, and wonders verified His Word. This demonstration brought the early Church into persecution. Although it was not the primary cause, it set the stage for the proclamation of *"in Jesus the resurrection from the dead"* (Acts 4:2). The healing of the lame beggar at the Gate Beautiful created a stir within the city of Jerusalem. Everyone heard about Jesus through physical demonstration.

Although these miracles impacted everyone, an equal miracle took place in the body of believers. Oneness in Jesus created a new approach to their materialism. Luke writes, *"Neither did anyone say that any of the things he possessed was his own, but that they had all things in common"* (Acts 4:32). This news should not shock us because Luke already reported this in the second chapter. *"Now all who believed were together, and had all things in common, and sold their possessions and goods, and divided them among all, as anyone had need"* (Acts 2:44-45). Miracles, wonders, and signs were a constant theme in the description of the early Church in Jerusalem. The inner sourcing of the Spirit of God demonstrated Himself in the physical realm of the believer's life.

The astounding aspect of this miracle was not in the physical demonstration of having *"all things in common,"* but this demonstration was in the believer's spiritual life. The believers did not view their possessions as their own. The miracle was the shift in how they perceived ownership. No one forced them; there was no obligation; they wanted to do this! Peter made this plain in what he said to Ananias when he referred to the property sold, and the money received. Peter said, *"Although it remained, was it not your own? And after it was sold, was it not in your own control? Why have you conceived this thing in your heart? You have not lied to men but to God"* (Acts 5:4).

Allow me to state this fact another way. The physical did not force their expression. The spiritual imposed this generous activity on the materialism of the early Church. There was no physical law written, no oral tradition. The early Church did not establish a standard for one to be a member in good standing. Their generosity was a spontaneous flow of God's nature and heart. Not everyone sold everything they had. The Lord directed each according to His will for the individual. Each believer would have been on a different level of spiritual maturity. God did not require the same amount or even the same percentage from each believer. They responded to God's heart in the area of materialism as they did in all other areas. The spiritual realm imposed itself on the materialistic realm of the believers.

We know that the bank account is the last thing we surrender to Jesus. It represents our efforts, earnings, and basis of security. The early Church demonstrated this shift! They moved from the security of this world to the security in the resurrected Lord. They were *"of one heart and one soul"* in what they believed, in worship and fellowship, but also materialism.

Organic Matter

What could be so dominant in the human life that even our view of materialism is affected? It is an organic matter. There are several definitions of "organic" given in the dictionary. As I travel the country, I regularly see signs advertising organic food. In large grocery stores, there are sections set aside to display and sell organic food, referring to "food produced or farming methods involving the production of food without the use of chemical fertilizer, pesticides, or other artificial agents." The price of such food is much higher because the cost of producing the product is much more. But it has become a strong desire for those focused on having good health to eliminate artificial elements from their diet.

To live organic in our spiritual lives is even more vital! Jeremiah was a great prophet of the Old Testament. He said the Lord spoke through him to announce the coming of a New Covenant. It would be different from the Old Covenant given when Israel came from the land of slavery. God said, *"But this is the covenant that I will make with the house of Israel after those days, says the Lord; I will put My law in their minds, and write it on their hearts; and I will be their God, and they shall be My people. No more shall every man teach his neighbor, and every man his brother, saying, 'Know the Lord,' for they all shall know Me, from the least of them to the greatest of them, says the Lord"* (Jeremiah 31:33-34). The written law of God had been like pesticides or chemical fertilizer attempting to create a pure heart in Israel. The New Covenant would be the inner law of God flowing as a natural part of the structure of the New Covenant person! The nature of God would merge with the spirit of man; the motive of man's heart would flow from the heart of God! God will completely change how the Kingdom person views materialism. It will be organic.

Another definition of "organic" in the dictionary is "denoting a relation between elements of something such that they fit together harmoniously as necessary parts of a whole," characterized by continuous or natural development, organic growth. This is a description of the merger between the nature of God and the nature of man, where God forms a new creature. The person is not placed on a life support system; instead, God fuses the new life of His Divine nature into his or her being. They come alive from within the core of their system. They are organic in unity with Jesus, a description of the early Church. They experienced unity with God and with each other. We cannot manufacture unity; laws cannot produce it. Religious training cannot cause it. It is organic. God created man to fit together harmoniously with His nature; these are two necessary parts of a whole!

The secret to the early Church is their intimacy with the fullness of the Spirit. The unity they experienced with each other came from the Spirit's infilling. This intimacy with Jesus produced their courage in the face of persecution. Intimacy with Jesus must be the focus of our lives!

Acts 4:32

STEWARDSHIP

"Now the multitude of those who believed were of one heart and one soul; neither did anyone say that any of the things he possessed was his own, but they had all things in common"
(Acts 4:32).

The unity of the early Church amazed the world. Luke considered the reality of this unity equal to "signs and wonders." The healing of the lame beggar was a miracle, demanding the attention of all Jerusalem and launching the persecution of the early Church. But equally as impressive is **"the multitude of those who believed were of one heart and of one soul"** (Acts 4:32). The power of Jesus' person is the only explanation for the lame beggar's healing and the unity of the early Church.

The early Church's demonstration of this unity was even more amazing! Their unity related directly to their materialism. In the original Greek text, the word "kai" immediately follows the declaration of their unity. "Kai" is not translated in most English versions but demonstrates a logical connection between the unity and what follows. Luke begins with a negative statement and follows with a positive statement. He points out what they did not do. **"Neither did anyone say that any of the things he possessed was his own"** (Acts 4:32). The conjunction **"but"** follows this statement. The common Greek word translated "but" is "de." Luke used the Greek word "alla," an emphatic antithesis after a full negation. It means "but," "but rather," "but on the contrary." In this case, it is at the beginning of the clause, which asserts the contrary to what precedes. Luke contrasted the negative with the positive. The early Church did not view their possessions as their own, ***"but they had all things in common"*** (Acts 4:32).

What does it mean to have ***"all things in common"***? The Greek word "koinos," translated ***"in common,"*** is used two ways in the New Testament. One meaning is unclean or impure. When a thing or activity does not properly achieve the standard of the Levitical law, it is "koinos." Peter expressed this in his vision of the sheet filled with all kinds of four-footed animals. Jesus instructed him to eat, but quickly replied, ***"Not so, Lord! For I have never eaten anything common*** (koinos) ***or unclean"*** (Acts 10:14). The second use of the word in our text is "koinos," which refers to property and the "community of goods" in the early Church. An example of this for comparison might be the fraternal community life of Jesus and His disciples (Luke 8:3; John 12:4-6; 13:29).

However, at no time in the early Church was there a "planned communistic economy, nor is it legal in the sense of constitutional socialization of property." Every evidence is that the early Christian practice was voluntary. Luke recorded the example of Barnabas' generosity (Acts 4:36-37) because he did not give out of obligation. The example of Ananias and Sapphira was not about the selling of their property. Peter clarified for Ananias that his sin was lying about his giving. The land remained his to do with as he pleased; he was under no obligation to give the proceeds to the church (Acts 5:4). There was no record he had transferred the ownership to any central governing body, no control of production or income, and no requirement to surrender one's property to the community. When the need arose for helping the widows, the solution was not apportioning each one's income or giving from a common fund. They had a charity fund for the needy (Acts 6:1-6). Another example was Mary, who still owned a home, had a maid, and Christians enjoyed the hospitality of her home (Acts 12:12), clearly no experiment in common ownership.

We must approach this passage from a Jewish context. The early Church was located only in Jerusalem and consisted of Jews. They continued their temple involvement, Jewish customs, and oral traditions. In the framework of the Old Testament, they had a fundamental teaching about materialism. All property was given to Israel by God. They did not own it! God appeared to Abram and said, *"To your descendants I will give this land"* (Genesis 12:7). God gave them their families and the future of their descendants. Their deliverance from Egyptian slavery focused on God's deliverance of the firstborn. After they came out of Egypt, the Lord spoke to Moses, *"Consecrate to Me all the firstborn, whatever opens the womb among the children of Israel, both of man and beast; it is Mine"* (Exodus 13:2). Every blessing they enjoyed in life resulted from God's provision. Are you surprised the members of the early Church understood the things they possessed were not their own?

They were stewards of God's provisions! A steward was a servant who managed the household affairs for the head of the family. The role of the early Church was to manage their materialism for God. Everything they possessed was a provision of Jesus. This awareness immediately invokes several ideas.

Ownership

Ownership is not an abstract concept. It is not possible to describe the significance of abstract spiritual realities. In his epistle to the Ephesians, Paul speaks of the *"heavenly realms"* where God has located all the spiritual blessings needed for life. God seats us in Christ in the *"heavenly realms"* (Ephesians 2:6). Spiritual blessings are real, but they are abstract. However, there is a measurable, physical, concrete realm, which is feeble, tangible, and seeable. Our verse is related to this physical realm. The early Church did not claim ownership of material things, but according to the passage, they *"possessed"* them. It is a translation of the Greek word "hyparcho." Luke uses this word fourteen times to describe something someone possesses.

The early Church recognized that God owned their material possessions. This should not be shocking to us in light of their response to the threats of the Sanhedrin. In unity, they prayed, **"Lord, You are God, who made heaven and Earth and the sea, and all that is in them"** (Acts 4:24). They address God as *"Lord"* (Despotes). He is a despot, a tyrant! He is sovereign in every way; everything belongs to Him! To claim ownership of what we possess is to infringe on God's sovereignty, degrading His position as God in our lives.

BUT I EARNED IT! Only a person who considers himself in charge would make such a statement. To say we earned our possessions places us in direct rebellion to God's sovereignty in our lives. Who gave you life, the ability to make money, and make your crops grow? Who provides the air you breathe and gives you energy? What do we have that God did not provide? Think of the haughty pride, the audacity, and the blaring arrogance of claiming anything as your own. We must see everything in light of God's ownership. Was it not here before I came? Will it not be here after I am gone? Death is the only thing I have ever earned. **"For the wages of sin is death"** (Romans 6:23).

BUT I BUILT IT! Where did you get your supplies? What material have you brought into existence from nothing? When did you sit on your throne and speak worlds into existence? Have you not simply manipulated the Divine provision? You may revel in the brilliancy of your idea or invention, but who supplied your mind? Does not every good thing come from God? Think of the stupidity of you producing anything apart from Him. One thought without His presence produces nothing but total evil.

BUT I BOUGHT IT! Who gave you the funds to own anything? You came into this world with nothing, and you will go out of this world with nothing. Are you not a steward of what has been given you in this life? In the spiritual realm, there is no merit, no coinage, no activity, nor any other thing that can purchase the redemption for my needy soul. Do I have anything in the physical that is selectively mine, anything that could sufficiently purchase even one item, anything that I could claim as exclusively mine? The only thing I have purchased is my destruction.

BUT I HAVE A RIGHT TO IT! The arrogance of self-centeredness always expresses itself in what we think we deserve. What physical item do you have a right to call your own? Even your life is not your own. Listen to the Biblical view of your physical body, *"Or do you not know that your body is the temple of the Holy Spirit who is in you, whom you have from God, and you are not your own? For you were bought at a price; therefore glorify God in your body and in your spirit, which are God's"* (1 Corinthians 6:19-20). This exhortation from Paul concerns sexual immorality. The members of your body are not yours. Therefore, you do not have ownership over them to dictate their activity. If this is true for your personal and private body, how much more is it true with everything your body claims to possess!

If we have no ownership, we are stewards, not owners. We must immediately renounce our ownership and acknowledge His exclusive ownership of all things, including us. *"But you are a chosen generation, a royal priesthood, a holy nation, His own special people, that you may proclaim the praises of Him who called you out of darkness into His marvelous light"* (1 Peter 2:9). The phrase *"His own special* (peripoiesis) *people"* is sometimes translated *"His own peculiar* (peripoiesis) *people."* "Peripoiesis" carries the sense of something of which a person has come into possession. Paul calls us the *"purchased possession"* (Ephesians 1:14). We are His! This is not a negative truth; it is a joyful, triumphant, exalting truth in which we rejoice. We are

His, and everything attached to us is His. There is nothing in or about our lives that is not under His ownership. The conclusion of the early Church was *"neither did anyone say that any of the things he possessed was his own, but they had all things in common"* (Acts 4:32).

Obligation

The members of the early Church did not view *"any of the things he possessed"* as personal possessions. If they did not own their possessions, who owned them? They knew Jesus owned everything they had, the context in which we must understand our passage. When the early Church came under persecution, they focused on the sovereignty of God! They understood God expressed His sovereignty in ownership. They amazingly used the personal pronoun *"Your"* eight times in their prayer response to the threat (Acts 4:24-30). They expressed God's ownership, *"Your servant David," "Your holy Servant Jesus," "Your hand," "Your purpose determined before to be done," "Your servants," "Your word," "Your hand,"* and *"Your holy Servant Jesus."*

Although the early Church recognized God's sovereign ownership, they also recognized His loving involvement. God was involved! God displayed His ownership in loving consideration. The early Church had a deep awareness of God's redemptive plan revealed through Jesus. They saw the suffering of Jesus as *"Your purpose determined before to be done."* The plan working in Jesus was also working in them. As Jesus belonged to the Father, so they belonged to Jesus! He was under no obligation as we usually understand obligation. We do not own God. We do not merit from Him, we have never earned a right to demand, and we should never have a sense of fairness or deserving. He is driven by love to include us in His plan!

Can we stand before God in the assurance that He needs

us? Have we earned a place in God's design? Can God survive without us? It is foolish to think or even suggest those thoughts. The angelic hosts could fulfill every task the Divine desires. His need for us is not in what we provide for His comfort; His need is in His love. God does not love us because He needs us; He needs us because He loves us. He delights in providing for us. He cares for us.

God's ownership gave the early Church security in life's difficulties. As long as God owned everything, all would be well. This security produced their unity and ability to share. No one held on to anything as if it were his. Each member of the early Church knew they owned nothing, and God who owned everything would replace everything they needed. This was Jesus' appeal in the Sermon on the Mount. Jesus gave the direct command, *"Do not worry"* (Matthew 6:25, 28, 31). The person who focuses on materialism, worries about clothing, food, water, or the physical aspects of life. What is the one basic premise concerning physical things? *"But seek first the Kingdom of God and His righteousness, and all these things shall be added to you"* (Matthew 6:33). However, this is all based on Jesus' previous statement, *"For your heavenly Father knows that you need all these things"* (Matthew 6:32).

The character of God's love drives, controls, and masters His ownership. He delights in providing for us. He is not a selfish king who demands service from his subjects. He wants to serve us. He does not need my provision to survive; He never lacks because I fail to provide. He owns all things, and graciously provides for me!

Opinion

Therefore, my life must become an expression of God's opinion to my world. How will anyone know what God is like unless they see a demonstration of it in and through my life? I become the physical expression of God's heart. When the early Church had *"one heart and one soul,"* their world could begin to grasp the loving heart of God. The Jewish world had lost this focus because of the constant weight of the law on them. The law was such a burden (Matthew 23:4), making them weary (Matthew 9:36). They could not see God reaching out to provide for them until the fullness of God's heart, demonstrated in Jesus, became visible in the early Church.

That is why the positive and negative illustrations given by Luke are so essential. Barnabas was the positive expression of God's heart! He demonstrated in the physical realm, an expression of the spiritual generosity and love of the redemptive Father. Luke writes, *"And Joses, who was also named Barnabas by the apostles (which is translated Son of Encouragement), a Levite of the country of Cyprus, having land, sold it, and brought the money and laid it at the apostles' feet"* (Acts 4:36). This verse emphasizes the completeness of the transaction expressing the heart. Therefore, the demonstration is not about money or land but reveals the heart of the Father. Barnabas became an expression of God's redemptive heart revealed in Jesus, who physically gave all because He had given all in the spiritual realm.

Ananias and Sapphira were negative examples of God's heart (Acts 5:1-11). The early Church included them in their fellowship. From all outward appearances, they were as committed as all other believers and considered a part of the attitude *"of those who believed were of one heart and one soul"* (Acts 4:32). The difficulty was with Ananias and Sapphira's physical demonstration of their spiritual state. Again, it was not about land or money. They revealed the deception of their heart's commitment in their deceit. But the physical expression always shows the spiritual condition of the heart. The heart of the Father, in my physical life, cannot be produced by law, obligation, or self-motivation, but results from *"those who believed."* Faith is "invoking the activity of the second party." The Father fills me with the Spirit of Jesus! He becomes the condition of my heart; I live in constant reliance on His action. His eyes become mine; His motives become mine. I am not the owner; He is! No wonder *"neither did anyone say that any of the things he possessed was his own but they had all things in common"* (Acts 4:32).

Acts 4:33

LOOKING RESURRECTED

"And with great power the apostles gave witness to the resurrection of the Lord Jesus. And great grace was upon them all" (Acts 4:33).

The members of the early Church were of **"one heart and one soul"** (Acts 4:32). This statement is significant as it describes the spiritual focus and unity of the believers. This powerful focus overruled and influenced their materialism. **"Neither did anyone say that any of the things he possessed was his own, but they had all things common"** (Acts 4:32). Their attitude toward materialism was a miracle on the level of other signs and wonders accomplished through the power of the Spirit. The following statement (verse 33) does not highlight the results of their approach to materialism, however, after this insert statement Luke writes, **"Nor was there anyone among them who lacked; for all who were possessors of lands or houses sold them, and brought the proceeds of the things that were sold"** (Acts 4:34). "Oude," translated *"Nor,"* is a continuative negative conjunction. *"Nor"* links with *"neither"* (Acts 4:32) connecting verses thirty-two and thirty-four.

Luke inserted verse thirty-three between the two verses to describe the early church's attitude toward materialism. It seems he wanted to be sure we knew that their spiritual witness, produced by the Spirit of God, created this attitude toward materialism. God unleashed the movement of the Spirit in them because of their attitude. *"And with great power the apostles gave witness to the resurrection of the Lord Jesus. And great grace was upon them all"* (Acts 4:33). The early Church was of *"one heart and one soul,"* causing what they believed (Acts 4:32) and shaping their attitude toward materialism (Acts 4:32, 34). But what did they believe? They believed in *"the resurrection of the Lord Jesus."*

We must understand that there was no requirement or obligation regarding materialism. The apostles forced no one to sell their property to join the early Church, and there was no indication the apostles expected or fostered such requirements. Their attitude toward materialism came from the same Spirit that produced the physical healings. The Spirit of God in the believer could not look at physical suffering without intervening, which resulted in signs and wonders. In like manner, this Spirit in the believers could not tolerate poverty and starvation. The Spirit of Jesus moved in the believers to make provision for those in need.

Perspective

The early Church believed in the resurrection of the Lord Jesus! The Holy Spirit used that belief to produce the perspective of these believers. Our passage verifies everything written in the previous chapters of Acts and is consistent with the continued truth throughout Luke's message. The central belief and message of the early Church was the resurrection of Jesus. Every sermon and exhortation throughout Acts highlight the truth of the resurrection. Think of how fresh this was in their lives. Most of them were in Jerusalem to participate in Jesus' crucifixion, a part of the crowd who screamed, "Crucify Him!" Peter addressed the gathering on Pentecost Day, fifty days after the crucifixion, during the Passover. The members of

Part 5: The Agreed Resolve

the early Church remembered the effect of Jesus' death when it impacted the city for days. They wondered if things would ever be normal again. Peter explained what God did in Christ and their participation in it. *"They were cut to the heart, and said to Peter and the rest of the apostles, 'Men and brethren, what shall we do?'"* (Acts 2:37). Repentance was the only answer. They rejected Jesus; they must now embrace Him! They crucified Jesus, but God resurrected Him from the dead! It was not enough that they believed the resurrection occurred, but they must embrace this Jesus who is alive and pressing their lives.

Peter's message at Solomon's Porch was even more pointed. A large crowd assembled after the healing of the lame beggar. Peter said, *"His Servant Jesus, whom you delivered up and denied in the presence of Pilate, when he was determined to let Him go. But you denied the Holy One and the Just, and asked for a murderer to be granted to you, and killed the Prince of life, whom God raised from the dead, of which we are witnesses"* (Acts 3:13-15). Peter reminded this crowd of their actions against Jesus. There was no other message!

Judas vacated his apostleship when he betrayed Jesus. After realizing his sin, Judas hanged himself. Before Pentecost, the Holy Spirit moved Peter and the 120 to replace Judas with one requirement only for the replacement. *"Therefore, of these men who have accompanied us all the time that the Lord Jesus went in and out among us, beginning from the baptism of John to that day when He was taken up from us, one of these must become a witness with us of the resurrection"* (Acts 1:21-22). The requirement was not that the person they would choose had witnessed Jesus in His resurrection presence, but that this person knew Jesus throughout His ministerial life. The resurrection was about this living Person, Jesus. They had to know Him!

The leaders of Israel were distressed by the ministry of the apostles. They were *"greatly disturbed that they taught the people and preached in Jesus the resurrection from the dead"*

(Acts 4:2). These leaders were not resistant to the apostles' preaching and teaching on the resurrection because the Pharisees and Sadducees had argued this doctrine forever. Their problem was not about the message of the early Church, but they hated the life of Jesus in the message. The apostles did not propose a theory. The Lord demonstrated Himself in and through them as they lived the resurrection! They looked resurrected! God resurrected them from the dead (Ephesians 2:1)!

The early Church lived the resurrected life, which created their attitude toward materialism. Therefore, Luke inserted the verse about the apostles' powerful witness of the resurrected Jesus between the two verses as an explanation of this attitude, making their treatment of materialism plausible. In a materialistic world, each person claims ownership of his property and guards it against others. The early Church did not have this attitude. The resurrection captured them, causing them to see through the eternal realm. Their lives were no longer dominated by physical comfort or swayed by safety and protection. The resurrected Jesus conquered death for them; they dwelt in an eternal realm, the resurrection. In the resurrected Christ, God resurrected the early Church!

After hearing of the threats of the leaders of Israel, these Christians did not pray for safety. They prayed, **"grant to Your servants that with all boldness they may speak Your word, by stretching out Your hand to heal, and that signs and wonders may be done through the name of Your holy Servant Jesus"** (Acts 4:29-30). How could this group become reckless about their physical existence? How did they reach a place where redeeming a world was more important than safety? It is not only that they saw the resurrected Lord, but they were seeing Him! They were living in the resurrection because of Him! They won their world by living the resurrected life. When they spoke of the resurrection of Jesus, the audience saw it! They looked resurrected!

Do I look resurrected, or do I cower in fear and cling to material things as if they save me? Do I live in anxiety and worry over physical issues that will not matter a hundred years from now? Why don't I look more resurrected in my attitude toward my materialism? Why do things capture my life, dictate my mood, and determine my relationships? I must encounter the resurrected Lord anew! He is my only chance. I do not need a theory about the resurrection; I need Jesus, the resurrected One!

Person

Who is the Person of the resurrection? *"And with great power the apostles gave witness to the resurrection of the Lord Jesus"* (Acts 4:33). All through the Book of Acts, the resurrection is always about the Person of Jesus! It is not about "an attesting of an event." They never bore witness to a fact or taught a doctrinal view. They did not propose a belief system or a new set of rules. There was a "Person" who conquered death. He was alive! They gave witness to this Person!

There are two facts about recognizing the Person of Jesus that have force in this setting. The first is the freshness of the early Church's encounter with the resurrected Lord. Most of them had experienced the crucifixion of Jesus, especially the 120 who lived in the disappointment of failed dreams until God filled them with the Spirit. They committed their lives to Jesus and the establishment of the Kingdom, but Jesus' death had devastated their dreams. The two men on the Emmaus Road said, *"We were hoping that it was He who was going to redeem Israel"* (Luke 24:21). These two men were overwhelmed with grief; they did not recognize Jesus when He stood before them (Luke 24:16).

The only thing that could remove the disappointment from those who grieved was an encounter with Jesus' resurrected

Person. There was no seminar, doctrine, theology, teaching, or preaching that could restore their hope. However, the Jesus they had believed in was now on the other side of the grave. Can you imagine the joy they felt as He spent 40 days with them? Luke calls this *"infallible proofs"* (Acts 1:3) translated from the Greek word "tekmerion," used in this verse only once in the New Testament. Dr. Luke was a scientist who would use this word, which means "proof beyond question." This proof is in the Person of Jesus. After 40 days of interaction with Jesus, the disciples did not question the resurrection. Jesus was real to them!

Pentecost was the second fact in recognizing the Person of Jesus. Pentecost marshaled the reality of His presence "in" them. What was real "to" them became real "in" them, the driving force of their witness. God raised Jesus from the dead, and this raised from the dead Jesus now indwelt them. He was as real now as He had been before His crucifixion. They witnessed to the resurrected Jesus living in them; He demonstrated Himself through their lives. Their witness launched the persecution of the early Church. ***"They taught the people and preached in Jesus the resurrection from the dead"*** (Acts 4:2). The Greek word *"en,"* translated "in," is the middle concept between "into" (eis) and "from" (ek). "Eis" and "ek" are movement terms depicting action, but "en" is a fixed state of dwelling. The resurrection moved from theory or academic fact to the state of being contained in a Person. Jesus became the resurrection. To witness about the resurrection was to witness about Jesus. To witness about Jesus was to witness about the resurrection. They were the same!

Those who recognized the Person of Jesus did not give witness to "an actual event." None of the apostles could testify to seeing Jesus' resurrection. Many Jews witnessed Lazarus' resurrection. Jesus ***"cried with a loud voice, 'Lazarus, come forth!' And he who had died came out bound hand and foot with grave clothes, and his face was wrapped with a cloth. Jesus said to them, 'Loose him, and let him go'"*** (John 11:43-44), but

Part 5: The Agreed Resolve

no one saw the resurrection of Jesus. The Trinity God involved mankind in every event in redemptive history. God used Mary and Joseph, human beings, at the birth of Christ. John the Baptist baptized Jesus, which facilitated God filling Jesus with His Spirit, a sign promised to John about the Messiah (John 1:32-34). Peter said, **"You have taken by lawless hands, have crucified, and put to death"** (Acts 2:23). Therefore, human hands wrought the crucifixion of Jesus. The disciples stood by and watched the ascension of Jesus (Acts 1:10), but humanity had no part in His resurrection. The stone of the tomb was rolled back, not to let Jesus out, but to let us in. No one saw Jesus depart the grave, and neither did any human eye behold the resurrection.

Because no human witnessed God raising Jesus from the dead, how do we know this is true? We have seen the resurrected Person! I believe the plan of God determined this. He knew the resurrection would capture us, and preachers would have sermon series on the resurrection, spending hours describing the activities around it. But this is not about an event; it is about the resurrected Person! How the resurrection happened is not our focus; Jesus is our focus. He is alive! The witness of the early Church was the story of the living Jesus, causing the Sanhedrin to threaten them. The threat was not that the apostles cease teaching and preaching the resurrection because the Sanhedrin did not care about this theology. As the Sanhedrin spoke among themselves, they said, **"But so that it spreads no further among the people, let us severely threaten them, that from now on they speak to no man in this name. So they called them and commanded them not to speak at all nor teach in the name of Jesus"** (Acts 4:17-18). The persecution on the early Church was not the resurrection, but was the resurrected Jesus!

The witness of the early Church was not "an activity exhibit." The resurrected Lord was living and moving through them to accomplish signs and wonders. The healing of the lame beggar, which triggered the persecution of the early Church, is a testimony to the power of Jesus' name. The prayer of the early Church in response to the threats of the Sanhedrin is significant. ***"Now, Lord, look on their threats, and grant to Your servants that with all boldness they may speak Your word, by stretching out Your hand to heal, and that signs and wonders may be done through the name of Your holy Servant Jesus"*** (Acts 4:29-30). Signs and wonders gave evidence to Jesus' presence among them, but that was not their witness of the resurrection. Signs and wonders attracted the attention of Jerusalem, so the witness of His resurrection could be proclaimed. However, the theme of their witness was not miracles but the resurrected Lord. If signs and wonders enamor us, we are like the child at Christmas, focused on the wrapping paper while ignoring the gift. Once again, the risen Lord draws us back. There is nothing beyond His person!

Platform

We must see this truth through the element of "platform." Applause resounds throughout the stadium for the baseball star who hits a home run. No one applauds the baseball field, the bat, or even the ball; they praise the athlete! The crowd sees all those things like the player's platform. The stage is the actor's platform, but no one applauds the stage; the audience applauds the performers. The early Church was careful in their witness, not allowing the focus to shift from the Person to the platform. They did not witness to signs, wonders, or miracles, the platform of the resurrected Person.

The early Church focused on Jesus, the resurrected Person, and would not allow materialism to grip them. The Jews of the Old Covenant loved materialism. The temple was the dwelling place of God, but the Jews made the buildings their center of attention. The temple ceremonies dominated their attention,

Part 5: The Agreed Resolve

while the person of God lost themselves in their worldly activities, which were required by law. Their self-centered hearts reverted to their achievements. However, even their materialistic and physical results were holograms at the end of all things.

Luke gives a classic example of this physical achievement in Acts Chapter 8. Simon lived in the city of Samaria and astonished the people with his magic, *"claiming that he was someone great"* (Acts 8:9), manipulating the people based on the physical. When Simon was converted and saw the apostles place their hands-on people as they received the Holy Spirit, he wanted to buy this ability (Acts 8:18). The apostles rebuked him for submerging himself in the physical pattern, witnessing to his own doing and the physical expression of power. Jesus will not be secondary to the platform of our materialistic gain.

Do I have a problem with my prayer life? I was sitting with a gathering of senior adults for prayer. Is it not good for senior adults to focus on prayer? The answer lies in their prayer focus, ten requests for themselves. Prayer can become a manipulation of God to foster my physical needs. Let us not argue about the right or wrong of their requests, because it is not wrong to make requests of God. However, we must not allow our needs to dominate our attention, becoming our witness instead of the resurrected Lord.

Paul gives a startling truth when he recites his birthright as a Jew. He said that he was *"circumcised the eighth day, of the stock of Israel, of the tribe of Benjamin, a Hebrew of the Hebrews; concerning the law, a Pharisee; concerning zeal, persecuting the church; concerning the righteousness which is in the law, blameless"* (Philippians 3:5-6). Paul offered this list to prove his ability and right to brag about the platform more than anyone else (Philippians 3:4). *"But what things were gain to me, these I have counted loss for Christ. Yet indeed I also count all things loss for the excellence of the knowledge of Christ Jesus my Lord, for whom I have suffered the loss of all things, and count them as rubbish, that I may gain Christ and be found in Him, not having my own righteousness, which is from the law, but that which is through faith in Christ, the righteousness which is from God by faith; that I may know Him and the power of His resurrection, and the fellowship of His sufferings, being formed to His death, if by any means, I may attain the resurrection from the dead"* (Philippians 3:7-11). It is the testimony of a person who sees materialism or physical things as a platform, but never loses sight of the actor on the stage, the resurrected Jesus!

The physical and the spiritual are not at war, but each is important in the function of life. The physical and spiritual accomplish a role in the fulfillment of God's plan for us. If there is a problem, it is in maintaining the position. The spiritual demonstrates itself on the physical platform, valid for the Christian and non-Christian, neither having a choice in the matter. You cannot be Christian and focus on the physical. The early Church focused on Jesus, and their witness to the resurrection of the Lord Jesus possessed them. In being captured by Him, they maintained all materialism as the platform for their witness. The physical resurrection became a platform to highlight Jesus.

Mastering materialism is an impossible task. Materialism is a survivor and will find a way to dominate you. Your problem is not materialism, but your focus on Jesus. Knowing Jesus will liberate us from materialism. Let's come back to Jesus!

Acts 4:33

WITH GREAT POWER

"And with great power the apostles gave witness to the resurrection of the Lord Jesus. And great grace was upon them all" (Acts 4:33).

Many Christians seem to long for the mighty days of the early Church. God's power was evident through the early Church's activities. Evangelism was not a strategy or methodology for the church, but it flowed through every encounter with their world. Winning the world was the nature of their existence as their daily lives touched the world with the power of God. No one was neutral; they either accepted or rejected Jesus and His nature. The power that flowed through the believers existed in the presence of the risen Jesus! As the early Church witnessed about the resurrection of Jesus, He was present and manifested Himself.

Our passage reads, ***"And with great power the apostles gave witness to the resurrection of the Lord Jesus. And great grace was upon them all"*** (Acts 4:33). The Greek word "dunamis," translated ***"power,"*** creates our word for "dynamite." The focus of "dunamis" is on the achievement or action of this power. There is the resource, and there is what the resource accomplishes. "Dunamis" highlights what the resource accomplishes, in contrast with "ischus." "Ischus" focuses on the ability while "dunamis" focuses on the achievement of the ability.

All of Scripture convinces us of the "ischus" power of God. Peter and John returned to the early Church, reporting the threats of the Sanhedrin. Speaking and teaching in the name of Jesus would bring an end to their lives. They immediately went to prayer. Their prayer begins with, **"Lord, You are God, who made heaven and earth and the sea, and all that is in them"** (Acts 4:24). The Greek word "Despotes" is translated **"Lord, You are God."** "Despotes" is our English word "despot." The early Church did not use this word as a negative term. God is a "tyrant, absolute ruler, a dictator!" Residing in Him is absolute sovereign power. It is a focus on "ischus."

The term "despot" is either negative or positive, based on the action (dunamis) of that power. Motive determines the effect. If God is love, we are safe; if He is not love, we are in trouble. Regardless of the conclusion concerning His motive, the truth remains that God is all-powerful (ischus), and His power affects (dunamis) our lives. In reality, we do not know the immensity of the "ischus" of God. We view the activity (dunamis) of His power and want to measure it. His creative activity displays His immense resource of power. The early Church experienced physical miracles, which were a display of His power. Although this is a physical measurement, how do we measure the spiritual power of God? The transformation in the lives of the early Church gave witness to the redeeming power of God. They gave **"witness to the resurrection of the Lord Jesus."** Their lives displayed the resurrected Lord!

The word "dunamis" is used many times in the first four chapters of Acts. It is in the promise Jesus gave to the apostles during His resurrection appearance. On the day He ascended to heaven, He said, **"But you shall receive power** (dunamis) **when the Holy Spirit has come upon you; and you shall be witnesses to Me in Jerusalem, and in all Judea and Samaria, and to the end of the earth"** (Acts 1:8). They will not receive the resource (ischus) of the Spirit apart from the Spirit. They

Part 5: The Agreed Resolve

cannot control this resource or use it as they choose. The Holy Spirit, who is the "ischus," will actively move through their lives (dunamis).

When God fulfilled this promise, and the power of the Holy Spirit came upon the apostles, Peter explained what happened. He cried, **"Men of Israel, hear these words: Jesus of Nazareth, a Man attested by God to you by miracles** (dunamis), **wonders, and signs which God did through Him in your midst, as you yourselves also know"** (Acts 2:22). Peter explained to the Jews who had gathered that the outpouring of the Holy Spirit on Pentecost is Jesus. The same Spirit of God (ischus), moving through (dunamis) Jesus, was now moving through them. He concludes that each of us can have this same "dunamis" moving through us!

One of these moments of "dunamis" was the miracle of the lame beggar's healing. Peter took hold of the beggar's right hand, lifted him to his feet, and said, **"In the name of Jesus Christ of Nazareth, rise up and walk"** (Acts 3:6). The temple crowd, gathered on Solomon's Porch, was amazed. Peter was horrified when he realized the crowd thought he was responsible for this miracle. He cried out, **"Men of Israel, why do you marvel at this? Or why look so intently at us, as though by our own power** (dunamis) **or godliness we had made this man walk"** (Acts 3:12)? Peter knew he did not control the "ischus," to perform the "dunamis" of such a miracle. He proclaimed the resurrected Jesus as the one who was the "ischus" and displayed the "dunamis" through the healed beggar.

Peter's proclamation that Jesus was the source of the beggar's healing disturbed the leaders of Israel (Acts 4:2). In court, they demanded, **"By what power** (dunamis) **or by what name have you done this"** (Acts 4:7)? The accusation against the apostles rested on "what was the resource (ischus) flowing through them (dunamis). The "ischus" is only in Jesus, the Resurrected One! The threats of the Sanhedrin focused on this flow. They could not deny the activity (dunamis) because they could see the result in the healed beggar. They demanded the apostles cease to be an expression of the "dunamis" of the resurrected Lord!

Now we come to our passage, ***"And with great power the apostles gave witness to the resurrection of the Lord Jesus"*** (Acts 4:33). The power (ischus) was the resurrected Lord; He gave an expression of Himself through the apostles (dunamis). They were filled with a resource that was not theirs and participated in a demonstration of that resource that they could not do, the typical Christian experience of the early Church. They lived beyond their resource and ability, and what Jesus displayed through them was supernatural. They did not propose a belief system, new theology, or philosophy of eternal life. They offered an amalgamation! Human life and the Divine life could merge and become one. The resource of God (ischus) could move through (dunamis) the life of man, displaying a new creature!

In our passage, Luke calls this power ***"great."*** It is the Greek word "megas," which refers to something that is beyond the ordinary. In the Book of Acts, "ordinary" is not considered Christian. Jesus referred to John the Baptist as the greatest man ever been born of woman (Matthew 11:11). But He went on to relate that any person living in the "dunamis" of the Spirit is greater than he. It is a reflection on the resource (ischus) of Jesus producing power (dunamis) in our lives. If we live out of our own "ischus," we are ordinary. Christianity is a call to the ***"great power,"*** and a display of the resurrected Jesus through our lives!

The apostles presented in their lives several elements in the context of our passage. These elements are not the "ischus" that is strictly in Jesus, and they are not the "dunamis" that can only come from Jesus. These elements are the stage on which Jesus can display His resurrection. The Spirit of God aids and participates with us to produce these elements, requiring our active involvement for the Spirit to move in and through us.

One of these elements is INTEGRITY! The English

dictionary suggests two meanings for the word "integrity." The first is "the quality of being honest and having strong moral principles," meaning "moral uprightness." The second is "the state of being whole and undivided." The combination of these two elements affects the physical and spiritual. If the "ischus" of Jesus flows through us (dunamis), the instrument (us) maintains the element of integrity.

Materialism

Luke now turns to the early Church's view of materialism. Their approach was *"neither did anyone say that any of the things he possessed was his own, but they had all things in common"* (Acts 4:32). He expands this idea saying, *"Nor was there anyone among them who lacked; for all who were possessors of lands or houses sold them, and brought the proceeds of the things that were sold"* (Acts 4:34). Luke sandwiched the verse of our study (Acts 4:33) between these two verses. The power of God flowed through the apostles and gave witness to the resurrection revealed in their attitude and approach to materialism. Then Luke illustrated this with a positive and a negative example.

The Spirit of God that flowed through Barnabas produced a *"Son of Encouragement"* (Acts 4:36). He sold his land and brought the money to the early Church, where the apostles distributed it to the needs of the people. In this manner, the Spirit of God displayed Himself through Barnabas' encouragement. The Spirit of God through Ananias and Sapphira resulted in death (Acts 5:1-11). They sold their land but kept part of the money for themselves. Peter reminded them they had a right to sell their land and keep the money. The problem was "integrity" in their materialism. They said they gave all their proceeds, but had not. They were deceptive! When a person experiences the active movement of God's Spirit, but is deceptive it results in death. The Spirit's righteousness and the unrighteousness of deception cannot survive in the same being.

The Spirit of God caused the early Church's attitude toward materialism; however, their response to this attitude opened the door for a movement of "dunamis" through them. We do not appeal for generosity in giving; we do not propose a health and wealth gospel. Our concern is for integrity with our materialism. Financial integrity is an absolute must for the *"great power"* of God to give *"witness to the resurrection of the Lord Jesus."*

One issue of materialism is "ownership." Luke wrote, **"Neither did anyone say that any of the things he possessed was his own"** (Acts 4:32). The core of their belief was in God's sovereignty. God is the Creator of all things (Acts 4:24); therefore, how could they claim anything as their own? Ownership bespeaks responsibility and control. They recognized they had responsibility for the existence of nothing and had no right to control, causing their openness for the *"great power"* of God to give *"witness to the resurrection of the Lord Jesus."*

The second issue of materialism is "opinion." The early Church was of *"one heart and one soul"* (Acts 4:32), referring to the believers' unity with Jesus. Their beings linked with Jesus caused their harmonious agreement with each other. This Divine mindset dictated their belief toward materialism. They owned nothing; they were stewards under God's direction and maintained His opinion of materialism. Jesus always sees the physical as a platform for redemption. The use of materialism for any other reason was to fight against His design. I want to merge with Him and think as He thinks, allowing my materialism to be an avenue for the *"great power"* of God to give *"witness to the resurrection of the Lord Jesus."*

The third issue of materialism is "obligation." Everyone who sold property brought the proceeds to the apostles, **"and they distributed to each as anyone had need"** (Acts 4:35). The early Church had a sense of obligation for their fellowman. They recognized those who *"had need,"* however, simply recognizing those with needs was not enough. They had the mind of Christ. Many people give to others because it makes them feel better, which is not the mind of Christ! Others give because it benefits them financially, which is also not the mind of Christ. When we merge with Jesus, we discover His mind. Merging my life with Jesus brings the *"great power"* of God, giving *"witness to the resurrection of the Lord Jesus."*

Morality

If we have integrity, we have honesty. The problem that destroys honesty is self-centeredness. If a helpless person does not admit he is helpless, he must use and manipulate every situation to benefit his life. What else can he do? He has to support himself. Again, we see this in the context of our passage (Acts 4:33) as Luke gives a positive and a negative illustration. The positive example is Barnabas, who embraced his helplessness and experienced the resource of the resurrected Lord. With God's resource, he could afford to be generous, not only in materialistic things but also in attitude. His generosity became so dominant in his life that the apostles called him *"Son of Encouragement."*

Luke's negative illustration is Ananias and Sapphira. They sold a possession and were under no obligation to give the money to the apostles. They could keep it all or part of it for themselves without criticism from others. The problem for them was their lack of honesty. They said they gave the full selling price, but they lied and kept part for their use. They were self-centered or self-sourcing. They did not embrace their helplessness; they did not rest in Jesus as their source. They manipulated the circumstance for personal benefit. They wanted the best they could get from the spiritual world, the Christian faith, but Ananias and Sapphira also wanted the best they could get from their self-sourcing. They were deceptive! Deception produces death!

Luke contrasts the dishonesty of Ananias and Sapphira with the honesty of the apostles under the threat of persecution. The Sanhedrin warned them, *"not to speak at all nor teach in the name of Jesus"* (Acts 4:18). Their action was an issue of life and death, not about their reputation or financial gain. A helpless man who does not admit his helplessness will, of necessity, manipulate the scene for his advantage. He will try to turn the circumstances to his benefit. The apostles' answer to the Sanhedrin's threat was, *"For we cannot but speak the things which we have seen and heard"* (Acts 4:20). This statement reveals their integrity. They were honest! They experienced the presence of the resurrected Jesus for 40 days, a presence so powerful Luke labeled it *"infallible proofs"* (Acts 1:3). The apostles received the indwelt presence of the resurrected Lord at Pentecost. All they had known of Jesus externally, they now knew internally. They merged with Jesus; everything He promised became a reality. Now the Sanhedrin wanted them to deny it all; they were never to speak of Jesus again. Their integrity would not allow such deception! Honesty with themselves and each other was their only response!

In the days that followed, after pondering their situation, the early Church continued in honesty. They were helpless in the face of their world; they embraced their helplessness and cried out to God, who is sovereign (Acts 4:24). Their confidence in the power of the resurrected Lord created their honesty. They needed not to manipulate the situation for survival, protection, or personal benefit. They relied entirely on Jesus, and because of this total honesty *"with great power the apostles gave witness to the resurrection of the Lord Jesus."* The power of the resurrected Lord flowed through their lives in ministry, creating this integrity, without which they might have the same results as Ananias and Sapphira. We must respond as the

Part 5: The Agreed Resolve

early Church did! Without the power of His presence, ministry becomes programs, maintenance, and crowd manipulation. His presence only operates on the platform of integrity.

Mastery

One greater than themselves mastered the members of the early Church. This enslavement to something beyond themselves was not without choice. They were committed to Jesus, the resurrected Lord. They would never again be in a Garden of Gethsemane asleep during prayer, and would never again run at the sight of threatening soldiers in the night hour. Christ, their Master, was so massive in their lives He mastered them. It was the merger. His nature caused what they thought, how they felt. They had His heart, mind, and emotions.

We see how Jesus mastered Peter and John in our passage. After a night in jail, the apostles must have imagined the worst of circumstances as the soldiers dragged them to the court site. After the crucifixion of Jesus, what would the Sanhedrin do to them? However, the boldness with which they spoke of Jesus caused the Sanhedrin to marvel (Acts 4:13). As Peter and John responded, there was no doubt in the minds of the Sanhedrin that Jesus was present in their midst! When the Sanhedrin demanded that Peter and John never preach or teach in the name of Jesus again, they replied, ***"Whether it is right in the sight of God to listen to you more than to God, you judge"*** (Acts 4:20).

We must now look at our hearts. We are helpless! Will we embrace and live in this helplessness so that Jesus can be our only resource? If we will not, our self-centeredness will manipulate every circumstance for our benefit. Our self-centered hearts will drown out the voice of Jesus as we adjust and compromise under pressure for our survival. We have no other choice if we have only our helplessness. If man merges with Jesus' nature, Jesus takes that man to a new level of living. This commitment to Him and Him alone allowed the *"great power"* in the apostles as they witnessed to the resurrection of the Lord Jesus. Commitment to Jesus is the platform on which God manifests His power. The early Church experienced this and changed their world.

Jesus calls each of us to experience a new commitment. When left alone, we rely on programs, organizational structure, and marketing schemes. We depend on our talents, education, and professionalism. We become mastered by psychological techniques, appeals to self, and our image. Jesus wants us to know the spiritual results of the early Church and experience the spiritual realities of their hearts. They knew Jesus. They did not know about Him; they knew Him.

This resurrected Jesus mastered their lives, and their materialism was at His disposal. They merged with His mind and heart until as Jesus lived free of the domination of materialism, so did they! **"Neither did anyone say that any of the things he possessed was his own"** (Acts 4:32). They possessed integrity that would not allow them to compromise truth. They would not shape their belief to fit the popular view of their day. They were uncompromising in the presentation of His resurrection presence. They were so mastered by Him and committed to Him that they became a platform for His demonstration. It was in this context that **"with great power the apostles gave witness to the resurrection of the Lord Jesus"** (Acts 4:33).

The demonstration of Jesus in the lives of the early Church has not changed for our day. It is as true for us as it was for them. Jesus has not changed; we will see Jesus again. Our families are desperate for such a demonstration through us. Please be mastered by Jesus' integrity and speak His truth to your world.

Acts 4:33

GREAT POWER - INVOLVEMENT

> *"And with great power the apostles gave witness to the resurrection of the Lord Jesus. And great grace was upon them all" (Acts 4:33).*

There is no new information in our passage. **"And with great power the apostles gave witness to the resurrection of the Lord Jesus"** (Acts 4:33). We are not astonished by the Holy Spirit's power demonstrated in miracles, boldness, and unity. This power was expected and assumed after the fulness of Pentecost. We are not shocked by the presence of God's power; we would be more shocked if the power were not present. After the early Church heard the threats of the Sanhedrin, they went to prayer. **"And when they had prayed, the place where they were assembled together was shaken; and they were all filled with the Holy Spirit, and they spoke the word of God with boldness"** (Acts 4:31). The "power of God" summarizes this report.

Through the **"witness to the resurrection,"** the church grew and impacted the city of Jerusalem. Everyone experienced the presence of Jesus within the witness. The witness was not telling about, but experiencing again, the reality of Jesus, which brought effective life change to those who crucified Jesus. No one could ignore the power of God flowing through the witness. If a person embraced such a witness, they were changed forever!

Therefore, as we view our passage, we wonder why Luke

repeated what, in essence, he had already said several times. Why does he waste the space trying to impress us with what has already gripped us? The value of the statement is not in its content but its location in the passage. Let me remind you of the opening verse of the paragraph: *"Now the multitude of those who believed were of one heart and one soul; neither did anyone say that any of the things he possessed was his own, but they had all things in common"* (Acts 4:32). It is a powerful statement of the early Church's perspective on materialism. Luke continues this explanation but not in the next verse. He writes, *"Nor was there anyone among them who lacked; for all who were possessors of lands or houses sold them, and brought the proceeds of the things that were sold"* (Acts 4:34). In the following verses, Luke gives both positive and negative illustrations concerning this view of materialism. You must note the words *"neither"* and *"nor,"* which connects verses 32 and 34. Why would Luke separate these two verses with verse 33, which is our passage?

"And with great power the apostles gave witness to the resurrection of the Lord Jesus" is surrounded by the early Church's view of materialism, and we must see it in that light. The early Church's generosity and their release of ownership of material things demonstrated the power of God's Spirit! Under the inspiration of the Holy Spirit, Luke communicated a spiritual truth. We do not demonstrate the power of God in isolation or apart from the interaction of human beings. The redemptive heart of God is redemptive through the human avenue. Redeemed humanity is the platform on which God acts to bring redemption to fallen humanity.

This truth is not new! A human being got us into the curse of sin (Romans 5:12); a human being must get us out of the curse of sin. The difficulty is that the redemptive human being must not be a part of the sin's curse (Romans 5:18). God looked for a righteous human being, but He could not find one (Romans 3:23). So, God became Man! Through Christ Jesus,

Part 5: The Agreed Resolve

the Man, God's redemptive heart, became active in our lives. Jesus, the Man, is the platform for the redemptive act of God toward humanity. Jesus extended redemption into the lives of the believers involved in God's nature, and they became an extension of God's redemptive heart. Therefore, Luke sandwiches the ***"great power"*** of God flowing through the ***"witness to the resurrection of the Lord Jesus"*** within the practical arena of material things.

We must keep a proper perspective in this discussion. The focus is on the power of God, not on the activity of man. It is the power of God that redeems, transforms, and restores. If we lose sight of this, all is lost. But our passage reminds us that God chose to manifest this redemptive power on the platform of human lives. There are several elements, within the context of our passage, present in the lives of the apostles. Jesus, the Man, is the platform for the redemptive action of God toward humanity. Jesus extended redemption into the lives of the believers involved in God's nature, and they became an extension of God's redemptive heart. The first element is INTEGRITY! We see this portrayed in the positive and negative illustrations given by Luke. Barnabas sold his land and generously gave it to the apostles to use for the early Church. He became a ***"Son of Encouragement,"*** an avenue of the redemptive heart of God (Acts 4:36). Ananias and Sapphira sold a possession; they reported giving all the proceeds but kept back some for themselves. Their deceitfulness became an avenue of destruction and ruin in their lives (Acts 5:1-11). God demonstrates His redemptive heart through the person of integrity!

The second essential element is INVOLVEMENT! Total surrender, consecration, total commitment, yielded, death to self, or crucifixion all are words used to express this element.

Complete Involvement

The expression, "I do my part, then God does His part," does not apply to involvement. I express the involvement element in "I have no part." In other words, I have nothing to contribute. It is difficult for most people to grasp because we focus on "doing." If language demands an expression of "my part," doing nothing is required, not a focus on inactivity but on sourcing. I have no part in sourcing, the activity, and yet my involvement is necessary. The best illustration of this concept is "the hand in a glove." Although this illustration may lack the actual saturation, integration, or merger of God and man in the activity of life, it does demonstrate involvement in the action without involvement in the sourcing. A glove is lifeless and useless; it sits without expression or movement; it has no energy or life. Suddenly a hand enters its existence and fills the glove. The glove begins to act with power in meaningful activity. How strong is the glove? It is as strong as the hand that indwells it! The glove does nothing and yet is involved in everything! The one need of the glove is that the hand fills it.

Our passage reveals the reality of the element. Everywhere in the context, there is assumed a complete involvement. Luke introduces our passage with, **"Now the multitude of those who believed were of one heart and one soul"** (Acts 4:32), an expression of completeness. The main verb of this sentence is **"were,"** a translation of the Greek word "eimi" a term of "being" not of "doing." It is an imperfect, indicative verb, describing a state of being that occurs in the past with no assessment of the completed state. In other words, it continues into the present. It is a state of **"one heart and one soul,"** Luke's description of their "completeness." Each person engaged completely in believing, and they linked with others completely involved in believing.

Part 5: The Agreed Resolve

Their belief is a repeat of the *"one accord"* that erupted from their lives in prayer (Acts 4:24). Peter and John reported to the early believers the threats of the Sanhedrin. They responded in prayer, focused on the sovereignty of God! They experienced the resurrection appearance of their crucified Lord. His presence completely engulfed them through Pentecost, and they all prayed the same prayer. Complete belief brought complete unity, giving complete expression to their complete focus on the resurrected Lord.

We have already discovered how this affected their view of materialism. Luke records, *"Neither did anyone say that any of the things he possessed was his own"* (Acts 4:32). The completeness of their surrender is evident. It was not a spiritual belief that had no expression in the physical. The spiritual and the physical came together in these believers as the Spirit of Jesus completely overwhelmed them. Perhaps this is the most verifiable evidence of their completeness.

The Rich Young Ruler realized he was not complete. He thought there was maybe one more thing he should do. Jesus told him that if he wanted eternal life, he must keep all the commandments. The young man quickly assured Jesus he had kept the commandments since his youth. So, what was it that hindered his completeness? His question was, *"What do I still lack?"* (Matthew 19:20). Jesus' answered, *"If you want to be perfect* (complete)*, go, sell what you have and give to the poor, and you will have treasure in heaven, and come, follow Me"* (Matthew 19:21). Although the Rich Young Ruler walked away sorrowfully, the early Church demonstrated their completeness by surrendering their materialism.

We can see this completeness in the negative and positive illustrations Luke gives following our passage. Barnabas becomes an illustration of complete involvement. He sold his land and brought the money to the apostles for the purpose of ministry. Because of his generous spirit, they named him,

"Son of Encouragement" (Acts 4:36). The negative illustration is heartbreaking. Ananias and Sapphira destroy and bring death to their lives, a direct result of incompleteness in their involvement, although they said they were involved. They did the same activities as the other believers. Even in the realm of materialism, they sold their possession and brought the money to the apostles (Acts 5:1). They gave an appearance of completeness, but they were incomplete, holding back part of the money for themselves. They lied and were not completely involved in truth. Instead of showing God's power through them and giving witness to the resurrection of the Lord Jesus, they demonstrated death.

When does the power of God display itself on the stage of our lives? God manifested His power on the platform of the apostles' lives, containing the element of "complete involvement." God ceases to demonstrate His power the moment this platform was not present. Christianity is never a part-time participation. We can never contain God's power by keeping a schedule of activities at church. God displays His power in complete involvement of the complete life. Jesus is Lord of all, or He is not Lord at all!

Core of Involvement

If we only have a surface view of the involvement of the early Church, we might get confused. These believers were involved in spiritual disciplines. Prayer was a consistent activity of their gatherings (Acts 4:31). They focused on proclaiming the Scriptures in boldness (Acts 4:31). There were many miracles, signs, and wonders, which they prayed would continue (Acts 4:30). They were consistent in evangelism, affecting their world and transforming lives in the power of Jesus' name. Our passage reveals their change in focus concerning materialism (Acts 4).

Part 5: The Agreed Resolve

Although all of these issues are present and of value, they are not the core of the early Church's involvement. Our passage gives us their focus, *"And with great power the apostles gave witness to the resurrection of the Lord Jesus"* (Acts 4:33). The core of their involvement was *"the Lord Jesus,"* giving witness through the miracles, signs, and wonders. Their bold proclamation of the Word verified Jesus. There was power manifested in their witness, but it was because of this Person! We cannot sidestep Jesus; He is never secondary. There is no substitute for His Presence.

The context of our passage will verify this truth. Listen again to the early Church's prayer: *"For truly against YOUR holy Servant Jesus, whom YOU anointed, both Herod and Pontius Pilate, with the Gentiles and the people of Israel, were gathered together, to do whatever YOUR hand and YOUR purpose determined before to be done. Now, Lord, look on their threats, and grant to YOUR servants that with all boldness they may speak YOUR word, by stretching out YOUR hand to heal, and that signs and wonders may be done through the name of YOUR holy Servant Jesus"* (Acts 4:27-30). Carefully note the pronouns! The core of their involvement is with Jesus, and they will not deviate from this involvement.

One of the battles the early Church fought with the Jewish Christians was their desire to add to Jesus. They followed the apostle Paul from place to place, proposing that His message about Jesus was right but not complete. They wanted to add specific Jewish laws to Jesus to make it complete. The Gospel message would not tolerate such an addition. The core of their involvement was Jesus alone, also valid for today. The message is not Jesus plus counseling, Jesus plus church attendance, Jesus plus the sacraments, Jesus plus Scripture reading, or Jesus plus being good. It is just Jesus! Each of the additions has its place, but they are not our focus. Jesus is our total involvement. Other things only have value because of Him!

When does the power of God display itself on the stage of our lives? It only happens when Jesus is the core of our involvement. We must not mix anything else with Him. Christianity is not a mixture; it is a single ingredient; it is Jesus! He is the platform on which God displays His power, and changes our world!

Certainty of Involvement

The context of our passage is the statement concerning *"those who believe"* (Acts 4:32). We might conclude that the early Church was simply in agreement about specific theological facts. They witnessed the crucifixion and the resurrected Jesus, and these events thoroughly convinced them. Therefore, their involvement in the events of the past caused their belief. Did they develop a doctrine around these events and persuade others of this belief system? That was not the case!

The event that decided the matter was Pentecost. The living Jesus came back from the dead and now lived in them. They did not proclaim an event, theology, or information; they presented a Person. The Person of Jesus Christ lived in them and caused the certainty of their involvement. We have defined faith or belief as "invoking the activity of the Second Party!" It is the consistent attitude or response of a person who refuses to be sourced by the first party (themselves). Jesus captured them; He moved in their lives; they merged with Him. Jesus was not a belief system, although they believed in Him. He was not a fact but a reality of their lives. They merged with Jesus until moment by moment He sourced their lives. They thought like Him, felt like Him, and had His desires.

When does the power of God display itself on the stage of our lives? It happens when we have a spiritual and physical involvement with the living Person of Jesus. The merger involvement is the platform for His display, not a performance, but a moment by moment interaction. We do not focus on

Part 5: The Agreed Resolve

events such as preaching or miracles, but we allow the power of God to flow through us, producing the essence of our lives. We have "sonship" living! We have the DNA of God's presence and produce His image. What a wonder!

Acts 4:33

GREAT POWER - INDULGENT

"And with great power the apostles gave witness to the resurrection of the Lord Jesus. And great grace was upon them all" (Acts 4:33).

The word "indulgent" is a negative term for most of us. It alludes to a parent who allows their child to do as he pleases without consequences, which we call "spoiled." No one approves of this and certainly would not accuse God of spoiling His children. However, let me quote the dictionary definition for indulgent, "having or indicating a tendency to be overly generous to or lenient with someone." The word originates from early sixteenth-century French or Latin. The French verb "indulgere" means "to give free rein to," which is not positive or negative.

If we take the positive view of the word, may we consider God "indulgent?" ***"But God demonstrates His own love toward us, in that while were still sinners, Christ died for us"*** (Romans 5:8). Is God's love not indulgent? A standard definition of "grace" is "the undeserved blessings of God freely bestowed on man." Every person in the human race knows the blessings of God. Paul declared Jesus the Creator of all things. Then He said, ***"And He is before all things, and in Him all things consist"*** (Colossians 1:17). ***"Consist"*** is translated from the Greek word, "sunistemi." "Sun" means "together with," and "histemi" means "to set." Jesus is the creator, and He holds all things together,

Part 5: The Agreed Resolve

sustaining what He made! God maintains the universal order so that everyone knows the generous indulgence of God.

The indulgence of God sustains the order of society. The sinful state of man would destroy human life if it were not for God's restraining power. Furthermore, God's prevenient grace has intervened in the life of every person. God gives us a conscience to know the difference between right and wrong, truth and falsehood, justice and injustice, and the awareness that we are accountable to Him and each other! Does this not explain His indulgence?

How do we describe the indulgence of God in the forgiveness of sin? The reality of God's forgiveness is a provision for every person, whether or not they embrace it. In the death of Jesus, God gave every person a position in Christ Jesus. We were chosen in Him, predestined to adoption as sons in Him, redeemed through His blood in Him, and accepted in Him (Ephesians 1:3-14). Thousands of people will ignore and reject their position; they will never know the full redemptive love of God. Why would God make such a provision knowing the mass rebellion of humanity? Does this not explain His indulgence?

Our passage reads, *"And great grace was upon them all"* (Acts 4:33), a statement of indulgence. The Biblical expression of God's indulgence is grace, translated from the Greek word "charis," a favor done without expectation of return. Grace is the free expression of God's loving kindness to man, finding love the only motive in the redemptive heart of God. Luke presents two views of grace in our passage. Many biblical scholars relate our passage to the favor given to the early Church by the populace of Jerusalem, a valid observation, which the Sanhedrin was concerned about (Acts 4:17). The Sanhedrin did not dare punish the apostles because of this acceptance, so they threatened them instead (Acts 4:21).

However, there is another consideration. The *"great grace"* is directly connected to the apostles' ministry and their witness to the resurrection of the Lord Jesus. Two indicators of this are the word *"great,"* connected to *"power,"* describing the witness, and *"grace"* experienced in the state of the witness. Another indication is the conjunction *"and,"* which generally would be a translation of the Greek word "kai," but in our passage, it is the Greek word "te." The Greeks used the conjunction "kai" when two ideas are connected, or one is the result of the other. "Te" is used to annex; it presents a fact that is not directly connected or resulting.

The *"great power"* in the witness of the apostles did not result in *"great grace."* Instead, *"great grace"* was an additional fact we must understand in light of the *"great power."* They knew the power because of grace. The state of grace is the platform on which God manifests His power. The Spirit of Jesus moved through the apostles as they proclaimed the resurrection of Jesus, a supernatural happening, beyond human ability, which controlled and influenced the proclamation of the resurrection. The apostles were not recounting an event, facts, or information. The resurrected Lord appeared to them, and they knew His presence. How or why did this happen? The *"great power"* was the platform of God's grace.

"Great power" and *"great grace"* are paralleled in the passage. "Megas" is the Greek word translated *"great,"* referring to remarkable, or out of the ordinary, in degree, magnitude, or effects. The movement of God caused their effective, resurrection witness, not because of talent, faithfulness, dedication, or organization. They did not earn God's movement in their lives, because His movement was a result of His grace. The early Church dwelt in a state of *"great grace,"* their platform for ministry. It is the same for us. Revival comes, people find salvation, and our society changes because of *"great grace."* We must dwell in such a state!

Part 5: The Agreed Resolve

Principle of Possession
"You cannot be an expression of grace unless you have grace."

Our passage gives validity to this principle. There was no way to measure the indulgence of God in the lives of the apostles. They experienced three years of "on the job training" with Jesus. They knew the Divine flow of grace daily through Jesus to the multitudes around them. Jesus was the expression of God's grace to them. From all the people of Israel, Jesus chose these twelve to be the inner circle of grace recipients. If Jesus based His choosing on qualifications, these men were least. But grace is the word that is consistently used by Jesus to qualify the Kingdom person. In comparing the Kingdom person to John the Baptist, Jesus said, ***"But he who is least in the kingdom of heaven is greater than he"*** (Matthew 11:11). The ***"poor in spirit"*** are the same as the "least" (Matthew 5:3). In the Jewish culture, these apostles were indeed the "least," yet they received the blessings of an indulgent Father.

Luke expresses this principle of grace in the broader context of our passage. Peter and John knew the grace of God ministering through them at the Gate Beautiful. A lame beggar, crippled from birth, asked them for money. In Jewish culture, he was far beyond the concern of God, prohibited from any redemptive interaction with God. He could not enter the temple or make sacrifices because he did not meet the religious requirements. He was unworthy. But God is an indulgent Father who cares about such people. Peter said to the lame beggar, ***"In the name of Jesus Christ of Nazareth, rise up and walk"*** (Acts 3:6). Is it not the grace of God bestowed on one who is unworthy?

However, the lame beggar was not the only unworthy person in the miracle. Peter was unworthy in ways beyond the beggar. He knew and believed in Jesus, yet denied Him three times in the crisis hour. His unfaithfulness is paramount in his record. He had no right to be included in the grace of God! But

Great Power - Indulgent | Acts 4:33

Jesus is an indulgent Father who forgives the worst of us. The grace of God flowed through this unworthy apostle because he knew God's grace in his life! A crowd gathered to see the healed beggar. Peter recognized they were attributing the miracle to him and was horrified at the thought because he was a recipient of the same grace. He responded to the crowd, *"Men of Israel, why do you marvel at this? Or why look so intently at us, as though by our own power or godliness we had made this man walk"* (Acts 3:12)? As Peter proclaimed the *"great grace"* of God through Jesus, God healed the lame beggar.

The leaders of Israel burst through the crowd to arrest Peter and John. After a night in jail, the leaders forced the apostles before the Sanhedrin, the 70 most powerful men in Israel. Peter and John were not on the educational level of these leaders. The political power of the nation did not rest in their decisions. Who were they to instruct the Sanhedrin? Yet, these influential leaders marveled at the boldness and strength of these unworthy Galileans. They *"perceived that they were uneducated and untrained men"* (Acts 4:13). But they recognized Jesus through them! Is this not the indulgence of the gracious Jesus pouring out His grace on and through the unworthy?

It is happening again in the city of Jerusalem. The apostles, having experienced the grace of an indulgent Father, yet ministered this grace to others. Grace is the "principle of possession." If you are a recipient of grace, you can minister in grace, the platform for all ministry. Education, intelligence, or talent are not the basis of ministry. When one beggar, who has found the bread of life shares with another beggar, where to find bread, then we know ministry! The depth of your brokenness is the depth of your ministry. In the awareness of your need, you discover the wonder of meeting the needs of others. There is no ministry in arrogance, cockiness, and self-sufficiency. Because God envelopes us in grace, we can minister grace! Always acknowledge His grace; live in the boundaries of His indulgence.

Part 5: The Agreed Resolve

Principle of Proclamation
"You cannot have grace unless you are an expression of grace."

We cannot minister grace to others unless we experience God in our lives. Our experience cannot be from the past but must be a present-tense awareness of grace. Grace cannot be a theological concept but must be the wonder of our life in awe of the abundant indulgence of God. Grace is the platform for ministry. However, it is also true that we cannot continue to experience this unmerited favor unless we are willing to share it with others. Grace always has a purpose. While God focuses His love on us, He looks beyond our lives to others He wants to communicate the same love. Personal grace experiences are always the platform for ministry. If we will not share this grace with others, personal grace diminishes.

The Scriptures consistently emphasize this principle of proclamation. Jesus proclaimed the Sermon on the Mount. This sermon communicated the principles of the Kingdom established in Jesus. The premise is one of a merger with Divine nature. We are poverty-stricken, ***"poor in spirit"*** (Matthew 5:3). If we embrace this helplessness, He will fill us with Himself (Matthew 5:4). God creates a new creature called the "Kingdom person," a merger between God and man. Such a merger is a state of grace; an indulgent Father resources His helpless creation producing a new level of righteousness. But it is not just about being right; it is about being redemptive.

Jesus used the illustration of ***"an eye for an eye and a tooth for a tooth"*** (Matthew 5:38) addressing the issue of fairness. The punishment should match the crime. A person should receive what they deserve. But this standard is not the heart of an indulgent Father. Jesus wrote, ***"But I tell you not to resist an evil person"*** (Matthew 5:39). God made it clear in the Scriptures that we are to resist evil. But how do you feel about the person who expresses evil? Jesus gave four examples to illustrate such a person. An evil person slaps you on the right cheek (Matthew 5:39). The purpose of the slap is not to cause physical harm, but to insult you. Will you live in the grace of an indulgent Father who reached into your life repeatedly, though you insulted Him? Will you be the extension of God's hand to the person insulting you?

The evil person wants to take advantage of you financially for his benefit (Matthew 5:40). Will you be the extension of God's hand in his life? Will you live in the grace embracing you, though you have taken advantage of God's blessing again and again? Someone demands that you go one mile with them in service (Matthew 5:41). Will you live in awe of the truth that an indulgent Father walked by your side during your rebellion? An evil person wants to borrow from you, taking advantage of you (Matthew 5:42). You are to live in the grace of the forgiveness of debt you can never repay.

If we refuse to extend the grace we are given, we will cease to experience its benefits. The Sanhedrin threatened the members of the early Church. But the grace of an indulgent Father through Jesus was so great in their lives, they could not heed the threats. They continued to share the grace of Jesus to their world. If they did not continue to give *"witness to the resurrection of the Lord Jesus,"* they would no longer experience the grace of the *"great power"* in which they lived. If we do not express grace, it will deteriorate.

Principle of Proportion
"You cannot express grace except to the degree grace is given."

We must return to the parallel between *"great power"* and *"great grace"* (Acts 4:33). The Greek word translated *"and"* connecting the two statements is "te," not used to connect two equal ideas or one thing resulting from another. It is an "annex." The main building has an annex. It may look similar to the main building, but it serves an additional purpose. In our passage, the main building is, *"And with great power the apostles gave witness to the resurrection of the Lord Jesus"* (Acts 4:33). Luke focused on the ministry of the apostles. As they witnessed about the resurrection, the resurrected Lord began to move. The power of Jesus' Spirit brought reality to everything the apostles said about His death and resurrection. Information and theology became living fact, a reference to the main building.

The main building is power, and the annex is *"great grace!"* Grace has the same proportion as the power. Their demonstration in ministry directly related to the movement of the indulgent Father in them. Think of it as the foundation of the main building. The strength of the foundation determines the height of the main building. The ministry of the apostles was in direct proportion to the indulgent Father's embrace. There is *"great power"* because there is *"great grace."*

Again, consider Peter's experience of the Father's indulgence. How could he face the resurrected Lord? He boasted of his faithfulness, saying, *"Even if I have to die with You, I will not deny You"* (Matthew 26:35). His failure overwhelmed him. How could this failure not overshadow any future relationship? Everyone would always see His position in ministry in light of his denial. But he encountered the indulgent resurrected Lord! Such grace flowed from Jesus; there were no walls. Jesus enhanced Peter's ministry, not diminished it. The *"great grace"* produced *"great power."*

We do not place a premium on failure, for we are all equal in this area. *"For all have sinned and fall short of the glory of God"* (Romans 3:23). If it took the death and suffering of Jesus to redeem me from sin, and the same death redeems you of yours, are we not equal in our sin? The indulgent Father extended *"great grace"* to us all. Perhaps the difficulty lies in our embrace and acknowledgment of His grace. God challenges us to embrace His grace. Anything else is a direct affront to His indulgent heart! Any reliance on talent, education, personality type, or tradition nullifies the *"great power"* for ministry. The power in ministry is directly proportionate to the measure of grace active in our lives. Oh, to be the instrument of an indulgent Father bestowing His grace on all!

Acts 4:33

I AM A DEBTOR

"And with great power the apostles gave witness to the resurrection of the Lord Jesus. And great grace was upon them all" (Acts 4:33).

The early Church, while experiencing persecution, embraced the challenge. Through prayer and surrender, **"they were all filled with the Holy Spirit, and they spoke the word of God with boldness"** (Acts 4:31). In the next verse, Luke describes the unity of the believers (Acts 4:32). Every believer's view of materialism affected their spiritual life, giving expression to **"one heart and one soul." "Neither did anyone say that any of the things he possessed was his own, but they had all things in common"** (Acts 4:32). Then Luke inserts this verse, **"And with great power the apostles gave witness to the resurrection of the Lord Jesus. And great grace was upon them all"** (Acts 4:33), to show a correlation between all of these facts. The power of their witness connected with the fulness of the Holy Spirit, and their unity centered on Jesus' indwelling. The sense of abundant grace permeates all these elements.

Luke uses unique words to describe the preaching of the apostles. He highlights the attitude of the apostles toward their ministry. They did not see their witness as a career move, though this had not always been true. Two of the apostles tried to secure the right and left-hand positions in Jesus' Kingdom

(Matthew 20:20-22). They witnessed the Rich Young Ruler's rejection of Jesus. All of them wondered what they would receive because of their faithfulness (Matthew 19:27), which proceeded with an argument about who would be greatest in the Kingdom of Heaven (Matthew 18:1). Something happened to their perspective!

Luke writes, *"And with great power the apostles gave witness to the resurrection of the Lord Jesus"* (Acts 4:33). The main subject of this verse is *"apostles."* The main verb is *"gave."* The Greek word "didomi," translated "give," is the ninth most frequently used verb in the New Testament (419 times). "Didomi" is the most common expression for the transfer of something to someone or something, making it available to the recipient. However, "didomi" is not the verb in our passage! The verb "gave" in this verse is the Greek word "apodidomi." "Apodidomi" is a compound Greek word giving added emphasis, but it includes this standard word for "give" (didomi).

Luke now gives us insight into the apostles' attitude as they ministered. "Apodidomi," used forty-eight times in the New Testament, basically means "to give or to do something necessary in the fulfillment of an obligation or expectation." The Greek word has the idea of debt, payback, or meeting an obligation. John used this word concerning the tree of life. *"In the middle of its street, and on either side of the river, was the tree of life, which bore twelve fruits, each tree yielding* (apodidomi) *its fruit every month"* (Revelation 22:2). This tree, in obligation to its nature, brings forth fruit monthly. The writer of Hebrews says the discipline of a father is unpleasant to the child. However, that discipline *"yields* (apodidomi) *the peaceable fruit of righteousness"* (Hebrews 12:11). The discipline of our heavenly Father is obligated to produce fruit in our lives, driven by the motive of righteousness. Other than these two occasions, "apodidomi" always refers to a person's actions.

Part 5: The Agreed Resolve

Paul stresses the obligation of a married couple to each other. *"Let the husband render to his wife the affection due* (apodidomi) *her, and likewise also the wife to her husband"* (1 Corinthians 7:3). Matthew uses this term seven times in the Parable of the Unforgiving Servant (Matthew 18:21-35). Jesus compares the Kingdom of Heaven to a king who settled accounts with his servants. He discovered one servant owed him $2,370,000. *"But as he was not able to pay* (apodidomi)*,"* the king was going to sell him, his wife, his children, and all his possessions so that *"payment be made* (apodidomi)*"* (Matthew 18:25). The servant pleaded with the king for patience, *"and I will pay* (apodidomi) *you all"* (Matthew 18:26). The king granted forgiveness to the servant. As the forgiven servant left with his master's forgiveness, he met a fellow servant who owed him $16.69. He grabbed him by the throat and yelled, *"Pay* (apodidomi) *me what you owe!"* (Matthew 18:28). The fellow servant begged for patience, saying, *"I will pay* (apodidomi) *you all"* (Matthew 18:29). The forgiven servant had no mercy but threw him in jail *"till he should pay* (apodidomi) *the debt"* (Matthew 18:30). Upon hearing of such a lack of forgiveness, the king turned the forgiven servant over *"to the torturers until he should pay* (apodidomi) *all that was due to him"* (Matthew 18:34).

All these accounts give us the intent of the verb. In our passage, Luke makes a statement about the apostles' motive and attitude toward ministry. They constrained themselves as if obligated. The apostles felt their indebtedness, which required a clear witness of the resurrected Jesus, regardless of the Sanhedrin's threats.

Obligation of Power

One aspect of the apostles' obligation came from knowing the power of God in and through their lives. *"And with great power the apostles gave witness to the resurrection of the Lord Jesus"* (Acts 4:33). The subject of this verse is *"apostles,"* and the verb is the action word *"gave"* in the imperfect tense. This verb tense is the writer's portrayal of action in the process that happened in the past with no assessment of the action's completion. Their witness did not occur on a particular Sunday morning but was the consistent activity of their lives. It was not a memorized speech, the sharing of data, but was the constant expression of their lives. They not only proclaimed the message, but they were the message. The accusative of the sentence is *"witness,"* like the direct object in the English language, receiving the action of the main verb. Therefore, the action used to pay back their obligation was their witness. It was their repayment!

The opening phrase of the sentence is, *"And with great power."* The power involved in their continual witness was *"great* (megas),*"* remarkable, beyond ordinary, magnitude, or extensive. It was supernatural! Luke attempted to describe the *"power."* This *"power"* (dynamis) is dative in the Greek language. The indirect object is similar in the English language, indirectly receiving the action of the main verb and connects to it in some way. In our verse, *"power"* is a dative of means used to express the means of an action, differing from the dative of instrumentality. Our dative is not an expressing agency but the course of action, not the tool but the process. Something was taking place through the apostles that was beyond them. The demonstration and expression were beyond their ability and educational level. They participated in what God was doing. Therefore, their obligation was in the great privilege of inclusion in God achieving His will.

You have heard it said, "God has a plan." Our lives will be changed forever if we embrace His plan. The Scriptures focus on this plan's reality, and God wants to accomplish His plan through humanity. But this plan is narrower than "humanity,"

Part 5: The Agreed Resolve

the plan is you! You are the instrument God chose to move His resource through to accomplish His plan. You, the instrument, come under an obligation to the process. The list of preparations for your involvement in this process is enormous. God invested in you, carefully planned your destiny, made you unique with DNA, fingerprints, and physical looks like no other. Listen to the Psalm of David.

> *"For You formed my inward parts,*
> *You covered me in my mother's womb.*
> *I will praise You, for I am fearfully and wonderfully made;*
> *Marvelous are Your works,*
> *And that my soul knows very well.*
> *My frame was not hidden from You,*
> *When I was made in secret,*
> *And skillfully wrought in the lowest parts of the earth.*
> *Your eyes saw my substance, being yet unformed.*
> *And in Your book they all were written,*
> *The days fashioned for me,*
> *When as yet there were none of them"*
> (Psalms 139:13-16).

The same reality is not only in His preparation involvement, but in His consistent concern and participation to fulfill my destiny. Think of the intimacy expressed in these words: **"Are not two sparrows sold for a copper coin? And not one of them falls to the ground apart from your Father's will. But the very hairs of your head are all numbered. Do not fear therefore; you are of more value than many sparrows"** (Matthew 10:29-31). We are indebted to God for His planning, fulfillment, and empowerment of the plan. If we pride ourselves in integrity and payment of what we owe, here is a debt worthy of payment. Do we stagger under the weight of such debt? Will it not take an eternity of giving **"witness of the resurrection of the Lord Jesus"** to even contribute to the deficit? Are we not extremely obligated? Dare we flippantly live as if we are self-made? Do we have the right to simply live for ourselves, achieving our desires, and reaping what we sow? The investment of God into your life demands a sense of obligation. Paul was correct when he said, *"Or do you not know that your body is the temple of the Holy Spirit who is in you whom you have from God, and you are not your own? For you were bought at a price; therefore glorify God in your body and in your spirit, which are God's"* (1 Corinthians 6:19-20).

Obligation of Person

The obligation is a fundamental truth! Our passage begins with, *"And with great power."* The obligation rests within this *"power."* We discovered it is a dative of means, compared to a dative of instrumentality. Therefore, the *"power"* is not a tool or agency by which the witness takes place, but the process or activity of resource within the instrument of the apostles.

The Greek word "ischus" means resource, focused not on the action or ability of that resource, but upon the resource. For instance, the omnipotence (ischus) of God is great! The statement does not address what God is doing but calls attention to God's mighty omnipotence. The Person of God contains the resource of power! The Greek word "dynamis" describes the action or result of that resource, the Greek word in our passage translated *"power."* The action of God's resource moved through the disciples and empowered their witness of the resurrection.

The apostles, instruments used by God's moving resource, were under obligation to repay with their witness. However, the obligation is to the Person (ischus) from which the movement comes. God never gives us His power apart from Himself. Our passage proceeds with the awareness of *"And when they had prayed, the place where they were assembled together was shaken; and they were all filled with the Holy Spirit, and they spoke the word of God with boldness"* (Acts 4:31). The fullness of the Spirit of Jesus was their obligation!

We highlight the reality that Jesus does not give us anything apart from Himself. Everything is in His person. He does not provide us with happiness; He is our happiness; we derive happiness from His person! He does not provide us with peace; He is our peace. He does not give us strength; He is our strength. God placed in Jesus every good thing He wants for us. **"Blessed be the God and Father of our Lord Jesus Christ, who has blessed us with every spiritual blessing in the heavenly places in Christ"** (Ephesians 1:3). While I am responsible for the resources and blessings I have, I am much more accountable to the One who is that resource! I am a debtor to Jesus!

Since we are honest people, should we not pay our bills? People of integrity meet their obligations. While we are conscious we can never repay Jesus, there is a growing awareness we must allow the action of His person to work through us. Our obligation is not in giving a witness for Him; our obligation is to allow Him to reveal His person through us. We must not become ministry driven; we must become Jesus driven! We must not become program focused; we must become alive with His Spirit. We must not be satisfied with the warm feelings of accomplishment; we must be hot with the embrace of His person. Our obligation is to love Him as He loves us! His embrace will activate circumstances in our lives, generating the *"witness to the resurrection of the Lord Jesus."* He is our obligation.

Obligation of Propriety

The apostles' witness, shown through their lives and declared through their voices, was the payment for their obligation. *"And with great power"* (Acts 4:33), is the focus of the obligation. The *"power"* (dynamis) is the active, flowing resource of God that moved through the apostles. They were God's instruments for the flow. The redemptive plan of God included the merger with God's nature, capturing their lives. God's nature flowed rivers of living water through them, giving an amazing demonstration of the resurrected Lord's presence, the privilege of participation. However, the resource is not something the Spirit of Jesus gave them. The flow of this power is the Holy Spirit, who is the Spirit of the resurrected Lord. Jesus came to fill them, and the initial filling happened at Pentecost (Acts 2:1-4). He lived within them, and people were able to see the Person of Jesus in and through the actions of the early Church (Acts 4:31). They were living in the influence of Jesus and were obligated and indebted to Him. Everything about them that was good, holy, and productive was dependent on Him. **"Neither did anyone say that any of the things he possessed was his own, but they had all things in common"** (Acts:32). Their indebtedness to His presence was extreme, affecting their attachment to material possessions! This indebtedness is the nature of the case, propriety!

A sense of indebtedness drove Paul. He cried, **"I am a debtor both to Greeks and to barbarians, both to wise and to unwise"** (Romans 1:14). The Greek word "opheiletes" is translated **"debtor,"** which means "debtor, one under obligation." The scope of his indebtedness reaches every person. As a Jew, he includes the Gentiles in those to whom he is indebted, to every individual regardless of status. The next verse says to what he owes. **"So, as much as is in me, I am ready to preach the gospel to you who are in Rome also"** (Romans 1:15). The Greek word "houto," translated **"so,"** means "thus, in this way." To pay my debt, I must, with all my being, give witness to the Gospel, Jesus! It is the nature of the case.

Paul made a case for his ministry when he wrote to the people of Corinth. Those who have a ministry live off that ministry. **"Do you not know that those who minister the holy things eat of the things of the temple, and those who serve at the**

Part 5: The Agreed Resolve

altar partake of the offerings of the altar" (1 Corinthians 9:13)? He gave other examples such as the shepherds who tend the flock of sheep drink the milk of the flock (1 Corinthians 9:7). But Paul said that he took nothing from the ministry. *"For if I preach the gospel, I have nothing to boast of, for necessity is laid upon me; yes, woe is me if I do not preach the gospel"* (1 Corinthians 9:16)*!* The Greek word "ananke," translated *"necessity,"* means "the state of being absolutely required," expressing the idea of inward compulsion. This statement relates directly to our passage (Acts 4:33). Notice that Paul's view of material things was dominated and shaped by his indebtedness. Jesus flowed His resource through Paul, capturing him and creating an obligation that affected his materialism. It is the nature of the case.

We pride ourselves on being honest people! Let us pay our debt, far more than our energy or resource can produce. Do we fill the obligation? Can we freely express the wonder of Jesus' resource (dynamis)? Does Jesus capture us?

Acts 4:34

SPIRITUAL FELLOWSHIP

"Nor was there anyone among them who lacked; for all who were possessors of lands and houses sold them, and brought the proceeds of the things that were sold" (Acts 4:34).

The New Testament epistles reveal that as the early Church expanded, they experienced severe problems. In 1 Corinthians, Paul wrote of these problems, which included divisions, immorality, marriage difficulties, legal proceedings for financial gain, eating of meat offered to idols, gluttony at the Lord's supper, and pagan practices drawn into an expression of spiritual gifts. It appears that the early Church was in desperate trouble. However, this was nothing new because the church experienced difficulty from its beginning. Before the church expanded into the Gentile world, the conflicts were evident. The hostility of the Sanhedrin threatened them from without, and the division of individual members threatened them from within. Ministry is messy!

In the context of our passage, the stability of the early Church was unshakable, despite the hostility of the world (Acts 4:31). The deception of Ananias and Sapphira resulted in their death (Acts 5:1-11). Ministry is messy! None of this describes the inner heart of the church. While an outsider might observe and criticize the church, Luke affirms the unity of the true church. He wrote, **"Now the multitude of those who believed were of one heart and one soul"** (Acts 4:32). **"Multitude,"** translated from the Greek word "pletho," comes from the root word "ple," meaning "fullness." Another version translates this verse as ***"Now the full number of those who believed were of one heart and one soul"*** (ESV). Ananias and Sapphire were a part of the church's fellowship but revealed their lack of belief. All who believed were in unity!

"Belief" in our cultural mindset rests in the mind rather than the whole being. It is for this reason I hesitate to emphasize the idea. We discovered in other studies the essence of belief for the early Church was the Person of Jesus, not their acceptance of ideas concerning His Person, but the full engagement of His presence in their lives. The life of Jesus' Person became their life! Therefore, to honestly believe, each member had to enter into a relationship with Jesus. The Person of Jesus enabled them to be of ***"one heart and one soul."***

Luke lists several things that resulted from this unity. In the spiritual realm, the early Church gave witness to Jesus' resurrection because the power of His Person filled them. Grace was in abundance on them all, which affected their physical world. Luke refers to the effect of unity on their materialism as ***"neither did anyone say that any of the things he possessed was his own"*** (Acts 4:32). He continued, ***"Nor was there anyone among them who lacked"*** (Acts 4:34). Many sold the property they owned and donated the proceeds to the church. All of these practices give content to Luke's statement, ***"they had all things in common"*** (Acts 4:32).

The Greek word "koinos," translated ***"in common,"*** is the root word for "koinonia." "Koinonia" is translated in a variety of ways because no single word can convey all its richness. "Koinonia" is translated fellowship, communion, communication, distribution, contribution, partners, and partakers. The translation "partner" expresses the idea of having things in common because of a business enterprise. Luke refers to James and John as ***"partners with Simon*** (Luke 5:10) in the business of fishing. In writing to the Church of Corinth, Paul said, *"If anyone inquires about Titus, he is my partner and fellow worker concerning you"* (2 Corinthians 8:23). There is no English word that can adequately express the depth of this idea contained in "koinonia." We often translate it "fellowship." However, in our thinking, there are various levels of fellowship. We have casual fellowship with many people in our neighborhood, but we do not link with them in business enterprise. This is not true with the body of Christ, the Church. We are linked together in a merger with Jesus in a phenomenal enterprise. Therefore, we are linked together with each other in an enterprise; we have *"all things in common."*

Paul wrote to the church at Corinth about buying the meat that had been offered to idols because it was less expensive. He makes it understandable that idols are nothing (1 Corinthians 8:4; 10:19). There is no life in idols, and they have no effect, also the meat offered to the idols merely is meat. The issue is far beyond the idol and the meat. He explains that the Gentiles made *"sacrifice to demons and not to God"* (1 Corinthians 10:20). He then pronounces the crucial issue, *"I do not want you to have fellowship* (partnership, koinonia) *with demons. You cannot drink the cup of the Lord and the cup of demons. You cannot partake* (synonym of koinonia) *of the Lord's table and the table of demons"* (1 Corinthians 10:20-21).

The Apostle Peter gives us another picture of "partnership" (koinonia). He begins his second epistle speaking of the Divine power of God. God's power is the author of all things that pertain to life and godliness (2 Peter 1:3). It is through this power *"precious promises"* have been put in place (2 Peter 1:4). These promises express the heart desire of God, that *"you may be partakers* (koinonia) *of the divine nature, having escaped the corruption that is in the world through lust"* (2 Peter 1:4). We enter into a partnership with God's heart, and His heart's enterprise becomes ours. We are in intimate fellowship with what makes Him who He is!

The writer of Hebrews tells us how God presented this partnership to us. In so doing, he gives an illustration of the union with God that we can experience, telling us of Christ. *"Inasmuch then as the children have partaken* (a form of koinonia) *of flesh and blood, He Himself likewise shared in the same, that through death He might destroy him who had the power of death, that is, the devil"* (Hebrews 2:14). A son becomes a partner with the nature of his father; Jesus became a partner with our humanity. The Greek word translated *"shared"* is a synonym of "koinonia." God became flesh. Thus, the incarnation is an illustration of the partnership God offers us. The Hebrew writer says God did this to destroy the devil who has the power of death, eliminating one partnership for the sake of another partnership.

The early Church entered into "koinonia!" *"They had all things in common"* (Acts 4:32). It was much more than potluck suppers or observing religious ceremonies. They united in an enterprise. Jesus was the enterprise! Their proclamation was Jesus, their only hope for salvation (Acts 4:12). The cornerstone of their building was Jesus (Acts 4:11). The Word they proclaimed was Jesus (Acts 4:29). The Trinity God herded together all the powers and peoples of the world (Acts 4:27). God allowed them to do whatever they desired, and they did *"whatever Your hand and Your purpose determined before to be done"* (Acts 4:28). The early Church was focused entirely on Jesus and experienced the resistance and persecution extended to Jesus. They were partners (koinonia) with Jesus in the enterprise of redemption! What a privilege!

The Procedure

Just the thought of the early Church's unity causes the heart to beat fast, creating a longing for *"all things in common"* to grip the inner being. It would be amazing to experience the power that flowed in the early Church resulting in evangelism. The signs and wonders verified the proclamation of their message and captured the imagination of every believer. The church must experience this again!

Luke presents a natural progression displayed throughout the Book of Acts, beginning at Pentecost! The Spirit birthed the early Church, Jesus indwelt them, and they were in one accord. Any attempt to produce the results of unity without the fullness of the Spirit of Jesus is ludicrous. You cannot legislate unity. The reason **"they had all things in common"** was not a requirement for membership. There was no proposal of written or unwritten rules for joining the early Church. Luke writes explicitly, **"And the Lord added to the church daily those who were being saved"** (Acts 2:47). "Koinonia" cannot be forced! You can see this in the sin and death of Ananias and Sapphira (Acts 5:1-11). Peter told Ananias the land was his before he sold it, and after the sale of the land, the money was his. There were no requirements placed on him. The problem was in his deception.

Our text confirms that birth in the Spirit creates unity and boldness in speaking the word of God. **"Now the multitude of those who believed were of one heart and one soul"** (Acts 4:32). The Greek word "de," translated **"now,"** is a continuative conjunction linking this statement with the proceeding verse. **"And they were all filled with the Holy Spirit, and they spoke the word of God with boldness"** (Acts 4:31). Nothing happens without the fullness of the Holy Spirit. Peter delivered a message to the Sanhedrin after a night in jail. Luke says, **"Then Peter, filled with the Holy Spirit, said to them"** (Acts 4:8). The message of Luke is that Jesus must fill us with His Spirit!

No one can live by the Sermon on the Mount without merging with the Spirit. Only those who are one with Jesus will think like Jesus, want what He desires, and express His nature of love. Our focus is not on the accomplishments of the Kingdom but on experiencing the Kingdom. You cannot legislate holiness;

we derive holiness from the indwelling nature of Christ. We may long for our community to live by Christian principles, have prayer in school, live in love, and renounce addictive behavior, but this will not be the experience of our community unless Jesus fills them! We begin with our focus on Jesus.

The Pattern

When we are filled with Jesus and focus on Him, our life produces a pattern. The physical living displays the spiritual life of a person. When we try to change this pattern, we alter the procedure. The physical life is the platform for the demonstration of the spiritual. We often blame our attitudes or spiritual responses to circumstances. When we do that, no one can adequately understand the pattern. C. S. Lewis wrote about rats in the basement. When do we see them? Sing as you go down the basement stairs, turn on all the lights, and noisily approach your destination. You will see no rats. When you tiptoe down the stairs and suddenly flip on the lights, then you see rats. Turning on the lights does not produce the rats. They were there all the time.

The physical circumstances of your life do not produce the "rats" of your spiritual life; the "rats" are there all the time. It is the physical circumstances that reveal our inner condition. I lose my temper when an unpleasant physical circumstance happens. The circumstance did not cause me to lose my temper because it is powerless to create anger in me. The circumstance is the platform that reveals my inner state.

The spiritual condition of the early Church was **"one heart and one soul,"** the pattern of the early Church. This spiritual state was a result of the procedure. They had encountered the resurrected Lord, and He filled them with His Spirit. Their physical circumstances had radically changed. The atmosphere of acceptance they received from the populace of Jerusalem caused the leadership of Israel to threaten them. These physical circumstances did not dictate the spiritual condition of the early Church! The threat revealed the spiritual state of the members living in the fullness of Jesus, seeing the spiritual enterprise clearer because of their physical circumstances. They linked with Jesus in the redemptive suffering for their world.

This pattern also revealed their view of materialism. The personal possessions and financial security of the early Church did not dictate their spiritual atmosphere. Their security was in Jesus, not in their possessions. The threat of persecution naturally changed their financial status did not affect their involvement in the enterprise. They had all things *"in common."* They linked with the sovereign God who herded nations together so they could do whatever His hand and purpose determined before to be done. They were now partners in His enterprise. Their financial security was not their concern; they belonged to Jesus! Therefore, their materialism did not determine their spiritual state; their spiritual state decided their materialism.

The Principle

The procedure (being filled with the Spirit and focusing on Jesus) and the pattern (physical circumstances reveal the spiritual condition) naturally give expression to the fundamental principle. The child of God only exists in birth. The nature of God births the life of God in the believer. Thus, the spiritual life of the believer gives expression to the enterprise of God's nature. All the resources of God's nature are available for the fulfillment of the enterprise of God dominating the focus and purpose of the believer. All the resources of the believer were now available to God's nature for the fulfillment of the enterprise.

We can say it another way. The fullness of the Spirit is

Part 5: The Agreed Resolve

a merger between the person of Jesus and the believer. The merger creates a "new creature." All of God and all of the believer becomes the new person, a son of God. This merged person thinks with the mind of Christ, acts with the resource of Christ, and wills with the desire of Christ. He is a manifestation of the nature of Christ! Jesus yields all His redemptive and loving nature to the believer. Christ's spiritual resource is available for the fulfillment of the merger. It is also true that the resource of the believer is now available for the fulfillment of the Divine enterprise. The believer is not an employee who punches a time clock, has days off, or goes on vacation. His life, with all of its physical aspects, is at the disposal of God to fulfill the enterprise. All the believer's time has one focus, he spends his energy for one accomplishment, and all his money or materialism exists for one purpose.

The "principle" is simple. All God's resources are available to the child of God; all the resources of God's child are open to God! We cannot violate this principle! What if the child of God decides to utilize the resources of God for personal benefit? After all, if God can do miracles, why not do miracles for me? If God can heal, I should never be sick; if God can prosper someone, I should have an abundance of materialism. If God can deliver from trying circumstances, why should I have a trial? If God is love, why should I encounter hate? I should expect the resource of God to produce life without pain, discomfort, or threat. But this nullifies the heart of the merger between God and man. The enterprise of the new creature would become a selfish, self-centered enterprise. He is not available for the accomplishment of God's plan. The believer begins to dictate to God how He should use His resource, which destroys the merger of God and man!

Luke gives two illustrations, one of a person who honored the principle and another of a couple who did not. God filled Barnabas with the Spirit. His materialism was at the disposal of the merger. He was engaged in the enterprise of God and became *"a Son of Encouragement"* (Acts 4:36). Ananias and Sapphire desired to use the resource of God for their enterprise (Acts 5:1-11). They wanted the benefits of belonging to the body of Christ, but also the benefits of their resources. The difficulty facing Ananias and Sapphire was deception. They thought the only way they could benefit from the resource of God and keep their resource was to be deceptive. It brought immediate death.

All the resources of God are available to the believer, and all the resources of the believer are available to God! This principle must dominate the relationship between God and man. There is no merger without it.

Acts 4:33

GREAT GRACE

"And with great power the apostles gave witness to the resurrection of the Lord Jesus. And great grace was upon them all" (Acts 4:33).

"Grace" has the sound of all good things. Who does not want grace, especially **"great grace?"** I am amazed that **"grace"** from the Greek word "charis" is a feminine noun originating from "chairo," meaning "to rejoice." God dwells in a state of rejoicing, so "chairo" relates to God's heart. Grace is a favor done without expectation of return, which is the nature of God's love. God freely expresses His loving kindness, His only motive in the bounty and benevolence of His giving heart, the state of His pure loving joy. **"Grace"** (charis) is in direct antithesis to works (erga); the two are complete opposites. Since man is helpless and no work he can achieve will produce his spiritual life, he must live in the state of grace. God must always flood man's life with the amazing grace of His love.

Is it any wonder that Luke declares God's grace as **"great grace?"** **"Great,"** translated from the Greek word "megas," means remarkable grace. This grace is beyond ordinary in degree, magnitude, and effort. God is greater than our universe, but that is by the measurement of our world. How much bigger is He than our universe? No one can measure God's immensity. His grace is who He is. How great is His grace? Sin is not a problem for **"*great grace.*"** God's forgiveness is abundant, and He assures victory in your life!

Some Bible scholars note that the phrase "of God" is missing. "The grace of God" is used throughout the New Testament. Luke did not identify the grace as "of God." Therefore, some see this grace coming from the Jewish community even though the Sanhedrin was threatening them. The miracles and generosity of the Christians moved the people of Jerusalem, and they saw these Christians with great favor. However, in the context of our passage, **"*great grace*"** comes from the nature of God. The power of God paralleled the grace received. With **"*great power,*"** the early Church gave witness to the resurrection of Jesus, and they experienced a state of **"*great grace.*"** With **"*great power,*"** they dwelt in **"*great grace*"** and expressed "great generosity."

In the passage of our study, Luke gives us distinct elements of God's grace. He paints a picture of the state in which we must abide as Spirit-filled believers.

Providence

The provision of God's grace comes from His heart and nature. The early Church founded their proclamation on the "sovereignty of God," the surety of their security. When the Sanhedrin threatened Peter and John, they returned to the early Church and **"*reported all that the chief priests and elders had said to them*"** (Acts 4:23). These Spirit-filled Christians responded with praise and worship, crying out, **"Lord, You are God, who made heaven and earth and the sea, and all that is in them"** (Acts 4:24). In a previous study, we discovered the Greek word "despotes" is translated, **"Lord, You are God."** It is our English word "despot," means God is a tyrant! God has absolute power over all that exists.

Part 5: The Agreed Resolve

The early Church measured God's sovereignty in terms of creation. All creation comes from God. He is the One who *"made"* the wonder of the heaven, earth, and the sea, but is also the One who created and controlled all that is in them. The Greek word" poieo" is translated *"made,"* depicting the creative flow from God's inner nature. All of creation manifests and declares the sovereign nature of God. While this gives us a sense of His great sovereignty, it does not adequately measure it. The early church believed God was greater than all He created. However, we do not know how much greater He is! Is He twice as great or perhaps three times as great? We do not have a method of measuring God's greatness.

God's greatness became the foundation for the early Church's experience of grace, coming from the sovereign hand of God that they could not measure. They only knew to refer to this grace as "great." You cannot measure the greatness of this grace any more than you can measure God. Therefore, grace is as sovereign as God is sovereign. There was never a problem, difficulty, or tragedy that the early Church faced that was beyond God's sovereign hand. They did not cry out to God for deliverance, and their prayers never gave a desire to escape discomfort. They yielded to the sovereign hand of God to accomplish His purpose.

All that was available to the early Church from the sovereign hand of God is also available to us. God provides for us unshakable stability for life. He brings rest, confidence, relaxation and boldness, and eliminates anxiety, depression, discouragement, bitterness, and the want to fight for those who abide in His sovereignty. We are unshakable in His sovereignty. When our principal focus is on Him, He is the fulfillment of His will in our lives, and there is no room for self-sovereignty. In the light of who Jesus is, we see who we are. He is sovereign!

If the sovereign God is total love, then we should not fear. It is frightening to believe that God is mean, hateful, and unpredictable.

However, the Scriptures declare that God is love (1 John 4:8, 16). His love can be real in our lives. The early Church understood God's love in the "strategy of God." His nature of love demanded His love action of redemption for the world. God's sovereignty is under the control of His love nature. God is still sovereign even though the nations of the earth raged like snorting horses, people plotted vain things, kings of the earth took their stand, and rulers gathered together to demand their rights (Acts 4:25-26).

God herded together the kings (**Herod**), the rulers (**Pontius Pilate**), the people of the world (**Gentiles**), and the Jews (**people of Israel**) (Acts 4:27). Although they came together to carry out their selfish desires, they did *"whatever Your hand and Your purpose determined before to be done"* (Acts 4:28). The crucifixion and suffering of Jesus was a fulfillment of the sovereign redemptive plan of God. The activities of evil men, who thought they were achieving their desires, were under the control of the sovereign, loving heart of God; they accomplished the possibility of their personal redemption.

God working His plan should force us to believe in God's goodness. *"And we know that all things work together for good to those who love God, to those who are the called according to His purpose"* (Romans 8:28). Surely we could fulfill the statement of James, *"My brethren, count it all joy when you fall into various trials, knowing that the testing of your faith produces patience. But let patience have its perfect work, that you may be perfect and complete, lacking nothing"* (James 1:2-4). God, who is sovereign, and His heart is love, fulfilled His sovereign plan! Is this not *"great grace"*?

Participation

The early Church was thrilled at the opportunity to participate in the sovereign God's unfolding plan. They

Part 5: The Agreed Resolve

considered themselves "servants of God." They prayed, *"Now, Lord, look on their threats and grant to Your servants that with all boldness they may speak Your word"* (Acts 4:29). The Greek word translated *"servants"* is "doulos," a description of one legally owned by another, whose entire livelihood and purpose are determined by that owner. Is not such the case, if God is sovereign?

The early Church referred to Jesus as *"Your holy Servant Jesus"* (Acts 4:27, 30). However, the Greek word is not "doulos," but "pais," which refers to a young person or son. All through the Scriptures, we are called "children" of God, and numerous verses refer to us a "sons." While God may view us as sons, in light of His sovereignty, we must see ourselves as "servants." What a great honor! We do not degrade or belittle ourselves when we assume such a position in light of God's sovereignty. We are privileged when God allows us to participate in the strategy of His great heart.

The early Church understood the sovereignty of God, as seen in the crucifixion and suffering of Jesus. God herded together all the nations and peoples of the earth to accomplish His will in Christ. His *"purpose determined before to be done"* was the redemption of the world. Jesus considered such sacrifice *"the joy set before Him"* (Hebrews 12:2), and the early church saw the threats and persecution they received from the Sanhedrin as an extension of this *"purpose determined before to be done."* They did not whimper or consider this unfair treatment. Their prayer was a plea for God to allow them to boldly continue speaking in the name of Jesus, which caused this persecution.

The sovereign God was so real in the disciples' lives, and Jesus' loving heart had so captured them, they wanted to participate in the fulfillment of God's plan. Do we want any less than that? If we demand our rights, do we not violate His sovereign heart? Why would I want to exert my self-will as if I am a god? That is the core of all sin. It is a privilege to be a servant of the most-high God!

The focus of the early Church's servanthood was the "speaking of God." They had to proclaim who God is. Luke records the answer to their prayer, *"And when they had prayed, the place where they were assembled together was shaken; and they were all filled with the Holy Spirit, and they spoke the word of God with boldness"* (Acts 4:31). God validated their speaking by healings, signs, and wonders (Acts 4:30). But Luke makes the proclamation's focus clear in our passage. *"And with great power the apostles gave witness to the resurrection of the Lord Jesus. And great grace was upon them all"* (Acts 4:33).

In previous studies, we have discovered the content of this speaking regarding the resurrection. Witnessing the event was not an issue because no one saw the resurrection of Jesus. The disciples were affected by the appearances of the resurrected Jesus, which was a result of the happening. But it was not the event that captured them. The message was not philosophical or theological. They did not declare a doctrine of resurrected life. They focused their proclamation on Jesus in the resurrection. Jesus is alive! He conquered death and the grave! Jesus is victorious!

The witness of Jesus being alive gave the apostles' proclamation power. Jesus made Himself known to the listeners. Something life-changing happened through the apostles as they witnessed. The crowds did not remember the date or information about the event, but they caught sight of the resurrected Jesus. The disciples' lives demonstrated the resurrection as they lived it. That is the reason they cried out for God to allow the people to see the resurrected Jesus in them, even in the threat of persecution.

God, in His sovereignty, dominated by His loving nature, birthed the plan of redemption, which came through Jesus' crucifixion and suffering. The disciples' participation in this suffering extended redemption to their world. Jesus filled them and was now portraying Himself through them in this redemption. Does Jesus not call us to this as well? Are we not as privileged as they were to know the same Christ with the same calling? How can we shrink from discomfort, filled with self-pity, when Jesus affords us the opportunity to redeem others?

Provision

Luke introduces the first and second sentences in our passage with the conjunction "And." However, the two usages of "and" are not the same word in the Greek language. ***"And with great power the apostles gave witness to the resurrection of the Lord Jesus"*** (Acts 4:33). The first ***"and"*** is a translation of the Greek word "kai," used to connect two equal ideas. The "great generosity" of the early church is equal and connected to the ***"great power"*** of the witness to the resurrection of the Lord Jesus. However, ***"And great grace was upon them all"*** (Acts 4:33) is a translation of the Greek conjunction "te," used when something is subjoined, which does not directly or necessarily follow. "Kai" connects and "te" annexes. The main church sanctuary is the building where ministry happens with people in worship and children in training. However, the gymnasium is an annex, which is also essential.

"Great grace" is the "supplementing of God." It is not so much what God is doing, healing, signs, and wonders, but is the atmosphere of His presence. God shook the place where they were assembled together. He filled the believers with Himself. He enabled them to speak the word of God with boldness. Even the generosity of the early church was a direct result of God's action upon and through them. The movement of God, within the believer, brings visible results in the lives of those around them. However, the believers live in a state of ***"great grace,"*** experiencing His presence, the stimulus of His nature.

We often focus on results in a physical demonstration without awareness that we dismiss God's presence. The wonder of His presence is beyond compare, the *"great grace"* to be cherished and honored above all. Paul starts his letter to the Ephesian people with, *"Blessed be the God and Father of our Lord Jesus Christ"* (Ephesians 1:3). *"Blessed"* is an adjective that modifies *"God."* Our God is a blessed God! He dwells in a state of blessedness. The source of this blessedness is Himself, flowing from deep within His nature, the core of His being. His blessedness escapes through the pores of His system and produces the atmosphere in which He dwells. Wherever He goes, this "blessedness" moves with Him. It is the *"great grace!"*

The unbelievable truth of our passage is that this *"great grace"* has come upon us! Listen to the passage. *"And great grace was upon them all"* (Acts 4:33), the "surrounding of God." The Greek word translated *"upon"* is "epi." There are two leading ideas, one of which is "to rest upon or in," the meaning in our passage. The presence of God, surrounding His people and resting upon them, is the amazing *"great grace"* of His nature. Beyond the miraculous physical results manifested through the disciples by God's power, the people experienced God's Divine Presence. The loving nature of God enfolded them, and they dwelt in the cloud of His strength and security. It is *"great grace."*

A second idea connected to "epi" is "of motion upon, to or toward." The fog of God's grace, emanating from His presence, steadily moved upon them. It is never stagnant. We can never get used to the various effects of God's presence upon our lives. He is consistently revealing Himself, and He moves us from one level to another in the wonder of His grace.

God's love nature floods and saturates His sovereignty. He demonstrates His plan, which He unfolded in the crucifixion of Jesus to redeem the world. He grants us the privilege to live in

Part 5: The Agreed Resolve

His fullness and participate in His plan. Although God's actions demonstrate His *"great power,"* those actions do not overshadow His *"great grace!"* He captures us, and we never escape the throb of His nature. *"And great grace was upon them all"* (Acts 4:33)

Acts 4:35

DIVINE NATURE EXPRESSED

"And laid them at the apostles 'feet; and they distributed to each as anyone had need" (Acts 4:35).

The "Divine nature expressed" is the proposition of Luke's writings. In his gospel account, Luke says the one Man, Jesus Christ, is the demonstration of this expression. Jesus was born through the power of the Holy Spirit (Luke 1:35), and the Holy Spirit filled Him (Luke 3:22). Jesus explained His ministry was a result of the Holy Spirit (Luke 4:18), and His death was a result of the Father's desire (Luke 22:42). The Trinity God planned Jesus' crucifixion and resurrection and wrote it into the Scriptures (Luke 24:45-46). Is this not why Paul cried, **"He is the image of the invisible God"** (Colossians 1:15)? Jesus is the expression of Divine nature!

In the Book of Acts, Luke proposes the same theme, "the Divine nature expressed." However, he expands the avenue of the expression to the believers. God poured out the Holy Spirit as promised by the prophet Joel (Joel 2:28-32). Peter explained the outpouring of the Holy Spirit at Pentecost in terms of Jesus (Acts 2:22). God's nature worked in Jesus; now, God's nature was working in the believers. We are **"the image of the invisible God."** Our lives are the platform for the "Divine nature expressed."

The creation story is an expression of this truth. God created the world to express who He is. **"For since the creation**

of the world His invisible attributes are clearly seen, being understood by the things that are made, even His eternal power and Godhead" (Romans 1:20). The physical, visible world is a display of the invisible, spiritual God. If this is true of nature, how much more is it true of His sons and daughters. The invisible God created a physical, visible human being He could indwell and demonstrate Himself through. We are the body of Christ, giving evidence of His nature to our world.

God clarified the heart of sin. He created you and me, to tell the truth about Him! When we do not merge our lives with His, we demonstrate ourselves. If God is not the source of what we express, we do not tell the truth about Him. When hatred fills our hearts and dominates our attitudes, we declare, "God is not love." The selfishness coming from our hearts proclaims that "God is selfish." We are lying about God! We are responsible for what others think about God. As human beings, we are the visibility of the invisible God to all His creation. God created us as vessels of revelation and wants to restore our redemption. We are His instruments for expressing His Divine nature!

As Luke recorded the activities of the early Church, He declared "the Divine nature expressed" repeatedly. Peter and John stood before the Sanhedrin for interrogation. Peter, filled with the nature of God, gave expression to the truth of God (Acts 4:8-12). The leaders of Israel recognized Jesus in the apostles' demonstration of God's nature (Acts 4:13). The same irritation the Sanhedrin felt when interacting with Jesus, they now experienced with Peter and John. They eliminated Jesus by crucifixion, but they were startled when they saw Him in the lives of the apostles.

The early church responded to the threats of the Sanhedrin remarkably. They prayed, ***"Now, Lord, look on their threats, and grant to Your servants that with all boldness they may speak Your word, by stretching out Your hand to heal, and that signs and wonders may be done through the name of Your*** *holy Servant Jesus"* (Acts 4:29, 30). They did not whine over the difficulties or threats, but their demonstration of the Divine nature continued and increased. Luke recorded the answer to their prayer. *"And when they had prayed, the place where they were assembled together was shaken; and they were all filled with the Holy Spirit, and they spoke the word of God with boldness"* (Acts 4:31). These believers, filled with the nature of God, revealed the Divine nature in a proclamation, both in word and in deed.

In our present paragraph of saturation (Acts 4:32-27), Luke gave details to this demonstration. He declared for a second time, the generous, unselfish attitude the early Church demonstrated regarding materialism. The structure of these verses magnifies the importance of the believer's selfless attitude toward materialism. *"Neither did anyone say that any of the things he possessed was his own, but they had all things in common"* (Acts 4:32). *"Nor was there anyone among them who lacked; for all who were possessors of lands or houses sold them, and brought the proceeds of the things that were sold"* (Acts 4:34).

Luke began with *"Neither"* and ended with *"Nor,"* connecting these two verses (Acts 4:32, 34). However, Luke separated these two verses with a powerful insert statement. *"And with great power the apostles gave witness to the resurrection of the Lord Jesus. And great grace was upon them all"* (Acts 4:33). You may recognize this distinction from previous studies. Its importance for this study is the value of the believer's demonstration of God's nature expressed through materialism. Their lives became the platform for clarity of the witness and experience of grace.

Luke concludes the focus of our present study with, *"and laid them at the apostles' feet; and they distributed to each as anyone had need"* (Acts 4:35). At first glance, there is nothing new in these statements. Many of the members of the early Church sold the land they owned and gave it to the apostles to distribute to the church body as needed. However, Luke reveals a pattern that is a pure expression of the Divine nature. When we show the Divine nature, others will discover this pattern, which never varies from the Old Testament through the New. Luke clarifies the pattern through three different connectional words, but never repeats himself.

"And (kai) **laid them at the apostles' feet; and** (de) **they distributed to each as** (kathoti) **anyone had need"** (Acts 4:35).

Resource

Luke begins the verse with the Greek word "kai," translated *"and,"* a conjunction used to connect two equal ideas. One idea is not subordinate to the other or has less importance. Luke joins "resource" and "release." Since the conjunction *"and"* is the first word in the Greek and English text, it connects us to the previous verse, presenting the "resource" of the early Church. Numerous people owned property. Luke gives the examples of landowners, Barnabas (Acts 4:36-37) and Ananias and Sapphira (Acts 5:1). From the tone of the passage, the number of people who owned and sold their land participated in meeting the needs of others.

Luke writes, *"laid them at the apostles' feet"* (Acts 4:35), suggesting the landowners "released" their "resource," without a demand. Ananias and Sapphira were free to do whatever they wanted with the proceeds from selling their land. Their problem was not in the sale or in what they did with the "resource." Their problem was deception, which made them different from all others in the early Church, whose generosity was the standard. **"Neither did anyone say that any of the things he possessed was his own, but they had all things in common"** (Acts 4:32).

The early Church demonstrated the same pattern in the spiritual realm, recognizing the spiritual "resource" of God. His sovereignty is beyond measure. God created the *"heaven and earth and the sea, and all that is in them"* (Acts 4:24). There is no "resource" above or beyond Him. God herded together the nations of the world *"to do whatever Your hand and Your purpose determined before to be done"* (Acts 4:28). Jesus is the redemptive resource, and He filled the believers. Without hesitation or consideration of the consequences, they "released" this "resource" upon their world. The main concern in their prayer was not that God deliver them from persecution, but that He allow them to continue in this pattern of Him "releasing" His "resource" through them (Acts 4:29-30). God quickly answered their prayer! God's spiritual "resource" shook the building where they met, renewed this "resource" through the filling of the Holy Spirit, and they released this "resource" by speaking the word of God with boldness (Acts 4:31).

Why was this pattern so prevalent in the early Church? God filled them with His Spirit, and they expressed His Divine nature. When each member merged with the Divine nature, they began to think as God thinks, feel like He feels, and want what He wants. The heart of God is one of great "resource." Paul described Him as *"Blessed be the God and Father of our Lord Jesus Christ"* (Ephesians 1:3). *"Blessed"* is an adjective modifying God, bespeaking the greatness, power, and glory that flows from His inner being. "Blessed" comes from God's nature and creates the atmosphere around His Divine person. When He moves, this atmosphere moves with Him. He dwells in this state of blessedness.

Paul proclaimed, *"Oh, the depth of the riches both of the wisdom and knowledge of God. How unsearchable are His judgments and His ways past finding out! For who has known the mind of the Lord? Or who has become His counselor? Or who has first given to Him and it shall be repaid to Him? For of Him and through Him and to Him are all things, to whom be glory forever. Amen"* (Romans 11:33-36). God "released" the "resource" of His person; God does not selfishly hoard His resource; He is not afraid to diminish His supply! He "released" all on behalf of redemption. When God releases His love upon the world, He does not reduce His amount of love. When God releases His forgiveness to us, His supply of forgiveness remains the same.

God affected the early Church by the wonder of His "resource," causing them to express this new attitude toward their materialism. They knew God! When they merged with Jesus, the supply of His person abundantly overwhelmed them in every area. They became as generous as the God who was sourcing them. They expressed the Divine nature!

Requirement

We do not use the word "requirement" as a law or demand but as a representation of need. The early Church had abundant "resource" available to them because they were owners of lands or houses. Many of these individuals sold their property, *"and"* (kai) "released" the proceeds; they *"laid them at the apostles' feet"* (Acts 4:35). Someone had to be responsible for distributing the funds to those in need. The obvious choice was the apostles; however, that quickly changed when the number of disciples increased. Luke refers to the growth of the early Church as *"multiplying"* (Acts 6:1). The apostles were too busy daily to distribute the funds adequately. They said, *"It is not desirable that we should leave the word of God and serve tables"* (Acts 6:2). The early Church selected seven men and commissioned them to serve by prayer and laying on of hands (Acts 6:6).

With the resource for distribution in place, Luke changed the conjunction *"and"* from the Greek word "kai" to "de," translated "but." *"And* (de) *they distributed to each"* (Acts 4:35). Luke created a contrast between the abundant resource and the abundant need. At the same time, the early Church recognized they had a precious resource, and they realized the need of many among them. We have some insight into the "resource." They sold their houses and land and contributed the money to meet the "requirement." However, Luke does not give us the details of the "requirement." He does provide some insight in the following chapters. They gave a *"daily distribution"* (Acts 6:1). The believers were meeting the "requirement" with their "resource."

God established the pattern of His Divine nature by expressing His nature through the early Church. He contained the abundance of "resource," a state of being. No one has ever been able to investigate the depth of this resource. We do know that the Trinity God "released" this "resource" in the Person of Jesus! The resource of God's nature working through Jesus "released" abundant power, forgiveness, glory, peace, mercy, and the list goes on. Paul said that Jesus **"has blessed us with every spiritual blessing in the heavenly places in Christ"** (Ephesians 1:3). God located the resource for our lives in this Person, Jesus!

"But" (de) there is a great need! However, it is not greater than the resource. We need not fear. Jesus assured us that He would forgive every sin. He guaranteed the resource of redemption is vast, and upon confession, He activates all forgiveness in our lives (1 John 1:9). Jesus never limits His forgiveness, and He gives complete victory. The Trinity God crushed the nature of sin by the sheer weight of Christ's redemption! We have no reason to be defeated. Regardless of how the circumstances look, **"all things work together for good to those who love God, to those who are the called according to His purpose"** (Romans 8:28). God made this a sure thing. He meets the "requirement" by "releasing" the "resource" of His Person through us.

Part 5: The Agreed Resolve

Response

Luke links the abundant "resource," and the "release" of that resource, with the conjunction *"and"* (kai). They *"brought the proceeds of the things that were sold, and* (kai) *laid them at the apostles' feet"* (Acts 4:34-35). Then he changed the conjunction to a contrast, they *"laid them at the apostle's feet; and* (de) *they distributed to each"* (Acts 4:35). The "resource" was "released," but (de) there was a "requirement." However, the "requirement" was not greater than the "resource." Luke focused explicity on the "response." What good is the "resource," "released" to meet the "requirement," if the apostles do not "respond" to the need? But the apostles do respond! In fact, *"they distributed to each as* (kathoti) *anyone had need"* (Acts 4:35). God had a "regulation" for "releasing" the "resource" to meet the "requirement," completing the "response!"

The Spirit of Jesus filled the early Church. They were the picture of the Divine nature! God was the resource they needed to meet their needs, and they became the instruments through which God expressed His Divine nature. Their pattern was God's pattern. They handled the needs among them precisely the way God's Divine heart engaged with them. Who can measure the "resource" in Jesus? Has Jesus not "released" His "resource" to meet the complete "requirement" of our lives? Is His "response" not under the "regulation" of His loving heart, bringing us to completion? Is this not "hope" on the highest level? There is no way we cannot be all we are to be! Jesus meets all our needs!

Can you imagine what you and I could be to our world? We can merge with this "Resource!" God wants to express His Divine nature through us. Is there any need that overwhelms Him? How can we then be overwhelmed by our needs? Our lives become the "resource" of His nature "released" to our world, meeting the "requirements" we face. The obstacles of the demonic forces are no match to the resource of His Person. The word "boldness" is attached repeatedly to the ministry of the early Church. They thrived amid intense adversity and ministered in the pattern and fullness of God. God expressed His Divine nature through them. Let us minister in this boldness! We are an expression of the Divine nature!

Acts 4:36

SON OF ENCOURAGEMENT

"And Joses, who was also named Barnabas by the apostles (which is translated Son of Encouragement), a Levite of the country of Cyprus" (Acts 4:36).

Luke introduces an essential person in our passage, who plays a significant role in the growth and ministry of the early Church. His name is **"Joses,"** but we know him as **"Barnabas."** Our passage says, **"And Joses, who was also named Barnabas by the apostles"** (Acts 4:36). The Greek word "epikaleo," translated **"named,"** is a compound word, "epi," meaning "upon," and "kaleo," meaning "call or surname." The apostles gave **"Joses"** a nickname, **"Barnabas."**

"Barnabas" means **"Son of Encouragement,"** though many scholars consider this a problem. In their view, **"Barnabas"** does not mean that. Arguments on either side are not worth our time. It becomes clear throughout the rest of the New Testament that Barnabas was an encourager in the early Church. Next to the apostle Paul, he was the most crucial person in a missionary role. His name occurs twenty-three times in the Book of Acts. Paul mentions Barnabas in three of his epistles, Corinthians, Galatians, and Colossians.

Barnabas befriends Saul of Tarsus after his radical conversion on the Damascus Road. **"And when Saul had come to Jerusalem, he tried to join the disciples; but they were all afraid** *of him, and did not believe that he was a disciple"* (Acts 9:26). It was Barnabas who brought Saul to the apostles to tell his story of conversion (Acts 9:27). Supporting Paul was the role of a *"Son of Encouragement."*

The persecution of Christians became strong after the stoning of Stephen. A group of Christians made their way to Antioch. They shared the Gospel with Hellenists, *"and a great number believed and turned to the Lord"* (Acts 11:21). When the church in Jerusalem heard of this revival, they sent Barnabas. *"When he came and had seen the grace of God, he was glad, and encouraged them all that with purpose of heart they should continue with the Lord. For he was a good man, full of the Holy Spirit and of faith. And a great many people were added to the Lord"* (Acts 11:23-24). These verses describe the work of a *"Son of Encouragement."*

As the church grew in Antioch, Luke listed Barnabas first among the leaders of the church. As these leaders sought God, the Holy Spirit spoke, *"Now separate to Me Barnabas and Saul for the work to which I have called them"* (Acts 13:2). Barnabas in leadership and activity became the core of the first recorded missionary endeavor. What better person could the church send than one who is a *"Son of Encouragement."*

Barnabas and Paul blazed the trail for the acceptance of the Gentiles into Christianity without restrictions. A choice between the traditions of Judaism and the transforming grace of Jesus faced the early Church. Would Christianity become a small Jewish sect or a worldwide movement? The Jerusalem Council discussed this decision. *"Then all the multitude kept silent and listened to Barnabas and Paul declaring how many miracles and wonders God had worked through them among the Gentiles"* (Acts 15:12). God used the *"Son of Encouragement"* to set the tone for a worldwide revival.

Conflict arose between Paul and John called Mark. Paul felt that Mark had not been faithful at crucial times in previous missionary outreach, and he refused to include John Mark in other missionary endeavors. Barnabas saw much good in John Mark and included him in the mission. It was then that Paul began missionary travels with Silas, and Barnabas continued with John Mark. As a *"Son of Encouragement,"* Barnabas could not allow someone who had made a mistake to be lost. He encouraged John Mark to reach his full potential.

Who would not admire the ministry and spirit of Barnabas? We cannot measure His influence on the early Church and its multitudes. Who would not want to be like him? But remember, all of this started in our passage! God released His Spirit through Barnabas because he was open to the Spirit's leadership in materialism. His attitude toward materialism was his springboard for ministry! Could this be a spiritual principle? A person's perspective about what he owns will determine the spiritual effect he has on others. If Jesus is not Lord in the realm of my possessions, He will not reign in the realm of ministry!

We see this fundamental spiritual truth repeated throughout the Scriptures. It is evident in Jesus' spiritual encounter with the Rich Young Ruler (Matthew 19:16-22), a young man who was filled with potential, having all the religious qualifications for ministry. His personality secured his leadership positions, and his resourcefulness had made him wealthy. The one thing he lacked was a proper attitude toward materialism. His attitude toward what he possessed blocked his possibility to be a disciple of Jesus. What might have been his ministry in the early Church if he had been willing to sell all he had?

Jesus marveled at the hold materialism had on those who wanted to be a part of the Kingdom of God. He pointed out the difficulty of a rich man entering the Kingdom of Heaven (Matthew 19:23). He said, *"it is easier for a camel to go through the eye of a needle than for a rich man to enter the kingdom of God"* (Matthew 19:24). Many biblical scholars have tried to soften what Jesus said by referring to the *"eye of a needle"* as the small gate by the main gates of Jerusalem. In response to Jesus' statement, the disciples cried, **"Who then can be saved?"** Jesus responded, **"With men this is impossible, but with God all things are possible"** (Matthew 19:26). With this clarification, we understand we cannot overcome the gripping power of materialism in our lives. Only God can set us free; it is a miracle of His grace!

Victory over materialism is God's miraculous power in the early Church. **"Neither did anyone say that any of the things he possessed was his own, but they had all things in common"** (Acts 4:32). Barnabas, **"Son of Encouragement,"** is an example of this deliverance. He demonstrated his victory over the things in His life throughout the coming chapters of the early Church's mission!

Connected to Scriptures

In the cultural setting of the New Testament, one person often referred to another as "son of," which could mean a son of your father. However, they also used it in speaking of a person's moral quality, the way **"Son of Encouragement"** is used in our passage. We must not interpret this as a personality trait. Although the personality of Barnabas tended toward the expression of encouragement, it was the Divine movement of God that gave expression through him.

The Greek word "paraklesis" is translated "encouragement," a feminine noun informing us is abstract. We cannot measure the "encouragement," and we cannot learn it through education. "Paraklesis" comes from the root word "parakaleo," which means "to beseech," the act of exhortation, encouragement, and comfort. All of Scripture is "paraklesis," encouragement consistently based upon and linked with the Scriptures. God gave the Scriptures to strengthen, exhort, admonish, and encourage the believer,

Part 5: The Agreed Resolve

strengthening and establishing him in the faith. Paul said, *"For whatever things were written before were written for our learning, that we through the patience and comfort* (paraklesis) *of the Scriptures might have hope"* (Romans 15:4). The Book of Hebrews ends with, *"And I appeal to you, brethren, bear with the word of exhortation* (paraklesis), *for I have written to you in few words"* (Hebrews 13:22).

Paul used the Greek word "paraklesis" often in his preaching. *"But even after we had suffered before and were spitefully treated at Philippi, as you know, we were bold in our God to speak to you the gospel of God in much conflict. For our exhortation* (paraklesis) *did not come from error or uncleanness, nor was it in deceit"* (1 Thessalonians 2:2, 3). When Paul attended the synagogue in Antioch on the Sabbath, the rulers of the synagogue said, *"Men and brethren, if you have any word of exhortation for the people, say on"* (Acts 13:15). While instructing Timothy, Paul said, *"Till I come, give attention to reading, to exhortation* (paraklesis), *to doctrine"* (1 Timothy 4:13).

Luke referred to Jesus, the coming Messiah, as *"the Consolation* (paraklesis) *of Israel"* (Luke 2:25). Jesus is the *"Word"* (John 1:1), the Living Word and the Written Word focused on encouragement. The Christian message is "Gospel," good news! Jesus did not come *into the world to condemn the world, but that the world through Him might be saved"* (John 3:17). The glory of its message is encouragement! In discouragement, where can we turn? We turn to the Scriptures! How can we look beyond our state of depression? We must come to the Living Word expressed through the Written Word. Positive thinking is not enough. At the heart of the universe is a sovereign God, expressing His aggressive love through His Word, Living and Written!

Joses was a *"Son of Encouragement,"* the truth of the Word gripping his heart. His life expressed the tone of the Scriptures. He consistently elevated people through the Word; his encouragement so dominant in his life, people nicknamed him Barnabas. His message still resounds in this hour. Will we fill our lives with the negative message of this world, or will we fill ourselves with the encouraging Word, both Living and Written?

Context of Salvation

Barnabas was the living demonstration of "encouragement." While the content of encouragement involves the Scriptures, we also see encouragement in the context of "salvation." I fear the meaning of salvation has changed from the biblical perspective. In our modern-day, we isolate salvation to a moment in time when a person repents, thinking God writes our name in the heavenly books, and our future home is heaven. The biblical view of salvation is much larger. Salvation includes an encounter with the Living God through repentance and faith and is relational in its content.

The Greek verb "sozo" means "to save," primarily denoting "saved from death or harm." The mocking crowd viewed Jesus as a false teacher because He saved others, but He could not save Himself from the cross (Luke 23:35). "Salvation" is a translation of the Greek "soteria," a feminine noun emphasizing the abstract element. We cannot measure salvation nor state it in a contract. The theme of the Scriptures is salvation, always the result of the Savior (soter), the one who saves. Peter called Jesus **"Lord and Savior"** (2 Peter 1:1; 2:20), and Paul called Jesus **"God and Savior"** (Titus 2:13).

The biblical view of "salvation" is the merger of God's saving life with the believer's lost life. As we said previously, salvation is not just a moment in time when a person repents. Paul said, **"For by grace you have been saved** (sozo) **through faith, and that not of yourselves; it is the gift of God"** (Ephesians 2:8). This

Greek verb "sozo" is in the perfect tense, used by the writer to describe a completed verbal action, occurring in the past, but produced in a state of being or a result that exists in the present. The perfect tense is not so much the past action as it is the present "state of affairs" resulting from the past action. In other words, salvation is not an event to view in the past only, but is a present living relationship with Jesus, saving us now. A proper translation of Paul's declaration might be, "For by grace you are being saved through faith."

Barnabas lived in this state of grace, the nature of which is encouragement, offering an extended period to those at the deadline. It is giving a renewed sense of hope to those who have lost all hope. But do not think of Barnabas always seeing the positive and expressing that to all people in every situation. The content of his encouragement was also the Scriptural message of Jesus saving wonder. His encouragement was not a "pep talk" or a "sales pitch." He consistently engaged those around him with the message of the Scriptures, which is salvation in Jesus!

The Scriptures are the only authentic words of encouragement. In the face of worsening circumstances, all other words crash on the rocks of despair. Where is the encouragement? When things in our lives are out of control, we do not need a pat on the back or a palm reader's advice. We need God to possess someone like Barnabas to speak truth to us through the Word.

Jesus, the Savior, is in charge and has a plan. A hate-filled world does not shake His love for me. The message of the angel to the shepherds rings true in this hour. ***"Do not be afraid, for behold, I bring you good tidings of great joy which will be to all people. For there is born to you this day in the city of David a Savior*** (Soter), ***who is Christ the Lord"*** (Luke 2:10, 11).

Character of Selflessness

Barnabas was a *"Son of Encouragement."* Do not picture him merely as a kind person, traveling to churches, speaking shallow but positive platitudes. Ingrained in the nature of encouragement is a character virtue, without which, the reality of encouragement is missing. The heart of authentic support only appears when the encourager desires nothing for himself but desires something for the person he addresses, meaning the context of encouragement is always personal with an emphatic concern for someone else.

We have many examples of this care and concern in the life of Paul. When he ministered in Ephesus, he was hated by those receiving financial gain from pagan worship. On one occasion, Paul wanted to speak to people gathered in a theater. *"Then some of the officials of Asia, who were his friends, sent to him pleading* (parakaleo) *that he would not venture into the theater"* (Acts 19:31). Paul's friends were concerned about his safety; their pleading established a platform for selfless encouragement. On another occasion, Agabus, a certain prophet, warned Paul that when he went to Jerusalem, he would be captured and delivered into the hands of the Gentiles. *"Now when we heard these things, both we and those from that place pleaded* (parakaelo) *with him not to go up to Jerusalem"* (Acts 21:12). Luke declared a selfless concern for Paul, which flowed into authentic encouragement.

"Encouragement" is at the heart of cross style. If Christianity is "never thinking about yourself," the Christian should flow with encouragement. Encouragement is not a trait we learn in a training seminar, not a spiritual gift granted to a few, but is the heart and soul of everyone who embraces their poverty, and God fills with His nature. Encouragement is engrained into the essence of the Christian. Without defense or rationalization, will

Part 5: The Agreed Resolve

you examine your life for this quality? How often are we negative regarding others? How often are we critical and judgmental, rather than encouraging? While there may be a variety of issues we do not approve, the attitude of expression makes the most significant impact. Should not the attitude of God be the attitude expressed through you? Oh, to be the expression of God's encouragement to my world!

Acts 4:37

ATTITUDE OF ENCOURAGEMENT

"Having land, sold it, and brought the money and laid it at the apostles' feet" (Acts 4:37).

In the proclamation of the resurrected Christ (Acts 4:33), Luke described the *"great power"* and *"great grace"* experienced by the early Church. The resurrected Person of Jesus shared in the proclamation. The believers did not testify to an eyewitness event, but they declared a Living Jesus! Everyone could see their attitude about materialism in their description of the risen Lord. Luke used one verse to describe the *"great power"* and *"great grace,"* but he used three verses of their attitude about their possessions (Acts 4:32, 34, 35). Luke linked the believers' attitude with the power of Jesus' presence. Did the early Church's victorious attitude toward materialism give them power and grace? Did power and grace allow them to have victory over materialism? The answer to both questions is "yes."

Luke gives two examples, one positive and one negative, to link this victorious attitude with the power of Jesus' presence. His positive example is his introduction of the main character in early Church evangelism. His name is Joseph, but the apostles nicknamed him, Barnabas, a translation of **"Son of Encouragement"** (Acts 4:37). Throughout the Book of Acts,

Part 5: The Agreed Resolve

you can read numerous accounts of Barnabas' ministry of encouragement. But in our passage (Acts 4:37), Luke writes about the content or ingredients of this character quality, using four verbs, *"having, sold, brought, and laid."*

Three of the verbs used by Luke, *"sold, brought, and laid,"* are in the aorist tense, but the first verb, *"having,"* is in the present tense. *"Having"* portrays an action in process or a state of being with no assessment of the actions' completion, which raises the issue of Barnabas selling all his land. Does this mean that Barnabas continued to own property after selling his land? Perhaps he did not sell all he owned? Whether he did or did not sell all he owned is not the focus of our passage. The state of materialism continually bombards the life with its claims and offers. Even if we sell all we own, we still live in a physical world, and we have needs we must meet. What I own does not determine the effect of material things on my life. Neither rich nor poor are exempt from this problem because we all dwell in a state of materialism.

The remaining verbs in our passage, **"sold, brought, and laid,"** are in the aorist tense, used by Luke to present the action of a verb as a "snapshot" event. The verb's action portrays in a summary fashion, without respect to any process. He does not refer to the past, present, or future. We will continually live in a state of physical materialism, and we must always surrender that materialism to Jesus. A trip to the altar, or an experience in a moment, is not the focus. The issue is in what state will we choose to live. We will always have things, but the Christian needs to yield those things to Jesus. Barnabas, **"Son of Encouragement,"** interacted with others from a state of victory over materialism. Living in this victory relates to any ministry in which we might be involved. Yielding our materialism affects the core character of the minister and establishes the platform for ministry.

Territory

"Having," the first verb in our verse, states the place where we dwell. It is the Greek word "hyparcho," the combination of two Greek words, "hupo" and "archo." "Hupo" means "under," and "archo" is the idea of "first, beginning, and to rule." Paul used the word "hyparcho," translated ***"principalities,"*** to describe the spiritual battle that engages us. "Hyparcho" has the same emphasis as "eimi," translated ***"I am,"*** highlighting the idea "to be, live, or exist." Regarding our verse, ***"having"*** means existing within the state of materialism. Does materialism have us or do we have materialism?

Peter, speaking to the lame beggar at the Gate Beautiful, said, ***"Silver and gold I do not have*** (huparcho), ***but what I do have*** (echo) ***I give to you"*** (Acts 3:6). We might question whether Peter was telling the complete truth. Did he not have funds available that he could share with the lame beggar? The point is that Peter made a distinction between having silver and gold and having the life of Jesus. The Greek word "echo," translated ***"have,"*** connects to Jesus, which paints a different picture. "Echo" defines something "one has in, or about him, including the idea of to bear, carries in oneself, as in the womb." Having silver and gold is similar to a veneer covering while having Jesus is more like pregnancy. What is present in you is not covering you, but is shaping, manifesting, and participating with you in life! It is the picture of the "merger" expressed by Jesus as the premise of the Sermon on the Mount.

We must not let materialism become the spiritual state of our being. We must not dwell in materialism. I want you to picture materialism as a house in which you live, a house existing to meet your needs. You arrange your living room and design your kitchen according to your needs and desires. You keep your house at a comfortable temperature for your pleasure. The house is not bad or evil, but it does perform a function. Materialism is this way. Material things are necessary, and no one proposes their elimination. However, let us broaden the picture, give the house life, and make it an organism. Instead of a house existing for you, it exists for itself, sucking the life from you for its survival. You exist to serve and minister to the needs of the living house. The house grows in power as you become weaker. The house determines your actions, and you contribute to the house. The house feeds off you, and you are worse than a slave.

We live in a physical materialistic world, and the threat of that materialism conquering us is constant. The things you own can be the platform upon which your spiritual life exists. God intended this in His creation. Sin is never original but twists the good God intended. Materialism can master us and dominate the way we live our lives. Luke projects a picture of the early Church's effectiveness in evangelism. What is the secret to living in the fullness of the Spirit? *"Neither did anyone say that any of the things he possessed was his own"* (Acts 4:32). Barnabas is a positive example of this verse! While he had material possessions, they did not have him. Whether he sold all of his land or part of it, he surrendered it all to Jesus and refused to live controlled by the physical world. We read about Barnabas' sacrifices and suffering in the Book of Acts, which is the basis for the accounts. His attitude in his sufferings is the reason the apostles called him a *"Son of Encouragement."*

Transaction

The second Greek verb in our passage is "poleo," translated "sold," means to exchange or deliver something for money or its equivalent. Barnabas "sold" the land he owned, gave it to the apostles, which was an expression of his attitude toward materialism. He had surrendered his materialism to Jesus. He refused to allow material things to dominate his life. Let me repeat once again; the leaders of the early church did not legislate this attitude or legally require it from their membership. Each person followed his heart under the direction of the Holy Spirit. Our passage is the first record of Barnabas' giving heart, the foundational attitude toward materialism. His transaction of selling his land and giving the proceeds to the apostles caused them to call him a *"Son of Encouragement."*

Barnabas' transaction was his expression of a fundamental principle. We cannot embrace what is to be until we surrender what has been. Many of us long for what might or could be. We dream about potential victory or the ministry we wish to have. Our present circumstances become our security because it is all we know. Will we risk that security for what could be?

John's Gospel records the feeding of the five thousand (John 6:1-14). At the heart of the story is a lad who had five barley loaves and two small fish. Given the multitude, such a small amount was meager; it was worthless. Can you see the disciples staring at this small amount of food? They could divide it among themselves; after all, they were the leaders among this group and must sustain their strength. Others can fall by the wayside, but they must not. How far will five loaves and two fish go among twelve grown men? Each will receive such a small portion they will hardly know they have eaten. Yet it is all they have! But if they will give what they have to Jesus, they can experience all that can be! Jesus can feed a vast multitude; the disciples can experience fullness in their lives; twelve baskets of leftovers come out of the abundance. But none of these things will happen unless they give up what has been.

Barnabas could choose to keep what he has and continue in that, however, what would happen if he sells his land, giving up what has been? Could he experience all God intends for him to be as a *"Son of Encouragement?"* What do you and I grasp as our own? Do we long for all that God dreams for us? We never know God's dreams for us unless we give up what has been to experience what is to be!

Transported

"Brought" is the third verb in our passage, a translation of the Greek word "phero," meaning "something is in the process of being taken or sent." From the definition, there is no new thought presented. However, it is vital to understand we never use this word without an intimate connection with the person or thing bringing it. Therefore, the focus in our verse is not that the apostles received the financial gift from the land's sale. The focus is on the heart and attitude of Barnabas, who *"brought"* the proceeds of the sale to the apostles. Luke expresses the merger of Barnabas and the Spirit of Jesus in physical activity, not the achievement of a task or a rule fulfilled.

Luke also uses "phero" in his negative illustration of Ananias and Sapphira (Acts 5:1-11). They also sold a possession. ***"And he kept back part of the proceeds, his wife also being aware of it, and brought*** (phero) ***a certain part and laid it at the apostles' feet"*** (Acts 5:2). As is always true with sin, it is not a matter of physical action. The intent of the heart carried out the physical act, revealing the intention of the heart. The self-centered, sinful nature of this couple demonstrated itself in what appeared a generous gift to the church. ***"But Peter said, 'Ananias, why has Satan filled your heart to lie to the Holy Spirit and keep back part of the price of the land for yourself? While it remained, was it not your own? And after it was sold, was it not in your own control? Why have you conceived this thing in your heart?'"*** (Acts 5:3-4).

Both uses of the verb "phero" are in the active voice, used to highlight that the subject is responsible for the action of the verb. Again, this attaches the verb's act directly to the person in action. Both Barnabas and Ananias gave expression to who they were as people, one positive, and one negative. In both instances, the work of the deed was generous; however, one produced life and the other death, determined not by the action of the deed but by the condition of the heart creating the deed.

Barnabas is a *"Son of Encouragement"* not because of training or counseling techniques for those in crisis. He recognized his existence in a materialistic world and refused to be dominated by materialism, regardless of its cost. His love for Jesus overpowered all physical claims on his life, and his merger with the Spirit of Jesus gave an expression of what he had become! He was a *"Son of Encouragement,"* an expression of his character. He was a demonstration of God's indwelling nature.

We never want to be judged by our actions or deeds in life. We do not want to become "white-washed tombs" as the Pharisees (Matthew 23:27). Are we filled with Jesus? Do we think as He thinks because we have His mind? Is He the source of our expressions? Do our actions reveal the reality of His controlling presence in our lives?

Tendered

At the climax of our passage, Barnabas brings the proceeds of his land sale to the apostles. However, carefully note how Luke describes this generous offering. Barnabas *"laid it at the apostles' feet."* The fourth verb, *"laid,"* is a translation of the Greek word 'tithemi,' meaning "to put in a place." Once again, the verb is in the active voice indicating the act comes from Barnabas' heart. His action is a result of his heart for Jesus.

The Greek word "tithemi" is used one hundred times in the New Testament, emphasized with strength in the Gospel

Part 5: The Agreed Resolve

accounts, used in a variety of settings. The significance in our passage is how John uses "tithemi," both in his Gospel and epistles. He uses it in connection with the sacrificial offering of Christ. He does not use it in the sense of "risking one's life" or "putting one's life at risk," but as "sacrificing one's life." It is the fulfillment of the Trinity God's heart, played out in Jesus' life, fulfilling Isaiah's prophecy. *"Yet it pleased the Lord to bruise Him; He has put Him to grief. When You made His soul an offering for sin, He shall see His seed, He shall prolong His days, and the pleasure of the Lord shall prosper in His hand"* (Isaiah 53:10).

John used "tithemi" many times in his Gospel. He recorded Jesus, saying, *"I am the good shepherd. The good shepherd gives* (tithemi) *His life for the sheep"* (John 10:11). *"As the Father knows Me, even so I know the Father; and I lay down* (tithemi) *My life for the sheep"* (John 10:15). *"Therefore My Father loves Me, because I lay down* (tithemi) *My life that I may take it again. No one takes it from Me, but I lay it down* (tithemi) *of Myself. I have power to lay it down* (tithemi)*, and I have power to take it again. This command I have received from My Father"* (John 10:17 18).

One of the most impressive of John's recordings is in his first epistle. *"By this we know love, because He laid down* (tithemi) *His life for us. And we also ought to lay down* (tithemi) *our lives for the brethren"* (1 John 3:16). These statements bring us to the declaration that *"God is love"* (1 John 4:8, 16). In other words, we know the heart of the Father because of Jesus' physical activity in the sacrificial giving of His life. The cross was a tangible demonstration of the inner merger of Jesus with the Father's heart.

Barnabas did not merely give a generous offering. He refused to be dominated by materialism but embraced the heart and nature of Jesus inwardly. Barnabas gave up what he had been to enter into the full expression of Christ's nature. The state of

Barbanas' merger with Jesus moved in an active demonstration in his life as he sacrificially offered himself for ministry. He was a *"Son of Encouragement."* Is this not the call of God in our lives? It is not a call to activities or rules, but a call to the full embrace of God's heart to demonstrate His style, cross style!

ABOUT THE AUTHOR

Stephen Manley has found through the saturation of the Word the message of the cross. It is beyond an event; it is a style. Thus, the cross is not a piece of wood or an emblem, but it is the heart of the person of Christ. Cross style is the Christ style. He must be central. As an international evangelist, Stephen has taken this message to the world.

After 41 years in itinerant evangelism, Stephen Manley felt a clear call from God to come off the road for the purpose of starting the Cross Style School of Practical Ministry. In 2009, Stephen launched and became the lead pastor of Cross Style Church in Lebanon, Tennessee to create the ministry platform for future students.

The Cross Style School of Practical Ministry was launched with a desire to not only train up men and women in the Word, but to give them practical hands-on experience in ministering to a lost and dying world.

Stephen's life, testimony, and preaching has been used throughout the last six decades to touch, influence, and transform the lives of countless people around the world. For Stephen, his life is wrapped up in a total saturation of Jesus and the Word of God. Time in the Word is more than an activity or duty to schedule in his day. It is the delight of his heart and the focus throughout his day because it draws him deeper into intimacy with Jesus Christ. He wants his "moment-by-moments" saturated with the Person of Jesus and the Word. He longs for Jesus to ever increase and expand in and through His life. As he once wrote:

"Jesus is present in every situation of my life. There is no conversation in which I do not feel His presence. He participates in all my recreation. He is everywhere I go. Who would want to be without Him? He is the protection for my life. He is the fragrance I constantly smell. He is the flow of my spiritual blood giving me life. He is my constant nutrition making me healthy. I cannot survive without Him. I am a Jesus pusher!!!!

I want to push Him on you.
I want you to join me in this obsession.
You do not have to work at it; it is not a discipline.
It is as natural as breathing.
Please let Him pull you to His heart."

Learn more about Stephen Manley
and the ministry of Cross Style at:
CrossStyle.org